Geopolitical Risk, Sustainability and "Cross-Border Spillovers" in Emerging Markets, Volume II

Michael I. C. Nwogugu

Geopolitical Risk, Sustainability and "Cross-Border Spillovers" in Emerging Markets, Volume II

Constitutional Political Economy, Pandemics-Governance And Labor-Oriented Bail-outs/Bail-ins

palgrave
macmillan

Michael I. C. Nwogugu
Enugu, Nigeria

ISBN 978-3-030-71418-5 ISBN 978-3-030-71419-2 (eBook)
https://doi.org/10.1007/978-3-030-71419-2

This Palgrave Macmillan imprint is published by the registered company Springer Nature Switzerland AG.
The registered company address is: Gewerbestrasse 11, 6330 Cham, Switzerland

Contents

List of Figures

List of Tables

CHAPTER 1

Introduction

This book is the second of a two-volume series, and focuses on *Cross-Border Spillovers* in Labor, Financial (e.g. stocks, bonds, derivatives), Finished-Commodity-Products and Commodities (e.g. electricity, agricultural products, basic necessities) markets and the *Preferences* of market-participants (primarily *Cross-Border Spillovers* from developed countries to Emerging Markets countries, and, to a lesser extent, across industries, in the same country).

This Volume II continues the Constitutional Law, Government and Economic Psychology orientation of Volume I, and in addition, analyzes Constitutional Political economy, Pandemics and Labor-Oriented Bail-outs/Bail-ins all of which are foundational issues that significantly affect Emerging Markets countries both individually and as a group. The book addresses issues relevant to economic policy, public policy, international political economy, ESG/Activist investing, portfolio management, and constitutional political economy, and can be helpful to countries that are developing their constitutions and/or capital markets. This book can also help improve Computer Science, Decision Sciences and Artificial Intelligence models that are used to identify or predict economic conditions, Crises, public policy, *Compliance* (as a physical phenomenon) and to

M. I. C. Nwogugu, *Geopolitical Risk, Sustainability and "Cross-Border Spillovers" in Emerging Markets, Volume II*,
https://doi.org/10.1007/978-3-030-71419-2_1

model Investment Portfolios[1], Financial Stability, Stock-market Fluctuations or Asset Pricing[2], (or are used within the context of Panel

[1] *See*: Kovarsky, P. (2019). *Fabozzi: Finance Must Modernize or Face Irrelevancy*. https://blogs.cfainstitute.org/investor/2019/06/03/fabozzi-finance-must-modernize-or-face-irrelevancy/#__prclt=C4ADXq9m. This article stated in part: "………Frank J. Fabozzi, CFA: My criticism of academic economics is that the models built by economists basically treat market agents as robots. They make decisions according to defined rules, and the constructed models are labeled "rational models." Since finance is a field within economics, the same criticism applies to the models built by financial economists. …….The "rational models" in finance have been attacked by the behavioral finance camp, which has demonstrated the disconnect between model behavior and real-world investor behavior. The concern with academic economics also comes from practitioners………The problem with relying on rational models and treating them as the foundation of finance is that new findings that are inconsistent with the bedrock theories are dismissed. This is the major point that Sergio M. Focardi and I made when we argued that economics in its current form does not describe empirical reality but an idealized rational economic world. It is revealing that in financial economics, deviations in empirical prices or returns from theoretical models are referred to as "anomalies." A true empirical science would revise its models so that they fit empirical data. Financial economics, however, takes the opposite approach and considers deviations from an idealized economic rationality to be anomalies of the true empirical price processes………In the 1970s and 1980s, an academic couldn't get published in a peer-reviewed finance journal if their research conflicted with prevailing theory, such as the capital asset pricing model (CAPM). For example, in the late 1970s, a prestigious financial journal sought papers written jointly by academics and practitioners. Thinking that the journal's editorial board was sincere, I co-authored a paper with then-chairman of Merrill Lynch White Weld, Tom Chrystie. Our thesis was that securities can be structured/customized for investors using the asset side of the balance sheet. Basically, it provided the general blueprint for structured finance. The review we received in response was short and went something like—the ideas in the paper did not make any sense because they were inconsistent with CAPM!……… The over-reliance on calculus is symptomatic of the subject's stagnation and a disservice to the students who aspire to work in asset management. Economists should combine sophisticated mathematical tools and empirical techniques while recognizing the limitations of a field where experiments are rarely possible…..Ultimately, calculus has not been effective in describing economic and financial phenomena…… Econometric models are utterly inappropriate to model the sheer complexity of economic systems……The paradox in economics is that researchers either use non-empirical tools—calculus and sophisticated math—or paleo-statistical tools that were designed before the advent of computers. ……. Other fields have embraced machine learning and other computational methods. But these methods are rejected in economic journals as "black boxes"……..In the idealized pseudo-rational world of current economic theory, there is no real place for major crises. Financial economics, in particular, is based on the assumption that economic quantities might deviate from their theoretical value, but that market forces will quickly realign them with theoretical values. This assumption has proved to be inadequate……….".

[2] *See*: Brunnermeier, Farhi, et al. (2021) which states in part: "…….In terms of asset pricing theory, an important avenue for future research is to develop models that explain which agency, behavioral, or regulatory frictions may give rise to sparse portfolios, low elasticities of

Vector Autoregressive models, Granger Causality, GARCH-type Models, Economic Modelling, Economic Forecasting, Political Decisions, Behavioral Macroeconomics, Behavioral Expectations, Peer Effects, sovereign debt crisis, VaR estimation; sovereign debt crisis, financial markets regulation, Tail Risk and so on).

With regard to public policy, business policy and affected populations, the issues addressed and the theories introduced in this proposed book affect or can affect more than three billion people worldwide, and more than $5 trillion of daily transactions (i.e. loans/mortgages/bonds/bills, credit transactions, trade finance transactions, money markets, swaps/ derivatives, real estate, stocks, commodities, etc.) and more than the equivalent of $280 trillion of corporate, government and household assets around the world. The approach in this book is entirely theoretical and the book uses and introduces concepts and theories in Economic Psychology,

demand, and volatile latent demand. ....Interestingly, the recent work on demand systems suggests that investors do not behave as our models suggest,....... Indeed, many of the salient policy and regulatory questions involve quantities: What is the impact of large-scale asset purchases by central banks? ......What is the impact of growing environmental, social, and governance (ESG) mandates on asset prices? What is the impact of changing the risk regulation of banks or insurance companies? The recent COVID-19 crisis has highlighted once more the importance of being able to answer these questions quantitatively..........By combining models of the asset demand system with models of corporate decision making, we obtain an integrated model of asset pricing and corporate finance.........Indeed, and despite decades of international financial integration, there are many more frictions in financial markets across countries than within countries. Third, currencies are more central to international finance than they are to finance......... Fourth, the role of governments is more central to international finance than it is to finance........Common long-standing problems include the identification of the economic determinants of beliefs Et, the economic determinants of risk premia or equivalently of stochastic discount factors $Xt,t+1$ and $X^{*}t,t+1$, the economic determinants of portfolios. They also include what I will call the "disconnect" problem: the fact that it seems difficult to connect the stochastic discount factor $Xt,t+1$ to an actual preference-based marginal rate of substitution $MRSt,t+1$ of a well-identified marginal investor .... Other common long-standing problems include the identification of the key market failures and externalities ....as well as the role and transmission of policy (monetary, fiscal, prudential, etc.).........International finance also faces specific challenges with no counterparts in finance. First, there is the *Mussa puzzle*,...... Second, there is covered-interest-parity (CIP) arbitrage violation, ...Third, there is the large degree of home bias in portfolios across countries. Fourth, there are the destabilizing effects of volatile capital flows in emerging markets. Fifth, there are the economic determinants of government behavior in these countries. Sixth, there are the economic determinants and implications of exchange rate regimes ...... Seventh and finally, there are the importance of the international monetary system and the special role of the United States......... as the world banker and the exorbitant privilege that comes with it, and the resulting pattern of global imbalances..........".

Constitutional Economics, Human-Computer Interaction (HCI) and Complex Systems theory.

The contributions of this book are as follows:

1. The scope of the book is international, and the theories developed are applicable in many countries.
2. Analysis and development of theories of group decision making and biases of decision makers that are facing risks in Transition Economies and responding to economic sanctions. This subject is a huge gap in the literature.
3. Analysis of the role of constitutional economics as a tool for national and global sustainable growth (i.e. economic, social, urban and environmental sustainability) and risk management.
4. Analysis of some of the financial and constitutional political economy crisis that occurred in Europe, Africa, Asia and the US during 2007–2020 including the COVID-19 Pandemic and associate government interventions.
5. Analysis of the often-symbiotic relationship between alternative sets of legal-institutional-constitutional rules that constrain the choices and activities of economic and political agents on one hand, and sustainable growth, financial regulation and the risk management of financial institutions within the context of the global digital economy.
6. Review of the effects of constitutions and legal institutions on market dynamics (e.g. volatility, market depth, liquidity) within the context of the global digital economy and Transition Economies.
7. Explains how constitutions can affect political processes, risk regulation, market volatility, bubbles and crashes, innovation and sustainable growth within the context of the global digital economy.
8. Explains how ISDA, FASB, GASB, IASB, SASB, ICMA Credit Rating Agencies and government bailouts/bail-ins are unconstitutional.
9. Explains how constitutions and risk regulations affect economic models within the context of the global digital economy.
10. Analyzes the unconstitutionality of, and weaknesses inherent in the Dodd-Frank Act (USA) and possible impact on sustainable growth.
11. Analyzes the economic and sustainability consequences of federalism.

1.1 Target Audience, US Dominance in International Trade/Finance, and This Book's Emphasis on US Laws

The subject/target countries for which this book debates the relationship among Sustainable Growth, the global digital economy, Constitutions, Economic Psychology and financial/economic risk are:

1. the 110+ countries whose constitutions and constitutional principles are based on, or are similar to the US Constitution.
2. all Commonwealth Countries that use common-law systems.
3. EU countries (especially those that use common-law systems).
4. Transition Economies (e.g. China; CIS countries; Nigeria; Egypt; India; Thailand; Saudi Arabia, UAE; Central/Eastern European countries; Libya; Morocco; Vietnam; Venezuela; etc.).
5. Countries that contribute substantially to the Global Digital Economy (and whose national broadband penetration rate exceeds 70%).

Obviously, the usefulness of this book to civil law countries is limited because the constitutional law analysis is done with US laws.

The more specific target audiences for this book are as follows:

1. University professors (in Finance, Computer Science, International Political Economy, Macroeconomics, Law-And-Economics, Law-And-Finance, Applied Math, Operations Research and Public Policy).
2. PhD and master's degree students (in Finance, Computer Science, International Political Economy, Macroeconomics, Law-And-Economics, Law-And-Finance, Applied Math, Operations Research and Public Policy).
3. PhD holders who work in industry, think-tanks, government agencies and financial services companies.
4. Research/Policy professionals that are involved in developing AI/ML/datascience models of Financial Stability, Systemic Risk, International Trade, *Complex Systems* (social, political and economic systems), *Compliance* (as a physical phenomenon), International Portfolio Management, Fiscal Policies, Macroeconomic Dynamics and Public Policy.

US laws are used throughout this book because of the following reasons:

1. More than eighty countries have copied the US Constitution (including Brazil),[3] and many countries have also copied US-style business processes, capital markets processes and financial regulations (e.g. China, Japan, India, Australia). The US Constitution and constitutional principles are similar to those of Commonwealth countries. Law and Versteeg (2012) noted that the US Constitution is similar to those of more than fifty countries including the following countries listed in Footnote-3. More than 110 countries created or amended their national constitutions during 1990–2020.
2. According to Amadeo (July 2020) and other sources, the US Dollar is the dominant international currency and as of 2018–2021,[4] the US Dollar was used in more than 50% of international transactions

[3] *See*: Go (2003). Law and Versteeg (2012) noted that the US Constitution is similar to those of many countries including the following countries: Albania, Armenia, Australia, Austria, Azerbaijan, Belgium, Bosnia and Herzegovina, Bulgaria, Canada, Croatia, the Czech Republic, Denmark, the Dominican Republic, El Salvador, Estonia, Fiji, Finland, France, Georgia, Germany, Greece, Honduras, Hungary, Iceland, Ireland, Italy, Japan, Jordan, Kazakhstan, Korea, Latvia, Lithuania, Luxembourg, Macedonia, Moldova, Mongolia, the Netherlands, New Zealand, Nicaragua, Norway, the Philippines, Poland, Portugal, Romania, Singapore, the Slovak Republic, Slovenia, Spain, Sweden, Switzerland, Thailand, Tonga, Turkey, Ukraine, and the United kingdom; Antigua and Barbuda, Bahamas, Bahrain, Bangladesh, Barbados, Belize, Botswana, Brunei, Cyprus, Dominica, Gambia, Ghana, Grenada, Guyana, India, Israel, Jamaica, Kenya, Kiribati, Lesotho, Liberia, Malawi, Malaysia, Maldives, the Marshall Islands, the Federated States of Micronesia, Namibia, Nepal, Nigeria, Pakistan, Papua New Guinea, American Samoa, Saudi Arabia, Sierra Leone, the Solomon Islands, Somalia, South Africa, Sri Lanka, St. Kitts and Nevis, St. Lucia, St. Vincent and the Grenadines, Sudan, Swaziland, Tanzania, Trinidad and Tobago, Uganda, the United Arab Emirates, the United Kingdom, Vanuatu, Zambia and Zimbabwe.

[4] *See*: "*Covid Crisis Shows Once Again Why US Dollar Is World's Dominant Currency – A Lack of Global Alternatives Helps Explain Some of The Dollar's Role. The Euro's Status As A Reserve Currency Remains Limited & China's Currency Is Still Subject To Capital Controls*". By Enda Curran and Finbarr Flynn; 23 October, 2020. https://theprint.in/economy/covid-crisis-shows-once-again-why-us-dollar-is-worlds-dominant-currency/529331/".

See: Gifford, C. (September 8, 2020). "The dominance of the US dollar is called into question". *World Finance*. https://www.worldfinance.com/markets/the-dominance-of-the-us-dollar-is-called-into-question.

See: Amadeo, K. (July 2020), "Why the US Dollar Is the Global Currency". *The Bottom Line*. July 23, 2020. https://www.thebalance.com/world-currency-3305931.

See: Federal Reserve Bank of New York. "Is the International Role of the Dollar Changing?" Page 6. https://www.newyorkfed.org/medialibrary/media/research/current_issues/ci16-1.pdf.

(finance and trade), used in about 90% of worldwide foreign exchange trading,[5] and accounted for more than 59% of central bank reserves[6] around the world (2000–2021), and more than 40% of existing debts/bonds around the world[7] were denominated in US Dollars See: Fig. 1.1. The global supply (and country-specific supply) of US dollars can be manipulated by changing the US Federal Reserve's US Dollar Swap Line and or by changing the Fed Funds Rate and/or by changing access to SWIFT (an international payments system that is controlled by the US). As of 2015–2021, at least sixty-five countries had officially pegged their domestic currencies to the US Dollar. Monetary Policy pertaining to the US dollar is set primarily by the US Federal Reserve. Fiscal Policy that substantially affects to the US Dollar is set primarily by the US Legislature and the US Treasury Department. As of 2018–2020, banks in the United Kingdom, France and Germany had more US Dollar-denominated liabilities than liabilities denominated in Euros and their own local currencies.[8] According to the Federal Reserve Bank of New York[9] and other research,[10] at various times during 2005–2020, more than half of the printed US dollars were circulating outside the United States, and a significant percentage of US dollars outside the US were circulating in Latin American countries and the former Soviet Union (CIS and CEE countries) (as of 2018 and December 2020, a total of about $1.671 trillion and $2.040 trillion of printed dollars respectively, were in circulation). At various times during the last thirty years, the US Dollar was used as the main currency in foreign countries (such as Poland, Zimbabwe, Panama, Ecuador, Turks and Caicos Islands, Guam, US and British Virgin Islands, El Salvador, Democratic Republic of Timor-Leste, American Samoa, Commonwealth of the

[5] *See*: XE. "*ISO 4217 Currency Codes*". http://www.xe.com/iso4217.php.

[6] *See*: International Money Fund. "*Table 1: World Currency Composition of Official Foreign Exchange Reserves.*" https://data.imf.org/regular.aspx?key=41175.

[7] *See*: International Monetary Fund (2019). "*Global Financial Stability Report*". https://www.imf.org/en/Publications/GFSR/Issues/2019/10/01/global-financial-stability-report-october-2019.

[8] *See*: Bank for International Settlements, "*The Geography of Dollar Funding of Non-US Banks*". https://www.bis.org/publ/qtrpdf/r_qt1812b.htm.

[9] *See*: Goldberg, L. (2010). Is the International Role of the Dollar Changing? *Federal Reserve Bank of New York – Current Issues in Economics & Finance*. https://www.newyorkfed.org/medialibrary/media/research/current_issues/ci16-1.pdf.

[10] *See*: U.S. Currency Education Program. "*U.S. Currency in Circulation.*" https://www.uscurrency.gov/life-cycle/data/circulation.

Northern Mariana Islands, Federated States of Micronesia, and Republic of Palau); and as of 2020, the US Dollar was used as quasi-currency or secondary-currency in many countries and territories (e.g. Canada, Mexico, Russia, Panama, Commonwealth of the Bahamas, Barbados, Bermuda, the Cayman Islands, Sint Maarten, St Kitts, and Nevis, the ABC Islands of Aruba, Bonaire, Curacao, the BES Islands, Sint Eustatius and Saba; Belize, Costa Rica, Philippines, Myanmar [Burma], Cambodia, Liberia, Nigeria [major cities only] and Vietnam [major cities only])—that involves more than 330 million people and more than $18 trillion of annual economic activity. The United States is the top export-destination of both Japan[11] and China,[12] and as of 2013–2020, each of China and Japan owned more than US$1 trillion of US government bonds/notes/bills. Given the foregoing, both the commodities-dependent Emerging Markets Countries are at significant risk if: (1) US dollar inflation increases and/or (2) there is increased U.S. deficit spending and printing of U.S. Treasury to support U.S. debt; and or (3) there are economic shocks that increase the value of US dollar denominated bonds or the US dollar; and or (4) the volume of outstanding/circulating US dollars declines; and or (5) US dollar interest rates change in ways that harm the local/national economies in these foregoing foreign countries that use large amounts of US dollars (See: Fig. 1.1).

3. The US has the most advanced and comprehensive financial/economic regulations and creates some of the most sophisticated financial products in the world. Many developing countries (and developed countries) copied their financial laws from US laws. For example, the Brazilian constitution is based on the US Constitution; and real estate investment trust (REIT) statutes worldwide are based on US REIT laws. Many countries have created variants of the Dodd-Frank Act and the Sarbanes Oxley Act (SOX). Mortgage/Foreclosure laws in many countries are very similar to US mortgage/foreclosure laws. Many developing countries and "transition" countries of Eastern Europe

[11] *See*: World Integrated Trade Solutions. "*Japan Exports By Country 2020*".

See: World Integrated Trade Solutions. "*US Exports By Country 2020*". https://wits.worldbank.org/countrysnapshot/en/USA.

[12] *See*: World Integrated Trade Solutions. "*China Exports By Country 2020.*" https://wits.worldbank.org/countrysnapshot/en/CHN.

See: World Integrated Trade Solutions. "*US Exports By Country 2020*". https://wits.worldbank.org/countrysnapshot/en/USA.

derived their mortgage/foreclosure laws from US laws. During the last twenty years, the US consistently had the largest national economy in the World; and the US economy directly/indirectly (through international trade, outsourcing, FDI, FI, Foreign Aid, etc.) supported the economies of other "First-Level Associated" countries (such as China, Japan, Brazil, Mexico, India) which, in turn, directly/directly supported (through international trade, outsourcing, loans, FDI, FI, Foreign Aid, etc.) the economies of "Second-Level Associated" countries (such as Russia, Nigeria, Philippines, Thailand, ASEAN countries, Pakistan, Central American countries, CIS countries).

4. During 1980–2021, the US was a major participant in major multilateral and bilateral trade agreements; and the US-China Trade War (2019–present) continues to have significant economic/social/psychological Multiplier Effects on many countries.
5. The US is a global technological innovation leader, and has consistently been a major contributor to, and beneficiary of the Global Digital Economy.
6. Labor Unions have been a significant factor in the US economy, in US legislative processes and in US Foreign Policy; and have also shaped MNCs, which in turn, sometimes propagated such influences and resultant effects around the world.
7. The US has the largest number of large MNCs, many of which operate in more than five countries and are highly influential in international trade and finance.
8. The US (and US law) is a fertile ground for the analysis of Geopolitical Risk, Constitutional Law, Economic Psychology and Regulation because:

   (a) The US has a federal-presidential system of government (many developing countries are shifting to this system of government). Federalism is a big issue in US politics and economy, as well as in an increasing number of developed and developing countries (such as Germany, Russia, India, Nigeria and Brazil).
   (b) US law was derived from English law (which is also the basis for laws in Commonwealth countries).
   (c) The US has a relatively diverse population, and relatively well-developed and deep capital markets.
   (d) The US has been at the forefront of mechanism design in both the private sector and in government.

(e) Securitization of assets/intangibles started in the US, and the securitization laws of many countries were derived from US securitization laws—which include mortgage/Foreclosure statutes.
(f) The US has one of the most advanced set of consumer protection laws in the world. The use of consumer credit is prevalent in the US economy—and is related to crime, willingness-to-comply and social order. Improper issuance and uses of consumer credit was a major cause of the 2006–2009 Subprime Crisis in the US which ballooned into the Global Financial Crisis of 2007–2014.
(g) In the US, individual wealth, Political Capital and social capital are very much linked together. This seems to be a growing trend in some developing countries and in some "transition" countries of Eastern Europe.
(h) Compared to other "developed" countries, US courts have been more willing to "experiment" in the areas of financial/economic regulation and the interpretation of the Constitution.
(i) US political/economic institutions and government agencies seem to be more concerned about various types of *inequality* (social, wealth, housing and income inequality) and sustainability (economic, environmental, social, etc.), compared to other countries.
(j) During 1980–2020, the US was a major cash contributor to, and exerted significant political influence at international organizations such as the United Nations, World Bank, WTO and WHO.

1.2 Causal Factors: Preferential Free Trade Agreements, "*Joint-Committees*" and Some of the Effects of "*US Dollar Dominance*" and "*US MNC Dominance*" in International Trade & Finance

Preferential Trade Agreements (PTAs) and *Joint-Committees* were summarized in Chap. 1 of Volume-I of this two-book series (Nwogugu 2021b). Repasi (July 2017), Lenk (2019) and Wright and Owen (2020) discussed the legitimacy, powers and roles of *Joint-Committees* (which can have significant effects on GVCs and International Trade & Finance). Thompson et al. (2019), Laurens and Morin (2019), and Mitchell et al. (2020) analyzed *Joint-Committees* that arose from international environmental agreements and international trade agreements. WTO (2019) and World Bank (July 2019) discussed International Trade and GVC (Global Value Chain) issues. Baccini (2019)[13] discussed *Preferential Trade Agreements*, which affect MNCs and GVCs. Because of their origins, objectives and structure, Preferential Trade Agreements (PTAs) and Joint-Committees directly affect a broad range of issues including the efficiency/effectiveness of domestic/international statutes (such as Dodd Frank Act and Sarbanes Oxley Act), the regulation of Credit Rating Agencies, international implications of government bailouts/bail-ins, coordinated responses to Pandemics/Epidemics, international impact of quasi-governmental agencies such as PCAOB, the development and implementation of accounting/derivatives standards, and so on.

One of the main motivations and thrusts of this book is the often inadequate responses of *Regulatory Mechanisms* (e.g. dominant, Labor-related and trade-related "federal" Financial/Governance statutes such as Dodd Frank Act and SOX in the USA; Government Bail-out/Bail-in processes/regulations; "emergency statutes"; etc.) to economic/financial crisis which in turn, can *Spillover* across national-borders through Trade Agreements and Joint-Committees.

International Trade and finance settlement systems are mostly developed and implemented by International Organizations and national/federal "*Joint Committees*" and administrative agencies in various countries. Thus, multilateral/bilateral International Trade & Finance settlement agreements have evolved into *International Constitutions* because of either the number of countries that are party to such formal and informal

[13] Baccini (2019) stated in part: "………According to the Desta dataset (Dür et al. 2014), there were a little more than one hundred PTAs in the 1990s, whereas there are more than seven hundred PTAs in force to date. Both developed and developing countries are heavily involved in preferential liberalization, and the number of North–South PTAs (i.e., PTAs between developed and developing countries) has boomed since the formation of the *North America Free Trade Agreement* (NAFTA). In summary, much of the trade liberalization that we have seen in the past twenty years is preferential rather than unilateral or multilateral. While impressive, the growing number of PTAs is not the most defining transformation in the global governance of trade. Rather, the most important change is that modern PTAs not only reduce tariffs but also regulate investment, intellectual property rights, competition policy, government procurement, and many other matters. In other words, PTAs remove barriers not only at the border but also behind the border, producing what has been referred to as deep integration between countries (Lawrence 1996). An illustration of this change is the contrast between the PTA that the European Union signed with Egypt in 1972, which is 92 pages long, and the 2016 Comprehensive Economic and Trade Agreement between Canada and the European Union, which is 1598 pages long. Since many of the provisions and regulations included in PTAs go beyond World Trade Organization commitments (Horn et al. 2010), it is fair to say that preferential liberalization shapes the global governance of trade in the twenty-first century…".

agreements, and or the significant annual volume of international trade/finance that is directly/indirectly affected. During 1990–2021, a substantial percentage (more than 50%) of International Trade/Finance was settled in the US Dollar, much to the great disadvantage of most Emerging Markets countries. Prasad (2019), Boz, et al. (2017), Gopinath (2018), Adler, et al. (2020), Druck, et al. (2015 July) and Zhang (2016 January) discussed the dynamics of *US Dollar Dominance*. Kim and Milner (2019) discussed the often-significant influence of MNCs (multinational corporations) on foreign policy and International Trade. Agbonika (2015) described various types of international trade/finance payment systems that were used in Africa. On optimal currency areas, see: Chari, Dovis, & Kehoe (2020), Bolton & Huang (2018), and Kunroo (2016).

The following are factors that continue to have significant negative effects on Emerging Markets economies:

1. *The significant dominance of the US Dollar in the settlement of international trade and finance transactions*—apparently, having recognized this significant risk, during 2005–2021, many "country-pairs" tried to break this near-monopoly by formally or informally agreeing to settle international trade/finance transactions between them in their own local currencies, and they include Russia-China, Russia-Iran, EU-Iran, China-Bangladesh, etc..
2. *The significant dominance of the US Dollar as a Reserve Currency*—as of 2000–2020 and 2021, the US dollar accounted for about 61%–64% and 59% respectively, of worldwide aggregate foreign currency reserves.
3. *The dominance of US MNCs (multinational corporations) in International Trade and finance*—which ultimately transmits/imposes US government and US MNCs' economic/political/legal/social policies and standards (such as SOX; Dodd Frank Act; corporate governance practices; etc.) around the world, often to the detriment of Emerging Markets countries, many of which have different cultures, government-revenues, priorities, social-welfare policies, enforcement-resources, compliance-patterns and usage-of-trade.

While various data (such as Fig. 1.1 below) indicate that the real purchasing power of the US dollar actually declined during 1900–2020, such data applies to purchasing power within the US (not in Emerging Markets, where the US dollar purchasing power has increased during the last few decades due to currency devaluation).

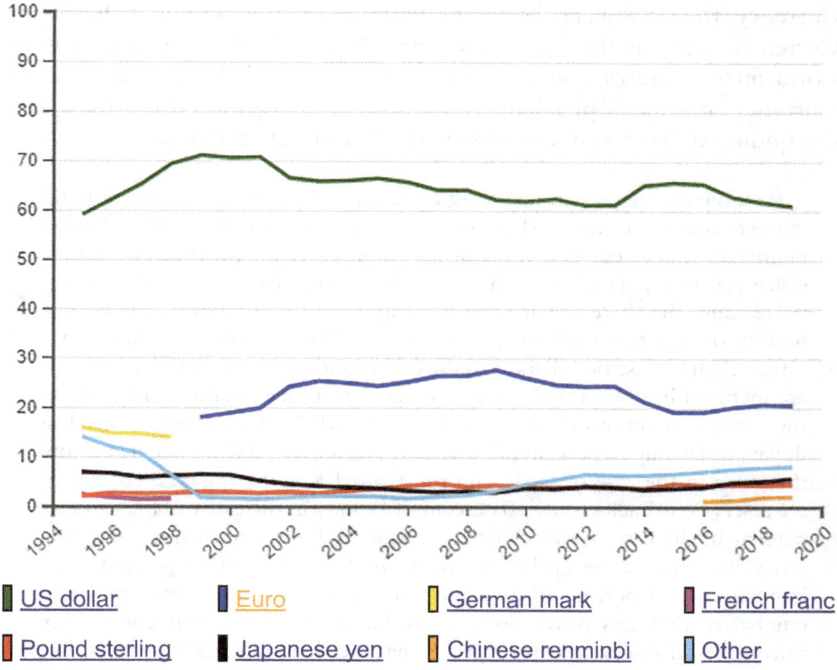

Fig. 1.1 Historical purchasing power of one US dollar within the US (1900–2021). (Source: https://www.in2013dollars.com/us/inflation/1900?amount=1)

According to Gopinath (2019) (quoting Bräuning & Ivashina (2017)), US dollar remains the dominant currency in international finance and accounted for 92% of loans by borrowers in emerging Africa (including Middle East), 87% of loans by borrowers in emerging Asia and Pacific, 76% of loans by borrowers in emerging Europe, 97% of loans by borrowers in the emerging Americas and 61% of loans by borrowers in developed countries. Gopinath (2018) explained: (i) why the *Mundell-Fleming Paradigm* (i.e. every country invoices its exports in its own currency; and the importance of a country's currency in international trade is closely and positively related to its share in world trade) is wrong; (ii) how many of the assumptions in international finance and trade are wrong; (iii) how the US dollar dominates both international finance and trade; (iv) how according to Gopinath and Stein (2018) the world can have a single Dominant

Currency (the US dollar) despite the existence of other potential Dominant Currencies such as the Euro or Chinese Yuan; (iv) how dollarization of world finance causes non-US companies to often suffer a balance sheet (currency) mismatch problem (those non-US companies don't have corresponding dollar revenues). Gopinath (2018) stated in part:

> …the dollar's share as an invoicing currency is 4.7 times its share in world imports and 3.1 times its share in world exports… Consequently, there is neither producer currency pricing nor local currency pricing, but mainly dollar pricing. … The Euro's share as an invoicing currency in world exports is 1.2 times the share of euro country exports. In other words, while some non-euro countries invoice exports in euros, this is of a much smaller magnitude than the use of dollars… In the case of India, 86 percent of its imports are invoiced in dollars while only 5 percent of India's imports originate in the United States. Similarly, 86 percent of India's exports are invoiced in dollars while only 15 percent of India's exports are to the United States…note that even in the case of Japan and the United Kingdom, whose currencies are reserve currencies, only 40 percent of exports in the case of Japan and 51 percent in the case of the United Kingdom are invoiced in their own currency. The real exception here is the United States, with 93 percent of its imports and 97 percent of its exports invoiced in its own currency. I also emphasize that this heavy dollar invoicing is not just about commodity prices like oil prices or copper prices that are denominated in dollars, but applies to a much wider set of goods…I document that dollar stickiness in the short run is indeed a feature of non-commodity prices in international trade. Boz, Gopinath, and Plagborg-Møller (2017b) find no evidence of the co-movement between nominal exchange rates and the terms of trade that is a central piece of the *Mundell-Fleming paradigm*…, the overwhelming share of world trade is priced/invoiced in a small set of currencies, with the dollar the dominant currency. Second, international prices in their currency of invoicing are not very sensitive to exchange rates at horizons of up to two years.… This finding is consistent with the fact that prices in international trade are sticky in a dominant currency, which is overwhelmingly the dollar … In the case of emerging markets, it has been long recognized that they rely heavily on foreign currency borrowing and that, too, in dollars, a phenomenon referred to as "*original sin*" …. There is a violation of uncovered interest parity (UIP) that favors the dollar as a cheap funding currency… Through a concerted policy push, the renminbi's share as a settlement currency in China's trade has grown from zero percent in 2010 to 25 percent in 2015.…" A consequence of dollarization of world finance is that firms outside of the United States often suffer a balance sheet (currency) mismatch problem. This is because dollar borrowing in many cases is done by firms that do not have corresponding dollar revenues,….

Some of the significant adverse effects of such three-pronged US dominance on Emerging Markets countries are as follows:

1. Its conjectured here that some significant and continuing devaluation of Emerging Markets currencies because of the following reasons:
   a. *US Dollar Dominance* and *US MNC Dominance* causes a "*Zero-Sum Dependency & Purchasing-Power Windfall*" that benefits the US and countries that have substantial US dollar reserves (the "*US-Dollar-Favored Countries*")—i.e. the *US-Dollar-Favored Countries* directly benefit (at the expense of Emerging Markets countries) from the currency devaluations/depreciations in Emerging Markets in the form of "*Continuing Import-Dependency*" and increased US dollar purchasing-power in Emerging Markets (that can be used to buy raw-materials, services, vehicles, finished-products and assets in Emerging Markets). "*Continuing Import-Dependency*" is a progressively worsening vicious cycle and "*Lock-in Effect*" wherein Emerging Markets countries that have weak/non-viable manufacturing sectors depend on imported finished-goods/machinery/vehicles for survival, but because of US dollar dominance dynamics and the resultant continuing devaluations/depreciation of their local currencies, they find it increasingly difficult to develop their manufacturing, infrastructure and power sectors and to import machinery/parts/fuels, and thus, they continue to increasingly depend on imports of finished-goods/equipment/parts/fuels. Prime examples are Nigeria, Venezuela and many African and Latin American countries.
   b. *US Dollar dominance* and *US MNC Dominance* causes unjustified artificially-high "*Current-Demand*" and "*Forward-Demand*" for the US dollar, and reduces demand for local currencies which in turn, devalues/depreciates such Emerging Markets currencies. "*Forward-Demand*" is Aggregate-Expectations-based, Aggregate-Regret-based and Risk-Perception-based demand for future supplies of the US dollar (that is also partly based on preferences for continuation of the status-quo as the *safest-option*). "*Current-Demand*" is based on current existing conditions wherein the US dollar is the most-popular settlement currency and reserve currency.

2. *US Dollar Dominance* creates a "*Zero-Sum Balance-of-Trade Purchasing-Power Windfall*" which is a progressively worsening vicious cycle and "*Lock-in Effect*" that benefits the US and *US-Dollar-Favored Countries*—in the form of "Continuing Import-Dependency" and increased US dollar purchasing power in Emerging Markets at the expense of Emerging Markets countries. The resulting and the Emerging Markets currency devaluations/depreciations occur in the following ways that increasingly harm their economies:
   a. Export-oriented Emerging Markets countries (that typically have significant trade surpluses against many countries) are often compelled to regularly and intentionally devalue their currencies in order for their goods/services to remain competitive in international markets (such as China and Brazil).
   b. Emerging Markets countries that are import-oriented (and have significant trade deficits with many countries) and are forced to use up most of their US dollar foreign currency reserves to import necessities (food, medicines, services, vehicles, equipment, etc.) which, in turn, devalues their local currency without any or much action by the *US-Dollar-Favored Countries* (such Emerging Markets countries become increasingly less able to "defend" their local currency).

   The negative impacts of both foregoing effects increase as such Emerging Markets countries increase their trade surpluses or trade deficits (which effectively puts them back in their previous positions where they increased their trade surpluses or trade deficits).
3. *US Dollar Dominance* creates a "*Zero-Sum Capital+Interest Windfall*" which is a progressively worsening vicious cycle and "*Lock-in Effect*" that benefits the US and "*US-Dollar-Favored Countries*" through "Continuing Import-Dependency" and increased US dollar purchasing power in Emerging Markets and in countries whose currencies are "cheap" with respect to the US dollar. Such increased purchasing power can be used to buy raw materials, services, vehicles, finished products and assets in Emerging Markets. That is, the *US-Dollar-Favored Countries* directly benefit (at the expense of Emerging Markets countries) in the following ways that increasingly harm Emerging Markets economies:
   a. Emerging Markets countries increase their interest rates in order to reduce inflation, to compensate for above-average credit risk and to attract dollar-based fixed-income foreign investors who

are usually promised easy repatriation of their interest/dividend payments and principal in US dollars, and when local or international shocks occur and such capital is repatriated in US dollars (at the pre-devaluation exchange rates), the local currency usually depreciates and/or is devalued (and as a result, "Continuing Import-Dependency" and US dollar purchasing power usually increases in that Emerging Markets country partly because domestic/local prices are not adjusted evenly across the country and are not adjusted at the same time).

b. The relatively high interest rates earned by foreign "traditional dollar investors" when they invest in Emerging Markets fixed-income instruments cause a psychological phenomenon, wherein such investment actually increases the perceived value of the US dollar and *Willingness-to-Pay* for the US dollar partly because local indigenes and third-party international investors attribute such investments (and investment opportunity) to US dollar dynamics and "efforts" of US dollar holders/investors (collectively, the "*Investment-Origin Appreciation Phenomenon*").

The negative impacts of these foregoing effects increase as such Emerging Markets countries increase their interest rates and or their volumes US dollar-based foreign investment (which effectively puts them back in their previous positions where they had to increase their interest rates or their volumes of US dollar-based foreign investment).

4. *US Dollar Dominance* creates a "*Zero-Sum Dollar-Liability Purchasing-Power and Interest Windfall*" which is a progressively worsening vicious cycle and "*Lock-in Effect*" that benefits the US and "*US-Dollar-Favored Countries*" in the form of increased US dollar purchasing power in Emerging Markets (and US dollar appreciation). That is, in export-oriented countries that have trade surpluses against many countries, and whose official aggregate dollar liabilities exceed their local-currency liabilities (the "*High-Dollar-Liability Countries*"), there are at least two resulting and progressively worsening dynamics:

a. The problem of reduced/declining domestic *business confidence*, "*government confidence*" and *consumer confidence* increases "*psychological devaluation*" of the local currency and *willingness-to-devalue* in favor of the US dollar, and the probability of actual devaluation in favor of the US dollar (all of which can affect both local US dollar pricing and local producer pricing due to *Expectations* and *Regret Minimization*).

b. The *high-dollar-liability countries* have strong incentives to reduce or are forced to reduce their benchmark interest rates to levels near, at or below US benchmark interest rates (which can result, and often results in appreciation of the US Dollar and depreciation of their local currency).

5. *US Dollar Dominance* creates a "*Zero-Sum Dollar-Hoarding Effect and Purchasing-Power Windfall*" which is a progressively worsening vicious cycle and "*Lock-in Effect*" that benefits the US and "*US-Dollar-Favored Countries*" in the form of "Continuing Import-Dependency" and increased US dollar purchasing power in Emerging Markets and US dollar appreciation. During 2000–2021, many African countries (mostly Emerging Markets) imported more than 50% of their aggregate annual imports from China, but most of such trade was settled in US dollars whereas China could have afforded to settle those trades either in Chinese Yuan or in the African countries' local currencies. Those are prime evidence of "*US Dollar Hoarding*" wherein "dollar-rich" countries (that have significant US dollar and dominant-currency reserves) intentionally hoard US dollars in order to gain international *influence*, global political power and economic power. Such US dollar hoarding reduces or can reduce Emerging Markets country's currency reserves, credibility, ability to defend their local currencies, sovereign ratings, ability to import critical necessities (food, medicines, vehicles, equipment and parts, services, refined fuels, etc.), quality of life and so forth, all of which devalues or can devalue their local currencies. Similarly, during 1970–1990, many "Pounds-Sterling-Rich" or "French-Francs-Rich" European countries that could afford to settle all or a percentage of their trades with African and Latin American countries insisted on settling trades with such countries in Pounds Sterling or French Francs.

6. For some Emerging Markets countries that have significant manufacturing capabilities (Eastern/Central European countries, Brazil, Thailand, Chile, Peru, Malaysia, South Africa, Egypt, Indonesia, etc.), *US Dollar Dominance* creates a harmful *Zero-Sum Demand-Based Devaluation and Purchasing Power Windfall* for *US-Dollar-Favored Countries* wherein:

8. *US Dollar Dominance* (combined with more advanced institutions, investor-protection and Corporate Governance in the US) creates significant "Relative uncertainty" and very-high currency devaluation risk in many Emerging Markets countries, which reduces most FDI and foreign investment (and some types of foreign aid) in such countries. Many of such Emerging Markets countries have historically low government and private sector expenditures on infrastructure, healthcare, food/agriculture, power and education. *US Dollar Dominance* and *US MNC Dominance* creates a "*Zero-Sum Investment-Bias and Purchasing-Power Windfall*" wherein due to concerns (about geopolitical risks, currency devaluations/depreciation, credit risk, corruption, weak institutions and low investor protection in Emerging Markets), the global derivatives and indexing markets strongly favor dollar-based and North America–domiciled structured products, index-products and ETPs which, in effect, increases the absolute volume of US dollar-based investments in securities/instruments and worldwide financial indices. Thus, cash that would have been invested in Emerging Markets is instead invested in US dollar-denominated structured products, ETPs and other "bets" on US and developed-country securities and index products (henceforth, the "*Investment-Concentration Effect*" which was noted in Nwogugu (2019c)). Such extreme concentration of "leveraged bets" (leveraged investments) in the securities, instruments and indices of the US (and, to a lesser extent, developed countries) exponentially increases financial instability and worldwide systemic risk. From the perspective of Emerging Markets countries, this windfall is a progressively worsening vicious cycle and "*Lock-in Effect*" that benefits the US and some European countries in the form of "Continuing Import Dependency", "Export Sub-contracting Dependency" and increased foreign investments "in the Dollar-Favored Countries) and US dollar purchasing power and also benefits "*US-Dollar-Favored Countries*" in the form of increased US dollar purchasing power.
   During 1995–2021, many African, Latin American and south Asian Emerging Markets currencies lost value against the US dollar by more than 30% (and in some cases such as Nigeria, by as much as 2000%). See Appendix 1, which lists the worsening US dollar exchange rates of many Emerging Markets countries during

1999–2019. The reality is that the resultant economic/social/psychological/environmental catastrophes in Emerging Markets far outweigh any benefits to the US and *US-Dollar-Favored Countries* (or both the US and developed countries). To understand just how important exchange rates are to Emerging Markets countries, consider the following: (i) during 2015–2020, more than 70% of drugs/medicines consumed in Nigeria were imported from China and India; (ii) most of the roads constructed in Nigeria are built with imported asphalt, equipment and road-laying machines; (iii) during 2015–2020, more than 90% of cars/trucks/buses/tankers/train-cars/boats and the associated vehicle-parts used in Nigeria were imported; (iv) during 2015–2020, more than 40% of the processed foods consumed in Nigeria were imported; (v) during 2015–2020, more than an estimated 90% of equipment, equipment parts and medical equipment purchased in Nigeria were imported; (vi) during 2015–2020, more than 70% of the refrigerators, air-conditioners and power generators used in Nigeria were imported; vii) during 2015–2020, more than 70% of the refined fuels (for cars, trucks, boats, buses and airplanes) used in Nigeria were imported despite the fact that Nigeria is an oil-gas producing country as of 2015–2021, Nigeria spent about forty percent of its currency reserves[14] on the import of petroleum products, fertilizers and petrochemicals. All these imports were paid for with foreign currency (mostly US dollars). These damaging effects of exchange rates and associated vicious cycles are some of the reasons why Emerging Markets countries had the biggest *brain drain* in their history during 1985–2015.

9. Its conjectured here that the resultant currency devaluations/depreciations in Emerging Markets (caused by US Dollar Dominance and or US MNV Dominance) had/has or can have the following *Multiplier Effects*:
   a. The affected Emerging Markets countries aren't able to provide desperately needed direct/indirect *subsidies* (for imported food, fuels, etc.) to households and companies which in turn, greatly reduces economic output, job-creation, quality-of-life and savings/incomes, and amplifies *Inequality*.

[14] *See*: "Emefiele: Nigeria Spends 40% of FX on Importation of Petrol, Others". *This Day* (Nigerian newspaper) October 15, 2021. https://www.thisdaylive.com/index.php/2021/10/15/emefiele-nigeria-spends-40-of-fx-on-importation-of-petrol-others/.

b. The affected Emerging Markets countries (many of whom don't have viable manufacturing industries) will be much less able to import machinery/equipment and spare-parts, which in turn greatly reduces economic output, job-creation, Business Confidence, Consumer Confidence, incomes, GDP and foreign currency earnings, which in turn causes and amplifies additional currency devaluation/depreciation and *Inequality*.
c. The associated reduced foreign currency earnings results in the declines of the affected Emerging Markets countrys' reported foreign-currency reserves, which in turn can reduce their sovereign credit ratings, government-credibility, Political-Capital, FDI and foreign investment.
d. The resultant/associated reduced government earnings, economic output and GDP, reduces Social Services and government expenditures, and increases *Inequality*, all of which can increase political-risk and social-unrest in Emerging Markets countries.

10. *US Dollar Dominance* and US MCN Dominance amplifies the costs of "*defending*" the local currencies of Emerging Markets countries (from arbitrageurs/speculators and temporary imbalances) especially for countries that don't export a lot of goods/services to the US (the "Low Dollar-Goods-Countries"). Such currency-defense often depletes the foreign currency reserves of many Emerging Markets countries, which in turn affects their sovereign credit ratings, government-credibility, government expenditures, FDI, etc. Some of the results and significant opportunity-costs are that such Emerging Markets countries cannot import much-needed machinery, equipment, parts, fuels, food, medicines, materials, etc., which in turn reduces economic output, job-creation, income, savings, quality-of-life, etc. Thus, in an era of *US Dollar dominance*, currency-defense by many Emerging Markets countries is increasingly less-useful (especially for Low-Dollar-Goods-Countries), and instead, Currency-Unions in geographical continents ("*Continental Currencies*" supported by increased intra-regional/continental trade) may be more viable for Emerging Markets.
11. The "*Original Sin*" *phenomenon* and the associated balance sheet mismatches (of Emerging Markets companies), increases the default rates, borrowing costs, profitability and growth prospects of Emerging Markets companies and financial institutions, which in turn negatively affects labor markets, job creation, household

dynamics, incomes, savings, employment, and both corporate and government expenditures on non-interest items and quality of life. *US Dollar Dominance* artificially increases the borrowing costs of other countries, and especially Emerging Markets countries because US dollar benchmarks and economic-trends are used to price, or are indirectly incorporated into prices of such foreign country debt, and the associated mis-matches.

12. *US MNC Dominance* causes over-reliance on US government and private-company policies (economic, social and political policies) which when combined with religious and cultural differences, can cause political turmoil, social unrest, *Inequality* and reduced government/corporate revenues, corporate/government spending, job-creation and quality-of-life in Emerging Markets countries. Emerging Markets countries' knowledge that *US Dollar Dominance* and/or *US MNC Dominance* is highly detrimental to them can drastically reduce their trust in US government policies and the credibility of the US government and can push such countries toward competing super-powers such as China, Russia and the EU (which puts the US at a significant disadvantage in global politics). That may have been confirmed by China's execution of bilateral local-currency settlement agreements with more than twenty countries during 2008–2020 (i.e. such country-pairs will use their own local currencies to settle bilateral finance and trade transactions).
13. *US Dollar Dominance* (and associated local currency volatility and devaluation) negatively affects the pricing of goods/services, price-discovery processes, product marketing/sales and corporate/product strategy in Emerging Markets (i.e. there is mostly US dollar-based pricing and not local currency pricing or producer-currency-pricing).
14. *US Dollar Dominance* amplifies the negative effects of Pandemics epidemics because: (1) it increases Emerging Markets countrys' costs of buying both imported and domestically-produced medicines and equipment; (2) it drastically increases the economic/social/psychological costs of international and domestic travel which in turn, reduces tourism, on which many Emerging Markets are heavily dependent for foreign currency and revenues; (3) it increases the domestic prices of goods/services which in turn, reduces overall day-to-day retail economic activity and the exports of commodities, on which many Emerging Markets are heavily dependent for foreign currency and revenues.

15. *US Dollar Dominance* (and associated local currency volatility and devaluation) creates two or three-tiers of cities in some low-manufacturing-capacity and high-manufacturing-capacity Emerging Markets countries wherein major cities are highly dollarized or more dollarized and have higher levels of US dollar pricing and higher real asset inflation and declining quality-of-life; whereas small/medium cities have less US dollar pricing and lower real asset prices. Some prime examples are Lagos, Abuja and Port Harcourt in Nigeria which are first-tier cities that have higher/above-average US dollar pricing—as a result, these cities attract low-skilled low-income migrants, and foster increasing slums/over-crowding, Inequality and public health problems. In Poland, Warsaw is a first-tier city that has above-average dollar pricing compared to other Polish cities. In Mexico, Mexico City, Cancun and border-cities (cities nearest to the US border) and some of the coastal cities cities/towns have above-average US dollar-pricing compared to other Mexican cities.
16. The dominance of US MNCs and the US dollar often extends/amplifies the harmful effects of *Economic Sanctions* to non-sanctioned countries (many of whom are weak-economy Emerging Markets countries). That is primarily because many sanctioned countries (such as Russia, China and Iran) are *Super-Powers* or "*Regional-Powers*" that (economically, financially and militarily) assist/assisted neighboring smaller dependent countries. Russia (CIS states, and the Baltics), China (ASEAN countries, Vietnam, Myanmar, Cambodia, Pakistan, Thailand and African countries) and Iran (Lebanon, Syria, Iraq, Pakistan, Azerbaijan, Afghanistan, Oman and Armenia) all have significant economic ties with their neighboring countries and "dependent" countries.
17. The economic/social/political damages inflicted on Emerging Markets countries by *US Dollar Dominance* and *US MNC Dominance* can reduce US MNCs' actual and potential currency-adjusted and inflation-adjusted revenues/profits from such Emerging Markets due to currency depreciation, reduced disposable income, rampant inflation, import tariffs, investment losses, asset deflation, job losses and increased personal/corporate bankruptcies in such Emerging Markets countries.
18. *US Dollar Dominance* is socially/psychologically/politically amplified by:

a. *US MNC dominance* in international trade and finance.
b. US military presence and controversial formal/informal military and political "*interventions*" around the world.
c. US foreign aid to Emerging Markets (some of which is delivered in US dollars).
d. US dominance in worldwide media and entertainment which provides trust (and acceptability of US culture and policies), hope, entertainment and aspiration to many around the world.
e. The US government's financing and dominance of international organizations that should have intervened (such as the United Nations, the World Bank and WTO).
f. The US Federal Reserve's large balance sheet, which has grown significantly since 1999 (see Chart 1), and such rapid growth coincided with the significant devaluations/depreciations of many Emerging Markets' local currencies versus the US dollar during the same time period as indicated in **Appendix-1** below (and in some cases depreciated by more than 4000% during that period). Also see Foerster and Leduc (2019). The strange and ironic phenomenon is that the US Fed's large-scale purchases of mortgage bonds, agency securities/instruments and US Treasuries (during 1999–2019) were supposed to increase the supply of US dollars in the global economy, and despite that, and as indicated in **Appendix-1**, many Emerging Markets currencies depreciated (versus the US dollar) mostly due to scarcity of US dollars in those Emerging Markets countries. That indicates that the incremental/extra supply of US dollars (released by QE in 1999–2019) didn't reach many Emerging Markets countries but instead were used or invested in the US and in countries (mostly developed countries) whose US dollar reserves increased and/or who sold their US bonds/notes to the US Federal Reserve. That phenomenon is henceforth referred to as the "*Preferred-Destination and Preferences Effect*" of monetary policy or quantitative easing (and it may confirm both the "*Zero-Sum Investment-Bias and Purchasing-Power Windfall*" and the *Investment-Concentration Effect* mentioned above and in Nwogugu (2019c)

19. *US MNC Dominance* and *US Dollar Dominance* often reduces human development, quality-of-life and "effective" household incomes/savings in Emerging Markets because: (1) it often trans-

fers low-income, dead-end low-skill non-transferable-skill labor-intensive jobs to Emerging Markets, and doesn't promote the acquisition of transferable-skills and high-tech skills; (2) it displaces local/domestic manufacturers—that is, the aggregate-jobs and aggregate-incomes created are often less than aggregate-jobs/aggregate-incomes/aggregate-motivation lost in several dimensions such as transferable-skills, high-tech skills, entrepreneurship, innovation, real-incomes (currency-adjusted, political-risk-adjusted and inflation-adjusted incomes), disposable-incomes, human aspirations; motivation; etc.; and (3) it often increases waste, over-crowding in cities and environmental pollution in Emerging Markets countries (most of which have low-regulation, low-enforcement and high-corruption regimes and weak environmental laws and don't have sufficient resources to enforce environmental and public health laws). Mexico, China, India and some southeast Asian countries are examples of these problems. "*Effective household incomes/savings*" in Emerging Markets means "net" incomes/savings after deducting the economic/financial/social costs of pollution, illness, mental health problems, over-crowding, travel, formal taxes, "informal" taxes, bribes, and so on; and the incremental Opportunity Costs of taking on such "imported" jobs that are directly/indirectly provided by US MNCs.

20. *US Dollar Dominance* is very likely to amplify/exacerbate the publicized harmful effects of cyptocurrencies in Emerging Markets countries[15] (e.g. money-laundering, human trafficking, illegal

[15] *See:* "*What the Chinese Bank Crackdown Means for Crypto Investors*". By Emma Newbery. May 20, 2021. https://www.fool.com/the-ascent/buying-stocks/articles/what-the-chinese-bank-crackdown-means-for-crypto-investors/?source=eptyholnk0000202&utm_source=yahoo-host&utm_medium=feed&utm_campaign=article.

See: "*China vows to crack down on bitcoin mining, trading activities*". May 21, 2021. https://finance.yahoo.com/news/china-says-crack-down-bitcoin-145443522.html.

See: Chaudhary, A. & Singh, S. (Sept. 17, 2020). "India Plans To Introduce Law To Ban Cryptocurrency Trading". *Economic Times Of India*. https://economictimes.indiatimes.com/news/economy/policy/government-plans-to-introduce-law-to-ban-cryptocurrency-trading/articleshow/78132596.cms.

See: India To Propose Cryptocurrency Ban, Penalising Miners, Traders—Source. By Aftab Ahmed and Nupur Anand. March 15, 2021.

See: Putin Says Russia Must Stop Illegal Cross-Border Crypto Transfers. By Anna Baydakova. Wed, March 17, 2021. https://finance.yahoo.com/news/putin-says-russia-must-stop-170337080.html.

gambling, extortion, prostitution; etc.) because: (1) Emerging Markets central banks don't have sufficient control of cryptocur-

See: "*Over 13% of all Proceeds of Crime in Bitcoin are Now Laundered Through Privacy Wallets*". 09 December, 2020. https://www.elliptic.co/blog/13-bitcoin-crime-laundered-through-privacy-wallet.

See: "*Ex-Microsoft Engineer Gets Prison Sentence For Bitcoin Tax Fraud*". By Shehan Chandrasekera. Nov 9, 2020. https://www.forbes.com/sites/shehanchandrasekera/2020/11/09/ex-microsoft-engineer-gets-prison-sentenced-for-bitcoin-tax-fraud/?sh=656419c062cd.

See: "*Top cryptocurrency scams of 2019—and how most hackers got away with it*". By Sophia Ankel and Prabhjote Gill. *Business Insider India*. Dec 27, 2019. https://www.businessinsider.com/the-biggest-cryptocurrency-scams-and-arrests-of-2019-so-far-2019-8?IR=T.

See: "*Romance fraud, cryptocurrency risks and money laundering in Asia Pacific*". July/August 2019. https://www.fraud-magazine.com/article.aspx?id=4295006266.

See: "*Chinese cryptocurrency scam ringleaders jailed in US$2.25 billion Ponzi scheme involving PlusToken platform*". By Sidney Leng. December 1, 2020. https://www.scmp.com/economy/china-economy/article/3112115/chinese-cryptocurrency-scam-ringleaders-jailed-us225-billion.

See: "*How Terrorists Use Cryptocurrency in Southeast Asia—The first transactions involving cryptocurrencies have been made recently by Islamic State-linked terrorist networks in the Philippines*". By V. Arianti and Kenneth Yeo Yaoren. June 30, 2020. https://thediplomat.com/2020/06/how-terrorists-use-cryptocurrency-in-southeast-asia/.

See: "*Two Chinese Nationals Charged with Laundering Over $100 Million in Cryptocurrency from Exchange Hack—Forfeiture Complaint Details Over $250 Million Stolen by North Korean Actors*". US Dept. Of Justice. March 2, 2020. https://www.justice.gov/opa/pr/two-chinese-nationals-charged-laundering-over-100-million-cryptocurrency-exchange-hack.

See: "*Lawsuits Filed Against Binance, Bitmex and Other Crypto Companies*". April 07, 2020. By M.D. Rockybul Hasan. https://atozmarkets.com/news/lawsuits-filed-against-binance-bitmex-other-crypto-companies/. ("US law firm, Roche Cyrulnik Freedman and Selendy & Gay PLLC, recently filed eleven class-action lawsuits. The firm has targeted many members of the crypto industry. The company, which represents crypto investors, has targeted a total of 42 defendants. Lawsuits filed against some of the biggest crypto exchanges, including Binance and BitMEX, as well as their founders and other officials.... Targeted companies operate in many countries around the world. This includes the United States itself, as well as Canada, China, Japan, Hong Kong, Switzerland, Israel and many others. The lawsuits also alleged that the defendants violated federal securities laws and misled investors by inducing them to buy unregistered assets.... Defendants include crypto issuers and exchanges, including KuCoin, BitMEX, Bprotocol, Status, Block.one, Civic and Binance. The class action names executives such as Block.one CTO Dan Larimer and Binance CEO Changpeng Zhao").

See: "*GemCoin Founder Sentenced to ten Years for $147M Crypto Scheme*". Danny Nelson. January 12, 2021. https://www.yahoo.com/finance/news/gemcoin-founder-sentenced-10-years-231228865.html.

See: "*Bitcoin exchange owner who helped scam eBay buyers sentenced to ten years in prison*". By Mariella Moon. January 13, 2021. https://www.yahoo.com/finance/news/bitcoin-exchange-owner-ebay-car-scam-sentenced-093009069.html.

See: "*Owner of Crypto Exchange RG Coins Gets 10 Years in Prison for Laundering $5Million*". By Sebastian Sinclair. January 13, 2021. https://www.yahoo.com/finance/news/bitcoin-exchange-owner-ebay-car-scam-sentenced-093009069.html.

See: "*Centra Tech Co-Founder Handed Prison Term for $25 Million Crypto Fraud*". By Tanzeel Akhtar. Dec 16, 2020. https://www.coindesk.com/centra-tech-co-founder-handed-prison-term-for-25m-crypto-fraud.

See: "*Criminals hide 'billions' in crypto-cash—Europol*". By Shiroma Silva. February 12, 2018. https://www.bbc.com/news/technology-43025787.

See: "*Terrorist Use of Cryptocurrencies: Technical and Organizational Barriers and Future Threats*". By Cynthia Dion-Schwarz, David Manheim and Patrick B. Johnston. https://www.rand.org/pubs/research_reports/RR3026.html.

See: "*Cryptoqueen: How This Woman Scammed The World, Then Vanished*". 24 November 2019. https://www.bbc.com/news/stories-50435014.

See: "*Illegal Online Gambling Proliferates In China's Digital Economy*". By Kapronasia. December 1, 2020. https://www.kapronasia.com/china-payments-research-category/illegal-online-gambling-proliferates-in-china-s-digital-economy.html. This article stated in part, "One key takeaway from the crackdown is that China's digital economy lacks sufficiently robust anti-fraud and anti-money laundering controls. Despite the widely touted technological capabilities of firms like Alipay and WeChat Pay, criminals appear to have moved massive amounts of illicit funds through the e-wallets with relative ease. Many of the suspicious transactions were somehow overlooked".

See: "*EU will make Bitcoin traceable and ban anonymous crypto wallets in anti-money laundering drive*". By Tom Bateman with Reuters. Updated: 26/08/2021. https://www.euronews.com/next/2021/07/21/eu-will-make-bitcoin-traceable-and-ban-anonymous-crypto-wallets-in-anti-money-laundering-d.

See: "Cryptocurrency: rise of decentralised finance sparks 'dirty money' fears—'Know your customer' rules for banks and brokers underpin anti-money laundering efforts but are at risk due to DeFi". *Financial Times.* By Gary Silverman, September 14, 2021. https://www.ft.com/content/beeb2f8c-99ec-494b-aa76-a7be0bf9dae6.

See: "Crypto crimes surge in Asia; Bitcoin cause for divorce in South Korea". *The Daily Forkast.* May 28, 2021. https://forkast.news/video-audio/crypto-crimes-surge-in-asia-bitcoins-reason-for-divorce-in-s-korea-the-daily-forkast/. This article stated in part, "As crypto grows in size and magnitude, we look deeper into scams right now that are landing some more victims. Police in South Korea have arrested 14 individuals in a cryptocurrency fraud case estimated to have cost 69,000 investors, a total of US$3.85 billion. That brings the country's losses due to crypto fraud to—get this—US$5 billion over the past five years. This accounts for an increase from 41 cases in 2017 to 333 last year. And that is a huge jump. This trend is not unique to Korea. In Singapore, police recorded 393 cases of crypto crimes last year. That's 60 more than South Korea".

See: "China says all cryptocurrency-related transactions are illegal and must be banned". By Manish Singh, September 24, 2021. https://techcrunch.com/2021/09/24/china-says-all-cryptocurrency-related-transactions-are-illegal/?guccounter=1&guce_referrer=aHR0cHM6Ly93d3cuZ29vZ2xlLmNvbS8&guce_referrer_sig=AQAAAICiG6PkR%2D%2D_7KkrIf_HX7v5jHUeN0RxVcNkvGn4t1a62QuOxeIDVJsQoM6EIPcRPBeKj_Payi_dv9K-spISOi-acV6Kd4UJjxKJaK5ZRd3LcfnsAghV-mldbEza0xkpSxhtsSDhQnrcuWkqGufy4A5AS-WrSArjGVKQ2DyViyYwQ8.

rency exchanges and US dollar flows (i.e. the average cryptocurrency investor's and cryptocurrency exchange's sources of US dollars are varied and sometimes unregulated); (2) as of June 2021, and unlike many large Emerging Markets countries, the US government, the Japanese government and governments of "cryptocurrency centers" hadn't statutorily banned cryptocurrencies and hadn't banned the use of US dollars in trading/settlement of cryptocurrencies (however, during September 2021, the Chinese government officially banned all types of cryptocurrency trading and mining); (3) most cryptocurrency exchanges are MNCs and use US dollars for settling trades.

21. Current Antitrust laws are often designed for, and are enforced within specific jurisdictions, and thus US antitrust and unfair-business-practices statutes often don't capture anti-competitive misconduct perpetrated by US MNCs in foreign countries. As of 2021, many Emerging Markets countries didn't have any or comprehensive antitrust and unfair-business-practices statutes. In the context of such regulatory-omissions (and the prevalence of corruption and weak-enforcement in Emerging Markets), US MNC dominance can harm Emerging Markets countries by US MNCs' perpetration of unfair business practices and antitrust/competition misconduct in those countries.
22. *US Dollar Dominance* and *US MNC dominance* compels Emerging Markets governments and MNCs to politically lobby US federal and state governments and to influence political-election processes in the US (and to illegally influence the US government, US judiciary and US law-enforcement systems), which in turn can significantly distort government policy-making, judicial decisions and electoral-processes in both the United States and such Emerging Markets countries. Some of the objectives of such multi-faceted lobbying and influence-seeking include but are not limited to access to US dollars, favorable US policies (monetary, trade and fiscal policies), reduction/waivers of economic sanctions, appointments of "favored politicians", and so forth. Under such increased "*Foreign Lobbying/Influence Burdens*", the risks of violations of the *Separation of Powers Doctrine*, the *Equal Protection Doctrine*, the *Freedom-Of-Speech Doctrine*, the *Right-To-Contract Doctrine*, the

See: "*China arrests 1,100 over cryptocurrency money laundering…China's bitcoin mines power nearly eighty percent of the global trade in cryptocurrencies*". June 10, 2021. https://www.straitstimes.com/asia/east-asia/china-arrests-1100-over-cryptocurrency-money-laundering.

Non-Delegation Doctrine and the *Due-Process Doctrines* increases significantly in both the United States and in such Emerging Markets countries. Because of their structure and policies, socialist and communist countries are more likely to be better able to handle such "*Foreign Lobbying/Influence Burdens*", than traditional "democratic systems". Also, because *US Dollar Dominance* and *US MNC Dominance* gives the US government an unfair advantage in international negotiations with foreign governments and countries, that increases the propensity for corruption and bribery among US government officials.

23. During 1995–2021, and partly through the *Continuing Import-Dependency* and the "*Zero-Sum Dependency & Purchasing-Power Windfall* phenomena, *US Dollar Dominance* increased the concentration of ownership of US dollars (and an increasing percentage of the total volume of global manufacturing activity) in the hands of relatively few countries that have very strong manufacturing sectors and are export-oriented (e.g. UK, USA, Mexico, Germany France, China, Japan, South Korea, Brazil, etc.). Thus, *US dollar dominance* progressively depletes the US dollar reserves of many Emerging Markets countries that don't have viable manufacturing sectors and are import-based economies which in turn, can negatively affect their FDI, sovereign credit ratings, growth prospects, quality of life, government credibility, savings/income, job creation and so forth. Similarly, *US Dollar Dominance* concentrated an increasing percentage of the total volume of global manufacturing activity in the hands of relatively few Emerging Markets countries (China, Indonesia, Mexico, Thailand, India, Brazil and South Korea) that have very strong manufacturing sectors, are export-oriented, but are low-regulation, low-enforcement, low-compliance, high-pollution countries. Thus, *US Dollar Dominance* has increased worldwide environmental pollution and improper waste management.
24. As *US Dollar Dominance* and *US MNC Dominance* increases, the *Purchasing Power Parity Theory* is increasingly invalidated primarily because of resultant artificially high demand for the US dollar and increased trade deficits/surpluses and increased dollar liabilities of foreign entities/countries, all of which occur in ways that violate logical relationships between exchange rates and purchasing power (and between exchange rates and interest rates), and the logical foundations of demand and supply.

25. During 1995–2021, and through the *Continuing Import-Dependency* and the "*Zero-Sum Dependency & Purchasing-Power Windfall* phenomena, *US Dollar Dominance* concentrated an increasing percentage of the total volume of global manufacturing activity in the hands of relatively few Emerging Markets countries (China, Indonesia, Mexico, Brazil, South Korea) that have very strong manufacturing sectors, are export-oriented, but are low-regulation low-enforcement low-compliance high-pollution countries. Thus, US dollar dominance has increased worldwide environmental pollution and improper waste-management.
26. *US Dollar Dominance* amplifies/exacerbates the *Global Pension Crisis* because: (1) as explained here, *US Dollar Dominance* devalues/depreciates the currencies of many countries which in turn, leads to decreased purchasing-power (of local currencies), leads to asset-deflation and un-realized/realized investment-losses in those countries, (2) *US Dollar Dominance* reduces the real purchasing-power of currencies of many countries; (3) outside the "top-ten major-currency" countries, most retirees hold the bulk of their assets in local currency and don't hedge their portfolios for currency and political risk; (4) outside the "top-ten major-currency" countries, a relatively small percentage of retirees hold dollar, pounds-sterling, Chinese-Yuan, Euro or Japanese-yen denominated assets; (5) as explained, *US Dollar Dominance* increases the default risks and currency mis-matches of foreign financial services companies (insurers, banks, investment-funds and securities brokers) that hold, insure or manage retirees' assets; (6) in many Emerging Markets, *US Dollar Dominance* negatively affects Consumer Confidence, Business Confidence, "*Government Confidence*" (confidence among government officials), government expenditures, corporate expenditures, income/savings, and so on; (7) the resulting low US dollar interest rates reduce cash interest/dividends paid to retirees (which affects consumer spending and quality of life) and compel retirees to rebalance their portfolios and invest in high-risk equities and alternative investments.
27. *US Dollar Dominance* amplifies/exacerbates market-volatility in stock and bond markets in many Emerging Market countries because: (1) as explained here, *US Dollar Dominance* devalues/depreciates the currencies of many countries which in turn, leads to significant currency-devaluation risk and political-risk, asset-deflation and un-realized/realized investment-losses that are often

priced into stock-prices and bond-prices in those countries, (2) *US Dollar Dominance* reduces the real purchasing-power of many legal currencies and also causes the *Continuing Import-Dependency* and the "*Zero-Sum Dependency & Purchasing-Power Windfall*"; (3) outside the "top-ten major-currency" countries, most investors hold a high percentage of their assets in local currency and don't hedge their portfolios for currency-risk and political risk; (4) outside the "top-ten major-currency" countries, a relatively small percentage of retail/institutional investors hold dollar, pounds-sterling, Chinese-Yuan, Euro or Japanese-yen denominated assets; (5) as explained, *US Dollar Dominance* increases the default risks and currency mis-matches of foreign financial services companies (insurers, finance companies, banks and securities brokers) that hold, insure or manage investors' assets; (6) US dollar dominance affects Consumer Confidence, Business Confidence, government expenditures, corporate expenditures, income/savings, etc.

28. *US Dollar Dominance* and *US MNC Dominance* can increase/amplify the negative actual and perceived psychological/social/political effects of Balance-of-Payments and/or Balance-of-Trade deficits in Emerging Markets. Such deficits can affect consumer confidence, business confidence, "*government confidence*", risk perception, regret minimization, expectations and so on.
29. *US Dollar Dominance* can cause "*Panic Policy-Formulation*" and "*Panic Dollarization*" in Emerging Markets countries, as exemplified by: (1) dollarization and subsequent reversal (de-dollarization) during 1990–2021 in Zimbabwe, Poland, Argentina, Peru and other countries, (2) strange Policy-Reversals (monetary, fiscal and social-welfare policies) during 1995–2021 in Emerging Markets such as Poland, Venezuela, Peru, Argentina, Nigeria, Zimbabwe, etc.; (3) volatile government subsidies and importation policies during 1990–2021 in Emerging Markets such as Nigeria; 4) inconsistent monetary policies during 1995–2021 in Emerging Markets (e.g. El Salvador, Nigeria, Zimbabwe, Zambia, Argentina, Venezuela, etc.); (5) domestic currency rebasing in Zambia and Zimbabwe and other Emerging Markets countries during 2000–2020.
30. *US Dollar Dominance* can reduce/dampen monetary transmission in Emerging Markets countries because: (1) it restricts the ability of Emerging Markets Central Banks to implement independent monetary policies; (2) it constrains US dollar supply that is needed for critical imports; (3) it increases the default-risk of, and reduces

the operating-flexibility of Emerging Markets banks, insurance companies and securities brokers, which in turn reduces their ability to comply with their Central Banks' monetary policies; (4) it distorts individuals' and corporate executives' Risk-Perception and decision-making processes (e.g. US dollar pricing, etc.).

31. *US Dollar Dominance* and *US MNC dominance* can increase Political Instability in both Emerging Markets and developed countries because it creates economic hardship, asset-deflation, Pension-Crisis, perceived dependency on a foreign country and social unrest that are often wrongly attributed to leading domestic politicians. For example: (1) the cumulative number of *Active Political-Reversals* in both developed countries and Emerging Markets countries during 1985–2015 more than twice exceeded the same metric during 1955–1984 (*Active Political-reversal* means a major adverse political event at the "national" level such as a vote-of-no-confidence in a Prime-Minister/President of a country, or the dissolution of the national parliament/congress, or a change of political power in Presidential/Prime-Minister elections, or a military coup or popular mass protest that results in the removal of a President/Prime-Minister or the national Parliament such as the *Arab Spring*; etc.); (2) the cumulative number of *Voter-reversals* in State Governor elections in the USA during 1990–2021 more than twice exceeded the same metric during 1960–1989 (*Voter-reversal* means that a different major political party—Democrats or Republicans—other than the incumbent party won a state governor election); (3) after both the 2016 and 2020 national elections in the USA, there were wide-spread accusations (by US government officials, US political party officials, PACs and individuals) of foreign interference in the elections by China and Russia.
32. *US Dollar Dominance* and *US MNC Dominance* can increase the negative effects of protectionist policies of large export-oriented economies such as the US, China, Japan and the EU.
33. *US Dollar Dominance* exaggerates/inflates the perceived/actual relative sizes/values of the national economies of the US and *US-Dollar-Favored Countries* because:
    a. The resultant "Windfalls" and currency devaluations/depreciations of Emerging Markets currencies (that benefit *US-Dollar-Favored Countries*) grossly understates the true values of Emerging Markets national economies.

b. Such calculations of sizes/values of national economies are usually done using exchange rates for conversion into US dollars for comparability.
c. Partly because of the "Windfalls" and associated changes in Risk-Perceptions, the exchange rates don't accurately reflect the economic activity, knowledge, resources, institutions, infrastructure, "*viable/sustainable technology*" and human capital of Emerging Markets countries. "*Viable/sustainable technology*" refers to the net-value and use-value of technology after considering its positive/negative impact on global sustainability.
d. Collectively, the foregoing is referred to as the "*Dollar Exchange Rate Illusion*".

34. As *US Dollar Dominance* increases, the size of the typical Emerging Markets Central Bank's balance sheet becomes increasingly irrelevant to the value/exchange rate of its home currency, and such Central Bank's ability to successfully defend its domestic currency (the "*Assets and Exchange-Rate Gap*"). That's because:
    a. *US Dollar Dominance* invalidates PPP in many circumstances;
    b. *US Dollar Dominance* causes companies/entities in Emerging Markets countries to settle significant percentages of both their imports and exports in US Dollars (which may contravene such country's official monetary policies) which generates artificially high demand for US dollars;
    c. *US Dollar Dominance* causes companies/entities and government agencies in Emerging Markets countries to issue increasing volumes of US dollar-denominated debt which typically have much lower interest rates (which may contravene such country's official monetary policies) and which causes artificially high demand for US dollars.
35. Each of *US Dollar Dominance* and *US MNC Dominance* can transmit increasing and amplified versions of US shocks (e.g. climate, political, public health/COVID, economic, financial and technology shocks, and collectively the "*Transmitted Shock Versions*") to Emerging Markets countries (and even developed countries). The "*Transmitted Shock Versions*" are more severe and are or can be amplified by any of the following factors:
    a. The scarcity of, or significant demand for US dollars, and the fact that most Emerging Markets companies don't earn significant dollar revenues (to match their formal/informal dollar liabilities and exposures).

b. Most Emerging Markets countries don't have the sophisticated financial instruments (e.g. local swaps/derivatives markets) to hedge such significant risks and don't have the credibility, credit ratings and contacts to efficiently access the global swaps/derivatives markets. "Local" swaps/derivatives markets are different from "global" swaps/derivatives markets in terms of size, liquidity, products sophistication, credit-rating requirements, collateral requirements, trust and so on.
c. Loss of business confidence, consumer confidence and government confidence in Emerging Markets.
d. Emerging Markets' doubts about global issues and geopolitical risks.
e. Domestic politics, corruption and tribalism/ethnic-strife, inequality, declining quality of life and religious conflicts in Emerging Markets.
f. Domestic regulations, policy conflicts and policy prioritization in Emerging Markets.

The results are often further economic damages and currency depreciations/devaluations and associated problems in Emerging Markets.

36. For most Emerging Markets borrowers, the purported cost savings from borrowing in US dollars are far exceeded by the sum of the following: (1) the associated currency-depreciation risk (for both short-term and long-term loans); (2) the documentation and legal risks and the increased transaction costs, monitoring costs and administrative costs for borrowing in US dollars; (3) the costs of political insurance and economic-risk insurance against shocks that originate in the US; (4) the costs of the currency-mismatch (most of such borrowers don't earn substantial dollar-based revenues); and (5) the costs of lower employee productivity due to associated social/economic/political problems.
37. For countries that have relatively very high debt-to-GDP ratios and import/consume a lot of products that were made in China/Japan/ASEAN (such as the US and the European Union), *US Dollar Dominance*:
    a. Increases such dependency on China/Japan/ASEAN and reduces the viability of locally manufactured products because it makes China/Japan/ASEAN goods much cheaper. The dependency also reduces consumer confidence and business confidence (and increases inequality because of the associated loss of US jobs).

b. Causes an associated loss of US/EU jobs and US/EU inflation-adjusted corporate profits due to "substitution" with foreign/China/Japan/ASEAN goods (hereafter, "*Foreign Displacement*"). Import tariffs don't seem to affect *Foreign Displacement*, which increasingly affects the stock-market values and credit ratings of US and EU companies and governments as the dependency increases.
c. Reduces US interest rates because of increased foreign demand for US dollars, which in turn increases the propensity for, and actual consumer borrowing, corporate borrowing and government borrowing in the US/EU (the "*Increased-Debt Bias*"). Such borrowing substantially increases foreclosures, loan defaults, inequality, personal/corporate bankruptcies, substance abuse, marital divorces and mental health problems.
d. Causes the prices of real assets (e.g. real estate) in the US to increase rapidly mostly due to historically low US interest rates. That often results in inequality and inflated property values and more foreclosures.
e. Causes a reduction in US/EU wage growth (and a resultant increase in inequality) wherein US/EU wages don't increase as fast as their domestic prices of goods/services partly because of *Foreign Displacement*, and US/EU firms' efforts to hold down wages in order to be able to compete with foreign companies.
f. Causes and increases "*Excess Localized Inflation*" in large cities such as New York City, Los Angeles, London and Frankfurt. "*Excess Localized Inflation*" means that inflation rates in US/EU large cities are higher than in their smaller cities partly because the larger cities disproportionately benefit more from low US interest rates and *Foreign Displacement*.
g. Causes a progressively worsening vicious cycle and lock-in effect wherein US/EU consumers/companies increase their borrowing due to lower domestic or US interest rates and buy more imported China/Japan/ASEAN goods, but are increasingly less able to repay their debts partly due to low wage growth, *Foreign Displacement*, *Increased-Debt Bias*, higher inflation and *Excess ocalized Inflation*, all of which causes them to further increase their borrowing (collectively, the "*Debt-GDP Lock-in Effect*").
h. Causes a progressively worsening vicious cycle and lock-in effect wherein US/EU consumers/companies buy homes at ever increasing prices, default on their mortgage loans, which causes

"mortgage redlining" which in turn reduces the values of neighborhoods and makes it more difficult for borrowers to refinance, which causes more mortgage defaults (the "*Mortgage Lock-in Effect*").

38. Given the foregoing, *US Dollar Dominance* (and associated local currency volatility and devaluation/depreciation) and *US MNC dominance* can negatively affect Consumer Confidence, Business Confidence, Risk-Perception, Corporate Expenditures, Government Expenditures, Social-Welfare policies, Quality-of-Life, perceptions of Government-Quality, personal-aspirations, and household dynamics in both the USA and many Emerging Markets.

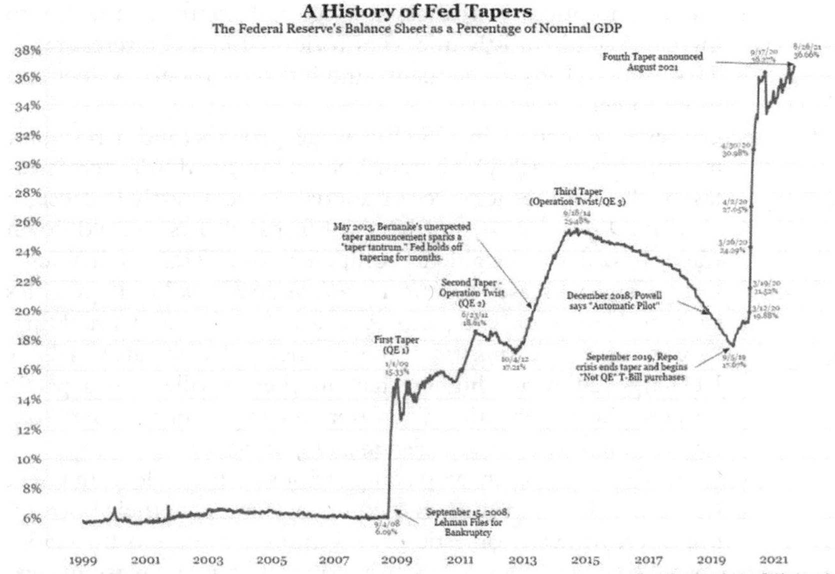

Chart-1: The US Federal Reserve Balance Sheet As A Percentage Of US Nominal GDP.

1.3 Possible Solutions For "US Dollar Dominance"

The main problems that existed in the global financial system during 1930–1975 are still recurring—such as significant and rapid currency devaluations, protectionism, illicit-money flows, disconnect between interest rates and currency rates, asymmetric adjustment (between the US and the rest of the world with regard to balance of payments) and unstable exchange rates. Merely devaluing the US dollar addresses the results (and not the root-causes) and will not solve the problems which can recur with another dominant currency such as the Euro or the Chinese Yuan. What's required are more comprehensive solutions that address the underlying imbalances, beliefs, biases, low regulation and restrictions that are causal factors. Some possible solutions for US dollar dominance are as follows:

1. Enter into a large-scale multilateral finance/trade settlement agreement wherein International Trade/Finance will be settled in any in any local-currency pair and or in any combinations of the top of five most-dominant currencies (ie. the US dollar, the Japanese Yen, the Chinese Yuan, and EU Euro and the UK Pound Sterling). There will be statutory "price-discounts" (in exchange rates) to encourage currency buyers/sellers to purchase/sell currency-baskets. There will be a mutually agreed upon method for determining the top-five global "Dominant Currencies" at the end of every five-year period. The multilateral settlement agreement will be strictly enforced by the United Nations (or a group of International Organizations such as the WTO and IMF).
2. Effect a large-scale multilateral finance/trade settlement agreement wherein (1) there will be "*Continental Currencies*" (such as the Euro) for each of Africa/MENA, Europe, US/Mexico/South-Americas, UK/Canada/Australia/New-Zealand and Asia/Pacific CIS; and (2) each of the five major-currency/Dominant-Currency countries (i.e. US dollar, the Japanese Yen, the Chinese Yuan, and EU Euro and the UK Pound Sterling) will contractually agree to provide "*Minimum Currency-Swap-Lines*" of a minimum amount in each calendar quarter for each of the four *Continental Currencies.* (3) International trade and finance transactions will be settled in any Continental Currency or in any local-currency pair and/or in any combinations of the top-five Dominant Currencies (i.e. the US dollar, the Japanese Yen, the Chinese Yuan, and EU Euro and the UK Pound Sterling). The quarterly volumes of the SwapLines can

only increase over time but cannot be reduced. Each continent will create and implement significant incentives and programs to increase intra-continental trade (and use of their *Continental Currency*) so that each *Continental Currency* will have sufficient and substantial underlying economic, social/cultural and political linkages and support to remain stable and "widely used". There will be a mutually agreed upon method for determining the top-five global "Dominant Currencies" at the end of every five-year period. The multilateral settlement agreement will be strictly enforced by the United Nations (or a group of International Organizations such as the WTO and IMF). Thus, countries in each continent will be more assured of sufficient amounts of "Dominant Currencies" for payments for critical foreign goods/services without the risks of ravaging currency devaluation. The "Continental Currencies" can be Central Bank Digital Currencies.

3. Enter into a large-scale multilateral settlement agreement wherein there will be a four-system "Currency-Area" regime and trade/finance originating in (buyer/issuer is based in) EU countries and the rest of Europe are settled in Euros; and finance/trade originating in (buyer/issuer is based in) Asian, Middle-East and African countries and Russia/CIS are settled in any of the "Top-Two Regional Currencies in that 'Currency-Area'" (i.e. Japanese Yen and Chinese Yuan); and finance/trade originating in (buyer/issuer is based in) US/Mexico/South-Americas are settled in any of the "Top-Two Regional Currencies in that 'Currency-Area'" (i.e. US Dollars or Canadian Dollars); and trade/finance originating in (buyer/issuer is based in) UK/Canada/Australia/New-Zealand/British-Caribbeans are settled in any of the "Top-Two Regional Currencies in that 'Currency-Area'" (i.e. Canadian Dollars or UK Pounds Sterling). Each of the five elected Dominant-Currency countries (the US dollar, the Japanese Yen, the Chinese Yuan, and EU Euro and the UK Pound Sterling) will contractually agree to provide "*Minimum Currency-Swap-Lines*" of a minimum amount in each calendar quarter for each of the other four Regional Currencies (to be shared among the respective countries in each such Currency-Area). The quarterly volumes of the swap lines can only increase over time. There will be a mutually agreed upon method for determining the "Regional Currencies" (in each designated Currency-Area) and the Dominant Currencies at the end of every five-year period. The multilateral settlement agreement will

be strictly enforced by the United Nations (or a group of International Organizations such as the WTO, IMF and BIS). The "*Regional Currencies*" and the Dominant Currencies can be Central Bank Digital Currencies.

4. Effect a large-scale multilateral finance/trade settlement agreement wherein all participating countries will agree that no one reserve currency will account for more than 25% of its total foreign currency reserves. This contractual provision can be achieved in the following ways:
    1. Each of the top-five Dominant Currency countries (i.e. US dollar, the Japanese Yen, the Chinese Yuan, EU Euro and the UK Pound Sterling) will enter into bilateral currency swaps with countries that are not in the top-ten Dominant Currency countries wherein it will pay its own currency and receive the counterparty's local currency. The net effect will be to increase holdings of the counterparty's currency.
    2. Each of the top-five Dominant Currency countries (i.e. US dollar, the Japanese Yen, the Chinese Yuan, EU Euro and the UK Pound Sterling) will enter into bilateral currency swaps with other top five countries except the US, wherein it will pay its own currency and receive the counterparty's local currency. The net effect will be to increase holdings of the counterparty's currency.
    3. If feasible and if the US participates, then each of the top-thirty dollar-reserve countries (that own the most US dollar reserves will enter into bilateral currency swaps with the US government wherein they will pay out their US dollars, and the US government will pay them foreign currencies.
    4. All participating countries will issue no more than 20% of their government bonds and corporate bonds/notes/bills and structured products in any one currency (except their local currency) in any calendar year (each country's government and companies can issue an unlimited amount of bonds/notes/bills in their local currency).
    5. All participating countries will bar/preclude their domestic institutional investors (on a consolidated basis), companies (on a consolidated basis) and banks (on a consolidated basis) from holding more than 25% of their assets and from holding more than 25% of their liabilities in any one currency (except their local currency) in any calendar year. Each country's institutional investors, banks and companies (all on a consolidated basis) can

hold an unlimited amount of assets and liabilities only in their local currency.

The rationale for such agreement is that in today's world, market share of currency reserves greatly affects global politics, economic power and *confidence* (consumer confidence, business confidence, government confidence and the credibility of governments).

5. Effect a large-scale multilateral finance/trade settlement agreement wherein each of the five Dominant-Currency countries (i.e. US dollar, the Japanese Yen, the Chinese Yuan, and EU Euro and the UK Pound Sterling) will contractually agree to provide "*Minimum Currency-Swap-Lines*" of a minimum amount in each calendar quarter to each country in Africa, Central/South America, Central/Eastern Europe Middle East, South-Asian countries and ASEAN (each a "Currency-Dependent Country"). For each Currency-Dependent Country, the quarterly volumes of the provided currency SwapLines: (1) can only increase over time but cannot be reduced; (2) will be indexed to both the trailing 18-month quarterly total import volume of such Currency-Dependent Country, and the trailing 18-month quarterly volumes of trade between the major-currency-country and such Currency-Dependent Country such that the Currency-Dependent Countries will have sufficient foreign currencies to import necessities without the risks of ravaging currency devaluation; (3) each participating Currency-Dependent Country will grant lower import-tariffs to each major-currency-country; (4) International finance/trade transactions will be settled in any local currency pair or in any one of the five Dominant Currencies. There will be a mutually agreed upon method for determining the top-five global "Dominant Currencies" at the end of every five-year period. The multilateral settlement agreement will be strictly enforced by the United Nations (or a group of International Organizations such as the WTO and IMF.
6. Effect a large-scale "two-scenario" multilateral finance/trade settlement agreement wherein:

   Option A:

   1. The bottom-performing fifty currencies (66% of whom must be Emerging Markets countries) that depreciated or were devalued most during the trailing ten years (the "Rebase Countries") will be rebased/revalued such that a "*Composite Exchange Rate*" (versus each such local currency) isn't less than 1:10 and such

currency rebasing will occur every two to four years (the "Rebase Term"). The *Composite Exchange Rate* is a trade-weighted and financial-transactions-weighted currency basket that consists of the top-five Dominant Currencies versus the Rebase Country's currency.

2. Each of the top-five Dominant Currencies will agree to provide ever-increasing quarterly volumes of currency swap lines to each of such Rebase Countries (perhaps indexed to their volumes of bilateral trade; and in adequate and ever-increasing quarterly volumes to eliminate ravaging currency devaluations).
3. International trade/finance will be settled in any local-currency pair and/or in any combinations of the top-five Dominant Currencies.
4. There will be a mutually agreed upon method for determining the top-five global "Dominant Currencies" at the end of every five-year period, and the multilateral settlement agreement will be strictly enforced by the United Nations (or a group of international organizations such as the WTO and IMF).
5. There will be the following additional adjustments:
   a. Each such Rebase Country will subsequently and statutorily adjust its export prices so that the effective prices of its exports remain stable.
   b. Each such Rebase Country will subsequently and statutorily adjust its labor prices (private and public sector employee salaries) so that the effective prices remain stable.
   c. Each such Rebase Country will subsequently and statutorily adjust prices of basic necessities (food, transportation, housing, healthcare) so that the effective prices remain stable.

Or, Option B:

1. The bottom-performing two Continental Currencies (50% of whom must be Emerging Markets currencies) that depreciated or were devalued most during the trailing ten years (the "Rebase-Continental Currencies") will be rebased/revalued such that a "*Composite Exchange Rate*" (versus each such Continental Currency) isn't less than 1:10 and such currency rebasing will occur every two to four years (the "Rebase Term"). The *Composite Exchange Rate* is a trade-weighted and financial-transactions-weighted currency basket that consists of the top-five Dominant Currencies versus the Rebase-Continental Currency.

2. Each of the top-five Dominant Currencies will agree to provide ever-increasing quarterly volumes of currency swap lines to countries in each continent covered by a Rebase Continental Currency (each a "Rebase Country") perhaps indexed to their volumes of bilateral trade, and in adequate and in ever-increasing quarterly volumes in order to eliminate ravaging currency devaluations.
3. International trade/finance will be settled in any local-currency pair and/or in any Continental Currency and or in any combinations of the top-five Dominant Currencies.
4. There will be a mutually agreed upon method for determining the top-five global "Dominant Currencies" at the end of every five-year period.
5. The multilateral settlement agreement will be strictly enforced by the United Nations (or a group of international organizations such as the WTO and IMF).
6. There will be the following additional adjustments:
    a. Each Rebase Country in each such Rebase Continent will subsequently and statutorily adjust its export prices so that the effective prices of its exports remain stable.
    b. Each Rebase Country in each such Rebase Continent will subsequently and statutorily adjust its labor prices (private and public sector employee salaries) so that the effective prices remain stable.
    c. Each Rebase Country in each such Rebase Continent will subsequently and statutorily adjust prices of basic necessities (food, transportation, housing, healthcare) so that the effective prices remain stable.

Some of the underlying premises of the above-mentioned solutions are that:

1. For any given currency, the *Willingness-to-provide-SwapLines* and the specific amount of currency SwapLines provided (by any of the top-five Dominant-Currency countries) is inversely proportional to the stability and "popularity" (number of users and absolute-volume of use) of the opposing currency. Thus, while each of the top-five-currency countries don't have much incentive to provide large currency SwapLines to most individual countries in Africa,

Latin America and Central/East Europe, the top-five-currency countries are more likely to provide much larger SwapLines to *Continental Currencies* and other top-five currency countries.
2. The advent and expected rapid growth of Chinese Central Bank "Digital Yuan" and the Japanese Central Bank "Digital Yen" may drastically change currency usage and finance/trade settlement patterns around the world.
3. Other possible or planned or pending Central Bank digital currencies (UK and EU) will also affect global currency usage and settlement patterns.

During 1995–2021, some countries such as China, Japan and India intentionally or unintentionally responded to *US MNC dominance* in the following ways:

1. Implementing *Import-Substitution* programs, and providing incentives for indigenes to buy locally manufactured goods.
2. Controlling foreign ownership in designated domestic industries.
3. Imposing import tariffs on imported products/services.
4. Forcing foreign companies to disclose their proprietary technology to domestic government agencies as a pre-condition for market-entry.
5. Changing their tax system.
6. In multi-stage negotiations during 2017–2020, Russia and China formally agreed to settle international trade and finance transactions between them in their own local currencies. China[16] has also

[16] *See*: "*China-Bangladesh Bilateral Currency Cooperation Enjoys Broad Prospects*". By Agencies. December 28, 2020. https://www.globaltimes.cn/page/202012/1211181.shtml. This article stated in part: "...In 2019, the cross-border RMB settlement between China and the neighboring countries registered RMB 3.6 trillion yuan, among which the trade in goods amounted to RMB 994.5 billion yuan, and the direct investment amounted to RMB 351.2 billion yuan. Furthermore, the total cross-border RMB payments and receipts between China and the countries along the B&R (Belt-And-road) reached over RMB 2.73 trillion yuan, among which the trade in goods amounted to RMB 732.5 billion yuan, and the direct investment to RMB 252.4 billion yuan.... Since 2008, China has signed the bilateral local currency settlement agreements with nine neighboring countries and the countries along the B&R such as Vietnam, Laos, Russia and Kazakhstan, and has signed the bilateral local currency swap agreements with the central banks or monetary authorities of twenty-three neighboring countries and the countries along the B&R such as Russia, Indonesia, the United Arab Emirates (the UAE), Egypt and Turkey. By the end of 2019, China's central bank, the People's Bank of China (PBC), had signed bilateral currency swap agreements with the central banks or monetary authorities of thirty-nine countries and regions, covering

signed other bilateral local currency settlement agreements with other neighboring countries such as Vietnam, Laos and Kazakhstan.

7. Signing long-term bi-lateral trade agreements with third-party countries and entities in third-party countries (e.g. Russia's oil/gas supplies to China; China's exports to African countries; etc.).
8. Each of China's and Japan's cumulative investment in US Treasuries exceeded US$1 trillion in each calendar year during 2010-2021, and that seems to have substantially lifted the international status, credibility, trustworthiness, Political Capital and Social Capital of their governments, Chinese MNCs and Japanese MNCs.
9. The Japanese and Chinese governments' 2010–2021 emphasis on corporate governance (a cornerstone of "*Abenomics*" in Japan) and strictly-enforced penalties for fraud and corruption have also substantially increased the international status, credibility, Political Capital and Social Capital of their governments, Chinese MNCs and Japanese MNCs.
10. More recently (1995–2021), India and China implemented programs to facilitate and drastically expand export-promotion, to develop their capital markets, and to encourage companies to list their shares in their domestic stock markets. Japan and South Korea implemented such programs earlier.

major developed and emerging economies in the world, as well as the major offshore RMB markets, totaling more than RMB 3.7 trillion yuan. In 2019, the PBC renewed the bilateral local currency swap agreements with the Centrale Bank van Suriname, Singapore Monetary Authority, Turkey Central Bank, European Central Bank and Hungary Central Bank, totaling RMB 683 billion yuan. In October, the Republic of Korea and China signed a deal to extend the bilateral currency swap agreement and expand the size to USD 59 billion. Though a late comer in the global reserve currency family, the RMB proved to be remarkably stable and resilient amid adverse and uncertain economic conditions in recent years, including during the Asian financial crisis in 1997 and the global financial crisis in 2008. Especially during the year of 2019 and 2020, despite headwinds from the ongoing trade tensions and unprecedented disruption caused by the Covid-19 pandemic, businesses globally are still increasing their use of RMB in international transactions…".

1.4 Causal Factors: Labor Regulations and Global-Value-Chains (GVCs)

The potentially significant effects of Labor regulations and GVCs (especially in MNCs and government agencies) on *Cross-Border Spillovers* were summarized in Chap. 1 of Volume-I of this two-book series (Nwogugu 2021b). Bargeron et al. (2015) and Aklamanu et al. (2016) analyzed the role of human resources management in post-M&A integration (and by extension, GVCs). Kim and Milner (2019)[17] discussed the influence of MNCs on foreign policy and International Trade (and by extension, on international labor markets and GVCs). Autor et al. (2017)[18] discussed changes in global labor dynamics.

[17] Kim and Milner (2019) noted that "………Multinational corporations (MNCs) play significant roles in shaping the global economy. For example, MNCs in the U.S., which has the world's largest economy, make disproportionate contributions to the national economy: they represent a very small number of total American firms (less than 1%), but a large fraction of GDP, exports, imports, research and development, and private-sector employee compensation; Specifically, U.S. MNC parent companies in 2016 constituted more than 24% of private sector GDP (value-added) and 26% of private-sector employee compensation (Bureau of Economic Analysis 2018a); U.S. MNCs are engaged in more than half of all U.S. exports and more than 40% of U.S. imports (Bureau of Economic Analysis 2018). Likewise, MNCs throughout the world dominate the global economy as well as their national economies. The OECD (2018) estimates that MNCs account for half of global exports, nearly a third of world GDP (28%), and about fourth of global employment. These firms all generate a significant share of their revenue from abroad as well. Importantly, their transnational activities have transformed the nature of international trade, investments, and technology transfers in the era of globalization. The extensive global value chains (GVCs) prevalent in today's world economy have been driven by how MNCs structure their global operations through outsourcing and offshoring activities. In fact, their decisions have enormous implications for a wide range of policy issues—such as taxation, investment protection, immigration—across many countries with different political and economic institutions. MNCs also may have strong political influence domestically. Indeed, their global economic dominance may go hand-in-hand with their powerful domestic political position……….".

[18] The abstract in Autor et al. (2017) states as follows: "………The fall of labor's share of GDP in the United States and many other countries in recent decades is well documented but its causes remain uncertain. Existing empirical assessments of trends in labor's share typically have relied on industry or macro data, obscuring heterogeneity among firms. In this paper, we analyze micro panel data from the U.S. Economic Census since 1982 and international sources and document empirical patterns to assess a new interpretation of the fall in the labor share based on the rise of "superstar firms." If globalization or technological changes advantage the most productive firms in each industry, product market concentration will rise as industries become increasingly dominated by superstar firms with high profits and a low share of labor in firm value-added and sales. As the importance of superstar firms increases, the aggregate labor share will tend to fall. Our hypothesis offers several testable

1.5 The Significant *Replicability/Reproducibility Crisis* in Academic Research

The significant *Replicability/Reproducibility Crisis* in academia was summarized in Chap. 1 of Volume I of this two-book series (Nwogugu 2021b), has been widely discussed in the academic literature, and renders most published academic research meaningless. Thus, all the empirical research cited in this book should be read with caution.

1.6 The Intentional Lack Of Emphasis On *Standards-of-Review* (Constitutional Law)

As in Nwogugu (2012), the constitutional law analysis in this book intentionally omits in-depth discussion of *standards-of-review* for constitutional law issues (i.e. *Rational-Basis* versus *Intermediate Scrutiny* versus *Strict Scrutiny* which is typical in US jurisprudence) because:

1. Such classifications by themselves are suspect and can introduce significant and unwarranted discretion and bias in judicial reasoning. The issue is that persons' rights should not be so varied in relevance or importance, and any such differences can be (or are already) accommodated in *Balancing-Of-Interests tests* and *Cost—Benefit Analysis*. That is, applying such classifications can result in "double-counting", repetition or mis-application (by judges and or juries) of criteria used in determining the appropriate *standard-of-review* or the constitutionality of events/statutes/transactions, much to the disadvantage of persons whose rights have been infringed.
2. Many judges are not technical experts in the matters and statutes being litigated and without such knowledge, it can be difficult to

predictions: industry sales will increasingly concentrate in a small number of firms; industries where concentration rises most will have the largest declines in the labor share; the fall in the labor share will be driven largely by between-firm reallocation rather than (primarily) a fall in the unweighted mean labor share within firms; the between-firm reallocation component of the fall in the labor share will be greatest in the sectors with the largest increases in market concentration; and finally, such patterns will be observed not only in U.S. firms, but also internationally. We find support for all of these predictions……". The decline in labor's share of GDP in many developed countries during 2000–2018 is significant evidence of Globalization, *Cross-Border Spillovers* and global *Market-Integration* (of international labor markets).

assign a specific *standard-of-review* to a statute or transaction or a group of persons.

3. Where a judge or a group of judges are not technical experts, they usually rely on experts who unfortunately, are or can be subject to lobbying, coercion and other influences and don't have the same physical protections as judges.
4. When applying *standards-of-review*, the costs of false-positives and false-negatives in such classifications can be significant.
5. Such classifications don't always advance the public interest, social welfare or individuals' rights.
6. Such classifications sometimes result in double-counting/repetition or mis-application (by judges and or juries) of criteria used in determining the appropriate *standard-of-review* or the constitutionality of events/statutes/transactions, much to the disadvantage of persons whose rights have been infringed.

1.7 Behavioral Bias Indicators

When aggregated at the national economy level, the Economic Psychology and Constitutional Political Economy factors/relationships introduced in this book combine to create a class of complex systems, behavioral operations research, MacroEconomic and MacroFinance indicators which are hereby referred to as the "Behavioral Bias Indicators". These indicators have not been properly recognized in the economics/finance, Internatioanl Political Economy, behavioral operations research or psychology literatures and are not tracked. Niamir et al. (2018), Nakagawa et al. (2012), Korniotis and Kumar (1993), Acquier et al. (2017), Schnellenbach and Schubert (2015), Stout (2017), Mirkina (Sept. 2018), Han (2018), Sen and Sinha (2017), Bather and Burnaby (2004), Sen and Sinha (2017), and Rosenbaum et al. (2012) concluded or implied that human biases can affect national economies, although the links they established or theorized were indirect and they didn't discuss the issue of *Behavioral Bias Indicators.*

1.8 Causal Factors: Franchising and Business-Opportunity Networks

Franchising and Business-Opportunity Networks are increasing in popularity around the world and account for more than 33% of the domestic retail industry in some countries such as the US. Because they are standardized, Franchising and Business-Opportunities are both Financial Stability and Cross-border Integration causal factors. Nwogugu (2009, 2019a, 2019b) analyzed franchising and Business-Opportunities.

1.9 Causal Factors: Social Capital and Social Networks

The extensive literature on Social Networks, Social Capital and Cross-border Spillover Effects are summarized in Volume I of this two-volume series.

1.10 New Sources of International Law (International Criminal Law and International Administrative Law)?

The traditional sources of International Law have been the following:

1. The rulings of contractually-accepted international adjudicative fora such as the International Criminal Court, the International Court of Justice (ICJ) and the Inter-American Court of Human Rights.
2. Laws/statutes that have been mutually agreed to by nations through conventions, agreements and treaties—including laws/regulations emanating from the United Nations and similar International Organizations.
3. "Customary" International Law.
4. Bilateral and multilateral international trade agreements.

In addition to the foregoing, and as a direct result of *Cross-Border Spillovers* and evolving geopolitical factors, the following can be deemed to be new classes of International Law:

1. Binding and non-binding "standards" and regulations that are created by internationally accepted non-governmental organizations and international Trade-Associations such as FASB (USA), IASB, SASB (USA), International Swap Dealers Association (ISDA), International Capital Markets Association (ICMA), and so on. Given their nature, functions and worldwide use and similarity to guidelines issued by government administrative agencies, and the

fact they are often incorporated into administrative laws, statutes and regulations, most of these are International quasi-Administrative Laws. Also, some countries have incorporated them into their Criminal Law statutes and case-law (i.e. as standards-of-behavior for evaluation of deviance).

2. Statutes and Administrative Law that are created by the national governments of economically or militarily dominant countries (such as the USA, United Kingdom, Russia, China and European Union), wherein such statutes are used extensively in International Trade, finance and business by MNCs, and are informally or formally adopted by other countries (especially neighboring or dependent countries and former colonial countries). Examples include the Dodd-Frank Act (USA), Sarbanes Oxley Act (USA), the EU's Patent/Trademark Laws, UK Company/Corporate Law, and the EU's Carbon Border-Adjustment Mechanism[19] (Climate-Change taxes), all of which affect MNCs and the many foreign companies that do business in the US, the UK and the EU.

1.11 The Chapters

This book: (i) analyzes problems in, and the current state of international risk regulation; and summarizes the problems in the institutions that monitor risk; and (ii) analyzes weaknesses in interpretation of constitutional laws, which may affect and are intertwined with risk management, Geopolitics and Cross-border Spillovers. One of this book's aims is to analyze *Complex Systems* and the "*Reasoning*" and "*Preferences*" of government and corporate actors in order to develop better Economic Psychology, Computer Science, Decision Science, and Artificial-Intelligence/ML models of Geopolitical Risk, Public Policy, banking policy and International Capital Flows, all of which are increasingly automated and are important decision factors for Investment Managers, Boards of Directors, research institutes and government officials.

Chapter 2 discusses the unconstitutionality and failure of the Dodd-Frank Act and its associated Economic Psychology effects. "Restoring American Financial Stability Act" of 2010 ("RAFSA" or the "Dodd-Frank

[19] *See*: European Union (2021). *Carbon Border Adjustment Mechanism*. https://ec.europa.eu/taxation_customs/green-taxation-0/carbon-border-adjustment-mechanism_en.

Act") was the first set of statutes in any country that attempted to simultaneously address the Global Financial Crisis, Global Financial Stability, Global Systemic risk, consumer protection, sustainable growth, the national securities law framework, the structure of the executive branch of the federal government and delegation of powers to federal government agencies (to the detriment of state governments). Other countries/jurisdictions have enacted statutes that are similar to RAFSA.[20] Canada, Brazil and Asian countries have also introduced similar statutes. The United Kingdom introduced the *Vickers Report*, which is similar to the *Volcker Rule* (the Vickers Report has the same purpose of the Volcker Rule but it has different methods, and is based on the ring-fence and not on the separation of commercial and investment banks). The EU also released the *Report of the European Commission's High-level Expert Group on Bank Structural Reform* (aka *Liikanen Group Report*) which addresses such differences. The European Union enacted the European Market Infrastructure Regulation (EMIR),[21] the Markets in Financial Instruments Directive II and Related Regulation (MiFID II and MIFIR),[22] the new Capital Requirements Directive and Regulation (CRD IV)[23] and other statutes. However, RAFSA and similar statutes in many countries/jurisdictions are inefficient, have not generated the expected sustainable growth and have failed to address the fundamental problems in financial systems; and parts of RAFSA are unconstitutional.

Chapter 3 analyzes the unconstitutionality of Credit Rating Agencies (CRAs) (and their ratings opinions) and government bailouts/bail-ins, and their associated Economic Psychology effects. Chapter 3 explains why government bailouts/bail-ins are motivated by Constitutional Political Economy issues, are unconstitutional and have not worked well (while US law is used, the same principles are applicable in most common-law

[20] *See*: Shearman & Sterling, *Dodd-Frank, UK, EU & Other Regulatory Reforms* (2013) at http://www.shearman.com/dodd-frank/ [Accessed July 1, 2013].

[21] *See*: Regulation 648/2012 on OTC derivatives, central counterparties and trade repositories [2012] OJ L201/1.

[22] *See*: FSA (UK) (2012), Review of The *Markets in Financial Instruments Directive II*. Available at: http://www.fsa.gov.uk/about/what/international/mifid.

See: DIRECTIVE 2008/10/EC OF THE EUROPEAN PARLIAMENT AND OF THE COUNCIL of 11 March 2008. Available at: http://eur-lex.europa.eu/LexUriServ/LexUriServ.do?uri=OJ:L:2008:076:0033:0036:EN:PDF.

[23] Directive 2006/48 relating to the taking up and pursuit of the business of credit institutions [2006] OJ L177/1.

countries). During 2007–2020 many governments implemented bailouts and bail-ins of both banks and companies in industry. Many of those bailouts[24] and bail-ins have proven to be very costly and inefficient because: (i) the operating performances of the bailed-out and bailed-in companies have been sub-par since the government interventions; (ii) the bailouts/bail-ins proved to be "cheap" capital at the expense of taxpayers; (iii) the bailouts and bail-ins were unconstitutional in most instances; (iv) the bailouts and bail-ins amplified the too-big-to-fail syndrome—and even the "orderly-liquidation" processes and principles set out in statutes such as the Dodd-Frank Act still facilitate the too-big-to-fail syndrome. Credit ratings around the world have been dominated by Moody's (USA), S&P (USA and Fitch (France) which together account for more than 85% of the credit ratings in the world. Around the world, credit ratings are pervasive and have significant and lasting effects in almost all aspects of sustainability, corporate growth and profitability, financial stability and national economies. Nwogugu (2021) and other researchers have argued that credit ratings and credit rating agencies (CRAs)[25] have been largely politicized because: i) through their licensing and regulation functions, government agencies can coerce rating agencies; and in addition, the business models of CRAs often distorts their ratings-accuracy; ii) through political lobbying, bribery and use of investment banks (that can steer issuers away from a CRA), issuers can influence CRAs; iii) the business/compensation models of CRAs often distorts their ratings-accuracy.[26] There have been significant debates about the unconstitutionality of unsolicited credit ratings. Credit Rating Agencies and their ratings also raise the constitutional law issues of the *Delegation Doctrine*, the *Equal Protection Doctrine*, the *Separation of Powers Doctrine* and the *Right-to-Contract Doctrine*. Nwogugu (2021a) and other researchers have argued for significant reform of CRAs; and have criticized credit rating agencies for their inaccuracy and inherent conflicts of interest in ratings.[27] Many parties have sued CRAs for

[24] *See*: Chwieroth and Walter (2020), Copelovitch et al. (2016), Carruthers (2013), and Banerji et al. (2018).

[25] *See*: Barta and Johnston (2017), Iyengar (2012), Mennillo and Sinclair (2019), Abdelal and Blyth (2015), Brummer and Loko (2014), Kiff et al. (2012), and Kruck (2016).

[26] *See*: Coffee (2011), Darbellay (2013), Amtenbrink and Heine (2013), European Commission (2015), Gaillard and Harrington (2016), Copelovitch et al. (2016), Nwogugu (2021) and Kruck (2016).

[27] *See*: "Financial Crisis Inquiry Commission – Final Report-Conclusions-January 2011". http://www.gpo.gov/fdsys/pkg/GPO-FCIC/pdf/GPO-FCIC.pdf.

inaccurate ratings and/or deception[28]—such as investors (e.g. pension

See: Casey, K. (February 6, 2009). "*In Search of Transparency, Accountability, and Competition: The Regulation of Credit Rating Agencies*". *Remarks at "The SEC Speaks in 2009"*. *US SEC*. http://www.sec.gov/news/speech/2009/spch020609klc.htm.

See: "Ratings agencies suffer 'conflict of interest', says former Moody's boss". Rupert Neate. *The Guardian*; 22 August 2011. https://www.theguardian.com/business/2011/aug/22/ratings-agencies-conflict-of-interest.

See: Kerwer (2004), Gaillard (2014), Frost (2007), Bartels and Weder di Mauro (2013), Blodget (2011), European Commission (2016), and Gärtner et al. (2011).

[28] *See*: "*SEC Sues Morningstar's Former Credit Ratings Agency*". By Bernice Napach. February 17, 2021. https://www.thinkadvisor.com/2021/02/17/sec-sues-morningstars-former-credit-ratings-agency/.

See: *US SEC vs. Morningstar Credit Ratings LLC* (US District Court for the Southern District Of New York, USA; Case #: 21-CV-1359). https://www.sec.gov/litigation/complaints/2021/comp-pr2021-29.pdf?utm_medium=email&utm_source=govdelivery.

See: *Jindal Power Limited vs. ICRA Limited* (Delhi High Court, India) (court stated the permitted basis for issuers to file lawsuits against CRAs; court stated that CRA regulations cannot be contracted away by CRAs and their clients). https://indiankanoon.org/doc/54995907/.

See: *SERI Infrastructure Finance Ltd. vs. Fitch Rating India Pvt. Ltd.* (Calcutta High Court; India). http://164.100.79.153/judis/kolkata/index.php/casestatus/viewpdf/APOT_380_2012_17092012_J_21_220.pdf.

See: *First Leasing Company of India vs. ICRA* (Madras High Court, India). https://www.lawyerservices.in/First-Leasing-Company-of-India-Limited-Versus-ICRA-Limited-2000-06-23.

See: *Credit Rating Agencies Dodge Investors' Lawsuits*. September 12th, 2016. By: Brad Fleming. http://ipjournal.law.wfu.edu/2016/09/credit-rating-agencies-dodge-investors-lawsuits/.

See: "*Litigation against Credit Rating Agencies: Delhi High Court Delineates the Scope*". September 8, 2020. https://indiacorplaw.in/2020/09/litigation-against-credit-rating-agencies-delhi-high-court-delineates-the-scope.html.

See: "Credit-rating agencies are back under the spotlight - This time is different from the financial crisis—sort of". *The Economist*. May 9, 2020. https://www.economist.com/finance-and-economics/2020/05/07/credit-rating-agencies-are-back-under-the-spotlight.

See: It Is High Time to Implement a Major Reform of Credit-Rating Agencies. *International Banker*. By Yuefen Li. June 16, 2021. https://internationalbanker.com/finance/it-is-high-time-to-implement-a-major-reform-of-credit-rating-agencies/.

See: "*First German decision holding credit rating agency liable to* ....". Allen and Overy. 2021. https://www.google.com/url?sa=t&rct=j&q=&esrc=s&source=web&cd=&ved=2ahUKEwj21omW7NvxAhUGV8AKHXH1Aqk4ChAWegQIBRAD&url=https%3A%2F%2Fwww.allenovery.com%2Fen-gb%2Fglobal%2Fnews-and-insights%2Fpublications%2Ffirst-german-decision-holding-credit-rating-agency-liable-to-investors&usg=AOvVaw2Kgmdf-HKgeT9ljIYWJGBKV.

See: *Why China Is Shaking Up Its Credit Ratings Industry: QuickTake*. Bloomberg. July 23, 2020. https://www.google.com/url?sa=t&rct=j&q=&esrc=s&source=web&cd=&c

funds that invested in collateralized bond obligations [CBOs]); the bankrupt Bear Stearns (for losses of $1.12 billion from alleged "fraudulently issuing inflated ratings for securities"); bond insurers and the US government (which sued S&P for $5 billion for "misrepresenting the credit risk of complex financial products"). This chapter addresses some of these issues.

Chapter 4 discusses the constitutionality of, and International Constitutional Political Economy and Sustainability issues inherent in Accounting and Derivatives Standards-Setting organizations; and their

ad=rja&uact=8&ved=2ahUKEwjapomH7dvxAhWhnVwKHfE8BGo4FBAWegQIDRAD&url=https%3A%2F%2Fwww.bloomberg.com%2Fnews%2Farticles%2F2020-07-23%2Fwhy-china-sought-help-with-credit-ratings-for-bonds-quicktake&usg=AOvVaw0qjmxyRB-D2yAe_6DMfYDT.

See: *Rating agencies braced for Calpers lawsuit - Risk.net*. 2021. https://www.google.com/url?sa=t&rct=j&q=&esrc=s&source=web&cd=&ved=2ahUKEwjapomH7dvxAhWhnVwKHfE8BGo4FBAWegQIDxAD&url=https%3A%2F%2Fwww.risk.net%2Frisk-management%2Fcredit-risk%2F1560780%2Frating-agencies-braced-calpers-lawsuit&usg=AOvVaw0XcaYVzgFSEJZwcSU4pj4V.

See: Nwogugu (2021a).

See: "*Liquidators of failed Bear Stearns funds sue rating agencies*". July 10, 2013. Reuters. https://www.reuters.com/article/2013/07/10/us-ratings-agency-lawsuit-idUSBRE9690QV20130710.

See: "*Bond Insurer Sues Credit-Rating Agencies*". July 17, 2013. http://www.wsj.com. https://www.wsj.com/article/SB10001424127887323993804578612212273026342.html.

See: Wayne, L. (15 July 2009). "Calpers Sues Over Ratings of Securities". *The New York Times*. https://www.nytimes.com/2009/07/15/business/15calpers.html?_r=1&partner=rss&emc=rss.

See: "S&P Lawsuit First Amendment Defense May Fare Poorly, Experts Say". 4 February 2013. *Huffington Post*. http://www.huffingtonpost.com/2013/02/04/sp-lawsuit-first-amendment_n_2618737.html.

See: "*Credit Rating Agencies Settle 2 Suits Brought by Investors*". Reuters. April 27, 2013. https://www.nytimes.com/2013/04/28/business/credit-rating-agencies-settle-lawsuits-over-debt-vehicles.html?_r=0.

See: Reuters (September 3, 2013). *"S.&P. Calls Federal Fraud Suit Payback for Credit Downgrade". New York Times.*

See: "*Corrupted credit ratings: Standard & Poor's lawsuit and the evidence*". Matthias Efing & Harald Hau; 18 June 2013. http://www.voxeu.org/article/corrupted-credit-ratings-standard-poor-s-lawsuit-and-evidence.

See: *Standard & Poor's Says Civil Lawsuit Threatened By DOJ Is Without Legal Merit And Unjustified*". https://Reuters.com. 2013/02/04. https://www.reuters.com/article/2013/02/04/ny-sp-doj-lawsuit-idUSnPnNY53856+160+PRN20130204.

See: "Analysis: Credit agencies remain unaccountable". Kathleen Day. *USA Today*. May 19, 2014. https://www.usatoday.com/story/money/business/2014/05/19/credit-rating-agencies-in-limbo/9290143/.

associated Economic Psychology effects. The IASB and FASB/GASB/SASB (USA), ISDA and ICMA perform important rule-making functions and affect accounting regulations, companies, financial institutions and government regulation around the world (many foreign countries raise capital or list their shares in the US markets; and many US companies operate in foreign countries). The PCAOB and Sarbanes Oxley Act of 2002 (SOX, USA) are also relevant institutions but are not analyzed in this book. The SASB, FASB, GASB, IASB, ISDA and ICMA and their standards are unconstitutional; and that can affect conventional and unconventional monetary policy, systemic risk, financial stability, consumer confidence, business confidence, risk perception and propensity for anti-competitive misconduct. Such un-constitutionality is also an element of structural changes in the global accounting/auditing industry and the global financial services industry. The magnitude of these effects/changes can vary drastically across countries/jurisdictions.

Chapter 5 explains why the Sarbanes-Oxley Act (USA) and the PCAOB (USA) and similar institutions are unconstitutional (and also discusses associated Economic Psychology issues).

Chapters 6 and 7 focus on global pandemics (with focus on the COVID-19 Pandemic of 2020-present), responses by national and state governments and associated Constitutional Law and Constitutional Political Economy issues, all of which constitute part of the "*Global Pandemic Economy.*"

Bibliography

Abdelal, R., & Blyth, M. (2015). *Just Who Put You in Charge? We Did: Credit Rating Agencies and the Politics of Ratings*. In A. Cooley & J. Snyder (Eds.), *Ranking the World: Grading States as a Tool of Global Governance* (pp. 39–59). Cambridge: Cambridge University Press.

Acquier, A., Daudigeos, T., & Pinkse, J. (2017). Promises and Paradoxes of the Sharing Economy: An Organizing Framework. *Technological Forecasting & Social Change, 125*, 1–10.

Adler, G., Casas, C., et al. (2020). *Dominant Currencies and External Adjustment*. IMF Staff Discussion Note. IMF, Washington, DC.

Agbonika, J. (2015). Methods of International Trade and Payments: The Nigerian Perspective. *Global Journal of Politics and Law Research, 3*(1), 21–60.

Aklamanu, A., Degbey, W., & Tarba, S. (2016). The Role of HRM and Social Capital Configuration for Knowledge Sharing in Post-M&A Integration: A

Framework for Future Empirical Investigation. *The International Journal of Human Resource Management, 27*(22), 2790–2822.

Amtenbrink, F., & Heine, K. (2013). Regulating Credit Rating Agencies in the European Union: Lessons from Behavioural Science. *The Dovenschmidt Quarterly, 2*(1), 2–15.

Autor, D., Dorn, D., et al. (2017). *The Fall of the Labor Share and the Rise of Superstar Firms.* NBER Working Paper Series, No. 23396. Retrieved from http://www.nber.org/papers/w23396.pdf.

Baccini, L. (2019). The Economics and Politics of Preferential Trade Agreements. *Annual Review of Political Science, 22*, 75–92.

Banerji, S., Duygun, M., & Shaban, M. (2018). Political Connections, Bailout in Financial Markets and Firm Value. *Journal of Corporate Finance, 50*, 388–401.

Bargeron, L., Lehn, K., & Smith, J. (2015). Employee–Management Trust and M&A Activity. *Journal of Corporate Finance, 35C*, 389–406.

Barta, Z., & Johnston, A. (2017). Rating Politics? Partisan Discrimination in Credit Ratings in Developed Economies. *Comparative Political Studies, 51*(5), 587–620.

Bartels, B., & Weder di Mauro, B. (2013). A Rating Agency for Europe – A Good Idea? *VOX* (CEPR's Policy Portal). Retrieved from https://voxeu.org/article/rating-agency-europe-good-idea.

Bather, A., & Burnaby, P. (2004). The Public Company Accounting Oversight Board: National and International Implications. *Managerial Auditing Journal, 21*(6), 657–663.

Blodget, H. (2011). *Moody's Analyst Breaks Silence: Says Ratings Agency Rotten to Core with Conflicts.* Retrieved from www.businessinsider.com/moodys-analyst-conflicts-corruption-and-greed-2011-8/?IR=T.

Bolton, P, & Huang, H. (2018). Optimal Payment Areas or Optimal Currency Areas? *AEA Papers and Proceedings*, 108, 505–508.

Boz, E., Gopinath, G., & Plagborg-Møller, M. (2017). *Global Trade and the Dollar.* NBER Working Paper 23988.

Brummer, C., & Loko, R. (2014). *The New Politics of Transatlantic Credit Rating Agency Regulation.* In T. Porter (Ed.), *Transnational Financial Regulation After the Crisis* (pp. 154–176). London/New York: Routledge.

Brunnermeier, M., Farhi, E., et al. (2021). Review Article: Perspectives on the Future of Asset Pricing. *The Review of Financial Studies, 34*, 2126–2160. https://doi.org/10.1093/rfs/hhaa129

Carruthers, B. (2013). From Uncertainty Toward Risk: The Case of Credit Ratings. *Socio-Economic Review, 11*(3), 525–551.

Chari, V., Dovis, A., & Kehoe, P. (2020). Rethinking Optimal Currency Areas. *Journal of Monetary Economics*, 111(C), 80–94.

Chwieroth, J., & Walter, A. (2020). Great Expectations, Financialization, and Bank Bailouts in Democracies. *Comparative Political Studies, 53*(8), 1259–1297.

Coffee, J. (2011). Ratings Reform: The Good, the Bad, and the Ugly. *Harvard Business Law Review, 1*, 231–278.

Copelovitch, M., Frieden, J., & Walter, S. (2016). The Political Economy of the Euro Crisis. *Comparative Political Studies, 49*(7), 811–840.

Darbellay, A. (2013). *Regulating Credit Rating Agencies.* Cheltenham: Edward Elgar Publishing.

Dellisanti, D., & Wagner, R. (2018). Bankruptcies, Bailouts, and Some Political Economy of Corporate Reorganization. *Journal of Institutional Economics, 14*, 833–851.

Druck, P., Magud, N., & Mariscal, R. (2015, July). *Collateral Damage: Dollar Strength and Emerging Markets' Growth.* IMF Working Paper. Western Hemisphere Department, IMF, Washington, DC.

European Commission. (2015). *Study on the Feasibility of Alternatives to Credit Ratings: Executive Summary.* Retrieved from https://ec.europa.eu/info/system/files/alternatives-to-credit-rating-study-01122015_en.pdf.

European Commission. (2016). *Study on the State of the Credit Rating Market: Final Report – Executive Summary.* Retrieved from https://ec.europa.eu/info/system/files/state-of-credit-rating-market-study-01012016_en.pdf.

Frost, C. (2007). Credit Rating Agencies in Capital Markets: A Review of Research Evidence on Selected Criticisms of the Agencies. *Journal of Accounting, Auditing & Finance, 22*(3), 469–492.

Gaillard, N., & Harrington, W. (2016). Efficient, Commonsense Actions to Foster Accurate Credit Ratings. *Capital Markets Law Journal, 11*(1), 38–59.

Go, J. (2003). A Globalizing Constitutionalism? Views from the Post-colony, 1945–2000. *International Society, 18*, 71–78.

Gopinath, G. (2018). *Dollar Dominance in Trade and Finance.* Chapter-2 in: Cochrane, J., Palermo, K., & Taylor, J., eds. (2019), "*Currencies, Capital And Central Bank Balances*" (Hoover Institution Press). Available at https://www.hoover.org/sites/default/files/research/docs/cochranepalermotaylor_currencies_ch2.pdf.

Han, B. (2018). The Role and Welfare Rationale of Secondary Sanctions: A Theory and a Case Study of the US Sanctions Targeting Iran. *Conflict Management and Peace Science, 35*(5), 474–502.

Kiff, J., Nowak, S., & Schumacher, L. (2012). *Are Rating Agencies Powerful? An Investigation into the Impact and Accuracy of Sovereign Ratings.* IMF Working Papers 12/23.

Kim, I., & Milner, H. (2019). *Multinational Corporations and their Influence Through Lobbying on Foreign Policy.* Retrieved from https://www.brookings.edu/wp-content/uploads/2019/12/Kim_Milner_manuscript.pdf.

Kruck, A. (2016). Resilient Blunderers: Credit Rating Fiascos and Rating Agencies' Institutionalized Status as Private Authorities. *Journal of European Public Policy, 23*(5), 753–770.

Kunroo, M. (2016). Theory of Optimum Currency Areas: A Literature Survey. *Review of Market Integration*, 7(2). https://doi.org/10.1177/0974929216631381.

Laurens, N., & Morin, J. (2019). Negotiating Environmental Protection in Trade Agreements: A Regime Shift or a Tactical Linkage. *International Environmental Agreements, 19*(6), 533–556.

Law, D., & Versteeg, M. (2012). The Declining Influence of the United States Constitution. *NYU Law Review, 87*, 762–826. Retrieved from http://www.nyulawreview.org/sites/default/files/pdf/NYULawReview-87-3-Law-Versteeg_0.pdf.

Lenk, H. (2019). Bilateral Committees in EU Trade and Investment Agreements. In F. Baetens (Ed.), *Legitimacy of Unseen Actors in International Adjudication* (pp. 591–610). Cambridge University Press.

Mennillo, G., & Sinclair, T. (2019). A Hard Nut to Crack: Regulatory Failure Shows How Rating Really Works. *Comparative Political Studies, 23*(3), 266–286.

Mirkina, I. (2018). FDI and Sanctions: An Empirical Analysis of Short- and Long-Run Effects. *European Journal of Political Economy, 54*(C), 198–225.

Mitchell, R., et al. (2020). What We Know (and Could Know) About International Environmental Agreements. *Global Environmental Politics, 20*(1), 103–110.

Nakagawa, R., Oiwa, H., & Takeda, F. (2012). The Economic Impact of Herd Behavior in the Japanese Loan Market. *Pacific-Basin Finance Journal, 20*(4), 600–613.

Niamir, L., Filatova, T., et al. (2018). Transition to Low-Carbon Economy: Assessing Cumulative Impacts of Individual Behavioral Changes. *Energy Policy, 118*, 325–345.

Nwogugu, M. (2009). Franchise Royalty Rates, Franchise Fees and Incentive Effects. *International Journal of Mathematics, Game Theory & Algebra, 17*(5/6), 303–316.

Nwogugu, M. (2012). *Risk in the Global Real Estate Market.* John Wiley.

Nwogugu, M. (2019a). Knowledge-Representation and Network Decisions in Franchising and Online-Retailing Under Combined MN-Transferable-Utility, WTAL, Perception and Regret-Minimization Regimes. In M. Nwogugu (Ed.), *Complex Systems, Multi-Sided Incentives and Risk Perception in Companies.* Palgrave Macmillan.

Nwogugu, M. (2019b). On Franchise Royalty Rates, Franchise Fees and Incentive Effects. In M. Nwogugu (Ed.), *Complex Systems, Multi-Sided Incentives and Risk Perception in Companies.* Palgrave Macmillan.

Nwogugu, M. (2019c). Chapter 13: Implications for Decision Theory, Enforcement, Financial Stability and Systemic Risk. In M. Nwogugu (Ed.),

Indices, Index Funds and ETFs: Exploring HCI, Nonlinear Risk and Homomorphisms. Palgrave Macmillan.

Nwogugu, M. (2021). Chapter 2: Financial Stability, Sustainable Growth, and the Global Quasi-Franchising/Business-Opportunity Industry. In M. Nwogugu (Ed.), *Complex Systems and Sustainability in the Global Auditing, Consulting, and Credit Rating Agency Industries*. IGI Global.

Nwogugu, M. (2021a). *Complex Systems and Sustainability in the Global Auditing, Consulting, and Credit Rating Agency Industries*. IGI Global Publishers.

Nwogugu, M. (2021b). Introduction. In M. Nwogugu (Ed.), *Geopolitical Risk, Sustainability and "Cross-Border Spillovers" in Emerging Markets, Volume-One*. Palgrave Macmillan.

O'Boyle, E., Banks, G., & Gonzalez-Mule, E. (2016). The Chrysalis Effect: How Ugly Initial Results Metamorphoze into Beautiful Articles. *Journal of Management, 43*(2), 376–399.

Prasad, E. (2019). *Has the Dollar Lost Ground as the Dominant International Currency?*. Working Paper. Brookings Institution. Retrieved from https://www.brookings.edu/wp-content/uploads/2019/09/DollarInGlobalFinance.final_.9.20.pdf.

Repasi, R. (2017, July). *Dynamisation of International Trade Cooperation: Powers and Limits of Joint Committees in CETA*. Retrieved from http://www.qil-qdi.org/forthcoming-2/.

Replicability Research Group. (2015). *Replicability vs. Reproducibility*. Tel Aviv University, Department of Statistics and Operations Research. Retrieved from http://www.replicability.tau.ac.il/index.php/replicability-in-science/replicability-vs-reproducibility.html.

Rosenbaum, S., Billinger, S., et al. (2012). Market Economies and Pro-Social Behavior: Experimental Evidence from Central Asia. *The Journal of Socio-Economics, 41*(1), 64–71.

Schnellenbach, J., & Schubert, C. (2015). Behavioral Political Economy: A Survey. *European Journal of Political Economy, 40B*, 395–417.

Sen, K., & Sinha, C. (2017). The Location Choice of US Foreign Direct Investment: How Do Institutions Matter? *Journal of Institutional Economics, 13*, 401–420.

Stanford Encyclopedia of Philosophy. (2018, December 3). *Reproducibility of Scientific Results*. Retrieved from https://plato.stanford.edu/entries/scientific-reproducibility/.

Stout, B. (2017). Sanctioned to Survive: How Foreign Firms Perform when Economic Sanctions Affect their Business Relationships—A Study of Contemporary Economic Sanction Actions and Their Impact. *Perspectives on Global Development and Technology, 16*(5), 501–538.

Świątkowski, W., & Dompnier, B. (2017). Replicability Crisis in Social Psychology: Looking at the Past to Find New Pathways for the Future. *International Review of Social Psychology, 30*(1), 111–124.

Thompson, A., Broude, T., & Haftel, Y. (2019). Once Bitten, Twice Shy? Investment Disputes, State Sovereignty, and Change in Treaty Design. *International Organization, 73*(4), 859–880.

Wright, G., & Owen, J. (2020). *Implementing Brexit: The Role Of The Joint Committee.* https://www.instituteforgovernment.org.uk/sites/default/files/publications/implementing-brexit-role-joint-committee_0.pdf.

Zhang, C. (2016, January). *International Currency Competition Redux.* Retrieved from https://voxeu.org/article/revisiting-international-currency-competition.

Appendix 1 Worldwide US Dollar Exchange Rates (1999–2019; the Value of One US Dollar in Foreign Currencies)

Country	*Currency*	*Code*	*2019[7]*	*2014[8]*	*2009*	*2006*	*2005*	*2004*	*2003*	*2002*	*2001*	*1989*
United Arab Emirates	Emirati dirham	AED	3.6725	3.673	3.673	3.6725	3.6725	3.6725	3.6725	3.6725	3.6725	3.6725
Afghanistan	Afghan afghani	AFN[9]	75.14	50.42	50.05	42.785	43.13	42.785	4.7	4.75	4.75	4.836
Albania	Albanian lek	ALL	108.931	79.546	92.668	140.16	102.93	115.918	143.71	137.69	150.63	148.92
Algeria	Algerian dinar	DZD	118.4	63.25	69.9	77.215	77.889	78.67	75.26	66.574	58.739	57.707
Angola[10]	Angolan kwanza	AOA	310.16	75.023	76.6	22.058	32.8716	73.8297	10.041	2.791	0.393	0.229
Anguilla, Antigua and Barbuda, Dominica, Grenada, Montserrat, Saint Kitts and Nevis, Saint Lucia, Saint Vincent and the Grenadines[11]	East Caribbean dollar	XCD	2.7	2.69	2.7	2.76	2.76	2.76	2.76	2.76	2.76	2.76
Argentina[12]	Argentine peso	ARS	59.9	8	3.1105	2.951	2.926	3.08	2.945	3.24	0.9994	0.9996
Armenia	Armenian dram	AMD	485.73	303.93	344.06	522.08	459.79	395.89	570.95	535.06	504.92	490.85
Aruba[13]	Aruban florin	AWG	1.79		1.8	1.79	1.79	1.8	1.79	1.79	1.79	1.79
Australia, Kiribati, Nauru, Norfolk Island, Tuvalu, Christmas Island, Cocos Island	Australian dollar	AUD	1.3994	1.2059	1.2137	1.932	1.9354	1.5361	1.7173	1.5497	1.5888	1.3439

Azerbaijan	Azerbaijani manat (old)	AZM	NA	NA	NA	4657	4804	4875.50	4474	4120	3869	3985
Azerbaijan	Azerbaijani manat	AZN	1.705	0.8219	0.8581	NA	NA	NA	NA	NA	NA	NA
The Bahamas	Bahamian dollar	BSD	1	1	1	1	1	1	1	1	1	1
Bahrain	Bahraini dinar	BHD	0.376	0.376	0.376	0.376	0.376	0.376	0.376	0.376	0.376	0.376
Bangladesh	Bangladeshi taka	BDT	83.891	68.554	69.893	55.807	57.756	58.15	52.142	49.085	46.906	43.892
Barbados	Barbadian dollar	BBD	2		2.02	2	2	2	2	2	2	2
Belarus[14]	Belarusian ruble	BYB/ BYR	NA	2130	2145	1531	Unk	2032.79	876.75	248.8	46.127	26.02
Belarus	Belarusian third ruble	BYN	2.06	NA	NA	NA	NA	NA	NA	NA	NA	NA
Belize	Belizean dollar	BZD	2	2	2	2	2	2	2	2	2	2
Benin, Burkina Faso, Central African Republic, Chad, Republic of the Congo, Ivory Coast, Equatorial Guinea, Gabon, Guinea-Bissau, Mali, Niger, Senegal, Togo[15]	CFA franc	XOF/ XAF	574.59	438.77	493.51	733.04	742.79	560	711.98	615.7	589.95	583.67
Bermuda	Bermudian dollar	BMD	1	1	1	1	1	1	1	1	1	1
Bhutan[16]	Bhutanese ngultrum/ Indian rupee	BTN/ INR	70.754		41.487	47.186	48.336	46.98	44.942	43.055	41.259	36.313

(*continued*)

Appendix 1: (continued)

Country	*Currency*	*Code*	*2019[7]*	*2014[8]*	*2009*	*2006*	*2005*	*2004*	*2003*	*2002*	*2001*	*1989*
Bolivia	Bolivian boliviano	BOB	6.912	7.253	7.8616	6.6069	6.8613	7.5719	6.1835	5.8124	5.5101	5.2543
Bosnia and Herzegovina	Bosnia and Herzegovina convertible mark	BAM	1.7132	1.3083	1.4419	2.161	1.6237	1.5579	2.124	1.837	1.76	1.734
Botswana	Botswana pula	BWP	10.5219	6.7907	6.2035	5.8412	6.8353	5.15464	5.1018	4.6244	4.2259	3.6508
Brazil[17]	Brazilian real	BRL	3.7404	1.8644	1.9516	2.358	2.378	2.9675	1.83	1.815	1.161	1.078
Brunei[18]	Bruneian dollar	BND	1.3562	1.4322	1.526	1.8917	1.8388	1.7346	1.724	1.695	1.6736	1.4848
Bulgaria[19]	Bulgarian lev	BGN	1.7132	1.3171	1.4366	2.1847	2.2147	1.654	2.1233	1.8364	1.7604	1.6819
Burundi	Burundi franc	BIF	1814.64	1198	1065	830.35	865.14	1052.8	720.67	563.56	477.77	352.35
Cambodia	Cambodian riel	KHR	4016.45	4070.94	4006	3918.50	3895.00	3950.00	3840.80	3807.80	3744.40	2946.30
Canada	Canadian dollar	CAD	1.3311	1.0364	1.0724	1.4963	1.5979	1.3866	1.452	1.5263	1.425	1.3737
Cape Verde	Cape Verdean escudo	CVE	96.58	73.84	81.235	104.617	123.556	108.95	115.877	102.7	98.158	93.177
Cayman Islands	Caymanian dollar	KYD	0.8333	0.8333	0.8333	0.82	0.8333	0.83	0.8189	0.81528	0.802	0.802
Chile	Chilean peso	CLP	675.38	509.02	526.25	618.7	651.9	545.5	535.47	508.78	460.29	419.3
China, People's Republic of	Renminbi	CNY	6.7888	6.9385	7.61	8.2771	8.2767	8.2768	8.2785	8.2783	8.279	8.2898
Colombia	Colombian peso	COP	3161.45	2302.90	2013.80	2299.63	2275.89	2856.80	2087.90	1756.23	1426.04	1140.96
Comoros[20]	Comorian franc	KOF	430.94	337.26	361.4	549.78	557.09	393.83	533.98	461.77	442.46	437.75
Congo, Democratic Republic of the[21]	Congolese franc	CDF	1628.74	459.175	437	305	420	437.962	21.82	4.02	1.61	1.31
Costa Rica	Costa Rican colon	CRC	603.78	529.62	519.53	328.87	343.08	395.29	308.19	285.68	257.23	232.6
Croatia	Croatian kuna	HRK	6.507	4.877	5.3735	8.34	8.452	6.4196	8.277	7.112	6.362	6.101

Cuba[22]	Cuban peso	CUP	1	0.9259	0.9259	1	1	1	1	1	1	1
Cyprus (Greek Cypriot area)	Cypriot pound	CYP	0.5127	NA	0.4286	0.6427	0.6518	0.49996	0.6208	0.5423	0.517	0.5135
Cyprus (Turkish Cypriot area)	Turkish lira	TRY	See Turkey			1.42234	1.34079	1.43111	1.49307	1.50548	1.22541	0.6237
Czech Republic	Czech koruna	CZK	22.468	17.037	20.53	38.035	36.325	26.645	38.598	34.569	32.281	31.698
Denmark, Faroe Islands, Greenland	Danish krone	DKK	6.5396	5.0236	5.4797	5.9911	5.9969	5.9468	6.5877	7.8947	8.3228	8.0831
Djibouti	Djiboutian franc	DJF	177.72	179.14	177.71	177.721	177.721	177.721	177.721	177.721	177.721	177.721
Dominican Republic	Dominican peso	DOP	50.501	34.775	33.113	16.952	17.31	27.1	16.415	16.033	15.267	14.265
East Timor	U.S. dollar	USD	1	1	1	Irr	1	1	Irr	Irr	Irr	Irr
Ecuador	U.S. dollar, Ecuadorian sucre	USD/ ECS	NA	NA	NA	25,000.00	25,000.00	25,000	24,988	11,787	5447	3988
Egypt	Egyptian pound	EGP	17.87	5.4	5.67	4.49	4.5	5.975	3.69	3.405	3.388	3.388
El Salvador	Salvadoran colon, U.S. dollar	SVC, USD	NA	NA	NA	8.755	8.75	8.75	8.755	8.755	8.755	8.755
Eritrea	Eritrean nakfa	ERN	15	15.38	15.5	Unk	15	9.65	9.5	7.6	7.2	Unk
Estonia	Estonian kroon	EEK	13.706	10.537	11.535	17.538	17.518	13.2625	16.969	14.678	14.075	13.882
Ethiopia	Ethiopian birr	ETB	28.39	9.57	8.96	8.314	8.455	8.4	8.314	8.134	7.503	6.864
Eurozone Countries	Euro	EUR	0.8934	0.6734	0.7345	0.8039	0.8038	0.7964	0.884	1.0575	1.1166	1.0827
Fiji	Fijian dollar	FJD	2.125	1.5986	1.6138	2.2766	2.2934	1.8653	2.1286	1.9696	1.9868	1.4437
French Polynesia, New Caledonia, Wallis and Futuna	Change Franc Pacifique	XPF	104.53	83.12	87.59	133.26	135.04	116.49	129.44	107.25	106.11	126.39

(*continued*)

Appendix 1: (continued)

Country	*Currency*	*Code*	*2019[7]*	*2014[8]*	*2009*	*2006*	*2005*	*2004*	*2003*	*2002*	*2001*	*1989*
The Gambia	Gambian dalasi	GMD	49.51	22.75	27.79	15	29.24	25	12.788	11.395	10.643	10.2
Georgia	Georgian lari	GEL	2.65	1.47	1.7	2.073	2.1888	2.1352	1.9762	2.0245	1.3898	1.2975
Ghana	Ghanaian cedi (old)	GHC	NA	NA	NA	7170.76	7195	8675	5455.06	2669.30	2050.17	5526.60
Ghana	Ghanaian cedi	GHS	4.91342	3.02469	1.54586	NA	NA	NA	NA	NA	NA	
Guatemala	Guatemalan quetzal	GTQ	7.729	7.5895	7.6833	7.8586	8.0165	7.925	7.7632	7.3856	6.3947	6.0653
Guinea	Guinean franc	GNF	9185.32	5500	4122.80	1950.60	1974.40	1963.14	1746.90	1387.40	1236.80	1095.30
Guyana	Guyanese dollar	GYD	209.01	203.86	201.89	187.3	189.5	179	182.4	178	150.5	142.4
Haiti	Haitian gourde	HTG	78.143	39.216	37.138	26.339	26.674	37.25	22.524	17.965	16.505	17.311
Honduras	Honduran lempira	HNL	24.271	18.983	18.9	15.9197	16.0256	17.26	15.1407	14.5039	13.8076	13.0942
Hong Kong	Hong Kong dollar	HKD	7.84	7.8	7.802	7.7994	7.798	7.7987	7.7918	7.7589	7.7462	7.7425
Hungary	Hungarian forint	HUF	280.13	165.89	186.16	286.49	275.92	209	282.179	237.146	214.402	186.789
Iceland	Icelandic króna	ISK	119.7	85.619	63.391	97.425	102.43	70.1	78.616	72.335	70.958	70.904
India	Indian rupee	INR	70.775	43.815	41.357	45.34	44.115	45.319	46.66	48.679	47.227	44.942
Indonesia	Indonesian rupiah	IDR	14,159.50	9558.10	9056	10,260.90	10,377.30	9183.77	–	7855.20	10,013.60	8374.50
Iran	Iranian rial	IRR	42,107.80	9142.80	9407.50	1750	7900	7900	1750	1750	1750	1750
Iraq	Iraqi dinar	IQD	1191	1202	1255	2000	1500.59	1516.50	1910	1815	1530	910
Israel, West Bank	new Israeli shekel	ILS	3.69	3.56	4.14	4.2057	4.2757	4.46685	4.1397	4.0773	3.8001	3.4494
Jamaica	Jamaican dollar	JMD	130.418	72.236	69.034	45.996	47.277	58.75	42.701	39.044	36.55	35.404
Japan	Japanese yen	JPY	108.92	103.58	117.99	121.529	125.388	115.933	107.765	113.907	130.905	120.991
Jordan	Jordanian dinar	JOD	0.709	0.709	0.709	0.709	0.709	0.709	0.709	0.709	0.709	0.709
Kazakhstan	Kazakh tenge	KZT	378.61	120.25	122.55	146.74	151.14	149.757	142.13	119.52	78.3	75.44
Kenya	Kenyan shilling	KES	101.54	68.358	68.309	78.563	78.597	73.5	76.176	70.326	60.367	58.732

North Korea	North Korean won	KPW	900.11	3400 (Oct) [34]	140	2.15	2.15	2.15	2.15	2.15	2.15	2.15
South Korea	South Korean won	KRW	1122.48	1101.70	929.2	1290.99	1317.01	1205.45	1130.96	1188.82	1401.44	951.29
Kuwait	Kuwaiti dinar	KWD	0.3032	0.2679	0.2844	0.3066	0.3075	0.299105	0.3067	0.3044	0.3047	0.3033
Kyrgyzstan	Kyrgyzstani som	KGS	69.835	36.108	37.746	48.378	47.972	44.0542	47.704	39.008	20.838	17.362
Laos	Lao kip	LAK	8549.18	8760.69	9658	8954.58	9467.00	7562	7887.64	7102.03	3298.33	1259.98
Lebanon	Lebanese pound	LBP	1507.50	1507.50	1507.50	1507.50	1507.50	1507.5	1507.50	1507.80	1516.10	1539.50
Lesotho, South Africa, Swaziland	South African rand (also, Lesotho loti, Swazi lilangeni)	ZAR, LSL, SZL	13.85	7.75	7.25	8.60918	11.58786	8.0154	6.93983	6.10948	5.52828	4.60796
Liberia	Liberian dollar	LRD	158.62	63.31	59.715	48.5833	46.04	57.149	40.9525	41.9025	41.5075	40
Libya	Libyan dinar	LYD	1.3898	1.2112	1.2604	0.6501	1.36495	1.2059	0.5403	0.5403	0.3785	0.3891
Lithuania	Lithuanian litas	LTL	3.0245	2.3251	2.5362	4	3.4946	2.93995	4	4	4	4
Macau	Macau pataca	MOP	8.07726	8.16567	8.011	8.034	8.033	8.0325	8.026	7.992	7.979	7.975
Madagascar	Malagasy franc	MGF	NA	NA	NA	6588.50	6531.40	5820.75	6767.50	6283.80	5441.40	5090.90
Madagascar	Malagasy ariary	MGA	3566.02	1654.78	1880	NA	NA	NA	NA	NA	NA	NA
Malawi	Malawian kwacha	MWK	730.99	419.6	155.5	72.1973	67.3111	91.8	59.5438	44.0881	31.0727	16.4442
Malaysia	Malaysian ringgit	MYR	4.117	3.33	3.46	3.8	3.8	3.8	3.8	3.8	3.9244	2.8133
Maldives	Maldivian rufiyaa	MVR	15.512	12.954	12.942	11.77	11.77	11.77	11.77	11.77	11.77	11.77
Malta	Maltese lira	MTL	NA	NA	0.3106	0.4499	0.4542	0.3632	0.4376	0.3994	0.3885	0.3857
Mauritania	Mauritanian ouguiya	MRO			267.66	254.35	273.72	261.2	238.923	209.514	188.476	151.853
Mexico	Mexican peso	MXN	19.182	11.016	10.8	9.3423	9.1614	10.247	9.4556	9.5604	9.136	7.9185

(*continued*)

Appendix 1: (continued)

Country	*Currency*	*Code*	*2019[7]*	*2014[8]*	*2009*	*2006*	*2005*	*2004*	*2003*	*2002*	*2001*	*1989*
Moldova	Moldovan leu	MDL	17.134	10.326	12.177	12.8579	Unk	14.1565	12.4342	10.5158	5.3707	4.6236
Mongolia	Mongolian tugrug	MNT	2650.51	1165.92	1170	1097.70	1101.29	1120.37	1076.67	1072.37	840.83	789.99
Morocco, Western Sahara	Moroccan dirham	MAD	9.535	7.526	8.3563	11.303	11.584	9.3135	10.626	9.804	9.604	9.527
Mozambique	Mozambique metical (old)	MZM	NA	NA	NA	20,703.60	23,314.20	23,180	15,447.10	13,028.60	12,110.20	11,772.60
Mozambique	Mozambique metical	MZN	61.72	24.125	26.264	NA	NA	NA	NA	NA	NA	NA
Myanmar	Myanma kyat	MMF	1531.78	1205	1296	6.7489	6.8581	Unk	6.5167	6.2858	6.3432	6.2418
Namibia	Namibian dollar, South African rand	NAD, ZAR	13.87	7.75	7.18	8.60918	11.58786	8.0154	6.93983	6.10948	5.52828	4.60796
Nepal	Nepalese rupee	NPR	113.14		118.14	74.961	76.675	74.83	71.094	68.239	65.976	58.01
Netherlands Antilles	Netherlands Antillean guilder	ANG	1.79	1.79	1.79	1.79	1.79	1.79	1.79	1.79	1.79	1.79
New Zealand, Niue, Cook Islands, Pitcairn Islands, Tokelau	New Zealand dollar	NZD	1.476	1.4151	1.3811	2.3776	2.3535	1.724	2.1863	1.8886	1.8632	1.5083
Nicaragua	Nicaraguan córdoba	NIO	32.533	19.374	18.457	13.37	13.88	14.9	12.69	11.81	10.58	9.45
Nigeria	Nigerian naira	NGN	360.9	117.8	127.46	133.56	115	136	101.697	92.338	21.886	21.886
North Macedonia	Macedonian denar	MKD	53.75	41.414	44.732	64.757	52.11	51.2467	65.904	56.902	54.462	50.004
Norway, Svalbard	Norwegian krone	NOK	8.5521	5.2338	5.8396	8.9917	8.9684	6.7156	8.8018	7.7992	7.5451	7.0734
Oman	Omani rial	OMR	0.3845	0.3845	0.3845	0.3845	0.3845	0.3849	0.3845	0.3845	0.3845	0.3845

Pakistan	Pakistani rupee	PKR	138.94	70.64	60.6295	61.927	60.719	57.8	53.648	49.118	44.943	40.918
Panama	U.S. Dollar, Panamanian balboa	USD, PAB	1	1	1	1	1	1	1	1	1	1
Papua New Guinea	Papua New Guinean kina	PGK	3.3653	2.6956	3.03	3.374	3.706	3.6036	2.765	2.539	2.058	1.434
Paraguay	Paraguayan guarani	PYG	6034.30	4337.70	5031	4107.70	4783.00	6265	3486.40	3119.10	2726.50	2177.90
Peru	Peruvian nuevo sol	PEN	3.3457	2.9322	3.1731	3.509	3.44	3.49185	3.49	3.3833	2.93	2.6642
Philippines	Philippine peso	PHP	52.454	44.439	46.148	50.993	51.201	53.255	44.192	39.089	40.893	29.471
Poland	Polish zloty	PLN	3.759	3.155	2.966	4.0939	4.0144	3.8045	4.3461	3.9671	3.4754	3.2793
Qatar	Qatari rial	QAR	3.64	3.64	3.64	3.64	3.64	3.64	3.64	3.64	3.64	3.64
Romania	Romanian leu	RON	4.122	2.5	2.43	3.26	2.91	2.81	3.32	3.3	2.91	2.16
Russia	Russian ruble	RUR/ RUB	66.84	24.3	25.659	29.0053	28.2885	27.0474	30.709	30.1372	28.16	27
Rwanda	Rwandan franc	RWF	884.73	550	585	442.99	456.81	520.385	389.7	333.94	312.31	301.53
Samoa	Samoan tala	WST	2.6		NA	3.4722	3.5236	3.0021	3.2712	3.012	2.9429	2.5562
São Tomé and Príncipe	São Tomé and Príncipe dobra	STD	21,461	14,900	13,700	8842.10	9009.10	9019.7	7978.20	7119.00	6883.20	4552.50
Saudi Arabia	Saudi riyal	SAR	3.75	3.75	3.745	3.745	3.745	3.7503	3.745	3.745	3.745	3.745
Serbia and Montenegro	Serbian dinar	RSD	103.67	56.14	54.5	58.96	65	57.6065	57.68	63.53	10	5.85
Seychelles	Seychellois rupee	SCR	13.65	8	6.5	5.8575	5.7458	5.618	5.7138	5.3426	5.2622	5.0263
Sierra Leone	Sierra Leonean leone	SLL	8584.71	3007.90	2800.86	1985.89	2212.47	2275	2092.13	1804.20	1563.62	981.48
Singapore	Singapore dollar	SGD	1.356	1.415	1.507	1.6902	1.6644	1.5819	1.7422	1.7906	1.7917	1.4848?
Slovakia	Slovak koruna	SKK	26.39	21.05	NA	47.792	31.087	35.173	46.035	41.363	35.233	33.616

(*continued*)

Appendix 1: (continued)

Country	*Currency*	*Code*	*2019[7]*	*2014[8]*	*2009*	*2006*	*2005*	*2004*	*2003*	*2002*	*2001*	*1989*
Slovenia	Slovenian tolar	SIT	NA	NA	NA	242.75	251.4	194.94	222.66	181.77	166.13	159.69
Solomon Islands	Solomon Islands dollar	SBD	8.1195	7.6336	7.6336	5.3728	7.629	7.3432	5.0889	4.8381	4.8156	3.7169
Somalia	Somali shilling	SOS	NA	1436	1423.73	Unk	Unk	2620	11,000	2620	Unk	7500
South Africa	South African rand	ZAR	13.87	7.9576	7.05	8.60918	11.58786	8.0154	6.93983	6.10948	5.52828	4.60796
Sri Lanka	Sri Lankan rupee	LKR	181.82	108.14	110.78	89.383	93.383	97.245	77.005	70.635	64.45	58.995
Sudan	Sudanese dinar	SDD	NA	NA	NA	258.7	261.44	257.41	257.12	252.55	200.8	157.57
Sudan	Sudanese pound	SDG	47.62	5.582	2.665	NA	NA	NA	NA	NA	NA	NA
Suriname	Surinamese dollar	SRD	7.458	3.271	3.225	2.1785	2.549	2.5024	2.1785	0.9875	0.401	0.401
Sweden	Swedish krona	SEK	8.9948	6.4074	6.7629	7.3489	7.4731	7.3783	8.0863	9.7371	10.3291	9.1622
Switzerland, Liechtenstein	Swiss franc	CHF	0.9906	1.0774	1.1973	1.6876	1.6668	1.3003	1.6888	1.5022	1.4498	1.4513
Syria	Syrian pound	SYP	515.03	46.5281	50.0085	51	52.98	41.79	46	52.29	46	41.9
Taiwan, Republic of China	New Taiwan dollar	TWD	30.83	31.47	32.84	34.49	34.6	34.699	33.08	31.4	32.22	32.05
Tajikistan	Tajik somoni	TJS	9.433	3.4563	3.4418	2.2	2.55	3.081	1550	998	Unk	350
Tanzania	Tanzanian shilling	TZS	2306.23	1178.10	1255	876.41	924.7	1038	800.41	744.76	664.67	612.12
Thailand	Thai baht	THB	31.81	33.37	33.599	43.432	43.982	41.695	40.112	37.814	41.359	31.364
Tonga	Tongan pa'anga	TOP	2.266	2.0747	2.0747	2.1236	2.192	2.151	1.7585	1.5991	1.492	1.2635
Trinidad and Tobago	Trinidad and Tobago dollar	TTD	6.7833	6.3228	6.3275	6.2332	6.2466	6.135	6.2998	6.2989	6.2983	6.2517
Tunisia	Tunisian dinar	TND	2.9607	1.211	1.2776	1.3753	1.44	1.26445	1.3707	1.1862	1.1387	1.1059
Turkey	Turkish lira (old)	TRL	NA	NA	NA	1,422,340	1,340,790	1,431,110	1,493,070	1,505,840	1,225,410	623,700
Turkey	New Turkish lira	TRY	5.375	2.1895	1.319	1.422	1.34	1.431	1.493	1.505	1.225	0.623

Turkmenistan	Turkmen manat	TMM	17,016	14,250	6250[45]	5200	5200	5200	5200	5350	Unk	4070
Uganda	Ugandan shilling	UGX	3703.09	1658.10	1685.80	1755.70	1738.70	2002.50	1644.50	1454.80	1240.20	1083.00
Ukraine	Ukrainian hryvnia	UAH	27.89	4.9523	5.05	5.3722	5.3126	5.3093	5.4402	4.1304	2.4495	1.8617
United Kingdom	Pound sterling	GBP	0.776	0.5302	0.4993	0.5462	0.55	0.5435	0.6125	0.6672	0.6947	0.6609
Falkland Islands	Falkland Islands pound	FKP										
Guernsey	Guernsey Pound	GGP										
Jersey	Jersey pound	JEP										
Saint Helena	Saint Helena pound	SHP										
Gibraltar	Gibraltar pound	GIP										
Uruguay	Uruguayan peso	UYU	32.6059	20.438	23.947	13.3191	14.3325	20.025	12.0996	11.3393	10.4719	9.4418
Uzbekistan	Uzbek som	UZS	8357.39	1317	1263.80	325	687	966.24	141.4	111.9	110.95	75.8
Vanuatu	Vanuatuan vatu	VUV	113.79	100.87	104.956	145.31	146.02	121.41	137.64	129.08	127.52	115.87
Venezuela	Venezuelan bolívar fuerte	VEF	#######	2.147	2.147	0.723.666	0.761225	2.15	0.679.96	0.605.717	0.547556	0.488635
Vietnam	Vietnamese đồng	VND	23,201.10	21,189	16,119	15,746	15,746	15,983	15,510	15,280	14,725	14,167.70
Yemen	Yemeni rial	YER	250.36	199.76	199.14	168.678	171.86	178.01	161.718	155.718	135.882	129.281
Zambia	Zambian kwacha	ZMK	11,937.15	3512.90	3990.20	4778.90	4463.50	3601.50	4733.30	4398.60	1862.07	1314.50
Zimbabwe	Zimbabwean dollar	ZWN[49]	322.33	361.9	30,000	5.729	77.965	162.07	0.824	0.055	0.055	0.038

(*continued*)

Appendix 1: (continued)

Source: https://en.wikipedia.org/wiki/Tables_of_historical_exchange_rates_to_the_United_States_dollar

Notes (Source: https://en.wikipedia.org/wiki/Tables_of_historical_exchange_rates_to_the_United_States_dollar):

(1) Financial Guide FX Fundamentals Retrieved on July 6, 2007 (http://www.financial-guide.net/markets-foreign_exchange-fx_fundamentals-page2.html).

(2) From November 1967 until June 1972, £1 was worth $2.40, making $1 = £0.41666, ±1%. see Linda Arch, The Regulation of the London Clearing Banks, 1946–1971: Stability and Compliance, pp. 72–73 (https://books.google.co.uk/books?id=hQJ2DwAAQBAJ&pg=PA73&lpg=PA73&dq=%22Bretton+woods%22+%22par+value%22+sterling+1946&source=bl&ots=tI0cDPri7N&sig=ACfU3U3qL6P8G5wy-1UWdRLOXoybe9Dkig&hl=en&sa=X&ved=2ahUKEwjRy5u_3croAhWFZMAKHehtDfAQ6AEwDHoECAwQKQ#v=onepage&q=%22Bretton%20woods%22%20%22par%20value%22%20sterling%201946&f=false).

(3) From September 1949 until November 1967, £1 was worth $2.80, making $1 worth £0.35714286, ±1%. see Linda Arch, The Regulation of the London Clearing Banks, 1946–1971: Stability and Compliance, pp. 72–73 (https://books.google.co.uk/books?id=hQJ2DwAAQBAJ&pg=PA73&lpg=PA73&dq=%22Bretton+woods%22+%22par+value%22+sterling+1946&source=bl&ots=tI0cDPri7N&sig=ACfU3U3qL6P8G5wy-1UWdRLOXoybe9Dkig&hl=en&sa=X&ved=2ahUKEwjRy5u_3croAhWFZMAKHehtDfAQ6AEwDHoECAwQKQ#v=onepage&q=%22Bretton%20woods%22%20%22par%20value%22%20sterling%201946&f=false).

(4) Exchange rates for the U.S. dollar vs 41 other currencies.

(5) Foreign Exchange Rates: Demand Draft (1893–1926).

(6) *Antweiler, Werner (2016). "Foreign Currency Units per 1 U.S. Dollar, 1948–2015" (PDF). Canada: University of British Columbia.* Retrieved June 25, 2016.

(7) *"Currency converter—fxtop.com". fxtop.com.* Retrieved January 4, 2020.

(8) https://www.cia.gov/library/publications/the-world-factbook/fields/2076.html.

(9) On January 1, 2003, the Afghan afghani was rebased. 1 new afghani equals 1000 AFA. In this table the AFN is used throughout.

(10) In December 1999 the Angolan kwanza was rebased. 1 new kwanza equals 1 million old kwanza. In this table the new kwanza is used throughout.

(11) The East Caribbean dollar has been pegged at a fixed rate of 2.76 to the dollar since 1976.

(12) The Argentine peso was pegged at equal parity to the U.S. dollar from January 1992 to January 2002. Since then it has been allowed to float freely.

(13) The Aruban florin has been pegged to the U.S. dollar since 1986.

(14) On January 1, 2000 the Belarusian ruble was rebased. One new ruble is worth 2000 old rubles. The new ruble is used throughout in this table.

(15) The Communaute Financiere Africaine franc is pegged to the euro. Before 1999, it was pegged to the French Franc.

(16) The Bhutan ngultrum is at par with the Indian rupee which is also legal tender.

(17) From October 1994 through 14 January 1999, the official Brazilian rate was determined by a managed float; since 15 January 1999, the official rate floats independently with respect to the U.S. dollar.

(18) The Bruneian dollar is at par with the Singaporean dollar.

(19) The Bulgarian lev was rebased on July 5, 1999. 1000 old levs are worth 1 new lev. New levs are used throughout this table.

(20) Prior to January 1999, the official rate was pegged to the French franc at 75 Comorian francs per French franc; since 1 January 1999, the Comorian franc is pegged to the euro at a rate of 491.9677 Comorian francs per euro

CHAPTER 2

Sustainable Growth, Financial Stability and the Failure/Unconstitutionality of the Dodd-Frank Act (USA) (and Similar Statutes Such as the Pre-2020 *European Union Sustainable Growth Regulations*)

"Restoring American Financial Stability Act" of 2010 (*RAFSA* or the Dodd-Frank Act) was the first set of statutes in any country that attempted to simultaneously address the Global Financial Crisis, financial stability, systemic risk, consumer protection, sustainable growth, the national securities law framework, the structure of the executive branch of the federal government and delegation of powers to federal government agencies (to the detriment of state governments). However, RAFSA and similar statutes in many countries/jurisdictions are inefficient, and have failed to address the fundamental problems in financial systems; and parts of RAFSA are unconstitutional. In July 2010, the US Congress enacted the Restoring American Financial Stability Act of 2010 (RAFSA or the Dodd-Frank

---

This chapter contains excerpts from the author Michael C. Nwogugu's articles that are cited as:

1. Nwogugu, M. (2015b). Un-Constitutionality of the Dodd-Frank Act. *European Journal of Law Reform*, 17, 185–190.
2. Nwogugu, M. (2015a). Failure of the Dodd-Frank Act. *Journal of Financial Crime*, 22(4), 520–572.

M. I. C. Nwogugu, *Geopolitical Risk, Sustainability and "Cross-Border Spillovers" in Emerging Markets, Volume II*,
https://doi.org/10.1007/978-3-030-71419-2_2

Act),[1] which consists of several individual distinct statutes and substantially changes the nature and effects of federalism and pre-emption in the United States—RAFSA grants more powers to the US federal government to regulate more financial services, but because the statute leaves critical details up to the US SEC and the US Federal Reserve System, sections of RAFSA may be challenged in court on constitutional grounds as void for vagueness.

Other countries/jurisdictions have enacted statutes that are similar to RAFSA.[2] Canada, Brazil and Asian countries have also introduced similar statutes. The United Kingdom introduced the Vickers Report, which is similar to the Volcker Rule (the Vickers Report has the same purpose of the Volcker Rule but it has different methods, and is based on the ring fence and not on the separation of commercial and investment banks). The European Union (EU) also released the *Report of the European Commission's High-level Expert Group on Bank Structural Reform* (aka *Liikanen Group Report*) which addresses such differences; and the European Union enacted the European Market Infrastructure Regulation (EMIR),[3] the Markets in Financial Instruments Directive II and related

[1] *See*: Summary of Financial Stability Act of 2010. Available at: http://banking.senate.gov/public/_files/FinancialReformSummaryAsFiled.pdf.

See: Davis Polk (2010). *Summary of the Restoring American Financial Stability Act, Passed by the Senate on 20 May 2010.* www.davispolk.com/sites/default/files/files/Publication/fc30f0b3-3db4-4181-a44e-3b3e54853b6f/Preview/PublicationAttachment/19c8367f-0467-4f3d-8492-010c9692578c/052210_Davis_Polk_Senate_Bill_as_Passed_Summary.pdf.

See: s.3217, 'Restoring American Financial Stability Act of 2010'. Available at: http://frwebgate.access.gpo.gov/cgi-bin/getdoc.cgi?dbname=111_cong_bills&docid=f:s3217as.txt.pdf.

See: http://dpc.senate.gov/docs/lb-111-2-64.html.

See: *Administration's Financial Regulatory Reform Bill, 2009 and 2010.* Available at: www.llsdc.org/Admin-Bill/.

See: '*Financial Overhaul Bill Has Many Rules*'. Available at: www.lvrj.com/business/bill-has-many-rules%2D%2Dcritics-97836159.html.

See: Jones, G., Klutsey, B. & Christ, K. (January, 2010). *Speed Bankruptcy: A Firewall to Future Crises.* Working Paper #10-02, Mercatus Center at George Mason University, USA.

See: Congressional Research Service (USA) (April 1, 2010). Summary of '*Restoring American Financial Stability Act of 2010*'. Financial Stability Act of 2010 (introduced on 15 April 2010).

[2] *See*: Shearman & Sterling, *Dodd-Frank, UK, EU & Other Regulatory Reforms* (2013) at http://www.shearman.com/dodd-frank/.

[3] *See*: Regulation 648/2012 on OTC derivatives, central counterparties and trade repositories [2012] OJ L201/1.

Regulation (MiFID II and MIFIR),[4] the new Capital Requirements Directive and Regulation (CRD IV)[5] and other statutes (collectively, the "EU Sustainable Growth Regulations").

Together, RAFSA and the EU Sustainable Growth Regulations have emerged as the new *Constitution of The Global Capital Markets.*

2.1 Existing Literature

According to David Polk (July 2016), as of July 19, 2016, 271 Dodd-Frank Act rulemaking deadlines were not met; and of those, 210 (77.5%) had been met with finalized rules and rules had been proposed that would meet 29 (10.7%) more; and rules had not yet been proposed to meet 32 (11.8%) missed rulemaking requirements. According to David Polk (July 2016), as of July 19, 2016, of the 390 total rulemaking requirements, 274 (70.3%) had been met with finalized rules and rules have been proposed that would meet 36 (9.2%) more; and rules had not yet been proposed to meet 80 (20.5%) rulemaking requirements.[6]

Nwogugu (2015a) analyzed the deficiencies in, and failures of, Dodd-Frank Act; and Nwogugu (2015b) explained why sections of Dodd-Frank Act are unconstitutional. While the Dodd-Frank Act has become pervasive around the world (via US multinational corporations, US international banks, cross-border swaps/derivatives and foreign companies whose shares/bonds are listed in US exchanges), its not clear that its being fully incorporated into quantitative models in published research (i.e. within the context of Panel Vector Autoregressive models, Granger Causality, GARCH-type models, Economic Modeling, Economic Forecasting, Political Decisions, Behavioral Macroeconomics, Behavioral Expectations, Peer Effects, sovereign debt crisis, VaR estimation, financial markets regulation, Portfolio Management, Tail Risk; etc.).

[4] *See*: FSA (UK) (2012), Review of The *Markets in Financial Instruments Directive II*. Available at: http://www.fsa.gov.uk/about/what/international/mifid.

See: DIRECTIVE 2008/10/EC of The European Parliament And of The Council of 11 March 2008. Available at: http://eur-lex.europa.eu/LexUriServ/LexUriServ.do?uri=OJ:L:2008:076:0033:0036:EN:PDF.

[5] Directive 2006/48 relating to the taking up and pursuit of the business of credit institutions [2006] OJ L177/1.

[6] *See*: Davis Polk (July 2013). *Dodd Frank Progress Report, July 2013*. Available at: www.davispolk.com/Dodd-Frank-Rulemaking-Progress-Report/.

Other researchers have also criticised Dodd Frank Act and noted the following weaknesses:

1. RAFSA does not eliminate the *too-big-to-fail phenomenon*—see: Noss and Sowerbutts (2012), Li et al. (2011), Otker-Robe et al. (International Monetary Fund) (2011), Brewer and Jagtiani (2013), Schmid (2012), Fisher (2013, June)[7] and Natter (2011, July).[8]
2. RAFSA failed and is inefficient, didn't generate meaningful economic growth and omitted various critical regulation—see Gordon and Muller (2011), Summe (2014), Peirce and Broughel (2012)[9] and Nwogugu (2015a).

[7] *See*: Fisher, R. (June 2013). *Correcting 'Dodd-Frank' To Actually End 'Too Big to Fail'*. Statement before the Committee on Financial Services, U.S. House of Representatives Hearing on "Examining How the Dodd-Frank Act Could Result in More Taxpayer-Funded Bailouts", Washington, D.C., June 26, 2013. Available at: www.dallasfed.org/news/speeches/fisher/2013/fs130626.cfm.

[8] *See*: Natter, R. (July 2011). *Does Dodd-Frank End Too Big to Fail?* (RAFSA did not end the too-big-to-fail phenomenon). Available at: www.bsnlawfirm.com/newsletter/OP0711_3.pdf.

[9] *See*: Peirce, H. & Broughel, J., (Eds.) (2012). *Dodd-Frank: What It Does and Why It's Flawed*. Mercatus Center, George Mason University, USA. Available at: http://mercatus.org/sites/default/files/publication/dodd-frank-FINAL.pdf. This document states that:

1. The US FSOC has not played an effective coordinating role in the crucial initial years of regulatory implementation of Dodd-Frank;
2. Designating specific firms as systemically important creates a market expectation that designated firms are too big to fail and thus dulls market discipline;
3. The US Federal Reserve's bank-centric regulatory model will not work for non-banks;
4. The structure of the OFR enables it to operate without the accountability expected to apply to government agencies and without adequate safeguards on data;
5. Once a company is in resolution, the FDIC has broad discretion, without effective checks, to determine how creditors' claims are handled;
6. Expansion of deposit insurance decreases effective market restraint of bank risk taking and may yield greater systemic instability;
7. Title III adds a new layer of bureaucracy at each financial regulator;
8. SEC resources will be diverted from monitoring advisers who manage the assets of average retail investors to monitoring the assets of wealthy investors who invest in private funds;
9. Regulators have devised an unnecessarily costly compliance regime for private funds, the costs of which will be passed on to investors;
10. Designating insurance companies as systemic aggravates the too-big-to-fail problem and introduces an inexperienced regulator in the insurance space without solving the insurance regulatory failures in evidence at entities like AIG;

3. RAFSA didn't sufficiently address the enforcement pf Goodwill/ Intangibles Rules and associated behavioral issues see Nwogugu (2015c).
4. RAFSA didn't sufficiently address "Netting" and the Liquidity Coverage Ratio and REITs' problems; and the US FSOC's (Financial Stability Oversight Council) non-SIFI (systemically important financial institution) criteria are wrong and misleading—see: Nwogugu (2014a, b).
5. RAFSA does not help to reduce systemic risk significantly (given that the Global Financial Crisis was caused by "universal banks" who incurred more than US$8 trillion of operating losses between 2007 and 2012, allowing large banks to remain large is probably an error)—see Sharfman (2011), Coffee (2012), Allen (2012), Labonte (2010) and Wilmarth (2009).
6. RAFSA increases transaction costs and compliance costs.[10]

11. Title VI consolidates an inordinate amount of regulatory power in the Fed, despite the Fed's past regulatory failures;
12. Title IV increases the likelihood that the US Federal Reserve and other regulators will prop up failing financial firms in the future;
13. Because the statutory language is ambiguous and the proposed rules are even more so, the Volcker Rule could make it difficult for banks to engage in legitimate hedging and market-making activities. Market liquidity could suffer;
14. Title VII fragments regulation of OTC derivatives markets by assigning responsibility to two regulatory agencies; and it imposes a regulatory scheme that better suits a highly liquid retail market;
15. Regulators' overly aggressive, uncoordinated, and inadequately analyzed approach to implementation of Title VII increases the likelihood that new rules will have harmful unintended effects).

[10] *See*: Accenture (2010). "US Financial Regulatory Reform: Cost or Opportunity?', Impact of The Dodd-Frank Wall Street Reform Act" (predicting that it will cost the US financial services industry $3–$5 Billion between 2010 and 2013 to implement RAFSA; and that the annual operating profits of the hardest hit firms could fall by 20%–30%; and that RAFSA will produce new operational challenges and pose significant strategic questions about how firms will prop up their return on equity while absorbing the cost of more reporting to regulators, a more expensive cost of capital and the loss of some of their most profitable businesses; and Accenture's June 2010 poll of 101 financial industry executives found that nearly half (49%) thought their profits would decrease as a result of RAFSA). Available at: www.accenture.com/SiteCollectionDocuments/PDF/Accenture_US_Financial_Regulatory_Reform.pdf.

See: Wallison, P. (July 20, 2014). 'Four Years of Dodd-Frank Damage'. *Wall Street Journal*, 20 July 2014. Available at: www.wsj.com/articles/peter-wallison-four-years-of-dodd-frank-damage-1405893333.

7. RAFSA effectively grants excessive power to the US Federal Reserve—see: Schnidman (2011).[11]
8. RAFSA did not make the US SEC a self-funded agency, and this limits the SEC's scope and powers.[12]
9. The US Congress can still limit RAFSA by underfunding it—see Carton (2011).[13]
10. RAFSA has not created any meaningful economic growth in the US—see Khademian (2013) and Nwogugu (2015).
11. RAFSA did not remedy the inefficiencies in executive compensation in financial services companies and SIFIs—see: Sepe (2014) and Nwogugu (2015).
12. RAFSA omitted some key legislation—see: Barr (2012) and Nwogugu (2015).
13. The orderly Liquidation Authority is inefficient—see: Lee (2011).
14. RAFSA makes it difficult for small companies to raise capital.[14]
15. RAFSA does not adequately address the members of the Boards of Directors' obligations that pertain to risk management—*see:* Johnson (2011).

See: The Economist (2012) (supra).

See: Switzer, L. & Sheahan-Lee, E. (May 2013). '*The Impact of Dodd-Frank Regulation of OTC Derivative Markets and the Volcker Rule on International Versus US Banks: New Evidence*' (RAFSA imposes costs on US banks while foreign international banks avoid such costs).

[11] *See*: Schnidman (2011) (noting that the post-crisis financial system structure fails to look dramatically different than before; and the major change in the post-crisis financial regulatory system is a US Federal Reserve that has excessive powers; and that there is a weaker Consumer Financial Protection Bureau that is housed in the US Federal Reserve rather than as a stand-alone agency). Available at: www.hblr.org/2011/06/why-the-federal-reserve-is-dodd-franks-big-winner/; or www.hblr.org/?p=1203.

[12] *See*: *Top Securities Lawyers Call for Self-Funded S.E.C.* Available at: http://dealbook.nytimes.com/2010/06/11/top-securities-lawyers-call-for-self-funded-s-e-c (noting that RAFSA failed to make the US SEC a self-funded agency, and the omission severely limits the SEC's scope and power).

[13] *See*: Carton, B. (2011). *How Can Congress Kill Dodd-Frank? By Underfunding It.* www.securitiesdocket.com/2011/01/20/how-can-congress-kill-dodd-frank-by-underfunding-it.

[14] *See*: "*Small Biz Has Big Stake in Dodd-Frank Changes*". Available at: www.hartfordbusiness.com/article/20130617/PRINTEDITION/306139922/small-biz-has-big-stake-in-dodd-frank-changes. The article states in part "The Small Business Capital Access and Job Preservation Act (H.R. 1105) seeks to modify certain aspects of the Dodd-Frank Wall Street Reform and Consumer Protection Act that are inappropriate for private equity firms, particularly middle market private equity firms. H.R. 1105 will address the many unintended consequences of Dodd-Frank that impede the flow of capital to small businesses and do not provide any protection to investors or the financial system as a whole".

16. Nwogugu (2012b)[15] noted that asset securitization was unconstitutional, and Nwogugu (2008c, d) noted that Asset Securitization is illegal; and Nwogugu (2014c) analyzed problems inherent in the LIBOR/EURIBOR/SHIBOR rate-setting mechanisms (these issues were not addressed by RAFSA).
17. RAFSA can reduce transparency and cause potentially harmful disclosure. See: Nazreth and Tahyar (2011).
18. RAFSA created an intolerable level of uncertainty as to whether information that financial services companies disclose to government agencies will be kept confidential.

Greene (2011) noted some of the problems inherent in RAFSA such as the following:

- RAFSA fails to deal with regulatory fragmentation which refers to having too many government agencies—however, Greene was not specific and did not state which government agencies should have been combined, restructured or eliminated;
- RAFSA fails to address *international coordination*—regulatory arbitrage remains an issue—and funding resolution and bailout expenditures have been a point of international divergence; there is also a serious question about whether Dodd-Frank will undermine the competitive position of major US financial institutions because some sections of the Dodd-Frank Act such as the Volcker Rule will not be followed in other key jurisdictions such as the European Union.
- RAFSA is overly optimistic in dealing with too-big-to-fail.
- RAFSA does not restrict size by growth, only by acquisition (but the five largest US financial institutions have grown 20% since the onset of the Global Financial crisis and as of 2011, they had over $6 trillion in assets).
- RAFSA implies that size is not necessarily the only concern but size can be critical, because of the contagion effect of failure.

[15] *See*: Nwogugu, M. (2012b). 'Asset Securitization Is Un-Constitutional and Should Be Banned'. Chapter in: Nwogugu, M. (2012a), *Risk in the Real Estate Markets* (John Wiley; 2012).

- The Swiss approach to regulation is based on the theory that capital assessment and organizational simplicity are the solution, not activity restriction or size limitations—RAFSA takes almost an opposite approach;
- RAFSA does not address the issue of moral hazard adequately—and despite the many provisions to monitor and reduce systemic risk, it remains unlikely that the US Government will allow an institution that is the size of one of the United States's five largest financial institutions to fail, especially in the absence of effective coordinated and consistent resolution mechanisms in key markets (and such firms will continue to have financing advantages that only increase the likelihood of their failure).

Nwogugu (2015b) explained why sections of Dodd-Frank Act are unconstitutional, but for reasons different from those stated in The Economist (2012), Simon (2012), Morrison & Foerster (2012), Gray & Shu (2010), Hall & Kazman (Feb. 13, 2013), Gray & Purcell (June 21, 2012), McTaggart & Silver (2011), Addington (2011)), Gray & Shu (2010), Barnett (2011), Rabinovitch [2013], and Van Oppen & Van Wert (Oct. 28, 2014).

Coffee (2012) reviewed various reasons why RAFSA has failed including moral hazard, executive compensation, excessive focus on the too-big-to-fail dilemma and cognitive deficits. American Action Forum (2010)[16] and Elliot (2010) questioned the extent of regulations of both the size of banks and trading of derivatives (two critical issues that led to the Global Financial Crisis). Schwarcz (2011) critiqued RAFSA's ability to reduce systemic risk. Rose and Walker (2013) noted the lack of adequate cost-benefit analysis for statutes like RAFSA.

2.1.1 Violations of the Appointments Clause, the Takings Clause, the Separation of Powers Doctrine *and* Article-Three *of the US Constitution*

The Economist (2012),[17] Simon (2012), Morrison and Foerster (2012),[18] Gray and Shu (2010), and other authors (see: Hall and

[16] *See*: American Action Forum (April 2010). The Senate Financial Regulatory Reform Bill. Available at: http://americanactionforum.org/files/FinRegBill1_0.pdf.

See: Elliot, D. (March 15, 2010). *Evaluating Key Aspects of Senator Dodd's Revised Financial Reform Bill*. The Brookings Institution.

[17] *See*: The Economist (2012) (supra).

[18] *See*: Morrison & Foerster (2012). '*The Dodd-Frank Act: A Cheat Sheet*'. Available at: www.mofo.com/files/Uploads/Images/SummaryDoddFrankAct.pdf.

Kazman 2013, February 13; McTaggart and Silver 2011; and Addington 2011)[19] stated that RAFSA may be unconstitutional (but for reasons different from those stated in this chapter), and that sections of RAFSA are vague (see: Gray and Shu 2010; and Rabinovitch 2013, December 22); and violate the *Appointments Clause* (Barnett 2011), the *Takings Clause* (Rabinovitch 2013)[20] the *Separation of Powers*

[19] *See*: Hall, C. & Kazman, S. (February 13, 2013). '*Eight More States Join Constitutional Challenge to Dodd-Frank Act: Eleven States Now Challenge Dodd-Frank's Orderly Liquidation Authority, Which Exacerbates "Too Big To Fail" and Puts State Pensions and Other Funds at Risk*'. Available at: https://cei.org/news-releases/eight-more-states-join-constitutional-challenge-dodd-frank-act.

See: Gray, C. & Purcell, J. (June 21, 2012). 'Why Dodd-Frank Is Unconstitutional: The Financial Regulations Signed into Law in 2010 Do Not Honor Checks and Balances. They Eliminate Them'. *Wall Street Journal*, 21 June 2012. Available at: www.wsj.com/articles/SB10001424052702304765304577480451892603234.

See: McTaggart, T. & Silver, M. (2011). *Constitutionality Analysis of Certain of the Dodd-Frank Wall Street Reform and Consumer Protection Act's Most Significant Grants of Regulatory Power*. Available at: www.pepperlaw.com/pdfs/McTaggart_CatoInstitutePresentation_021511.pdf.

See: US House Hearing, 113 Congress (July 9, 2013). *Examining Constitutional Deficiencies and Legal Uncertainties in The Dodd Frank Act*, Hearing before the Subcommittee on Oversight and Investigations of the Committee on Financial Services. US House of Representatives, One Hundred Thirteenth Congress, First Session, 9 July 2013. Available at: www.gpo.gov/fdsys/pkg/CHRG-113hhrg82859/html/CHRG-113hhrg82859.htm.

See: Addington, D. (2011). *Congress Should Promptly Repeal or Fix Unwarranted Provisions of the Dodd-Frank Act*. www.heritage.org/research/reports/2011/10/congress-should-promptly-repeal-or-fix-unwarranted-provisions-of-the-dodd-frank-act.

[20] *See*: Rabinovitch (2013) (discussing the violation of the *Takings Clause* that is inherent in the *Durbin Amendment*).

See: *Federal Republic of Germany* et al. vs. *Philipp* et al. (No. 19–351; February 3, 2021; US Supreme Court). https://www.supremecourt.gov/opinions/20pdf/19-351_o7jp.pdf.

See: *Bolivarian Republic of Venezuela vs. Helmerich & Payne Int'l Drilling Co.*, 581 U.S. _____ (2017, US Supreme Court).

See: *Cedar Point Nursery vs. Hassid*, ____ US ____ (US Supreme Court; pending as of 2021).

See: *Cedar Point Nursery vs. Sheroma*, ____ F.3d. ____ (US Ninth Circuit Court of Appeals).

See: *PennEast Pipeline Co. vs. New Jersey*, ___ US ____ (US Supreme Court; pending as of 2021).

See: *Murr vs. Wisconsin*, 137 S.Ct. 1933 (US Supreme Court; 2017).

See: *California Bldg. Industry Ass'n vs. City of San Jose, Calif.*, 136 S.Ct. 928 (US Supreme Court; 2016).

See: *Koontz vs. St. Johns River Water Management District*, 570 U.S. 2588 (US Supreme Court; 2013).

See: *Lucas vs. South Carolina Coastal Council*, 505 U.S. 1003 (US Supreme Court; 1992).

Doctrine (Van Oppen and Van Wert 2014, October 28;[21] Nwogugu 2012a, 264–265;[22] and Rabinovitch 2013[23]) and Article-Three of the US Constitution (Horton 2011). RAFSA didn't eliminate the adjudicatory powers of the US SEC. Several authors noted that RAFSA violates the Non-delegation Doctrine because it unconstitutionally delegates legislative power to the US Financial Stability Oversight Council (FSOC) and the CFPB in contravention of Article-One of the US Constitution. RAFSA violates the *Separation of Powers Doctrine* because it grants both rule-making and enforcement powers to the US FSOC and to the Consumer Financial Protection Bureau (CFPB), and grants adjudicative powers to the CFPB.

2.1.2 Dodd-Frank Act As Major International Criminal Law And Administrative Law Reform: Unconstitutionality of the Criminal Provisions of the Dodd-Frank Act

Dodd-Frank Act significantly amended existing US federal criminal law statutes and added new major criminal law provisions that can have substantial impact on litigation in US federal and state courts and in foreign countries (see the section in Chap. 1 about new sources of International Law). These new Dodd-Frank Act criminal provisions are likely to have substantial economic and psychological *Multiplier Effects*—in terms of Willingness-To-Comply, Consumer Confidence, Consumer Debt, Business Confidence, Litigation costs, Transaction Costs and so on. Heritage Foundation and National Association of Criminal Defense

[21] *See*: Van Oppen and Van Wert (2014, October 28) (questioning the constitutionality of the US SEC's adjudicatory powers and in-house courts).

[22] *See*: Nwogugu (2012a: 264–265) (noting that the US SEC's and the US IRS's rule-making and adjudicatory powers constitute violations of the *Separation of Powers Doctrine*).

See: *Collins vs. Yellen*, ___ US ___ (No. 19-422; US Supreme Court; pending as of 2021).

See: *Collins vs. Mnuchin*, ____ US ____ (Docket No. 19-422; US Supreme Court; pending as of 2021).

See: *Seila Law LLC vs. Consumer Financial Protection Bureau*, ____ US ____ (Case#: No. 19-7; US Supreme Court; 2020) (the Consumer Financial Protection Bureau's single-Director structure violates the *Separation of Powers Doctrine*, and the proper remedy is to sever the Director's statutory for-cause removal restriction).

See: *Humphrey's Executor vs. United States*, 295 U.S. 602 (US Supreme Court; 1935).

See: *PHH Corp. vs. CFPB*, 839 F.3d 1 (2016) *on rehearing enbanc*, 881 F.3d 75 (D.C. Cir., 2018) (en banc).

[23] *See*: Rabinovitch 2013 (noting that RAFSA violates the *Separation of Powers Doctrine*).

Lawyers (NACDL) (2010),[24] NACDL (2010a),[25] NACDL (2010b)[26] and Joslyn (2010) criticized the criminal law provisions in RAFSA and found them to be unconstitutional. While most of their Constitutional Law arguments are reasonable, they focused on the *Mens Rea* and *Intent*

[24] *See*: Heritage Foundation and National Association of Criminal Defense Lawyers ("NACDL") (2010). *Without Intent: How Congress Is Eroding the Criminal Intent Requirement in Federal Law*. Available at: www.nacdl.org/withoutintent.

[25] *See*: National Association of Criminal Defense Lawyers ("NACDL") (2010a). *NACDL on HR 4173–Recommendations* (recommendations for reforming Dodd-Frank Conference Report [HR 4173]). Available at: www.nacdl.org/public.nsf/86871e9e0d470e318525 7006006e5f55/b5224f126c7e41cb8525773f00741 36f/$FILE/NACDL%20on%20 HR4173.pdf. Also available at: www.nacdl.org/criminaldefense.aspx?id=9920. NACDL (2010a) criticized specific sections of RAFSA as follows:

1. Section 202(a)(1)(C)—is over-criminalized and has inadequate *Mens Rea* requirement and should be deleted.
2. Section 741—covers material that is already covered in the federal mail fraud and wire fraud codes; and weakens the *Mens Rea* requirements; and should be deleted.
3. Section 747(B)(5)—does not provide adequate notice; is somewhat vague; and has inadequate *Mens Rea* requirement and should be deleted.
4. Section 747 (amends 7 USC 6c(a) by adding "(7) use of swaps to Defraud")—this statute duplicates existing federal aiding-and-abetting and conspiracy statutes; weakens the men area requirement and should be deleted.
5. Section 1036(3)—this statute duplicates existing federal aiding-and-abetting and conspiracy statutes; does not have adequate men area requirement and should be deleted.
6. The following statutes lack adequate *Mens Rea* requirements: Section 723; Section 768(b); Section 724; Section 728; Section 731; Section 733; Section 975(a)(1); Section 764; Section 753(b); Section 746; Section 747; Section 724(a); Section 730; Section 929; Section 975(a)(5); and Section 1036(1;2;3).
7. The following sections of RAFSA are over-broad or vague: Section 746; Section 975; and Section 934.
8. The following sections of RAFSA constitute inappropriate regulatory criminalization: Section 730; Section 929 and Section 1036.
9. Sections that require conforming amendments—Sections 763 and 764 at pages 387 and 409 repeat many of the aforementioned offenses, and should be amended to conform to recommended changes.

[26] *See*: National Association of Criminal Defense Lawyers ('NACDL') (2010b). *Criminal Provisions in HR 4173* (list of the criminal provisions in Dodd-Frank Conference Report [HR 4173]).

requirements of criminal liability. NACDL (2010a, 2010b) critiqued some specific criminal sections of Dodd-Frank Act—see herein and below.)[27]

2.1.3 *Omissions of In-depth Analysis of Constitutionally Granted* Right-to-Contract, Equal Protection *and* Right-of-Association *in the Labor Regulation and Labor Economics Literatures: A Critique Of Mwakagali (2018)*

It's notable that in the Labor Economics and Labor Regulation literatures, most studies have completely omitted (or didn't adequately analyze) constitutional analysis[28] of workers' *Right-to-Contract*, *Right-of-Association* and *Equal Protection* rights. These three constitutional rights are central to workers' rights and ability to negotiate working conditions and to push for implementation of Collective Bargaining agreements, both of which account for a significant percentage of Labor-related litigation and economic Multiplier Effects.

Even studies such as Mwakagali (2018) that take the legal approach have failed to fully analyze the Constitutional Law and Constitutional Political Economy implications of workers' *Right-to-Contract* and *Right-of-Association*.

[27] *See*: Joslyn, T. (Dec. 10, 2010). Criminal Provisions in the Dodd-Frank Wall Street Reform & Consumer Protection Act. *The Federalist Society*. https://fedsoc.org/commentary/publications/criminal-provisions-in-the-dodd-frank-wall-street-reform-consumer-protection-act.

[28] *See*: "*Unions, retirees sue to block Chicago pension changes*". By Karen Pierog. December 16, 2014. https://www.reuters.com/article/usa-chicago-pensions-lawsuit/update-2-unions-retirees-sue-to-block-chicago-pension-changes-idUSL1N0U01MO20141216 (states in part: "The lawsuit asks the court to declare the law void and illegal because pensions will be reduced in violation of a constitutional provision prohibiting the diminishment or impairment of public employee retirement benefits. A similar argument by unions and others led to a November 21 Sangamon County Circuit Court ruling that tossed Illinois' 2013 pension reform law for being unconstitutional. The Illinois Supreme Court will hear arguments in March over the state's appeal of that ruling. Illinois has the worst-funded state pension fund, while Chicago is struggling with a huge pension funding burden. Moody's Investors Service has said the city is an "extreme outlier" among U.S. local governments it rates, citing a $32 billion adjusted net pension liability that is equal to eight times operating revenue. A hearing on a temporary restraining order to stop the January 1 implementation of Chicago's pension law is set for December 29, according to AFSCME spokesman Anders Lindall. He said last month's ruling on Illinois' law, along with a state supreme court ruling in July over state retiree health care, have reinforced constitutional protections for retirement benefits").

2.1.4 *Dodd-Frank Act as* "Super" *Labor Regulation*

The Dodd-Frank Act has functioned as both a modifier and an enactment of labor regulations that can have cross-border *Multiplier Effects*. The *Legislative-Intent*, history, wording and application/implementation of Dodd-Frank Act clearly indicates an intent to directly/indirectly regulate or modify or affect the following issues that pertain to the global labor market:

1. Existing labor/employment regulations (especially in the banking/financial-services industry).
2. Workers' rights (including complaints and appeals) and consumer financial protection (i.e. the Consumer Financial Protection Bureau).
3. Financial matters that affect pension funds and mutual funds (workers' retirement savings).
4. Whistleblower protections[29] and working conditions.

[29] *See*: The U.S. Securities and Exchange Commission (2011). *Implementation of the Whistleblower Provisions of Section 21F of the Securities Exchange Act of 1934*. https://www.sec.gov/rules/final/2011/34-64545.pdf.

See: "*New Record for Dodd-Frank Whistleblowers – Employment Law This Week*". By Epstein Becker & Green, P.C. on April 11, 2018. https://www.workforcebulletin.com/2018/04/11/new.-record-for-dodd-frank-whistleblowers-employment-law-this-week/.

See: Malone, A. & Jones, R. (December 6, 2010). "*Revealed: Inside the Chinese suicide sweatshop where workers toil in 34-hour shifts to make your iPod*". Daily Mail (London). Available at: http://www.dailymail.co.uk/news/article-1285980/Revealed-Inside-Chinese-suicide-sweatshop-workers-toil-34-hour-shifts-make-iPod.html.

See: "*Chinese Factory asks for 'no suicide' vow*". MSNBC. May 26, 2010. Available at: http://www.msnbc.msn.com/id/37354853/ns/business-world_business/?ns=business-world_business.

See: Carlson, N. (April 7, 2010). "*What It's Like To Work In China's Gadget Sweatshops Where Your iPhones And iPads Are Made*". *Business Insider*. Available at: http://www.businessinsider.com/what-its-like-to-work-if-chinas-gadget-sweatshops-where-your-iphones-and-ipads-are-made-2010-4?utm_source=Daily+Buzz&utm_campaign=81432d578c-nl_emv_db_04082010_a&utm_medium=email.

See: "*Apple denies claims it broke Chinese labor laws in iPhone factory*". September 8, 2019. Saheli Roy Choudhury. https://www.cnbc.com/2019/09/09/apple-appl-claims-it-broke-china-labor-laws-at-iphone-factory-mostly-false.html.

See: "*Apple's 2019 supplier report shows progress on labor and health issues*". Jeremy Horwitz. March 6, 2019. https://venturebeat.com/2019/03/06/apples-2019-supplier-report-shows-progress-on-labor-and-health-issues/.

See: "*Apple and Foxconn broke Chinese Labour law to build new iPhones – US tech group and manufacturing partner admit using too many temporary workers*". Louise Lucas. September 9, 2019. https://www.ft.com/content/19fefd86-d2c3-11e9-8367-807ebd53ab77.

See: Chen, B. (May 14, 2010), "*Workers Plan to Sue iPhone Contractor Over Poisoning*", *Wired*. https://www.wired.com/gadgetlab/2010/05/wintek-employees-sue/.

See: "*Apple under fire again for working conditions at Chinese factories*". *The Guardian*. December 19, 2014. https://www.theguardian.com/technology/2014/dec/19/apple-under-fire-again-for-working-conditions-at-chinese-factories?CMP=EMCNEWEML66 19I2.

See: "Study Casts Doubts on Apple's Ethical Standards". *China Labor Watch*. February 24, 2016. http://www.chinalaborwatch.org/report/113.

See: "*Poor Working Conditions Persist at Apple Supplier Pegatron*". *China Labor Watch*. October 22, 2015. http://www.chinalaborwatch.org/report/109.

See: Perlin, R. (2013). "Chinese Workers Foxconned". *Dissent*, 60(2), 46–52.

See: Armitage, J. (July 30, 2013). "*'Even worse than Foxconn': Apple rocked by child labour claims*". *The Independent*. London.

See: Mozur, P. (December 19, 2012). "Life Inside Foxconn's Facility in Shenzhen". *The Wall Street Journal*. https://blogs.wsj.com/chinarealtime/2012/12/19/life-inside-foxconns-facility-in-shenzhen/.

See: "*Apple suppliers maintain tight security to avoid leaks: Foxconn said to have 'special status' in China*". MacNN, February 17, 2010. Available at: http://www.macnn.com/articles/10/02/17/foxconn.said.to.have.special.status.in.china/.

See: *Apple's Recent Strike in Suzhou is Sign of Continued Bad Labor and CSR Practices in China*. *All Roads Lead to China*, January 21, 2010. Available at: http://www.allroadsleadtochina.com/2010/01/21/will-apple-be-the-next-nike-or-will-they-take-labor-compliance-seriously/.

See: "*Apple – Supplier Responsibility*" (PDF). Apple. Available at: http://images.apple.com/supplierresponsibility/pdf/L418102A_SR_2010Report_FF.pdf.

See: Blodget, H. (April 7, 2010). "*Apple-Supplier Factory Worker Tries to Kill Herself – That's 4 in 4 Weeks*". Business Insider. Available at: http://www.businessinsider.com/henry-blodget-another-apple-supplier-factory-worker-tries-to-kill-herself-thats-4-in-4-weeks-2010-4.

See: *Apple Loses Lawsuit Over a Company Policy Tim Cook Didn't Know About*. By Sissi Cao. February 14, 2020. https://observer.com/2020/02/apple-lose-lawsuit-retail-employee-security-check-pay/. ("Apple has a lost a class-action lawsuit brought by its Apple store employees regarding a seemingly miscellaneous company policy at the retail level that CEO Tim Cook wasn't even aware of. The plaintiffs filed the class-action suit in 2013, revealing that Apple would require its retail employees to go through a security check after they clocked out every day to make sure that no company assets or trade secrets were stolen. The exit check would typically take 10 to 20 minutes and involved searches of employees' purses, briefcases and personal iPhones").

See: *Apple sued by employees over labor issues*. by James O'Toole. July 23, 2014. https://money.cnn.com/2014/07/23/technology/apple-labor/. ("The company is facing a lawsuit certified as a class action this week from employees who say they were denied meal breaks

5. Employee-costs (i.e. compliance costs, employee salaries, employee taxes, etc.) of banks and financial services companies.
6. Increased compliance processes and documentation that pertain to work-processes and workers in the financial services industry.
7. The restructuring or Orderly Liquidation of financially or operationally distressed financial institutions—and without such Dodd-Frank Act processes, such distress can cause significant job losses and workers' psychological distress not only at the troubled financial institution, but also at its competitors.
8. Diversity and fair inclusion of minorities and women.[30]

and rest periods in violation of California labor law. Attorneys for the plaintiffs estimate that more than 20,000 current or former Apple employees from the retail to corporate level have been affected by the alleged violations. Among other things, the lawsuit claims Apple employees were forced to work for stretches of five hours or more without meals, and didn't get breaks on shorter shifts").

See: "Class complaint for injunctive relief and damages, in the United States District Court for the District of Columbia, 15 December 2019; Major tech companies respond to lawsuit over mining deaths". ComputerWeekly.com. https://www.business-humanrights.org/en/latest-news/lawsuit-against-apple-google-tesla-and-others-re-child-labour-drc/ ("Snapshot: In 2019, IRAdvocates, a US-based NGO filed a class action lawsuit against Apple, Google, Tesla, Alphabet, Microsoft, and Dell alleging the corporations profited from child labour in their cobalt supply chains in the Democratic Republic of Congo. Plaintiffs are either guardians of children killed in cobalt mining tunnels or children who were maimed while working in the mines").

See: *The Other Side Of Apple II: Pollution Spreads Through Apple's Supply Chain*. Institute of Public and Environmental Affairs, August 31, 2011. http://www.ipe.org.cn/Upload/Report-IT-V-Apple-II.pdf.

See: Barboza, D. (2012). Apple Cited as Adding to Pollution in China. *The New York Times*, September 1, 2011. Accessed March 26, 2012. https://www.nytimes.com/2011/09/02/technology/apple-suppliers-causing-environmental-problems-chinese-group-says.html?_r=1.

See: Watts, Jonathan, Apple secretive about 'polluting and poisoning' supply chain, says report. The Guardian, January 19, 2011. https://www.theguardian.com/environment/2011/jan/20/apple-pollution-supply-chain.

See: Jobs, Steve, A Greener Apple. Apple, Inc. https://www.apple.com/hotnews/agreenerapple/.

See: Greenpeace. "*Hazardous Materials Found in Apple's iPhone: Chemicals Include those Banned in Children's Toys in EU*". Greenpeace International. Greenpeace. http://www.greenpeace.org/usa/en/media-center/news-releases/hazardous-materials-found-in-a/.

[30] *See*: "*Dodd-Frank Wall Street Reform Act Requires Federal Financial Agencies to Address Diversity and Fair Inclusion of Minorities and Women*". By Stephanie Wilson. October 20, 2010. https://www.employmentlawwatch.com/category/employment-us/workplace-laws-and-regulations/.

9. Statutorily mandated bounties and Anti-Retaliation provisions[31] (employer-retaliation in the workplace).
10. *Say-on-Pay* (mandatory disclosure of *income inequality*) by exchange-traded companies in the USA.
11. Consumers' perceptions of fairness of the financial system and working conditions—which in turn affects worker motivation and morale, Consumer/Corporate Tax Compliance, Consumer Confidence, Business Confidence, productivity, and so on. See the comments in: Hardardottir (2017), Dixon et al. (2014), Debelle (2004), Garcia et al. (2020) and Nguyen and Claus (2013).
12. Hansberry (2012) noted that RAFSA distorted the US Foreign Corrupt Practices Act (FCPA).[32] The FCPA requires US firms (and some foreign companies that issued securities in the USA) to maintain proper accounting records and bars them from engaging in corruption. The FCPA is enforced by the US SEC and the US DOJ. Under the US SEC's whisteblower program, whistleblowers can report violations of the FCPA to the US SEC for prosecution. However, a significant percentage of the corruption that is regulated by the FCPA pertains to, or can be attributed to, labor issues and labor costs.

Nwogugu (2015a, b), Lee (2011), Johnson (2011), Gordon and Muller (2011), Summe (2014), Peirce and Broughel (2012), Rabinovitch (2013, December 22), Barnett (2011), Horton (2011) and Smith and Muniz-Fraticelli (2013) critiqued the Dodd-Frank Act. Feldman et al. (2013) and Dolar and Dale (2020) discussed some of the impact of the Dodd-Frank Act. Kenadjian et al. (2013), Cervone (2017), Godwin et al. (2017) and Greene and Potiha (2013) focused on the cross-border impact of Dodd-Frank Act.

[31] *See: Financial Regulators Set Out to Get Their Man: Federally Mandated Bounties and Anti-Retaliation Provisions Designed to Regulate the Financial Services Industry.* By David Krulewicz and Stephanie Wilson. October 26, 2010. https://www.employmentlawwatch.com/category/employment-us/.

[32] *See*: "*The International State of Corruption: Why the Foreign Corrupt Practices Act Continues to be the Most Successful Mechanism Available to Fight Corruption*". Tuesday, October 27, 2020. https://www.natlawreview.com/article/international-state-corruption-why-foreign-corrupt-practices-act-continues-to-be.

On Economic Psychology of international Labor-Market institutions, see: Ochsen and Welsch (2012), Haferkamp et al. (2009) and Pántya et al. (2016).

See the comments in MacDonald (2013). While Mwakagali (2018)[33] focuses on "IFIs" (such as World Bank, EBRD, Asian Development Bank, IBRD), some large international banks such as Citigroup, HSBC and JP Morgan function as informal "International Financial Institutions" (IFIs). Freeman (2011) critiqued the US National Labor Relations Act and suggested characteristics and additional components of new labor regulations for the twenty-first century. The Dodd-Frank Act effectively reduces the probability of unionization and Collective Bargaining in the financial services industry and in ancillary industries (such as computer hardware/software, transportation, building services, electrical services) in the following ways:

1. By statutory creation of the Consumer Financial Protection Bureau which encourages and handles individual-consumer complaints (but not collective-action by worker-consumers)—such as group complaints, or lawyer-represented class-action[34] complaints or union-

[33] States in part: "Today, labor rights stand at a crossroads. The traditional stance where labor law and regulation rested in the state as the lawmaker, enforcer and implementer, with international labor standards as the minimum standards has, with time, been hampered by the activities of other actors, such as multinational corporations, international non-governmental organizations, paramilitary groups, international financial institutions (IFIs) and international organizations, that have inadvertently had an impact on labor standards and their governance. Here, the boundaries between domestic and international are increasingly blurred as issues which were once solely under the purview of domestic law and politics, such as environmental standards and labor regulation, are influenced and affected by such actors".

[34] *See: You Still Can't Sue Your Bank. So What Can You Do? How to make arbitration work in disputes with your financial institution*". By Tobie Stanger. October 25, 2017. https://www.consumerreports.org/contracts-arbitration/you-still-cant-sue-your-bank-arbitration-cfpb/. This article states in part: "The Senate's recent vote to let forced-arbitration language remain in consumer contracts with banks and other financial institutions means that consumers will continue to have limited legal options when they believe they've been harmed by companies like Wells Fargo and Equifax. Now, as before, consumers with complaints about financial companies will in most cases be forced to settle the dispute in arbitration, an out-of-court procedure that often favors deep-pocketed companies and usually can't be appealed. With Vice President Mike Pence casting the tie-breaking vote, the Senate voted 51 to 50 to eliminate a rule, finalized in July by the Consumer Financial Protection Bureau, that would have made it easier for consumers to join class-action lawsuits to fight alleged misconduct by financial institutions. Under the *Congressional Review Act*, lawmakers can vacate government agency regulations 60 legislative days after their introduction. The House already voted against the rule, so it is effectively dead. It would have gone into full effect in 2018.

represented complaints about workers' pension funds[35] (e.g. pension payments), workers' 401K and IRA accounts, workers' social security deductions; workers' contractual non-pension benefits (including benefits obtained from or through a labor union); workers' student-debt[36] administration; workers' mortgages obtained under a labor union's mortgage programs; etc. CFPB defines a consumer complaint as "submissions that express dissatisfaction with, or communicate suspicion of wrongful conduct by, an identifiable entity

Consumers Union, the policy and mobilization division of Consumer Reports, had strenuously supported the CFPB's rule to give consumers the option to join in class actions against financial institutions".

[35] *See*: *Are California pensions 'sacrosanct?' State Supreme Court hears challenge to Jerry Brown's law*. By Wes Venteicher. May 05, 2020. https://www.sacbee.com/news/politics-government/the-state-worker/article242524421.html.

See: *Harzewski vs. Guidant Corporation*, 489 F.3d. 799 (2007, US Seventh Circuit Court of Appeals) (under ERISA, former employees can sue pension plans). https://www.casemine.com/judgement/us/59146e09add7b0493432e5b3.

See: *"Unions, retirees sue to block Chicago pension changes*". By Karen Pierog. December 16, 2014. https://www.reuters.com/article/usa-chicago-pensions-lawsuit/update-2-unions-retirees-sue-to-block-chicago-pension-changes-idUSL1N0U01MO20141216. (states in part: "The lawsuit asks the court to declare the law void and illegal because pensions will be reduced in violation of a constitutional provision prohibiting the diminishment or impairment of public employee retirement benefits. A similar argument by unions and others led to a November 21 Sangamon County Circuit Court ruling that tossed Illinois' 2013 pension reform law for being unconstitutional. The Illinois Supreme Court will hear arguments in March over the state's appeal of that ruling. Illinois has the worst-funded state pension fund, while Chicago is struggling with a huge pension funding burden. Moody's Investors Service has said the city is an 'extreme outlier' among U.S. local governments it rates, citing a $32 billion adjusted net pension liability that is equal to eight times operating revenue. A hearing on a temporary restraining order to stop the January 1 implementation of Chicago's pension law is set for December 29, according to AFSCME spokesman Anders Lindall. He said last month's ruling on Illinois' law, along with a state supreme court ruling in July over state retiree health care, have reinforced constitutional protections for retirement benefits").

[36] *See*: "*Consumer Protection Agency Is Failing Student Loan Borrowers, Lawsuit Says*". November 25, 2019. https://www.npr.org/2019/11/25/782460891/consumer-agency-failed-to-protect-student-loan-borrowers-lawsuit-says. This article states in part: "A non-profit student loan group is suing the nation's most powerful consumer watchdog agency. The lawsuit, first obtained by NPR, alleges that the Consumer Financial Protection Bureau has abandoned its obligation to oversee companies that manage student loans, in particular a troubled loan forgiveness program. 'We are suing the Department of Education and the CFPB because they are not doing their jobs,' says Natalia Abrams, the founder of Student Debt Crisis. Abrams' group works both on policy issues and directly with borrowers".

related to a consumer's personal experience with a financial product or service". See: Porter (2012).

2. Dodd-Frank Act is large and politically and psychologically dominating. Otherwise-relevant matters that Dodd-Frank Act omits may be considered irrelevant or less important by some people. Dodd-Frank Act expressly omitted statutes/regulation that would facilitate/strengthen unionization and Collective Bargaining in the financial services industry and associated/ancillary industries, such as the following:
   (a) Expressly omitted (in the Orderly Liquidation statutes) statutes/regulations that would facilitate union intervention or union-participation and Collective Bargaining in financially/operationally distressed financial institutions. That omission can be deemed intentional (i.e. a product of political lobbying by the financial services industry) and is critical because some financial services companies become financially or operationally distressed because of high labor-related costs (sometimes as much as 60% of total annual operating expenses of financial services companies). Thus, Dodd-Frank's Orderly Liquidation regulations can be avoided by Collective-Bargaining.
   (b) Expressly omitted (in the Derivatives statutes) statutes/regulation that would facilitate union intervention or union-participation and Collective-Bargaining. That omission can be deemed intentional (i.e. a product of political lobbying by the financial services industry) and is critical because many Derivatives trading is done by humans who can collude and they face labor-intensive manual-compliance regulations. Thus, costs, errors and Antitrust in Derivatives trading can be reduced or avoided by Collective Bargaining.
   (c) While Dodd-Frank Act statutorily implemented *Say-on-Pay* regulations,[37] it omitted labor union (or other employee-group) participation in establishing or correcting compensation stan-

[37]This refers to the mandatory disclosure of *Pay-Ratios* which is required by Section 953(b) of the Dodd-Frank Wall Street Reform and Consumer Protection Act of 2010 (United States, 2017). Under this regulation, each exchange-traded company must disclose its "*Pay-Ratio*" (the ratio of its CEO's compensation to its median employee salary). The US government also created a "Say on Pay" mandatory-disclosure requirement for companies that obtained funds from the US government's *Troubled Asset Relief Program* (TARP)—the regulation grants shareholders (of such investee-companies) the right to vote on executive compensation issues.

dards for executives and in setting/implementing corporate governance and sustainability standards in financial services companies. *Wealth Inequality* and *Income Inequality* are major concerns for Labor Unions and employees. See: Jacob (2011) and Mitchell and Erickson (2005).

3. Dodd-Frank Act's *Volcker Rule*[38] bars banks from some proprietary investment/trading activities (for their own accounts) and limits their dealings with hedge funds and private equity funds ("covered funds"). That effectively: (i) bars any affected services labor unions (unions for hedge funds and private equity professionals—e.g. bankers, technology staff, electricians, administrative staff) from being active in banks; (ii) limits the ability of hedge funds and private equity professionals to engage in industry-wide collective bargaining.
4. Dodd-Frank Act facilitates non-compliance with International Labor Standards (e.g. ILO's) by creating and enforcing an "alternate" regulatory framework that doesn't expressly or impliedly incorporate or consider international labor regulations and standards.
5. Some researchers deem the US National Labor Relations Board (NLRB) and the National Labor Relations Act (US statute) to be outdated and ineffective (see: Freeman 2011; and MacDonald 2013), and Dodd-Frank Act doesn't effectively incorporate, update or amend the National Labor Relations Act and related/similar US statutes (at both the state and federal government levels), even though the Dodd-Frank Act regulates labor relations issues.
6. Dodd-Frank Act doesn't effectively regulate FINRA (Financial Industry Regulatory Authority) which handles all or most labor (employee-employer) disputes in the US securities industry. FINRA is a self-regulated entity that: (a) ideally, should be regulated by the US SEC, NLRB and the US Department of Labor; (b) should provide a right-of-appeal to the labor resolution processes of the US Department of Labor and NLRB.[39]

[38] *See*: Barlas, S. (June 2012). Volcker Rule: Unleashes Stream of Complaints: Chastened by Criticism from a Variety of Sources – Including Financial Executives Worried About Its Impact on Access to Capital – Federal Banking Regulators Say They Will Miss the July 21 Deadline for Finalizing the '*Volcker Rule*,' Part of the Sweeping Dodd-Frank Act. *Financial Executive*, 28(5).

[39] *See*: *You Still Can't Sue Your Bank. So What Can You Do? How to make arbitration work in disputes with your financial institution*". By Tobie Stanger. October 25, 2017. https://www.consumerreports.org/contracts-arbitration/you-still-cant-sue-your-bank-arbitration-cfpb/.

7. As explained in this chapter, sections of Dodd-Frank Act infringe the Rights-of-Association of workers.
8. As mentioned above, the National Association of Criminal Defense Lawyers (NACDL) (2010a) noted that sections of Dodd-Frank Act over-criminalize employee conduct—those regulations can be used to prevent or hinder collective bargaining and unionization.
9. Dodd-Frank Act doesn't map or properly define the labor requirements and labor-related disclosure requirements for Global Supply Chains[40] in the financial services industry.

2.2 Geopolitical Risk and Some Economic Psychology[41] and *Cross-Border Spillover Effects* of the Sub-Prime Crisis, the Global Financial Crisis and the *Dodd-Frank Act* (Cross-Border Spillovers into Emerging Markets)

2.2.1 Cross-Border Spillovers and Economic Psychology Effects

The extensive literatures on *Social Networks, Social Capital* and Cross-border *Spillover Effects* are summarized in Volume-1 of this two-volume series. The significant and negative global effects of the US Subprime Mortgage Crisis of 2006–2012, and the resulting Global Financial Crisis of 2007–2014, are extensive and are well documented in the literature—see the comments in Martikainen et al. (2013). The US government dominated the coordinated post-2008 global financial reform efforts and the G20/G30 recommendations of 2010–2013. The Dodd-Frank Act and the G20/G30 recommendations of 2010 and the Financial Stability Board

[40] *See*: Phillips, N., LeBaron, G. & Wallin, S. (June 2018). *Mapping and Measuring the Effectiveness of Labor-Related Disclosure Requirements for Global Supply Chains.* International Labour Office, Research Department Working Paper No. 32. https://www.ilo.org/wcmsp5/groups/public/%2D%2D-dgreports/%2D%2D-inst/documents/publication/wcms_632120.pdf.

[41] On associated Economic Psychology and Behavioral IPE (International Political Economy) issues, see the comments in: Hardardottir (2017), Birz (2017), Dixon et al. (2014), Ochsen and Welsch (2012), Debelle (2004), Schniter et al. (2020), Garcia et al. (2020), Bavetta et al. (2020), Nguyen and Claus (2013), Pántya et al. (2016), Haferkamp et al. (2009), Banker et al. (2020), Blaufus et al. (2019), Kenadjian et al. (2013), Cervone (2017), Martikainen et al. (2013), Hämäläinen and Martikainen (2015), Noss and Sowerbutts (2012), Brewer and Jagtiani (2013), Coffee (2012), Nwogugu (2012a, 2014a, c), Rose and Walker (2013), Ben-Ishai and Lubben (2011), Goddard (2011), and Gordon and Muller (2010).

(based in Basel, Switzerland) eventually became the foundation for new financial statutes/regulations that were enacted and implemented in many countries during 2009–2019.

Kenadjian et al. (2013), Cervone (2017), Godwin et al. (2017) and Greene and Potiha (2013) discussed some of the global effects of RAFSA. RAFSA and similar regulations in the European Union (e.g. the Liikanen Group Report, EMIR, MiFID II, MIFIR and CRD IV; and, collectively, the "EU Sustainable Growth Regulations") and other developed countries had, and continue to have, worldwide *Multiplier Effects* because of the following:

1. RAFSA and the *EU Sustainable Growth Regulations* regulate US and EU multinational corporations (MNCs) which have significant global operations and are influential in international trade—and many of these US and EU MNCs have major suppliers that are located in Emerging Markets countries (e.g. Mexico, Brazil, India, Philippines, Chile, Peru, China, ASEAN countries) that essentially have to comply with US and/or EU business/legal/operations standards. Also, MNCs' operations in foreign countries are a transmission channel for cross-border *Corporate Governance Contagion* and *Operations Policies Contagion*—see Hämäläinen and Martikainen (2015) and Kinnunen et al. (2016). "Secondary-Level Emerging Markets countries" such as Nigeria, Thailand, Indonesia and Russia benefit from these US- and EU-influenced international trade/financial relationships—for example: (1) Nigeria sells its petroleum products to India, imports large volumes of goods from China and borrows large amounts from China; and (2) Thailand exports substantial volumes of goods/services to China; (3) Russia sells substantial amounts of oil/gas and military technology/equipment to China.
2. RAFSA and the EU Sustainable Growth Regulations are "core" regulation for the global capital markets and the global derivatives markets—see: Greene and Potiha (2013).
3. Other countries (such as Canada, France and the UK) have copied parts of the Dodd-Frank Act, or have enacted statutes/regulations that are similar to, or have the same objectives as RAFSA. Such *Regulatory Contagion* can amplify the effects of RAFSA in Emerging Markets countries.

4. RAFSA and the EU Sustainable Growth Regulations regulate foreign companies that do business in the US and EU, and/or whose shares and/or debt are traded on US and EU financial exchanges; and foreign companies that raise money in the US and/or EU.
5. RAFSA and the EU Sustainable Growth Regulations can have significant worldwide economic *Multiplier Effects* and *Spillover Effects* across national borders because they affect and regulate the financing of international trade, international capital flows, capital raising, financial regulation and so on.
6. As of 2020 (and for much of 2010–2020), more than 50% of worldwide international trade[42] was conducted with the US dollar and about 60% (sixty percent) of government reserves around the world were held in US Dollars; about 40% (forty percent) of the world's debt was issued in dollars; and about 90% of worldwide forex trading involved the U.S. dollar. Thus the economies of many Emerging Markets countries are sensitive to fluctuations of US dollar exchange rates, which affect most transactions that

[42] *See*: "*Why the US Dollar Is the Global Currency*". July 23, 2020. https://www.thebalance.com/world-currency-3305931. This article states in part: "As of 2018, the U.S. had US$1671 billion in circulation. As much as half that value is estimated to be in circulation abroad. Many of these bills are in the former Soviet Union countries and in Latin America. They are often used as hard currency in day-to-day transactions. In the foreign exchange market, the dollar rules. Around 90% of forex trading involves the U.S. dollar. The dollar is just one of the world's 185 currencies according to the International Standards Organization List, but most of these currencies are only used inside their own countries … Almost 40% of the world's debt is issued in dollars. As a result, foreign banks need a lot of dollars to conduct business. This became evident during the 2008 financial crisis. Non-American banks had $27 trillion in international liabilities denominated in foreign currencies. Of that, $18 trillion was in U.S. dollars. As a result, the U.S. Federal Reserve had to increase its dollar swap line. That was the only way to keep the world's banks from running out of dollars. The financial crisis made the dollar even more widely used. In 2018, the banks of Germany, France and Great Britain held more liabilities denominated in dollars than in their own currencies. Additionally, bank regulations enacted to prevent another crisis have made dollars scarce, and the Federal Reserve has increased the fed funds rate. That decreases the money supply by making dollars more expensive to borrow".

See: "*Share of Currencies in Global Foreign Exchange Reserves From 2009 to 2019*". https://www.statista.com/statistics/233674/distribution-of-global-currency-reserves/.

See: "*Dominant Currencies and the Limits of Exchange Rate Flexibility*". July 20, 2020. By Gustavo Adler, Gita Gopinath and Carolina Osorio Buitron. IMF. https://blogs.imf.org/2020/07/20/currencies-and-crisis-how-dominant-currencies-limit-the-impact-of-exchange-rate-flexibility/.

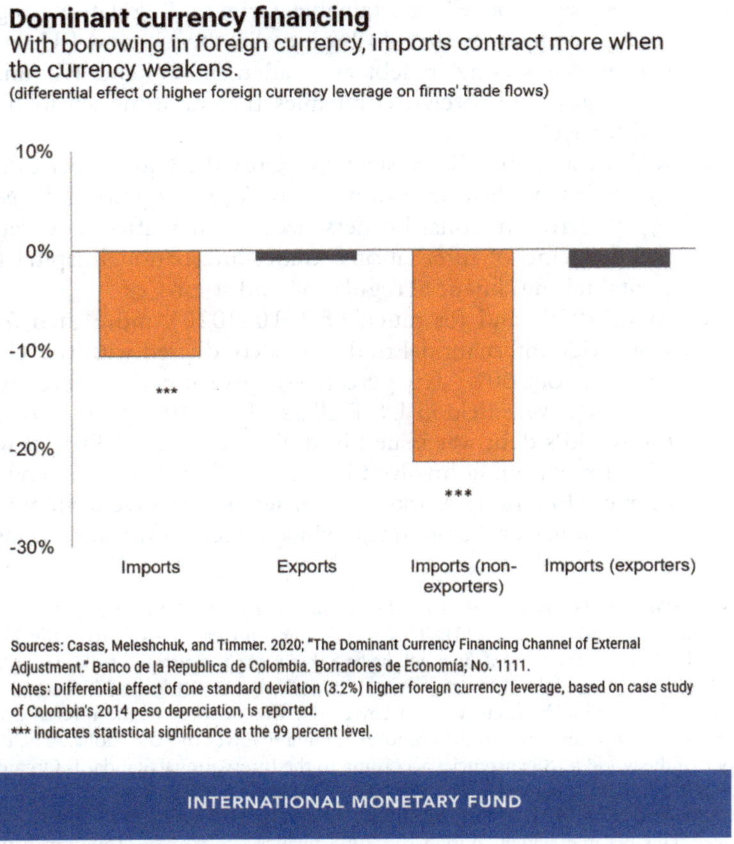

Source: https://blogs.imf.org/2020/07/20/currencies-and-crisis-how-dominant-currencies-limit-the-impact-of-exchange-rate-flexibility/

are critical for the survival of Emerging Markets countries—such as commodities transactions, oil/gas sales, issuance of government and corporate debt, payments transactions, imports of finished goods/machinery, and so on. RAFSA's statutes directly affect US monetary policies, fiscal policies and money supply. Around the world, the US Dollar exchange rate is also factored into firms' prices and employee compensation/benefits which ultimately affect Consumer Expenditures, Consumer Confidence, Business Confidence, Corporate Expenditures, Government

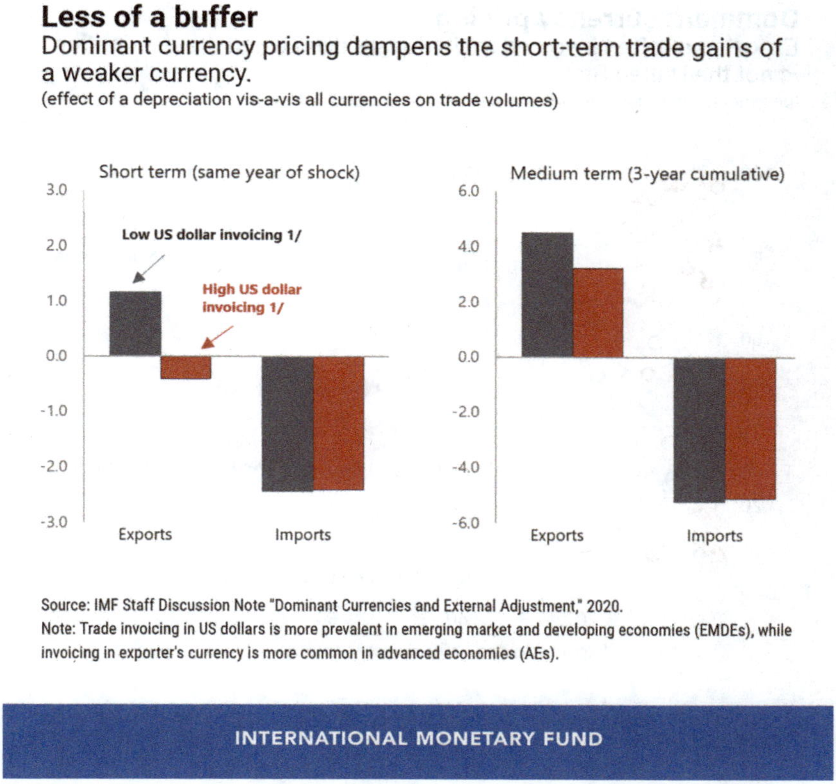
Less of a buffer
Dominant currency pricing dampens the short-term trade gains of a weaker currency.
(effect of a depreciation vis-a-vis all currencies on trade volumes)
Short term (same year of shock)
3.0
2.0
1.0
0.0
-1.0
-2.0
-3.0
Low US dollar invoicing 1/
High US dollar invoicing 1/
Exports
Imports
Medium term (3-year cumulative)
6.0
4.0
2.0
0.0
-2.0
-4.0
-6.0
Exports
Imports
Source: IMF Staff Discussion Note "Dominant Currencies and External Adjustment," 2020.
Note: Trade invoicing in US dollars is more prevalent in emerging market and developing economies (EMDEs), while invoicing in exporter's currency is more common in advanced economies (AEs).
INTERNATIONAL MONETARY FUND

Source: https://blogs.imf.org/2020/07/20/currencies-and-crisis-how-dominant-currencies-limit-the-impact-of-exchange-rate-flexibility/

expenditures and Risk-Perception. The US dollar is managed by the US Federal Reserve and the large international US banks, all of which are significantly regulated by RAFSA. During 2005–2020, the US Federal Reserve emerged as the central bank to the world because of the significant and continuing worldwide impact of its activities and economic policies. However, during 2017–2020, Russian, China and Iran entered into agreements to use their own domestic currencies to settle trade among themselves. Some Emerging Markets countries use or have used the US dollar as their official currencies—these countries include Poland, Ecuador, El Salvador, Zimbabwe, Timor-Leste,

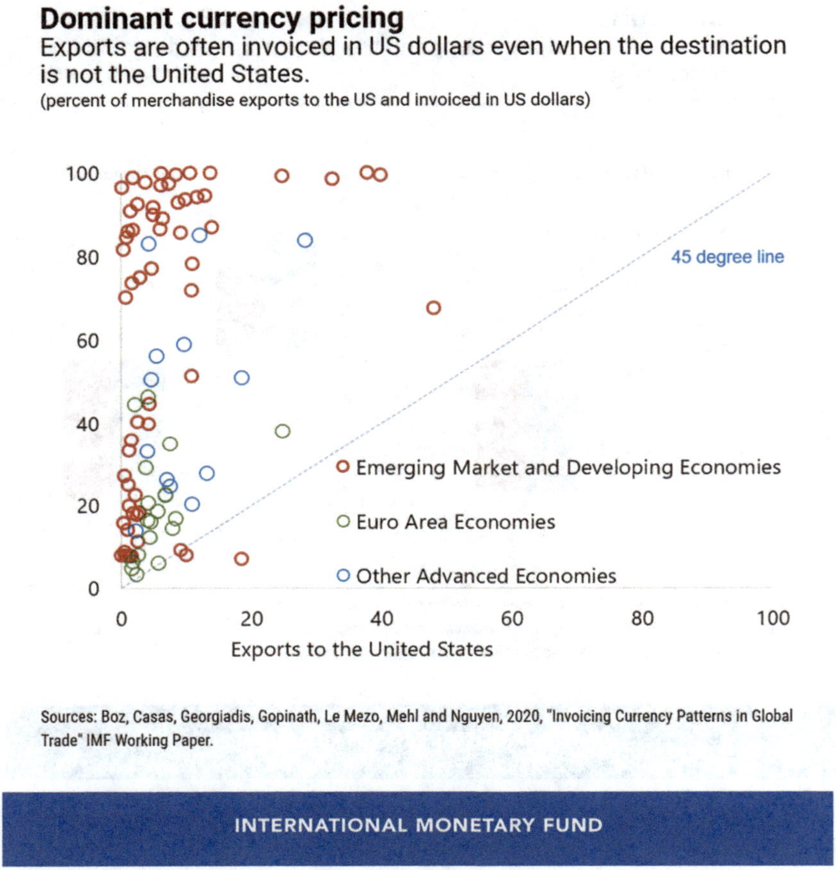

Source: https://blogs.imf.org/2020/07/20/currencies-and-crisis-how-dominant-currencies-limit-the-impact-of-exchange-rate-flexibility/

Micronesia, Palau and the Marshall Islands. The following countries/regions also widely use the US Dollar simultaneously with their own local currencies—Bahamas, Barbados, St. Kitts and Nevis, Belize, Costa Rica, Nicaragua, Panama, Myanmar, Cambodia and Liberia, as well as several Caribbean territories; and British territories in the Caribbean (Turks and Caicos and the British Virgin Islands).

7. RAFSA regulates and has substantial effects on non-financial industries that are global industries—such as hotel chains, restaurant chains, insurance and logistics/distribution.
8. RAFSA regulates and has substantial effects on non-financial industries that employ significant numbers of immigrants such as hotel-chains, restaurants, construction, retail-trade, business services, and healthcare/home-health services. These immigrants send remittances to, and make investments in, Emerging markets countries. Also, immigrant expenditures are not tied to their countries of origin—for example Philippines/Filipino immigrants in the United Kingdom can send remittances to relatives in Sri Lanka or UAE or South Africa; and/or make investments in Kenya or Uganda (where there are substantial immigrant communities). RAFSA regulates and has major effects on the financing of construction activity around the world. Construction activity metrics (e.g. Housing Starts) are major economic indicators in most developed and developing countries. In many developed and developing countries, the construction industry imports significant volumes of finished/semi-finished products from Emerging Markets countries, and the construction industry employs a significant number of immigrants who, in turn, send remittances and knowledge/human capital to Emerging Markets countries, all of which affect the GDP/exports/productivity of those countries.
9. RAFSA and the EU Sustainable Growth Regulations have affected, and are likely to continue to affect, legislation and adjudication in many countries because many such countries' constitutions are based on the US and/or EU constitution (and were either enacted or amended within the last thirty years). RAFSA may also be relevant to Commonwealth countries because, like the USA, their legal systems and constitutional principles are based on the British legal system. The governments and citizens of the United Kingdom, Canada, India and other Commonwealth countries have significant investments in the USA, and US commercial and investment banks (which are subject to RAFSA) are very active in the UK capital markets and in many Commonwealth countries. The shares of many companies based in Commonwealth countries are listed in the USA. The global financial crisis of 2007–2014 affected many Commonwealth countries (like the United Kingdom, India, Canada and Australia).

10. As mentioned herein and above, other countries have enacted statutes that are similar to RAFSA[43] and the EU Sustainable Growth Regulations—and that is likely to make RAFSA more acceptable around the world.
11. RAFSA has introduced significant Economic Psychology effects in both the financial services industry and nonfinancial industries. Much more documentation is now required in many areas of global financial services, and in some nonfinancial industries. RAFSA has changed or can change the risk perception of capital markets participants, corporate executives and government regulators around the world. The FSOC SIFI/non-SIFI requirements/criteria, and the Consumer Protection bureau have all affected corporate executives and consumers. The litigation costs that arose solely from the enactment of the Dodd-Frank Act has been significant. Kleymenova and Zhang (2020, April) noted that RAFSA made banks less likely to disclose bad news. DeFusco et al. (2020) analyzed how lenders responded to Dodd-Frank Act's ATR Rule which was only partially implemented in 2014 (and remains so until 2021). They noted that the ATR Rule changed the ways that mortgage lenders provide mortgages, and provide a way for borrowers to sue lenders for predatory lending. This split the mortgage market in two: a regulated portion of the market and another where the regulation never happened. These foregoing factors can affect the following variables in both developed countries and Emerging Markets countries: international capital flows to emerging markets, risk perceptions, lending to immigrants in developed countries, remittances to Emerging Markets, Consumer Confidence, Business Confidence, Consumer expenditures, Corporate Expenditures, Government Expenditures, savings/investments, FDI, foreign Investment, Foreign Aid and so on.
12. As explained herein, Dodd-Frank Act directly and indirectly affects governments' Fiscal Policy (corporate taxation; government's revenues from fees, levies and fines; cost of corporate financial distress and bankruptcy; litigation costs; Foreign Corrupt Practices Act; compliance reporting; etc.) and Monetary Policy (earnings management and market volatility; stock market

[43] *See*: Shearman and Sterling (2013). *Dodd-Frank, UK, EU, & Other Regulatory Reforms.* Available at: www.shearman.com/dodd-frank/.

crashes; money supply; liquidity in financial markets; bubbles; stock market-driven inflation/deflation; risk perception [corporate bonds, stocks, etc.]; derivatives compliance reports; economic models and capital-adequacy models; contagion; etc.), all of which can have cross-border *Multiplier Effects* in Emerging Markets countries through the channels explained in this book. The US Federal Reserve and many of the regulations issued by the US government are directly and substantially affected by RAFSA; and a significant percentage of international investors are directly/indirectly affected by RAFSA. A significant portion of international Derivatives transactions are affected by RAFSA and are documented and settled in US Dollars. As explained in Chap. 1 in this book, the US dollar remains the dominance currency in International Trade and Finance.

13. The US has the most advanced and comprehensive financial regulations and creates some of the most sophisticated financial products in the world. The US has been at the forefront of enactment of financial/economic laws at both the federal and state levels. Many developing countries (and developed countries) copied their financial laws from US laws. For example, the Brazilian constitution is based on the US Constitution; and REIT statutes worldwide are based on US REIT laws. Many countries have created variants of the Dodd-Frank Act and the Sarbanes Oxley Act (SOX). Mortgage/Foreclosure laws in many countries are very similar to US mortgage/foreclosure laws. Many developing countries and "transition" countries of Eastern Europe derived their mortgage/foreclosure laws from US laws.
14. During the last twenty years, the US consistently had the largest national economy in the world; and the US economy directly/indirectly (through international trade, outsourcing, FDI, FI, Foreign Aid, etc.) supported the economies of other "First-Level Associated" countries (such as China, Japan, Brazil, Mexico, India) which in turn, directly/directly supported (through international trade, outsourcing, loans, FDI, FI, Foreign Aid, etc.) the economies of other "Second-Level Associated" countries (such as Russia, Nigeria, Philippines, Thailand, ASEAN countries, Pakistan, Central American countries, CIS countries).

During 1980–2020, the US was a major participant in major multilateral and bilateral trade agreements; and the US-China

Trade War (2019–present) continues to have significant economic/social/psychological *Multiplier Effects* on many countries. The use of the terms "First-Level Associated" countries and "Second-Level Associated" countries is introduced here as a "mutual-dependency" classification of countries as a way to better reflect the often symbiotic relationships between countries with regard to international trade and international capital flows.

15. RAFSA and the EU Sustainable Growth Regulations are major geopolitical risk factors and their actual effects on a specific country can vary dramatically across countries due to several factors including but not limited to the following:
    (a) Whether the subject country is a member of the WTO.
    (b) The terms of any treaties between the US and EU on one hand, and the subject country.
    (c) The volume of trade and balance-of-trade between the US and EU on one hand, and the subject country.
    (d) The existing financial regulation framework in the subject country.
    (e) Interpretations of international law and conflict-of-laws.
    (f) The volumes of FDI, FI and Foreign Aid and other international capital flows between the US and EU on one hand, and the subject country.

2.2.2 Dodd-Frank Act and Fiscal Policy, Monetary Policy, Trade Policy and Foreign Policy

The Dodd-Frank Act directly and indirectly affects governments' Fiscal Policy in the following ways:

1. Accurate and timely disclosures of corporate tax and real estate tax liabilities (i.e. Tax Avoidance, Tax Evasion, International Taxation, etc.).
2. government's revenues from fees, fines, taxes, permits and levies.
3. costs of corporate financial distress and bankruptcy (most of which are borne by governments).
4. US Government's Litigation costs (economic, legal, social, psychological, environmental and political costs).
5. US Government's enforcement costs.
6. Accuracy of National Income Accounting.
7. The costs of consumers' complaints against government agencies.

8. Compliance reporting.
9. Foreign Corrupt Practices Act (US statute).
10. Consumer Financial Protection Bureau (US government agency)—that is, the CFPB's activities, costs and *Multiplier Effects.*
11. The *Volcker Rule* (which can affect US government's tax revenues).
12. The Lincoln Amendment (prohibits entities that participate in swaps transactions from receiving assistance from the US government).
13. *Regulatory Consolidation* (which affects Government Expenditures by reducing the number of government agencies).

The Dodd-Frank Act directly and indirectly affects Monetary Policy in the following ways (and the Dodd-Frank Act may be unique for its significant effects on Monetary Policy):

1. US companies and foreign companies that operate in the USA must comply with the Dodd-Frank Act. Many of these companies are MNCs that have significant international operations, and thus propagate the Dodd-Frank Act and US standards/compliance around the world.
2. Earnings management and market volatility; Crash-risk and Bubbles in stock, bond and commodities markets of stock markets—through implementation/propagation of, or non-compliance with the Dodd-Frank Act around the world.
3. Money supply and liquidity in financial markets—that is: (1) requirements and standards for stress testing, leverage ratios, capital buffers and liquidity; (2) restrictions on the US Federal Reserve's emergency lending powers; and (3) the Dodd-Frank Act compels the US Federal Deposit Insurance Corporation to obtain permission from the US Congress before providing temporary liquidity guarantees.
4. Validity and accuracy of the asset base of financial institutions, some of which are used as collateral for trading and loans.
5. International Financial Contagion—through international propagation/implementation of, or non-compliance with, the Dodd-Frank Act.
6. Economic models and capital-adequacy standards for SIFIs, non-financial SIFIs and financial institutions—both of which are substantially affected by Dodd-Frank Act provisions.

7. Collateral for Derivatives, derivatives compliance reports, Derivatives exchanges and clearing (and verification of derivatives trading processes), all of which are substantially affected by Dodd-Frank Act provisions (oversight and transparency).
8. Stock market-driven inflation/deflation.
9. The risk perception of both domestic and foreign investors (corporate bonds, stocks, etc.).
10. Interest rates—through banks' and non-bank financial institutions' cost-of-operations and compliance costs (which are factored into their lending rates), and so on.
11. The US Fed's Open market transactions such as *Quantitative Easing*—through compliance reports; accuracy of pricing of financial instruments, and so on.
12. Financial Stability—(1) higher prudential standards; (2) the single-point-of-entry resolution authority (resolution of failed SIFIs); (3) greater transparency and oversight of derivatives; (4) requirements and standards for leverage ratios, capital buffers, stress testing, (5) liquidity requirements and (6) more independence for the Financial Stability Oversight Council and the Office of Financial Research.
13. The *Volcker Rule*.
14. The *Lincoln Amendment* (prohibits entities that participate in swaps transactions from receiving assistance from the US government).
15. *Regulatory Consolidation* (of statutes and or government administrative agencies)—which affects policy-making and rule-making at government agencies that develop, monitor or implement domestic/international monetary policy.
16. "*Netting*", the *Liquidity Coverage Ratio* and The US FSOC's *Non-SIFI Criteria* and *SIFI Criteria* are affected by Dodd-Frank Act—see Nwogugu (2014d).
17. As noted in Nwogugu (2014e), REIT Shares/Interests are Derivatives Instruments, and REITs are SIFIs (Systemically Important Financial Institutions).

The Dodd-Frank Act can directly and indirectly affect both foreign policy and trade policy in the following ways:

1. US companies and foreign companies that operate in the USA must comply with the Dodd-Frank Act. Many of these companies are MNCs that have significant international operations, and thus propagate the Dodd-Frank Act and US standards/compliance around the world.
2. Bubbles and the Crash-risk of stock markets, commodities markets and bond markets—through implementation/propagation of, or non-compliance with, the Dodd-Frank Act around the world.
3. International Financial/Economic Contagion—through implementation/propagation of, or non-compliance with, the Dodd-Frank Act around the world.
4. Money supply and liquidity in international financial markets (see above).
5. Validity and accuracy of the asset base of financial institutions, some of which is used as collateral for trading and loans; and Collateral for Derivatives; derivatives compliance reports and verification of derivatives trading processes.
6. Stock market-driven inflation/deflation.
7. Risk perception of international investors (corporate bonds, stocks, etc.).
8. Calculation of Foreign Aid, FDI, import taxes and export taxes.
9. Compliance reporting in international finance and international trade.
10. Foreign Corrupt Practices Act (US statute).
11. Consumer Financial Protection Bureau.
12. The *Volcker Rule*—which also affects foreign financial institutions that have offices in the USA.
13. *Regulatory Consolidation* (of statutes and or government administrative agencies)—which affects policy-making and rule-making at government agencies that develop, monitor or implement Monetary Policy and associated Foreign Policy.
14. The US Financial Stability Oversight Council (FSOC).
15. International perceptions of the *Political Capital* and *Enforcement-Commitment* of the US government.

This chapter explains how the Dodd-Frank Act can affect Labor Policy. All of the foregoing effects on Public Policy can have cross-border *Multiplier Effects* in Emerging Markets countries through the channels explained in this book.

2.3 The Nwogugu (2015a) Critique of the *Dodd-Frank Act*

Nwogugu (2015a) explained the following weaknesses of RAFSA (these critiques also apply to the *European Union Sustainable Growth Regulations*):

1. RAFSA did not provide sufficient regulation of rating agencies, although RAFSA lowered the standards under which rating agencies may be sued for outright fraud and also for reckless behavior.
2. RAFSA did not provide adequate regulation of non-bank companies that provide financial services—such as retailing companies and pay-day loan companies.
3. RAFSA failed to create a system of transparent penalties for companies and individuals that increase systemic risk.
4. RAFSA did not address the many problems inherent in Real Estate Investment Trusts (REITs)
5. RAFSA did not address the problem of bank liquidity, and weaknesses inherent in the Liquidity Coverage Ratio and the net stable funding ratio.
6. RAFSA does not address the internal decision processes of financial services companies (and "covered financial companies") for the repayment of obligations and for compliance with financial laws, as well as for interaction with the Federal Deposit Insurance Corporation (FDIC), US Fed and the US Treasury.
7. RAFSA did not address "Earnings Management Contagion".
8. RAFSA did not address "Corporate Governance Contagion".
9. RAFSA does not provide adequate regulation of insurance and reinsurance companies. It has become evident that in most markets, risk is not eliminated but is merely transferred to other parties in the economic system—such as insurance companies.
10. RAFSA does not sufficiently address Fannie Mae and Freddie Mac, which remain major elements of the US mortgage/housing industry and account for more than US$5 trillion of mortgages. Fannie Mae and Freddie Mac should be substantially re-organized.
11. RAFSA failed to address the many known weaknesses in antitrust regulation and enforcement in the USA.
12. RAFSA didn't sufficiently address asset securitization issues which affect executive compensation and vice versa, and that symbiotic relationship can amplify systemic risk.

13. RAFSA does not prevent depository commercial banks from trading over-the-counter (OTC) derivatives as principals.
14. RAFSA failed to physically consolidate the activities of the FDIC, the Federal Housing Finance Authority (FHFA), the Office of the Comptroller of the Currency and the US Federal Reserve System. These entities have duplicitous functions which cause coordination problems.
15. RAFSA failed to abolish the dual regulatory structure in the US banking industry—all banks in the USA should be regulated at the federal level to ensure consistency, regulatory efficiency, lower transaction costs and better monitoring of systemic risk.
16. RAFSA does not address the systemic risk that arises from organizational form (of companies).
17. RAFSA is conjectured here to be likely to amplify some of the behavioral biases that were defined in Nwogugu (2012b), Zagorski (2012) and Nwogugu (2010) and psychological effects introduced in Nwogugu (2008e, f). RAFSA has also not solved many of the issues raised in Chaps. 6, 7, 8 and 12 in Nwogugu (2012a).
18. RAFSA penalizes primarily non-failing banks for the costs of failure of failing banks at or around the time of failure. Such penalties are likely to jeopardize "non-failing" banks because of significant reputation effects and systemic risks in the financial services industry.
19. RAFSA failed to ban banks and insurance companies from owning any equity stakes in hedge funds and private equity funds.
20. RAFSA failed to provide regulations for the "prime brokerage" services of commercial banks and investments banks.
21. Although RAFSA bars depository banks from acting as principals in securities trades (and such banks can only function as "agents"), RAFSA does not state any meaningful criteria for inventory of securities that depository banks need to function as agents.
22. Federally insured banks should be barred from proprietary trading and derivatives trading, but the independent derivatives trading companies should not be allowed to become CCHs (central clearing houses) and should not have access to the Fed's discount window—Bear Stearns, AIG and Lehman Brothers failed partly because they became opaque quasi-clearing-houses.
23. Executive and incentive compensation at banks and insurance companies was not fully addressed and regulated in RAFSA.

24. Executive and incentive compensation at non-bank and non-insurance companies were not sufficiently regulated in RAFSA.
25. RAFSA failed to amend the (securities law) disclosure rules for private companies.
26. RAFSA failed to eliminate the dual regulatory scheme for franchising and business opportunities in the USA.
27. RAFSA failed to adequately address the issue of auditor liability for material misstatements in financial statements.
28. RAFSA failed to extend "suitability" requirements and "fraud" standards to the derivatives market (Rosenthal 1995). These two standards now exist in US federal and state securities laws.
29. RAFSA did not adequately address the accounting/disclosure for leases and pension liabilities, which remains a major source of systemic risk that affects many industries in the USA
30. RAFSA failed to:
    (a) implement a national property title system which will also resolve the existing conflicts between the state uniform commercial code statutes and local/municipal mortgage/title systems;
    (b) enact title statutes that will preempt state and municipal title systems;
31. RAFSA failed to statutorily change the structure of insurance contracts. One of the big problems in insurance is that if a catastrophe occurs, one or a few insurance companies are deluged with claims and eventually file for bankruptcy because it cannot pay claims, as it was not able to accurately calculate required premiums and/or did not allocate enough reserves for losses.
32. Central Clearing-Houses (CCHs) (for clearing of financial and commodity derivatives) remain inadequately regulated after RAFSA.
33. RAFSA focused excessively on the financial sector and neglected the real sector—even though a significant amount (if not the majority) of systemic risk in developed economies arises from their real sectors. RAFSA did not do enough to explore and enact measures that foster real economic growth and sustainability. Inequality continues to increase in the USA.
34. RAFSA failed to provide sufficient regulation of, and limitations on, non-bank, non-insurance companies that offer retail loan products—such as credit cards, car loans, home equity loans and general unsecured loans to consumers.

35. RAFSA did not limit or reduce the amount, availability and sources of excessive consumer credit, and did not develop a system of incentives and penalties for financial services companies that provide consumer credit.
36. RAFSA did not fully address the insulation of financial services companies from political interference.
37. The economic relationship between the US federal government and the state governments affects the constitutionality of many of the new statutes in RAFSA (FSA), and vice versa. Ideally, RAFSA should have been neutral to and should have reduced the magnitude of this phenomenon, and such reduction could have reduced transaction costs and compliance costs.
38. RAFSA does not provide any meaningful policies, criteria or guidelines for the management of the debt of US states and their deficit. States like California and New York have recently had significant financial difficulties
39. RAFSA does not provide any meaningful policies, criteria or guidelines for the management of US sovereign debt and the US federal deficit. "Several authors have noted that the US Government has been insolvent since 2006 (Kotlikoff 2006; Thakor 2007; Roubini 2009; Walker 2006; Pelerin 2013; Casey 2012)".
40. RAFSA failed to address the choice that companies make between executing strategic alliances (and joint ventures [JV]) or effecting mergers/acquisitions (M&A) (Nwogugu 2003, 2008d), and the choice has both monetary policy and fiscal policy implications.
41. RAFSA failed to address the excessive US military budget and expenditure, which now accounts for more than 35% of total global military expenditures.
42. RAFSA failed to address excessive outstanding student loans in the USA. Most US indigenes repay their student loans completely in four to fifteen years. Thus, student loans essentially bind a large percentage of US graduates to a form of indentured servitude and suboptimal behaviors.
43. RAFSA does not address the many deficiencies inherent in national income accounting.
44. RAFSA does not address the efficiency and accuracy of market indices for stocks, bonds and commodities. These indices are the foundations for trillion of dollars of daily trading in cash securities, index funds, Exchange Traded Funds, derivatives and swaps in many countries.

45. RAFSA did not sufficiently address problems inherent in the US bankruptcy code and in judicial proceedings. Historically, the rates of false negatives (weak and distressed companies that were dismissed from bankruptcy proceedings or for which pre-packaged bankruptcy plans were approved by the court) and false positives (healthy companies that were liquidated and/or reorganized in bankruptcy) in the USA have been relatively high. There remain substantial differences among the patterns holdings/judgments of US bankruptcy court judges. Procedural issues in bankruptcy courts have also been interpreted and adjudged differently by US bankruptcy courts.
46. Authors cited in Nwogugu (2015a) noted various problems in implementing the Bankruptcy Abuse Prevention and Consumer Protection Act of 2005 in the USA. "Primo and Green (2011) and Mathur (2013) analyzed the link between bankruptcy and entrepreneurship (and, thus, economic growth). Li et al. 2011), Eggum et al. (2008) and Morgan et al. (2012) argued that the reform of US consumer bankruptcy statutes in 2005 caused mortgage defaults to rise in the USA (and was a major cause of the mortgage crisis and the current recession)". Using a separate dataset for prime and subprime mortgage foreclosures, Morgan et al. (2008) concluded that for subprime mortgages in states with higher, but not unlimited, homestead exemptions, foreclosure rates increased more after bankruptcy reform in states with higher or unlimited homestead exemptions. "Mann (2007) and White (2007) attempted to relate consumer credit card debt to bankruptcy law reforms". Thus, the Bankruptcy Abuse Prevention and Consumer Protection Act is somewhat inefficient.
47. RAFSA didn't sufficiently address the mandatory exemption of derivatives contracts from automatic stays in bankruptcy courts in many countries/jurisdictions (as recommended by International Swap Dealers Association guidelines). Such exemption has not improved the efficiency or transparency of derivatives markets and may not reduce systemic risk or limit the disruption of financial markets as illustrated by the global financial crisis of 2008–2013.
48. RAFSA does not address weaknesses in state corporation laws, conditions for *Preemption* of state corporation laws and the issue of shareholder activism. Shareholders' rights affect sustainability, financial stability and systemic risk substantially. Executive

employment agreements can also cause "manager–shareholder gap" (distinct from pure principal-agent issues), wherein the objectives of managers and shareholders not only become less aligned but managers become more likely to frustrate shareholder activism. While RAFSA appears to shift the balance of power from the board to shareholders, the reality is that shareholders do not have real power to direct or influence matters that were traditionally decided by BOD under state law. Although Dodd-Frank seems to increase the scrutiny on BOD through enhanced disclosure obligations and advisory votes, one critical factor is that there is no independent/external coordination of these efforts and the management team (the persons who stand to either gain most or lose most) are the team charged with coordinating these efforts and also implementing any shareholder recommendations that are adopted by the company. Thus, RAFSA has provided management teams with substantially greater incentives to engage in collusion, fraud and deceit to hedge their careers, base compensation and incentive compensation.

49. In the current regulatory environment, the US Government is a quasi-shareholder of banks and financial companies because state and federal banking statutes grant the US Fed and the FDIC rights and powers that are very similar to, and sometimes stronger than, rights granted to shareholders by state corporation laws (the same applies to governments in common-law countries that enacted statutes that are similar to the Dodd-Frank Act). However, these factors are not reflected in RAFSA and many regulations.
50. Many authors and researchers have noted that the US Government's Troubled Asset Relief Program (TARP) and HAMP programs have failed, and the Dodd-Frank Act did not sufficiently address such market failures.

2.4 A Critique of *Roe* (2013)

Roe (2013) attempted to analyze the problems inherent in *Central Clearing Houses* ('CCHs') within the context of RAFSA. The following are the errors and omissions in the Roe (2013) study:

- The analysis of setoff is almost irrelevant in this context because: (1) in the US, the application of setoff varies across different US bankruptcy courts (there has not been consistency) and US Bankruptcy Courts have broad discretion to grant or deny setoff,[44] and to rescind setoffs that occur within the ninety-day period immediately before the filing of bankruptcy; (2) in the US, the applicability of setoff varies according to state law (some states have a common-law right of setoff), particularly in cases or circumstances where state law is deemed to *preempt* sections of the US Bankruptcy Code; (3) the efficiency and applicability of setoff also depends on the percentage of claims held by each party, that is, unsecured and secured; (4) the efficiency of setoff depends on the liquidity of assets and claims of the CCH customers and the transparency of financial statements and disclosures of CCH customers; (5) as noted in the existing literature, the application of setoff creates the potential for inequitable and/or impermissible improvement of the position of some creditors to the detriment of other creditors (in terms of priority).

- The analysis does not cover the issue of collateral deposits required from clients by CCH members.
- The analysis does not cover the effects of "intermediation" and "selective transaction processing" by CCH members and the associated social welfare costs. Selective transaction processing discriminates among clients of CCH members.
- The study does not analyze the effects of credit ratings on collateral requirements—that is, collateral sought by both the CCH (from CCH members) and CCH members (from clients). The rating agency lags in updating credit ratings and absolute errors in credit ratings affect the efficiency of CCHs.
- While the study insists that CCHs merely "re-distribute" risk in the financial system, the study does not trace the path of such re-distribution in both the financial system and the real economy.
- Contrary to Roe (2013), a substantial portion of systemic risk arises from the real economy. A significant percentage (both by absolute number and by transaction volume) of clients of CCH members are companies in the real sector.

[44] *See*: *In Re: HAL*, Inc., 122 F.3d. 851 (CA9, 1997).

See: Caughey, B. (2011). *A Creditor's Right to Setoff: When Does a Creditor Impermissibly Improve Its Position?* Available at: www.icemiller.com/publications/Creditor%27s_Right_to_Setoff_ABI.pdf.

- Roe (2013) repeats much of what already exists in the literature—there is no new information. The Roe analysis does not offer any solutions to the weaknesses of CCHs.

2.5 A Critique of *Gray and Shu* (2010)

Gray and Shu (2010) is relevant because it attempted to show that RAFSA is unconstitutional, but it misconstrued some issues (and other common-law jurisdictions that enacted statutes similar to RAFSA are likely to face the same constitutional law questions). Gray and Shu (2010) focused on three of RAFSA's most central grants of regulatory power which are as follows:

- the Financial Stability Oversight Council (FSOC) and its powers in Title-I;
- the Federal Deposit Insurance Corporation's (FDIC)-related liquidation authority in Title-II; and
- the Bureau of Consumer Financial Protection (BCFP) in Title-X.

Gray and Shu (2010) significantly misconstrued the following:

- The amount and scope of power granted to Article-Three courts (and such powers cannot be overridden by statutes, particularly whereas in the case of matters covered by RAFSA, common-law commercial rights are involved).
- The difference between administrative rule-making and legislation (particularly where administrative agency rule-making is subject to review by courts).
- The nature of "delegation" among the executive, legislative and judicial branches of government (particularly where the matters are specialized and complex, and transaction costs time spent can be reduced by delegation with the possibility of judicial review, and/or delegation reduces/eliminates knowledge gaps (where the adjudicator has insufficient expertise); and/or delegation substantially reduces harmful contagion and information effects.
- The differences between "adjudication" and "judicial power"—not all "adjudication" requires an exercise of judicial power; in many instances, the exercise of Article-Two "executive power" and "judicial power" are functionally and legally the same.

The legislative history of, and the stated purposes of, RAFSA indicates that the US Congress did not intend that RAFSA function as an amendment of the US Constitution; only a Constitutional Amendment can reduce or modify the powers of Article-Three courts in the US in the ways that Gray and Shu (2010) have alleged. Article-Three of the US Constitution bars the US Congress from establishing under its Article-One powers "legislative courts" (or government agencies that have adjudicative powers) to exercise jurisdiction over all matters arising under the bankruptcy laws or similar financial laws.

The Gray and Shu (2010) conclusion that the powers of the FSOC are excessive and that its procedures may violate substantive and procedural due process rights, and that a court is unlikely to find an FSOC action to be arbitrary and capricious under the Act's prima facie language, is very much false and unfounded. These assertions presume and/or imply that the federal district courts are biased. The discretions granted to the FSOC by RAFSA are not materially different from the statutory discretions that similarly placed government agencies are granted. Such discretion does not overly interfere or burden commerce, fairness and financial stability, and any abuses of discretion can be corrected by federal district courts which have Article-Three powers. The FSOC's power to limit and control transactions (such as mergers and acquisitions) by both bank and non-bank financial companies is necessary to maintain financial stability, and any abuse of discretion is subject to review in federal courts which can declare all or parts of the statute to be unconstitutional and can also decide on its own scope of judicial review regardless of the scope of judicial review that the statute prescribes. The Gray and Shu (2010) claim that Title-I is likely to prompt disputes over several issues such as the amount and scope of legislative power, which the Act delegates to others, is also inaccurate because that statement does not differentiate between permitted and normal administrative agency rule-making on one hand, and on the other hand, regular legislation. It is normal for legislatures that don't have the detail or expertise required to establish complete specialized standards, to delegate such rule-making to government agencies for further rule-making.[45] Contrary to Gray and Shu (2010), the FSOC does not have any executive powers, does not "legislate" (distinct from administrative rule-

[45] *See*: The Administrative Procedure Act, 5 U.S.C.§551.
See: *Vermont Yankee Nuclear Power Corp. vs. Natural Resources Defense Council*, 98 S.Ct. 1197; 435 U.S. 519 (1978).

making), and does not have adjudicative powers. Thus, there is no issue of violation of the separation of powers clause.

According to Gray and Shu (2010), Title-II appears to preclude or restrict the federal courts' jurisdiction over claims brought by the shareholders and creditors of a company that has been seized under the Orderly Liquidation Authority (OLA). On the contrary, most elements of OLA do not violate procedural due process and the reality is that in some circumstances:

- The risk posed by such entities to the financial system may require immediate and time-constrained resolution which courts typically cannot provide.
- The risk posed by such entities to the financial system can far outweigh any benefit that can be gained from litigation, particularly where litigation has adverse information effects (i.e. news about litigation reduces the reputation, or credit ratings, or perceived credit quality, or stock prices of companies in the industry) or where litigation takes a long time to resolve and can cause harmful contagion.
- Litigation is socially, psychologically and economically expensive and can significantly increase transaction costs in financial transactions and the financial services industry.
- Each of the government agencies that are charged with exercising OLA powers have in-house counsel and economists that are very knowledgeable about the financial services industry and systemic risk (sometimes more knowledgeable than courts). Hence, the theory of delegation (from the judicial branch to the executive branch) can be said to apply and is justifiable.[46] *See*: Stern (1998), Hessick (2018, 2019) and Smith (_____).

Contrary to Gray and Shu (2010), any restrictions on Article-Three jurisdiction and review that are imposed by RAFSA generally and Title-II specifically do not contravene the separation of powers clause of the US Constitution but, in the worst case, may violate the procedural due process clause of the US Constitution. Furthermore, Article-Three grants US federal district courts the power to review such statutes on their terms and

[46] *See*: *Crowell vs. Benson*, 285 U.S. 22, 36–37 (1932; US Supreme Court).
See: *Whitman vs. Am Trucking Ass'ns Inc.*, 531 U.S. 457, 473 (2011; US Supreme Court).
See: Smith, L. (n.d.). *A Note on Non-Article III Courts*. Available at: www.heritage.org/constitution/#!/articles/3/essays/106/a-note-on-non-article-iii-courts.

according to their chosen standards, to determine whether they are unconstitutional.[47] Indeed Gray and Shu (2010) stated that "The key principle is that Article-Three is likely to require the judiciary's close attention if the statute in question addresses rights which have been traditionally viewed as common-law commercial rights, but not require the same level of attention if the statute in question addresses regulatory issues which the federal statute created". Many matters covered by RAFSA address common-law commercial rights.

Contrary to Gray and Shu (2010):

- Title-II of RAFSA does not strip Article-Three courts of the right to review whether the US Treasury's designation of receivership for FDIC resolution is consistent with RAFSA or the Constitution. RAFSA cannot limit the US district court to arbitrary and capricious review or any type of review. Article-Three courts can review cases based on their own chosen standards and can declare all or part of the statute to be unconstitutional.
- Although RAFSA requires the US district court to conduct the review of Title-II actions in secret and complete it within twenty-four hours, the US federal district court has the power to unilaterally extend the time within which it will perform such reviews (and the court can request that the US Treasury waive the twenty-four-hour requirement). Any alleged abuse of discretion or violation of Title-II by the federal district court is subject to appeal in the US federal appeals courts.
- While RAFSA states that it strips the federal district court of its usual authority to grant a stay pending appeal, such court has the power to declare such measure to be unconstitutional.
- While RAFSA states that it prevents the courts from reviewing the US Treasury's factual determination about whether a financial company's default will affect the financial stability of the United States as a condition of seizing the financial company, under Article-Three and *Northern Pipeline Construction Co. v. Marathon Pipe Line Co*, the federal district courts have the power to review such actions, regardless of what RAFSA states.

[47] *See*: *Northern Pipeline Constr. Co. vs. Marathon Pipe Line Co*, 458 U.S. 50, 73 (1982; US Supreme Court).

- RAFSA states that the courts are not authorized to review whether the FSOC has correctly interpreted the Act, and also specifically states that courts must apply interpretations of provisions (to the extent that an interpretation of the BCFP exists) as if the BCFP "was the only agency authorised to apply, enforce, interpret, or administer the provisions of such Federal consumer financial law". *Kucana v. Holder*[48] can be distinguished from cases and issues that pertain to RAFSA, which can be highly complex and specialized (and require the expert knowledge of economists).
- The public disclosure or announcement of pending or actual liquidation of financial services firms often has adverse information effects and financial contagion effects (as shown in the bankruptcy of Lehman Brothers) which may far outweigh any benefits of government intervention. In fact, it is more likely that public announcement of government intervention (mandated by OLA) will create panic and drastically reduce liquidity and asset prices in financial markets, all of which would defeat the aims of the government.
- Contrary to Gray and Shu (2010), RAFSA is not potentially unconstitutional under *Northern Pipeline*[49] because RAFSA's actual or implied restrictions on, or preclusion of the US bankruptcy code and its judicial review options, can be reviewed by and declared unconstitutional by an Article-Three court. Furthermore, given the significant social welfare, psychological and economic costs of corporate bankruptcy in the United States and the possible resulting financial contagion that exacerbates systemic risk (and the fact that the typical US Bankruptcy Judge and US Bankruptcy Trustee are also functional equivalents of the "agency bureaucrats" or "political appointees" that Gray and Shu (2010) described) and given the fact that such "agency bureaucrats" have specialized knowledge about the financial services industry (which bankruptcy courts often don't have), any implicit delegation of quasi-judicial authority to government agencies by RAFSA may be justified. Corporate bankruptcy carries substantial stigma which affects not only the subject company

[48] *See*: *Kucana vs. Holder*, 130 S.Ct. 827 (2010; US Supreme Court) (implying that through the enactment of statutes, the US Congress can limit the jurisdiction of the federal courts).

[49] *See*: *Northern Pipeline Constr. Co. vs. Marathon Pipe Line Co.*, 458 U.S. 50, 73 (1982; US Supreme Court).

> but its major suppliers and similarly situated companies in the same industry. Lawsuits take a long time to resolve, and dissemination of news about lawsuits (and bankruptcy cases in particular) tends to increase cost-of-capital and the perceived risks of both transactions and companies. Lawsuits also directly and indirectly increase the government's monitoring and enforcement costs, and perpetrators will typically change their tactics to avoid detection.

The Gray and Shu (2010) comment to the effect that the activities of Bureau of Consumer Financial Protection are unconstitutional is also unwarranted. The delegation of rule-making and quasi-adjudication to the BCFP is justifiable because the matters are complex, judicial review may cause or increase financial contagion, courts may not have adequate knowledge or resources to handle such matters, and overall social welfare can be improved by such delegation (and the US Congress can withdraw such delegation).

The Gray and Shu (2010) assertions that key sections of RAFSA are possibly void for vagueness are unwarranted and completely unsupported. *First*, while the *Void-for-vagueness Doctrine* is used only in the context of criminal law statutes, Gray and Shu (2010) erroneously applied this doctrine to parts of RAFSA that are not criminal statutes. *Second*, the history and legislative intent of RAFSA indicates that many sections of RAFSA were not intended to be final directives, but rather, in its various sections, RAFSA was "transient" or "temporary" legislation that specifically requested that US federal government agencies conduct further studies and enact additional rules and statutes. Some of these additional rules/statutes presumably require specialized knowledge and deliberation that were not available in, or could not be effectively done within, the US Congress. *Third*, even where the sections of RAFSA mentioned by Gray and Shu (2010) (as being void for vagueness) were intended to be a "statutory directive", RAFSA defines which persons are regulated, the prohibited conduct and the applicable penalties, and the procedures that should be followed in enforcement and/or adjudication. *Fourth*, any actual or implied delegation of authority by RAFSA to government agencies is typically subject to judicial review by Article-Three courts, and any authority delegated to federal district courts is also subject to review by federal appellate courts. *Fifth*, historically and in most instances, the US Supreme Court has found statutes to be void-for-vagueness only where the application of the statute in question has also caused an ancillary violation of a person's civil rights or personal liberty. *Hoffman Estates vs. The Flipside, Hoffman Estates, Inc.*;[50] *Gonzales vs. Carhart* (2007);[51] *Hill vs. Colorado* (2000);[52] *Tuilaepa vs. California* (1994);[53] *Gentile vs. State Bar of Nev.* (1991);[54] *City Of Mesquite vs. Aladdin's Castle, Inc.*[55] and Hadfield (1994) all addressed the *Void-for-Vagueness Doctrine*. *Sixth*, Gray and Shu (2010) seem to take issue with the degree of specification or definitiveness of RAFSA—but that is really a matter of semantics and not function, and in such circumstances and context (i.e. Global Financial Crisis; political bickering, budget deficits, public-approval ratings, etc.), it may have been difficult to develop better definitions.

2.6 The Dodd-Frank Act Contravenes Various Constitutional Law Principles

This section discusses how RAFSA violates various Constitutional Law principles that are well accepted in common-law countries. See: Downs et al. (2013). Under the US Constitution, the relevant *State Actions* are as follows:

- the enactment of RAFSA and
- the required mandatory compliance with sections of RAFSA.

As stated above, Joslyn (2010) summarized some possible constitutional law problems which are as follows: (1) RAFSA is constitutionally suspect to the extent it creates crimes but allows the precise contours of the criminal conduct to be defined by unelected regulatory authorities; (2) in the US, traditional police powers reside at the state-government level, which makes US states more appropriate enforcers of criminal penalties (rather than federal investigative/police agencies such as the FBI); (3) many of the criminal provisions in RAFSA were drafted in an overly broad

[50] *See*: *Hoffman Estates vs. The Flipside, Hoffman Estates, Inc.*, 455 U.S. 489 (1982; US Supreme Court).

See: *Skilling vs. United States*, 130 S. Ct. 2896, 2934 (2010; US Supreme Court).

[51] *See*: *Gonzales vs. Carhart*, 550 U.S. 124, 168 (2007; US Supreme Court).

[52] *See*: *Hill vs. Colorado*, 530 U.S. 703 (2000; US Supreme Court).

[53] *See*: *Tuilaepa vs. California*, 512 U.S. 967 (1994; US Supreme Court).

[54] *See*: *Gentile vs. State Bar of Nevada*, 501 U.S. 1030 (1991; US Supreme Court).

[55] *See*: *City of Mesquite vs. Aladdin's Castle, Inc.*, 455 U.S. 283 (1982; US Supreme Court).

or vague manner, which creates the problems of fair notice and violations of the due process clauses of the US Constitution.

2.6.1 *The* Non-Delegation Doctrine

The "Non-Delegation Doctrine" is derived from Article-One of the US Constitution which states that "[a]ll legislative Powers herein granted shall be vested in a Congress of the United States". In a rather strange and open-ended manner, RAFSA unconstitutionally delegated legislative powers to many US federal government agencies. These are statutes/regulations that should have been enacted by the US Congress but with substantial input from federal agencies—primarily because: (i) the US Constitution expressly grants "Spending Powers" to the US Congress and many of the regulations that the Dodd-Frank Act delegated to federal agencies involve substantial expenditures of cash and human capital; (ii) according to various estimates, RAFSA requires more than 250 (two hundred and fifty) new formal rule-makings by eleven different federal government agencies, with at last twenty-five new rules to be enacted by the BCFP and at least fifty new rules by the FSOC, and at least ninety new rules by the SEC. However, it seems that it has been generally acceptable for US federal government agencies (such as the US SEC) to create rules based on statutes (that may be considered open-ended) enacted by the US Congress.[56]

This unconstitutional delegation by the US Congress raises the questions of:

1. The differences between congressionally enacted statutes and administrative law created by US federal government agencies.
2. the power and effectiveness of federal administrative law.
3. Preemption issues.[57]

[56] *See*: *PennEast Pipeline Co. vs. New Jersey*, ___ US ___ (No. 19-1039; US Supreme Court; pending as of 2021).

See: *Seila Law LLC vs. Consumer Financial Protection Bureau*, ____ US ____ (Case#: No. 19-7; US Supreme Court; 2020) (the Consumer Financial Protection Bureau's single-Director structure violates the *Separation of Powers Doctrine*, and the proper remedy is to make the Director removable by the President at will.).

[57] See the existing US Supreme Court *preemption* criteria that is summarized in Nwogugu (2012c: 127–135); and the *preemption* criteria introduced in Nwogugu (2012c: 135–138).

See: *Rutledge vs. Pharmaceutical Care Management Association*, ___ US ___ (No. 18-540; US Supreme Court; pending as of 2021).

2.6.2 *The* Substantive Due Process Doctrine

The federal government has an affirmative duty to enact effective laws, risk regulations and statutes that will reduce bankruptcy risk, systemic risk and financial contagion; and the government breached this duty by enacting RAFSA. Under the *State Action* and Constitutional Tort theories explained and/or introduced in Tushnet (2003), Kania (1983), Gardbaum (2006), Jamison (2008), Ellman (2001), Heinzerling (1986), Burnham (1989), Nwogugu (2012c)[58] and Currie (1986), the failure of RAFSA to enact the various statutes that are required for the protection of investors and for overall financial stability constitutes actionable Constitutional Torts.

The Financial Stability Act of 2010 (FSA) contravenes Substantive Due Process principles because it grants the US Federal Reserve the power to liquidate financial institutions (deemed to be in default or in danger of default, and whose failure will have adverse consequences on the US economy) in a special proceeding in the US District Court for the District of Columbia (the "Orderly Liquidation Authority" or "OLA")[59] (Financial Stability Act of 2010). Karmel (2011) and Fisher (2013) noted some of the weaknesses in OLA. The FSOC selects financial companies that are subject to seizure by the government. In OLA, the US Treasury, the FDIC and the US Federal Reserve can agree to put a financial institution into an orderly liquidation process in a US District Court for the District of Columbia wherein the Court must agree that the company is insolvent within twenty-four hours, in order for the liquidation process to begin. OLA is essentially an alternative insolvency regime (an alternative to traditional bankruptcy processes), and Court proceedings under OLA are filed under seal and in a petition brought to the United States District Court

[58] *See*: Nwogugu, M. (2012c). *Risk in the Global Real Estate Market* (John Wiley; 2012) (introducing the "*Substitution Theory*" [p. 198] and the "*Substantial Inducement Theory*" [p. 9]).

[59] *See*: 12 U.S.C. § 5394 (Dodd-Frank Act § 214) (this clause prevents any future government bailouts for troubled financial institutions).

See: Woo (2011), Ben-Ishai and Lubben (2011), Smolinsky (2011), Goddard (2011), Paulus (2011), Sivon and Natter (2011), Gordon and Muller (2010), Noss and Sowerbutts (2012), Otker-Robe et al. (2011), Schmid (2012), Gordon and Muller (2011), Jackson (2009), Cihak and Nier (2012), Reeves and Stucke (2011), and Brewer and Jagtiani (2013).

See: Markham (2011) (noting that "Antitrust law could make a greater contribution in resolving this public-policy problem if Congress enacted or the judiciary forged more robust rules preventing and dismantling unwieldy corporate size in excess of any plausible scale efficiency justification").

for the District of Columbia (the US District court for the District of Columbia has changed its local rules—to effectively modify OLA).[60] Where the expedited twenty-four-hour US District Court process is used, OLA attempts to eliminate stays or injunctions, the US District court can extend the twenty-four-hour deadline (or rule that the twenty-four-hour deadline is unfair), and although the subject company and its creditors don't participate in the US District Court proceedings, a party can appeal the US District court's decision to a US Federal Court of Appeals on the basis that the actions of the FDIC, the US Federal Reserve and the US Treasury were arbitrary and/or constitutes abuse of discretion.

OLA grants the US Fed and the US Treasury excessive power and discretion over financial institutions and non-bank business entities—OLA is somewhat vague and does not state specific minimum criteria for selection of business entities for liquidation, and the US Fed's and the US Treasury's interpretation of "management of systemic risk" and "threat to financial stability" may be politically motivated and/or may deviate from the US Congress's legislative intent when OLA was drafted. Because many financial institutions rely heavily on their reputation and brand equity, it is likely that OLA will compel government agencies and courts to:

- focus on business entities that have substantial reputation and brand equity—and neglect less visible financial institutions that are sometimes more relevant, and
- focus on "direct financial contracts" which are more easily provable in court, rather than the often more important "indirect financial contracts" and chains-of-insurance.

The FSA contravenes Substantive Due Process because it grants the US Federal Reserve the power to break up firms that are deemed to be too large and that pose a risk to the financial system (the "Break-up Procedure"). In the cases of the both the OLA and the Break-up Procedure, the government's interest in regulating the economy to reduce systemic risk is far outweighed by the following:

[60] The United States District Court for the District of Columbia has adopted *Local Civil Rule 85*. Available at: www.dcd.uscourts.gov/dcd/sites/dcd/files/DFWSR.pdf. It may be argued that these procedures in Local Civil Rule 85 effectively modify OLA and provide for procedural and substantive due process.

- the subjectivity and vagueness inherent in the FSA (OLA and the Break-up Procedure),
- potentially disastrous consequences of liquidating or breaking up a firm that does not pose a threat to the economy; and
- the Liquidation Procedure and the Break-Up Procedure have substantial information effects that can adversely affect the credit ratings, perceived credit quality and stock prices of associated companies or companies in the same industry.[61]

2.6.3 *The* Procedural Due Process Doctrine

The *Break-up Procedure* grants the US Fed excessive discretion over financial institutions. The key issue is that while firms may pose a risk due to their perceived or actual economic impact, the FSA does not establish objective standards for determining the adverse economic impact of a firm. Also, some authors have stated that there has been inadequate cost-benefit analysis in processes for enactment of financial regulations/laws[62]—and such inadequacies may also exist in application of RAFSA. See the discussions of the *Procedural Due Process Clause* of the US Constitution in Nwogugu (2012c). In the cases of both the *Liquidation Procedure* and the *Break-up Procedure*, the government's interest in regulating the economy to reduce systemic risk is far outweighed by the following:

[61] *See*: *Washington v. Glucksberg*, 521 U.S. 702, 719 (US Supreme Court; 1997) ("The Due Process Clause guarantees more than fair process, and the 'liberty' it protects includes more than the absence of physical restraint.").

See: *Obergefell vs. Hodges*: 576 U. S. 644 (US Supreme Court; 2015).

See: *Lawrence vs. Texas*, 539 U. S. 558 (US Supreme Court; 2003).

See: *United States vs. Vaello-Madero*, _____ US ____ (Case#: 20-303; US Supreme Court; pending as of 2021).

See: *DeNolf vs. U.S.*, _____ US _____ (US Supreme Court; pending as of 2021) (https://static1.squarespace.com/static/5b660749620b85c6c73e5e61/t/608d544886d55300e492a619/1619874888658/2021-22+AMCA+Case.pdf).

See: *DeNolf vs. U.S.*, (Case#: 01-76320; US 14th Circuit, 2020) (https://static1.squarespace.com/static/5b660749620b85c6c73e5e61/t/608d544886d55300e492a619/1619874888658/2021-22+AMCA+Case.pdf).

See: *Planned Parenthood of Southeastern Pennsylvania v. Casey*, 505 U.S. 833, 848 (1992) ("Neither the Bill of Rights nor the specific practices of States at the time of the adoption of the Fourteenth Amendment marks the outer limits of the substantive sphere of liberty which the Fourteenth Amendment protects").

[62] *See*: Rose and Walker (2013) (supra).

- potentially disastrous consequences of breaking up a firm that does not pose a threat to the economy,
- the *Break-up Procedure* has, or can have, substantial information effects (that can adversely affect the credit ratings, perceived credit quality and stock prices of associated companies or companies in the same industry) and
- the potential for abuse of discretion by the US Treasury, US Federal Reserve and/or the FDIC.

2.6.4 The Right-to-Contract *Doctrine*

The OLA and the *Break-up Procedure* constitute violations of the Right-to-Contract Clause[63] because they prevent companies from contracting as they see fit and force companies into legal processes that reduce or eliminate their rights to contract with others. These legal processes also reduce these subject companies' opportunity set. The Government's interest in facilitating financial stability and reducing systemic risk is far outweighed by the adverse subjectivity of the *Liquidation Procedure* and the *Break-up Procedure*, and the damaging effects of false-positives (healthy firms are forcibly liquidated or broken up; and/or liquidations and break-ups are biased or politically motivated) and the adverse information affects the Liquidation Procedure and the Break-up Procedure. In the financial services industry, liquidations and break-ups have substantial information content (because many firms are linked by financial contracts) and are very likely to result in a significant decline in liquidity of markets (as occurred during the Global Financial Crisis of 2008–2010). The government's interest in regulating institutions and companies is far outweighed by the following factors:

- The potentially destructive effects of the wide discretion granted to the US Fed to liquidate or break up firms.
- The potentially adverse effects of the Liquidation Procedure and the Break-up Procedure on competition in financial services industry and other industries. These processes are likely to reduce competi-

[63] *See* the discussions of the *Right-to-Contract Clause* in Nwogugu (2012c) (supra).
See: *Energy Reserves Group, Inc. vs. Kansas Power and Light Co.*, _____ US ____ (US Supreme Court; 1983).
See: *Sveen vs. Melin*, ___ US ____ (US Supreme Court; 2018).

tion and, instead, can promote collusion, price-fixing and refusals-to-deal.

- The potentially destructive effects of financial contagion when certain firms (with good reputations and/or many contracts with other firms) are liquidated or broken up.

There are other alternatives for the government to control or limit the size of large "risky" firms—such as the following: (1) increasing the minimum-capital requirements for both financial institutions and non-financial firms that sell financial products (and perhaps physically segregating all or a portion of such capital at the US Federal Reserve or the US Treasury); (2) limitations on the scope of activities of banks and non-bank "financial companies"; or (3) implementing a system of penalties for financial services companies that increase systemic risk and implementing a system of incentives for companies that reduce systemic risk. Similarly, there are other alternatives to outright liquidation of firms that are deemed to be financially distressed or too risky.

RAFSA violates the *Contracts Clause* of the US Constitution because it amends the Securities Exchange Act of 1934 to expressly require that sponsors of securitizations must retain at least 5% of the risk of the assets and ABS. This *Retention Requirement* restricts firms from contracting with third parties. The *Retention Requirement* is ineffective. For example, a sponsor firm has a pool of US $500 million of bad assets and wants to get rid of the assets via securitization, and the sponsor sells all the resulting ABS. Regardless of whether the sponsor retains 5% or 50% of the risk of the US $500 million pool, the sponsor has achieved its objective of transferring the risk of bad risky assets to investors. Hence, the *Retention Requirement* serves no purpose. The *Retention Requirement* provides substantial incentives for sponsors to increase systemic risk because it compels them:

- to seek and purchase third-party credit enhancement for the underlying loans/assets or of the retained ABS (which simply distributes the risk within the financial system and creates a credit-chain)—and the sponsor's mere searches for third-party credit enhancement has, or can have, substantial information content that can cause harmful financial contagion,
- to include the riskiest assets in the ABS tranches that are sold to investors—and retain 5% of the tranches backed by the least-risky assets;

- to inflate ABS prices, and to inflate the prices of collateral sold to the Securitization Trust (in order to reduce the true quantities/volumes of ABS that they have to retain); and
- to treat the *Retention Requirement* as merely a cost of doing business rather than a deterrence measure that can have punitive effects.

The above-mentioned restrictions on contract rights of persons do not serve any meaningful purpose and are far outweighed by the distorted and adverse incentives that they create.

The Consumer Financial Protection Act of 2010 (CFPA; USA) violates the *Contracts Clause* because it amends the Truth in Lending Act (TILA; USA) to prohibit certain prepayment penalties. Lenders incur transaction costs and monitoring costs to originate, monitor and service loans and prepayment penalties are designed to ensure that lenders retain the economic benefits of providing loans. Without adequate prepayment penalties, lenders will have much less incentives to provide loans, and their profit margins can decline substantially. In such circumstances, these lenders are more likely to increase interest rates they charge for loans, in order to maintain their profits. Most banks/lenders generate most of their profits from net interest margins. Hence, eliminating prepayment penalties will have adverse economic effects on banks/lenders, prospective borrowers and the economy, all of which will outweigh the government's interest in regulating financial institutions and financial services. This prohibition on prepayment penalties effectively restricts firms and lenders from contracting with third parties, and unfairly discriminates between: (1) lenders of different sizes and reputations—in terms of their ability to afford and absorb the risk of lack of prepayment penalties; (2) any pair of lenders that have different quality of assets (3) lenders that have the knowledge and capability to pass on prepayment penalties in other forms to borrowers and the lenders that do not have such knowledge and capability; and (4) lenders that have the knowledge and capability to hedge prepayment risk and the lenders that do not have such knowledge.

2.6.5 *The* Equal Protection Doctrine

The *Liquidation Procedure* and the *Break-up Procedure* of the FSA violates the *Equal Protection Doctrine*[64] of the US Constitution because:

- the procedures unfairly discriminate between financial institutions and non-financial services firms (who sell financial products and whose default may have adverse consequences on the economy—such as large retailing companies, captive finance subsidiaries of international conglomerates, captive insurance subsidiaries etc.);
- the procedures unfairly discriminate between firms that focus on or provide financial services, and firms that provide other non-financial services/products (whose financial distress or default may have adverse consequences on the economy);
- the procedures unfairly discriminate between large and visible financial institutions that are subject to reputation penalties and smaller or less-visible financial institutions that may have the same economic impact;
- the procedures unfairly discriminate between large financial services firms that pose a threat to financial stability and small financial services firms that pose the same magnitude of threat/risk to financial stability.

RAFSA's express protection of the existing dual banking system in the United States constitutes a violation of the *Equal Protection Doctrine* because RAFSA:

- causes unfair discrimination between banks that are registered in different states and, thus, are subject to different banking laws;
- unfairly discriminates between large national/international banks and small/local/regional banks that are often subject to different sets of regulations but provide the same or similar services to individuals and organizations (unfairly discriminates between federally

[64] *See* the discussions of the *Equal Protection Clause* of the US Constitution in various contexts in Nwogugu (2012c).

See: *United States vs. Vaello-Madero*, _____ US ____ (Case#: 20-303; US Supreme Court; pending as of 2021).

See: *Espinoza vs. Montana Department of Revenue*, _____ US ____ (US Supreme Court; pending as of 2021).

chartered and state-chartered banks that provide the same or similar services to individuals and organizations); and
- unfairly discriminates between banks that afford the transaction costs of interstate commerce and those that cannot.

RAFSA (Private Fund Investment Advisers Registration Act of 2010—PFIARA) requires that some types of hedge funds register with the US SEC and be subject to SEC regulation (i.e. hedge funds that have more than $100 million of assets). The PFIARA's registration requirement for hedge funds violates the Equal Protection Clause because:

- It unfairly discriminates between hedge funds that have more than $100 million in assets but have low economic impact on markets and hedge funds that have less than $100 million of assets but have large economic and psychological impact on markets and/or large trading volumes.
- It unfairly discriminates between hedge funds that have more than $100 million of assets and non-financial companies that trade substantially in derivatives and securities (such as commodities firms, agriculture companies, energy companies, large retailers that offer financial products) but are not deemed to be hedge funds.
- It unfairly discriminates between hedge funds that have more than $100 million of assets and securities brokerage firms that have less than $100 million of assets—but act as agents and have the same or greater trading volume and economic impact as the regulated/qualifying hedge funds.
- It unfairly discriminates between hedge funds that have more than $100 million of assets but have different capital structure—that is, one hedge fund may be using 1: 50 debt leverage (achieved by borrowing and/or shorting bonds and/or trading derivatives), while the other hedge fund may have only a 1:1 leverage (trades in only cash market without leverage).

The current oligopoly in the global accounting/auditing industry has adverse effects on risk regulation and global financial stability. See the comments in Nwogugu (2021). RAFSA's failure to break up the oligopoly in the accounting/auditing industry constitutes a violation of the Equal Protection doctrine. The omission in RAFSA unfairly discriminates between:

- companies that can afford the services of the Big-Four accounting firms and companies that cannot afford to hire the Big-Four accounting firms; and
- companies in industries where auditor reputation is critical and, on the other hand, companies in industries where auditor reputation is not critical; and
- small accounting firms who do not enjoy the benefits of the prevailing "reputation-based auditing" and, on the other hand, the Big-Four accounting firms.

The Consumer Financial Protection Act of 2010 (CFPA) of RAFSA violates the Equal Protection Contracts Clause because it amends the Truth in Lending *Act* ('TILA') to prohibit certain prepayment penalties. Lenders incur transaction costs and monitoring costs to originate, monitor and service loans, and prepayment penalties are designed to ensure that lenders retain the economic benefits of providing loans. Without adequate prepayment penalties, lenders will have much less incentives to provide loans, and their profit margins will decline substantially—most banks generate most of their profits from Net Interest Margins. Hence, eliminating prepayment penalties will have adverse economic effects on banks. The prohibition on prepayment penalties unfairly discriminates between (1) borrowers whose loans have prepayment penalties and borrowers whose loans do not have such provisions, (2) banks that focus on providing loans with prepayment penalties (mostly small and mid-sized banks and banks that rely in interest income) and banks that do not provide loans with prepayment penalties (typically larger banks with more diversified sources of income).

Nwogugu (2014a) explained weaknesses inherent in the US FSOC's non-bank SIFI criteria, and also introduced more efficient criteria. The US FSOC's non-bank SIFI Criteria do not address asset management companies and REITs—but as explained in Nwogugu (2014b), REIT shares/interests are derivatives and can cause systemic risk; and as explained in Nwogugu (2008a, b), REITs have inherent Corporate Governance deficiencies. The US FSOC's "non-bank SIFI Criteria" violates the Equal Protection Doctrine because the criteria can cause a high probability of false negatives and false positives (as explained above), and:

1. The *Absolute Size Criteria* (i.e. the US FSOC's minimum size cutoff for non-bank SIFIs is $50 billion of assets) unfairly discriminate

between firms whose annual revenues are less than $50 billion (more than $50 billion) but otherwise are systemically very important, as explained above, and firms whose revenues are below $50 billion (more than $50 billion) and are not systemically important, as explained above.

2. The *Absolute Debt Burden Criteria* (*i.e.* $20 billion of debt is the FSOC's minimum cut-off for non-bank SIFIs) unfairly discriminate between firms whose total debts are less than $20 billion (more than $20 billion) but otherwise are systemically very important, as explained above, and firms whose total debts are above 20 billion (less than $20 billion) and are not systemically important, as explained above.
3. The outstanding Derivatives liabilities Criteria (the US FSOC's cut-off for derivatives liabilities is a minimum of $3.5 billion after accounting for cash collateral and netting agreements) unfairly discriminate between firms whose total debts are less than $20 billion (more than $20 billion) but otherwise are systemically very important, as explained above, and firms whose total debts are above 20 billion (less than $20 billion) and are not systemically important, as explained above.
4. The *CDS Criteria* ($30 billion or more in gross notional credit default swaps for which the company is a party) unfairly discriminate between firms whose CDS contracts have a combined notional value that is less than $30 billion (more than $30 billion) but are systemically very important, as explained in the section on FSOC criteria, and firms whose CDS contracts have a notion value that is more than 30 billion (less than $30 billion) and are not systemically important, as explained above.
5. The *Leverage Criteria* (an assets-to-equity leverage ratio that exceeds 15:1) unfairly discriminates between firms whose assets-to-equity leverage ratio is less than 15:1 (more than 15:1) but otherwise are systemically very important, as explained herein in the section on FSOC criteria, and firms whose assets-to-equity leverage ratio exceeds 15:1 (less than 15:1) but are not systemically important, as explained above.
6. The *Short-term Debt Criteria* (the ratio of short-term debt to total consolidated assets exceeds 10%) discriminates between firms whose short-term-debt-to total-assets ratio is less than 10% but otherwise are systemically very important, as explained above, and firms whose

short-term-debt-to total-assets ratio is greater than 10% and are not systemically important, as explained above.

2.6.6 *The* Dormant Commerce Clause Doctrine (USA Only)

A section of RAFSA named EFISSA (*Enhancing Financial Institutions Safety and Soundness Act of 2010*—EFISSA) expressly prohibits the issuance of charters for federal savings and loan (S&L) associations, and thus violates the Dormant Commerce Clause Doctrine, because:

- EFISSA unduly burdens interstate commerce by subjecting S&Ls and their customers to state regulation of S&Ls.
- EFISSA shifts the regulation of S&Ls to states and hence creates discrimination between S&Ls that are regulated by and/or registered in different states (in terms of transaction costs, compliance costs and opportunity set).
- EFISSA prevents and limits the growth of savings and loan banks.

See the discussions of the Dormant Commerce Clause Doctrine of the US Constitution in Nwogugu (2012c).[65] The express protection of the current dual banking system by RAFSA constitutes a violation of the Dormant Commerce Clause Doctrine, because it increases transactions costs of banks and their customers that are located in different states, and it increases transaction costs and compliance costs of banks that are involved in interstate commerce.

Given that banking (even at the local level) is very much an international business, and the direct/indirect links/contracts among banks are continuing to increase, the RAFSA/EFISSA provisions substantially limit interstate commerce.

[65] *See*: Nwogugu (2012c) (supra).

See: *DeNolf vs. U.S.*, _____ US _____ (US Supreme Court; pending as of 2021) (https://static1.squarespace.com/static/5b660749620b85c6c73e5e61/t/608d544886d55300e492a619/1619874888658/2021-22+AMCA+Case.pdf).

See: *DeNolf vs. U.S.*, (Case#: 01-76320; US 14th Circuit, 2020) (https://static1.squarespace.com/static/5b660749620b85c6c73e5e61/t/608d544886d55300e492a619/1619874888658/2021-22+AMCA+Case.pdf).

See: *Perez vs. United States*, 402 U.S. 146, 150 (1971) (Congress can ban loansharking that threatens interstate commerce).

See: *Gonzales vs. Raich*, 545 U.S. 1, 18 (US Supreme Court; 2005).

The CFPA's prohibition of prepayment penalties burdens interstate commerce because it creates or can create adverse tax consequences for: (1) lenders that are located in states where the costs of hedging prepayment risk and/or losses from early prepayment are classified as tax-deductible expenses, or are not classified as such; (2) lenders that are located in states where the existence or non-existence of prepayment penalties affects the classification of the loan for tax or accounting purposes; (3) lenders that are located in states where prepayment penalties are treated as capital gains or taxable income, or are not treated as such; and/or (4) lenders that are located in states where the existence or non-existence of prepayment penalties affects the contract rights of the lenders and borrowers.

RAFSA's express protection of the existing "dual banking" system in the US (i.e. different banking laws at both the federal government and state government levels) also burdens interstate commerce because: (1) it creates different amounts of transaction costs, compliance costs, and operating costs for state-chartered and federally chartered banks that are otherwise similar; (2) it discriminates between banks that have only in-state operations and banks that have multi-state operations; and (3) it discriminates between banks that combine banking and insurance services and banks that do not.

2.6.7 The Takings Doctrine

The above-mentioned discriminatory classifications inherent in RAFSA also constitute violations of the *Takings Doctrine*[66] with respect to the associated *Protected Classes*. See the *Takings* theories introduced in Nwogugu (2012c).[67] The *Takings* involved include the traditional

[66] *See*: *Federal Republic of Germany* et al. vs. *Philipp* et al. (No. 19–351; February 3, 2021; US Supreme Court). https://www.supremecourt.gov/opinions/20pdf/19-351_o7jp.pdf.

See: *Republic of Austria v. Altmann*, 541 U. S. 677 (US Supreme Court).

See: *Bolivarian Republic of Venezuela vs. Helmerich & Payne Int'l Drilling Co.*, 581 U. S._____ (2017; US Supreme Court).

[67] *See*: Nwogugu (2012c: 109, 144, 190 & 246).

See: *Cedar Point Nursery vs. Hassid*, ____ US ____ (US Supreme Court; pending as of 2021).

See: *Cedar Point Nursery vs. Sheroma*, ____ F.3d. ____ (US Ninth Circuit Court of Appeals).

See: *PennEast Pipeline Co. vs. New Jersey*, ___ US ____ (US Supreme Court; pending as of 2021).

Regulatory Takings Doctrine (when the government's excessive regulation of the use of property directly or indirectly results in a deprivation of rights).

2.6.8 Unconstitutionality of the Consumer Financial Protection Bureau *(CFPB)*

The sections of RAFSA that created the *Consumer Financial Protection Bureau* (CFPB) violate the US Constitution because the US Congress (which has exclusive *Spending Power* pursuant to the US Constitution) doesn't appropriate the budget of the CFPB (and the CFPB performs functions that should be regulated and overseen by the US Congress).[68]

Separately and in 2018, the US Supreme Court held that the structure of the Consumer Financial Protection Bureau was unconstitutional[69] and violated the *Separation of Powers Doctrine*.[70]

See: *Murr vs. Wisconsin*, 137 S.Ct. 1933 (US Supreme Court; 2017).

See: *California Bldg. Industry Ass'n vs. City of San Jose, Calif.*, 136 S.Ct. 928 (US Supreme Court; 2016).

See: *Koontz vs. St. Johns River Water Management District*, 570 U.S. 2588 (US Supreme Court; 2013).

See: *Lucas vs. South Carolina Coastal Council*, 505 U.S. 1003 (US Supreme Court; 1992).

[68] *See*: *Trump v. Sierra Club*, ___ US ___ (US Supreme Court; pending as of 2021).

See: *National Federation of Independent Business v. Sebelius*, 567 U.S. 519 (2012; US Supreme Court).

See: *South Dakota v. Dole*, ____ US _____ (US Supreme Court; 1987).

[69] *See*: *Seila Law LLC vs. Consumer Financial Protection Bureau*, ____ US ____ (Case#: No. 19-7; US Supreme Court; 2020) (the Consumer Financial Protection Bureau's single-Director structure violates the *Separation of Powers Doctrine*, and the proper remedy is to sever the Director's statutory for-cause removal restriction).

[70] *See*: *Collins vs. Yellen*, ___ US ___ (No. 19-422; US Supreme Court; pending as of 2021).

See: *Collins vs. Mnuchin*, ____ US _____ (Docket No. 19-422; US Supreme Court; pending as of 2021).

See: *Humphrey's Executor vs. United States*, 295 U.S. 602 (US Supreme Court; 1935).

See: *PHH Corp. vs. CFPB*, 839 F.3d 1 (2016) *on rehearing enbanc*, 881 F.3d 75 (D.C. Cir., 2018) (en banc).

2.7 Conclusion

Given the foregoing, RAFSA is not only operationally, politically and economically deficient but also many parts of RAFSA are unconstitutional and should be substantially modified. RAFSA (and the US$600+ billion that the US government invested in the US economy during 2009–2013) has not created much needed economic growth in the US and has not stimulated US capital markets. Instead, sections of RAFSA have increased uncertainty, transaction costs and compliance costs for financial services companies, non-financial companies, and federal and state governments. In hindsight, sections of RAFSA continue to be a tax on corporate entities and a fee-bonanza for Washington D.C. lobbyists, law firms and financial services consultants. While the concepts, legislative intent and initiative embodied in RAFSA are laudable and perhaps were overdue, the benefits of some parts of RAFSA remain questionable and are yet to emerge.

Bibliography

Addington, D. (2011, October 13). *Congress Should Promptly Repeal or Fix Un-Warranted Provisions of the Dodd-Frank Act*. Heritage Foundation – Backgrounder #2615. Retrieved from www.heritage.org/research/reports/2011/10/congress-should-promptly-repeal-or-fix-unwarranted-provisions-of-the-dodd-frank-act.

Allen, J. (2012). Derivatives Clearinghouses and Systemic Risk: A Bankruptcy and Dodd-Frank Analysis. *Stanford Law Review, 64*(4). (States that Under RAFSA, Central Clearing Houses Can Increase Systemic Risk).

American Action Forum. (2010, April). *The Senate Financial Regulatory Reform Bill*. Retrieved from http://americanactionforum.org/files/FinRegBill1_0.pdf.

Banker, S., Bhanot, S., & Deshpande, A. (2020). Poverty Identity and Preference for Challenge: Evidence from the U.S. and India. *Journal of Economic Psychology, 76*, in press.

Barnett, K. (2011). The Consumer Financial Protection Bureau's Appointment with Trouble. *American University Law Review, 60*, 1459–1463.

Barr, M. (2012). The Financial Crisis and the Path of Reform. *Yale Journal on Regulation, 29*(1), 91–119.

Bavetta, S., Li Donni, P., & Marino, M. (2020). How Consistent Are Perceptions of Inequality? *Journal of Economic Psychology, 78*, in press.

Ben-Ishai, S., & Lubben, S. (2011). A Comparative Study of Bankruptcy as Bailout. *Brooklyn Journal of Corporate, Financial & Commercial Law, 6*(1), 79–102.

Birz, G. (2017). Stale Economic News, Media and the Stock Market. *Journal of Economic Psychology, 61*, 87–102.

Blaufus, K., Möhlmann, A., & Schwäbe, A. (2019). Stock Price Reactions to News About Corporate Tax Avoidance and Evasion. *Journal of Economic Psychology, 72*, 278–292.

Brewer, E., & Jagtiani, J. (2013). How Much Did Banks Pay to Become Too-Big-to-Fail and to Become Systemically Important? *Journal of Financial Services Research, 43*(1), 8–12. Retrieved from http://link.springer.com/content/pdf/10.1007%2Fs10693-011-0119-6.pdf.

Burnham, W. (1989). Separating Constitutional and Common Law Torts: A Critique and a Proposed Constitutional Theory of Duty. *Minnesota Law Review, 73*, 515–525.

Casey, D. (2012, January). *The US Government Is Bankrupt*. Retrieved from http://www.caseyresearch.com/articles/us-government-bankrupt.

Caughey, B. (2011). *A Creditor's Right to Setoff: When Does a Creditor Impermissibly Improve Its Position?* Retrieved from www.icemiller.com/publications/Creditor%27s_Right_to_Setoff_ABI.pdf.

Cervone, E. (2017). The Final Volcker Rule and Its Impact Across the Atlantic: The Shaping of Extraterritoriality in a World of Dynamic Structural Banking Reforms. In G. Adinolfi, F. Baetens, J. Caiado, A. Lupone, & A. Micara (Eds.), *International Economic Law* (pp. 233–251). Cham: Springer.

Cihak, M., & Nier, E. (2012). The Need for Special Resolution Regimes for Financial Institutions – The Case of the European Union. *Harvard Business Law Review, 2*, 398–408. Retrieved from www.hblr.org/wp-content/uploads/2012/11/HLB206_Special-Resolution.pdf.

Coffee, J. (2012). The Political Economy of Dodd-Frank: Why Financial Reform Tends to Be Frustrated and Systemic Risk Perpetuated. *Cornell Law Review, 97*, 1019–1029. Retrieved from www.lawschool.cornell.edu/research/cornell-law-review/upload/Coffee-final-2.pdf.

Congressional Research Service (USA). (2010, April 1). Summary of '*Restoring American Financial Stability Act of 2010*'. Financial Stability Act of 2010 (introduced on 15 April 2010).

Currie, D. (1986). Positive and Negative Constitutional Rights. *University of Chicago Law Review, 53*(3), 864–890.

Debelle, G. (2004). Household Debt and the Macroeconomy. *BIS Quarterly Review*. Retrieved from http://ssrn.com/abstract=1968418.

DeFusco, A., Johnson, A., & Mondragon, J. (2020). Regulating Household Leverage. *Review of Economic Studies, 87*(2), 914–958.

Dixon, R., Griffiths, W., & Lim, G. (2014). Lay People's Models of the Economy: A Study Based on Surveys of Consumer Sentiments. *Journal of Economic Psychology, 44*, 13–20.

Dolar, B., & Dale, B. (2020). The Dodd–Frank Act's Non-Uniform Regulatory Impact on the Banking Industry. *Journal of Banking Regulation, 21*, 188–195.

Downs, H., Salser, M., & Long, D. (2013). *Recent Constitutional Challenges to Dodd-Frank.* Retrieved from www.johnstonbarton.com/wp-content/uploads/2013/04/Recent-Constitutional-Challenges-to-Dodd-Frank.pdf.

Eggum, J., Porter, K., & Twomey, T. (2008). Saving Homes in Bankruptcy: Housing Affordability and Loan Modification. *Utah Law Review, 2008*(3), 1123–1168.

Elliot, D. (2010, March 15). *Evaluating Key Aspects of Senator Dodd's Revised Financial Reform Bill.* The Brookings Institution.

Ellman, S. (2001). Constitutional Confluence: American "State Action; Law and the Application of South Africa's Socio-Economic Rights Guarantees to Private Actors". *New York Law School Law Review, 45.*

Feldman, R., Schmidt, J., & Heinecke, K. (2013). Quantifying the Costs of Additional Regulation on Community Banks. *Federal Reserve Bank of Minneapolis Economic Policy Papers, 13*(3), 1–23.

Fisher, R. (2013, June 26). *Correcting 'Dodd-Frank' to Actually End 'Too Big to Fail'.* Statement Before the Committee on Financial Services, U.S. House of Representatives Hearing on "Examining How the Dodd-Frank Act Could Result in More Taxpayer-Funded Bailouts", Washington, DC. Retrieved from www.dallasfed.org/news/speeches/fisher/2013/fs130626.cfm.

Freeman, R. (2011). What Can We Learn from the NLRA to Create Labor Law for the Twenty-First Century? *ABA Journal of Labor & Employment Law, 26*(2), 327–343.

FSA (UK). (2012). *Review of the Markets in Financial Instruments Directive II.* Retrieved from www.fsa.gov.uk/about/what/international/mifid.

Garcia, F., Opromolla, L., & Marques, A. (2020). The Effects of Official and Unofficial Information on Tax Compliance. *Journal of Economic Psychology, 78*, in press.

Gardbaum, S. (2006). Where The (State) Action Is. *International Journal of Constitutional Law, 4*, 760–779.

Goddard, B. (2011). The New World Order: Financial Guaranty Company Restructuring and Traditional Insurance Insolvency Principles. *Brooklyn Journal of Corporate, Financial & Commercial Law, 6*(1), 137–170.

Godwin, A., Ramsay, I., & Sayes, E. (2017). Assessing Financial Regulatory Coordination and Integration with Reference to OTC Derivatives Regulation. *Capital Markets Law Journal, 12*(1), 38–65.

Gordon, J., & Muller, C. (2010). *Avoiding Eight-Alarm Fires in the Political Economy of Systemic Risk Management.* Columbia Law & Economics Working Paper No. 369. European Corporate Governance Inst. Finance Working Paper No. 277. Retrieved from http://ssrn.com/abstract_id=1553880.

Gordon, J., & Muller, C. (2011). Confronting Financial Crisis: Dodd-Frank's Dangers and the Case for a Systemic Emergency Fund. *Yale Journal on Regulation, 28*, 151–191.

Gray, B., & Shu, J. (2010, December). The Dodd-Frank Wall Street Reform & Consumer Protection Act of 2010: Is It Constitutional? *Engage: Journal of the Federalist Society's Practice Groups, 11*(3). Retrieved from www.fed-soc.org/doclib/20101209_BoydenShuDoddFrankWP.pdf.

Greene, E. (2011). Dodd-Frank and the Future of Financial Regulation. *Harvard Business Law Review, 2*, 79–89.

Greene, E., & Potiha, I. (2013). Issues in the Extraterritorial Application of Dodd–Frank's Derivatives and Clearing Rules, the Impact on Global Markets and the Inevitability of Cross-Border and US Domestic Coordination. *Capital Markets Law Journal, 8*(4), 338–394.

Hadfield, G. (1994). Weighing the Value of Vagueness: An Economic Perspective on Precision in the Law. *California Law Review, 82*, 541–550.

Haferkamp, A., Fetchenhauer, D., et al. (2009). Efficiency Versus Fairness: The Evaluation of Labor Market Policies by Economists and Laypeople. *Journal of Economic Psychology, 30*(4), 527–539.

Hämäläinen, S., & Martikainen, M. (2015). Foreign Direct Investments Affecting Accounting Quality in Transitional Economies of Europe. *International Journal of Business Innovation and Research, 9*(3), 295–310.

Hansberry, H. (2012). Spite of Its Good Intentions, the Dodd-Frank Act Has Created an FCPA Monster. *Journal of Criminal Law & Criminology, 102*(1).

Hardardottir, H. (2017). Long Term Stability of Time Preferences and the Role of the Macroeconomic Situation. *Journal of Economic Psychology, 60*, 21–36.

Heinzerling, L. (1986). Actionable Inaction: Section 1983 Liability for Failure to Act. *University of Chicago Law Review, 53*, 1048–1061.

Heritage Foundation and National Association of Criminal Defense Lawyers (NACDL). (2010). *Without Intent: How Congress Is Eroding the Criminal Intent Requirement in Federal Law*. Retrieved from www.nacdl.org/withoutintent.

Hessick, F. (2018). *Consenting to Adjudication Outside the Article III Courts*. Retrieved from https://scholarship.law.unc.edu.

Horton, B. (2011). How Dodd-Frank's Orderly Liquidation Authority for Financial Companies Violates Article III of the United States Constitution. *Journal of Corporation Law, 36*(4), 869.

Jackson, T. (2009). Chapter 11F. In K. E. Scott, G. P. Schultz, & J. B. Taylor (Eds.), *A Proposal for the Use of Bankruptcy to Resolve Financial Institutions, in Ending Government Bailouts As We Know Them* (p. 217).

Jacob, S. (2011). Executive Pay and Labor's Shares: Unions and Corporate Governance from Enron to Dodd-Frank. *Accounting, Economics, and Law: A Convivium, 10*(3).

Jamison, F. (2008). State Constitutional Law – Freedom of Speech – A Tightening of the Reins. *Rutgers Law Journal, 39*, 969–979.

Johnson, K. (2011). Addressing Gaps in the Dodd Frank Act: Directors' Risk Management Oversight Obligations. *University of Michigan Journal of Law Reform, 45*(1), 55–65.

Joslyn, J. (2010, December). Criminal Provisions in the Dodd-Frank Wall Street Reform & Consumer Protection Act. *Engage: The Federalist Society for Law and Public Policy Studies.* Retrieved from www.fed-soc.org/doclib/20101210_NFIPCrimProvisionsinDoddFrank.pdf.

Kania, R. (1983). A Theory of Negligence for Constitutional Torts. *Yale Law Journal, 92*, 683–693.

Karmel, R. (2011). An Orderly Liquidation Authority Is Not the Solution to Too-Big-to-Fail. *Brooklyn Journal of Corporate, Financial & Commercial Law, 6*(1), 1–46.

Kenadjian, P., Nazareth, A., & Rosenberg, G. (2013). *Chapter-9: The Cross-Border Impact of the Dodd-Frank Act.* Davis Polk & Wardwell LLP. Retrieved from https://www.davispolk.com/files/The.Cross-border.Impact.of_.the_.Dodd-Frank.Act_.pdf.

Khademian, A. (2013). The Financial Crisis: A Retrospective. *Public Administration Review, 71*(6), 841–849.

Kinnunen, J., Martikainen-Peltola, M., Kallunki, J.-P., & Mikkonen, J. (2016). *Insider Trading and Earnings Management: A Cross-Country Comparison.* Proceedings of Nordic Accounting Conference 2016.

Kleymenova, A., & Zhang, L. (2020, April). *The Impact of Banking Regulation on Voluntary Disclosures: Evidence from the Dodd-Frank Act.* Working Paper.

Kotlikoff, L. J. (2006). Is the United States Bankrupt? *Federal Reserve Bank of St Louis Review, 88*(4), 235–249. Retrieved from http://research.stlouisfed.org/publications/review/06/07/Kotlikoff.pdf

Labonte, M. (2010, August). *CRS Report for Congress Prepared for Members and Committees of Congress – The Dodd-Frank Wall Street Reform and Consumer Protection Act: Systemic Risk and the Federal Reserve.* Retrieved from www.llsdc.org/attachments/files/240/CRS-R41384.pdf.

Lee, P. (2011). The Dodd Frank Act Orderly Liquidation Authority: A Preliminary Analysis and Critique – PART II. *The Banking Law Journal, 128*(10), 867–915.

Li, Z., et al. (2011). Quantifying the Value of Implicit Government Guarantees for Large Financial Institutions. *Moody's Analytics, 14.*

MacDonald, I. (2013). Towards Neoliberal Trade Unionism: Decline, Renewal and Transformation in North American Labor Movements. *British Journal of Industrial Relations, 52*(4).

Mann, R. (2007). Bankruptcy Reform and the 'Sweat Box' of Credit Card Debt. *Univ. of Illinois Law Review, 2007*(1), 375–404.

Markham, J. (2011). Lessons for Competition Law from the Economic Crisis: The Prospect for Antitrust Responses to the "Too Big to Fail" Phenomenon. *Fordham Journal of Corporate & Financial Law, 16*, 261–262.

Martikainen, M., Nikkinen, J., & Saleem, K. (2013). Transmission of the Subprime Crisis: Evidence from Industrial and Financial Sectors of BRIC Countries. *Journal of Applied Business Research, 29*(5), 1469–1478.

Mathur, A. (2013). Beyond Bankruptcy: Does the Bankruptcy Code Provide a Fresh Start to Entrepreneurs. *Journal of Banking & Finance, 37*(11), 4198–4216.

Mitchell, D., & Erickson, C. (2005). Not Yet Dead at the Fed: Unions, Worker Bargaining, and Economy-Wide Wage Determination. *Industrial Relations, 44*(4), 565–566.

Morgan, D. P., Iverson, B., & Botsch, M. (2008). *Seismic Effects of the Bankruptcy Reform.* Staff Report no. 358, Federal Reserve Bank of New York.

Morgan, D., Iverson, B., & Botsch, M. (2012). Subprime Foreclosures and the 2005 Bankruptcy Reform. *Federal Reserve Bank of New York Economic Policy Review, 18*(1), 47–57.

Mwakagali, M. (2018). *International Financial Institutions and Labor Standards: A Legal Study into the Role of These Institutions in the Promotion and Implementation of Freedom of Association and Collective Bargaining.* PhD thesis, Stockholm University, Sweden. Retrieved from https://su.diva-portal.org/smash/get/diva2:1189029/FULLTEXT01.pdf.

National Association of Criminal Defense Lawyers (NACDL). (2010a). *NACDL on HR 4173–Recommendations (Recommendations for Reforming Dodd-Frank Conference Report [HR 4173]).* Retrieved from www.nacdl.org/public.nsf/86871e9e0d470e3185257006006e5f55/b5224f126c7e41cb8525773f0074136f/$FILE/NACDL%20on%20HR4173.pdf. Also Retrieved from www.nacdl.org/criminaldefense.aspx?id=9920.

National Association of Criminal Defense Lawyers (NACDL). (2010b). *Criminal Provisions in HR 4173* (List of the Criminal Provisions in Dodd-Frank Conference Report [HR 4173]).

Natter, R. (2011, July). *Does Dodd-Frank End Too Big to Fail?* (RAFSA Did Not End the Too-Big-to-Fail Phenomenon). Retrieved from www.bsnlawfirm.com/newsletter/OP0711_3.pdf.

Nazreth, A., & Tahyar, M. (2011). Transparency and Confidentiality in the Post Financial Crisis World – Where to Strike the Balance? *Harvard Business Law Review, 1*, 145–155. Retrieved from www.hblr.org/download/HBLR_1_1/Nazareth_Tahyer-Transparency_Confidentiality.pdf.

Nguyen, V., & Claus, E. (2013). Good News, Bad News, Consumer Sentiment and Consumption Behavior. *Journal of Economic Psychology, 39*, 426–438.

Noss, J., & Sowerbutts, R. (2012). *The Implicit Subsidy of Banks.* Bank of England Financial Stability Paper No. 15, p. 6. Retrieved from www.bankofengland.co.uk/publications/Documents/fsr/fs_paper15.pdf.

Nwogugu, M. (2003). Corporate Governance, Credit Risk And Legal Reasoning: The Case Of Encompass Services Inc. *Managerial Auditing Journal, 18*(4), 270–291.

Nwogugu, M. (2008a). Some Corporate Governance Problems Pertaining To REITs—Part One. *Journal Of International Banking Law & Regulation, 23*(2), 71–89.

Nwogugu, M. (2008b). Some Corporate Governance Problems Pertaining To REITs—Part Two. *Journal of International Banking Law & Regulation, 23*(3), 142–162.

Nwogugu, M. (2008c). Securitization Is Illegal: Racketeer Influenced And Corrupt Organizations, Usury, Antitrust and Tax Issues. *Journal Of International Banking Law & Regulation, 23*(6), 316–332.

Nwogugu, M. (2008d). Illegality of Securitization, Bankruptcy Issues and Theories of Securitization. *Journal of International Banking Law & Regulation, 23*(7), 363–375.

Nwogugu, M. (2008e). Prospective Home-Buyers' Propensity-To-Buy in the Housing Industry. *Chaos & Complexity Letters, 3*(2), 169–190.

Nwogugu, M. (2008f). On the Choice Between Renting and Buying In The US Housing Industry. *Chaos & Complexity Letters, 3*(2), 191–208.

Nwogugu M. (2010). *Some Economic Psychology Issues in the Operations of REITs and Companies That Own substantial Real Estate—Parts One & Two.* Retrieved from www.ssrn.com. https://ssrn.com/abstract=874647.

Nwogugu, M. (2012a). *Risk in the Global Real Estate Markets.* John Wiley.

Nwogugu, M. (2012b). Asset Securitization Is Un-constitutional and Should Be Banned. In M. Nwogugu (Ed.), *Risk in the Global Real Estate Markets.* John Wiley.

Nwogugu, M. (2012c). *Risk in the Global Real Estate Market.* John Wiley.

Nwogugu, M. (2014a). "Netting", The Liquidity Coverage Ratio; And the US FSOC's Non-SIFI Criteria, and New Recommendations. *Banking Law Journal, 131*(6), 416–420.

Nwogugu, M. (2014b). REIT Shares/Interests Are Derivatives Instruments; And REITs Are SIFIs. *Pratt's Journal of Bankruptcy Law, 10*(3), 242–246.

Nwogugu, M. (2014c). A Critique of LIBOR/EURIBOR/SHIBOR Rate-Setting Processes; and New Recommendations. *Journal of International Banking Law & Regulation, 29*(4), 208–228.

Nwogugu, M. (2015a). Failure of the Dodd-Frank Act. *Journal of Financial Crime, 22*(4), 520–572.

Nwogugu, M. (2015b). Un-Constitutionality of the Dodd-Frank Act. *European Journal of Law Reform, 17*, 185–190.

Nwogugu, M. (2015c). Real Options, Enforcement of Goodwill/Intangibles Rules and Associated Behavioral Issues. *Journal of Money Laundering Control, 18*(3), 330–351.

Ochsen, C., & Welsch, H. (2012). Who Benefits from Labor Market Institutions? Evidence from Surveys of Life Satisfaction. *Journal of Economic Psychology, 33*(1), 112–124.

Otker-Robe, I., et al. (International Monetary Fund). (2011). *The Too-Important-to-Fail Conundrum: Impossible to Ignore and Difficult to Resolve.* USA: International Monetary Fund. Retrieved from www.imf.org/external/pubs/ft/sdn/2011/sdn1112.pdf.

Pántya, J., Kovács, J., et al. (2016). Work Performance and Tax Compliance in Flat and Progressive Tax Systems. *Journal of Economic Psychology, 56*, 262–273.

Paulus, C. (2011). The New German System of Rescuing Banks. *Brooklyn Journal of Corporate, Financial & Commercial Law, 6*(1), 171–181.

Peirce, H., & Broughel, J. (Eds.). (2012). *Dodd-Frank: What It Does and Why It's Flawed.* USA: Mercatus Center, George Mason University. Retrieved from http://mercatus.org/sites/default/files/publication/dodd-frank-FINAL.pdf.

Pelerin, M. (2013, July). *The Government Is Bankrupt and Will Destroy the Economy.* Retrieved from http://www.americanthinker.com/2012/08/the_government_is_bankrupt_and_will_destroy_the_economy.html.

Porter, K. (2012). The Complaint Conundrum: Thoughts on the CFPB's Complaint Mechanism. *Brooklyn Journal of Corporate Finance & Commercial Law, 7*, 57–77.

Primo, D., & Green, S. (2011). Bankruptcy Law and Entrepreneurship. *Entrepreneurship Research Journal, 1*(2), 5–15.

Rabinovitch, A. (2013, December 22). Constitutional Challenges to Dodd-Frank. *Antitrust Bulletin, 58*(4), 635–640.

Reeves, A., & Stucke, M. (2011). Behavioral Antitrust. *Industrial Law Journal, 86*, 1527–1541.

Roe, M. (2013). The Dodd-Frank Act's Maginot Line: Clearinghouse Construction. *California Law Review.*

Rose, P., & Walker, C. (2013). Dodd-Frank Regulators, Cost-Benefit Analysis, and Agency Capture. *Stanford Law Review Online, 66*, 9–16.

Rosenthal, J. (1995). Incorporation May Not Mean Sophistication: Should There Be a Suitability Requirement for Banks Selling Derivatives to Corporations? *Chicago Kent Law Review, 71*, 1249–1269.

Roubini, N. (2009, March). *The US Financial System Is Effectively Insolvent.* Retrieved from http://www.forbes.com/2009/03/04/global-recession-insolvent-opinions-columnists-roubini-economy.html.

Schmid, L. (2012). Living Wills: Will They Fail to Remedy "Too Big to Fail"? *The Columbia Journal of European Law Online, 18*, 69–79. Retrieved from www.cjel.net/wp-content/uploads/2012/09/Schmid_69-80.pdf.

Schnidman, E. (2011). Why the Federal Reserve Is Dodd-Frank's Big Winner. *Harvard Business Law Review Online, 1*, 88–93.

Schniter, E., Shields, T., & Sznycer, D. (2020). Trust in Humans and Robots: Economically Similar but Emotionally Different. *Journal of Economic Psychology, 78*, in press.

Schwarcz, S. (2011). Identifying and Managing Systemic Risk: An Assessment of Our Progress. *Harvard Business Law Review Online, 1*, 94–103. Retrieved from www.hblr.org/?p=1412.

Sepe, S. (2014). Making Sense of Executive Compensation. *Delaware Journal of Corporate Law, 36*, 189–199.

Sharfman, B. (2011). Using the Law to Reduce Systemic Risk. *Journal of Corporation Law, 36*(3), 607–634. Retrieved from http://works.bepress.com/bernard_sharfman/19.

Simon, A. (2012, July). Dodd-Frank at Two: Bad for Business and the Constitution. *National Review*. Retrieved from https://www.nationalreview.com/bench-memos/dodd-frank-two-bad-business-and-constitution-ammon-simon/.

Smith, L., & Muniz-Fraticelli, V. (2013). Strategic Shortcomings of the Dodd-Frank Act. *The Antitrust Bulletin, 58*(4), 617–622.

Smolinsky, J. (2011). Retooling General Motors: Defending an Innovative Use of the Bankruptcy Code to Save America's Auto Industry. *Brooklyn Journal of Corporate, Financial & Commercial Law, 6*(1), 103–136. Retrieved from www.brooklaw.edu/~/media/PDF/LawJournals/CFC_PDF/cfc_vol_6i.ashx.

Stern, C. (1998). What's a Constitution Among Friends? Un-Balancing Article III. *University of Pennsylvania Law Review, 146*, 1043–1053.

Summe, K. (2014). An Evaluation of the U.S. Regulatory Response to Systemic Risk and Failure Posed by Derivatives. *Harvard Business Law Review, 4*(76). Retrieved from www.hblr.org/?p=3779.

Switzer, L., & Sheahan-Lee, E. (2013, May). *The Impact of Dodd-Frank Regulation of OTC Derivative Markets and the Volcker Rule on International Versus US Banks: New Evidence* (RAFSA Imposes Costs on US Banks While Foreign International Banks Avoid Such Costs).

Thakor A. (2007). Commentary: Is the US Bankrupt? (July/August 2006). *Federal Reserve Bank of St. Louis Review*.

Tushnet, M. (2003). The Issue of State Action/Horizontal Effect in Comparative Constitutional Law. *International Journal of Constitutional Law, 1*(1), 79–98.

Van Oppen, M., & Van Wert, D. (2014, October 28). *There's No Place Like Home: The Constitutionality of the SEC's In-House Courts*. Retrieved from http://blogs.orrick.com/securities-litigation/2014/10/28/theres-no-place-like-home-the-constitutionality-of-the-secs-in-house-courts/ (Questioning the Constitutionality of the US SEC's Adjudicatory Powers).

Walker, D. (2006). *Government Accountability Office Report (2006)*. Retrieved from http://fms.treas.gov/fr/06frusg/06gao2.pdf.

White, M. (2007). Bankruptcy Reform and Credit Cards. *Journal Of Economic Perspectives, 2007*, 175–199.

Wilmarth, A. (2009). The Dark Side of Universal Banking: Financial Conglomerates and the Origins of the Subprime Financial Crisis. *Connecticut Law Review, 41*, 963–983.

Woo, T. (2011). A Comparison of Liquidation Regimes: Dodd-Frank's Orderly Liquidation Authority and the Securities Investor Protection Act. *Brooklyn Journal of Corporate, Financial & Commercial Law, 6*(1), 47–78.

Zagorski, B. (2012). How Does the Dodd-Frank Act Impact the Appraisal Process? *Secondary Marketing Executive*. Retrieved from https://www.creditplus.com/site/user/files/41/Secondary_Market_Executive___October_2011.pdf.

CHAPTER 3

Economic Psychology, Geopolitical Risk and The Unconstitutionality of Private-Sector Credit Rating Agencies, Ratings Opinions and Government Bailouts/Bail-ins

This chapter: (i) explains why private-sector Credit Rating Agencies (CRAs) and their ratings opinions are unconstitutional (with emphasis on CRAs that rate corporate, municipal and government financial-instruments); (ii) explains why government bailouts/bail-ins are motivated by Constitutional Political Economy issues, are unconstitutional and have not worked well; (iii) explains the unconstitutionality of "Obamacare" (the healthcare statutes enacted by the Obama administration in the USA), the European Union bailouts, the bailout of the US auto industry, the Nigerian banking industry and the Nigerian power industry. While US law is used in this chapter, the same legal principles are applicable in most common law countries.

During 2007–2020, many governments implemented bailouts and bail-ins of both banks and companies in industry. Many of those bailouts and bail-ins have been very costly and inefficient because: (i) the enabling statutes were inefficient and not comprehensive; (ii) the legislative process and implementation of the governing statutes were highly politicized; (iii) the enabling statutes didn't account for the economic and psychological impact on households and companies—and, in many instances, there were public protests; (iv) the management teams and the operating performances of the bailed-out/bailed-in companies have been sub-par since the government interventions; (v) the bailouts/bail-ins provided "cheap"

M. I. C. Nwogugu, *Geopolitical Risk, Sustainability and "Cross-Border Spillovers" in Emerging Markets, Volume II*,
https://doi.org/10.1007/978-3-030-71419-2_3

capital at the expense of tax payers; (vi) the bailouts and bail-ins were unconstitutional in most instances; (vii) the bailouts and bail-ins amplified the too-big-to-fail syndrome—and even the "orderly-liquidation" processes and principles set out in statutes such as the Dodd-Frank Act still facilitate the too-big-to-fail syndrome.

There have been significant debates about the unconstitutionality of Credit rating Agencies (CRAs) and unsolicited credit ratings. Credit Rating Agencies and their ratings also raise the constitutional law issues of the *Delegation Doctrine*, *Equal Protection Doctrine*, *Separation of Powers Doctrine* and the *Right-to-Contract Doctrine*.

Most of the government bailouts/bail-ins discussed in this chapter were disguised bailouts/bail-ins wherein such bailout/bail-in was "clothed" in legislative reform. In most instances, the disguised bailouts/bail-ins significantly affected other industries that were related to the subject-industry (financial services, manufacturing, logistics/distribution, utilities/energy, consumer durables, etc.).

The common element is that CRAs, Ratings-Opinions and Government Bailouts-Bail-ins are significant geopolitical risks because their impact, sustainability effects and duration can vary drastically across countries/jurisdictions, and they can create Economy Psychology and *Cross-border Spillover* effects.

3.1 Existing Literature

The literature on the *International Political Economy* of CRAs[1] is significant, and notes that the credit-ratings process has been politicized and is discriminatory especially in Emerging Markets—many researchers have critiqued CRAs' processes,[2] fee models and ratings opinions. There is very scant literature on the constitutional political economy and unconstitutionality of CRAs. Similarly, the literature on the *International Political*

[1] *See*: Barta and Johnston (2018); Iyengar (2012); Mennillo and Sinclair (2019); Abdelal and Blyth (2015); Amtenbrink and Heine (2013); Barducci and Fest (2011); Bartels and Weder di Mauro (2013); Blodget (2011); Brummer and Loko (2014); Carruthers (2013); Coffee (2011); European Commission (2015); European Commission (2016); Gaillard (2014); Gaillard and Harrington (2016); Gärtner et al. (2011); Kiff et al. (2012); Kruck (2016); Archer et al. (2007); Nwogugu (revised 2013; 2021a; 2021b; 2021c) and Copelovitch et al. (2016).

[2] *See*: Bai (2010), Bar-Isaac and Shapiro (2014), Bolton et al. (2012), Bongaerts (2013), Deb et al. (2011), Fourie and Botha (2015), Frost (2009), Gudzowski (2010), White (2019), Gaillard (2014), Gaillard and Harrington (2016), Nwogugu (revised 2013) and Kruck (2016).

Economy of government bailouts[3] is significant, and notes that government bailout/bail-in decisions have been politicized, are discriminatory (especially in Emerging Markets) and often have *Multiplier Effects* across national borders. There is also very scant literature on the constitutional political economy and unconstitutionality of government bailouts/bail-ins—but some researchers concluded that the bailouts of financial institutions in the US during 2008–2010 were unconstitutional.

3.1.1 Economic Policy

On the Economic Policy dimensions of bailouts/bail-ins, see Guynn (2012), Lubben (2013), Jackson and Skeel (2012), Vanberg (2011), Eicher et al. (2018) and Crawford (2018). On Bail-ins, see: Ventoruzzo and Sandrelli (2019), Bodellini (2018), Vanberg (2011), Eicher et al. (2018) and Somer (2015). Some researchers have also commented on the trade implications of accounting regulations and government bailouts—see comments in Trujillo (2010); Poretti (2009); Delimatsis (2012) and International Institute for Sustainable Development (March 2009). Nwogugu (2014) analyzed AMCON and the bailout/bail-in of the Nigerian banking industry.

3.1.2 Government Bailout/Bail-in Programs as Labor Regulation

The history, wording and Legislative-Intent of many Government bailouts/bail-ins in common law countries indicate or imply an intent to directly/indirectly affect

1. Labor statutes.
2. Workers' rights and working conditions.
3. Labor unions, industry associations and collective bargaining processes. That is, Labor Unions and Industry Associations are subject to state/location Executive Orders, regulations and agreements that pertain to bailouts/ail-ins.

[3] *See*: Chwieroth and Walter (2020); Bechtel (2009), Wang et al. (2019); Wang and Sui (2019); Hung et al. (2017); Hazera et al. (2017); Chi and Li (2019); Williams (2014); Uddin et al. (2020), Shukla (2014), Gradstein and Kaganovich (2019), Banerji et al. (2018), Kim (2019), Calò (2019), Blau et al. (2013), Vaugirard (2007), Pancrazi et al. (2020), Caliendo et al. (2018), and Berger and Roman (2020).

See: 12 U.S.C. § 5394 (Dodd-Frank Act § 214) (this clause prevents any future US government bailouts for troubled financial institutions).

4. Trade agreements that have Labor-Market components.
5. Existing federal/state/local regulations (such as OSHA and its state- and municipal-level equivalents in the USA).
6. Consumers' perceptions of Government bailouts/bail-ins—which, in turn, can affect employee morale, Tax Compliance, employee motivation, Consumer Confidence, Business Confidence and so on.
7. Labor mobility.
8. Employers' ability to recruit employees.
9. Employers' exposure to labor costs (employee salaries/commissions, employee taxes, employee benefits, other employee payment/deductions, social security taxes, etc.)—all of which can also affect workers' morale and motivation.
10. Allocation of labor resources across industries and industry sectors.

Some examples are as follows:

1. The US government's (Obama administration) bailout/bail-in of the Auto Industry was negotiated and enacted as legislation with input from Labor Unions, Industry Trade Associations and auto companies and their suppliers, and most of these parties hired political lobbyists.
2. The US government's (Obama administration) bailout/bail-in of the US healthcare industry (Obamacare) was negotiated and enacted as legislation with input from Labor Unions, Industry Trade Associations and HMOs/PPOs/Hospitals, and most of these parties hired political lobbyists.
3. The Nigeria government's bailout/bail-in of the Nigerian Banking Industry (the AMCON Acts of 2010, 2015 and 2019) was negotiated with Industry Trade Associations and banks, who hired political lobbyists.
4. The Nigeria government's bailout/bail-in of the Nigerian Power Industry was negotiated with Industry Trade Associations, prospective purchasers of government-owned power assets and banks.

See the comments in: Ochsen and Welsch (2012), Haferkamp et al. (2009), Qian et al. (2019), Torgler and Schneider (2009), Vanberg (2011), Eicher et al. (2018) and Pántya, Kovács, et al. (2016).

3.2 Geopolitical Risk and Some Economic Psychology[4] and Cross-Border *Spillover Effects* of The Big-3 CRAs and Foreign Government Bailouts/Bail-ins in Emerging Markets

The significant literatures on Social Capital, Social Networks and Cross-border *Spillover Effects* are discussed in Chap. 2 of this book. "Emerging Markets" refers to primarily underdeveloped countries and, to a lesser extent, some developing countries (Mexico, China, Brazil, Peru, Chile, Thailand, UAE, ASEAN countries, etc.).

3.2.1 Credit Rating Agencies

There can be *Spillover Effects* of credit ratings from developed countries (and from Emerging Markets countries such as India, China, South Korea, Mexico and South Africa) to "typical" underdeveloped/developing countries primarily because of the following reasons:

1. Credit ratings around the world have been dominated by Moody's (USA), S&P (USA) and Fitch (France) which together account for more than 85% of global credit ratings.
2. Around the world, credit ratings are pervasive and have significant and lasting effects on many aspects of sustainability, international trade, corporate growth and profitability, financial stability, household economics and national economies. Credit ratings affect interest rates, savings/investments, remittances (to Emerging Markets), loan-volumes (to Emerging Markets), FDI/Foreign-Investment/Foreign-Aid, Consumer Confidence, Consumer Expenditures, Business Confidence, Corporate Expenditures, Government Expenditures, Risk-Perception and so on.

[4] On associated *Economic Psychology* and *Behavioral IPE (International Political Economy)* issues, see: Hardardottir (2017), Birz (2017), Dixon et al. (2014), Qian et al. (2019), Debelle (2004), Ochsen and Welsch (2012), Vanberg (2011), Eicher et al. (2018), Abdelal and Blyth (2015), Amtenbrink and Heine (2013), Barta and Johnston (2018), Bechtel (2009), Chwieroth and Walter (2020), Blendon and Benson (2017), Schniter et al. (2020); Garcia et al. (2020); Bavetta et al. (2020); Torgler and Schneider (2009); Nguyen and Claus (2013); Haferkamp et al. (2009); Banker et al. (2020); and Mennillo and Sinclair (2019).

3. Many researchers have argued that both CRAs and credit ratings[5] have been largely politicized—that is, through their licensing, oversight and rule-making functions, government agencies can coerce and or collude with CRAs. This implies that the US and French governments effectively exert direct and indirect control over nations and foreign companies through their regulation ("Primary CRA Regulation") of the Big-three CRAs, even though many countries have their own CRA regulations ("Secondary CRA Regulation"). There are obvious Cross-border *Spillover Effects* from such *Primary CRA Regulation* in terms of actual policies/procedures of CRAs and their ratings products. Furthermore, because many emerging markets countries depend on developed countries for capital, FDI (foreign direct investment), FI (foreign investment), technology/human capital/knowledge transfers, the roles, influence and *Spillover Effects* of the Big-three CRAs becomes even more dominant in Emerging Markets countries.
4. The worldwide transaction volumes and amounts of debt-issuances and debt-related swaps/derivatives by Emerging Markets companies and government agencies increased significantly during 2005–2020. Almost all such transactions are based on Credit Ratings and involve due diligence and reviews by CRAs. Most of such transactions are priced/valued on a "relative-value" basis which facilitates cross-border *Spillovers* and market integration.
5. The worldwide transaction volumes and amounts of commodities transactions and commodities-related swaps/derivatives by Emerging Markets companies and government agencies increased significantly during 2005–2020. Almost all such transactions are based on credit ratings and involve due diligence and reviews by CRAs. Most of such transactions are priced/value on a "relative-value" basis which facilitates cross-border *Spillovers* and market integration.
6. CRAs and their ratings opinions and associated Social Networks have or can have significant effects on government tax policies, *perceived*

[5] *See*: Barta and Johnston (2018); Frost (2009); Iyengar (2012); Mennillo and Sinclair (2019); Abdelal and Blyth (2015); Amtenbrink and Heine (2013); Barducci and Fest (2011); Bartels and Weder di Mauro (2013); Blodget (2011); Brummer and Loko (2014); Carruthers (2013); Coffee (2011); European Commission (2015); European Commission (2016); Gaillard (2014); Gaillard and Harrington (2016); Gärtner et al. (2011); Kiff et al. (2012); Kruck (2016); Archer et al. (2007); Bechtel (2009); Block and Vaaler (2004); Copelovitch et al. (2016), and Chwieroth and Walter (2020).

Tax Equity, *Tax-Sensitivity* and *Tax Compliance* (by individuals and companies); all of which can affect savings/investments, remittances (to Emerging Markets), loan volumes (to Emerging Markets), FDI/ Foreign-Investment/Foreign-Aid, Consumer Confidence, Consumer Expenditures, Business Confidence, Corporate Expenditures, Government Expenditures, Risk-Perception and so on.

7. During 2005–2021, more than 50% of international trade was conducted in US dollars. The credit terms for international trade and the supply/demand for US dollars are influenced by credit ratings. During 2017–2020, China, Iran and Russia entered into agreements to use their local currencies for the settlement of international trade and financing, and that may reduce the dominance of the US dollar.
8. CRAs and their ratings create *Social Networks* and their success/failure is partly based on *Social Capital* (Reputation; Influence, etc.). Such Social Networks and Social Capital often transcend national borders and regulations to create *Spillovers* and market integration.
9. CRAs and their ratings opinions have significant influence on sovereign debt, which in turn affect many economic and political variables that can cause cross-border spillovers.
10. CRA *Influence* and *Reputation* are likely to be significant in Emerging Markets countries that: (1) use or have used the US dollar as their official currency or their "secondary currency", (2) were former colonies of the UK and France; (3) are major international trade partners of, or have significant Trade Imbalances with the US and European countries. This is because country credit ratings and corporate credit ratings are more likely to affect the terms of international trade and associated financings in such countries. See below—countries that have used the US Dollar as their official currency or as their "secondary-currency".
11. The headquarters of two of the big-three CRAs (Moody's and S&P) are in the US, and are regulated by US government agencies. Many of the regulations issued by the US government are or were directly/ directly based on corporate credit ratings. A significant percentage of international investors still rely on Big-3 CRA corporate credit ratings to evaluate investments. A significant portion of international trade and international Derivatives transactions are documented and settled in US Dollars, and formally or informally use Big-3 CRA credit ratings. Thus, the Big-3 CRAs affect or can affect Trade Policy, Labor Policy, Monetary Policy and Fiscal Policy in many countries. The US

Dollar is the dominant international currency as explained in Chap. 1 in this book.
12. The US has the most advanced and comprehensive financial regulations and creates some of the most sophisticated financial products in the world. The US has been at the forefront of enactment of financial/economic laws at both the federal and state levels. Many developing countries (and developed countries) copied their financial laws from US laws. For example, the Brazilian constitution is based on the US Constitution; and REIT statutes worldwide are based on US REIT laws. Many countries have created variants of the Dodd-Frank Act and the Sarbanes Oxley Act (SOX). Mortgage/Foreclosure laws in many countries are very similar to US mortgage/foreclosure laws. Many developing countries and "transition" countries of Eastern Europe derived their mortgage/foreclosure laws from US laws.
13. During the last twenty years, the US consistently had the largest national economy in the world; and the US economy directly/indirectly (through international trade, outsourcing, FDI, FI, Foreign Aid, etc.) supported the economies of other "First-Level Associated" countries (China, Japan, Brazil, Mexico, India, etc.) which, in turn, directly/directly supported (through international trade, outsourcing, loans, FDI, FI, Foreign Aid, etc.) the economies of other "Second-Level Associated" countries (Russia, Nigeria, the Philippines, Thailand, ASEAN countries, Pakistan, Central American countries, CIS countries, etc.).

During 1980–2020, the US was a major participant in major multilateral and bilateral trade agreements, and the US-China Trade War (2019–present) continues to have significant economic/social/psychological *Multiplier Effects* on many countries. The use of the terms "First-Level Associated" countries and "Second-Level Associated" countries is introduced here as a "mutual-dependency" classification of countries as a way to better reflect the often symbiotic relationships between countries with regard to international trade and international capital flows.

3.2.2 Government Bailouts/Bail-ins

There can also be *Spillover Effects* of bailouts/bail-ins from developed countries and from upcoming Emerging Markets countries such as India, China, South Korea, Mexico and South Africa (the "Primary Bailing Countries") to "typical" underdeveloped countries:

1. Government expenditures on bailouts/bail-ins in *Primary Bailing Countries* often results in lower Foreign Aid, FI (foreign investments) and FDI (foreign direct investments) by such *Primary Bailing Countries* in Emerging Markets countries, which in turn reduces GDP/GNP/productivity of Emerging Markets countries.
2. Government expenditures on bailouts/bail-ins in *Primary Bailing Countries* often results in lower social welfare expenditures (food stamps, healthcare benefits, housing assistance, etc.) in such countries which tends to directly affect immigrants and low-income households in those countries, which in turn reduces remittances to Emerging Markets, purchases of goods imported from Emerging Markets countries, and GDP/GNP/productivity of Emerging Markets countries.
3. Bail-ins/bailouts can reduce private sector investments and or cause "Credit Contagions" (declines of the perceived credit quality of other companies in the same industry) in specific industries that traditionally hire many immigrants (retailing, restaurants, hotels, hospitals, business services, distribution/logistics, etc.), all of which can have negative *Multiplier Effects* on Emerging Markets countries (exports, aggregate productivity, remittances, availability of credit, consumer confidence, business confidence, etc.).
4. Financially/operationally distressed and bailed-out companies are very likely to reduce staff and to implement more automation, close foreign offices/factories, and reduce purchases of goods/services imported from Emerging Markets countries; and that also reduces consumer spending which often directly and indirectly affects low-income and immigrant households that work in consumer goods/services sectors, all of which, in turn, reduce remittances to Emerging Markets and GDP/exports/productivity of Emerging Markets countries.
5. Bailouts/bail-ins can reduce needed technology/human-capital transfers to Emerging Markets countries.
6. Bailouts/bail-ins can reduce construction activity if real estate developers anticipate economic downturns—that is especially relevant if the subject industry is property-intensive (hospital-chains, hotels/lodging, manufacturing, retailing, distribution/logistics, etc.). Construction activity metrics are major economic indicators in most developed and developing countries. In many developed and developing countries, the construction industry employs a significant number of immigrants who, in turn, send remittances and knowledge/human capital to Emerging Markets countries. Also, immigrant expenditures are not

tied to their countries-of-origin—for example, Philippines/Filipino immigrants in the United Kingdom can send remittances to their relatives in Sri Lanka or UAE or Caribbean countries, and or make investments in Kenya or Uganda (where there are substantial immigrant communities).

7. Bailouts/bail-ins create *Social Networks* and their success/failure is partly based on *Social Capital* (reputation, influence, etc.). Such *Social Networks* and *Social Capital* often transcend national borders and regulations to create spillovers and market integration.
8. Bailouts/bail-ins and their associated Social Networks have or can have significant effects on government tax policies, perceived Tax Equity, *Tax-Sensitivity* (individuals and companies) and Tax *Compliance* (by individuals and companies), all of which can affect savings/investments, remittances (to Emerging Markets), loan volumes (to Emerging Markets), FDI/Foreign-Investment/Foreign-Aid, Consumer Confidence, Consumer Expenditures, Business Confidence, Corporate Expenditures, Government Expenditures, Risk-Perception and so on.

3.2.3 Central Bank Independence and Central Bank Governance Models

For most of the government bailouts/bail-ins discussed in this chapter (and in other government bailouts/bail-ins around the world), the deliberation and legislation processes that resulted in the government interventions were heavily politicized seemed to reduce the independence of national central banks.

During 2000–2020, the rule-making processes and associated enforcement that pertained to CRAs almost completely omitted central banks in many countries. That was strange given that in many countries, it's the central banks that bear a significant portion of losses and social welfare payouts that arise from failures of regulation of CRA, and from inflated credit ratings and misuse of ratings opinions (economic/financial crisis, corporate bankruptcies market crashes, inflation, etc.).

3.3 Unconstitutionality of Private-Sector Credit Rating Agencies (CRAs) and Ratings Opinions (Emphasis on Ratings of Corporate, Municipal and Government Financial-Instruments)

There have been significant debates about the unconstitutionality of both private-sector CRA and their credit ratings, which raises the constitutional law issues of the *Delegation Doctrine*, *Due Process*, *Equal Protection Doctrine*, *Separation of Powers Doctrine* and the *Right-to-Contract Doctrine*.

Many parties have criticized CRAs for their inaccuracy and the inherent conflict of interest in ratings,[6] and many parties have sued CRAs for inaccurate ratings and or deception[7]—such as investors (e.g. pension funds

[6] *See*: "Financial Crisis Inquiry Commission—Final Report-Conclusions-January 2011". http://www.gpo.gov/fdsys/pkg/GPO-FCIC/pdf/GPO-FCIC.pdf.

See: Casey, K. (Feb. 6, 2009). *"In Search of Transparency, Accountability, and Competition: The Regulation of Credit Rating Agencies". Remarks at "The SEC Speaks in 2009". US SEC.* http://www.sec.gov/news/speech/2009/spch020609klc.htm.

See: "Ratings agencies suffer 'conflict of interest', says former Moody's boss". Rupert Neate. *The Guardian*; 22 August 2011. https://www.theguardian.com/business/2011/aug/22/ratings-agencies-conflict-of-interest.

See: Kerwer, D. (2004). *Holding Global Regulators Accountable The Case of Credit Rating Agencies.* Technical University of Munich, Germany. https://www.ucl.ac.uk/political-science/publications/downloads/spp-wp-11.pdf.

See: CFR Staff (Feb. 2015). *The Credit Rating Controversy.* https://www.cfr.org/backgrounder/credit-rating-controversy.

See: Kambayashi, S. (May 2020). Credit-rating agencies are back under the spotlight: This time is different from the financial crisis—sort of. *The Economist.* https://www.economist.com/finance-and-economics/2020/05/07/credit-rating-agencies-are-back-under-the-spotlight.

See: Blodget, H. (2011). *Moody's Analyst Breaks Silence: Says Ratings Agency Rotten To Core With Conflicts.* Available at: www.businessinsider.com/moodys-analyst-conflicts-corruption-and-greed-2011-8/?IR=T (accessed 1 February 2015).

See: Freifeld, K. (July 10, 2013). *Liquidators of failed Bear Stearns funds sue ratings* agencies. Reuters—http://www.reuters.com/article/2013/07/10/us-ratings-agency-laws uitidUSBRE9690QV20130710.

[7] *See*: *"LiquidatorsoffailedBearStearnsfundssueratingagencies". July10,2013. Reuters. https://www.reuters.com/article/2013/07/10/us-ratings-agency-lawsuit-idUSBRE9690QV20130710.*

See: "*Bond Insurer Sues Credit-Rating Agencies*". July 17, 2013. www.wsj.com. https://www.wsj.com/article/SB10001424127887323993804578612212273026342.html.

See: Wayne, L. (15 July 2009). *"Calpers Sues Over Ratings of Securities". The New York Times.* https://www.nytimes.com/2009/07/15/business/15calpers.html?_r=1&partner=rss&emc=rss.

that invested in CBOs); the bankrupt Bear Stearns (for losses of $1.12 billion from alleged "fraudulently issuing inflated ratings for securities"); bond insurers, CRAs' shareholders, CDO/ABS/MBS holders, corporate issuers, state attorney generals, the US SEC and the US government (which sued S&P for US$5 billion for "misrepresenting the credit risk of complex financial products").

The "State-Actions" are as follows: (i) the US SEC's and other national governments' licensing/appointment and active support of CRAs as the only corporate credit rating agencies; and (ii) the federal government's failure to directly regulate the CRA processes, where the government definitely has a duty to do so (it's well established in the literature that failure of the government to act where it has a duty to act creates Constitutional Torts—see Nwogugu [2012]). In addition, the *Substantial Control Theory*[8] and the *Substitution Theory* apply (these theories were introduced in Nwogugu [2012] as alternatives to the *State Action* requirement).

See: *"S&P Lawsuit First Amendment Defense May Fare Poorly, Experts Say"*. February 4, 2013. Huff Post. http://www.huffingtonpost.com/2013/02/04/sp-lawsuit-first-amendment_n_2618737.html.

See: "*Ohio Jumps On The Rating Agency Lawsuit Bandwagon*". By Daniel Indiviglio. *TheAtlantic.com*. Nov 20, 2009. https://www.theatlantic.com/business/archive/2009/11/ohio-jumps-on-the-rating-agency-lawsuit-bandwagon/30602/.

See: *"Credit Rating Agencies Settle Two Suits Brought by Investors"*. Reuters. April 27, 2013. https://www.nytimes.com/2013/04/28/business/credit-rating-agencies-settle-lawsuits-over-debt-vehicles.html?_r=0.

See: *Reuters (September 3, 2013)*. "S.&P. Calls Federal Fraud Suit Payback for Credit Downgrade". *New York Times*.

See: Snyder, P. (July 18, 2013). *"Federal judge denies credit rating agency's motion to dismiss fraud lawsuit"*. http://jurist.org/paperchase/2013/07/us-district-court-denies-standard-and-poors-motion-to-dismiss-in-fraud-lawsuit.php.

See: "*Corrupted credit ratings: Standard & Poor's lawsuit and the evidence*". By Matthias Efing & Harald Hau. June 18, 2013. http://www.voxeu.org/article/corrupted-credit-ratings-standard-poor-s-lawsuit-and-evidence.

See: "*Standard & Poor's Says Civil Lawsuit Threatened By DOJ Is Without Legal Merit And Unjustified*". Reuters.com. 2013/02/04. https://www.reuters.com/article/2013/02/04/ny-sp-doj-lawsuit-idUSnPnNY53856+160+PRN20130204.

See: "Analysis: Credit agencies remain unaccountable". Kathleen Day. *USA Today*. May 19, 2014.

https://www.usatoday.com/story/money/business/2014/05/19/credit-rating-agencies-in-limbo/9290143/.

[8]The *Substantial Inducement theory* and the *Substitution Theory* (which are alternatives to the *State Action* requirement in Constitutional Law) were introduced in Nwogugu (2012: 9 & 198).

The Dodd-Frank Act of 2010 (USA) expressly imposed liability on CRAs for their erroneous ratings; and during December 2011 (and as part of Dodd-Frank Act–mandated rule-making) the US FDIC proposed the removal of all credit ratings from risk-based capital requirements for banks (http://www.fdic.gov/news/news/financial/2011/fil11075.html.3). Several US congressional investigations have concluded that the rating agencies played a significant role in, and were responsible for, the global financial crisis[9] of 2007–2014. Gudzowski (2010) discussed the need for government-operated Mortgage Securities CRAs. Nwogugu (2010; revised 2013) introduced a business-model for a government-operated credit rating agency. CRAs' activities constitute quasi-rule-making, enforcement and quasi-adjudication because:

1. CRAs effectively function as rule-makers and create industry-wide standards for evaluation of credit risk. These standards and credit ratings are widely used (formally and informally) in policy-making in industries and government. That is, Research/Credit Analysts outside CRAs use CRAs' ratings standards and procedures in their research.
2. CRAs effectively function as formal and informal private enforcement agencies (enforcement of accounting regulations and securities laws)—they have both an implied and statutory duty to report violations of accounting regulations and securities laws to government agencies (such as the US SEC), and the Big-3 CRAs process large numbers of ratings opinions annually.
3. CRA perform quasi-adjudicatory functions by issuing ratings opinions. Ratings opinions are highly debated and controversial topics that have significant implications and *Multiplier Effects* in the global capital markets and policy-making (in industry and governments).
4. The costs of CRAs' ratings errors (false positives, false negatives, intentional deflate/inflated ratings, etc.) are critical, have global *Multiplier Effects* and greatly reduce social welfare.
5. National and state governments often ultimately bear the costs of CRA errors in the form of bailouts, welfare payments to households, tax

[9] *See*: Financial Crisis Inquiry Commission, "*The Financial Crisis Inquiry Report: Final Report of the National Commission on the Causes of the Financial and Economic Crisis in the United States*" (Washington: GPO, January 2011).

See: U.S. Senate Permanent Subcommittee on Investigations, Majority and Minority Staff Report, "*Wall Street and the Financial Crisis: Anatomy of a Financial Collapse*" (Washington: U.S. Senate, April 13, 2011).

credits issued to companies and households; reduced tax revenues; extra government spending on healthcare and housing; loss of export revenues and so on.

Cahill Gordon and Reindel LLP (July 2005) sufficiently discussed the constitutionality of the "Credit CRA Duopoly Relief Act of 2005". Nwogugu (2021a), Nwogugu (2021b) and Nwogugu (2021c) analyzed various aspects of the global Credit Rating Agency industry including Antitrust/Competition issues.

3.3.1 Violation of the Free Speech Clause *(First Amendment Issues in the USA)*

In the USA, the liability standards in *Free Speech* cases were developed by the U.S. Supreme Court in *The New York Times Co. vs. L. B. Sullivan*, 376 U.S. 254 (1964) and *Milkovich vs. Lorain Journal Co.*, 497 U.S. 1 (1990). Husisian (1990) erroneously states that this standard should be applied in *Free Speech* litigation against CRAs. Hager (1991) noted that in *Milkovich vs. Lorain Journal Co.*, the US Supreme Court eliminated First Amendment Opinion Privilege.

The issue of the constitutionality of unsolicited ratings opinions has been widely debated—and the pre-2009 consensus in the US seems to be that ratings agency opinions didn't violate the *Free Speech* clause of the US Constitution[10] (the same principles may be applicable in common-law and other commonwealth jurisdictions). See: U.S. Department of Justice (Oct. 2009). Zhou and Kumar (April 2012) discussed economic and legal factors in litigation against CRAs.

However, Gaillard and Waibel (2018), Nästegård (2016) and Nagy (2009) noted that the US Senate discovered that CRAs were issuing inflated corporate credit ratings (which in turn caused the US Subprime Mortgage Crisis of 2006–2010 and the Global Financial Crisis of 2007–2014), and that CRAs lost their regulatory and judicial "quasi-immunity" during

[10] *See*: U.S. Department of Justice (Oct. 2009). *Constitutionality of Mandatory Registration of Credit Rating Agencies*. http://www.justice.gov/olc/2009/opinion-letter-treasury.pdf. *See*: *Americans for Prosperity Foundation vs. Bonta*, ____ US ____ (US Supreme Court; pending as of 2021). *See*: *Mahanoy Area School District vs. B.L.*, ____ US ____ (No. 20-255; US Supreme Court; pending as of 2021) (free speech that occurs outside area-of-influence). *See*: *Houston Community College System vs. Wilson*, ____ US ____ (Case#: 20-804; US Supreme Court; pending as of 2021). *See*: *Fulton vs. City of Philadelphia*, ____ US ____ (US Supreme Court; pending as of 2021). *See*: *Thomas More Law Center vs. Bonta*, ____ US ____ (No. 19-255; US Supreme Court; pending as of 2021).

2008–2018 (through a series of court decisions and US congressional investigations in the USA). Nästegård (2016) also analyzes the *Free Speech* issue from a European Law perspective. Indeed, the series of widely publicized US court cases against CRAs during 2008–2020 confirms that—and the US courts ruled that CRAs were liable for their ratings opinions[11]. The Staff of the US Senate Committee on Governmental Affairs[12] correctly noted that: "'the fact that the market seems to value the agencies' ratings mostly as a certification (investment grade vs. non-investment grade) or as a benchmark (the ratings triggers in agreements) and not as information, and the fact that the law, in hundreds of statutes and regulations, also uses their work that way, seems to indicate that their ratings are not the equivalent of editorials in The New York Times. The Staff was of the opinion that the fact that the rating agencies have received First Amendment protection for their work should not preclude greater accountability.'"

The Dodd-Frank Act of 2010 (USA) expressly imposed liability on CRAs for their erroneous ratings—and that has far-reaching worldwide *Multiplier Effects* because it applies to S&P and Moody's ratings businesses around the world, and to Fitch's ratings of US companies.

It's clear that the CRA argument that they are essentially members of the press and thus have *Free Speech* protections has no basis in fact or law, because: (i) as explained herein and above, CRAs perform quasi-governmental functions, for which the costs of CRAs' ratings errors (false positives, false negatives and intentionally fraudulent ratings) are significant, critical and greatly reduce social welfare; and (ii) governments often ultimately bear the costs of CRA errors in the form of bailouts, welfare payments/transfers to households and companies (e.g. vouchers and tax credits), reduced tax revenues, extra government spending on healthcare, transportation and housing, loss of export revenues and so on; (iii) the

[11] *See: Abu Dhabi Commercial Bank et. al. vs. Morgan Stanley & Co. Incorporated et al*, No. 08 Civ. 7508 (SAS) (S.D.N.Y.; USA; September 2, 2009).

See: California Public Employees' Retirement System vs. Moody's Corp., et. al., No. CGC-09-490241, (Cal. App. Dep't. Super. Ct.; USA; May 24, 2010).

See: Genesee County Employee's Retirement System, et. al. vs. Thornsburg Mortgage Securities Trust 2006-3, et. al., No. CIV 09-0300 (U.S. District Court, District of New Mexico, USA; November 12, 2011).

[12] The Staff of the Senate Committee on Governmental Affairs (October 8, 2002). *Financial Oversight of Enron: The SEC and Private-Sector Watchdogs.* Report of the Staff to The Senate Committee on Governmental Affairs, United States Senate (October 8, 2002), at 124.

Substantial Inducement Theory[13] and the *Substitution Theory* (which were introduced in Nwogugu [2012] and summarized in Chap. 1 in this book) apply in this circumstance, and impose liability on CRAs both for their existence/operations and for ratings opinions.

3.3.2 *Constitutionality of Mandatory Registration of CRAs*

U.S. Department of Justice (October 2009) affirmed the constitutionality of mandatory registration of CRAs. See: Cahill Gordon & Reindel LLP (July 2005), and Nagy (2009).

3.3.3 *Un-Constitutional Interference with Presidential Powers and The* Non-**Delegation Doctrine** *(Unconstitutional Delegation of CRA Regulation to Government Agencies in the USA and the EU)*

A critical issue which has not been directly and sufficiently addressed by United States courts is whether the issuance of credit ratings is a government function that has been unconstitutionally delegated to CRAs in violation of constitutional principles like the *Delegation Doctrine* of the US Constitution. As explained herein and above, CRAs perform quasi-governmental (rule-making, adjudicatory and enforcement) functions. Also, the *Substantial Inducement Theory*[14] and the *Substitution Theory* (which were introduced in Nwogugu [2012] and summarized in Chap. 1 in this book) apply in this circumstance, and impose liability on CRAs both for their existence/operations and for ratings opinions. Nwogugu (2010; revised 2013) and Gudzowski (2010) discussed the need for government-operated CRAs. On the *Non-Delegation Doctrine*, see: *PennEast Pipeline Co. vs. New Jersey*, _____ US _____ (No. 19-1039; US Supreme Court; pending as of 2021); and *Seila Law LLC vs. Consumer Financial Protection Bureau*, _____ US _____ (Case#: No. 19-7; US Supreme Court; 2020).

One view is that by ruling that CRA opinions don't violate the *Free Speech Clause* of the US Constitution, US Courts have implicitly ruled that issuance of credit ratings doesn't violate the *Non-Delegation Doctrine*. Many of these court rulings were issued during 1970–2009 when capital markets were not very large or so interconnected across national borders (but since then, Cross-Border Spillovers and Cross-Border Market-Integration have

[13] *See: Tulsa Professional Collection Services vs. Pope*, 485 US 478 (1988; US Supreme Court).

[14] *See: Tulsa Professional Collection Services vs. Pope*, 485 US 478 (1988; US Supreme Court).

increased around the world), and when regional economies and national economies were less sensitive to the credit ratings of large multinational companies (today, a change in the credit rating of a US multinational company that is worth $240 billion can affect the capital markets in a Latin American or Asian or CIS/CEE or African country whose annual GDP is only $10 billion).

CRAs represent a detrimental and unconstitutional interference with Presidential powers. For example, in the US, some of the functions performed by CRAs are reserved for the executive branch of the US government by statute (Securities Act of 1934), but on the contrary, the US government and most national governments have minimal real control over CRAs. (the Dodd Frank Act doesn't sufficiently regulate CRA).

CRAs effectively usurp the powers of the executive branch of the government (in democracies) by their ratings and quasi-rule-making activities. In the US, although US Congress enacted the Securities Act of 1934 and the Dodd Frank Act of 2010, which in turn empower the US SEC to enact accounting rules and to regulate markets, and the US SEC apparently formally delegated such powers to CRAs (through the licensing requirement), the CRAs effectively perform executive and congressional functions because CRAs' non-binding rules and ratings have substantial economic effects on, and regulate interstate commerce and foreign commerce.

A rational school of thought is: i) that the subprime crisis and the Global Financial Crisis of 2007–2014 and the associated bailouts/bail-ins of financial institutions and companies by governments in several countries suggest that credit ratings are of national importance and should be handled by the legislature and or the executive branch of national governments, and ii) that delegation of credit ratings to the agencies in the executive branch of government violates the *Non-Delegation Doctrine.*

3.3.4 *The* Interstate Commerce Doctrine And The Dormant Commerce Clause Doctrine *(US Only)*

CRAs represent an unconstitutional interference with the constitutional/statutory powers of the US Congress and other national legislatures to regulate interstate commerce – and examples are as follows:

1. The *Dormant Commerce Clause Doctrine*[15] – CRAs' ratings opinions burden interstate commerce and create substantial false positives/false negatives errors and compliance costs—that is, the costs of ratings errors and ratings-related compliance exponentially increases as the subject issuer-company's volume of interstate commerce increases.

[15] *See: DeNolf vs. U.S.*, _____ US _____ (US Supreme Court; pending as of 2021) (https://static1.squarespace.com/static/5b660749620b85c6c73e5e61/t/608d544886d55300e492a619/1619874888658/2021-22+AMCA+Case.pdf)

See: DeNolf vs. U.S. (Case#: 01-76320; US 14th Circuit, 2020) (https://static1.squarespace.com/static/5b660749620b85c6c73e5e61/t/608d544886d55300e492a619/1619874888658/2021-22+AMCA+Case.pdf) *See: Perez vs. United States*, 402 U.S. 146, 150 (1971) (Congress can ban loansharking that threatens interstate commerce). *See: Gonzales vs. Raich*, 545 U.S. 1, 18 (US Supreme Court; 2005). *See: United States vs. Lopez*, 514 U.S. 549 (US Supreme Court; 1995).

See: Dennis vs. Higgins, 498 U.S. 439, 447 -450 (1991; US Supreme Court); *Metropolitan Life Ins. Co. vs. Ward*, 470 U.S. 869 (1985; US Supreme Court); *Oregon Waste Systems, Inc.* vs. *Department of Environmental Quality of Oregon*, 511 U. S. 93 (______; US Supreme Court); *Hughes* v. *Alexandria Scrap Corp.*, 426 U. S. 794 (______; US Supreme Court); *Reeves, Inc.* vs. *Stake*, 447 U.S. 429 (______; US Supreme Court); *Edgar vs. MITE*, 457 U.S. 624 (state law declared unconstitutional); *Dynamics Corp. Of America vs. CTS Corp.*, 679 F.Supp. 1022 (*affirmed*) 794 F2d 250 (*reversed*) 481 U.S. 69 (state law declared unconstitutional); *Department of Revenue Of Kentucky et. al. vs. Davis et. ux.*, (May 19, 2008; No. 06-666; US Supreme Court); *Pike vs. Bruce Church, Inc.*, 397 U.S. 137, 142 (US Supreme Court); *New Energy Co. of Ind.* vs. *Limbach*, 486 U.S. 269 (1988); *Fulton Corp.* vs. *Faulkner*, 516 U.S. 325 (1996; US Supreme Court); *Oklahoma Tax Comm'n* vs. *Jefferson Lines, Inc.*, 514 U.S. 175 (1995; US Supreme Court); *Hughes* vs. *Oklahoma*, 441 U.S. 322 (1979; US Supreme Court); *Garcia* vs. *San Antonio Metropolitan Transit Authority*, 469 U.S. 528 (1985; US Supreme Court); *Philadelphia* vs. *New Jersey*, 437 U.S. 617 (1978; US Supreme Court); *Alexandria Scrap,* 426 U.S., at 810 (the "*market participant*" exception); *Reeves,* 447 U.S. at 436 (the "*market participant*" exception); *White* vs. *Massachusetts Council of Construction Employers, Inc.*, 460 U.S. 204 (1983; US Supreme Court) (the "*market participant*" exception); *Dean Milk Co.* vs. *Madison*, 340 U.S. 349 (1951; US Supreme Court); *Hunt* vs. *Washington State Apple Advertising Commission,* 432 U.S. 333 (1977; US Supreme Court); *C & A Carbone, Inc.* vs. *Clarkstown*, 511 U.S. 383 (1994; US Supreme Court); *Philadelphia* vs. *New Jersey*, 437 U.S. 617 (1978; US Supreme Court); *Hughes* vs. *Oklahoma*, 441 U.S. 322 (1979; US Supreme Court); *New England Power Co.* vs. *New Hampshire*, 455 U.S. 331 (1982; US Supreme Court); *Bacchus Imports, Ltd.* vs. *Dias*, 468 U.S. 263 (1984; US Supreme Court).

Contrast: Bonaparte vs. *Tax Court*, 104 U.S. 592 (_____; US Supreme Court).

Compare: United Haulers Assn., Inc. vs. *Oneida-Herkimer Solid Waste Management Authority*, 550 U.S. ___, ___-___ (2007; US Supreme Court) (the *Pike* vs. *Bruce Church* scrutiny).

Compare: Northwest Central Pipeline Corp. vs. *State Corporation Comm'n of Kansas*, 489 U.S. 493 (1989; US Supreme Court) (the *Pike* v. *Bruce Church* scrutiny).

Compare: Minnesota v. *Clover Leaf Creamery Co.*, 449 U.S. 456 (1981; US Supreme Court) (the *Pike* v. *Bruce Church* scrutiny).

2. The *Dormant Commerce Clause Doctrine* – Credit ratings issued by CRAs have greater information effects for exchange-traded companies (who generally have larger volumes of interstate commerce) compared to non-listed companies—and thus CRAs and their ratings are or can be discriminatory.
3. CRAs and their ratings violate or can violate the *Interstate Commerce Doctrine* because they jointly reduce or can reduce the number of audit firms that are willing and able to audit publicly traded companies.[16] CRAs and their ratings opinions burden interstate commerce by imposing onerous requirements (the ratings opinion) on accounting/auditing firms and thus, reduce competition among auditing firms. That is, auditing firms that issue audit opinions that contravene a Big-three CRA ratings opinions incur the significant risk of offending their audit clients and loss of their audit contracts and or harmful litigation.
4. CRAs have taken over some functions that are statutorily reserved for the legislatures of some countries – such as what amounts to:

   i. regulation of interstate commerce (i.e. enactment of guidelines for the issuance of securities/instruments);
   ii. enactment of soft-law (CRAs' processing and ratings opinions can be construed as, and sometimes function as "soft law" in some circumstances (and CRAs' ratings opinions have been incorporated into statutes in some jurisdictions);
   iii. oversight and investigation—CRAs' processing and research (and structuring securitizations) activities can be construed as, and sometimes function as "oversight" and investigation in capital markets transactions.

5. The *Dormant Commerce Clause Doctrine* (in only USA) – During the last twenty years (and especially after the US Subprime Mortgage Crisis), CRAs' ratings opinions and their requirements have drastically increased the costs of obtaining insurance coverage[17]—for some types of corporate insurance policies in the USA (such as Directors-And-Officers policies and Business-Interruption policies, and many insurance companies in the US now offer only limited insurance contracts with limited pay-outs). In the US, insurers are regulated by state gov-

[16] *See*: Gifford, R. & Howe, H. (2009). *Regulation and Unintended Consequences: Thoughts on Sarbanes-Oxley. The CPA Journal.* http://www.nysscpa.org/cpajournal/2004/604/perspectives/p6.htm.

[17] *See*: Gifford & Howe (2009) (supra).

ernments and thus their operating costs vary across states; and the foregoing limited insurance contracts may burden interstate commerce.

6. *Interstate Commerce Doctrine*—in the US, state-level Insurance statutes sometimes incorporate Ratings-Opinions. When affected insurance policies control or determine outcomes in industries that are regulated (in whole or part) by the US government, that can interfere with the US Congress's power to regulate interstate commerce.

3.3.5 *The* Substantive Due Process Doctrine

As explained herein and above, CRAs perform quasi-governmental (rule-making, adjudicatory and enforcement) functions. Also the *Substantial Inducement Theory* and the *Substitution Theory* (which were introduced in Nwogugu [2012]) apply in this circumstance, and impose liability on CRAs both for their existence/operations and for ratings opinions. Nwogugu (2010; revised 2013) and Gudzowski (2010) discussed the need for government-operated CRAs.[18]

The existence and current activities of CRAs in many countries constitute violations of the *Substantive Due Process Doctrine*, because:

1. The cost of CRA errors (false positives, false negatives, inflated ratings, fraudulent ratings; etc.) are significant, unregulated and excessive for issuers, investment banks and households.
2. The "*Tie-Breaker Phenomenon*", "Actual/Perceived Antitrust/Collusion" and the excessive "Influence" of the Big-three CRAs are

[18] *See*: *Washington v. Glucksberg*, 521 U.S. 702, 719 (US Supreme Court; 1997) ("The Due Process Clause guarantees more than fair process, and the 'liberty' it protects includes more than the absence of physical restraint."); *Obergefell vs. Hodges*, 576 U.S. 644 (US Supreme Court; 2015); *Lawrence vs. Texas*, 539 U.S. 558 (US Supreme Court; 2003); *United States vs. Vaello-Madero*, ____ US ____ (Case#: 20-303; US Supreme Court; pending as of 2021); *DeNolf vs. U.S.*, ____ US ____ (US Supreme Court; pending as of 2021) (https://static1.squarespace.com/static/5b660749620b85c6c73e5e61/t/608d544886d55300e492a619/1619874888658/2021-22+AMCA+Case.pdf); *DeNolf vs. U.S.* (Case#: 01-76320; US 14th Circuit, 2020) (https://static1.squarespace.com/static/5b660749620b85c6c73e5e61/t/608d544886d55300e492a619/1619874888658/2021-22+AMCA+Case.pdf); *Planned Parenthood of Southeastern Pennsylvania vs. Casey*, 505 U.S. 833, 848 (1992) ("Neither the Bill of Rights nor the specific practices of States at the time of the adoption of the Fourteenth Amendment marks the outer limits of the substantive sphere of liberty which the Fourteenth Amendment protects").

essentially unregulated and remain major problems in the global CRA industry and the global capital markets.

3. In many countries (such as the US and the UK), the statutes that purport to regulate CRAs are grossly inadequate, and have not solved or reduced the many problems in the CRA industry.
4. As explained herein and above, the CRAs' activities constitute quasi-rule-making processes that deprive certain constituencies (small companies, companies in regulated industries, and companies who cannot afford to hire lobbyists, etc.) of their rights to contract, and rights to privacy (due to improper disclosure). The government's interest is far outweighed by the many documented critiques of CRA, and inadequate/inefficient regulation of CRAs, and their adverse effects on small and medium sized companies.

3.3.6 *The* **Procedural Due Process Doctrine**

As explained herein and above, CRAs perform quasi-governmental functions. Also, the *Substantial Inducement Theory*[19] and the *Substitution Theory* (which were introduced in Nwogugu [2012]) apply in this circumstance, and impose liability on CRAs both for their existence/operations and for ratings opinions.

The existence and current activities of CRAs in many countries constitute violations of the *Procedural Due Process Doctrine*, because the government securities regulatory agencies in many countries (such as the US SEC) illegally delegated the issuance of corporate credit ratings to CRAs, but the CRA ratings processes and quasi-rule-making procedures are inefficient and highly politicized (as documented in articles cited herein). The government's interest is far outweighed by the many documented disadvantages of CRA processes, and their adverse effects on large-, small and medium sized companies and the capital markets.

The existence and current activities of CRAs in many countries constitute violations of the *Procedural Due Process Doctrine*, because:

1. CRAs' ratings processes and ratings opinions have been shown to be biased and politicized—see Nwogugu (2021) and the articles cited herein and above.

[19] *See: Tulsa Professional Collection Services v. Pope*, 485 US 478 (1988).

2. CRAs' fee models (e.g. issuer-pay versus investor-pay) have been empirically shown to affect their ratings opinions which constitutes a major bias—see Nwogugu (2021) and the articles cited herein and above.
3. The cost of CRA errors (false positives, false negatives, etc.) are significant and excessive for issuers, investment banks and households.
4. The "*Tie-Breaker Phenomenon*", "Actual/Perceived Antitrust/ Collusion" and the excessive "Influence" of the Big-three CRAs remain major problems in the global CRA industry and haven't been addressed by existing laws.
5. In many countries (such as the US and the UK), the statutes that purport to regulate CRAs are grossly inadequate, and have not solved or reduced the many problems in the CRA industry.

3.3.7 Violation of the Equal Protection Doctrine

The requisite *State Action* is the licensing of CRAs by government agencies. Also, the *Substantial Inducement Theory* and the *Substitution Theory* (which were introduced in Nwogugu [2012] as an alternative to the *State Action* requirement) apply in this circumstance, and impose liability on CRAs both for their existence/operations and for ratings opinions. CRAs and the applicable regulatory regimes in most countries inherently discriminate against the following classes of "persons":

1. Companies that cannot afford ratings fees.
2. Companies that will be prejudiced by unsolicited credit ratings. There is evidence in the literature that CRAs issue lower credit ratings to companies in unsolicited ratings, than in regular paid ratings.
3. Special Purpose Vehicles which don't have any real operating business and are usually organized and represented by investment banks and their agents.
4. The CRA procedures unfairly discriminate between large companies that can afford to hire investment banks and lobbyists to influence credit-ratings processes, and small companies that cannot afford to influence their rule-making processes.

These foregoing persons are among protected classes of persons. The inherent discrimination by CRAs harms the protected classes. There are other regulatory alternatives that governments can implement. These foregoing discriminatory classifications don't serve any meaningful purpose; and the government's interest is far outweighed by the adverse effects of the discriminatory classifications that are directly and indirectly imposed.[20]

3.3.8 *Violation of the* Separation of Powers Doctrine

As explained herein and above, CRAs perform quasi-governmental functions (rule-making, adjudicatory and enforcement). Also the *Substantial Inducement Theory* and the *Substitution Theory* (which were introduced in Nwogugu [2012] as alternatives to the *State Action* requirement) apply in this circumstance, and impose liability on CRAs both for their existence/operations and for ratings opinions. Nwogugu (2010; revised 2013) and Gudzowski (2010) discussed the need for government-operated CRAs. Thus, CRAs' activities constitute an unconstitutional delegation of duties of the executive branch and legislative branch of national governments.

CRAs violate the *Separation of Powers Doctrine* because: i) the *Substantial Inducement Theory* and the *Substitution Theory* apply, and CRAs combine rule-making and enforcement and quasi-adjudicatory functions, ii) CRAs' functions were unconstitutionally delegated to them by the legislative and executive branches of national governments.[21]

3.3.9 *Violation Of The* Right-To-Contract Doctrine

As explained herein and above, CRAs perform quasi-governmental functions (rule-making, adjudicatory and enforcement). Also, the *Substantial Inducement Theory* and the *Substitution Theory* (which were introduced in Nwogugu [2012] as alternatives to the *State Action* requirement) apply in this circumstance, and impose liability on CRAs both for their existence/

[20] *See*: *United States vs. Vaello-Madero*, _____ US _____ (Case#: 20-303; US Supreme Court; pending as of 2021); *Espinoza vs. Montana Department of Revenue*, _____ US _____ (US Supreme Court; pending as of 2021).

[21] *See*: *Collins vs. Yellen*, _____ US _____ (No. 19-422; US Supreme Court; pending as of 2021).

See: Collins vs. Mnuchin, _____ US _____ (Docket No. 19-422; US Supreme Court; pending as of 2021).

See: Seila Law LLC vs. Consumer Financial Protection Bureau, _____ US _____ (Case#: No. 19-7; US Supreme Court; 2020).

See: Humphrey's Executor vs. United States, 295 U.S. 602 (US Supreme Court; 1935)

See: *PHH Corp. vs. CFPB*, 839 F.3d 1 (2016) *on rehearing enbanc*, 881 F.3d 75 (D.C. Cir., 2018) (en banc).

operations and for ratings opinions.[22] As before, the *State Action* is the governments' licensing of CRAs (and alternatively, the *Substantial Inducement Theory and the Substitution Theory* apply). CRAs violate the *Right-to-Contract clauses* of national constitutions where:

1. A CRA's rating opinion is grossly wrong, and causes an issuer-company to lose a contract (e.g. a contract with an investment bank or investor to raise capital) or to breach a contract (e.g. a loan contract or a securitization contract).
2. The CRA's payment model (e.g. issuer-pays or investment-bank-pays or investor-pays) causes a bias in the CRA's ratings opinion that affects the issuer's or investor's *Right-to-Contract* or *Opportunity-to-Contract.*
3. The CRA's unsolicited ratings opinion (which is typically done without complete information or permission from the subject issuer) causes a bias in the CRA's ratings opinion that affects the issuer's or investor's *Right-to-Contract* or *Opportunity-to-Contract.*

The issuer's or investor's interests and the government's interest in maintaining fair and efficient financial markets far outweigh CRAs' knowing or unintentional interference in contractual rights, *Opportunity-to-Contract* and "Opportunity Sets" of issuers, investors and investment banks.

3.4 Government Bailout/Bail-In Programs: International Trade Aspects

During 2000–2021 and around the world, most government bailouts have focused on the financial services industry (banks, insurance companies and securities brokers). Government bailouts/bail-ins have, or can have "global" *Multiplier Effects*, and critically affect how international trade is conducted, recorded and its disputes resolved—see the articles cited herein and above. Swaps/derivatives trading is global and ISDA and ICMA critically affect how it's conducted, recorded and its disputes resolved. The deliberations of the World Trade Organization Working Party on Professional Services and GATS also pertain to swaps/derivatives sales and trading. The standardization/harmonization of swaps/derivatives regulations across countries and market access for foreign banks and

[22] *See*: *Energy Reserves Group, Inc. vs. Kansas Power and Light Co.*, ____ US ____ (US Supreme Court; 1983). *See*: *Sveen vs. Melin*, ____ US ____ (US Supreme Court; 2018).

securities firms remain important elements of foreign trade negotiations. See Cattaneo et al. (2010)[23] and Cornford (June 2009).[24]

Government bailouts raise significant international trade issues of illegal subsidies and protectionism by member/signatory countries in international trade agreements and agencies. The coordinated efforts of national governments to resolve the global financial crisis of 2007–2013 indicate the relevance of international trade factors. Whether a given bailout package (and associated subsidies) contained therein is WTO-compliant depends on the *Agreement on Subsidies and Countervailing Measures* (SCM Agreement). The disturbing issue is that many government bailouts that occurred during 2008–2016 were illegal (contravened WTO's regulations) but many WTO members chose not to complain. See the comments in Trujillo (2010); Poretti (2009); Delimatsis (2012) and International Institute for Sustainable Development (March 2009).

3.5 Government Bailout/Bail-In Programs: Antitrust Issues, Complexity and Rule-of-Law[25] (and a New Administrative Law Regime?)

The unconstitutionality of government bailout programs for financial institutions, and healthcare reform in the US are elements of structural changes in those industries, and have significant implications for competition and antitrust policy for several reasons including but not limited to the following.

First, government bailouts/bail-ins can create and or reinforce oligopolies, duopolies and quasi-monopolies that are encouraged and unreviewed by governments (as in the US government's bailouts of financial services companies during 2008–2014, and US auto manufacturing

[23] *See*: Cattaneo, O., Engman, M., Saez, S. & Stern, R., eds. (2010). *International Trade in Services: New Trends and Opportunities for Developing Countries* (World Bank).

[24] *See*: Cornford, A. (June 2009). *Statistics For International Trade In Banking Services: Requirements—Availability And Prospects.* UNCTAD. Working paper No. 194. http://unctad.org/en/docs/osgdp20092_en.pdf.

[25] *See*: Andrews et al. (2017); Byrne and Callaghan (2014); Bamberger et al. (2016); Kirman (2016); Salzano and Colander (2007); OECD (2016); Finch (2013); Durlauf (2012), Bayoumi et al. (2016), Room (2011), Kuhlman and Mortveit (2014), Melnik et al. (2013), Miklashevich (2003), Perc et al. (2013), Post and Eisen (2000), Ruhl and Ruhl (n.d.); Williams and Arrigo (2002), Cooper (2011), Datz (2013) and Arthur (1999).

companies during 2008-2009)—and that can result in foreclosure,[26] tying[27] (bundling of financial products or financial services), price-fixing[28] and increases in the volumes of exclusive contracts[29] in capital markets. These two entities are very much subject to lobbying and influence-peddling by the private sector. Capital markets standards obviously affect the nature of competition especially in the financial services industry and in regulated industries.

Second, government bailout/bail-in programs in various countries affected the nature of competition and the propensity for antitrust violations in several industries such as the financial services industry. The bailout/bail-in programs literally placed many banks under government control, subsidized financial institutions (in ways that could have caused or increased vertical foreclosure and market-entry costs) and caused instances of ***inefficient continuance*** wherein banks, finance companies and insurance companies that should have been liquidated were allowed to continue operations.

Third, during 1990–2015, the global swaps/derivatives sector experienced significant structural changes. Furthermore, the timing, structure and effects of the government bailouts of financial institutions in various countries especially during 2007–2010 represent a major structural change in the global financial services industry. The structural changes in the swaps/derivatives sector of the financial services industry included but were not limited to the following: (i) industry consolidation of swaps/derivatives dealers and increased market concentration in the securities industry; (ii) new regulations in many countries such as the US (e.g. the Dodd-Frank Act; SOX), EU, the UK, China, India and Japan; (iii)

[26] *See: Otter Tail Power Co.*, 410 U.S. at 372-375.

[27] *See*: *Eastman Kodak Co. vs. Image Technical Services* (1992) 504 U.S. 451; *Jefferson Parish Hospital vs. Hyde*, 466 U.S. 2 (1984); and *Zenith Radio Corp. vs. Hazeltine Research*, 395 U.S. 100 (1969).

See: Economides (2012a, b) and Economides (1998).

[28] *See*: *Business Electronics Corp. vs. Sharp Electronics Corp.*, 485 U.S. 717 (1988); *Copperweld Corp. vs. Independence Tube*, 467 U.S. 752 (1984); *Monsanto Co. vs. Spray-Rite Service Corp.*, 465 U.S. 752 (1984); *US vs. Arnold, Schwinn, et. al.*, 388 U.S. 365 (1967); *Brown v. Pro Football*, 518 U.S. 213 (1996); *Allied Tube & Conduit Corp. vs. Indian Head, Inc.*, 486 U.S. 492 (1998; US Supreme Court); *Phonetele*, 664 F.2d at 728; *Jacobi vs. Bache & Co.*, 520 F.2d 1231 (CA2, 1975).

[29] *See*: *Standard Oil Co vs. US*, 337 U.S. 293 (1949; US Supreme Court); *US vs. Griffith*, 334 U.S. 100 (1948; US Supreme Court); *Brooke Group Ltd. vs. Brown & Williamson Tobacco*, 509 U.S. 209 (1993; US Supreme Court).

regulatory convergence such as the increasing adoption of ISDA/ICMA standards an SOX-type regulations in many countries; (iv) technological progress and the increased use of technology in trading and record-keeping (combined with increased automation of finance/accounting functions within audit clients); (v) increased participation of companies in the swaps/derivatives markets; (vi) the global financial crises and the bankruptcies of swaps/derivatives dealers; (vii) the growth of the credit default swaps (CDS) market and associated regulations (in some jurisdictions like New York State, CDS are deemed to be insurance products).

Fourth, the Obama administration's (US) healthcare reform of 2010 has significant effects on competition and liquidity in most sectors of the US healthcare industry (which accounts for more than 20% of US annual GDP) and increases the propensity for antitrust violations in the US healthcare industry. More specifically, it increases or can increase the propensity for tying by insurance companies; exclusive contracts[30] by insurance companies; vertical foreclosure and increased market-entry costs in the health insurance sector; price-fixing and or price discrimination[31] by insurance companies and group-boycotts by insurance companies.

Fifth, there is an increasing and symbiotic relationship between the unconstitutionality and the anti-competition effects of these foregoing "institutions"—that is, the greater their anti-competition effects, the greater their unconstitutionality and vice versa.

Sixth, these foregoing "institutions" cause and propagate *network effects* which affect the nature of competition in industries.

The complexity pertaining to these issues is, or can be, manifested in the following ways:

1. Nonlinearity in relation to rule of law development.
2. Self-organization of institutions and organizations; and self-organization in enforcement of laws by private and or public entities.

[30] *See*: *Standard Oil Co vs. US*, 337 U.S. 293 (1949; US Supreme Court).

See: *US v. Griffith*, 334 U.S. 100 (1948; US Supreme Court).

See: *Brooke Group Ltd. v. Brown & Williamson Tobacco*, 509 U.S. 209 (1993; US Supreme Court).

[31] *See: Texaco vs. Hasbrouck*, 496 U.S. 543 (1990; US Supreme Court); *J. Truet Payne Co. vs. Chrysler Motors*, 451 U.S. 557 (1981; US Supreme Court); *Great Atlantic & Pacific Tea Co. vs. Federal Trade Commission*, 440 U.S. 69 (1979; US Supreme Court); *US vs. United States Gypsum*, 438 U.S. 422 (1978; US Supreme Court); *FTC vs. Sun Oil Co.*, 371 U.S. 505 (1963; US Supreme Court).

3. Change and theories of change.
4. Nonlinearity in relation to deadweight losses in the demand for, and enforcement of, laws.
5. Nonlinearity in relation to compliance with statutes and enforcement of laws.
6. Complex networks.
7. Network effects and the associated growth-and-evolution effects (on the mechanism/system and the users and their usage patterns).

The legal and economic environment in which derivative standards organizations function (defined by standards organizations, regulations, regulators, financial institutions, customers, internet systems, etc.) is a complex adaptive system because it has some or all of the following attributes:

1. The relations between the system and its environment are non-trivial and or nonlinear.
2. The system can be influenced by, or can adapt itself to, its environment.
3. The system has feedback or memory, and can adapt itself according to its history or feedback.
4. The system is highly sensitive to initial conditions.
5. The number of parts (and types of parts) in the system and the number of relations between the parts are non-trivial.

During 2010–2019, various new US, European, Latin American and Asian government agencies emerged (thus creating various categories of "regulatory fragmentation") and have issued new regulations that pertain to systemic risk and financial stability which in hindsight, have not been effective. Furthermore, entities such as ISDA and ICMA have significant influence over companies, governments and the regulation of systemic risk and financial stability in various countries because their rules/regulations are widely accepted, incorporated into government regulations and operating procedures of financial services companies, and are implemented as international standards—hence, a new cadre of international "express" and "adopted" administrative law is emerging.[32] The term "emerging" is used because globalization evolved and rapidly increased during

[32] *See*: Kingsbury (2009); Cassese (2005); Kingsbury et al. (2005); Zaring (2005, 2008); Barr and Miller (2006). *See*: http://www.iilj.org/GAL/.

2005–2020. *Express International Administrative Law* refers to regulations that are directly enacted by government administrative agencies where such regulations affect entities, persons and governments in various countries (such as regulations enacted by the US SEC, the FSA in the UK and the Chinese securities regulatory agency). *Adopted International Administrative Law* refers to generally accepted regulations/rules/norms that are enacted by non-governmental entities that have international impact (e.g. regulations of ICMA and ISDA) and are supported by international coalitions (e.g. ISDA, G20, G30) but are adopted by administrative agencies (US SEC, US CFTC, etc.) and are incorporated into administrative regulations and statutes in various countries. The constitutionality of these entities and international coalitions and how they fit into national or regional regulatory frameworks has important ramifications for systemic risk, financial stability, accounting disclosure, contagion and the functioning of markets in various countries.

As noted by Lawson (2010), the modern administrative state in various countries has veered from their constitutions. As noted by some authors, the evolution of government bailouts and these accounting/derivatives standards organizations in various countries constitutes structural changes in the financial services industry and other industries. See: Nwogugu (2013/2015).

3.6 The Dodd-Frank Act Government Bailout Programs in the US

The US government's bailout programs for financial institutions (under the Emergency Economic Stabilization Act of 2008 and related statutes)[33] have been properly and sufficiently criticized as unconstitutional by vari-

[33] *See*: Levy (2008); Rahn (2008), Vermeule (2009), Shah (2009), Posner and Vermeule (2009), Unterman (2009), Fettig (Dec. 2002), Gersen (2007), and Lawson (2010).

See: Emergency Economic Stabilization Act of 2008 ("the EESA").

See: Krey P. (Nov. 2008). The bailout and the Constitution: the $700 billion bank bailout plan will use taxpayer money to purchase troubled assets. How does this stack up against the limited federal powers granted by the Constitution? *The New American* (stating that the bailout is unconstitutional). http://www.thenewamerican.com/index.php/economy/commentary-mainmenu-43/512.

See: American Recovery and Reinvestment Act of 2009, Pub. L. No. 111–5, 123

Stat. 115 (2009) (appropriating an additional several hundred billion dollars in tax cuts and spending programs).

ous authors such as Lawson (2010), Levy (2008), Lunder, Meltz and Thomas (Congressional Research Service) (March 25, 2009), Nwogugu (2015a, b) and FreedomWorks Foundation (January 13, 2009).[34,35]

3.7 The US Government's Bailout/Bail-in of the Auto Industry Was Unconstitutional

During 2006–2009, the US auto industry was operationally and financially distressed (and had suppliers that were located all over the world). By December 2008, the Bush administration enacted a bailout regulation for the US auto industry (which would have provided about $17 billion of aid). During 2006–2009, the US auto industry heavily lobbied the US Congress and the executive branch of the US government for financial/economic aid and new protectionist statutes. By April 2009, General Motors (GM) and Chrysler were faced with imminent

See: Davis, C. (Nov. 2008). "Fast Track" Parliamentary Procedures of the Emergency Economic Stabilization Act. http://www.policyarchive.org/handle/10207/bitstreams/18792.pdf.

See: Vermeule (2009) ("[W]here judges perceive an emergency … standards of rationality, statutory clarity, evidence, and reasonableness all become more capacious and forgiving").

See: Hannan, J (2008). A Tale of Two Streets: *(Re)presenting Economic Value during the Creation and Passage of the Emergency Economic Stabilization Act.* Available at: http://www.natcom.org/NCA/files/ccLibraryFiles/Filename/000000002294/Hanan%20-%20A%20Tale%20of%20Two%20Streets.pdf.

See: Grey, B. (June 2009). *The GM Bankruptcy and the Supreme Court.* http://www.americanthinker.com/2009/06/the_gm_bankruptcy_and_the_supr.html.

See: Bianco K & Pachkowski J (2008). *The Economic Bailout: An Analysis of the Economic Emergency Stabilization Act.* http://www.cch.com/press/news/CCHWhitePaper_Bailout.pdf.

[34] *See*: FreedomWorks Foundation (Jan. 13, 2009). *Constitutional Infirmities of the Emergency Economic Stabilization Act of 2008 ("EESA"): A Legal Analysis from Freedom Works Foundation.* Available at: Constitutional Infirmities of the Emergency Economic Stabilization Act of 2008 ("EESA"), A Legal Analysis from FreedomWorks Foundation. http://www.freedomworks.org/files/policyanalysis.pdf.

[35] White House—http://www.whitehouse.gov/wallstreetreform. US Congress—the *Dodd-Frank Wall Street Reform And Consumer Protection Act*—http://financialservices.house.gov/Key_Issues/Financial_Regulatory_Reform/Financial_Regulatory_Reform062910.html. US Senate Banking, Housing and Urban Affairs Committee: http://banking.senate.gov/public/.

Financial Services Roundtable: http://www.fsround.org/. Consumer Federation of America: http://www.consumerfed.org/.

See: Questions About The $700 Billion Emergency Economic Stabilization Funds. http://cop.senate.gov/documents/cop-121008-report.pdf. http://business.msstate.edu/bizservices/pdf/2009-1-EESA.pdf.

bankruptcy, while Ford Motors survived because it had raised money (had issued debt) during 2007. In 2009, the US (Obama administration) and Canadian governments provided bailout loans (about US$85 billion) to both GM and Chrysler and both companies filed for Chapter 11 bankruptcy by June 1, 2009. GM emerged from bankruptcy as a new company majority-owned by the United States Treasury, while Chrysler emerged from bankruptcy with the United Auto Workers union and Italian automaker Fiat S.p.A. as its majority owners. As part of their bankruptcy filings, GM and Chrysler terminated agreements with hundreds of their dealerships and GM discontinued several of its brands. The government bailouts raise the issues of international trade law violations (protectionism, anti-competitive conduct) and preferential treatment of industries (which affects competition), the Equal Protection Doctrine and other Constitutional Law problems.

It's noteworthy that it was only after the US Senate rejected the Bush administration's proposed bailout for GM and Chrysler in late 2008 that the Bush administration (and after January 2009, the Obama administration) decided to use TARP funds to unconstitutionally bailout GM and Chrysler by Presidential Orders. That move effectively and unconstitutionally eliminated the statutory requirement for congressional/legislative approval for such bailout—but the US Constitution expressly grants all "Spending Powers" to the US Congress.[36]

The US government's intervention in GM and Chrysler was both: i) a bailout because about $85 billion of US government funds were invested in GM and Chrysler; and ii) a bail-in because the US government's intervention occurred within the context of bankruptcy proceedings wherein the US government loans took priority over some of GM's and Chrysler's debts/obligations; and some of GM's and Chrysler's creditors' debts were restructured or converted into equity; and GM's/Chrysler's pension obligations and contracts were also changed or cancelled.

Grey (2009)[37] properly noted that the Obama administration's bailout of GM and Chrysler were unconstitutional and stated that: "the heart of

[36] On the Spending Powers Clause *see: Trump v. Sierra Club*, _____ US _____ (US Supreme Court; pending as of 2021); *National Federation of Independent Business v. Sebelius, 567 U.S. 519* (2012; US Supreme Court); and *South Dakota v. Dole*, _____ US _____ (US Supreme Court; 1987).

[37] *See*: Grey, B. (June 20, 2009). The GM Bankruptcy and the Supreme Court. *The American Thinker*. http://www.americanthinker.com/2009/06/the_gm_bankruptcy_and_the_supr.html.

the individual bondholders' objections to the Obama Administration's plan to save GM is that it is a *Sub Rosa* and unconstitutional effort to do an end-run around the bankruptcy code and to enrich the coffers of the UAW, a key political ally of President Obama. In vacating its brief stay in the Chrysler case, the Supreme Court refused to address the merits of similar allegations, but limited its order to the facts at hand and arguably left open the possibility for a return trip with GM bondholders".

Grey (2009) also correctly noted that *Medellin vs. Texas*[38] (US Supreme Court case) and *Hamdan vs. Rumsfeld*[39] (US Supreme Court case) shows that the US Supreme Court had a history of ruling against excessive use of presidential powers that were not moderated/checked by legislative or constitutional authority. The implication is that the US Supreme Court would have struck down the Obama administration's bailout of GM and Chrysler if the bailout/bail-in had been properly challenged in the US Supreme Court.

Other authors have also concluded that the US government's bailout of the auto industry was unconstitutional.[40]

[38] *See: Medellin vs. Texas*, (US Supreme Court).

[39] *See: Hamdan vs. Rumsfeld*, (US Supreme Court).

[40] *See: "Auto Bailout Unconstitutional?"* By Kristin Jones. Dec. 11, 2008. https://www.propublica.org/article/auto-bailout-unconstitutional-1211.

See: "*Debating the Legality of the Bailout*". By Dennis K. Berman. Dec. 7, 2010. https://www.wsj.com/articles/SB10001424052748703471904576003880475807692.

See: "*Car Dealers Press Case Against U.S. Over Bailout, Citing Constitution*". By Emily Maltby And Angus Loten. Updated April 26, 2012. https://www.wsj.com/articles/SB10001424052702304811304577366292306078480.

See: *Bush Auto Bailout Illegal, Bailout Supporter Admits*. Hans Bader. December 20, 2008. https://cei.org/blog/bush-auto-bailout-illegal-bailout-supporter-admits

See: "TARP: Now A Slush Fund for Detroit?" By Andrew M. Grossman. December 12, 2008. https://www.dailysignal.com/2008/12/12/tarp-now-a-slush-fund-for-detroit/.

See: Dominique (November 22, 2008). "*Ten Reasons not to Bailout the Auto Industry*". https://web.archive.org/web/20090215061128/http://anunlikelyperspective2.squarespace.com/aup2/2008/11/22/ten-reasons-not-to-bailout-the-auto-industry.html.

See: "*Illegal, Unfair Auto Bailout That Harms Retirees and Taxpayers Challenged in Chrysler Bankruptcy*" by Hans Bader, June 4, 2009. https://cei.org/blog/illegal-unfair-auto-bailout-harms-retirees-and-taxpayers-challenged-chrysler-bankruptcy. This article stated in part: "The bailouts are doing no good. General Motors and Chrysler would actually have been better off if they had filed for bankruptcy last year, rather than taking federal money, since the bailouts have come with costly political strings attached, such as dropping opposition to costly CAFE regulations and other federal mandates, and bowing to political meddling in fundamental corporate decision making, and have left the automakers with higher labor costs than if they had just ripped up their collective bargaining agreements in a standard bankruptcy, endangering their long-run competitiveness. Indeed, the politicized auto bailouts resemble the failed British auto bailouts of the 1970s. The Obama and

The reality is that the US government's bailout of the auto industry was unconstitutional and violated the following Constitutional Law doctrines.

3.7.1 *The* Takings Doctrine[41] *(The Fifth Amendment of the US Constitution)*

The bailout was implemented as part of the bankruptcy process of GM and Chrysler, and the bailout effectively and illegally placed the US

Bush Administrations used money from the $700 billion financial system bailout for an auto industry bailout. To do that, they have seized on the fact that the bailout statute contains a broad definition of 'financial institution,' which the Administration claims includes virtually any institution, financial or not. The bailout statute defines 'financial institutions' eligible for the bailout as 'including, but not limited to, any bank, savings association, credit union, security broker or dealer, or insurance company.' Never mind that Congress listed as examples of 'financial institutions' only entities that were banks, insurance companies, or financial institutions, not automakers. During the debate over the auto bailout legislation, the Treasury Department admitted that automakers are not financial institutions covered by the bank bailout statute ... Legal scholars at the Heritage Foundation, former Labor Secretary Robert Reich and many other commentators have argued that this violates the financial bailout statute under the principle of statutory construction known as *Ejusdem Generis*, which says that when a term's definition includes examples that are all of a similar kind, it limits the meaning of the term to things similar in kind to such examples. But if that's not so, and the bailout was just a big slush fund for the Administration to dispense with as it chooses, then the bailout law itself was unconstitutional, since it conferred unbridled discretion in the hands of the President to do whatever he wanted with it".

See: "*GM's Main Street Bondholders Would Lose, Lawyer Says*". Bloomberg. https://www.bloomberg.com/apps/news?pid=20601103&sid=aVXocPtIYXOA&refer=us.

See: Haberman, M. (Oct. 2011). "New Hampshire debate: Mitt Romney talks against auto bailout". *Politico*, October 11, 2011. http://www.politico.com/news/stories/1011/65699.html.

See: *Big Three Spending Millions On Lobbying*. CBS News, December 3, 2008. http://www.cbsnews.com/stories/2008/12/03/cbsnews_investigates/main4646424.shtml.

See: *Big Three auto CEOs flew private jets to ask for taxpayer money*. CNN, November 19, 2008. http://www.cnn.com/2008/US/11/19/autos.ceo.jets/?iref=hpmostpop.

See: "*Bush unveils $17.4bn car bail-out*". BBC. December 19, 2008. http://news.bbc.co.uk/2/hi/business/7791999.stm.

See: *Auto Industry Financing and Restructuring Act*. US House Of Representatives Financial Services Committee, Dec. 10, 2008. http://crossovercars.org/wp-content/uploads/2008/12/automakerbailoutbillpacakage.pdf.

[41] *See*: *Cedar Point Nursery vs. Hassid*, _____ US _____ (US Supreme Court; pending as of 2021)

See: *Cedar Point Nursery vs. Sheroma*, _____ F.3d. _____ (US Ninth Circuit Court of Appeals).

See: *PennEast Pipeline Co. vs. New Jersey*, _____ US _____ (US Supreme Court; pending as of 2021).

See: *Murr vs. Wisconsin*, 137 S.Ct. 1933 (US Supreme Court; 2017).

government ahead of all of other creditors of GM and Chrysler with regard to debt-seniority and liquidation preference. That was a violation of the US Bankruptcy Code,[42] and constituted an unconstitutional *Takings*. The harmed protected class included pension funds, insurance companies and mutual funds (and associated dependent senior citizens) who were creditors and or shareholders of GM or Chrysler and were harmed by the terms of the US government's bailout loan. See the *Takings* theories introduced in Nwogugu (2012: 109-112; 144-145; 190-191; 246-247). The *State Action* consisted of the use of TARP funds to bailout GM and Chrysler, and the bailout statutes enacted by the US Congress and the Presidential Orders issued by the Bush administration and the Obama administration. The US government's interest in stabilizing the US economy and preventing job losses were far outweighed by: (1) the negative effects of raw and publicized *protectionism* in the global auto industry (which eventually resulted in similar protectionist responses in the auto industry and other industries by China, India and Japan); (2) the anti-competitive effects of such loans; (3) the uncertainty surrounding the future prospects of GM and Chrysler, which in turn increases volatility of stock markets; (4) the

See: *California Bldg. Industry Ass'n vs. City of San Jose, Calif.*, 136 S.Ct. 928 (US Supreme Court; 2016).

See: *Koontz vs. St. Johns River Water Management District*, 570 U.S. 2588 (US Supreme Court; 2013).

See: *Lucas vs. South Carolina Coastal Council*, 505 U.S. 1003 (US Supreme Court; 1992).

See: *Federal Republic Of Germany Et Al.* vs. *Philipp Et Al.* (No. 19–351; February 3, 2021; US Supreme Court). https://www.supremecourt.gov/opinions/20pdf/19-351_o7jp.pdf.

See: Republic of Austria v. Altmann, 541 U. S. 677 (US Supreme Court).

See: Bolivarian Republic of Venezuela vs. Helmerich & Payne Int'l Drilling Co., 581 U. S. _____ (2017; US Supreme Court).

[42] *See*: "*Illegal, Unfair Auto Bailout That Harms Retirees and Taxpayers Challenged in Chrysler Bankruptcy*" by Hans Bader, June 4, 2009. https://cei.org/blog/illegal-unfair-auto-bailout-harms-retirees-and-taxpayers-challenged-chrysler-bankruptcy. This article stated in part: "cheating Chrysler's lenders, the government's plan discourages lending, and sets a dangerous precedent that makes it harder for companies like Chrysler to raise money to create jobs in the future, as newspapers like USA Today have noted. The federal government's poorly-conceived bailouts will also endanger Indiana jobs in the long run by leaving Chrysler and General Motors with uncompetitive work rules and compensation. Earlier, a panel of the U.S. Court of Appeals for the Second Circuit, including Chief Judge Dennis Jacobs, and Judges Amalya Kearse and Robert Sack, entered a temporary stay of the bankruptcy judge's ruling rubberstamping the government's plans for Chrysler, in an appeal brought by the Indiana State Teachers' Retirement Fund".

See: *In re Chrysler, LLC* (US Second Circuit; Docket #: 09-2311-mb) (US Federal Appeals Court case).

effects of retaliation by other countries such as South Korea, China and Japan (which are major players in the global auto industry); (5) the damaging long-term effects of the intense and expensive political lobbying by GM, Chrysler and the US auto industry which sets a very bad precedent for other US industries; (6) the fact that both GM and Chrysler could have been safely liquidated and sold to other and more stable US auto companies.

3.7.2 *The* Right-to-Contract Doctrine

The US government's bailout of GM and Chrysler effectively and illegally placed the US government ahead of all of other creditors of GM and Chrysler with regard to debt-seniority and liquidation preference. That constituted an unconstitutional interference with other GM/Chrysler creditors' *Right-to-Contract*. The *State Action* was the bailout statutes enacted by the US Congress and the Presidential Orders issued by the Obama administration. As stated herein and above, the US government's interest in stabilizing the US economy and preventing job losses were far outweighed by other factors.[43]

3.7.3 *The* Equal Protection Doctrine

The US government's bailout violated the *Equal Protection Doctrine* because: (1) the US government didn't provide similar bailouts/bail-ins/aid to other non-financial industries, and to small/medium companies; (2) the bailout disadvantaged US companies that were competitors of GM and Chrysler; (3) the bailout changed the nature and intensity of competition in the US auto industry. Thus, the US government's bailout unfairly discriminated against: (1) other non-financial industries in the US, and 2) small/medium sized non-financial companies that didn't have the wealth or capacity to lobby the US government for financial aid; (3) pension funds and insurance companies (and associated dependent senior citizens) who were bond-holders or shareholders of GM and or Chrysler, and were affected/prejudiced by the terms of the bailout loans. As stated herein and above, the US government's interests in stabilizing the US economy and preventing job losses were far outweighed by other factors.[44]

[43] *See*: *Energy Reserves Group, Inc. vs. Kansas Power and Light Co.*, _____ US _____ (US Supreme Court; 1983); and *Sveen vs. Melin*, _____ US _____ (US Supreme Court; 2018).

[44] *See*: *PennEast Pipeline Co. vs. New Jersey*, _____ US _____ (No. 19-1039; US Supreme Court; pending as of 2021); and *Seila Law LLC vs. Consumer Financial Protection Bureau*, _____ US _____ (Case#: No. 19-7; US Supreme Court; 2020).

3.7.4 The Separation of Powers Doctrine

The US government's bailout violated the *Separation of Powers Doctrine* because it was by the Obama administration's Executive Orders that authorized the bailout (of GM and Chrysler) which clearly violated the TARP statutes. In *A.L.A. Schechter Poultry Corp. v. United States*, 295 U.S. 495 (1935), the US Supreme Court ruled that that giving the executive branch of the government unchecked powers violates the *Separation of Powers Doctrine* by giving the president essentially legislative powers (which was what happened in the 2009 US bailout). The *State Action* was the Presidential Executive Orders and the use of TARP funds. As stated herein and above, the US government's interests in stabilizing the US economy and preventing job losses were far outweighed by other factors.

3.7.5 The Spending Powers Clause

The US Constitution expressly granted to the US Congress, the power over all spending by the US federal government. Automakers don't meet the definition of financial institutions in the TARP statutes. The TARP statute was enacted many months before the bailout/bail-in of GM and Chrysler. Thus the US Executive Branch's use of TARP funds for the bailout/bail-in of GM and Chrysler without express and specific authorization of the US Congress constituted a violation of the *Spending Powers Clause.*[45]

3.7.6 The Non-Delegation Doctrine

The US Executive Branch's use of TARP funds for the bailout/bail-in of GM and Chrysler without express and specific authorization of the US Congress constituted a violation of the *Non-Delegation Doctrine* (the US Congress didn't expressly or impliedly delegate its Spending Clause powers to the US Executive branch which illegally authorized the use of TARP funds for the bailout/bail-in).[46]

[45] *See: Trump v. Sierra Club*, _____ US _____ (US Supreme Court; pending as of 2021); *National Federation of Independent Business v. Sebelius, 567 U.S. 519* (2012; US Supreme Court); and *South Dakota v. Dole*, _____ US _____ (US Supreme Court; 1987).

[46] *See: PennEast Pipeline Co. vs. New Jersey*, _____ US _____ (No. 19-1039; US Supreme Court; pending as of 2021); and *Seila Law LLC vs. Consumer Financial Protection Bureau*, _____ US _____ (Case#: No. 19-7; US Supreme Court; 2020).

3.8 *Obamacare* Was a Government Bailout/Bail-In and was Unconstitutional: Sections Of The US Supreme Court's Ruling in *National Federation of Independent Businesses vs. Sebelius* Were Error

The US Congress and the Obama administration enacted the Affordable Care Act of 2009[47] (Obamacare) which has changed, restructured and bailed-out/bailed-in the US healthcare system. McIntyre and Song (2019) noted that almost ten years after its enactment, Obamacare remains a highly contentious/controversial issue in policy debates. Obamacare was both a *bailout* (Obamacare increased the US federal government and state government investment/expenditures in the healthcare industry) and a *bail-in* (Obamacare changed the allocations of capital, payments, rights and interests among healthcare industry participants such as patients, insurance companies, HMOs/PPOs, hospitals/providers, suppliers and government agencies).

Obamacare's main achievement was to expand insurance coverage (which could have the effects of reducing risk, losses, high debt levels and cash shortages at hospitals and healthcare facilities and also benefit ancillary industries that support the healthcare industry). In the US, healthcare-related expenditures account for more than 15% of the US GNP. Prior to 2008, the US healthcare industry was troubled—i) there were excessive costs; many hospitals were financially/operationally distressed, and healthcare bankruptcies were increasing; ii) many US residents didn't have

[47] *See*: H.R.3200—*America's Affordable Health Choices Act of 2009*. Available at: http://www.opencongress.org/bill/111-h3200/show.

See: Health Care Reform Bill Summary—http://www.ccisco.org/media/news/38_Health%20Reform%20Bill%20Summary%206_09%20_4_.pdf.

See: Summary of National Health Care Reform Legislation And Reconciliation Amendment Changes (Updated March 30, 2010). Available at: http://www.cpehn.org/pdfs/Summary%20of%20National%20Health%20Care%20Reform%20Legislation%20-%20Community%20Catalyst.pdf.

See: Summary of the healthcare reform bill (http://www.cbsnews.com/8301-503544_162-20000846-503544.html)

See: *California vs. Texas*, _____ US _____ (No. 19-840; US Supreme Court; pending as of 2021).

See: *Texas vs. California*, _____ US _____ (No. 19-1019; US Supreme Court; pending as of 2021).

See: *National Federation of Independent Business v. Sebelius, 567 U.S. 519* (2012; US Supreme Court).

sufficient insurance coverage; iii) healthcare was and remains relatively very expensive (compared to developed and developing countries); iv) there was rampant insurance and billing fraud. In effect, the US healthcare industry could have collapsed before Obamacare was enacted.

Given the continuing unaffordability of healthcare services in many developed countries (and especially in the USA), healthcare costs are an ongoing Financial Instability Risk, systemic risk and sustainability problem that has or can have Multiplier Effects on households (savings, personal bankruptcies, disposable income, earning capacity, etc.), companies (cost of employees, productivity, etc.) and governments (tax revenues, welfare transfers, etc.). Such systemic risk also affects overall financial stability because much of the healthcare system in many developed countries (and an increasing number of Emerging Markets countries such as Mexico, Brazil, ASEAN countries, etc.) heavily relies on availability of financing, insurance, energy and consumer durables. Patients often have to finance healthcare expenditures out-of-pocket, and that reduces their disposable income, savings, Remittances and Consumer Confidence; and also can affect Risk Perception. In addition, large healthcare costs are shocks that can impose substantial debts on households and cause mental health problems. High healthcare costs often have disproportionate effect on immigrants, many of whom are not covered by insurance. Healthcare costs are a primary cause of consumer bankruptcy in the US. High healthcare costs often have disproportionate effect on immigrants, many of whom are not covered by insurance. Clinics and diagnostic labs have to either lease equipment or borrow to purchase equipment. Hospitals routinely borrow to finance day-to-day operations and capital expenditures. Healthcare costs are a primary cause of consumer bankruptcy in the US; and are an ongoing Systemic Risk and Sustainability problem that has or can have *Multiplier Effects* on households (savings; personal bankruptcies; disposable income; earning capacity; etc.), companies (cost of employees; productivity; etc.) and governments (tax revenues; welfare transfers; etc.).

Obamacare has been subjected to several legislative and judicial challenges[48] during both the Obama administration and the Trump

[48] McIntyre and Song (2019) stated in part: "........... For example, terminating funding for cost-sharing reductions, which are supplemental subsidies available to some low-income enrollees, led to fears about destabilizing the markets and increasing the ranks of the uninsured. Cutting resources allocated to enrollment outreach and education have raised similar concerns. Recent changes to insurance regulations will likely make plans that bypass the ACA's consumer protections more common. Moreover, the administration has made it

administration. See: Blendon and Benson (2017) and Gostin (2019). As of January 2020, the US Supreme Court had ruled at least twice that parts of *Obamacare* were constitutional; but as correctly explained in Barnett (March 2010)[49], Gostin (2019), Epstein (December 2009)[50] and Epstein

easier for states to modify their Medicaid programs in ways that could lower enrollment (by requiring nondisabled beneficiaries to work in order to qualify for benefits, for example). Its proponents have championed these changes as efforts to promote consumer choice and state innovation. Other serious threats to the law's sustainability have come from the courts. A landmark 2012 Supreme Court decision scaled back the Medicaid expansion from a nationwide mandate to a state option. To date, fourteen states have declined to expand their Medicaid programs (although this number has gradually decreased in recent years). Another challenge sought to roll back subsidies on the ACA (Affordable Care Act) marketplaces. Still other litigation concerning regulations related to contraceptive coverage is ongoing. Perhaps the ACA's greatest lingering existential threat comes from a late-2018 district court ruling in Texas. The judge in this case ruled that the zeroed-out mandate is unconstitutional—and, moreover, that the mandate is not severable from the rest of the ACA, meaning that the rest of the law would need to fall with it. The case is now within the appeals process and could end up before the Supreme Court ....".

See: *National Federation of Independent Business vs. Sebelius* 132 S.Ct. 2566 (US Supreme Court case; #11-393; 2012) (upheld the ***individual mandate*** as within Congress's power to tax).

See: *Texas vs. United States of America* (4:18-cv-00167, 2018; US District Court, N.D. Texas) (***on appeal at the US Supreme Court as of July 2020 as California vs. Texas***) (US District Court invalidated the entire *Affordable Care Act*). https://www.courtlistener.com/docket/6321938/texas-v-united-states-of-america/?page=1.

See: National Conference of State Legislatures. State legislation and actions challenging certain health reforms, 2011-2012 (updated August 10, 2012). http://www.ncsl.org/issues-research/health/state-laws-and-actions-challenging-aca.aspx.

See: National Conference of State Legislatures. 25 states consider health compacts to challenge federal PPACA (updated July 26, 2012). http://www.ncsl.org/issues-research/health/state-laws-and-actions-challenging-aca.aspx.

See: O'Keefe, E. (2014). "The House has voted fifty-four times in four years on Obamacare. Here's the full list". *The Washington Post.* Available from: https://www.washingtonpost.com/news/the-fix/wp/2014/03/21/the-house-has-voted-54-times-in-four-years-on-obamacare-heres-the-full-list/.

[49] *See*: *Confiscatory Insurance Regulation: Yet Another Constitutional Attack, Rebutted.* Available at: http://oneillhealthreform.wordpress.com/2010/01/02/confiscatory-rates-yet-another-constitutional-attack-rebutted/.

See: Barnett, R. (March 2010). *Is Healthcare Reform Constitutional?* Available at: http://www.washingtonpost.com/wp-dyn/content/article/2010/03/19/AR2010031901470.html.

See: *Is The Health Care Law Unconstitutional?* (July 2010). Available at: http://roomfordebate.blogs.nytimes.com/2010/03/28/is-the-health-care-law-unconstitutional/.

[50] See: Epstein, R. (December 2009). "Impermissible Ratemaking in Health-Insurance Reform: Why the Reid Bill is Unconstitutional" (arguing that the Healthcare Reform Bill

and Hyman (Feb. 2010), parts of Obamacare are unconstitutional. See: Thompson et al. (2018), Blake (2012) and Esfeld and Loup (2011).

Clinics and diagnostic labs usually either lease equipment or borrow to purchase equipment. Hospitals routinely borrow to finance regular operations and capital expenditures.

Given those foregoing comments, the sections of the US Supreme Court's Ruling in *National Federation of Independent Businesses vs. Sebelius*[51] that upheld the following were error:

1. US Congress's power to enact most provisions of the *Patient Protection and Affordable Care Act* ("ACA" or "Obamacare") and the *Health Care and Education Reconciliation Act* (HCERA).
2. The requirement for most Americans to pay a penalty for forgoing health insurance by and after 2014 (the US Supreme Court upheld the individual mandate as within the US Congress's power to tax).
3. The *Anti-Injunction Act* did not apply.

During June 2021, the US Supreme Court decided *California versus Texas* (Case #: 19–840; June 17, 2021; US Supreme Court) and *Texas versus California* (Case #: 19–1019; June 17, 2021; US Supreme Court) (collectively, the "Obamacare III 2021 Cases"). The Court noted that Obamacare (*Patient Protection and Affordable Care Act* of 2010) required "minimum essential health insurance coverage" for which Obamacare had originally imposed an income-scaled monetary penalty, but the US Congress changed the penalty to $0 in 2017, but to become effective beginning in 2019[52] (the "*2017 Amendment*"). See *Tax Cuts and Jobs Act of 2017*, Pub. L. 115–197, §11081, 131 Stat. 2092 (codified in 26 U. S. C. §5000A(c)). In the *Obamacare III 2021 Cases*, the US Supreme Court politically avoided the issue of the unconstitutionality of Obamacare, and instead ruled that Texas and California didn't have "standing" to sue, which was error because of the following reasons:

enacted by the Obama administration is unconstitutional). http://www.pointoflaw.com/columns/archives/2009/12/impermissible-ratemaking-in-he.php.

[51] *See*: *National Federation of Independent Business vs. Sebelius* (US Supreme Court case; #11-393; 2012).

[52] *See*: §11081, 131 Stat. 2092.

See: the "*Obamacare III 2021 Cases*" quoting: IRS, Publication 5187, Tax Year 2019, p. 5 ("... Form 1040 ... will not have the 'full-year health care coverage or exempt' box and Form 8965, Health Coverage Exemptions, will no longer be used as the shared responsibility payment is reduced to zero...").

1. The US Supreme Court's constant attempts to separate the *§5000A(a) Minimum Coverage Requirement* from the associated monetary penalty when trying to evaluate *Standing* and harm was moot, unnecessary and clear error (the issue of penalty was eliminated by the US Congress).
2. Given the significant economic and political effects of the US Supreme Court's ruling in *California versus Texas* and *Texas versus California*, even if it wasn't mentioned in the arguments or in the lower courts, the US Supreme Court should have resolved the issue of *Standing* and constitutionality with regards to other statutes in Obamacare other than §5000A(a). Both issues have been very controversial, and delaying their resolution merely increases *Costly Uncertainty*, litigation costs and litigation backlog in US courts.
3. Both the pre-2019 and post-2018 monetary penalties and the *Minimum Essential Coverage Requirement* (MECR) aren't severable from the rest of Obamacare. It is reasonably inferable from the wording and legislative intent of Obamacare that US Congress intended all sections of Obamacare to work together and to depend on each other. This position is supported by the following. First, the *2017 Amendment* didn't expunge or perpetually remove the monetary penalty but merely reduced it to zero. Second, sections of Obamacare reference and depend on other sections of Obamacare. Third, the costs and the economic, social and psychological impact of sections of Obamacare depend on the interpretations of other sections of Obamacare. Fourth, there are psychological effects of the post-2018 MECR which create the same or similar effects as the pre-2019 MECR—and some of these are explained below.
4. The *Minimum Essential Coverage Requirement* (MECR) (with or without the monetary penalties) harms state governments in the following specific ways:

    a. For households that chose to comply for whatever reason, the post-2018 MCR reduces the after-tax incomes of low-income and mid-income households (that are required to file federal tax returns but have relatively low disposable incomes), which in turn reduces their ability to pay for basic expenses such as rent/housing, education, travel, food, housing maintenance, auto insurance; and so on, which in turn, harms state governments by increasing their expenditures on (and legal liabilities for) these items and related costs (such as crime; auto accidents; emergency hospital visits; food and housing for low-income households, etc.) (collectively, the "*Incremental Costs*"). Furthermore, even without monetary penalties, the mere existence of MECR is very likely to compel more individuals to enroll in state-operated programs such as Medicaid. The facts/circumstances in *Lujan*, 504 U. S., at 562 (quoting *Allen*, 468 U. S., at 758) and *Clapper*, 568 U. S., at 414 (expressing "…reluctance to endorse *Standing* theories that rest on speculation about the decisions ofindependent actors…") are distinguishable from this instance.

b. For households that chose not to comply with post-2018 MECR but need healthcare services, the post-2018 MCR is likely to increase the incidence of fraud (misclassification of medical treatment by providers and patients that use medicaid; false/falsified applications/enrollment for Medicaid insurance and similar programs; etc.) and over-billing in state-operated Medicaid systems (see 42 U. S. C. §§1396–1396w), and similar programs such as the Children's Health Insurance Program (CHIP) (see §1397aa), and health insurance programs for state employees (collectively, the "*Incremental Costs*"), and all that directly harms state governments. In the context of over-billing, the foregoing provides significant incentives for healthcare providers to collude with low-income individuals to over-bill for non-existent or improperly classified medical conditions, where in some instances, the patient can be paid side-payments (cash or other consideration) or granted free treatments in exchange for participating in such misconduct. The facts/circumstances in *Lujan*, 504 U. S., at 562 (quoting Allen, 468 U. S., at 758) and *Clapper*, 568 U. S., at 414 are distinguishable from this instance.

c. It compels or encourages some eligible low/moderate income households to buy relatively unaffordable insurance in private markets. The net result is that they have to depend on state government financial aid for their other non-health expenses.

d. The US Supreme Court's main argument is that MECR compels individuals to buy insurance coverage. However, MECR has no means of enforcing it and without such enforcement or threat of enforcement, there cannot be any harm to the plaintiffs. The reality is that "*Actual Enforcement*" of the monetary penalties (the "Enforcement Requirement") is not required in order for the plaintiffs to suffer harm from the MECR. The US Supreme Court's "*Enforcement Requirement*" argument is wrong because of the following reasons:

- The US Supreme Court completely omitted the analysis of the statutory construction of the *2017 Amendment* and the resulting effects. In this context, a stated monetary penalty of $0 is very different from absence/non-mention of any monetary penalty. The wording and construction of the *2017 Amendment* leaves open the possibility that the US Congress may in the future, increase the penalty to an amount above $0 (e.g. after a change of control of the US Congress; or if the US incurs greater-than-normal budget deficits; or if the US government exceeds its *Debt-Ceiling*; etc.). That argument is supported by the fact the US Congress didn't simply expunge and perpetually cancel the monetary penalty, but merely reduced it to $0. Any such future increases of the monetary penalty will directly harm the state governments who will incur both the costs that they stated (the "State Costs")[53] and the *Incremental Costs* explained herein and above as a result, and thus there is *Traceability* and the plaintiff state governments have *Standing* to sue. The wording and construction of the *2017 Amendment* also leaves open the possibility that the US Congress may in the future, retroactively increase the monetary penalty and retroactively apply it to a section of eligible households for any reason. That will directly harm the state governments by causing them to incur the "State Costs" and the *Incremental Costs*, and thus there is *Traceability* and the plaintiff state governments have *Standing* to sue.
- The US Supreme Court completely omitted the psychological/social/political effects of the *2017 Amendment*. In this context, a stated monetary penalty of $0 is very different from absence/non-mention of any monetary penalty. As statutorily constructed, the *2017 Amendment* (of the MECR, i.e. without monetary penalties) raises the specter and fear among households that the US government or even private companies may use data about non-compliant households (who didn't comply with MECR) in decisions about them; just like consumer credit scores are used for a

[53] According the to the US Supreme Court, the "State Costs" are as follows: "...they allege an indirect injury in the form of the increased use of (and therefore cost to) state-operated medical insurance programs. Second, they claim a direct injury resulting from a variety of increased administrative and related expenses required, they say, by the minimum essential coverage provision, along with other provisions of the Act that, they add, are inextricably "'interwoven'" with it....".

broad range of decisions about US adults in the US. It also raises the issue of *Regret-minimization* or *Regret-Aversion* by eligible households which causes them to comply with post-2019 MECR (without monetary penalties). Such *Induced Compliance* or *Fear/ Anxiety Driven Compliance* directly harms the state governments by causing them to incur the *State Costs* and the *Incremental Costs* and both costs are direct and "but-for" causal relationships between Government action and the plaintiffs' injury (the costs), and thus state governments have *Standing* to sue. Unfortunately, the US Supreme Court's ruling and indeed past US Supreme Court cases[54] didn't address or consider Behavioral Economics, Risk-Perception and Psychology issues that pertain to *causality* and injuries. See Nwogugu (2006, 2009).

- Separately, the combination of the MECR and the *2017 Amendment* by itself is a non-monetary *Psychological Penalty* and or *Moral-Altruism Penalty* and or *Nationalism-Oriented Penalty* which (without any statutory monetary penalties), compels individuals to comply with the MECR. That in turn directly harms the state governments by causing them to incur the *State Costs* and the *Incremental Costs*, and those are direct and but-for causal relationships between the government's action and the plaintiffs' injury (the costs), and thus the plaintiffs have *Standing* to sue.
- The cases cited by plaintiff in support of their position[55] were decided before the *2017 Amendment*, but the *2017 Amendment* didn't affect the holdings of those cases because of the following reasons. First, there are psychological effects of the post-2018 MECR which create the same or similar effects as the pre-2019 MECR—those are explained herein and above. Second, as explained above, the MECR and the monetary penalty are not severable from the rest of Obamacare.

[54] Cases cited by the US Supreme Court to support its position such as: *Allen vs. Wright*, 468 U.S. 737 (1984); *DaimlerChrysler Corp. vs. Cuno*, 547 U.S. 332 (2006); *Lujan vs. De-fenders of Wildlife*, 504 U. S. 555, 560–561 (1992); *Babbitt vs. Farm Workers*, 442 U.S. 289, 298 (1979); *Susan B. Anthony List v. Driehaus*, 573 U. S. 149, 164 (2014); *Clapper vs. Amnesty Int'l USA*, 568 U. S. 398, 414 (2013); and *Virginia vs. American Booksellers Assn., Inc.*, 484 U.S. 383, 392 (1988).

[55] See the "Obamacare III 2021 Cases" which cited: *Florida ex rel. Atty. Gen. vs. United States Dept. of Health and Human Services.*, 648 F.3d 1235 (CA11; 2011); *Thomas More Law Center vs. Obama*, 651 F.3d 529 (CA6 2011); and *Virginia ex rel. Cuccinelli vs. Sebelius*, 656 F. 3d 253, 266–268 (CA4 2011).

	Going concern supervision/Crisis prevention	⇦ Scope of the Crisis Management Communication ⇨		
		Early intervention	Bank resolution	Insolvency framework
Current situation	Capital Requirements Directive 3 pillar approach (CRD) Colleges National authorities Committee of European Banking Supervisors (CEBS) Stress testing	CRD (Art. 130 + 136) Colleges Emergency Liquidity Assistance by National Central Banks (NCBs) 2008 MoU	2008 MoU – determines who (e.g. finance ministries, NCBs) coordinates actions with other competent authorities (coordination via cross-border stability groups)	Winding up Directive: Winding-up of a cross-border branches takes place under insolvency procedures of country of parent bank. Winding up of cross-border subsidiaries takes place according to procedures where subsidiary is licensed.
Possible changes for consideration	Establish European Systemic Risk Board (ESRB) and European Banking Authority (EBA) Leverage ratio Management of risks (remuneration structures) Quantity and Quality of capital Enhanced capital requirements Supervision of liquidity Preparation of Wind-down plans	European Banking Authority New powers towards bank management Joint assessment framework Restoration plans Asset transferability framework Expanded common tools for supervisors (CEBS) Clarify home/host branch supervision (Art. 33 CRD)	New bank resolution tools New framework for cooperation Broader changes to the legal framework in support of new bank resolution tools Mechanisms to finance cross-border resolutions (including possible role for DGS) Application of wind-down plans	Facilitate integrated winding up of a group: – Coordination framework for insolvency proceedings – Lead insolvency administrator – Integrated resolution by a single authority – Asset transfers under post commencement financing

Table 4. Amounts Pledged or Utilized for Financial Sector Support
(In percent of 2009 GDP unless otherwise noted)1/

	Capital Injection		Purchase of Assets and Lending by Treasury 2/		Direct Support 3/	Guarantees 4/	Asset Swap and Purchase of Financial Assets, including Treasuries, by Central Bank
	(A)		(B)		(A+B)	(C)	(D)
	Pledged	Utilized	Pledged	Utilized	Pledged	Pledged	Pledged
Advanced Economies							
Australia	0.0	0.0	0.0	0.0	0.0	13.2	0.0
Canada	0.0	0.0	9.1	4.4	9.1	0.0	0.0
France	1.3	1.1	0.2	0.0	1.5	16.9	0.0
Germany	3.4	1.2	0.0	3.7	3.4	17.2	0.0
Italy	1.3	0.3	0.0	0.0	1.3	0.0	2.7
Japan	2.5	0.1	4.1	0.1	6.6	7.2	0.0
Korea	1.2	0.4	1.5	0.1	2.7	11.6	0.0
United Kingdom	8.2	6.4	3.7	0.1	11.9	40.0	28.2
United States	5.1	2.9	2.3	1.9	7.4	7.5	12.1
Emerging Economies							
Argentina	0.0	0.0	0.0	0.0	0.0	0.0	0.0
Brazil	0.0	0.0	0.8	0.3	0.8	0.5	0.0
China	0.0	0.0	0.0	0.0	0.0	0.0	0.0
India	0.0	0.0	0.0	0.0	0.0	0.0	0.0
Indonesia	0.0	0.0	0.0	0.0	0.0	0.0	0.0
Mexico	0.0	0.0	0.0	0.0	0.0	0.0	0.0
Russia	7.1	3.1	0.5	0.0	7.7	0.0	0.0
Saudi Arabia	0.0	0.0	0.0	0.0	0.0	0.0	0.0
South Africa	0.0	0.0	0.0	0.0	0.0	0.0	0.0
Turkey	0.0	0.0	0.0	0.0	0.0	0.0	0.0
G-20 Average	2.6	1.3	1.4	0.9	4.0	6.4	4.6
Advanced Economies	3.8	2.0	2.4	1.4	6.2	10.9	7.7
In billions of US$	1,220	639	756	461	1,976	3,530	2,400
Emerging Economies	0.7	0.3	0.1	0.0	0.8	0.04	0.0
In billions of US$	90	38.4	18	5.0	108	7	0

- The facts/circumstances in *Lujan*, 504 U. S., at 562 (quoting *Allen*, 468 U. S., at 758) and *Clapper*, 568 U. S., at 414 (expressing "…reluctance to endorse *Standing* theories that rest on speculation about the decisions of independent actors….") are distinguishable from this instance.

5. The US Supreme Court's argument about *redressability* lacks merit and constituted "avoidance-of-responsibility" because given the clearly significant economic, social and psychological impact of the outcome of the "Obamacare III 2021 Cases" on tens of millions of Americans (and associated economic *Multiplier Effects* on foreign countries and actual/ potential conflicting judicial rulings of lower US courts):

    a. The US Supreme Court should have treated the "Obamacare III 2021 Cases" as *quasi Class-action cases* even if the litigants didn't expressly state that in their pleadings. The state governments that are and aren't litigants in the case will be bound to apply the US Supreme Court's rulings to millions of their indigenes.
    b. The US Supreme Court should have considered plaintiff's theories that were not raised in the lower courts or in the *certiorari stage.*
    c. The facts and dispute satisfy Article-III's *case-or-controversy* requirement, as explained herein and above; and the US Supreme Court should have extended declarative and injunctive relief to the broad class of persons affected by Obamacare. The results of not doing so include increased cost-of-capital (of healthcare companies and local/ state governments), *Costly-Uncertainty*, negative economic *Multiplier-Effects*, excessive and distorting Political Lobbying, increased litigation costs and litigation backlog in lower US courts.
    d. The US Supreme Court misconstrued the uses of Medicaid and similar healthcare payment programs (operated by state governments) that for many low-income and moderate-income persons are alternatives to the minimum essential coverage provision of §5000A(a).
    e. As stated above in this chapter, sections of the US Supreme Court's Ruling in *National Federation of Independent Businesses vs. Sebelius*[56] were error.

[56] *See*: *National Federation of Independent Business vs. Sebelius* (US Supreme Court case; #11-393; 2012).

6. See the US District Court's ruling in *Texas vs. United States*, 340 F. Supp. 3d 579,593–595 (ND Tex.; 2018). See the US Court of Appeal's ruling in *Texas vs. United States*, 945 F.3d 355, 377–393 (CA5; 2019) (plaintiffs had *Standing* to sue; but the US District Court's severability analysis was "incomplete").

It's clear that the enactment, implementation and judicial/legislative challenges of Obamacare were highly politicized (involved deep divisions along political-party lines; and significant political lobbying by different groups/interests), and implicate significant constitutional law and constitutional political economy issues which are yet to be resolved. See the comments in Thompson et al. (2018).

3.9 The 2010 Bailouts by the European Union

On May 2, 2010, Euro-zone countries announced that they had agreed to provide up to €80 billion in loans to Greece over a three-year period. On May 11, 2010, the EU Council adopted Regulation 407/2010 which established a European Financial Stabilization Mechanism (the EFSF is the €60 billion European financial stabilization mechanism). On June 7, 2010, the EU members signed the "European Financial Stabilization Facility" (EFSF) agreement, pursuant to which EU member states pledged to make available an additional €440 billion.[57] Although they

[57] *See*: *Germany's Constitutional Court Gets Into the Mix Over the Future of Europe*. http://seekingalpha.com/article/208806-germany-s-constitutional-court-gets-into-the-mix-over-the-future-of-europe.

See: Eurobank EFG (June 2010). The Greek Economy And its Stability Programme. *Eurobank Research—Economy & Markets*, 5(3), ________. http://www.eurobank.gr/Uploads/Images1024/EconomyStabilityProgramNew.pdf.

See: EU (2010). *European Stabilization Mechanism To Preserve Financial Stability*. http://www.consilium.europa.eu/uedocs/cms_data/docs/pressdata/en/ecofin/114324.pdf.

See: EU Debt Office, Authority For Bank Resolution Funds & European Financial Stabilization Mechanism. http://www.asymptotix.eu/content/eu-debt-office-authority-bank-resolution-funds-european-financial-stabilisation-mechanism.

See: Commission of The European Communities (Oct. 2009). *An EU framework for Cross-Border Crisis Management in the Banking Sector*. http://ec.europa.eu/internal_market/bank/docs/crisis-management/091020_communication_en.pdf.

Source: http://ec.europa.eu/internal_market/bank/docs/crisis-management/091020_communication_en.pdf.

Source: IMF—*World Economic & Financial Surveys—Navigating the Fiscal Challenges Ahead* (May 14, 2010). http://www.imf.org/external/pubs/ft/fm/2010/fm1001.pdf.

were unsuccessfully opposed in legislatures of EU member states and challenged in European constitutional courts, collectively, these three financial mechanisms represent a circumvention of the EU Constitution based on the same principle of lack of "unified action" by EU member states (use of "inter-governmental" agreements rather than reliance on, or reference to any specific EU Treaty provision). However, the economic substance of these three mechanisms is that the EU member states are essentially either guaranteeing obligations of other member states or providing loans to member states, all of which contravene the EU constitution. On May 6, 2010, the European Central Bank decided to accept as collateral debt issued or guaranteed by the Greek government and on May 20, 2010, the ECB announced new "non-standard" liquidity measures (USD swap facilities, Euro long-term refinancing operations [LFTOs] and interventions in the European public and private debt securities markets). Currie et al. (July 2010),[58] Wadhwa et al. (J. P. Morgan)

[58] *See*: Currie, A., Fountoukakos, K., Gale, S., Pullen, K., Spahlinger, A. Van den Hende, L. (Herbert Smith Gleitz Stibbe Lutz) (July 2010). *European financial stability measures and EU law.* (analyzing the constitutionality of the EU's bailout loans to Greece, and the European Financial Stabilization Mechanism, and the European Financial Stabilisation Facility). Available at: http://www.herbertsmith.com/NR/rdonlyres/BA7C5FA2-BBB5-4B8D-9971-23AF97BBB678/08339Europeanfinancialstabilitymeasuresbriefing.pdf. Currie, Fountoukakos, Gale, et. al. (July 2010) states in part: "Although managed by the Commission and conditional on respect for a Council decision, the loans themselves do not have any strict EU legal basis. Rather, they are based primarily on an inter-governmental agreement ... Since several articles of the Treaty on the Functioning of the European Union ('TFEU') specifically forbid certain types of financial assistance to Member States, it needs to be considered whether the Member State loans to Greece are in compliance with EU law. Relevant articles include:

• *Article 123(1) TFEU which generally prohibits either the ECB or the national banks of Member States from providing credit facilities to or purchasing debt instruments from Member States*

• *Article 124 TFEU which prohibits measures providing EU institutions or Member State entities privileged access to financial institutions; and*

• *Article 125(1) TFEU which generally prohibits either the EU or Member States from being liable for or assuming the obligations of other Member States.*

Although Article 123(1) prohibits credit facilities, including loans like those provided to Greece, its provisions only apply to the ECB and Member State national banks. At this stage, available information indicates that the loans are provided by Member States rather than national banks. Therefore, the loans do not appear to be prohibited by Article 123(1). It has also been suggested that the loans could be contrary to Article 125(1) TFEU (often referred to as the '*No bailout clause*'). The Member States are only providing loans and not grants or guarantees. Furthermore, there is no evidence that the

(May 14, 2010)[59] and Lefeuvre (Natixis—Research) (May 2010)[60] explain some of the practical legal, macroeconomic and rating-agency ramifications of these actions by the EU.

Member States are otherwise assuming or becoming directly liable for Greece's debt obligations. Therefore, it is doubtful that Article 125(1) would prohibit the Member State loans to Greece ... Like the loans to Greece, the EFSF is based on an inter-governmental agreement rather than any specific EU Treaty provision .... It is in any event noteworthy that a member of the German Parliament has challenged Germany's participation in the EFSF in the German Constitutional Court on the basis that the EFSF violates Article 125 TFEU ... The ECB's decision to accept Greek debt in the course of its credit operations is explicitly based on Article 18.1 of the Statute of the European System of Central Banks and of the European Central Bank ('ESCB Statute') ... Although the ECB's May 6, 2010 decision complies with Article 123(1) TFEU, there may be questions as to whether the decision could potentially violate Article 18.1 of the ESCB Statute ....

[59] *See*: Wadhwa, P., Belton, T., Chang, J., Mackie, D. & Marrese, M. (J. P. Morgan) (May 14, 2010). ***European Rates Strategy: The European Stabilization Mechanism.*** https://mm.jpmorgan.com/stp/t/c.do?i=E0271-555&u=a_p*d_414788.pdf*h_ajfko049. Wadhwa, Belton, Chang, Mackie & Marrese (May 14, 2010) states in part: "In proposing the SPV, the EU is attempting to create a separate legal entity backed solely by the 16 members of the EMU. This is in contrast to the existing BoP facility which is backed by all 27 members of the EU, and allows EU countries to lend to each other ... When rating a structure, rating agencies may focus on *1)* the probability of loss, without regard to the potential size of the loss, or *2)* the expected loss on the assets in the SPV. Under the first methodology, the "severally liable" feature would imply that the probability of loss would be determined by the weakest country, Greece, currently rated BB+ by S&P. Thus, debt issued by the SPV under this methodology could be rated sub-investment grade, assuming no credit enhancement". .... "These loans (the EU Balance-of-Payments (BoP) facility) are financed in the capital markets by means of European Commission (EC) bonds, which are effectively backed by the EU budget and the 27 EU member states ... Indeed, all EU member states are jointly and severally liable for any payments due on these bonds; for this reason, EC bonds in the 5-Year sector trade around Libor flat. Investors are therefore exposed only to the credit risk of the EU, and not the beneficiary country ... Although we believe that SPV debt guarantees require parliamentary approval of the 16 EMU countries, we expect this to occur over the next several weeks, with German parliamentary approval expected within the next two weeks ... One outstanding risk for parliamentary approval of the SPV is the potential for a constitutional challenge in Germany. Because German law precludes the government from guaranteeing the debt of another sovereign, the constitutionality of the SPV may be challenged in court. However, because the guarantee is on an SPV rather than a sovereign, we expect that the guarantee can be structured in a way that meets the requirements of German law".

[60] *See*: Lefeuvre E (Natixis—Research) (May 11, 2010). *Special Report—Economic Research: Markets Implications of the Support Packages.* http://cib.natixis.com/flushdoc.aspx?id=53032.

3.10 Central Bank Independence, Central Bank Governance Models and the Unconstitutionality of AMCON (Asset Management Corporation of Nigeria), the *AMCON Act of 2010*, the *AMCON Amendment Act of 2019*, and the Associated Bailout/Bail-in

In response to extremely high *non-performing loan rates* (NPL rates) and a *credit-crunch* (both of which were national political campaign issues in Nigeria during 2006–2010), significant political pressures and allegations of fraud and corruption in the Nigerian banking industry, the Nigerian federal legislature and the Obasanjo administration enacted the AMCON Act of 2010 (the "*AMCON Act*" or the "*AMCON Act of 2010*") which changed, restructured and bailed-out/bailed-in banks in Nigeria. The AMCON Act of 2010 created AMCON (Asset Management Corporation of Nigeria), the government-owned *asset-management corporation* for resolution of non-performing loans. Roughly ten years after its enactment, the AMCON Act and AMCON have failed and NPL rates have risen again in the Nigerian banking industry (i.e. during 2017–2021), and several Nigerian banks became financially and operationally distressed during 2016–2019. For example: i) Diamond Bank became financially and operationally distressed and was sold to Access Bank;[61] ii) during 2018, Skye Bank[62] was seized by the Central Bank of Nigeria; (iii) during 2021, the Central Bank of Nigeria[63] sacked the entire board of

[61] *See*: "How Distressed Oil Sector Loans Damaged Diamond Bank". *This Day* (Nigerian Newspaper). May 20, 2019. https://www.thisdaylive.com/index.php/2019/05/20/how-distressed-oil-sector-loans-damaged-diamond-bank/.

See: "How intrigues, lapses, losses caused Diamond Bank's fall". *The Guardian* (Nigerian newspaper). By Chijioke Nelson, Asst. Editor, Finance/Economy. 24 December 2018. https://guardian.ng/business-services/how-intrigues-lapses-losses-caused-diamond-banks-fall/.

[62] *See*: Nigeria's Central Bank takes over Skye Bank. *Premium Times* (Nigerian Newspaper). By Bassey Udo. September 21, 2018. https://www.premiumtimesng.com/news/headlines/284921-breaking-nigerias-central-bank-takes-over-skye-bank.html.

See: "Management contributed to collapse of Nigeria's Skye Bank – deposit insurer". *Reuters*. By Reuters Staff. November 12, 2018. https://www.reuters.com/article/nigeria-skye-bank-idUSL8N1XN6HW.

[63] *See*: "First Bank directors fired to protect customers, minority shareholders—CBN". *Punch* (Nigerian Newspaper). By Okechukwu Nnodim, Abuja. April 30, 2021. https://punchng.com/first-bank-directors-fired-to-protect-customers-minority-shareholders-cbn/.

directors of First Bank's holding company; and (iv) Keystone Bank, Mainstreet Bank and Polaris Bank were "re-launched" and "re-branded", but were products of bank seizures and restructurings by Central Bank Of Nigeria.[64] As explained in Nwogugu (2014) both AMCON and the AMCON Act of 2010 changed the nature of competition in, and the structure of the Nigerian banking industry (and, by extension, the African banking industry, because many Nigerian banks are pan-African banks).

The creation of both AMCON and the AMCON Act was both a *bail-out* (AMCON and the AMCON Act increased the Nigerian federal government's investment/expenditures in the African banking industry) and a *bail-in* (AMCON and the AMCON Act changed the allocations of capital, payments, liquidation priorities, rights and ownership-interests in Nigerian banks). On bailouts, see: Harry and Madume (2018).

The AMCON Act of 2010 was amended several times by the following statutes:

See: *"Removal of Bank Directors by the Central Bank of Nigeria: The Recent Case of First Bank of Nigeria Limited and FBN Holdings Plc"*. By Jackson Etti & Edu. May 2, 2021. https://jee.africa/removal-of-bank-directors-by-the-central-bank-of-nigeria-the-recent-case-of-first-bank-of-nigeria-limited-and-fbn-holdings-plc/.

[64] *See: "Recouping revenues: Restructuring efforts are helping to recover past losses"*. By Oxford Business Group. https://oxfordbusinessgroup.com/analysis/recouping-revenues-restructuring-efforts-are-helping-recover-past-losses. This article stated in part: "...Three failed banks—AfriBank, SpringBank and Bank PHB—were taken over by the Nigerian Deposit Insurance Corporation (NDIC) in 2011, restructured as temporarily publicly held banks—Mainstreet, Enterprise and Keystone Banks, respectively—and transferred to AMCON for resale to strategic investors. ...In total, AMCON has acquired 12,000 individual NPLs, according to the IMF, with average maturities of five years. In 2013, AMCON claims to have restructured some 40% of the NPLs on its books, of which around half had returned to performing status by June 2013. While recoveries stood at 112% of the eligible banking assets' purchase prices, AMCON's target over the full course of resolution is for the recovery of 80% of NPLs' purchase price...... With interest on the part of both foreign investors and mid-tier domestic banks in the three sanitised banks held by AMCON, the first and smallest bank, Enterprise Bank, was put up for sale in June 2013. Having injected some N318.6bn ($2.01bn) into Afribank (Mainstreet), N296.9bn ($1.87bn) into Bank PHB (Keystone) and N121.4bn ($764.82m) into Spring Bank (Enterprise)—worth a combined N736.9bn ($4.64bn)—AMCON expects to gross some N341bn ($2.15bn) in the sale of the three banks. As of October 2013, AMCON was seeking buyers for Enterprise, and expected all of the sales to be completed by September 2014...".

1. The AMCON Amendment Act of 2015[65] (the "2015 Act" or the "2015 AMCON Act") was enacted in 2015 and it amended Sections 2(3), 34(1;2),16(5), 35, 46(2); 48; 60; 61 & 62 of the AMCON Act of 2010. The AMCON Amendment Act of 2015 made into statute, the mandatory contributions by banks to the AMCON Resolution Cost Fund (RCF); and it created a Board of trustees for the RCF which consists of "two representatives of the Central Bank of Nigeria, whom shall be appointed by the Central Bank of Nigeria from among its Deputy- Governors ... (b) four representatives of Eligible Financial Institutions to be appointed by the Eligible Financial Institutions ... (c) and 2 (two) ex-officio members, one each to be nominated by the Federal Ministry of Finance, and the Nigerian Deposit Insurance Corporation, from among their respective officers". However, the 2015 AMON Act doesn't solve the problems inherent in the original AMCON Act, some of which are discussed herein.
2. The AMCON Amendment Act of 2019[66] (the "2019 Act" or the "2019 AMCON Act") was enacted in 2019 and it introduced some new sections to, and amended some sections of the AMCON Act of 2010. The 2019 Act amended Sections 6, 10, 19, 31, 33, 34, 35, 39, 43, 45, 47, 48, 49, 50, 51, 52, 53, 55, 60 and 61 of the AMCON Act of 2010, and introduced Sections 33A, 50A and 50B.

According to data from the World Bank[67] and CEIC[68] (a Euromoney company) and other sources, as of 2017–2021, non-performing loan rates remained relatively high (above 8%) in many Emerging Markets countries and have become a major economic indicator and political controversy in India and China. Such high NPL rates have dragged

[65] *See*: The "*AMCON Amendment Act of 2015*". https://amcon.com.ng/downloads/AMCON_(Amendment)_Act_2015.pdf.

[66] *See*: "*Nigeria: The Revised AMCON Debt Recovery Approach Vis-A-Vis The AMCON Special Powers—A Critical Review Of AMCON Amendment Act 2019*". March 17, 2020. By AAA Chambers. http://www.aaachambers.com/articles/the-revised-amcon-debt-recovery-approach-vis-a-vis-the-amcon-special-powers-a-critical-review-of-amcon-amendment-act-2019/?utm_source=Mondaq&utm_medium=syndication&utm_campaign=LinkedIn-integration.

[67] *See*: World Bank, "*Bank Non-performing Loans To Total Gross Loans %*". http://data.worldbank.org/indicator/FB.AST.NPER.ZS.

[68] *See*: https://www.ceicdata.com/en/indicator/malaysia/non-performing-loans-ratio.

down economic growth and sustainability efforts globally, have reduced international capital flows (specifically foreign investment and FDI)—NPL rates are key economic indicators for foreign investors. *Second*, in most democratic countries and even in socialist countries, high NPL rates have political ramifications especially during elections; and asset management corporations (AMCs) such as AMCON and high NPL rates are often precipitated by, and or amplify, constitutional political economy issues. High NPL rates can have significant negative psychological effects in terms of consumer confidence, business confidence, interest rates, consumer spending, intra-household disagreements and so on. More specifically, and since 2015, the economies of India, China and Russia have been significantly affected by high NPL rates of banks and finance companies. In most countries (both socialist and democratic), the use of either private or government-controlled AMCs often triggers economic psychology issues in several dimensions—such as pricing, estimation of risk, risk perception and liquidity. High NPL rates are a major geopolitical risk (because their magnitude, economic impact and political effects vary across countries). The sometimes symbiotic relationship between international capital flows and NPL rates is often omitted in studies of both phenomena, as was the case in Forbes, Warnock and Francis (2012). That is, international capital flows affect the supply of capital and loans, and corporate profitability; and conversely, NPL rates affect in-bound and out-bound capital flows. Morais et al. (2015) noted that US and European monetary policies affect the supply of credit from foreign banks to local firms in Mexico. Some AMCs raise capital from international investors for use in purchasing NPLs in their home countries. See the comments in Baskaya et al. (2017); De Bock and Demyanets (2012); and Beck et al. (2013). Like Nigeria, many emerging markets countries and some developed countries have bank-based or bank-driven economies, which often amplify the economic and sustainability effects of high NPL rates. During the last forty years and in most countries, the resolution of high NPL rates has taken the form of the creation of public AMCs and associated enabling statutes; but there have been mixed reviews of the effectiveness of AMCs whose performance seems to depend on its independence, the national legal framework, constitutions, the accountability within banks, effectiveness of the central bank and macro-prudential policies, politics and the nature of the banking system. Thomson (2010), Cassell and Hoffmann (2009) and Klingebiel (2000) surveyed various "asset management corporations" used for resolution of bank NPLs in various countries. Klingebiel (2000) concluded that in more than 66% of cases, AMCs were not efficient in corporate-loan or bank-loan restructuring, and also suggested that banks are better positioned to resolve NPLs than centralized AMCs.

Like many similar AMCs, AMCON's main purpose was to acquire defaulted loans from Nigerian banks, takeover troubled banks and infuse cash into both troubled borrowers and banks as a way of stabilizing the financial system. AMCON was created in 2010 by the AMCON Act of 2010, a federal statute (with the approval of the Nigerian President) even though there was evidence that very similar AMCs in other countries (specifically Ireland and Malaysia AMCs which AMCON had copied) had only a 33% (thirty-three percent) chance of succeeding—that is, there was substantial risk of constitutional political economy problems. Alford (2010, 2012) and Ogun (2012) discussed the enabling statutes and operations of AMCON (Nigeria).

3.10.1 AMCON's Power to Unilaterally Takeover Banks Without Third-Party Review Is Unconstitutional

Because the AMCON Act gives AMCON the power to take over any bank that it deems to be failing, and to purchase any bank asset at AMCON's discretion and without any judicial review or approval by another independent government agency or independent non-government entity (Section 30 of the *AMCON Act*), the AMCON Act constitutes a violation of *Procedural Due Process* rights, *Takings*[69] rights, *Substantive Due Process* rights and *Equal Protection* rights of banks and their shareholders. The relevant *State Actions* are the enactment of the AMCON Act and AMCON's activities. The government's interest in reducing banks' NPLs and stabilizing the banking sector is far outweighed by the negative information effects (e.g. contagion) and the economic, political and social harm caused by AMCON's takeover powers, and the deprivation of constitutional rights of banks, banks' shareholders and depositors, and borrowers of such banks. In the US, the Dodd-Frank Act empowers the US FSOC to take over banks

[69] *See*: *Federal Republic Of Germany Et Al.* vs. *Philipp Et Al.* (No. 19–351; February 3, 2021; US Supreme Court). https://www.supremecourt.gov/opinions/20pdf/19-351_o7jp.pdf.

See: Republic of Austria v. Altmann, 541 U. S. 677 (US Supreme Court).

See: Bolivarian Republic of Venezuela vs. Helmerich & Payne Int'l Drilling Co., 581 U. S. _____ (2017; US Supreme Court).

and large companies that are deemed to pose threats to financial stability but such takeover can be executed only after a court has reviewed the request.

3.10.2 The AMCON Act *of 2010 Is Constitutionally Void Because It's Very Vague*

The *Void-for-Vagueness* doctrine of constitutional law is usually applied to criminal statutes (USA). However, it's applied in the civil context here because of the following:

1. The *Substantial Control Doctrine* applies here, and there has been significant corruption in Nigeria (Nigeria ranks in the lowest fifth percentile among all countries based on various indices of corruption);
2. the significant ramifications of the AMCON Act; and
3. dealings between AMCON on one hand and banks and borrowers often involved criminal misconduct and fraud—and so there is a "derivative" triggering of criminal laws.

Collectively, the foregoing is henceforth referred to as the "*derivative applications theory*" and it can be applied in any field of law where the applicability of a legal doctrine is limited. The AMCON Act is constitutionally void because it's very vague about the following important issues:

1. the key elements and criteria for AMCON's takeover of distressed companies.
2. protection of due process rights of borrowers.
3. transparency of AMCON's activities.
4. elimination of political partisanship in AMCON's activities and in the appointment of AMCON's officers and Board Members.
5. checks and balances to prevent political manipulations and targeting of opposing political parties by AMCON.
6. the scope of activities and business life of AMCON.
7. the specific activities for which AMCON is completely "independent" from oversight or interference from any part of the government—independence is an issue because the CBN and the MoF have substantial direct/indirect influence and control over AMCON's operations and funding.

The AMCON Act expressly makes AMCON subject to any guidelines provided by the CBN. The AMCON Act expressly states that the MoF (Federal Ministry of Finance) and or the CBN can request that AMCON report to them at any time on any matter that concerns AMCON's business. Furthermore, the AMCON Act (AMCON Act, Part I, § 10, sub-section (d)) expressly grants the President of Nigeria the power to remove any AMCON Board member [upon recommendation by the CBN Governor] "if ... (d) his removal appears to be necessary or expedient for the effective performance of the functions of the Corporation". This term is clearly vague and does not contain the necessary qualifications to narrow the basis of removal to specific misconduct or conditions. The relevant *State Actions* are the enactment of the AMCON Act and AMCON's activities.

3.10.3 Burden on Interstate Commerce

Because the 2010 AMCON Act (and the 2015 AMCON Act and the 2019 AMCON Act) and AMCON's activities substantially increased bank's transaction costs and operating losses in Interstate Commerce, the amended AMCON Act constitutes a burden on interstate commerce, and thus is unconstitutional.

Since the AMCON Act does not compel AMCON to implement a uniform rule for selection of defaulted loans for purchase (but rather, allows selling banks to which of their loans that they will sell to AMCON which, in turn, creates *adverse selection*, *incentive deflation* and moral hazard), the AMCON Act constitutes a significant burden on interstate commerce, and also is a violation of the *Substantive Due Process rights* of banks' shareholders; and the AMCON Act reduces the government's property interest in ensuring the viability of banks and markets.

As explained herein, the *AMCON Tax* is unconstitutional and burdens banks, and since that tax is a major element of AMCON's activities and also defines a substantial portion of AMCON's socio-psychological impact on financial markets, bankers and credit rating agencies, AMCON and the AMCON Act are unconstitutional, and constitute burdens on commerce. The size of the AMCON Tax is proportional to the asset sizes of Nigerian banks without regard to their NPL rates and actual loan portfolios, and almost all the big banks in Nigeria are headquartered in Lagos State. Thus the AMCON Tax unfairly discriminates against the big Nigerian banks.

3.10.4 *The* Right-to-Contract Doctrine

The AMCON Act of 2010 (and the 2015 AMCON Act and the 2019 AMCON Act) is unconstitutional because it impairs or can impair the *Right-to-Contract* of various persons:

1) it impairs or can impair the *Right-to-Contract* of debtor banks/companies in the following ways: i) there is no mechanism for independent verification of AMCON's decision to take over a defaulting borrower company; ii) there is no mechanism for independent verification of AMCON's decision to take over a bank that is deemed to be financially distressed; iii) a false-positive decision or false-negative decision by AMCON to initiate prosecution/court-cases can have disastrous economic consequences—that is, the cost of AMCON errors is too high.
2) Under the AMCON Act of 2010, private companies were not allowed to purchase loans from banks under the same or similar terms as AMCON.
3) The right of AMCON (under the AMCON Act of 2010 and the AMCON Amendment Act of 2019) to file for ex parte court orders and to gain access to third-party bank accounts, cellphones/computers and mechanical devices has adverse information affects that can infringe on the alleged debtors rights-to-contract and opportunity set. Ideally such orders should be granted after a court-hearing for the alleged debtor.

The relevant *State Actions* are the enactment of the AMCON Act and the 2019 AMCON Act and AMCON's activities.

3.10.5 *The* Separation of Powers Doctrine

The AMCON Act of 2010, the 2015 AMCON Act and the 2019 AMCON Act violate the *Separation of Powers Doctrine* because AMCON acts as both a quasi-adjudicator (AMCON's decisions to take over borrowers or banks) and as enforcer of statutes (AMCON's use of creditor-debtor statutes, the AMCON Act and bankruptcy statutes); and as a rule-maker (AMCON enacted its own internal rules which are administrative laws). The relevant *State Actions* are the enactment of the AMCON Act and AMCON's activities. The government's interest in reducing NPLs and the perceived benefits of "delegation" of loan-recovery to AMCON are far outweighed by the economic and psychological losses caused by AMCON's activities.

3.10.6 AMCON's Loan Forbearance Process (Under The AMCON Act of 2010*) Is Unconstitutional*

AMCON's power to forgive/forbear any debt shall be exercisable only with approval of the Nigerian Federal Minister of Finance, and upon recommendation of the CBN. This process is deficient and is subject to political manipulation because there is no independent or judicial review of the decision. Thus, AMCON's loan forbearance approval process constitutes violations of the *Procedural Due Process*, *Substantive Due Process* and *Equal Protection* rights of banks and their shareholders, and defaulting borrowers. The relevant *State Actions* are the enactment of the AMCON Act and AMCON's activities. The government's interest in reducing NPLs and the perceived benefits loan forbearance by AMCON are far outweighed by the economic and psychological losses caused by AMCON's activities and unconstitutional loan-forbearance procedures.

3.10.7 The Takings[70] Doctrine*: The Regulatory Rent-Extraction Inherent in AMCON's Operations Is Unconstitutional*

Banks' shareholders and depositors (especially those that lost money because their banks were taken over by AMCON or were sold) are not shareholders of AMCON. If AMCON recovers the face values of the NPLs that it purchased at significant discounts, then these two groups would have suffered unnecessary losses and the government (the CBN and the MoF) will reap a windfall. In such circumstances and given the arbitrary process used (by banks and AMCON) for selecting bank-loans for purchase by AMCON, this type of regulatory "rent-extraction" is unconstitutional and constitutes a violation of the *Substantive Due Process* rights and *Takings* rights of such bank shareholders and depositors. The

[70] *See*: *Federal Republic Of Germany Et Al.* vs. *Philipp Et Al.* (No. 19–351; February 3, 2021; US Supreme Court). https://www.supremecourt.gov/opinions/20pdf/19-351_o7jp.pdf.

See: Republic of Austria v. Altmann, 541 U. S. 677 (US Supreme Court).

See: Bolivarian Republic of Venezuela vs. Helmerich & Payne Int'l Drilling Co., 581 U. S. _____ (2017; US Supreme Court).

relevant *State Actions* are the enactment of the AMCON Act and AMCON's activities. The government's interest in reducing NPLs and stabilizing the banking industry are far outweighed by the economic and psychological losses caused by AMCON's activities.

3.10.8 The Equal Protection Doctrine

The relevant *State Actions* are the enactment of the AMCON Act and AMCON's activities.

Given the amount of resources of the Central Bank and the Nigerian federal government that were and are to be devoted to AMCON, the AMCON Act of 2010 unfairly discriminated between the banking industry on one hand, and other industries that were bailed out by the Nigerian government (e.g. securities brokerage industries; and the GENCOs/DISCOs in the power industry) because companies in those industries were not subjected to similar harsh bailout terms. Similarly, the AMCON Act unfairly discriminates against other troubled Nigerian industries that weren't bailed-out by the Nigerian government. Thus, the AMCON Act violates the *Equal Protection rights* of Nigerian banks and their shareholders and companies in other troubled Nigerian industries.

AMCON's power to forgive/forbear any debt shall be exercisable only with approval of the Minister of Finance, and upon recommendation of the CBN. This process is deficient and is subject to political manipulation because there is no independent or judicial review of the decision. Thus, AMCON's loan forbearance approval process constitutes violations of the *Equal Protection rights* of banks and their shareholders, and the affected borrowers. The government's interest in reducing NPLs and the perceived benefits loan forbearance by AMCON are far outweighed by the economic and psychological losses caused by AMCON's activities and loan-forbearance procedures.

3.10.9 AMCON's Activities (Under The AMCON Act of 2010 *and The Amendments of 2015 and 2019) Violated the* Non-Delegation Doctrine *(Unconstitutional Delegation)*

The Nigerian Deposit Insurance Corporation (NDIC) was created by the Nigeria Deposit Insurance Corporation Act of 1990, and is a government agency that reports to the Nigerian Federal MoF. The NDIC's statutory mandate includes: i) advising the CBN in the liquidation of distressed banks, and the management of distressed banks' assets until they are fully liquidated, and ii) joint supervision of insured banks (with CBN), and iii) the prevention of perceived or actual financial instability caused by bank-runs and loss of depositors' confidence. The NDIC is a member of the Financial Reporting Council of Nigeria. Under the AMCON Act of 2010, AMCON effectively took over some of the functions of the NDIC (i.e. the AMCON Act preempted the Nigeria Deposit Insurance Corporation Act of 1990). The alternative would have been for the Nigerian Legislature to have granted the NDIC more powers and significant independence from both the CBN and the MoF—that is, (i) the statutory powers to purchase defaulted loans and or to create a subsidiary that is similar to AMCON; and (ii) the power to liquidate troubled and insolvent banks; and power to enact rules/regulations that supplements CBN rules pertaining to banks' accounting disclosures; (iii) the power to fine non-compliant banks; (iv) the power to oversee NPL management and collateral management. Thus, this type of *Regulatory Delegation* to AMCON is redundant and may be deemed unconstitutional because: (i) as explained herein, AMCON's activities reduce or restrict the *Due Process, Equal Protection* and *Takings* rights of various persons; (ii) such delegation can increase transaction costs and enforcement costs of affected persons, banks and government agencies; (iii) it reduces or can reduce the government's interest in maintaining or increasing financial stability (i.e. as explained herein, AMCON is inefficient). Furthermore, the high NPL problem in Nigerian banks began around 2006–2007 but the AMCON Act was enacted in June 2010, which was approximately one year before the 2011 Nigerian elections (for local, state and federal positions). The implication or reasonable inference is that the creation of AMCON may have been wholly or partly motivated either by political considerations or by the need to shift blame or to cover up mistakes. The relevant *State Actions* are the enactment of the AMCON Act and AMCON's activities. The government's interest in reducing NPLs and improving Financial Stability, as well as the perceived benefits of delegation to AMCON are far outweighed by the economic and psychological losses caused by AMCON's activities.

3.10.10 Unconstitutional Preemption

As stated in Ofo (2011), the AMCON Act conflicted with, or modified or preempted sections of the Nigerian *Companies and Allied Matters Act* (bankruptcy law), the *Land-use Act* and some procedural laws in Nigeria. Specifically, Ofo (2011) noted the following conflicts:

1. *Company And Bankruptcy Law*—Ofo (2011) stated in part:
   "First, under Nigerian company law, there are basically three modes of winding up a company provided for by the *Companies and Allied Matters Act*. These are by the court, voluntarily, and subject to the supervision of the court. Section 408 of the CAMA further provides for five grounds for the winding up of a company by the court. One of the grounds for the winding up of a company by the court is 'where the company is unable to pay its debts'. Section-409 of the CAMA defines the circumstances when a company may be deemed to be unable to pay its debts. However, section 52 of the AMCON Act has extended the circumstances when a company may be deemed to be unable to pay its debts for the purposes of winding up proceedings against a debtor company. In addition, by virtue of section-54(4) of the AMCON Act, it is contended that an additional ground for winding up by the court has been introduced into Nigerian company law for affected companies. According to section-54(4) of the AMCON Act, the fact of the conviction of a company for any of the offences provided for in section-54(1) & (2) of the AMCON Act is a ground for the winding up of such a company. This fact of conviction can now be regarded as a sixth ground for winding up by the Court … In relation to a company defaulting in its debt obligations, section-290 of the CAMA recognizes the personal liability of directors and officers of a company where the company received loan or other property for a particular purpose but the money or property was fraudulently diverted for other purposes … This straightforward provision appears to have been substantially modified by the AMCON Act where the debt concerned is owed to an EFI. This could be the basis for a bankruptcy proceeding against a director of the company under section-51 of the AMCON Act. Also, by virtue of section-49(1) of the AMCON Act, possession of the movable and immovable property of a director of such debtor company may, upon an ex parte application made to the court, be granted to the AMCON. The extension of the provisions of Sections 49(1) & 51 of the AMCON Act to directors of a debtor company is achieved by the definition of the terms 'debtor' and 'debtor company' in section-61 of the AMCON Act."
2. The Nigerian *Land Use Act* of 1978—under the Nigerian *Land Use Act*, a Governor's consent is mandatorily required before any land/improvements that is transferred via assignment, mortgage, charge

and so on, is formally registered (i.e. Certificate of Occupancy). Ofo (2011) presented two conflicting groups of statutes within the AMCON Act, and noted that under the *AMCON Act*, it's not clear whether a Governor's consent is required for the transfer of Eligible Bank Assets (EBAs) that are land, to AMCON. Ofo (2011) states that the first group of statutes within the AMCON Act require the Governor's consent for land transfers—such as Section 34(1;2) and Section 34(4) of the AMCON Act (which makes the Eligible Financial Institution [EFI] a "bare trustee" of such land for the sole benefit of AMCON; and Section 12(c)(iii) of the Asset Management Corporation of Nigeria Guidelines No. 1 of 2010 (which empowers AMCON to appoint third party service providers to perfect AMCON's rights and interests in any collateral or other security). Also the Land Use Act isn't listed in Section 60(1) of the AMCON Act which lists the statutes whose provisions shall not apply to AMCON. Conversely, Ofo (2011) noted that the opposing (second) group of statutes consists of Section 45 of the AMCON Act, pursuant to which the Governor's consent isn't required for land transfers—that section states that where an EBA has been acquired by AMCON, AMCON shall not be required to become registered as owner of any security that is part of that EBA but in the interim, AMCON shall have the powers and rights of a registered owner of such security under any law; and at its discretion, AMCON may elect to register any interest capable of registration.

3. *Procedural Law*—Section 53 of the AMCON Act of 2010 empowered the Chief Judge of the Federal High Court to designate any Judge of the Federal High Court to exclusively adjudicate only lawsuits/claims for the recovery of debts owed to AMCON or an EFI and other matters arising from the AMCON Act for such period as may be determined by the Chief Judge. There is only one Federal High Court in Nigeria but it has numerous Judicial Divisions all over the country. Also under Section 55 of the AMCON Act of 2010, only the Attorney general of Nigeria can prosecute offences punishable under the AMCON Act (the Police and the state Attorney Generals cannot prosecute).

Although Ofo (2011) did not address the administrative law issues (that pertain to the NDIC) or constitutional law issues, such conflicts of law or preemption are or may be unconstitutional because they interfere with the *Equal Protection*, *Takings*, *Procedural Due Process* and *Substantive Due Process* rights of companies and individuals whose loans were purchased by AMCON; or who were contacted by AMCON as a prelude to purchasing their loans. The relevant *State Actions* are the enactment of the AMCON Act of 2010 and AMCON's activities.

3.10.11 The Nigerian President's Removal Option in the AMCON Act *of 2010 Is Unconstitutional*

Under Section 14(2) of the AMCON Act, the President of Nigeria has the power to remove any member of the Board of Directors of AMCON—this *Removal Option* eliminates any and all independence from AMCON's operations. Under generally accepted common law constitutional law principles, this *Removal Option* is unconstitutional because: i) it is overbroad and grants the President excessive powers; ii) it eliminates the independence of AMCON and makes AMCON subject to political manipulation and or the constant threat of political manipulation, and damage to careers of AMCON BOD members; iii) it eliminates the checks and balances that are a core principle of the Nigerian democratic system (and most other democratic systems) wherein none of the three arms of government (executive, judicial and legislative branches) are allowed to wield excessive power; iv) it unfairly interferes with the Due Process rights and Equal Protection rights of such AMCON BOD members and the companies whose assets have been purchased or taken over by AMCON. The relevant *State Actions* are the enactment of the AMCON Act and AMCON's activities.

The government's interest in reducing banks' NPLs (nonperforming loans) and improving Financial Stability by creating AMCON is far outweighed by the economic, political and social harm caused by AMCON's loan-buying, foreclosure and restructuring activities, some of which are described herein.

3.10.12 The Right-to-Privacy Doctrine

The relevant *State Actions* are the enactment of the AMCON Act and AMCON's activities.

The AMCON Amendment Act of 2019 grants AMCON (through ex-parte court orders) extensive rights to place bank accounts of alleged debtors under surveillance and to access computer/mechanical devices of alleged debtors (in search of assets and debts). Such unprecedented powers may constitute a violation of Section 37 and Section 45(1) (privacy)[71] of the 1999 Constitution of Nigeria, and violation of the *Privacy Rights* of such alleged debtors.

3.10.13 The **Procedural Due Process Doctrine**

The AMCON Act of 2010 and the AMCON Amendment Act of 2019 both contain constitutionally suspect procedural deficiencies that may violate the *Procedural Due Process Doctrine.* For example, the AMCON Amendment Act of 2019 grants AMCON (through ex parte court orders) extensive rights to place bank accounts of alleged debtors under surveillance and to access computer/mechanical devices of alleged debtors (in search of assets and debts). Such unprecedented powers may constitute a violation of Section 37 of the Nigerian Constitution, and violation of the *Procedural Due Process* rights of such alleged debtors.

The AMCON Act of 2010 and the AMCON Amendment Act of 2019 both contain statutes that permit court to grants ex parte orders in favor of AMCON based only AMCON's allegations of indebtedness and without a fair hearing for the alleged debtor. That seems to violate Section-36[72] of the 1999 Constitution of Nigeria.

AMCON's power to forgive/forbear any debt shall be exercisable only with approval of the Minister of Finance, and upon recommendation of the CBN. This process is deficient and is subject to political manipulation because there is no independent or judicial review of the decision. Thus, AMCON's loan forbearance approval process constitutes violations of the *Procedural Due Process rights* of banks and their shareholders, and the affected borrowers. The government's interest in reducing NPLs and Financial Instability, and the perceived benefits loan forbearance by AMCON are far outweighed by the economic and psychological losses caused by AMCON's activities.

[71] *See: "AMCON (amendment #2) Act, 2019 And Its Weighty Flaws"*. Oct. 15, 2019. https://www.pressreader.com/nigeria/thisday/20191015/281887300072887.
See: Gbejuade vs. Gbejuade, LPELR-419977 (2017).
See: Okolonji vs. Mbanefo, LPELR-41887 (2017).
See: Spiess vs. Oni, LPELR-40502 (2016).
See: Achebe vs. Mbanefo, LPELR-41886 (2017).

[72] *See: Garba vs. University of Maiduguri* (1986) 1 NWLR Pt 18 pg. 55O SC.
See: Mai Rai vs. Bauchi Native Authority (1957) N.R.N.LR. 115 at 116.

During 2019, a Lagos high court declared Section 34(6)[73] of the AMCON Amendment No. 2 Act of 2019 to be unconstitutional, primarily because it barred the court from issuing injunctions against AMCON. Other persons have also claimed that the AMCON Amendment Act of 2019 is unconstitutional.[74]

3.10.14 The Substantive Due Process Doctrine

The AMCON Act of 2010 and the AMCON Amendment Act of 2019 both contain constitutionally suspect substantive deficiencies. Both statutes unfairly discriminate between alleged debtors that that have sufficient social capital and social networks to prevent AMCON investigations and ex-parte orders, and those that don't.

Banks' shareholders and depositors (especially those that lost money because their banks were taken over by AMCON or were sold) are not shareholders of AMCON. If AMCON recovers the face values of the NPLs that it purchased at significant discounts, then these two groups would have suffered unnecessary losses and the government (the CBN and the MoF) will reap a windfall. In such circumstances, this form of regulatory "Rent-Extraction" is unconstitutional and constitutes a violation of the *Substantive Due Process* rights of such shareholders and depositors.

Since the AMCON Act does not compel AMCON to implement a uniform rule for the selection of defaulted loans for purchase, but rather, allows selling banks to select their loans for sale to AMCON (which, in turn, creates Adverse Selection, Incentive-Deflation and Moral Hazard), the AMCON Act constitutes a violation of the *Substantive Due Process rights* of banks' shareholders; and the AMCON Act reduces the government's property interest in ensuring the viability of banks and markets.

AMCON's power to forgive/forbear any debt shall be exercisable only with approval of the Minister of Finance, and upon recommendation of

[73] *See: Court Declares Section 36(4) Of AMCON (Amendment 2) Unconstitutional.* Oct 29, 2019. https://www.miyettilaw.com/blog/court-declares-section-364-of-amcon-amendment-2-unconstitutional/. ("AMCON had opposed the application by relying on Section 34(6) of the AMCON(Amendment No. 2) Act, 2019, which states that no injunction shall be made against it. But in her ruling, Justice Jose invalidated AMCON's reasoning and granted the prayer. The judge held that the said AMCON provision was unconstitutional as it sought to curtail the powers of the court".)

[74] *See: "AMCON (amendment #2) Act, 2019 And Its Weighty Flaws".* Oct. 15, 2019. https://www.pressreader.com/nigeria/thisday/20191015/281887300072887.

the CBN. This process is deficient and is subject to political manipulation because there is no independent or judicial review of the decision. Thus, AMCON's loan forbearance approval process constitutes violations of the *Substantive Due Process rights* of affected banks and their shareholders, and the affected borrowers. The government's interest in reducing NPLs and the perceived benefits loan forbearance by AMCON are far outweighed by the economic and psychological losses caused by AMCON's activities.

The relevant *State Actions* are the enactment of the AMCON Act and AMCON's activities.

3.10.15 The Inefficient and Unconstitutional **AMCON Tax**

The inefficient annual "AMCON Tax" on banks in Nigeria is used to fund the *Resolution Cost Fund*—and is an annual cash payment equal to 0.5% of each bank's total assets plus 0.5% of 33% of their off-balance-sheet items. Under generally accepted common law principles of constitutional law, the *AMCON Tax* is unconstitutional for the following reasons.

The *AMCON Tax* does not provide sufficient incentives for banks and borrowers to address the issue of loan/securities defaults because it's over-broad (and not narrowly tailored to achieve the objective of reducing credit risk and loan losses) and targets both potentially harmful assets (e.g. loans, bonds and guarantees) and non-harmful assets (intangibles/goodwill, PP&E, cash, cash-equivalents, prepaid expenses, etc.). That is: i) the AMCON Tax taxes all of a bank's activities instead of taxing only its lending activities which are the primary cause of NPLs; ii) the AMCON Tax is uniform across all banks instead of being based on each bank's historical and current NPL rates and the actual risk of their loan portfolios (which varies drastically across banks as confirmed by AMCON's loan buying activities). Such over-broadness reduces banks' incentives to diversify their assets, invest in cash-equivalents and increase their non-interest income.

The AMCON Tax is discriminatory because most companies in other industries that were bailed out by the Nigerian government (e.g. securities brokerages, and the GENCOs/DISCOs in the power generation industry) were not subjected to such taxes. The AMCON Tax causes big banks (the Tier-One banks which control a substantial percentage of assets in the Nigerian banking industry) to subsidize the risk-taking of smaller, less-efficient or badly managed Nigerian banks. The AMCON Tax unfairly discriminates between banks for whom loans constitute a low percentage of their total assets, and banks for whom loans constitute a high percentage of their total assets. The AMCON Tax unfairly discriminates between banks that have effective credit policies (they pay proportionately higher taxes—discriminatory over-payment) and banks that don't (they pay proportionately lower taxes—discriminatory under-payment). Thus the AMCON Tax infringes banks' *Right-to-Contract* and violates the *Substantive Due Process Rights* and *Equal Protection* rights of banks and their shareholders.

The AMCON Tax increases financial instability partly because it constitutes a substantial portion of the bank's operating incomes, and it causes psychological and economic effects that create or foster financial contagion within markets and contagion among credit rating agencies. The AMCON Tax unfairly and discriminately burdens Nigerian banks and amounted to 6%–13% of each bank's annual operating profits during 2013–2016 and hampers banks' flexibility, operating results and current/future credit ratings. Thus, the AMCON Tax is a substantial incentive for banks to engage in earnings management and fraud.

The AMCON Tax was not the best way of handling past or future loan/credit losses of banks. This is confirmed by the relatively low credit ratings assigned to Nigerian banks by Moody's/S&P/Fitch during 2011–2020. The inefficiencies and harm caused by the AMCON Tax far outweigh the government's interest in NPL resolution. As noted herein and below, there are more efficient alternatives to the AMCON Tax.

Feasible alternatives to the AMCON Tax include but are not limited to the following:

1. Having the banks issue exchange-traded preferred stock and or shares to AMCON which will sell such shares in the open market until it realizes an equivalent amount of cash—and perhaps the AMCON zero-coupon bonds should have been convertible in whole or part into baskets of some of such shares.
2. Reserving a portion of the total monthly compensation of lending/credit officers and senior management of banks for up to six years, and using such cash to offset any future loan losses.
3. Imposing a mandatory "Borrower tax" on all borrowers which will be paid as a percentage of loan proceeds plus a percentage of the amount of all their existing bank loans; adjusted by a "multiplier" (e.g. of 1.0-1.25) that varies inversely with the bank's credit-quality or asset-quality.
4. Imposing a mandatory "Lender-Tax" on all lenders which will be paid as a percentage of interest income earned from loans plus a percentage of their existing loan portfolios; adjusted by a "multi-

plier" (e.g. of 1.0–1.25) that varies inversely with the bank's credit quality or asset quality. A portion of this lender tax can also be deducted from the compensation of bank executives and loan officers.

5. Imposing a mandatory "investment tax" on all securities investors which will be a percentage of all paid cash interest income earned from all non-government fixed-income investments (and remitted to the Central Bank).
6. Imposing a mandatory "auditor tax" on all external auditors of individuals/companies that borrow amounts that exceed a threshold level, from a bank or finance company. The tax will be a percentage of all paid audit fees earned from such individuals/companies, adjusted by a "multiplier" (e.g. of 1.0–1.25) that varies inversely with the borrower's asset quality or credit quality (and should be remitted to the Central Bank).

The foregoing proposed taxation models are based on the following general principles:

1. Direct/Indirect Causation—In the context of reduction of social welfare caused by loan defaults, the external auditors, borrowers and lenders can be deemed to be joint-tortfeasors or joint-perpetrators of criminal activities, but with different proportions of liability.
2. *Proportionality*—the taxation models can account for changes in both loan/bond volume and changes in the credit quality and risk-management processes of the bank.
3. Temporal and financial matching.
4. *Incentive neutrality*—the taxation models have minimal impact on incentive effects of incentive compensation;
5. *Size neutrality*—the taxation models implicitly adjust for differences in size of banks (measured by loan-portfolio, asset-size or book equity).
6. *Specificity*—the taxes are narrowly tailored to address the issues of improper due diligence, inefficient lending procedures and fraudulent borrower misconduct.

3.11 The Failure and Government Bailout/Bail-in of the Nigerian Power Industry: Some Constitutional Political Economy Problems

During 2005, the Nigerian federal legislature enacted the Electric Power Sector Reform Act 2005 (the EPSRA or Power Statute) for the simultaneous bailout/bail-in and privatization of the Nigerian power industry which at the time was controlled by one government-owned monopolist (NEPA).

EPSRA was a politically motivated bailout because: i) during 2000–2005, inadequate power supply had become a national political campaign issue that couldn't be ignored by political parties (many complainants, the popular press and politicians linked Nigeria's poor economy, low industrial output, high unemployment, crime and other problems to inadequate power supply); ii) NEPA was highly inefficient and unprofitable and couldn't supply adequate and constant power to Nigerian households, companies and government agencies, iii) EPSRA called for significant investments in the Nigerian power industry by the Nigerian government. The EPSRA and the associated privatization were also a politically motivated bail-in because: (i) EPSRA changed both the industry structure and the ownership structure in the Nigerian Power industry, and introduced "DISCOs" (electricity distribution companies) and "GENCOs" (power generation companies), many of which were partly owned by the Nigerian federal government; (ii) EPSRA introduced the Nigerian Electricity Regulatory Commission (NERC), the Transmission Company of Nigeria (TCN; which retained ownership of the power transmission network) and the NBET, all of which were initially subsidiaries of the federal Ministry of Power & Works; (iii) EPSRA and the associated privatization directly and indirectly imposed debts on, and changed the allocation of rights, obligations and payments in the Nigerian power industry. See the comments in: Olalere (2014), Oriakhogba and Odiase-Alegimenlen (2011), Adedeji (2017), Ukoha and Agbaeze (2018), Ajumogobia and Okeke (2015).

Inadequate power supply in Nigeria has had significant psychological effect on the indigenes as evidenced by articles in newspapers and events—such as, (i) general disillusionment and depression, (ii) low consumer confidence and business confidence; (iii) changes in risk perception; iv) high youth unemployment which increases crime; v) relatively low entrepreneurship (compared to developed countries).

The privatization of the Nigerian power industry became effective in 2013, but the entire process (i.e. legislative process, the post-legislation design of the new industry structure and the implementation of the statutes and the new industry structure) was controversial, and most of the resulting

DISCOs (electricity distribution companies) and GENCOs (power generation companies) were awarded to politicians or politically connected business professionals through questionable bidding processes. During 2013–2020, it was widely rumored in Nigeria that many of these politician-owners were giving bribes to members of the Nigerian federal legislature in order to avoid government investigations and prosecution. During 2013–2020, there were significant volumes of consumer and corporate complaints about unfair business practices, overbilling and fraud by DISCOs. The GENCOs also complained about unfair business practices by DISCOs.

Some of the constitutional law problems inherent in EPSRA,[75] the associated privatization process and orders/notices issued by both the federal Ministry of Power (formerly and until 2019, the federal Ministry of Power, Works & Housing) and NERC are as follows:

1. The *Equal Protection Doctrine*—the Nigerian government discriminated against other financially/operationally distressed industries that deserved the same government bailouts/interventions.
2. The *Separation of Powers Doctrine*—The Federal Ministry of power (formerly and until 2019, the federal Ministry of Power, Works & Housing) and its subsidiary agencies (such as NERC) have been serving as rule-makers, enforcement agents and adjudicators in the Nigerian power industry, which violates the *Separation of Powers Doctrine*.
3. The *Right-to-Contract Doctrine*—the EPSRA and the enforcement and adjudication activities of the federal ministry of power and the NERC infringe the Rights-to-Contract of owners/operators of GENCOs and DISCOs, and consumers, by: (1) the NERC's and the federal ministry's issuance of orders/regulations that conflict with the privatization contracts and or EPSRA, (2) the NERC and the federal ministry of Power directly or indirectly imposing additional costs on DISCOs and GENCOs; (3) restrictions of the strategic and contracting options/

[75] *See: "Conflicting Laws Keep Nigeria's Electricity Supply Unreliable"*, August 23, 2017, by Professor Yemi Oke. https://theconversation.com/conflicting-laws-keep-nigerias-electricity-supply-unreliable-81393 ("Nigeria's energy sector is regulated centrally by the Nigerian Electricity Regulatory Commission. This has created the conditions for corruption to thrive. The result is that the supply of electricity is unstable and cannot support economic development. Decentralised regulation is the solution, but has been prevented by conflicting laws … The result is corruption, poor service delivery and use of substandard equipment. Gas pipelines are sometimes vandalised by frustrated citizens whose local needs are not understood or met").

opportunities of DISCOs and GENCOs by NERC and or the federal Ministry of Power; (4) directly or indirectly imposing additional costs on customers (e.g. permitting DISCOs to illegally pass on costs to customers, such as the costs of meters and poles).

4. The *Procedural Due Process Doctrine*—the implementation of EPSRA (and subsequent regulations by the federal Ministry of Power) discriminated against the eventual owners of DISCOs and GENCOs—for example by: (1) denying them their area-franchising rights; (2) imposing additional costs on them; (3) violating EPSRA and the privatization agreements; and so on. The Nigerian government apparently didn't disclose the full state of the GENCOs and DISCOs to prospective buyers, or the prospective buyers didn't conduct thorough due diligence, or they weren't allowed to complete due diligence and the Nigerian government hasn't complied with all the terms of the privatization contracts and hasn't invested the capital that it promised to invest in the power industry as part of the privatization.
5. The *Substantive Due Process Doctrine*—the EPSRA and the ongoing regulations/Orders/Notices issued by the federal Ministry of Power and NERC during 2005–2018 were often vague, were sometimes conflicting and not sufficient to address the many post-privatization problems that have arisen in the Nigerian power industry. The implementation of EPSRA (and subsequent regulations by the federal Ministry of Power) discriminated against the eventual owners of DISCOs and GENCOs—for example by: (1) denying them their area-franchising rights; (2) imposing additional costs on them. The foregoing constituted violations of the Substantive Due Process rights of GENCOs, and/or DISCOs and or their customers.
6. The *Non-Delegation Doctrine*—it appears that the federal Ministry of Power (formerly and until 2019, the federal Ministry of Power, Works & Housing) and NERC have been enacting regulations and Executive Orders which they weren't authorized to enact, and/or which were within the exclusive jurisdiction of the Nigerian federal legislature (and the legislature didn't delegate any such rule-making powers to them), and/or which contravened EPSRA and the privatization contracts. For example, during May 2017, both the Nigerian federal minister for power and the NERC announced that GENCOs were free to supply power directly to four types of end-users beginning from May 15, 2017 and pursuant to Section-27 of the Electric Power Sector Reform Act 2005 (EPSRA)—that move was criticized by Nigerian legal scholars as

being in bad faith and not in accordance with the law[76]—it violated the EPSRA and the privatization contracts.

7. Burden On *Interstate Commerce*: the EPSRA and the NERC's regulations/Orders could be deemed to have burdened interstate commerce because: (1) the application of EPSRA and the NERC's Orders to GENCOs and DISCOs across Nigerian states differed in terms of magnitude/severity, costs and impact on customers; (2) the application of the orders of NERC and the federal Ministry Of Power differed across the states and had non-uniform impact on different GENCOs and DISCOs based on their location; (3) the application of EPSRA and the NERC's Orders to GENCOs and DISCOs across Nigerian states had or could have had different economic and psychological impact on customers depending on their geographical location in various Nigerian states. Some customers in some Nigerian states were made to bear the costs of meters and poles, and were subjected to "estimated billing" while customers in other states weren't.
8. *Preemption Doctrine—Preemption* remains an issue because there are conflicts of laws between Nigerian federal and state statutes/regulations that pertain to the power industry. Some researchers have noted that such conflicts makes the NERC (and/or some of its activities)[77] unconstitutional.

[76] *See*: "*Don Faults FG On Direct Sale Of Electricity To End Users*". May 23, 2017. *The Guardian* (Nigerian newspaper), page-27. https://guardian.ng/business-services/don-faults-fg-on-direct-sale-of-electricity-to-end-users/.

[77] *See*: "*Conflicting Laws Keep Nigeria's Electricity Supply Unreliable*", August 23, 2017, by Professor Yemi Oke. https://theconversation.com/conflicting-laws-keep-nigerias-electricity-supply-unreliable-81393 ("The Act provides for the establishment of the Rural Electrification Agency. This administers a Rural Electrification Fund which is meant to provide, promote and support rural electrification programmes. The roles played by the agency (NERC) and the fund conflict with the Constitution. This is because the Constitution assigns these roles to the states. The Constitution gives states the powers to regulate off-grid electric power. And rural electricity is off-grid power. .... There is a third problem with the act. It gives the Nigerian Electricity Regulatory Commission ('NERC' or the 'Commission') the power to make regulations for the granting of permits for 'captive power' generation. The objective is to streamline the procedure for those who want to generate more than one megawatt of power for their own use. This power should ordinarily vest in state governments. Like rural electricity, captive electricity generation is off-grid, and should be regulated by state governments as the Constitution intended. The commission's (NERC's) powers are therefore unconstitutional").

The privatization of the Nigerian power industry has failed,[78] and as of 2021, that industry remained at risk of collapsing. After 2013, the Nigerian government and the Nigerian Central Bank repeatedly bailed out the Nigerian power industry through loans and subsidies. Most of the structural agreements that underpin the privatization have either been breached or are not in place.[79] The 2016–2021 industry structure is as follows. Each

[78] *See*: "Woeful Performance Of DISCOs". http://nationalmirroronline.net/new/woeful-performance-of-discos/.

July 18, 2014.

See: "*NERC Bows To Consumers' Pressure, Sets Target For DISCOs*". Mar 23, 2014. *This Day*. http://www.thisdaylive.com/articles/nerc-bows-to-consumers-pressure-sets-target-for-discos/174317/.

See: Oni, M. (Mayer Brown) (2014). *Power Sector Privatization In Nigeria: Opportunities And Challenges*. https://www.mayerbrown.com/files/uploads/Documents/PDFs/2014/Energy-Review.pdf?utm_source=Mondaq&utm_medium=syndication&utm_campaign=View-Original.

See: Banwo & Ighodalo (2013). *The Nigerian Power Sector Legal/Regulatory Framework—Key Financing Considerations*. http://www.banwo-ighodalo.com/assets/resources/378fdcdef57c4be50d521a2c2c8c4ea5.pdf.

See: Adesina, K. (2016). "*An Operator's Perspective of the Nigerian Power Sector*". https://www.google.com.ng/url?sa=t&rct=j&q=&esrc=s&source=web&cd=18&ved=0ahUKEwibg82GlbHSAhWHvRoKHZ3nCUE4ChAWCEgwBw&url=http%3A%2F%2Fwww.lbs.edu.ng%2FLBSBreakfastClub%2FAn%2520Operator%27s%2520View%2520of%2520the%2520Power%2520Sector.pdf&usg=AFQjCNEBK3o0ygVhSD6bgHrgR4Ontm7gJQ&sig2=0BmSsjDBJqb0hwQird3iJw.

See: Latham & Watkins (2016). *Nigerian Power Sector: Opportunities and Challenges for Investment in 2016—A summary of the existing power sector in Nigeria, current key initiatives, and opportunities and challenges for developers, investors and lenders*. https://www.lw.com/thoughtLeadership/lw-nigerian-power-sector-opps-and-challenges.

See: Ajumogobia and Okeke (2015). *Nigerian Energy Sector: Legal & Regulatory Overview (2015)*. http://www.ajumogobiaokeke.com/assets/media/1656f5aded41ecbbbb7e451a778c5e1d.pdf.

See: *Energy Situation Report—West Africa*. http://e4sv.org/wp-content/uploads/2016/10/West-Africa-Energy-Report-AW-Draft-3-200516-V3_MT.pdf.

See: "*Power: Liquidity crisis, same old story in 2020?—FG will bear a financial burden of N544.894 billion in 2020 being the cumulative shortfall in electricity tariffs of the eleven DISCOs*". January 6, 2020. By CSL Stockbrokers. https://nairametrics.com/2020/01/06/power-liquidity-crisis-same-old-story-in-2020/.

See: SERAP (August 2017). "*From Darkness to Darkness: How Nigerians are Paying the Price for Corruption in the Electricity Sector*" (Socio-Economic Rights and Accountability Project (SERAP); Lagos, Nigeria). http://serap-nigeria.org/wp-content/uploads/2017/08/CORRUPTION-IN-ELECTRICITY-REPORT-A4.pdf.

[79] *See*: "Nigerian Power Sector Is In Crisis!" By Odion Omonfoman. *Premium Times*, June 28, 2016.

GENCO and DISCO is restricted to a specific region. GENCOs (buy gas from suppliers and) generate power which they sell to NBET, and the DISCOs buy power from NBET and distribute power to, and collect fees from customers, while TCN (a government entity) does the transmission. NBET is a government entity (NBET was capitalized with more than US$800 million; and during 2020, NBET was moved from the federal ministry of Power & Works into the federal ministry of Finance) and contractually guarantees payment to GENCOs for power that they supply. It seems that NBET has not been performing its guarantee to the GENCOs. There seems to be a mismatch wherein: (i) DISCOs are not generating sufficient revenues to pay GENCOs; (ii) DISCOs have been rejecting power supplied by GENCOs;[80] (iii) these two trends have left NBET regularly incapable of meeting its financial obligations to GENCOs. The DISCOs provided letters of credit to NBET to cover their power purchases and in August 2016, NBET authorized GENCOs to draw-down on those

http://opinion.premiumtimesng.com/2016/06/28/173605/. This article states in part: "Recently, two Federal High Courts granted separate restraining orders against the Nigerian Electricity Regulatory Commission (NERC) and the Nigerian Bulk Electricity Trading Plc (NBET) at the instance of some electricity distribution companies (DISCOs) who took both NERC and NBET to court. The DISCOs are praying the courts to compel NERC and NBET from enforcing the commercial terms of the various industry contracts they entered into at the conclusion of the privatization of successor PHCN companies. ...The power sector is yet to attain a contractual market status. Under the Electric Power Sector Reform Act (EPSRA) 2005, the electricity market in Nigeria would be administered by a number of industry contracts and market rules. The declaration of the Transitional Electricity Market (TEM) would signal the commencement of these contracts. In 2015, TEM was declared but the conditions for declaring it are still far away. Without effective contracts—Power Purchase Agreements (PPA), Ancillary Agreements, Gas Supply Agreements (GSA), Vesting Contracts between DISCOs and NBET and other industry contracts—TEM cannot be said to have taken off ... One of the key requirements for the declaration of TEM was the posting of payment securities in the form of back-to-back letters of credit (L/C) between DISCOs and NBET under the Vesting Contracts, and between NBET and GENCOs under the PPA. To date, a number of DISCOs have not posted their payment securities. This is a fundamental breach of the Performance Agreement between the Core Investors and the Bureau of Public Enterprises (BPE) as it is a clear indication of the lack of financial capacity of Core Investors in DISCOs to adequately provide capital (equity and/or long-term debt) to fund DISCO operations. In addition, NBET is yet to activate the PPAs with GENCOs. However to its credit, NBET has just completed a securitization process that would enable it post its own L/Cs to GENCOs. Hopefully, that would lead to the activation of the PPAs soon".

[80] *See:* "Baru: DISCOs' Rejection Of Power Hinders Evacuation Of 4,500MW—Over 4,000 Nigerian Cars Run On Gas". March 7, 2017. *This Day* (Nigerian newspaper) page 21.

letters of credit for payment for power supplied[81] (payment depended on the liquidity and willingness of Nigerian banks who already had substantial NPL exposures to the power sector; and that also increased DISCOs' insolvency). The World Bank provided partial payment guarantees to some GENCOs but such guarantees were to become applicable only if NBET doesn't pay the GENCO and if the GENCO cannot collect from the associated DISCO's letters of credit. Contrary to suggestions by some industry consultants, having NBET borrow funds (most probably in foreign currency) for payment for electricity wasn't and isn't feasible; it exposes NBET to significant currency and liquidity risks, and it will encourage DISCOs to become more irresponsible. Many DISCOs and GENCOs in Nigeria haven't been able to raise adequate capital for expansion and upgrade of equipment. Some DISCOs and GENCOs complained that the condition of equipment/facilities that they purchased were worse than they expected which raises question about: i) whether DISCOs conducted due diligence; and ii) the credibility of the Nigerian government's process for the selection of companies that purchased the DISCOs and GENCOs. During 2014–2021, most DISCOs and GENCOs were unprofitable and technically insolvent and needed to be financially and operationally restructured—their liabilities exceed their assets and their *debt/assets ratios* were typically between 2:1 and 4:1. It was only in March 2017 (at least two and a half years after the financial/operational distress became obvious) that the Nigerian federal Ministry of Power, Works & Housing requested that the DISCOs and GENCOs submit their audited financial statements to the ministry. As of 2014–2021, the DISCOs owed unpaid and overdue debts to their banks, their vendors, NBET and the GENCOs; and the GENCOs owed unpaid and overdue debts to their banks, their gas suppliers and their other vendors; and NBET owed money to the GENCOs. As of 2014–2021, some vesting contracts had not been signed—including supply guarantees. The current industry structure precludes inter-regional and intra-Nigeria (within Nigeria) supply and subsidization (privatized GENCOs and DISCOs generally cannot operate outside their designated regions).

As of 2021, more than 90% (ninety percent) of existing and planned power generation plants in Nigeria were gas-powered plants. Severely

[81] *See: "Bulk Trader Empowers GENCOs to Access DISCOs' Letters of Credit"*. August 23, 2016. *This Day Live*(Nigerian newspaper). https://www.thisdaylive.com/index.php/2016/08/23/bulk-trader-empowers-gencos-to-access-discos-letters-of-credit/.

limited gas supply/processing/transmission has constrained growth in West Africa's power sector; and that may take a long time to resolve due to vandalism/arson (of gas lines, and transmission equipment), limited domestic gas processing; outstanding debts owed by GENCOs (to gas suppliers); lack of capital to build gas lines and agitation by separatists and community activists in the Niger Delta (which is the source of most gas supplies in Nigeria). Contrary to the suggestions of some consultants and industry participants, it's not economically and logistically feasible to deliver LNG to gas-fired power generation plants using trucks or trains on a daily basis[82] (some power plants will require 500+ truck-loads of LNG per day). In 2014, the Nigerian government directed the Central Bank of Nigeria to create a special-purpose vehicle to restructure about ₦25 billion debts owed to gas suppliers but that hasn't worked well.

As of 2021, Nigeria's existing power transmission network was small, dilapidated and severely limited and had significantly constrained growth in Nigeria's and West Africa's power sector; and that may take a long time to resolve due to vandalism/arson (of transmission lines and equipment), outstanding debts; lack of capital to repair and/or build power transmission lines; and agitation by terrorists, separatists and community activists in the Niger Delta and Northern Nigeria. The power transmission system in West Africa is insufficient and outdated. As of 2020, Nigeria had transmission capacity for less than 5800MW and its transmission capacity has never exceeded 6500MW,[83] while demand has always exceeded 16,000MW. Previous attempts to engage the Nigerian government and Transmission Company of Nigeria (TCN) to build additional transmission capacity have not been successful (e.g. unsuccessful negotiations between TCN and Manitoba Hydro for the investment of US$8 billion in the transmission network but with a sovereign guarantee, and a reported proposal by the China State Grid to invest in, operate and transfer the transmission network back to the government within an agreed timeframe). Thus, as of 2021, even if

[82] *See*: Fabiyi, M. (2016). "*Fashola—Let There Be Light: three Challenges And three Solutions Needed To Transform The Power Sector*". Available at: http://saharareporters.com/2016/03/13/fashola-%E2%80%93-let-there-be-light-3-challenges-and-3-solutions-needed-transform-power-sector.

[83] *See*: "*Obsolete Transmission Facilities Worsens Power Supply*". *The Punch* (Nigerian newspaper). April 16, 2017.

there is additional power supply, it cannot be distributed regionally or nationally.

In Nigeria, due to their inability or unwillingness to raise capital, many DISCOs have not been able to execute their ATCC (*Aggregate Technical Commercial and Collection*) loss reduction plans, and that in turn affects the solvency and liquidity of many GENCOs and DISCOs:[84] There have

[84] *See*: KPMG (Feb. 2021). *Nigeria's Electricity Supply Industry Highlights*—February 2021 Power Sector Watch | Edition 2021—Q1. https://assets.kpmg/content/dam/kpmg/ng/pdf/tax/power-sector-watch-edition-2021%E2%80%93q1.pdf. This document stated in part: "...In 2020, NERC had set a minimum market remittance threshold payable by the DisCos across the country and mandated the DisCos to make remittances to the Transmission Company of Nigeria's (TCN) Market Operator in line with the threshold, repay loans to CBN and remit some percentage to Nigerian Bulk Electricity Trading Company (NBET) monthly. In addition, CBN directed money deposit banks to take charge of the collection of electricity bill payments. This was in a bid to ensure that payments are made into a dedicated account and disbursed depending on priority, beginning with loan repayment and service charge to TCN. It was also expected to lead to cash flow management discipline in the NESI. However, the Discos failed in remitting ₦416.94 billion between January and September 2020, according to data published by NBET. The cumulative revenue lost by the power sector in 2020 is estimated at ₦645.15billion. This shortfall in funding has resulted in little or nothing left for capital improvements of the distribution network. The lack of significant capital investment in the distribution sector makes it difficult for the sector to cope with generation and transmission capacity. The FG has demonstrated fresh impetus in its efforts to invest in the sector by allocating ₦1.5 billion for the distribution expansion programme projects to utilize the stranded power from the grid. However, it would be interesting to see how the cost of these FG led distribution expansion projects would be treated in the books of the Discos: whether as equity or as a payable to the FG given that the programme is expected to be driven by the private sector.... Other notable projects include the ₦1.5billion allocated for the distribution expansion programme projects to utilize the stranded power from the grid and approval of the counter-part funding for the Siemens AG Power Agreement which is expected to increase the distribution capacity to 7000MW by the end of 2021...".

See: Price Waterhouse (2019). *Solving the Liquidity crunch in the Nigerian Power Sector*. White Paper presented at Power Sector Roundtable Conference hosted by Mainstream Energy Solutions Limited on September 24, 2019, at Kainji Dam Hydropower Plant, Niger State, Nigeria. https://www.pwc.com/ng/en/assets/pdf/solving-liquidity-crunch-nigerian-power.pdf. This paper stated in part: "...However, the country's current operational capacity stands at less than 4,000MW, less than 8,400 MW projection for 2018 in Multi-Year Tariff Order (MYTO). The installed capacity of 7,000MW is also less than the pre-privatization target of 11,879MW by 2012 and post-privatization target of 14,218MW and 40,000MW by 2013 and 2020 respectively. The bulk of electricity generated comes from thermal sources (gas-fired power plants). As a result, the inadequate gas supply often affects power generation.... Essentially, many of the DISCOs have been unable to collect a significant proportion of the total billings to customers as total revenue collected by all the DISCOs

been informal and formal reports of prevalent fraud at DISCOs wherein revenue collection is selective (some influential customers don't pay bills), and shareholders illegally siphon money to pay off politicians. Due to difficulties in raising capital, some of the DISCOs illegally passed on their direct expenses to electricity consumers[85] at various times during 2014–2020. Many DISCOs have been facing a *shadow price-cap* because of the following reasons:

for energy distributed still significantly lags the total billings. Collection efficiency improved by about 10% from 55.3% in Q3'2017 to 65.6% by Q3'2018. This implies that about N3.4 out of every N10 billed to customers are not paid to DISCOs as at when due... Liquidity crunch is the biggest challenge of the Nigerian electricity sector today. The eleven DISCOs have been struggling to meet their obligations to the Nigerian Bulk Electricity Trading Plc (NBET) and Market Operators (MO) as evidenced in their low remittances to NBET and MO.... In Q1'2019, only about 28% of the N190 billion invoice (comprising invoice of 161.4 billion for energy purchased from NBET and an invoice of N28.8 billion for administrative services from MO) of DISCOs were remitted.... In one year (Q1'2018–Q1'2019), DISCOs' outstanding remittance to NBET and MO stood at about N523.8 billion and N80.3 billion respectively.... Consequently, NBET have in turn been unable to meet their obligation to the generation companies (GENCOs) thus creating a liquidity challenge that has plagued the electricity industry since the privatization exercise in 2013...".

[85] *See*: *Mixed feelings trail power sector privatization*. August 16, 2015. *The National Mirror* (Nigerian newspaper). http://nationalmirroronline.net/new/mixed-feelings-trail-power-sector-privatisation/. (This article stated in part: "These were part of the resolutions passed by the Senate after the debate on a motion entitled: '*Unfair Trade Practices of Electricity Distribution Companies (DISCOs) in Nigeria*,' which was sponsored by Senators Sam Egwu (PDP Ebonyi North) and David Umaru (APC Niger East) ... 'NERC should make a regulation to mandate the DISCOs to discontinue the practice of making consumers pay for meters, poles and transformers which by law, are properties of the DISCOs, but where the consumers purchase those items, they should give notice of the purchase to the DISCOs and should be entitled to recover their expenses from subsequent consumption of electricity, ...' lawmakers added. In his concluding remarks, the Senate President, Bukola Saraki, lamented that after the unbundling of the Nigerian power sector, there is yet to be any noticeable change in the power situation in the country. Saraki also said there is something fundamentally wrong with the privatization program, hinting that either those that bought the distribution companies lack the financial capacity to deliver or the regulatory body is ignoring them. '...This is a very important topic. The people have not seen any benefits from this privatization exercise. If it needs to be reversed, it must be reversed in the interest of Nigerians. The period of impunity is over...', Saraki said. .... Senator Ben Bruce (PDP, Bayelsa East), who described the situation as a big scam, accused the government of being guilty as well. 'What is happening is a big scam. This is the biggest fraud I have ever seen. This process must be investigated. The Federal Government is as guilty as those who are extorting us,'" he alleged".)

1. They cannot increase the prices charged to a large percentage of the population (either because of regulation/price-controls or because of "reported" low per-capita income which often does not include the "black market" or informal economy).
2. Historically and for many power customers in West Africa, demand for electricity is *super-elastic* and above certain prices, retail and corporate demand can quickly drop to zero or even below zero (e.g. vandalism of infrastructure).
3. High inflation and continuing currency devaluation limits prices.
4. DISCOs experience collection losses.
5. GENCOs often deliver power to neighborhoods where residents are much less likely to pay their electricity bills.

GENCOs have also been facing a *shadow-price-cap* because, for example:

1. NBET typically does not pay GENCOs their full billings and NBET owed about N400 billion to DISCOs and GENCOs as of March 2017.[86] On average (and during 2014–2018), GENCOs collected only about 40% of their billings from NBET, but needed to collect at least 60% of their billings in order to remain solvent.[87]
2. DISCOs remitted only about 45% of their collected revenues to NBET (for power purchased), instead of the contractual targeted minimum of 65%[88] (that has led to DISCOs' accumulation of debts and non-payment of GENCOs).
3. Although in 2016, NBET instructed GENCOs to draw-down on letters of credits of DISCOs, actual collection was doubtful.

The irony and a key variable is that these *shadow-price-caps* are directly proportional to the volume of "commercial power" that is supplied to the

[86] *See*: "Power Operators Decry N400 Billion NBET debt, Poor Gas Supply—Egbin Threatens To Shut Down Operations". *The Guardian* (Nigerian newspaper). March 31, 2017.

[87] *See:* "Developing A Liquidity Solution For The Nigerian Power Sector (Part-1)". August 23, 2016. *This Day* (Nigerian newspaper). https://www.pressreader.com/nigeria/thisday/20160823/282140700794328.

[88] *See: Poor Power Supply: DISCOs Can't Account For The Bulk Of Revenue From Electricity Consumers — NBET MD*. December 18, 2016. *Vanguard* (Nigerian newspaper). http://www.vanguardngr.com/2016/12/poor-power-supply-discos-cant-account-bulk-revenue-electricity-consumers-nbet-md/.

Nigerian economy which is good—that is, the greater the volume of commercial power consumed, the greater the absolute magnitude of the prices that DISCOs can charge consumers because such "commercial" (separate from "retail/household") power consumption boosts manufacturing and economic activity and can reduce expensive imports and capital flight.

The continuing, but perhaps reasonable, threats by some Nigerian federal Senators to reverse the privatization of the power industry and the Buhari administration's announcement in November 2015 that it had begun a review of the power industry created additional and significant uncertainty and probably reduces the willingness of GENCOs and DISCOs to invest additional monies in their facilities, and the willingness of foreign investors to invest in, or lend to the, Nigerian power industry. However, it's possible and perhaps most efficient to expand and stabilize the power sector by structuring and implementing joint ventures and strategic alliances that will be as immune as possible to new regulations and changes to the privatization statutes.

As of May 2017, the Nigerian federal government had not released the N100 billion subsidy that it had contractually promised to buyers of DISCOs and GENCOs in the 2013 privatization[89] of the Nigerian power industry—this fact combined with NBET's significant debts that are owed to GENCOs erodes the credibility of the Nigerian federal government—such credibility is a necessary ingredient of economic stability and growth. The federal statute (EPSRA) that enabled the privatization of the Nigerian power industry is clearly inefficient, because the resulting industry structure:

1. does not promote growth or accountability;
2. imposes under-capitalized, troubled and low-credibility companies on specific regional markets with little opportunities for substitution, true competition or supplementation;
3. is not flexible enough to accommodate cross-fertilization among DISCOs/GENCOs; and supplementary power generated by, and the distribution capacities of third parties;
4. does not facilitate or provide incentives for additional investment or compliance with important agreements (e.g. NBET-GENCO agreements and NBET-DISCO agreements).

[89] *See*: "FG Fails To Release N100 Billion Subsidy, Say Power Firms". The *Punch* (Nigerian newspaper). Page 24. April 25, 2017. https://punchng.com/fg-fails-to-release-n100bn-subsidy-say-power-firms/

In April 2017, the Nigerian federal government announced that it intends to: i) create an escrow account into which DISCOs' revenues will be paid;[90] and ii) stipulate minimum capital requirements for DISCOs and GENCOs. These measures were opposed by DISCOs in several articles in Nigerian newspapers. In May 2017, the Managing Director of Eko Electricity Distribution Company (EKEDC, a DISCO)[91] stated that: i) EKEDC buys power from power generation companies at an implied exchange rate of about N308 per US$1, and sells power to consumers at an implied exchange rate of N198.98 per US$1; ii) some of the equipment that EKEDC uses were sixty years old (as of 2017) and needed to be replaced. That seems to be typical of most DISCOs in Nigeria.

During May 2017, the federal minister of Power, Works & Housing (Mr. Fashola) suddenly made an about-turn and a major policy shift when he publicly announced that "no DISCO has exclusive rights over any area and its ability to retain an area must be consistent with the ability to provide service to the area".[92] The federal minister's statement contravened the privatization contracts, and was also self-contradictory because it stated that DISCOs don't have any specific franchise-areas, but also simultaneously says that having a franchise-area is contingent on the DISCO being able to provide services to such area. During May 2017, both the Nigerian Federal Minister for power and the NERC announced that GENCOs were free to supply power directly to four types of end-users beginning from May 15, 2017 and pursuant to Section 27 of the Electric Power Sector Reform Act 2005 (EPSRA)—that move was criticized by Nigerian legal scholars as being in bad faith and not in accordance with the law[93]—it violated the EPSRA and the privatization contracts.

Many Nigerian banks that financed the 2013 privatization of the Nigerian power sector have significant loan exposures that are now NPLs (which, in turn, may affect their solvency) and they have drastically reduced lending to the power sector. In that privatization, about 70% of the purchase prices of the GENCOs and DISCOs were financed with loans from

[90] *See*: "GENCOs, DISCOs Disagree Over Proposed Escrow Revenue Accounts". *The Guardian* (Nigerian newspaper). April 26, 2017. Page 9.

[91] *See*: "DISCOs: We Buy Electricity At N305 Per Dollar, Sell At N198.98". *This Day* (Nigerian newspaper). May 1, 2017.

[92] *See*: Anyaogu, I. (May 12, 2017). "FG Signals Policy Shift On Exclusive DISCO Franchise Rights". *Business Day* (Nigeria).

[93] *See*: "*Don Faults FG On Direct Sale Of Electricity To End Users*". May 23, 2017. *The Guardian* (Nigerian newspaper), page-27.

Nigerian banks. Those loans were clearly error because the privatization model was bound to fail from the beginning.

During 2019, the Nigerian federal government proposed repurchasing the DISCOs from the buyers[94] of DISCOs (in the 2013 privatization)—and that offer was rumored to be politically motivated.

The series of government bailouts of the Nigerian power sector was counter-productive, doesn't address the core structural problems in the Nigerian power industry and will remain unsuccessful without additional private or public restructuring of the industry. The Central Bank of Nigeria's (CBN) efforts to stabilize the power industry are not adequate.[95] As of January 2016, the CBN had provided a N213 billion Electricity Market Stabilization Facility in order to settle outstanding debts and address revenue shortfalls in the power industry (legacy debts and significant revenue shortfalls during the *Interim Rule Period*). As of January 2016, at least N56 billion had been disbursed to five GENCOs and five DISCOs. The CBN has also made available a N300 billion *Real Sector Support Facility* which targets the manufacturing, agriculture and some services industries. Those amounts are grossly inadequate to address the problems in the targeted industries. In March 2017, it was announced that the

[94] *See:* "FG'll pay '*failed investors*' N736 billion to repossess Discos: Eleven distribution firms declared technically insolvent; Review power sale but don't politicize exercise—ECAN". *The Punch* (Nigerian newspaper). By Everest Amaefule and 'Femi Asu. August 15, 2019. https://punchng.com/fgll-pay-failed-investors-n736bn-to-repossess-discos/. (*The Punch* had on Friday reported that 17 of the nation's 27 power stations had been forced to shut down some of their units on the back of low demand by Discos, worsening the blackout being experienced by millions of customers across the country. .... Five and a half years after privatization, the eleven Discos have been described as 'technically insolvent.'

The ministry, in its new '*Power Sector Policy Directives and Timelines*,' said there was an urgent need to recapitalize the Discos. It described the inability of the Discos to improve customer service and meet operational costs as a direct consequence of their inability to raise capital. The Bureau of Public Enterprises said in October 2018 that the five-year performance agreement with the core investors in the Discos, with the exception of Kaduna Disco, became effective on January 1, 2015 and the fifth anniversary for final performance review would therefore be December 31, 2019. The ministry said the Discos' accumulated debts to the Nigeria Bulk Electricity Trading Plc and the Market Operator had made them technically insolvent. On the option of repossessing the distribution assets, it said, 'To do so within the provisions of the Share Sale Agreement will require a sum in the region of $2.4 billion, some of which will be paid as compensation to the failed investors. This is not a desirable outcome. It is noteworthy that government is yet to pay the investor in Yola Disco for its negotiated return to government.'.)

[95] *See*: Nweze, C. (Jan. 26, 2015). "Stimulating Economic Development With Banking Regulations". *The Nation* (Nigerian daily newspaper).

federal government had approved a N702 billion electricity market bailout fund for NBET[96]—but such bailouts are unlikely to work: i) because they provide the wrong incentives to industry participants, and they inefficiently shield DISCOs/GENCOs from market forces; ii) there is a culture of corruption in both the government and the industry and the funds are unlikely to be spent efficiently; and iii) the bailout doesn't address the core structural problems in the power industry. Most, if not all, of the DISCOs and GENCOs have substantially outdated and or inadequate equipment and face vandalism/arson, and thus have significant capital expenditure requirements and foreign currency requirements (they will have to import new equipment and parts, and pay for maintenance contracts).

In West Africa, alternative modes of consumption of electricity among retail and corporate customers have not been developed or tried. Given the pervasive power production (and distribution) constraints in the power industry, the *consumption side* of the industry can be reorganized to achieve more efficient consumption (group consumption, hybrid consumption, etc.) that maximizes aggregate productivity/output and social welfare. That is, given a limited X units of available electricity that has to be allocated among Y persons/entities each of which has different capital constraints, cost-structures, product-market risk, efficiency and risk profiles; how do you allocate power and charge prices to each of these entities to maximize their combined/overall productivity, profits and cash balances? Most efforts of the Nigerian government, many West African governments and the private sector have erroneously focused on expanding the *production side* (power generation capacity) and in the wrong way (focus on gas-powered plants), hoping that would increase consumption revenues and boost power generation companies and manufacturing companies. However, during 2019–2021, the Nigerian government made limited efforts to increase power distribution capacity. It's very likely that increased efficiency in consumption can stimulate and help to rapidly expand the *production side* of the industry, rather than the other way around. Despite much human and financial capital that has been committed to the Nigeria power industry during the last four decades, Nigeria's "reported actual" commercial power generation capacity (not including on-site generators owned by households and companies) has never exceeded 7500MW and Nigeria's power transmission capacity has never exceeded 6500MW while its actual power demand has always exceeded 16,000 MW. If current trends continue, there won't be any change due to

[96] *See: "A New Bailout For Ailing Power Sector"*. March 7, 2017. *ThisDay*. Page 24.

logistics constraints, inadequate domestic gas-processing and gas-transmission, capital constraints, vandalism/arson (destruction of gas lines, transmission equipment, etc.) and the federal government's correct refusal to provide sovereign guarantees for power projects. Some of the huge gap between demand and supply of power in Nigeria (and West Africa) has been filled with a large volume of small portable on-site household power generators and industrial generators (for companies/facilities), all of which use expensive diesel, petrol and other liquid fuels (most of which was imported during 1990–2020; and importation of such fuels accounts for at least 30% of foreign currency expenditures in Nigeria). Most of those small generators are not documented in power sector statistics. The Nigerian government and the power sector do not provide any incentives for such consumers to purchase most of their electricity from DISCOs—for example, some type of consumption-prioritization scheme for customers that absolutely need steady power (or will pay a premium for steady power supply) and customers that need power.

In West and Central Africa, other non-gas power generation methods (such as waste-to-energy, wind power, nuclear power, solar power, joint venture power generation), electricity-trading and contract power generation have not been fully explored. Also, alternative methods of distribution have not been fully explored.

In Nigeria and as of 2019, none of the ten *national integrated power projects* (NIPPs)[97] (which were to have been completed in 2013) were operating. To date, more than US$5 billion has been invested in the NIPPs which are gas-powered plants that would have added 4774MW of power generation capacity to the national grid (most or all of those funds should have been used to expand and upgrade the Nigerian transmission network). The commencement of NIPPs' operations has been delayed by lack of gas supply, many court injunctions that block transmission; encroachments on transmission facilities (in Imo, Enugu, Abia, Akwa-Ibom and Cross River states) which have disrupted the delivery of power; and theft and arson (destruction of generation and transmission infrastructure). It's estimated that the ten NIPPs need 1295 million standard cubic feet per day (mmscufd) of gas, but at least 50% of that required supply cannot be guaranteed even when gas pipelines are completed, and as a

[97] *See: "Weighty crises crushing N1 trillion NIPPs as 4,800MW power hangs"*. Sep. 28, 2015. *The Daily Trust*. http://www.dailytrust.com.ng/news/business/weighty-crises-crushing-n1trn-nipps-as-4-800mw-power-hangs/112821.html.

result, NBET cannot execute PPAs with most of the NIPPs. As of 2015, the ten NIPPs were valued at US$7.1+ billion, the associated gas assets at US$0.5 billion, the associated transmission assets at US$2+ billion and the associated distribution assets at US$1.5+ billion. The Nigerian government stated that it intends to sell the NIPPs via auctions.

In Nigeria, existing and planned *independent power projects* (IPPs) are scheduled to add more than 4000MW of new power generation capacity by 2022. However, most of those IPPs are gas-powered plants and will have the same problems as NIPPs (arson/vandalism of gas pipelines; low transmission capacity; unreliable or non-existent gas supply; no PPAs; litigation about construction of transmission lines; etc.).

During March 2017, the NNPC (Nigeria)[98] announced that it will engage in power generation and transmission in Nigeria, and that Nigeria has enough gas to produce 8000MW of power annually. It's most likely that such new power plants will be gas-powered and will have the same problems as NIPPs (arson/vandalism of gas pipelines; litigation about construction of transmission lines; etc.).

During 2013, US President Obama announced "Power Africa", a US government initiative to add 30,000 MW of electricity generation capacity in six African countries; and the World Bank committed to invest US$5 billion to support "Power Africa". In 2014, US President Obama announced a US government commitment to invest US$14 billion in Africa—which is grossly insufficient, given Africa's infrastructure needs. The Obama administration's cash commitment was subsequently reduced to US$1 billion; and in 2017, the Trump administration mentioned that it will significantly reduce USAID's budget. A substantial portion of the World Bank's commitment is likely to be used on feasibility studies, creation of enabling environments, consulting and ancillary issues. So far those initiatives have not made much difference; and they are unlikely to produce tangible results unless followed up with meaningful action. Again, inefficient management of both the consumption side and production side of the power sector and delays in obtaining PPAs may have affected such initiatives.

Partly due to the perceived troubled state of the power industry in West Africa and lack of understanding of the industry dynamics, opportunities

[98] *See*: Nnodim, O. (March 30, 2017). NNPC plans to generate, transmit electricity. *The Punch*. http://punchng.com/nnpc-plans-to-generate-trasmit-electricity/.

and risks, most venture capital and private equity funds have not invested in the sector.

According to Palekar (2013),[99] the following are some of the problems of the Nigerian GENCOs, and many of these problems still exist:

- Shortage of gas supply has continuously hindered the availability of new gas-fired power stations to generate electricity in sufficient quantities.
- The regulatory environment is restrictive (government approval is required for planned CAPEX spends; and annual tariff filings are required).
- The existing maintenance culture is inclined toward post-breakdown maintenance rather than scheduled preventive maintenance.
- The existing generation assets are old and over-loaded and require significant operating and maintenance costs; and there has been limited new capacity added in recent years. The existing transmission network is also inadequate, fragile and not reliable. The average availability of generators during 2005–2013 was 35%.
- Many GENCOs and DISCOs haven't been able to raise capital for expansion and/or construction of new plants; and the slow execution of PPAs hinders IPPs from raising required funding.
- The payment guarantees to be provided by vesting contracts and PPAs are not clear and are open to different interpretations.

According to Palekar (2013),[100] the following are some of the problems of the Nigerian DISCOs (and some of these problems still exist):

- The distribution network (injection sub-stations, distribution substation transformers, conductors, wooden cross arms and poles) is largely weak, overloaded and in very poor condition.
- Inadequacy of skilled technical staff, and significant training costs.
- The labor unions remain a major factor.

[99] *See*: Palekar, C. (2013). *Transformational Issues For GENCOs And DISCOs*. https://www.pwc.com/ng/en/assets/pdf/pwc-round-table-post-privatisation.pdf.

[100] *See*: Palekar (2013)(*supra*).

As confirmed by the NIPC (Nigerian Investment Promotion Commission), the investment opportunities in the Nigerian power sector include but are not limited to the following:

- Expansion of existing facilities in generation, transmission and distribution
- Manufacturing of wires, cables, transformers and other auxiliary equipment
- Building new integrated power plants (IPPs) greenfield
- Expansion of existing transmission lines
- Production and distribution of metering devices
- Provision of operations and maintenance services

On a separate note and during 2009, the Indonesian government enacted a new statute to promote privatization and market-based rules in the Indonesian Power industry (the "2009 Electrification Law"). Subsequently, two Indonesian energy unions (SP Perjuangan PLN Persero and Pesatuan Pegawai Indonesia Power) challenged the statute on the basis that it would lead to a reduction of the state's role in electricity supply (there was a constitutional requirement that electricity supply must be controlled by the Indonesian government). During 2017, the Indonesian Constitutional Court[101] declared that the 2009 Electrification Law was unconstitutional. Attempts by the Indonesian government to revise that statute in 2020 led to widespread protests by labor unions and the general public.[102]

[101] *See: "Indonesian Court Judges Electricity Privatization Unconstitutional*". 14 February 2017. https://www.google.com/search?q=Don+Faults+FG+On+Direct+Sale+Of+Electricity+To+End+Users&sxsrf=ALeKk00NwtdYS-whuPt72UlYPZ1clbIdJg:1599168662418&ei=lmBRX6-WGdPzgAbsp7TQBw&start=10&sa=N&ved=2ahUKEwivubzA983rAhXTOcAKHewTDXoQ8NMDegQIDBA-&biw=1278&bih=694.

[102] *See*: "*Electricity Trade Unions Oppose Omnibus Bill Revisions Over Privatization Concerns*". By Norman Harsono. *The Jakarta Post*.

https://www.thejakartapost.com/news/2020/07/14/electricity-trade-unions-oppose-omnibus-bill-revisions-over-privatization-concerns.html. ("Major electricity industry trade unions are considering public protests and strikes to opposite revisions to the 2009 Electrification Law in the controversial omnibus bill on job creation, mainly over concerns that the country's electricity supply chain will be privatized. The unions are particularly opposed to the addition of Article-10(2) and Article-11(1) to the omnibus bill, which appear to give more room for private enterprises to enter Indonesia's electricity industry. Article-11(1) of the bill states that electricity for the public interest can be provided by state

According to Dubash and Rajan (April 2001), the statutory reform of the power sector in India during 1991–1996 raised significant political and constitutional law questions—and the Indian federal Home Ministry argued that the Orissa Electricity Reform Act (enacted by the State of Orissa) was unconstitutional.

Basañes et al. (September 1999) analyzed a series of post-privatization disputes and renegotiations that occurred in the Chilean power industry between the late 1980s and 1999—some of these disputes were resolved by the Chilean courts and its Antitrust Commission and involved both antitrust and constitutional law issues.

In Canada and decades ago, constitutional political economy issues (e.g. separation of powers; allocation of powers between state and federal governments) also limited the development of energy generation facilities—see Valentine (2010) and Goldstein (1981).

These constitutional political economy issues directly/indirectly affect the attractiveness of both new and re-development/refurbishment power generation projects to foreign investors (which are increasingly a major source of funds for such projects), which in turn affects other foreign investors' perceptions of other industries in Emerging Markets countries. On FDI, Foreign Investment and constitutional law issues, also see Jensen and McGillivaray (2005), Ginsburg (2005) and Nwogugu (2012).

The foregoing problems in the Nigerian power industry are compounded by the fact that households, companies and government agencies often compensate for inadequate power supply by: (i) buying generators that are fueled by diesel and petrol, most of which are imported and cause substantial environmental pollution; and (ii) using wood and potentially toxic plastics to build fires. Such importation (of electricity generators,

enterprises, municipally owned firms, private enterprises, cooperatives and the community. Under existing regulations, private entities can only act as power producers, and entails building power plants, while state-owned electricity firm PLN has a monopoly on the transmission, distribution and sale of electricity, which involves the construction of significant amounts of electricity infrastructure".)

petrol and diesel) consumes scarce foreign exchange which leads to further devaluation of the Naira. During 2020/2021, some federal legislators proposed a new statute to ban the purchase and use of such generators, but the law hasn't been enacted, and even if enacted will be very difficult to enforce because of habits, convenience of generators, significant mistrust of the government/DISCOs/GENCOs, high enforcement costs, tribalism; and so on.

The laws and constitutions of many emerging markets countries (such as India, Indonesia and Chile) are based on US, UK and Spanish laws/constitutions. Verkuil (2006) discussed constitutional law problems in privatizations.

3.12 Conclusion

Around the world, government bailouts/bail-ins are significant geopolitical risks (their political origins, basis for legitimacy, duration and effects can vary drastically across countries), have been politicized and are usually implemented in difficult economic/social circumstances and under political pressures, and they raise significant political, social, economic and constitutional law questions which have not been addressed correctly or fully in some circumstances/countries.

In their current states, both CRAs and their credit ratings are unconstitutional, and CRAs' functions should be delegated to national government agencies (with global coordination for standards-setting) and or *international organizations* that have broad membership (such as the United Nations, the WTO, the World Bank, the Financial Stability Board). The significant antitrust problems in the CRA industry were analyzed in Nwogugu (2013, 2021), are significant and reduce the credibility of credit ratings and can cause negative effects (excessive market volatility, shocks, market crashes, harmful contagion, etc.), cross-border spillovers and integration in global financial, Labor, Information and finished-commodity-goods markets.

Bibliography

Abdelal, R., & Blyth, M. (2015). Just Who Put You in Charge? We Did: Credit Rating Agencies and the Politics of Ratings. In A. Cooley & J. Snyder (Eds.), *Ranking the World: Grading States as a Tool of Global Governance* (pp. 39–59). Cambridge: Cambridge University Press.

Adedeji, A. (2017). Privatisation and Performance of Electricity Distribution Companies in Nigeria. *Journal of Public Administration and Governance, 7*(3), 190.

Ajumogobia, O., & Okeke, B. (2015). *Nigerian Energy Sector: Legal and Regulatory Overview*. Nigerian Energy Sector Reforms.

Alford, D. (2010). Nigerian Banking Reform: Recent Actions and Future Prospects. *Journal of International Banking Law & Regulation, 25*, 337–347.

Alford, D. (2012). *Reform of the Nigerian Banking System—Assessment of the Asset Management Corporation of Nigeria (AMCON) And Recent Developments.* Working Paper, University of South Carolina, USA. Retrieved from http://www.researchgate.net/publication/228119565_Reform_of_the_Nigerian_Banking_System__Assessment_of_the_Asset_Management_Corporation_of_Nigeria_(AMCON)_and_Recent_Developments.

Amtenbrink, F., & Heine, K. (2013). Regulating Credit Rating Agencies in the European Union: Lessons from Behavioural Science. *The Dovenschmidt Quarterly, 2*(1), 2–15.

Andrews, M., Pritchett, L., & Woolcock, M. (2017). *Building State Capability: Evidence, Analysis, Action.*

Archer, C., Biglaiser, G., & DeRouen, K. (2007). Sovereign Bonds and the "Democratic Advantage": Does Regime Type Affect Credit Rating Agency Ratings in the Developing World? *International Organization, 61*, 341–365.

Arthur, W. B. (1999). Complexity and the Economy. *Science, 284*, 107–109.

Bai, L. (2010). On Regulating Conflicts of Interest in the Credit Rating Industry. *NYU Journal Of Legislation And Public Policy, 13*, 253–263.

Bamberger, M., Vaessen, J., & Raimondo, E. (2016). Dealing with Complexity In Development Evaluation: A Practical Approach.

Banerji, S., Duygun, M., & Shaban, M. (2018). Political Connections, Bailout in Financial Markets and Firm Value. *Journal of Corporate Finance, 50*, 388–401.

Banker, S., Bhanot, S., & Deshpande, A. (2020). Poverty Identity and Preference for Challenge: Evidence from the U.S. and India. *Journal of Economic Psychology, 76*, 1.

Barducci, M., & Fest, T. (2011). *Evaluation of the Regulations of Credit Rating Agencies in the United States and the European Community.* Retrieved August 29, 2016, from http://papers.ssrn.com/sol3/papers.cfm?abstractid=1803132.

Bar-Isaac, H., & Shapiro, J. (2014). Ratings Quality Over the Business Cycle. *Journal of Finance*.

Barnett, R. (2010, March). *Is Healthcare Reform Constitutional?* Retrieved from http://www.washingtonpost.com/wp-dyn/content/article/2010/03/19/AR2010031901470.html.

Barr, M., & Miller, G. (2006). Global Administrative Law: The View from Basel. *European Journal of International Law, 17*, 15–25.

Barta, Z., & Johnston, A. (2018). Rating Politics? Partisan Discrimination in Credit Ratings in Developed Economies. *Comparative Political Studies, 51*(5), 587–620.

Bartels, B., & Weder di Mauro, B. (2013). A Rating Agency for Europe—A Good Idea? *VOX*. Retrieved May 15, 2018, from https://voxeu.org/article/rating-agency-europe-good-idea.

Basañes, F., Saavedra, E., & Soto, R. (1999, September). *Post-Privatization Renegotiation and Disputes in Chile*. IADB. Washington, DC. September 1999—N° IFM-116.

Baskaya, Y., & Di Giovanni, J., et al. (2017). *Capital Flows and the International Credit Channel*. Working paper. https://econ-papers.upf.edu/papers/1557.pdf.

Bavetta, S., Li Donni, P., & Marino, M. (2020). How Consistent Are Perceptions of Inequality? *Journal of Economic Psychology, 78*, 1.

Bayoumi, T., Pickford, S., & Subacchi, P. (2016). *Managing Complexity: Economic Policy Cooperation after the Crisis*. Washington, DC: Brookings Institution Press.

Bechtel, M. (2009). The Political Sources of Systematic Investment Risk: Lessons from a Consensus Democracy. *The Journal of Politics, 71*, 661–677.

Beck, R., Jakubik, P., & Piloiu, A. (2013). *Non-Performing Loans: What Matters in Addition to the Economic Cycle?* European Central bank. Working paper series, No. 1515. Available at.

Berger, A., & Roman, R. (2020). *Conditions That Generally Bring About Bank Bailouts, Bail-ins, and Other Resolution Methods*. Chapter-2 in: "TARP and other Bank Bailouts and Bail-ins around the World" (2020; Pages 43-56).

Bianco, K., & Pachkowski, J. (2008). *The Economic Bailout: An Analysis of the Economic Emergency Stabilization Act*. http://www.cch.com/press/news/CCHWhitePaper_Bailout.pdf.

Birz, G. (2017). Stale Economic News, Media and the Stock Market. *Journal of Economic Psychology, 61*, 87–102.

Blake, V. (2012). The Constitutionality of the Affordable Care Act: An Update. *Virtual Mentor, 14*(11), 873–876.

Blau, B., Brough, T., & Thomas, D. (2013). Corporate Lobbying, Political Connections, and the Bailout of Banks. *Journal of Banking & Finance, 37*(8), 3007–3017.

Blendon, R., & Benson, J. (2017). Public Opinion about the Future of the Affordable Care Act. *New England Journal of Medicine, 31*(377(9)), e12. https://doi.org/10.1056/NEJMsr1710032.

Block, S., & Vaaler, P. (2004). The Price of Democracy: Sovereign Risk Ratings, Bond Spreads and Political Business Cycles in Developing Countries. *Journal of International Money and Finance, 23*, 917–946.

Blodget, H. (2011). *Moody's Analyst Breaks Silence: Says Ratings Agency Rotten to Core With Conflicts.* Retrieved February 1, 2015, from www.businessinsider.com/moodys-analyst-conflicts-corruption-and-greed-2011-8/?IR=T.

Bodellini, M. (2018). To Bail-in, or to Bail-out, That Is the Question. *European Business Organization Law Review.*

Bolton, P., Freixas, X., & Shapiro, J. (2012). The Credit Ratings Game. *Journal of Finance, 67*, 85–112.

Bongaerts, D. (2013). *Can Alternative Business Models Discipline Credit CRAs?* Working Paper.

Brummer, C., & Loko, R. (2014). *The New Politics of Transatlantic Credit Rating Agency Regulation.* In T. Porter (Ed.), *Transnational Financial Regulation After the Crisis* (pp. 154–176). London / New York: Routledge.

Byrne, D., & Callaghan, G. (2014). Complexity Theory and the Social Sciences: The State of the Art.

Cahill Gordon & Reindel LLP. (2005, July). Memorandum on the Constitutionality of H.R. 2990, the "Credit CRA Duopoly Relief Act of 2005". Retrieved from http://www2.standardandpoors.com/spf/pdf/media/Exhibit_2.pdf.

Caliendo, F., Guo, N., & Smith, J. (2018). Policy Uncertainty and Bank Bailouts. *Journal of Financial Markets, 39*, 111–125.

Calò, S. (2019). Bailouts: The Lesser of Two Evils? *Journal of Policy Modeling, 41*, 84–98.

Carruthers, B. (2013). From Uncertainty Toward Risk: The Case of Credit Ratings. *Socio-Economic Review, 11*(3), 525–551.

Casey, K. (2009, February 6). *In Search of Transparency, Accountability, and Competition: The Regulation of Credit Rating Agencies.* Remarks at "The SEC Speaks in 2009". US SEC, Washington, DC. Retrieved from http://www.sec.gov/news/speech/2009/spch020609klc.htm.

Cassell, M., & Hoffmann, S. (2009). *Managing a $700 Billion Bailout: Lessons from the Home Owners' Loan Corporation and the Resolution Trust Corporation. IBM Center for the Business of Government, Financial Management Series.* Washington: IBM Center for the Business of Government 2009.

Cassese, S. (2005). Administrative Law without the State? The Challenge of Global Regulation. *New York University Journal of International Law and Politics, 37*, 663–673.

Cattaneo, O., Engman, M., Saez, S., & Stern, R. (Eds.). (2010). *International Trade in Services: New Trends and Opportunities for Developing Countries.* Washington DC: World Bank.

Chari, V., et al. (2008). *Facts and Myths About the Financial Crisis of 2008.* Federal Reserve Bank of Minnesota Research Department, Working Paper No. 666. Retrieved from http://www.minneapolisfed.org/publications_papers/pub_display.cfm?id=4062.

Chi, Y., & Li, X. (2019). Beauties of the Emperor: An Investigation of a Chinese Government Bailout. *Journal of Financial Markets, 44*, 42–70.

Chwieroth, J., & Walter, A. (2020). Great Expectations, Financialization, and Bank Bailouts in Democracies. *Comparative Political Studies*, in-press.

Coffee, J. (2011). Ratings Reform: The Good, the Bad, and the Ugly. *Harvard Business Law Review, 1*, 231–278.

Commission of The European Communities. (2009, October). *An EU framework for Cross-Border Crisis Management in the Banking Sector.* http://ec.europa.eu/internal_market/bank/docs/crisis-management/091020_communication_en.pdf.

Cooper, M. (2011). Complexity Theory After the Financial Crisis—The Death of Neoliberalism or the Triumph of Hayek? *Journal Of Cultural Economy, 4*(4), 371–385.

Copelovitch, M., Frieden, J., & Walter, S. (2016). The Political Economy of the Euro Crisis. *Comparative Political Studies, 49*(7), 811–840.

Cornford, A. (2009, June). *Statistics For International Trade In Banking Services: Requirements—Availability And Prospects.* UNCTAD. Working paper No. 194. http://unctad.org/en/docs/osgdp20092_en.pdf.

Crawford, J. (2018). Resolution Triggers for Systemically Important Financial Institutions. *Nebraska Law Review, 97*, 65–85.

Currie, A., & Fountoukakos, K., et al. (Herbert Smith Gleitz Stibbe Lutz) (2010, July). *European Financial Stability Measures and EU Law.* Available at: http://www.herbertsmith.com/NR/rdonlyres/BA7C5FA2-BBB5-4B8D-9971-23AF97BBB678/0/8339Europeanfinancialstabilitymeasuresbriefing.pdf.

Datz, G. (2013). The Narrative of Complexity in the Crisis of Finance: Epistemological Challenge and Macroprudential Policy Response. *New Political Economy, 18*(4), 459–479.

Davis, C. (2008, November). *Fast Track Parliamentary Procedures of the Emergency Economic Stabilization Act.* http://www.policyarchive.org/handle/10207/bitstreams/18792.pdf.

De Bock, R., & Demyanets, A. (2012). *Bank Asset Quality in Emerging Markets: Determinants and Spillovers*. IMF working paper, 12/71. (Washington: International Monetary Fund). Retrieved from https://www.imf.org/external/pubs/ft/wp/2012/wp1271.pdf.

Deb, P., Manning, M., Murphy, G., Penalver, A., & Toth A. (2011). *Whither the Credit Ratings Industry?* Financial Stability Paper #9, Bank of England, England.

Debelle, G. (2004). Household Debt and the Macroeconomy. *BIS Quarterly Review*, available at SSRN: http://ssrn.com/abstract=1968418.

Delimatsis, P. (2012). *Of Bailouts and Rescue Measures: Subsidies in Financial Services*. Working Paper No 2012/24. Swiss National Center of Competence In Research. http://www20.iadb.org/intal/catalogo/PE/2012/12020.pdf.

Dixon, R., Griffiths, W., & Lim, G. (2014). Lay People's Models of the Economy: A Study Based on Surveys of Consumer Sentiments. *Journal of Economic Psychology, 44*, 13–20.

Dubash, N., & Rajan, S. (2001, April). *The Politics of Power Sector Reform in India*. http://pdf.wri.org/power_politics/india.pdf.

Durlauf, S. (2012). Complexity, Economics, and Public Policy. *Politics, Philosophy & Economics.*

Economides, N. (1998). The Incentive for Non-price Discrimination by an Input Monopolist. *International Journal of Industrial Organization, 16*, 271–284.

Economides, N. (2012a). *Tying, Bundling, and Loyalty/requirement Rebates*. Book Chapter in Elhauge, E., ed. (2012), "Research Handbook of the Economics of Antitrust Law" (Edward Elgar; 2012). http://www.stern.nyu.edu/networks/Economides_Tying_Bundling_and_Loyalty_Requirement_Rebates.pdf.

Economides, N. (2012b). *Antitrust Issues in Network Industries*. Book chapter in Kokkoris, I., & Lianos, I., eds. (2008), "The Reform of EC Competition Law" (Kluwer; 2008). http://www.stern.nyu.edu/networks/Economides_Antitrust_in_Network_Industries.pdf.

Eicher, T., Garcia-Penalosa, C., & Kuenzel, D. (2018). Constitutional Rules as Determinants of Social Infrastructure. *Journal of Macroeconomics, 57*, 182–209.

Epstein, R. (2009, December). Impermissible Ratemaking in Health-Insurance Reform: Why the Reid Bill Is Unconstitutional. http://www.pointoflaw.com/columns/archives/2009/12/impermissible-ratemaking-in-he.php.

Epstein, R., & Hyman, D. (2010, February). *Controlling the Costs of Medical Care: A Dose of De-regulation*. University Of Chicago Law & Economics, Olin Working Paper No. 418; University Of Illinois Law & Economics Research Paper No. LE08-023. Available at SSRN: http://ssrn.com/abstract=1158547.

Esfeld, L., & Loup, A. (2011). Constitutional Challenges to the Patient Protection and Affordable Care Act—a Snapshot. *Virtual Mentor, 13*(11), 787–791.

EU. (2010). *European Stabilization Mechanism To Preserve Financial Stability*. http://www.consilium.europa.eu/uedocs/cms_data/docs/pressdata/en/ecofin/114324.pdf.

EU Debt Office, Authority For Bank Resolution Funds & European Financial Stabilization Mechanism. http://www.asymptotix.eu/content/eu-debt-office-authority-bank-resolution-funds-european-financial-stabilisation-mechanism.

Eurobank EFG (2010, June). The Greek Economy and Its Stability Programme. *Eurobank Research—Economy & Markets, 5*(3). Retrieved from http://www.eurobank.gr/Uploads/Images1024/EconomyStabilityProgramNew.pdf.

European Commission. (2015). *Study on the Feasibility of Alternatives to Credit Ratings: Executive Summary*. Retrieved March 21, 2018, from https://ec.europa.eu/info/system/files/alternatives-to-credit-rating-study-01122015_en.pdf.

European Commission. (2016). *Study on the State of the Credit Rating Market: Final Report—Executive Summary*. Retrieved March 21, 2018, from https://ec.europa.eu/info/system/files/state-of-credit-rating-market-study-01012016_en.pdf.

Fettig, D. (2002, December). Lender of More Than Last Resort. *The Region*. Retrieved from http://www.minneapolisfed.org/publications_papers/pub_display.cfm?id=3392.

Finch, J. (Ed.). (2013). *Complexity and the Economy—Implications for Economic Policy*. Cheltenham: Edward Elgar.

Forbes, K. J., & Warnock, F. E. (2012). Capital Flow Waves: Surges, Stops, Flight, and Retrenchment. *Journal of International Economics, 88*(2), 235–251.

Fourie, L., & Botha, I. (2015). Sovereign Credit Rating Contagion in the EU. *Procedia Economics and Finance, 24*, 218–227.

FreedomWorks Foundation. (2009, January 13). *Constitutional Infirmities of the Emergency Economic Stabilization Act of 2008 ("EESA"): A Legal Analysis from FreedomWorks Foundation*. Available at: Constitutional Infirmities of the Emergency Economic Stabilization Act of 2008 ("EESA") A Legal Analysis from FreedomWorks Foundationhttp://www.freedomworks.org/files/policy-analysis.pdf.

Frost, C. (2009). Credit CRAs in Capital Markets: A Review of Research Evidence on Selected Criticisms of the Agencies. *Journal of Accounting, Auditing & Finance, 22*(3), 469–492.

Gaillard, N. (2014). How and Why Credit Rating Agencies Missed the Eurozone Debt Crisis. *Capital Markets Law Journal, 9*(2), 121–136.

Gaillard, N., & Harrington, W. (2016). Efficient, Commonsense Actions to Foster Accurate Credit Ratings. *Capital Markets Law Journal, 11*(1), 38–59.

Gaillard, N., & Waibel, M. (2018). The Icarus Syndrome: How Credit Rating Agencies Lost Their Quasi Immunity. *Southern Methodist University Law Review, 71*, 1077.

Garcia, F., Opromolla, L., & Marques, A. (2020). The Effects of Official and Unofficial Information on Tax Compliance. *Journal of Economic Psychology, 78*, 1.

Gärtner, M., Griesbach, B., & Jung, F. (2011). PIGS or Lambs? The European Sovereign Debt Crisis and the Role of Rating Agencies. *International Advances in Economic Research, 17*(3), 288–299.

Gersen, J. (2007). Temporary Legislation. *University of Chicago Law Review, 74*, 247–268.

Ginsburg, T. (2005). International Substitutes for Domestic Institutions: Bilateral Investment Treaties and Governance. *International Review of Law and Economics, 25*(1), 107–123.

Goldstein, W. (1981). Canada's Constitutional Crisis: The Uncertain Development of Alberta's Energy Resources. *Energy Policy, 9*(1), 4–13.

Gostin, L. (2019). *Texas vs. United States*: The Affordable Care Act Is Constitutional and Will Remain So. *JAMA, 321*(4), 332–333.

Gradstein, M., & Kaganovich, M. (2019). Legislative Restraints in Corporate Bailout Design. *Journal of Economic Behavior & Organization, 158*, 337–350.

Grey, B. (2009, June). *The GM Bankruptcy and the Supreme Court*. http://www.americanthinker.com/2009/06/the_gm_bankruptcy_and_the_supr.html.

Gudzowski, M. (2010). Mortgage Credit Ratings and the Financial Crisis: The Need for a State-Run Mortgage Securities CRAs. *Columbia Business Law Review, 10*, 245–255.

Guynn, R. (2012). Are Bailouts Inevitable? *Yale Journal on Regulation, 29*, 121–135.

Haferkamp, A., Fetchenhauer, D., et al. (2009). Efficiency Versus Fairness: The Evaluation of Labor Market Policies by Economists and Laypeople. *Journal of Economic Psychology, 30*(4), 527–539.

Hager, T. (1991). Recent Development: *Milkovich vs. Lorain Journal Co.*: Lost Breathing Space Supreme Court Stifles Freedom of Expression by Eliminating First Amendment Opinion Privilege. *Tulane Law Review, 65*, 944. at 946-947.

Hannan, J. (2008). *A Tale of Two Streets: (Re)presenting Economic Value during the Creation and Passage of the Emergency Economic Stabilization Act*. Retrieved from http://www.natcom.org/NCA/files/ccLibraryFiles/Filename/000000002294/Hanan%20-%20A%20Tale%20of%20Two%20Streets.pdf.

Hardardottir, H. (2017). Long Term Stability of Time Preferences and the Role of the Macroeconomic Situation. *Journal of Economic Psychology, 60*, 21–36.

Harry, D., & Madume, W. (2018). State Intervention/Bailout and Economic Stabilisation in Nigeria: Some Lessons from the United States. *Mediterranean Journal of Social Sciences, 9*(3), 71–77.

Hazera, A., Quirvan, C., & Triki, A. (2017). Too Big to Fail and Bank Loan Accounting in Developing Nations: Evidence from the Mexican Financial Crisis. *Research in Accounting Regulation, 29*, 109–118.

Hung, C., Jiang, Y., & et al. (2017). Bank Political Connections and Performance in China. *Journal of Financial Stability, 32*, 57–69.

Husisian, G. (1990). What Standard Of Care Should Govern the World's Shortest Editorials?: An Analysis of Bond Rating Agency Liability. *Cornell Law Review, 75*, 460–461.

International Institute For Sustainable Development. (2009, March). *Will Government Bailouts Lead to Trade Wars?* https://www.iisd.org/gsi/news/will-government-bailouts-lead-trade-wars.

Iyengar, S. (2012). The Credit Rating Agencies — Are They Reliable? A Study of Sovereign Ratings. *Comparative Political Studies, 37*(1), 69–82.

Jackson, T., & Skeel, D. (2012). Dynamic Resolution of Large Financial Institutions. *Harvard Business Law Review.*

Jensen, N., & McGillivaray, F. (2005). Federal Institutions and Multinational Investors: Federalism, Government Credibility, and Foreign Direct Investment. *International Interactions, 31*(4), 303–325.

Kerwer, D. (2004). *Holding Global Regulators Accountable The Case of Credit Rating Agencies.* Technical University of Munich. Retrieved from https://www.ucl.ac.uk/political-science/publications/downloads/spp-wp-11.pdf

Kiff, J., Nowak, S., & Schumacher, L. (2012). *Are Rating Agencies Powerful? An Investigation into the Impact and Accuracy of Sovereign Ratings.* IMF Working Papers 12/23.

Kim, H. (2019). Information Spillover of Bailouts. *Journal of Financial Intermediation*, In press.

Kingsbury, B. (2009). The Concept of "Law" in Global Administrative Law. *European Journal of International Law, 20*, 23–33.

Kingsbury, B., Krisch, N., & Stewart, R. (2005). The Emergence of Global Administrative Law. *Law & Contemporary Problems, 68*, 15–30.

Kirman, A. (2016). Complexity and Economic Policy: A Paradigm Shift or a Change in Perspective? A Review Essay on David Colander and Roland Kupers's *Complexity and the Art of Public Policy. Journal of Economic Literature, 54*(2), 534–572.

Klingebiel, D. (2000, Feb). *The Use of Asset Management Companies in the Resolution of Banking Crises—Cross-Country Experiences.* Worldbank Working Paper #002284, Washington, DC, USA. Retrieved from http://www1.worldbank.org/finance/assets/images/wp002284.pdf.

Krey, P. (2008, November). The Bailout and the Constitution: the $700 Billion Bank Bailout Plan Will Use Taxpayer Money to Purchase Troubled Assets. How Does This Stack Up Against the Limited Federal Powers Granted by the

Constitution? *The New American*. Retrieved from http://www.thenewamerican.com/index.php/economy/commentary-mainmenu-43/512.

Kruck, A. (2016). Resilient Blunderers: Credit Rating Fiascos and Rating Agencies' Institutionalized Status as Private Authorities. *Journal of European Public Policy, 23*(5), 753–770.

Kuhlman, C., & Mortveit, H. (2014). Attractor Stability in Non-uniform Boolean Networks. *Theoretical Computer Science, 559*, 20–33.

Lawson, G. (2010). Burying the Constitution Under A Tarp. *Harvard Journal of Law and Public Policy,* 33.

Lefeuvre, E. (Natixis—Research) (2010, May 11). *Special Report—Economic Research: Markets Implications of the Support Packages.* http://cib.natixis.com/flushdoc.aspx?id=53032.

Levy, R. (2008, October 20). *Is the Bailout Constitutional?* Cato Institute, USA. http://www.cato.org/pub_display.php?pub_id=9729.

LoPucki, L. (1997). The Systems Approach to Law. *Cornell Law Review, 82*, 479–483.

Lubben, S. (2013). Resolution, Orderly and Otherwise: B of A in OLA. *University Of Cincinnati Law Review, 81*, 485–495.

Lunder, E., Meltz, R., & Thomas, K. (Congressional Research Service) (2009, March 25). *Retroactive Taxation of Executive Bonuses: Constitutionality of H.R. 1586 and S. 651.*

McIntyre, A., & Song, Z. (2019). The US Affordable Care Act: Reflections and Directions at the Close of a Decade. *PLoS Med, 16*(2), e1002752.

Melnik, S., Ward, J., Gleeson, J., & Porter, M. (2013). Multi-stage Complex Contagions. *Chaos, 23*, 013124. https://doi.org/10.1063/1.4790836.

Mennillo, G., & Sinclair, T. (2019). A Hard Nut to Crack: Regulatory Failure Shows How Rating Really Works. *Comparative Political Studies, 23*(3), 266–286.

Miklashevich, I. (2003). Mathematical Representation of Social Systems: Uncertainty and Optimization of Social System Evolution. *Non Linear Phenomena in Complex Systems, 6*(2), 678–686.

Morais, B., Peydro, J., & Ruiz, C. (2015). *The International Bank Lending Channel of Monetary Policy Rates and QE: Credit Supply, Reach-for-Yield, and Real Effects.* International Finance Discussion Papers 1137.

Nagy, T. (2009). Credit Rating Agencies and the First Amendment: Applying Constitutional Journalistic Protections to Subprime Mortgage Litigation. *Minnesota Law Review, 479*, 140–160.

Nästegård, E. (2016). *Credit Rating Agencies and the First Amendment Defence in the US.* Nordic & European Company Law Working Paper No. 16-17, Available at SSRN: https://ssrn.com/abstract=2893564

Nguyen, V., & Claus, E. (2013). Good News, Bad News, Consumer Sentiment and Consumption Behavior. *Journal of Economic Psychology, 39*, 426–438.
Nwogugu, M. (2005a). Towards Multifactor Models of Decision Making and Risk: Critique of Prospect Theory and Related Approaches, Part One. *Journal of Risk Finance, 6*(2), 150–162.
Nwogugu, M. (2005b). Towards Multifactor Models of Decision Making and Risk: Critique of Prospect Theory and Related Approaches, Part Two. *Journal of Risk Finance, 6*(2), 163–173.
Nwogugu, M. (2005c). Towards Multifactor Models of Decision Making and Risk: Critique of Prospect Theory and Related Approaches, Part Three. *Journal of Risk Finance, 6*(3), 267–276.
Nwogugu, M. (2006). Regret Minimization, Willingness-To-Accept-Losses and Framing. *Applied Mathematics & Computation, 179*(2), 440–450.
Nwogugu, M. (2009). Entrepreneurship and New Theories of Equity-Based Incentives Taxation. *International Tax Review, 37*(4), 270–275.
Nwogugu, M. (2010, Revised 2013). *Problems Inherent in the Compensation and Business Models of Credit Rating Agencies.* Available at: www.researchgate.com and www.ssrn.com.
Nwogugu, M. (2012). *Risk in the Global Real Estate Markets.* John Wiley.
Nwogugu, M. (2013/2015). *Structural Changes, Competition And Financial Stability: Accounting Firms, Credit Rating Agencies (CRAs) And Allocation Mechanisms.*
Nwogugu, M. (2014). *Group-Decisions, Systemic Risk and Politics: The Resolution of Non-Performing Loans.* Available at SSRN: https://ssrn.com/abstract=2537102 or https://doi.org/10.2139/ssrn.2537102.
Nwogugu, M. (2021a). Chapter 4: A Comparison of CRAs (Credit Rating Agencies), Management Consulting Firms, Environmental Auditing Firms, Tax Consulting Firms, and Auditing/Accounting Firms. In M. Nwogugu (Ed.), *Complex Systems and Sustainability in the Global Auditing, Consulting, and Credit Rating Agency Industries.* IGI Global.
Nwogugu, M. (2021b). Chapter 7: The Existing and Proposed Credit Rating Agency (CRA) Business Models and Compensation Models Are Inefficient. In M. Nwogugu (Ed.), *Complex Systems and Sustainability in the Global Auditing, Consulting, and Credit Rating Agency Industries.* IGI Global.
Nwogugu, M. (2021c). Chapter 8: Complex Systems, Competition/Antitrust, and Legal Problems in the Global Credit Rating Agency Industry. In M. Nwogugu (Ed.), *Complex Systems and Sustainability in the Global Auditing, Consulting, and Credit Rating Agency Industries.* IGI Global.

Ochsen, C., & Welsch, H. (2012). Who Benefits from Labor Market Institutions? Evidence from Surveys of Life Satisfaction. *Journal of Economic Psychology, 33*(1), 112–124.

OECD, ed. (2016). *New Approaches to Economic Challenges—Insights into Complexity and Policy*. 29-30 September 2016. OECD Headquarters, Paris. https://www.Oecd.Org/Naec/Insights%20into%20Complexity%20and%20Policy.Pdf.

Ofo, N. (2011). *Is the Asset Management Corporation of Nigeria Designed to Fail?*. Retrieved from SSRN: http://ssrn.com/abstract=1751459 or https://doi.org/10.2139/ssrn.1751459.

Ogun, O. (2012). *An Appraisal of the Asset Management Corporation of Nigeria (AMCON) Act, 2010*. http://topeadebayollp.wordpress.com/2012/02/28/an-appraisal-of-the-asset-management-corporation-of-nigeria-amcon-act-2010/.

Olalere, P. (2014). Privatization of Electricity Industry in Nigeria: Lessons from Europe and United States of America. *Renewable Energy Law and Policy Review, 5*(2), 136–149.

Oriakhogba, D., & Odiase-Alegimenlen, O. (2011). Regime for the Regulation of the Electricity Market in Nigeria: An Appraisal. *Ahmadu Bello University Journal of Public and International Law*, 1(5), 116-133. Available at SSRN: https://ssrn.com/abstract=3283101.

Pancrazi, R., Seoane, H., & Vukotić, M. (2020). Welfare Gains of Bailouts in a Sovereign Default Model. *Journal of Economic Dynamics and Control, 113*, 1.

Pántya, J., Kovács, J., et. al. (2016). Work Performance and Tax Compliance in Flat and Progressive Tax Systems. *Journal of Economic Psychology*, 56, 262-273.

Palekar, C. (2013). *Transformational Issues For GENCOs And DISCOs*. Retrieved from https://www.pwc.com/ng/en/assets/pdf/pwc-round-table-post-privatisation.pdf.

Perc, M., Donnay, K., & Helbing, D. (2013). Understanding Recurrent Crime as System-Immanent Collective Behavior. *PLOS ONE, 8*(10), e76063.

Poretti, P. (2009). *The Regulation of Subsidies within the General Agreement on Trade in Services—Problems and Perspectives* (Kluwer Law International, 2009).

Posner, E., & Vermeule, A. (2009). Crisis Governance in the Administrative State: 9/11 and the Financial Meltdown of 2008. *The University of Chicago Law Review, 76*, 1613–1626. http://lawreview.uchicago.edu/issues/archive/v76/76_4/PosnerVermeule.pdf.

Post, D. G., & Eisen, M. (2000). How Long Is the Coastline of the Law? Thoughts on the Fractal Nature of Legal Systems. *Journal of Legal Studies, 29*, 545–555.

Qian, F., McQuade, T., & Diamond, R. (2019). The Effects of Rent Control Expansion on Tenants, Landlords, and Inequality: Evidence from San Francisco. *American Economic Review, 109*(9), 3365–3394.

Rahn, R. (2008, November 5). *Is It Constitutional?* Cato Institute, USA. http://www.cato.org/pub_display.php?pub_id=9772.

Rajan, R. (2000). Government Bailouts and Monetary Disequilibrium: Common Fundamentals in the Mexican and East Asian Currency Crises. *The North American Journal of Economics and Finance, 11*(2), 123–135.

Room, G. (2011). *Complexity, Institutions, and Public Policy.*

Ruhl, J. & Ruhl, H. (n.d.). The Arrow of the Law in Modern Administrative States: Using Complexity Theory to Reveal the Diminishing Returns and Increasing Risks the Burgeoning of Law Poses to Society. *University of California Davis Law Review*, 30, 405-426 (explaining the various kinds of attractors).

Salzano, M., & Colander, D. (2007). *Complexity Hints for Economic Policy.* London: Springer.

Scheuerman, W. (2000). Exception and Emergency Powers: The Economic State of Emergency. *Cardozo Law Review, 21*(1869), 1883–1884.

Schniter, E., Shields, T., & Sznycer, D. (2020). Trust in Humans and Robots: Economically Similar But Emotionally Different. *Journal of Economic Psychology, 78*, 1.

Shah, A. (2009). Note: Recent Developments: Emergency Economic Stabilization Act of 2008. *Harvard Journal on Legislation, 46*, 570–575. http://www.harvardjol.com/wp-content/uploads/2009/09/569-584.pdf.

Shukla, S. (2014). Emerging Issues and Challenges for HRM in Public Sectors Banks of India. *Procedia—Social and Behavioral Sciences*, 358–363.

Somer, J. (2015). Why Bail-in? And How! *Economic Policy Review.*

Thompson, F., Gusmano, M., & Shinohara, S. (2018). Trump and the Affordable Care Act: Congressional Repeal Efforts, Executive Federalism, and Program Durability. *Publius: The Journal of Federalism, 48*(3), 396–424.

Thomson, J. (2010). *Cleaning Up the Refuse from a Financial Crisis: The Case for a Resolution Management Corporation.* Federal Reserve Bank of Cleveland Working Paper 10-15 of September 2010.

Torgler, B., & Schneider, F. (2009). The Impact of Tax Morale and Institutional Quality on the Shadow Economy. *Journal of Economic Psychology, 30*(2), 228–245.

Trujillo, E. (2010). International Trade and the Financial Crisis. *Proceedings of the Annual Meeting (American Society of International Law), 104*, 438–443.

U.S. Department of Justice (2009, October). *Constitutionality of Mandatory Registration of Credit Rating Agencies.* Retrieved from http://www.justice.gov/olc/2009/opinion-letter-treasury.pdf.

Uddin, A., & Chowdhury, M., et al. (2020). Revisiting the Impact of Institutional Quality on Post-GFC Bank Risk-taking: Evidence from Emerging Countries. *Emerging Markets Review*, in-press.

Ukoha, K., & Agbaeze, E. (2018). Deregulation of the Nigerian Power Sector on Performance: A Review. *European Journal of Scientific Research, 148*(3), 377–385.

Unterman, A. (2009). Innovative Destruction — Structured Finance and Credit Market Reform in the Bubble Era. *Hastings Business Law Journal, 5*, 53–77.

Valentine, S. (2010). Canada's Constitutional Separation of (Wind) Power. *Energy Policy, 38*(4), 1918–1930.

Vanberg, G. (2011). Substance vs. Procedure: Constitutional Enforcement and Constitutional Choice. *Journal of Economic Behavior & Organization, 80*(2), 309–318.

Vaugirard, V. (2007). Bank Bailouts and Political Instability. *European Journal of Political Economy, 23*(4), 21–837.

Ventoruzzo, M., & Sandrelli, G. (2019). O Tell Me the Truth About Bail-in: Theory and Practice. *Journal of Business & Technology Law Proxy.*

Verkuil, P. (2006). Public Law Limitations on Privatization of Government Functions. *North Carolina Law Review, 84*, 397–415.

Vermeule, A. (2009). Our Schmittian Administrative Law. *Harvard Law Review, 122*, 1095–1140.

Wadhwa, P., Belton, T., Chang, J., Mackie, D., & Marrese, M. (J. P. Morgan) (2010, May 14). *European Rates Strategy: The European Stabilization Mechanism.* https://mm.jpmorgan.com/stp/t/c.do?i=E0271-555&u=a_p*d_414788.pdf*h_ajfko049.

Wang, L., Menkhoff, L., et al. (2019). Politicians' Promotion Incentives and Bank Risk Exposure in China. *Journal of Banking & Finance, 99*, 63–94.

Wang, R., & Sui, Y. (2019). Political Institutions and Foreign Banks' Risk-taking in Emerging Markets. *Journal of Multinational Financial Management, 51*, 45–60.

Webel, B. & Murphy, E. (2008, November 25). *The Emergency Economic Stabilization Act and Current Financial Turmoil: Issues and Analysis.* Retrieved from http://www.fas.org/sgp/crs/misc/RL34730.pdf.

White, L. (2019). The Credit Rating Agencies and Their Role in the Financial System. Chapter- in. In E. Brousseau et al. (Eds.), *Oxford Handbook on Institutions, International Economic Governance, and Market Regulation.* Oxford: Oxford University Press.

Williams, B. (2014). Bank Risk and National Governance in Asia. *Journal of Banking & Finance, 49*, 10–26.

Williams, C., & Arrigo, B. A. (2002). *Law, Psychology and Justice: Chaos Theory And New (Dis)Order.* Albany: State University of New York Press.

Young, T. (1997). The ABCs of Crime: Attractors, Bifurcations and Chaotic Dynamics. In D. Milanovic (Ed.), *Chaos, Criminology and Social Justice: The New Orderly (Dis)Order.* Praeger Publishers.

Zaring, D. (2005). Informal Procedure, Hard and Soft, in International Administration. *Chicago Journal of International Law, 5*, 547–557.

Zaring, D. (2008). Rulemaking and Adjudication in International Law. *Columbia Journal of Transnational Law, 46*, 563–573.

Zhou, B., & Kumar, P. (2012). *Economic Considerations in Litigation Against the Credit Rating Agencies.* The Brattle Group, Inc. Retrieved from https://brattlefiles.blob.core.windows.net/files/8177_economic_considerations_in_litigation_against_credit_rating_agencies_apr_2012.pdf

CHAPTER 4

International Constitutional Political Economy and Sustainability Issues Inherent in Accounting and Derivatives Standards-Setting Organizations

The FASB (Financial Accounting Standards Board, USA), IASB (International Accounting Standards Board), GASB (Government Accounting Standards Board, USA), the International Auditing and Assurance Standards Board (IAASB)), Partnership for Carbon Accounting Financials (PCAF), SASB (Sustainability Accounting Standards Board, USA), the ISDA (International Swap & Derivatives Association; http://www.isda.org/) and the ICMA (International Capital Market Association; http://www.icmagroup.org/) and FINRA (USA) are among a class of very powerful trade associations that have "Quasi-Executive Powers" (similar to powers of the executive branch of the federal governments of countries) even though they are not part of the government (but are implicitly supported and encouraged by governments). IASB/FASB/GASB/SASB/PCAF perform important rule-making functions and affect accounting regulations, companies, Climate Policy, Sustainability efforts, ESG investing, financial institutions and government regulation around the world (many foreign countries raise capital or list their shares in the US markets, and many US companies operate in foreign countries). The FASB, GASB, SASB, IAASB, PCAF, ICMA, ISDA and IASB and their

M. I. C. Nwogugu, *Geopolitical Risk, Sustainability and "Cross-Border Spillovers" in Emerging Markets, Volume II*,
https://doi.org/10.1007/978-3-030-71419-2_4

standards are unconstitutional and that can affect responses to accounting/derivatives regulations and standards and general economic activity.

FINRA (and similar self-regulatory industry-associations in other countries), ISDA and ICMA perform important rule-making functions and affect accounting regulations, companies, financial institutions and government regulation around the world. The ISDA and ICMA and their standards are unconstitutional and that affects or may affect responses to accounting standards and also general economic activity. Government bailouts of financial institutions are also unconstitutional. Government bailouts/bail-ins and sustainability/ESG investing are largely based on regulatory, accounting and swaps/derivatives standards that are developed by ISDA, ICMA, IASB, IAASB, PCAF, GASB, FASB and SASB and FINRA-type associations. The unconstitutionality of these "institutions" can affect conventional and unconventional monetary policy; can increase actual and potential systemic risk, propensity for anti-competitive misconduct and financial instability; and are elements of structural changes in those industries.

The Sarbanes Oxley Act of 2002 (SOX) was enacted by the US government in response to corporate governance and earning management problems (SOX isn't discussed in this book). Other countries and jurisdictions have enacted statutes that are very similar to SOX—such as the United Kingdom's Companies (Audit, Investigations and Community Enterprise) Act of 2004. The EU enacted the Financial Services Action Plan (www.financial-services-action-plan.com); and the European Union's 8th Company Law Directive on Statutory Audit (Directive 2006/43/EC) (www.8th-company-law-directive.com). India enacted Clause-49. The China Securities Regulatory Commission (CSRC) passed the Company Law and the Securities Law, both of which became effective in May 2006. Japan's Financial Instruments and Exchange Act was enacted on June 14, 2006, and became effective in April 2008. The Canadian government enacted "Policy 52-109", and Ontario (Canada) enacted "Keeping the Promise for a Strong Economy Act (Budget Measures) of 2002". Australia's government enacted the "CLERP-9".

Accounting and sustainability standards setting are usually done at the national level in most countries—by: (i) a government agency that sets the standards via regulations; or (ii) a government agency that expressly adopts accounting/sustainability standards set by a non-governmental entity; or (iii) by government agencies that incorporate into their regulations, accounting/sustainability standards created by a non-governmental entity. The IASB is based in the UK and coordinates the harmonization of accounting principles across many countries. Many countries have either adopted IASB's IFRS or have supplemented their national accounting regulations with parts of IFRS. The IASB coordinates the development of the IFRS accounting standards. FASB, SASB and GASB are based in the US and they develop GAAP accounting standards for use in the US—however, many countries have also copied FASB/GASB/SASB standards; and companies that want to list their stocks or bonds on the US financial exchanges and foreign companies that are required to file regulatory reports in the US also have to comply with FASB and SASB. India's accounting standards were created by the Ministry of Corporate Affairs and are similar to International Financial Reporting Standards (IFRS). These accounting standards are formulated by Accounting Standards Board of Institute of Chartered Accountants of India. On July 13, 2007, the Securities and Exchange Commission of Brazil—Comissão de Valores Mobiliários, or CVM (www.cvm.gov.br)—issued Rule No. 457 which requires listed companies to publish their consolidated financial statements according to IFRS, starting with reporting periods that ended in 2010. In December 2009, the Brazilian Accounting Pronouncements Committee (CPC) adopted a Portuguese version of the IFRS for SMEs as an option for SMEs in Brazil. The CPC's SME standard was endorsed by the Brazilian Federal Accounting Council (CFC) by enactment of Resolution-1255 of 2009. The new Chinese accounting standards and the IFRS are almost 90–95% similar. The Chinese accounting standard systems is composed of the Basic Standard (38 specific standards) and application guidance. The IFRS Foundation made the following observations (in 2016) about the adoption of IFRS around the world:

1. There has been significant acceptance of IFRS and 95% of the sixty-six jurisdictions that were surveyed have publicly committed to the concept of a single set of high-quality global accounting standards and to IFRS standards.
2. More than 80% of the respondents stated that IFRS have been adopted and almost all were exchange-traded companies.
3. The jurisdictions that have adopted IFRS claim to have made very few modifications to the standards (the modifications were often described as limited, temporary and of little impact).

This chapter uses the US Constitution and case law to analyze issues, but the principles and conclusions are also applicable in most common law countries and in the 70+ countries whose constitutions are similar to the US Constitution.[1]

4.1 Existing Literature

The IASB's IFRS standards have been widely adopted or copied in many Emerging Markets countries and thus the politicization of IASB standards-setting directly affects Emerging Markets countries. See: Temiz and Gulec (2017), Rehman and Shahzad (2014), Melgarejo (2017) and Dima, Dima, et al. (2014).

Some researchers have also commented on the trade implications of accounting regulations and government—see comments in Trujillo (2010), Poretti (2009), Delimatsis (2012) and International Institute for Sustainable Development (March 2009). The literature on *International Political Economy* of Accounting Standards Setting is significant—see: Camfferman (2020), Botzem (2012), Gäumann and Dobler (2019), Giner and Mora (2019), Jorissen et al. (2013), Sokolov (2016), Walton (2020), Königsgruber (2010, 2014, 2017), Weiss and Gronewold (2020), Morley (2016), De Luca and Prather-Kinsey (2018), Dobler and Knospe (2016), Chiapello and Mediad (2009), Fleckner (2008), Gros and Worret (2016), Konigsgruber (2013), Hoffmann and Zülch (2014), Konigsgruber and Palan (2015), and Li and Soobaroyen (2020). On the *International Political Economy*[2] of the ISDA and ICMA, see: Dinov (2017), Biggins and Scott (2012), Menkes (2019) and Liu, Lejot and Arner (2012).

While the Accounting/Derivatives Standards Setting Organizations are pervasive around the world (via Multinational Corporations, international/local banks and insurance companies; cross-border swaps/derivatives and foreign companies whose shares/bonds are listed in foreign financial exchanges), it's not clear that the dynamics and Multiplier Effects of these

[1] *See*: Go (2003) ("Many of the post-colonial constitutions in existence in 2000 were written in the 1990s").

See: Law and Versteeg (2012). The Declining Influence Of The United States Constitution. *NYU Law Review*, 87, 762–826. http://www.nyulawreview.org/sites/default/files/pdf/NYULawReview-87-3-Law-Versteeg_0.pdf. This article notes that the US Constitution is similar to those of many countries.

[2] *See*: ICMA (2015). *ICMA Response to ESMA CSD Regulatory Level 2 Consultation Paper*. February 19th 2015. Available: http://www.icmagroup.org/Regulatory-Policy-and-Market-Practice/short-term-markets/Repo-Markets/erc-contribution.

See: ISDA (2017). *ISDA response To The Fair And Effective Markets Review Consultation*. Available: http://www.bankofengland.co.uk/markets/Documents/femr/isda.pdf.

organizations are being fully incorporated into quantitative models in published research (i.e. within the context of Panel Vector Autoregressive models, Granger Causality, GARCH-type Models, Economic Modelling, Economic Forecasting, Political Decisions, Behavioral Macroeconomics, Behavioral Expectations, Peer Effects, sovereign debt crisis, VaR estimation; sovereign debt crisis, financial markets regulation, Portfolio Management, Tail Risk, etc.).

There is very scant literature on the constitutional political economy and un-constitutionality of IASB, GASB, SASB, FASB, ICMA and ISDA and FINRA-type associations. However, the literature notes that IASB, FASB, GASB and US SEC rule-making has been and remains heavily politicized with significant political lobbying. Nwogugu (2010) noted that the existence and activities of non-governmental Accounting and Derivatives standards-setting organizations (such as FASB, GASB, SASB, IAASB, PCAF, IASB, ICMA and ISDA) were unconstitutional.

Its notable that in the Labor Economics and Labor Regulation literatures, most studies have completely omitted (or didn't adequately analyze) constitutional analysis of workers' *Right-to-Contract, Right-of-Association* and *Equal Protection* rights. These three constitutional rights are central to workers' rights and ability to negotiate working conditions and to push for implementation of Collective Bargaining agreements, both of which account for a significant percentage of labor-related litigation and economic Multiplier Effects. Even studies such as Mwakagali (2018) that take the legal approach have failed to fully analyze the Constitutional Law and Constitutional Political Economy implications of workers' *Right-to-Contract* and *Right-of-Association*. Some researchers have also commented on the trade implications of accounting regulations and government bailouts—see comments in Trujillo (2010), Poretti (2009), Delimatsis (2012) and International Institute for Sustainable Development (March 2009).

The literature on associated institutional law and economics is well developed. Kunst and Wagner (2011) discussed the concept of constitutional framework and its role in ordering society. Metelska-Szaniawska (2010) found substantial positive correlations between constitutional rules and the economic reform process in post-socialist countries of Europe and Asia after 1989. Metelska-Szaniawska (2010) is among many studies that have confirmed similar relationships in developed countries. Doring and Schnellenbach (2010) compared federalism in Germany and the US, and concluded that a constitutional framework of competitive federalism does not prevent the long-term centralization of competencies; that formal institutions affect the pathways of government centralization and that informal political institutions may have a substantial effect on the preservation of state and local autonomy. These "*informal political institutions*" include trade associations, standards organizations (such as FASB, IASB, ISDA, IAASB, SASB, PCAF, ISDA and ICMA), specific statutes (such as Sarbanes Oxley Act), quasi-government agencies, and so on. Blomquist and Ostrom (2009), and Witt and Schubert (2009) analyzed various elements of Constitutional Political Economy. Mistri (2007) analyzed the constitutional political economy of the creation of the Euro, and noted that the inherent conflict among the monetary systems of the constituent countries has been acted out according to the single states' collective preference functions, wherein both employment and price stability are major elements of said preference functions. Similarly, risk measurement and risk management in the global financial system involve substantial standardization of processes and most financial institutions use similar risk models; and the emergent consensus standards (ISDA, BIS, Basel-III, IASB/IFRS/ICMA/SASB/PCAF) are a function of conflicts among the regulatory systems of various countries and preference functions of both government regulators and managers of large financial institutions.

The FASB standards and the IASB's IFRS standards and ISDA/ICMA derivatives standards have been widely adopted or copied in many Emerging Markets countries and thus the politicization of accounting/derivatives standards setting directly affects Emerging Markets countries. See: Temiz and Gulec (2017), Rehman and Shahzad (2014), Melgarejo (2017) and Dima et al. (2014).

4.1.1 Omissions of In-depth Analysis of Constitutionally Granted Right-to-Contract, Equal Protection *and* Right-of-Association *in the Labor Regulation and Labor Economics Literatures: A Critique of Mwakagali (2018)*

Its notable that in the Labor Economics and Labor Regulation literatures, most studies have completely omitted (or didn't adequately analyze) constitutional analysis[3] of workers' *Right-to-Contract*, *Right-of-Association* and *Equal Protection* rights. These three constitutional rights are central to workers' rights and ability to negotiate working conditions and to push for implementation of Collective Bargaining agreements, both of which

[3] *See*: "*Unions, Retirees Sue To Block Chicago Pension Changes*". By Karen Pierog. Dec. 16, 2014. https://www.reuters.com/article/usa-chicago-pensions-lawsuit/update-2-unions-retirees-sue-to-block-chicago-pension-changes-idUSL1N0U01MO20141216.

account for a significant percentage of Labor-related litigation and economic Multiplier Effects.

Even studies such as Mwakagali (2018) that take the legal approach have failed to fully analyze the Constitutional Law and Constitutional Political Economy implications of workers' *Right-to-Contract* and *Right-of-Association*.

4.2 Geopolitical Risk and Some Economic Psychology[4] and Cross-Border *Spillover Effects* of FASB/GASB/SASB/IASB/IAASB/PCAF, ICMA and ISDA (*Cross-Border Spillovers* into Emerging Markets)

4.2.1 Some Cross-Border Spillovers and Economic Psychology Effects

The significant literatures on social networks, social capital and cross-border *spillover effects* are summarized in Chap. 2 of this book. FASB/GASB/SASB/IASB/IAASB/PCAF and ICMA/ISDA had and continue to have worldwide *Multiplier Effects* because of the following in addition to other factors:

1. The evolution of accounting and derivatives standards-setting organizations in various countries can be deemed to constitute global structural changes in the financial services industry and other industries.[5]
2. Given the foregoing, accounting standards organizations and derivatives standards organizations have become important financial intermediation/disintermediation (i.e. disintermediation of traditional financial institutions) mechanisms partly because: (1) they dictate the relationship between issuers and investors, and between parties to derivatives contracts; (2) they significantly affect the disintermediation of financial services companies; (3) they affect the relationships between consumers and financial services

[4] On associated *Economic Psychology* and *Behavioral IPE* issues, see: Hardardottir (2017), Birz (2017), Dixon et al. (2014), Ochsen and Welsch (2012), Debelle (2004), Schniter et al. (2020), Garcia et al. (2020), Torgler and Schneider (2009), Nguyen and Claus (2013), Banker et al. (2020), and Blaufus et al. (2019).

[5] *See*: Nwogugu (2015).

companies and consumers' disintermediation decisions; (4) they affect the savings rates, expenditures, risk-perception and investment patterns of households, companies and parties to derivatives contracts. Government bailout programs are also types of financial intermediation.

3. During 2010–2020, various new US, European, Latin American and Asian government administrative agencies emerged and in combination with entities such as IASB, FASB, SASB, IAASB, PCAF, ISDA, ICMA and GASB have created various categories of "*regulatory fragmentation*" and "regulatory capture" and new "administrative laws".
4. The "modern administrative state" (as exemplified by IASB/FASB/SASB/GASB/IAASB/PCAF and ISDA/ICMA) in various countries has veered from their constitutions—as noted by Lawson (2010).
5. In July 2010, the International Monetary Fund (IMF) issued a set of recommendations for strengthening risk regulation in the US, in the light of the Emergency Economic Stabilization Act of 2008 (EESA; USA) and the then pending Financial Stability Act of 2010 (Dodd-Frank Act). *See*: IMF (July 9, 2010). The G20 and G30 and other regulatory entities also issued their own recommendations for financial stability. *See*: G20 (April 2, 2009), Group of Thirty (2009), de Larosière et al. (2009), Lord Turner (2009). All these recommendations and statutes have not been effective,[6] partly because they didn't restructure (or didn't require the government takeover of) the IASB/GASB/FASB/IAASB/PCAF, ISDA and ICMA. *See*: Norton (2009), Bertezzolo (2009), Meyer (2009), Verdier (2009), Hamann and Fabri (2008), Piccioto (2008), Norton (1995), Arner (2007) and Weber and Arner (2008).

[6] *See:* Arner and Taylor (2009) which states in part: "The FSB and the BIS currently serve the primary role in coordination of the process of standard-setting. As noted, the FSF was established under the auspices of a G7 mandate in February 1999, with a threefold purpose: (1) promote international financial stability; (2) improve the functioning of markets; and (3) reduce systemic risk through enhanced information exchange and international cooperation in financial market supervision and surveillance. The FSF, as originally constituted, included five different types of members: national authorities, international financial institutions, other international organizations, international financial organizations and committees of central bank experts … The FSF agreed upon twelve key standards areas (See http://www.financialstabilityboard.org/cos/key_standards.htm)".

6. There are important international trade considerations and ramifications of accounting and derivatives standards setting and government bailouts. The Global Financial Crisis of 2007–2014 has highlighted the need for the re-evaluation and restructuring of incentives, traditional institutions and analysis of institutions. Analysis in Institutional Economics has been largely defined by formal models and cost-benefit analysis, which collectively have not solved many modern problems inherent in institutions. Spiegler and Milberg explained how this traditional approach to Institutional Economics has been insufficient, and state that there is more explanatory power in "quasi-models" which are a vaguer, nuanced and narrative version of the formal models of Institutional Economics. *See*: Milberg and Piegler (2009), Boettke and Aligica (2009), Vanberg (2005).
7. The unconstitutionality of IASB, FASB, GASB, SASB, IAASB, PCAF, ISDA and the ICMA creates or can create *deadweight losses* in: (1) the demand and supply of legal enforcement around the world; (2) the demand and supply of auditing services around the world; (3) the pricing of securities.
8. FASB/GASB/SASB/IASB/IAASB/PCAF and ICMA/ISDA directly and indirectly regulate US and EU and East Asian multinational corporations (MNCs) which have significant global operations and are influential in international trade—and many of these US and EU and East Asian MNCs have major suppliers that are located in Emerging Markets countries (e.g. Mexico, Brazil, India, Philippines, Chile, Peru, China, African countries, ASEAN countries) that essentially have to comply with US and/or EU or East Asian business/legal standards. Also, MNCs' operations in foreign countries are a transmission channel for cross-border *Corporate Governance Contagion* and *Operations Policies Contagion*. "Secondary-level emerging markets countries" such as Nigeria benefit from these US-, EU- and East Asian–influenced international trade/financial relationships—for example Nigeria sells its petroleum products to India, imports large volumes of goods from China and borrows large amounts from China.
9. FASB/GASB/SASB/IASB/IAASB/PCAF and ICMA/ISDA standards/regulations are "core" regulations for the global capital markets and the global derivatives markets, and thus they can affect market volatility, pricing of financial instruments, market integration and spillovers.

10. Many countries have copied parts of FASB/GASB/SASB/IASB/IAASB/PCAF and ICMA/ISDA standards/regulations or have enacted statutes/regulations that are similar to them, or have the same objectives. Such *regulatory contagion* amplifies the effects of FASB/GASB/SASB/IASB/IAASB/PCAF and ICMA/ISDA and makes them more acceptable in Emerging Markets countries.
11. FASB/GASB/SASB/IASB/IAASB/PCAF and ICMA/ISDA directly and indirectly regulate foreign companies that do business in the US, EU and East Asia, and/or whose shares and/or debt are traded on US and EU financial exchanges; and those that raise money in the US or EU.
12. FASB/GASB/SASB/IASB/IAASB/PCAF and ICMA/ISDA have significant worldwide economic *Multiplier Effects* and *spillover effects* across national borders because they affect and regulate the financing of international trade, international capital flows, capital raising, financial regulation and so on.
13. During 2010–2020, more than 50% of international trade was conducted with the US dollar and an average of about 59% of governments' foriegn currency reserves around the world were held in US Dollars. The US dollar is managed by the US Federal Reserve and the large international US banks, all of which are significantly affected by, and also affect, FASB/GASB/SASB/IASB/IAASB/PCAF and ICMA/ISDA. During 2005–2020, the US Federal Reserve emerged as the central bank to the world because of the worldwide impact of its activities and policies.
14. FASB/GASB/SASB/IASB/IAASB/PCAF and ICMA/ISDA directly and indirectly regulate and have substantial effects on non-financial industries that are global industries—such as hotel chains, restaurant chains, insurance, logistics/distribution, technology/Internet, and telecommunications.
15. Around the world, sustainability and ESG-investing standards and measurements are based in part on environmental audits, accounting audits and compliance with FASB/GASB/SASB/IASB/IAASB/PCAF regulations—all of which affect international capital flows, FDI (foreign direct investment), FI (foreign investment) and foreign aid.
16. The domestic and international capital flows that determine sustainability and economic growth around the world are partly based on ICMA/ISDA regulations/standards.

17. FASB/GASB/SASB/IASB/IAASB/PCAF and ICMA/ISDA directly and indirectly regulate and have substantial effects on non-financial industries that employ significant numbers of immigrants such as hotel-chains, restaurants, construction, agriculture, retail-trade, business services and healthcare/home-health services. These immigrants send remittances to, and make investments in Emerging markets countries. Also immigrant-expenditures are not tied to their countries-of-origin—for example Philippines/Filipino immigrants in the United Kingdom can send remittances to relatives in Sri Lanka or UAE or South Africa; and/or make investments in Kenya or Uganda (where there are substantial immigrant communities). FASB/GASB/SASB/IASB/IAASB/PCAF and ICMA/ISDA regulate and have significant effects on the financing of construction activity around the world. Construction activity metrics are major economic indicators in most developed and developing countries. In many developed and developing countries, the global construction industry imports significant volumes of finished/semi-finished products from Emerging Markets countries, and the construction industry employs a significant number of immigrants who, in turn, send remittances, investments and knowledge/human capital to Emerging Markets countries, all of which affect the GDP/exports/productivity of those countries.
18. FASB/GASB/SASB/IASB/PCAF/ISDA/ICMA are likely to be influential in emerging markets countries that use or have used the US dollar or the EU euro as their official currencies—these countries include Poland, Ecuador, El Salvador, Zimbabwe, Timor-Leste, Micronesia, Palau and the Marshall Islands. The following countries/regions also widely use the US Dollar and/or the Euro simultaneously with their own local currencies—Bahamas, Barbados, St. Kitts and Nevis, Belize, Costa Rica, Nicaragua, Panama, Myanmar, Cambodia and Liberia, as well as several Caribbean territories; and British territories in the Caribbean (Turks and Caicos and the British Virgin Islands).
19. FASB/GASB/SASB/IASB and ICMA/ISDA have affected and are likely to continue to affect legislation and adjudication in many countries because many such countries' statutes/regulations expressly or impliedly incorporate FASB/GASB/SASB/IASB and ICMA/ISDA standards/regulations.

20. The accounting and economics literature notes that accounting regulations have significant effects on international trade—and thus have significant effects on Emerging Markets countries, many of whom have trade-based and/or commodities-based economies. During the last ten years, the WTO (World Trade Organization) created working committees to analyze accounting regulations and accounting standards setting. Similarly, swaps/derivatives standards (ICMA and ISDA) and regulations have significant effects on international capital flows and financing in Emerging Markets countries, and the number of contracts and dollar volumes of swaps/derivatives trading in Emerging Market countries have increased significantly during the last twenty years.
21. Accounting and derivatives standards and associated standards-setting organizations, social networks and social capital dynamics have or can have significant effects on government tax policies, perceived tax equity, tax sensitivity and tax compliance (by individuals and companies), all of which can affect savings/investments, remittances (to Emerging Markets), loan volumes (to Emerging Markets), FDI/foreign investment/foreign aid, consumer confidence, consumer expenditures, business confidence, corporate expenditures, government expenditures, risk-Perception and so on.
22. Accounting/Derivatives Standards directly and indirectly affect governments' fiscal policy (corporate taxation; government's revenues from fees, levies and fines; cost of corporate financial distress and bankruptcy; litigation costs; compliance reporting; incorporation of Accounting/Derivatives Standards in regulations/statutes; etc.) and monetary policy (earnings management and market volatility, stock market crashes, money supply, liquidity in financial markets, bubbles; stock market–driven inflation/deflation, risk perception [corporate bonds, stocks, etc.]; economic models and capital-adequacy models; derivatives compliance reports; contagion; etc.), all of which can have cross-border Multiplier Effects in emerging markets countries through the channels explained in this book. Many of the regulations issued by the US government are based on FASB/SASB/IAASB/PCAF accounting standards, and FASB accounting standards are very similar to IASB/IFRS standards. A significant percentage of international investors use FASB and IASB/IFRS accounting standards to evaluate investments—

that is, FASB accounting standards (US corporate accounting standards) are widely used around the world (by both foreign companies and international investors). A significant portion of international Derivatives transactions are documented and settled in US Dollars, and are based on ICMA and ISDA standards. The global dominance of the US dollar was discussed in Chap. 1 of this book.

23. The US has the most advanced and comprehensive financial regulations and creates some of the most sophisticated financial products in the world. The US has been at the forefront of enactment of financial/economic laws at both the federal and state levels. Many developing countries (and developed countries) copied their financial laws from US laws. For example, the Brazilian constitution is based on the US Constitution, and REIT statutes worldwide are based on US REIT laws. Many countries have created variants of the Dodd-Frank Act and the Sarbanes Oxley Act (SOX). Mortgage/foreclosure laws in many countries are very similar to US mortgage/foreclosure laws. Many developing countries and "transition" countries of Eastern Europe derived their mortgage/foreclosure laws from US laws.
24. FASB accounting standards (US corporate accounting standards) are widely used around the world (by both foreign companies and international investors). During the last twenty years, the US consistently had the largest national economy in the world, and the US economy directly/indirectly (through international trade, outsourcing, FDI, FI, foreign aid, etc.) supported the economies of other "First-Level Associated" countries (such as China, Japan, Brazil, Mexico, India) which, in turn, directly/directly supported (through international trade, outsourcing, loans, FDI, FI, foreign aid, etc.) the economies of other "Second-Level Associated" countries (such as Russia, Nigeria, the Philippines, Thailand, ASEAN countries, Pakistan, Central American countries, CIS countries).
25. During 1980–2020, the US was a major participant in major multilateral and bilateral trade agreements; and the US-China Trade War (2019–present) continues to have significant economic/social/psychological *Multiplier Effects* on many countries. The use of the terms "First-Level Associated" countries and "Second-Level Associated" countries is introduced here as a "mutual-dependency" classification of countries as a way to better reflect the often symbi-

otic relationships between countries with regard to international trade and international capital flows.

26. The un-constitutionality of accounting and derivatives standards-setting organizations can have substantial direct/indirect effects on any of the following:

    - The harmonization of ESG (such as CSR, sustainability) reporting across firms and countries.
    - Mandatory ESG reporting.
    - Effects of ESG reporting on the efficiency, valuation and disclosure of Climate Finance instruments (such as green bonds, pollution permits, Carbon trading).
    - Effects of ESG reporting on environmental compliance and waste management.
    - Enforcement of sustainability/ESG reporting standards by governments and private persons.
    - Use of financial statements and ESG reports for performance evaluation, organizational design, capital allocation, incentives and compensation in organizations.
    - The uses of ESG disclosures in decision-making by investors, regulators and other stakeholders.
    - The functions, processes and powers of accounting/derivatives standards-setting organizations.
    - The powers and functions of audit committees (in organizations) and external auditors.
    - The Real-Sector effects of ESG/sustainability reporting.
    - Liability for ESG reporting (i.e. inadequate or inaccurate disclosures).
    - Effects of ESG reporting on corporate credit ratings and legal-liability of credit-rating agencies.

27. FASB/GASB/SASB/IASB and ICMA/ISDA are major geopolitical risk factors and their actual effects on a specific country can vary dramatically across countries due to several factors including but not limited to the following:

    a. Whether the subject country is a member of the WTO.
    b. The terms of any treaties between the US and EU on one hand, and the subject country.

c. The volume of trade and balance-of-trade between the US and EU on one hand, and the subject country.
d. The existing financial, derivatives and accounting regulation frameworks in the subject country.
e. Interpretations of international law and conflict of laws.
f. The volumes of FDI, FI and foreign aid and other international capital flows between the US, EU and China on one hand, and the subject country.
g. The political structure and processes in the subject country, and the relative power/influence of the top political parties.
h. The regulation, if any, of political lobbying in the country.

4.2.2 Accounting/Derivatives Standards-Setting Organizations: Monetary Policy, Fiscal Policy, Trade Policy and Foreign Policy

Accounting/Derivatives Standards directly and indirectly affect both fiscal policy and trade policy in the following ways:

1. Accurate and timely disclosures of corporate tax and real estate tax liabilities (i.e. tax avoidance, tax evasion; international taxation, etc.).
2. Government's revenues from fees, fines, taxes, permits and levies.
3. Costs of corporate financial distress and bankruptcy (most of which are borne by governments).
4. Costs of derivatives/swaps disputes.
5. Governments' litigation costs and enforcement costs (economic, legal, social, psychological, environmental and political costs).
6. Accuracy of National Income Accounting and governments' statistical/economic data.
7. Regulation of accounting/audit firms.
8. Compliance reporting.
9. Calculation of import taxes, export taxes and so on.
10. Government accounting standards (e.g. GASB standards in the USA).
11. Incorporation of Accounting/Derivatives Standards in regulations/statutes.
12. Cash management by government agencies.

Accounting/derivatives standards directly and indirectly affect monetary policy in the following ways:

1. Earnings management and market volatility.
2. Crash-risk and Bubbles in stock, bond and commodities markets—through accounting disclosures.
3. Money supply and liquidity in financial markets.
4. Validity and accuracy of the asset base of financial institutions, some of which is used as collateral for trading and loans.
5. International Financial/Economic Contagion—through international propagation of, or non-compliance with, accounting/derivatives standards.
6. Economic models and capital-adequacy models—Accounting/Derivatives Standards are sometimes incorporated into these models.
7. Collateral for Derivatives, derivatives compliance reports and verification of derivatives trading processes—Accounting/Derivatives Standards are used for these documents.
8. Stock market–driven inflation/deflation.
9. Risk-Perception (corporate bonds, stocks, etc.).
10. Derivatives compliance reports.
11. Cash management by government agencies.

Accounting/Derivatives Standards can directly and indirectly affect both foreign policy and trade policy in the following ways:

1. US companies and foreign companies that are listed on stock exchanges around the world must comply with Accounting/Derivatives Standards. Many of these companies are MNCs that have significant international operations and thus propagate Accounting/Derivatives Standards around the world.
2. Bubbles and the Crash-risk of stock markets, commodities markets and bond markets—through accounting disclosures.
3. Money supply and liquidity in international financial markets.
4. Validity and accuracy of the asset base of financial institutions, some of which is used as collateral for trading and loans; and Collateral for Derivatives, derivatives compliance reports and verification of derivatives trading processes.
5. Stock market–driven inflation/deflation.

6. The risk perception of international investors (corporate bonds, stocks, etc.).
7. Calculation of foreign aid, FDI, import taxes and export taxes.
8. National Income Accounting.
9. International Financial/Economic Contagion—through international propagation of, or non-compliance with, Accounting/Derivatives Standards.
10. Government accounting standards (GASB standards in the USA)—which can affect the government's expenditures on foreign affairs.
11. International perceptions of the *political capital* of US political parties and the *enforcement-commitment* of the US government.

All of the foregoing effects on public policy can have cross-border *Multiplier Effects* in Emerging Markets countries through the channels explained in this book.

4.2.3 Geopolitical Risks *and* Cross-Border Spillover Risks: *Antitrust Issues and Rule-of-Law*[7] *(and a New Administrative Law Regime?)*

The antitrust issues discussed in this section also constitute *geopolitical risks* and *cross-border spillover risks* and the *transmission channels* include but are not limited to the following; (i) accounting and derivatives regulations; (ii) "global-effect" statutes such as the Dodd-Frank Act (USA); (iii) corporate governance standards; (iv) business contracts; (v) bilateral agreements and so on.

The unconstitutionality of accounting and derivatives standards-setting organizations and SOX are elements of structural changes in those industries, and have significant implications for competition and antitrust policy for several reasons including but not limited to the following.

First, accounting standards-setting organizations (i.e. FASB, IASB and GASB, IAASB, PCAF) have quasi-monopolies that are encouraged and un-reviewed by governments. These entities are very much subject to

[7] *See*: Andrews et al. (2017), Byrne and Callaghan (2014), Bamberger et al. (2016), Kirman (2016), Salzano and Colander (2007), OECD (2016), Finch (2013), Durlauf (2012), Bayoumi et al. (2016), Room (2011), Kuhlman and Mortveit (2014), Melnik et al. (2013), Miklashevich (2003), Perc et al. (2013), Post and Eisen (2000), Williams and Arrigo (2002), Cooper (2011), and Datz (2013).

lobbying and influence peddling by the private sector. Accounting firms have substantial input in the development of accounting standards. Accounting standards obviously affect the nature of competition especially in regulated industries. Accounting standards affect the cost structure and profitability of accounting/auditing firms, and hence the nature of competition in the auditing industry.

Second, capital markets standards-setting organizations (i.e. ISDA and ICMA) have quasi-monopolies that are encouraged and un-reviewed by governments—and that can result in foreclosure,[8] tying (bundling of financial products or financial services—see: Economides (2012a, b); and Economides [1998]), price-fixing[9] and increases in the volumes of *Exclusive Contracts*[10] in capital markets. These two entities are very much subject to lobbying and influence-peddling by the private sector. Capital markets standards obviously affect the nature of competition especially in the financial services industry and in regulated industries.

Third, SOX (and similar statutes in other countries) affects the cost structures, strategy and corporate governance of companies and, thus, affects the nature of competition especially in regulated industries and for listed companies. SOX also affects the cost structure of, and competition among, accounting/auditing firms. ICMA and ISDA affect the cost structures, strategy and corporate governance of companies and, thus, affect the nature of competition especially in regulated industries and for listed companies.

Fifth, during 1990–2019, the global auditing/accounting industry and the swaps/derivatives sector experienced significant structural changes. The structural changes in the global accounting/auditing industry included but were not limited to the following:

[8] *See: Otter Tail Power Co.*, 410 U.S. at 372–75.

[9] *See*: *Business Electronics Corp.* vs. *Sharp Electronics Corp.*, 485 U.S. 717 (1988; US Supreme Court); *Copperweld Corp.* vs. *Independence Tube*, 467 U.S. 752 (1984; US Supreme Court); *Monsanto Co.* vs. *Spray-Rite Service Corp.*, 465 U.S. 752 (1984; US Supreme Court); *US* vs. *Arnold, Schwinn*, et al., 388 U.S. 365 (1967; US Supreme Court); *USPS* vs. *Flamingo Industries*, #02–1290 (2004); *Brown* vs. *Pro Football*, 518 U.S. 213 (1996; US Supreme Court); *Federal Trade Commission* vs. *Ticor Title Insurance Company*, 60 U.S.L.W. 4515 (1992); *Allied Tube & Conduit Corp.* vs. *Indian Head, Inc.*, 486 U.S. 492 (1998; US Supreme Court); *Phonetele*, 664 F.2d at 728; *Jacobi* vs. *Bache & Co.*, 520 F.2d 1231 (CA2, 1975).

[10] *See*: *Standard Oil Co* vs. *US*, 337 U.S. 293 (1949; US Supreme Court); *US* vs. *Griffith*, 334 U.S. 100 (1948; US Supreme Court); *Brooke Group Ltd.* vs. *Brown & Williamson Tobacco*, 509 U.S. 209 (1993; US Supreme Court).

1. industry consolidation and the emergence of the *Big-four oligopoly*;
2. the increasing use of joint ventures and strategic alliances among auditing firms in some countries (e.g. China)—which has become problematic;
3. new regulations in many countries such as the US, EU, the UK, China, India and Japan;
4. increased *regulatory convergence* such as the increasing adoption of IASB/IFRS standards and the harmonization of accounting regulations in many countries;
5. increased intra-firm cross-border collaboration within audit firms;
6. changes in the pricing of audit services and non-audit services (which were partly influenced by regulations);
7. technological progress and the increased use of technology in audits and quality control (combined with increased automation of finance/accounting functions within audit-clients);
8. introduction of SOX in the US and similar statutes in other countries.

The structural changes in the swaps/derivatives sector of the financial services industry included but were not limited to the following:

1. industry consolidation of swaps/derivatives dealers and increased market-concentration in the securities industry;
2. new regulations in many countries such as the US (e.g. the Dodd-Frank Act; SOX), EU, the UK, China, India and Japan;
3. *regulatory convergence* such as the increasing adoption of ISDA/ICMA standards an SOX-type regulations in many countries;
4. technological progress and the increased use of technology in trading and record-keeping (combined with increased automation of finance/accounting functions within audit-clients);
5. increased participation of companies in the swaps/derivatives markets;
6. the global financial crises and the bankruptcies of swaps/derivatives dealers;
7. the growth of the credit default swaps (CDS) market and associated regulations (in some jurisdictions like New York State, CDS are deemed to be insurance products).

Sixth, there is an increasing and symbiotic relationship between the unconstitutionality and the anti-competition effects of these foregoing "institutions"—that is, the greater their anti-competition effects, the greater their unconstitutionality and vice versa.

Seventh, these foregoing "institutions" cause and propagate *network effects* which affect the nature of competition in industries.

The complexity pertaining to these issues is, or can be, manifested in the following ways:

1. Nonlinearity in relation to rule of law development.
2. Self-organization of institutions and organizations; and self-organization in enforcement of laws by private and/or public entities.
3. Change and theories of change.
4. Nonlinearity in relation to deadweight losses in the demand for, and enforcement of, laws.
5. Nonlinearity in relation to compliance with statutes and enforcement of laws.
6. Complex networks.
7. Network effects and the associated growth-and-evolution effects (on the mechanism/system and the users and their usage patterns).

The legal and economic environment in which accounting/derivative standards organizations function (defined by standards organizations, regulations, regulators, financial institutions, customers, internet systems, etc.) is a complex adaptive system because it has some or all of the following attributes:

1. The relations between the system and its environment are non-trivial and/or nonlinear.
2. The system can be influenced by, or can adapt itself to, its environment.
3. The system has feedback or memory, and can adapt itself according to its history or feedback.
4. The system is highly sensitive to initial conditions.
5. The number of parts (and types of parts) in the system and the number of relations between the parts are non-trivial.

During 2010–2019, various new US, European, Latin American and Asian government agencies emerged (thus creating various categories of "regulatory fragmentation") and have issued new regulations that pertain to systemic risk and financial stability which have not been effective. Furthermore, entities such as IASB/FASB/SASB/GASB/IAASB/PCAF, ISDA and ICMA have significant influence over companies, governments and the regulation of systemic risk and financial stability in various countries because their rules/regulations are widely accepted, incorporated into government regulations and are implemented as international standards—hence, a new cadre of international "express" and "adopted" administrative law is emerging.[11] See: Kingsbury (2009), Cassese (2005), Kingsbury et al. (2005), Zaring (2005, 2008) and Barr and Miller (2006). The term "emerging" is used because globalization evolved and rapidly increased during 2005–2019. *Express International Administrative Law* refers to regulations that are directly enacted by government administrative agencies where such regulations affect entities, persons and governments in various countries (such as regulations enacted by the US SEC, the FSA in the UK and the Chinese securities regulatory agency). *Adopted International Administrative Law* refers to generally accepted regulations/rules/norms that are enacted by non-governmental entities that have international impact (e.g. regulations of FASB, IASB, GASB, IAASB, PCAF, ICMA and ISDA) and are supported by international coalitions (e.g. ISDA, G20, G30) but are adopted by administrative agencies (US SEC, US CFTC, etc.) and are incorporated into administrative regulations and statutes in various countries. The constitutionality of these entities and international coalitions and how they fit into national or regional regulatory frameworks has important ramifications for systemic risk, financial stability, accounting disclosure, contagion and the functioning of markets in various countries. As noted by Lawson (2010), the modern administrative state in various countries has veered from their constitutions. As noted by some authors, the evolution of government bailouts and these accounting/derivatives standards organizations in various countries constitutes structural changes in the financial services industry and other industries. See: Nwogugu (2015).

[11] *See*: http://www.iilj.org/GAL/.

4.3 Accounting/Derivatives/Securities Standards-Setting Organizations and Regulations as "*Super*" International Labor Institutions

Accounting/Derivatives Standards-Setting Organizations and Regulations have intentionally or unintentionally functioned as both modifiers and enactment of labor regulations that can have cross-border *Multiplier Effects*, as evidenced by their rule-making history, wording and application/implementation with regard to the following issues in the global Labor Market:

1. Existing labor/employment regulations (especially in the accounting/consulting industry and the banking/financial services industry).
2. Workers' obligations and rights (including complaints and appeals) and consumer financial protection (i.e. the Consumer Financial Protection Bureau).
3. Financial/disclosure matters that affect workers' pension funds and mutual funds (workers' retirement savings).
4. Whistleblower protections[12] and working conditions (i.e. prohibited or reportable working conditions at directly regulated organizations such as banks and securities brokerages, and indirectly regulated

[12] *See*: The U.S. Securities and Exchange Commission (2011). *Implementation of the Whistleblower Provisions of Section 21F of the Securities Exchange Act of 1934* https://www.sec.gov/rules/final/2011/34-64545.pdf.

See: The whistleblower regulations of FINRA and similar non-governmental self-regulatory industry trade associations in other countries.

See: Malone, A. & Jones, R. (December 6, 2010). "*Revealed: Inside the Chinese suicide sweatshop where workers toil in 34-hour shifts to make your iPod*". Daily Mail (London). Available at: http://www.dailymail.co.uk/news/article-1285980/Revealed-Inside-Chinese-suicide-sweatshop-workers-toil-34-hour-shifts-make-iPod.html.

See: "*Chinese Factory asks for 'no suicide' vow*". MSNBC. May 26, 2010. Available at: http://www.msnbc.msn.com/id/37354853/ns/business-world_business/?ns=business-world_business.

See: Carlson, N. (April 7, 2010). "*What It's Like To Work In China's Gadget Sweatshops Where Your iPhones And iPads Are Made*". *Business Insider*. Available at: http://www.businessinsider.com/what-its-like-to-work-if-chinas-gadget-sweatshops-where-your-iphones-and-ipads-are-made-2010-4?utm_source=Daily+Buzz&utm_campaign=81432d578c-nl_emv_db_04082010_a&utm_medium=email.

See: "*Apple denies claims it broke Chinese labor laws in iPhone factory*". September 8, 2019. Saheli Roy Choudhury. https://www.cnbc.com/2019/09/09/apple-appl-claims-it-broke-china-labor-laws-at-iphone-factory-mostly-false.html.

See: "Apple's 2019 supplier report shows progress on labor and health issues". Jeremy Horwitz. March 6, 2019. https://venturebeat.com/2019/03/06/apples-2019-supplier-report-shows-progress-on-labor-and-health-issues/.

See: "*Apple and Foxconn broke Chinese Labour law to build new iPhones—US tech group and manufacturing partner admit using too many temporary workers*". Louise Lucas. September 9, 2019. https://www.ft.com/content/19fefd86-d2c3-11e9-8367-807ebd53ab77.

See: *"Apple—Supplier Responsibility" (PDF). Apple.* https://images.apple.com/supplierresponsibility/pdf/L418102A_SR_2010Report_FF.pdf.

See: Chen, B. (May 14, 2010), "*Workers Plan to Sue iPhone Contractor Over Poisoning*", *Wired*. https://www.wired.com/gadgetlab/2010/05/wintek-employees-sue/.

See: "Apple under fire again for working conditions at Chinese factories". *The Guardian*. December 19, 2014. https://www.theguardian.com/technology/2014/dec/19/apple-under-fire-again-for-working-conditions-at-chinese-factories?CMP=EMCNEWEML6619I2

See: "Study Casts Doubts on Apple's Ethical Standards". *China Labor Watch*. February 24, 2016. http://www.chinalaborwatch.org/report/113.

See: "Poor Working Conditions Persist at Apple Supplier Pegatron". *China Labor Watch*. October 22, 2015. http://www.chinalaborwatch.org/report/109.

See: Perlin, R. (2013). "Chinese Workers Foxconned". *Dissent*, 60(2), 46–52.

See: Armitage, J. (July 30, 2013). "'Even worse than Foxconn': Apple rocked by child labour claims". *The Independent*. London.

See: Mozur, P. (December 19, 2012). "Life Inside Foxconn's Facility in Shenzhen". *The Wall Street Journal*. https://blogs.wsj.com/chinarealtime/2012/12/19/life-inside-foxconns-facility-in-shenzhen/.

See: "*Apple suppliers maintain tight security to avoid leaks: Foxconn said to have 'special status' in China*". MacNN, February 17, 2010. Available at: http://www.macnn.com/articles/10/02/17/foxconn.said.to.have.special.status.in.china/.

See: *Apple's Recent Strike in Suzhou is Sign of Continued Bad Labor and CSR Practices in China. All Roads Lead to China*. January 21, 2010. Available at: http://www.allroadsleadto-china.com/2010/01/21/will-apple-be-the-next-nike-or-will-they-take-labor-compliance-seriously/.

See: "*Apple—Supplier Responsibility*" (PDF). Apple. Available at: http://images.apple.com/supplierresponsibility/pdf/L418102A_SR_2010Report_FF.pdf.

See: Blodget, H. (April 7, 2010). "Apple-Supplier Factory Worker Tries To Kill Herself—That's 4 In 4 Weeks". *Business Insider*. Available at: http://www.businessinsider.com/henry-blodget-another-apple-supplier-factory-worker-tries-to-kill-herself-thats-4-in-4-weeks-2010-4.

See: *Apple Loses Lawsuit Over a Company Policy Tim Cook Didn't Know About*. By Sissi Cao. Feb. 14, 2020. https://observer.com/2020/02/apple-lose-lawsuit-retail-employee-security-check-pay/. ("...Apple has a lost a class-action lawsuit brought by its Apple store employees regarding a seemingly miscellaneous company policy at the retail level that CEO Tim Cook wasn't even aware of. The plaintiffs filed the class-action suit in 2013, revealing that Apple would require its retail employees to go through a security check after they clocked out every day to make sure that no company assets or trade secrets were stolen. The

organizations such as issuer-entities and non-financial derivatives counter-parties).

5. Employee costs (i.e. compliance costs; employee salaries; employee taxes) of banks and financial services companies.
6. Increased compliance processes and documentation that pertain to work processes and workers in the financial services industry.
7. *Say-on-Pay* (mandatory disclosure of *Income Inequality*) by exchange-traded companies in the USA.

exit check would typically take 10 to 20 minutes and involved searches of employees' purses, briefcases and personal iPhones…").

See: *Apple sued by employees over labor issues.* by James O'Toole. July 23, 2014. https://money.cnn.com/2014/07/23/technology/apple-labor/. ("…The company is facing a lawsuit certified as a class action this week from employees who say they were denied meal breaks and rest periods in violation of California labor law. Attorneys for the plaintiffs estimate that more than 20,000 current or former Apple employees from the retail to corporate level have been affected by the alleged violations. Among other things, the lawsuit claims Apple employees were forced to work for stretches of five hours or more without meals, and didn't get breaks on shorter shifts. …").

See: "*Class complaint for injunctive relief and damages, in the United States District Court for the District of Columbia, 15 Dec 2019; Major tech companies respond to lawsuit over mining deaths*". ComputerWeekly.com. https://www.business-humanrights.org/en/latest-news/lawsuit-against-apple-google-tesla-and-others-re-child-labour-drc/. ("…Snapshot: In 2019, IRAdvocates, a US-based NGO filed a class action lawsuit against Apple, Google, Tesla, Alphabet, Microsoft, and Dell alleging the corporations profited from child labor in their cobalt supply chains in the Democratic Republic of Congo. Plaintiffs are either guardians of children killed in cobalt mining tunnels or children who were maimed while working in the mines…").

See: *The Other Side Of Apple II: Pollution Spreads Through Apple's Supply Chain.* Institute of Public and Environmental Affairs, August 31, 2011. http://www.ipe.org.cn/Upload/Report-IT-V-Apple-II.pdf.

See: Barboza, D. (2012). Apple Cited as Adding to Pollution in China. *The New York Times*, September 1, 2011. Accessed March 26, 2012. https://www.nytimes.com/2011/09/02/technology/apple-suppliers-causing-environmental-problems-chinese-group-says.html?_r=1.

See: Watts, J., "Apple secretive about 'polluting and poisoning' supply chain, says report". *The Guardian*, January 19, 2011. https://www.theguardian.com/environment/2011/jan/20/apple-pollution-supply-chain .

See: Jobs, S., "A Greener Apple". Apple, Inc. https://www.apple.com/hotnews/agreenerapple/.

See: Greenpeace, "*Hazardous Materials Found in Apple's iPhone: Chemicals Include those Banned in Children's Toys in EU*". Greenpeace International. Greenpeace. http://www.greenpeace.org/usa/en/media-center/news-releases/hazardous-materials-found-in-a/.

See: Chen, B. (May 14, 2010), "Workers Plan to Sue iPhone Contractor Over Poisoning", *Wired*. https://www.wired.com/gadgetlab/2010/05/wintek-employees-sue/.

8. Consumer's perceptions of fairness of the financial system and working conditions—which in turn affects worker motivation and morale, Consumer/Corporate Tax Compliance, Consumer Confidence, Business Confidence, productivity, and so on.

Unfortunately, the ILO (International Labor Organization), the national labor agencies (such as the National Labor Relations Board in the USA) don't sufficiently regulate or coordinate the activities of (and don't work closely with) Accounting/Derivatives standards-setting organizations.

On Economic Psychology of international Labor-Market institutions, see: Ochsen and Welsch (2012), Haferkamp et al. (2009) and Pántya et al. (2016).

While Mwakagali (2018)[13] focuses on "*International Financial Institutions*" ("IFIs"; such as World Bank, EBRD, Asian Development Bank; IBRD), many large international banks such as Citigroup, HSBC and JP Morgan function as informal IFIs. Freeman (2011) critiqued the US *National Labor Relations Act* and suggested characteristics and additional components of new labor regulations for the twenty-first century.

4.4 International Trade

There are important international trade considerations and ramifications. Accounting is the most global of all professional services, and critically affects how international trade is conducted, recorded and its disputes resolved. The World Trade Organization (WTO) Working Party on Professional Services and the General Agreement on Trade in Services

[13] Mwakagali (2018) stated in part: "...Today, labor rights stand at a crossroads. The traditional stance where labor law and regulation rested in the state as the lawmaker, enforcer and implementer, with international labor standards as the minimum standards, has with time, been hampered by the activities of other actors, such as multinational corporations, international non-governmental organizations, paramilitary groups, international financial institutions (IFIs) and international organizations, that have inadvertently had an impact on labor standards and their governance. Here, the boundaries between domestic and international are increasingly blurred as issues which were once solely under the purview of domestic law and politics, such as environmental standards and labor regulation, are influenced and affected by such actors...".

(GATS) has prioritized the accounting sector and its deliberations also cover SOX and similar statutes in other countries (which often apply to companies involved in cross-border finance and/or business). The standardization/harmonization of accounting regulations across countries and market access for foreign accounting firms remain important elements of foreign trade negotiations. See White (2001), WTO (2017) and Cattaneo et al. (2010). The coordinated efforts of national governments to resolve the global financial crisis of 2007–2013 indicate the relevance of international trade. Whether a given bailout package (and associated subsidies) contained therein is WTO compliant depends on the *Agreement on Subsidies and Countervailing Measures* (SCM Agreement). The disturbing issue is that most government bailouts that occurred during 2008–2011 were illegal but many WTO members chose not to complain. See comments in Trujillo (2010), Poretti (2009) and International Institute for Sustainable Development (March 2009).

Similarly, derivatives and government bailouts have "global" effects, and critically affects how international trade is conducted, recorded and its disputes resolved. The deliberations of the World Trade Organization Working Party on Professional Services and GATS also pertain to swaps/derivatives sales and trading. The standardization/harmonization of swaps/derivatives regulations across countries and market access for foreign banks and securities firms remain important elements of foreign trade negotiations. See Cattaneo et al. (2010)[14] and Cornford (June 2009).[15] Government bailouts of banks and financial services companies raise significant international trade issues of illegal subsidies and protectionism by member/signatory countries in international trade agreements and agencies. The coordinated efforts of national governments to resolve the global financial crisis of 2007–2013 indicate the relevance of international trade. Whether a given bailout package (and associated subsidies) contained therein is WTO compliant depends on the *Agreement on Subsidies and Countervailing Measures* (SCM Agreement). The disturbing issue is that most government bailouts that occurred during 2008–2011 were illegal but many WTO members chose not to complain. See comments in Trujillo

[14] *See*: Cattaneo, O., Engman, M., Saez, S. & Stern, R., eds. (2010) *International Trade in Services: New Trends and Opportunities for Developing Countries* (World Bank).

[15] *See*: Cornford, A. (June 2009). *Statistics For International Trade In Banking Services: Requirements—Availability And Prospects.* UNCTAD. Working paper No. 194. http://unctad.org/en/docs/osgdp20092_en.pdf.

(2010),[16] Poretti (2009),[17] Delimatsis (2012)[18] and International Institute for sustainable development (March 2009).[19]

4.5 Systemic Risk, Financial Instability and Networks

4.5.1 *Emergence and Nonlinearity: Systemic Risk, Financial Instability, Networks and the* Network Effects *of IASB/GASB/FASB/SASB/IAASB/PCAF*

It's conjectured here that the worldwide acceptance of regulations enacted by IASB/GASB/FASB/SASB/IAASB/PCAF: (i) has created global networks that have significantly increased the psychological, political and social interconnectedness among companies and institutions but without implementation of appropriate controls and buffers that reduce systemic risk and financial instability—such "virtual" connectedness is sometimes more important than actual physical/transactional connectedness because they govern human perceptions of risk; (ii) has created *network effects*[20] in the global financial services industry, in financial systems and in derivatives markets. See: Ahdieh (2003), Awrey (2014) and Yu and Wahid (2014). Ironically, the problem is that such network effects are negative because they increase the probability of transmission of shocks across industries and countries, and they decrease financial stability because they increase the probability that failure of one or a few companies will cause the failure

[16] *See*: Trujillo, E. (2010). International Trade and the Financial Crisis. *Proceedings of the Annual Meeting (American Society of International Law)*, 104, 438–443.

[17] *See*: Poretti, P. (2009). "*The Regulation of Subsidies within the General Agreement on Trade in Services—Problems and Perspectives*" (Kluwer Law International, 2009).

[18] *See*: Delimatsis, P. (2012). *Of Bailouts and Rescue Measures: Subsidies in Financial Services*. Working Paper No 2012/24. Swiss National Center of Competence In Research. http://www20.iadb.org/intal/catalogo/PE/2012/12020.pdf.

[19] *See*: International Institute For Sustainable Development (March 2009). *Will Government Bailouts Lead To Trade Wars?* https://www.iisd.org/gsi/news/will-government-bailouts-lead-trade-wars.

[20] *See*: Ramanna and Sletten (2014) ("We find that perceived network benefits increase the degree of IFRS harmonization among countries, and that smaller countries have a differentially higher response to these benefits … Further, economic ties with the European Union are a particularly important source of network effects. The results, robust to numerous alternative hypotheses and specifications, suggest IFRS adoption was self-reinforcing during the sample period, which, in turn, has implications for the consequences of IFRS adoption").

of others. Kingston and Caballero (2009) compared various theories of institutional change in terms of causes, process and outcomes of institutional change, habit, learning and bounded rationality, and institutional inertia and path-dependence.

As mentioned, entities such as IASB/GASB/FASB/SASB/IAASB/PCAF can have significant influence over companies, governments and the regulation of systemic risk and financial stability in various countries because their rules/regulations are widely accepted, incorporated into government regulations and are implemented as international standards. The unconstitutionality of these entities can increase financial instability and/or systemic risk.

4.5.2 Emergence and Nonlinearity: Systemic Risk, Financial Instability, Networks and the Network Effects *of ICMA and ISDA*

Similar to the foregoing, its conjectured here that the worldwide acceptance of regulations enacted by ICMA And ISDA: (i) has created global networks that have significantly increased the psychological, political and social interconnectedness among companies and institutions but without implementation of appropriate controls and buffers that reduce systemic risk and financial instability—such "virtual" connectedness is sometimes more important than actual physical/transactional connectedness because they govern human perceptions of risk; (ii) has created *network effects*[21] in the global financial services industry, in financial systems and in derivatives markets. Ironically, the problem is that such network effects are negative because they increase the probability of transmission of shocks across industries and countries; and they decrease financial stability because they increase the probability that failure of one or a few companies will cause the failure of others. Kingston and Caballero (2009) compared various theories of institutional change in terms of causes, process and outcomes of institutional change, habit, learning and bounded rationality, and institutional inertia and path-dependence.

Furthermore, as mentioned, entities such as ISDA and ICMA have significant influence over companies, governments and the regulation of systemic risk and financial stability in various countries because their rules/

[21] *See*: Ramanna and Sletten (2014), Ahdieh (2003), Awrey (2014), and Yu and Wahid (2014).

regulations are widely accepted, incorporated into government regulations and loan/derivatives contracts and are implemented as international standards. The unconstitutionality of these entities can increase financial instability and/or systemic risk.

4.6 The *Substantial Control Theory*

The diffusion of power inherent in the FASB, IASB, GASB, SASB, PCAF, the International Swap & Derivatives Association (ISDA, http://www.isda.org/), and the International Capital Market Association (ICMA, http://www.icmagroup.org/) and FINRA (USA) creates a diffusion of accountability and lack of appropriate oversight, which effectively subverts the powers of the executive branch of the federal government in many countries. Through their rule-making functions, the FASB, GASB, IAASB, PCAF, and IASB have "quasi-executive powers" even though they are not part of the government (but are implicitly supported and encouraged by governments). FASB, GASB, IAASB, PCAF, and IASB receive substantial input on accounting regulations from, and are lobbied by the private sector. Thus, FINRA, FASB, IASB, GASB, SASB, IAASB, PCAF, ICMA, and ISDA have "federal-government type" power and influence over capital markets, securities brokers and disclosure patterns, and such power is essentially the same as government control and/or "state action" required to prove violations of the US Constitution. Hence a new doctrine of constitutional analysis named "*substantial control*" is introduced here an alternative to the "state action"[22] requirement of constitutional law. *See*: Ellman (2001), Gardbaum (2003), Tushnet (2003), Gardbaum (2006) and Currie (1986). The elements of the *substantial control* doctrine are as follows: (a) a private entity; (b) that is a national or international or local or state organization; and (c) market participants that are not affiliated with this organization will find it difficult, but not impossible, to conduct business in the industry; (d) the rules of the organization are binding on its members and/or on the general public; (e) the rules of the organization

[22] *See: Evans* vs. *Newton*, 382 U.S. 296 (1966; US Supreme Court).
See: Evans vs. *Abney*, 396 US 435 (1970; US Supreme Court).
See: Burton vs. *Wilmington*, 365 U.S. 715 (US Supreme Court).
See: Moose Lodge vs. *Irvis*, 407 U.S. 163 (1972; US Supreme Court).
See: *Edmonson* vs. *Leesville Concrete*, 500 US 614 (1991; US Supreme Court).
See: Marsh vs. *Alabama*, 326 U.S. 501 (1946; US Supreme Court).
See: Screws vs. *US*, 325 U.S. 91 (1945; US Supreme Court).

are implicitly or explicitly sanctioned by, and are often adopted by, federal, state or local governments. The *Substantial Control Theory* is an alternative to the *State Action* requirement of constitutional law, and is different from the *Substantial Inducement Theory* and the *Substitution Theory* (both are alternatives to the *State Action* requirement) which were introduced in Nwogugu (2012).[23] The *Substantial Control Theory* and the *Substitution Theory* can also be applied in Antitrust Law. See the comments in: Meyer (2009).

4.7 The Unconstitutionality of the International Accounting Standards Board (IASB), the Financial Accounting Standards Board (FASB), SASB, IAASB, PCAF and the Government Accounting Standards Board (GASB)

The Financial Accounting Standards Board (FASB) and the Government Accounting Standards Board (GASB), IAASB, PCAF and SASB are private non-governmental organizations that are based in the US.[24] FASB was incorporated in 1973, and replaced the Committee on Accounting Procedure (CAP) and the Accounting Principles Board (APB) of the American Institute of Certified Public Accountants (AICPA). The FASB's and GASB's primary purpose is to develop generally accepted accounting principles (GAAP) within the United States and to foster debate about accounting principles. Under the US Securities Exchange Act of 1934, the US SEC has sole legal authority to establish financial accounting and reporting standards for publicly held companies. However, the US SEC has always relied on either the private sector or non-profit organizations

[23] *See*: Nwogugu (2012), p. 198.

[24] See: Governmental Accounting Standards Board (2008). *Facts About GASB*. Available at: http://www.gasb.org/facts/facts_about_gasb.pdf.

See: National Association of State Auditors, Comptrollers and Treasurers. http://www.nasact.org.

See: Securities Industry and Financial Markets Association. http://www.sifma.org.

See: American Accounting Association. http://www.aaahq.org.

See: Institute of Management Accountants. http://www.imanet.org.

See: American Institute of Certified Public Accountants. http://www.aicpa.org.

See: Chartered Financial Analyst Institute. http://www.cfainstitute.org.

See: Financial Executives International. http://www.financialexecutives.org.

See: Government Finance Officers Association. http://www.gfoa.org.

for primary accounting rule-making. The US Securities and Exchange Commission (SEC) formally appointed the FASB and GASB as the organizations responsible for developing accounting standards for public companies and government agencies, respectively, in the U.S.

FASB functions primarily through a series of internal committees and hybrid committees (made up of FASB staff, industry professionals, practicing accountants and regulators). GASB also functions primarily through a series of internal committees and hybrid committees (made up of GASB staff, industry professionals, practicing accountants and regulators). The IASB has a similar structure and recruits representatives from accounting rule-making entities in various countries. FASB is subject to oversight by the Financial Accounting Foundation (FAF) in the US. FAF selects the members of the FASB and the Governmental Accounting Standards Board and funds both organizations. The Board of Trustees of the FAF, in turn, is selected in part by a group of organizations including: National Association of State Auditors, Comptrollers and Treasurers; American Accounting Association; Securities Industry Association, American Institute of Certified Public Accountants; CFA Institute; Institute of Management Accountants; Financial Executives International; and the Government Finance Officers Association.

Note that the orientation and emphasis of FASB (and similar organizations in other countries) has always been toward the creation of accounting rules for "public companies". FASB is pursuing a convergence project with the International Accounting Standards Board (IASB) and International Financial Reporting Standards (IFRS), which also focuses on accounting rules for public companies.[25] This continuing "Regulatory Emphasis Gap" has proven to be destructive because: (a) most entities are either private or non-profit entities, (b) most new jobs are created by private or non-profit entities, (c) these private and non-profit entities have much more economic impact on society and the economy than the public companies—hence, risk regulation should actually focus on rules for private companies, (d) the suppliers and customers of these private companies and non-profit companies are more prone to cause systemic risk than those of public companies.

[25] Financial Accounting Standards Board and International Accounting Standards Board (2002). *Memorandum of Understanding, "The Norwalk Agreement"*.
See: Fleckner (2008).

Similarly, in most countries, the federal governments have appointed organizations similar to FASB as the dominant accounting rule-making entity, and/or have approved the IASB as a supplemental rule-making entity. In most countries, the government does not have any specific powers (oversight, reports, appointment of executives or committee members, vetting of accounting rules, feedback from enforcement, etc.) over these accounting rule-making entities. The relationship between IASB and governments of various countries is not very clear—except that the securities regulators in many countries accept filings, financial statements and documents that use IASB accounting standards.

Clearly accounting regulations have economic effects[26] and also affect the cost structure of, and competition among, accounting firms. See: Durocher et al. (2015), OECD (2009). Within the context of the Global Financial Crisis of 2007–2013 and recessions in various countries during 2008–2017 (which are partly attributable to accounting rules including "mark-to-market" rules and goodwill/intangibles rules), the lack of direct government oversight or control over FASB/GASB and IASB is detrimental. Various authors have extensively documented the political economy and over-politicized processes of accounting rule-making in the FASB and IASB which can and did have adverse consequences on financial stability in the US economy and the global economy.[27] FASB and IASB have repeatedly compromised their independence and have been susceptible to external influence[28]—and the fact that their accounting rules are non-binding does not help. Corporate commitment to, and compliance with, non-binding accounting rules are quite different to what can be obtained if the accounting rules are formally binding and made mandatory by the government.

Hence, similar constitutional law issues that arose in the case of the PCAOB (US) also apply to FASB, GASB and IASB. The "state actions" are as follows: (i) the US SEC's appointment and active support of FASB and GASB as the primary accounting rule-making entities in the US; and (ii) the federal government's tacit support of FASB, IASB, IAASB, PCAF,

[26] *See*: Allee et al. (2008), Pererea and Baydoun (2007), and Sunder (2011).

[27] *See*: Königsgruber (2010), Konigsgruber (2017), Konigsgruber (2014), Ramanna (2013), Jamal and Sunder (2014), Carmona & Trombetta (2008), Wagenhofer (2011), Konigsgruber (2013), Hoffmann and Zülch (2014), Konigsgruber and Palan (2015), Mohammadrezaei & Mohd-Saleh (2012), Dobler and Knospe (2016), Prochazka (2015), and Gros and Worret (2016).

[28] *See*: Fleckner (2008), and Chiapello and Mediad (2009).

SASB and GASB (and incorporation of their accounting standards in regulations/statutes) in many countries; and the government's failure to directly regulate the accounting rule-making process, where the government definitely has a duty to do so (it's well established in the literature that failure of the government to act where it has a duty to act, creates constitutional torts[29]); (iii) the *Substantial Control Theory*[30] and the *Substitution Theory* apply. FASB, IASB, SASB, IAASB, PCAF, and GASB are unconstitutional because of the following reasons.

4.7.1 Unconstitutional **Delegation**

FASB, IASB, SASB, IAASB, PCAF, ISDA, ICMA and GASB represent a violation of the *Non-Delegation Doctrine* and a detrimental and unconstitutional interference with presidential powers. Also in some countries such as the US, some of the functions performed by FASB, IASB, SASB, IAASB, PCAF and GASB are statutorily reserved for US Congress (regulation of interstate commerce; enactment of laws—the accounting/derivatives regulations are often used as laws; and oversight/investigations) and the executive branch of the US government (Securities Act of 1934), but on the contrary, the US government has no or minimal control over FASB, SASB, IASB, IAASB, PCAF and GASB.[31]

FASB, IASB, SASB, IAASB, PCAF and GASB effectively usurp the powers of the legislature by their rule-making activities. In the US, although US Congress enacted the Securities Act of 1934, which in turn empowers the US SEC to enact accounting rules, and the US SEC can be deemed to have informally delegated such powers to FASB/GASB/

[29] *See*: Nwogugu (2012: 198).

[30] On the *Substantial Inducement Theory* and the *Substitution Theory* (which are alternatives to the *State Action* requirement in constitutional law), see Nwogugu (2012: 9 & 198).

[31] On the Non-delegation Doctrine, *see*: *PennEast Pipeline Co. vs. New Jersey*, ___ US ___ (No. 19-1039; US Supreme Court; pending as of 2021); *see*: *Seila Law LLC vs. Consumer Financial Protection Bureau*, ____ US ____ (Case#: No. 19-7; US Supreme Court; 2020). On the Interstate Commerce Clause, see: *DeNolf vs. U.S.*, _____ US _____ (US Supreme Court; pending as of 2021) (https://static1.squarespace.com/static/5b660749620b85c6c73e5e61/t/608d544886d55300e492a619/1619874888658/2021-22+AMCA+Case.pdf); *DeNolf vs. U.S.* (Case#: 01-76320; US 14th Circuit, 2020) (https://static1.squarespace.com/static/5b660749620b85c6c73e5e61/t/608d544886d55300e492a619/1619874888658/2021-22+AMCA+Case.pdf); *Perez vs. United States*, 402 U.S. 146, 150 (1971) (Congress can ban loansharking that threatens interstate commerce); *Gonzales vs. Raich*, 545 U.S. 1, 18 (US Supreme Court; 2005) and *United States vs. Lopez*, 514 U.S. 549.

IASB/IAASB/PCAF/SASB, the FASB/GASB/IASB/IAASB/PCAF/SASB effectively perform congressional functions because their non-binding rules have substantial economic effects on, and regulate, interstate commerce and foreign commerce. A somewhat extreme school of thought is that the subprime crisis and the Global Financial crisis and the bailout of financial institutions by governments in several countries suggest that accounting rule-making is of national importance and should be handled by the legislature, and that delegation to the agencies in the executive branch of government violates the Non-Delegation Doctrine.

4.7.2 *The* Procedural Due Process Doctrine

The existence and activities of FASB, IASB, SASB, IAASB, PCAF and GASB constitute violations of the Procedural Due Process doctrine, because the government securities regulatory agencies in many countries (such as the US SEC) illegally delegated accounting rule-making to FASB/GASB/IASB, IAASB/SASB/PCAF but the SASB/FASB/GASB/IASB rule-making procedures are inefficient and highly politicized (as documented in articles cited herein).

4.7.3 *The* Substantive Due Process Doctrine

The existence and activities of FASB, IASB, SASB, IAASB, PCAF and GASB constitute violations of the Substantive Due Process doctrine, because:

1. The FASB/GASB/SASB/IASB/IAASB/PCAF rule-making processes deprive certain constituencies (small companies; companies in regulated industries who cannot afford to hire lobbyists; etc.) of their rights to contract, and rights to privacy (due to improper disclosure).
2. In many instances, the regulations/standards are one-size-fits-all and don't account for heavy industry-regulation.
3. These regulations/standards sometimes create conflicts-of-interests and Externalities—as illustrated in Nwogugu (2003, 2015).
4. These regulations are sometimes very inefficient—as illustrated in Nwogugu (2003, 2015, 2021).

These foregoing discriminatory classifications don't serve any meaningful purpose and always don't advance the government's interests in fair regulation.

In some countries, the government's failure to adequately regulate or directly manage the functions of ISDA and ICMA (and private trade groups such as FINRA in the US) also constitutes violations of substantive Due Process rights of investors and the general public (in the US, the due process clauses of the Fifth and Fourteenth Amendments to the US Constitution). This is because: (i) the functions of the FASB/GASB/SASB/IASB/IAASB/PCAF are critical and affect a wide range of persons; (ii) the government's policy of permitting FASB/GASB/SASB/IASB/IAASB/PCAF to exist and regulate capital markets without appropriate oversight can result in deprivation of persons' right to contract, right to free-speech and right of association. These rights arise from norms and expectations. The government's interest in maintaining orderly capital markets is far outweighed by the actual and potential harm caused by the inadequate government oversight of FASB/GASB/SASB/IASB/IAASB/PCAF. The relevant state-actions are as follows: (i) the failure of the governments to regulate and/or directly manage the functions of FASB/GASB/SASB/IASB/IAASB/PCAF and to enact capital markets regulations, where the governments definitely has a duty to do so; (ii) the *Substantial Control Theory* and the *Substitution Theory* apply.

4.7.4 The Equal Protection Doctrine

In some instances, the FASB, SASB, IAASB, PCAF and IASB rule-making procedures and the application of their standards/regulations unfairly discriminates between.

1. Large companies that can afford to hire lobbyists to influence such processes, and small companies that cannot afford to influence their rule-making processes.
2. Large companies that can afford to hire lawyers and economists to decipher such regulations and to litigate them at government administrative agencies (such as the US IRS), and small companies and individuals that cannot afford to do so.
3. Companies whose current and former employees/agents serve on the board and advisory-boards of these rule-making entities, and companies that don't have that

These foregoing discriminatory classifications don't serve any meaningful purpose and always don't advance the government's interests in fair regulation; and the government's interest is far outweighed by the adverse effects of the discriminatory classifications that are directly and indirectly imposed.

4.8 The Unconstitutionality of Private-Sector (Non-governmental) Corporate Governance Standards and Associated Standards Organizations

In many countries, private organizations (stock exchanges, trade associations, etc.) have enacted Corporate Governance guidelines and "regulations" that formally/mandatorily or informally (non-binding) apply to their members. For the same reasons mentioned herein and above, these private corporate governance standards and standards organizations (created by private entities or trade associations) in many countries are also unconstitutional.

4.9 International Political Economy and the Unconstitutionality of the ISDA, ICMA and Private-Sector Securities-Regulation Trade Associations (Such as FINRA in the USA)

Securities-Regulation Trade Associations (Such as FINRA in the USA). The Dodd Frank Act (or "FSA"; a US statute) and government financial/economic regulations in the EU and other countries have failed to sufficiently curtail or modify the activities of the International Swap & Derivatives Association ("ISDA"; http://www.isda.org/) and the International Capital Market Association ("ICMA"; http://www.icmagroup.org/) and private sector securities-regulating industry-associations (such as FINRA (USA), Investment Industry Regulatory Organization of Canada ("IIROC"; Canada), which are collectively and henceforth referred to as "FINRA-Type Associations"). See the comments in: Arner and Taylor (2009), Riles (2009), Partnoy (2010), Johnson and Hazen (2004), Wilmarth (2009), Johnson (1997) and Barkbu and Ong (2010). Various researchers have analyzed the political economy of capital markets standards setting and regulation. See: Biggins and Scott (2012). The ISDA and ICMA are private trade associations (similar to the NAIC) that exert excessive control over the international derivatives markets. The Global Financial Crisis of 2007–2014 and the subprime crisis in the US (2007–2010) have now confirmed that the ISDA and ICMA and their standard documents/agreements have not been effective and exert adverse control over derivatives trading. Given the national security importance and significant effects of derivatives markets, most of the regulatory functions of the ISDA should have been statutorily transferred to a government-controlled entity—in the US, perhaps the US SEC or the US Treasury (or to a combined entity that will result from the merger of the OCC, FDIC, FHFA and OTS). In essence, any form of self-regulation is not a viable option for derivatives markets.

A similar issue arose in *Free Enterprise Fund* vs. *Public Company Accounting Oversight Board*[32] (US Supreme Court case). A similar constitutional question has also emerged with regard to the unconstitutionality of NAFTA Article 19—under NAFTA Article-19, a bi-national panel (some members are appointed by foreign governments and no members can be removed by the President, for good cause or otherwise) that is not subject to review or control by any U.S. executive or judicial branch officials, is empowered to review (and/or override) US government agency enforcement of US trade laws.[33]

[32] *See*: *Free Enterprise Fund* vs. *Public Company Accounting Oversight Board*, 561 US ___ (2010; US Supreme Court case) (the court stated that "That arrangement is contrary to Article II's vesting of the executive power in the President … Without the ability to oversee the Board, or to attribute the Board's failings to those whom he can oversee, the President is no longer the judge of the Board's conduct … The diffusion of power carries with it a diffusion of accountability … By granting the Board executive power without the Executive's oversight, this Act subverts the President's ability to ensure that the laws are faithfully executed—as well as the public's ability to pass judgment on his efforts").

[33] *See*: *International Agreements Without Senate Approval*. Available at: http://caselaw.lp.findlaw.com/data/constitution/article02/12.html.

Compare: *Dames & Moore* vs. *Regan*, 453 U.S. 654 (1981) (Court sustained a series of implementing actions by the President pursuant to executive agreements with Iran in order to settle the hostage crisis; and found that Congress had delegated to the President certain economic powers underlying the agreements and that his suspension of claims powers had been implicitly ratified over time by Congress's failure to set aside the asserted power).

See: *United States Security Agreements and Commitments Abroad*—Hearings Before a Subcommittee of the Senate Foreign Relations Committee, 91st Congress, 1st sess. (1969).

See: *U.S. Commitments to Foreign Powers*—Hearings Before the Senate Foreign Relations Committee on S. Res. 151, 90th Congress, 1st session (1967).

See: *Unit Owners Assoc.* vs. *Gillman*, 223 V.A. 752 (1982) (the Virginia Supreme Court held that the power to fine is a governmental power).

The relevant *State Actions* are as follows: (i) the failure of the governments to regulate ISDA and ICMA and to enact capital markets regulations, where the government definitely has a duty to do so (it's well established in the literature that failure of the government to act where it has a duty to act, creates constitutional torts[34]); (ii) the *Substantial Control Theory*[35] and the *Substitution Theory* apply.

4.9.1 *The* Privileges & Franchises Clause *and the* Privileges & Immunities Clause *(USA Only)*

In the US, both the failure of the EESA of 2008 (USA) and the Dodd Frank Act of 2010 (FSA) to expressly regulate or limit the ISDA, ICMA and FINRA and the implicit government support of, and coordination with, the ISDA, FINRA and ICMA may constitute violations of the *Privileges & Franchises Clause*[36] in Section 9 and the *Privileges & Immunities Clause* in Section 13[37] of the US Constitution (and similar clauses in the Constitutions of foreign countries, Brazil and the EU).

4.9.2 *The* Substantive Due Process Doctrine

In some countries, the government's failure to adequately regulate the ISDA and ICMA (and FINRA-Type Associations) also constitutes

See: James Foley vs. *Osborne Court Condominium*, et al., 724 A.2d 436, 1999 R.I. LEXIS 55 (C.A. No. 96–360, Superior Court of Rhode Island, Newport; 1999) (Rhode Island Supreme Court asked the lower court to determine if fining represents an unconstitutional delegation of judicial or police power to the association).

Compare: *Constitutional Litigation Clinic Wins Landmark Decision Guaranteeing Free Speech Rights to Residents of Homeowner Associations.* Available at: http://www.ahrc.com/new/index.php/src/news/sub/pressrel/action/ShowMedia/id/2667.

Compare: *Committee For A Better Twin Rivers,* Et Al Vs. *Twin Rivers Homeowners' Association* et al., Case No: A-4047-03 T24047-03 T2, Feb. 7, 2006. Available at: http://www.ahrc.se/new/index.php/src/courts/sub/lawsuit/action/display/id/135.

Compare: McKenzie (1994).

[34] *See*: Nwogugu (2012: 198).

[35] On the *Substantial Inducement Theory* and the *Substitution Theory* (which are alternatives to the *State Action* requirement in constitutional law), see Nwogugu (2012: 9 & 198).

[36] Section-9 states in part: "Section 9. No law granting irrevocably any privilege, franchise, or immunity shall be enacted".

[37] Section-13 states in part: "No law shall be enacted granting to any citizen, class of citizens, or corporation other than municipal, privileges or immunities which, upon the same terms, shall not equally belong to all citizens or corporations".

violations of substantive Due Process rights of investors and the general public (in the US, the due process clauses of the Fifth and Fourteenth Amendments to the US Constitution). This is because: (i) the functions of the ICMA, ISDA and FINRA-Type Associations are critical and affect a wide range of persons; (ii) the government's policy of permitting ISDA, ICMA and FINRA-Type Associations to exist and regulate capital markets without appropriate oversight can result in deprivation of persons' *Right-to-Contract*, *Right-to-Free Speech* and *Right-of-Association*; (iii) The ISDA and ICMA and FINRA-Type Associations' rule-making processes deprive certain constituencies (small companies; companies in regulated industries who cannot afford to hire lobbyists; etc.) of their rights to contract, and rights to privacy (due to improper disclosure); (iv) In many instances, the regulations/standards are one-size-fits-all and don't account for heavy industry-regulation. These rights arise from norms and expectations. The government's interest in maintaining orderly capital markets is far outweighed by the actual and potential harm caused by the inadequate government oversight of ISDA, ICMA and FINRA-Type Associations.[38] The relevant *State Action* are as follows: (i) the failure of the governments to regulate ISDA and ICMA and to enact capital markets regulations, where the government definitely has a duty to do so; (ii) the *Substantial Control Theory* and the *Substitution Theory* apply. These foregoing discriminatory classifications don't serve any meaningful purpose and always don't advance the government's interests in fair regulation.

[38] *See*: *Railway Express* vs. *New York*, ____US___(1949; US Supreme Court); *Kotch* vs. *Bd. of River Port Pilot Commissioners*, ___ US ___(1947; US Supreme Court); *Loving* vs. *Virginia*, ____US ____ (1967; US Supreme Court); *Washington* vs. *Davis*, ____ US ___ (1976; US Supreme Court); *Arlington Heights* vs. *MHDC*, _____US ____ (1977; US Supreme Court); *City of Phoenix* vs. *Kolodziejski*, 399 U.S. 204 (1970; US Supreme Court). *See*: *Washington v. Glucksberg*, 521 U.S. 702, 719 (US Supreme Court; 1997) ("The Due Process Clause guarantees more than fair process, and the 'liberty' it protects includes more than the absence of physical restraint."); *Obergefell vs. Hodges*, 576 U.S. 644 (US Supreme Court; 2015); *Lawrence vs. Texas*, 539 U.S. 558 (US Supreme Court; 2003); See: *United States vs. Vaello-Madero*, _____ US ____ (Case#: 20-303; US Supreme Court; pending as of 2021); *DeNolf vs. U.S.*, _____ US _____ (US Supreme Court; pending as of 2021) (https://static1.squarespace.com/static/5b660749620b85c6c73e5e61/t/608d544886d55300e492a619/1619874888658/2021-22+AMCA+Case.pdf); and *DeNolf vs. U.S.* (Case#: 01-76320; US 14th Circuit, 2020) (https://static1.squarespace.com/static/5b660749620b85c6c73e5e61/t/608d544886d55300e492a619/1619874888658/2021-22+AMCA+Case.pdf); and *Planned Parenthood of Southeastern Pennsylvania v. Casey*, 505 U.S. 833, 848 (1992).

4.9.3 The **Procedural Due Process Doctrine**

In some countries, the well-documented politicization of ICMA, ISDA and FINRA-Type Associations Standards Setting process constitutes violations of the Procedural Due Process rights of users of the accounting standards issued by ICMA, ISDA and FINRA-Type Associations. The government's failure to adequately regulate ICMA, ISDA and FINRA-Type Associations also constitutes violations of the Procedural Due Process rights of users (who are a protected class) of the accounting standards issued by ICMA, ISDA and FINRA-Type Associations. The *Substantial Control Theory*, the *Substantial Inducement Theory* and the *Substitution Theory* apply. The *State Action* is: (i) the government's failure to properly regulate ICMA, ISDA and FINRA-Type Associations; (ii) the government's implied or express delegation of rule-making to ICMA, ISDA and FINRA-Type Associations; (iii) the government's implied or actual use of standards/regulations created by ICMA, ISDA and FINRA-Type Associations. The government's interest in regulating capital markets far outweighs any benefits from the actual or implied delegation of accounting/derivatives standards setting to ICMA, ISDA and FINRA-Type Associations.

4.9.4 The **Equal Protection Doctrine**

In some countries, the well-documented politicization of ICMA, ISDA and FINRA-Type Associations constitutes violations of the equal protection rights of users of the accounting standards issued by ICMA, ISDA and FINRA-Type Associations. The government's failure to adequately regulate the ICMA, ISDA and FINRA-Type Associations also constitutes violations of the equal protection rights of users of accounting data and derivatives, investors and funds (who are a protected class). The *Substantial Control Theory*, the *Substantial Inducement Theory* and the *Substitution Theory* apply. The *State Action* is: (i) the government's failure to properly regulate ICMA, ISDA and FINRA-Type Associations; (ii) the government's implied or express delegation of rule-making to ICMA, ISDA and FINRA-Type Associations; (iii) the government's implied or actual use of standards/regulations created by ICMA, ISDA and FINRA-Type Associations. The government's interest in regulating capital markets and inability to regulate these standards-setting organizations are far outweighed by the actual/potential harm that can result from the continuing existence and operations of these standards-setting organizations.[39]

4.9.5 *The* Non-Delegation Doctrine

The *Substantial Control Theory*, the *Substantial Inducement Theory* and the *Substitution Theory* apply. The *State Action* is: (i) the government's failure to properly regulate ICMA, ISDA and FINRA-Type Associations; (ii) the government's implied or express delegation of rule-making to ICMA, ISDA and FINRA-Type Associations; (iii) the government's implied or actual use of standards/regulations created by ICMA, ISDA and FINRA-Type Associations. The government's interest in regulating capital markets and inability to regulate these standards-setting organizations are far outweighed by the actual/potential harm that can result from the continuing existence and operations of these standards-setting organizations.[40] The ICMA, ISDA and FINRA-Type Associations perform governmental rule-making functions:

1. The functions of the ICMA, ISDA and FINRA-Type Associations' are critical and affect a wide range of persons and social welfare across many countries.
2. Many governments have incorporated into their statutes/ regulations, various ICMA, ISDA and FINRA-Type Associations' standards/regulations.
3. The standards-setting organizations' errors (false positive, false negatives, etc.) can have wide-ranging and *Multiplier Effects* across countries.
4. The costs of standards-setting organizations' errors are significant, long-lasting and are usually borne by governments (in the form of bailouts/bail-ins, subsidies, tax credits, welfare transfers to households and companies, etc.).

[39] *See*: *United States vs. Vaello-Madero*, _____ US ____ (Case#: 20-303; US Supreme Court; pending as of 2021). *See*: *Espinoza vs. Montana Department of Revenue*, _____ US ____ (US Supreme Court; pending as of 2021).

[40] *See*: *PennEast Pipeline Co. vs. New Jersey*, ___ US ___ (No. 19-1039; US Supreme Court; pending as of 2021); and *Seila Law LLC vs. Consumer Financial Protection Bureau*, ____ US ____ (Case#: No. 19-7; US Supreme Court; 2020).

In many modern democracies such as the USA, the national legislature has the exclusive right to regulate interstate commerce. The functions and rule-making performed by the ICMA, ISDA and FINRA-Type Associations' clearly involve the regulation of interstate commerce which should be done by the legislature or delegated by the legislature to government agencies. The government's policy of permitting these accounting and derivatives standards-setting organizations to exist and regulate businesses and capital markets without appropriate oversight can result in deprivation of persons' constitutional *Rights-to-Contract*, *Right-to-Free Speech* and *Right-of-Association*.

4.9.6 *The* Right-to-Contract Doctrine

The well-documented politicization of the ICMA, ISDA and FINRA-Type Associations and their Standards Setting process, and the governments' failure to adequately regulate or directly manage the functions of ICMA and ISDA (and private trade groups such as FINRA in the US), constitute discriminatory and unjustified interferences with the *Rights-to-Contract* of the users of swaps/derivatives and accounting regulations around the world. Such persons are a protected class.[41] The *Substantial Control Theory*, the *Substantial Inducement Theory* and the *Substitution Theory apply*. The *State Action* is: (i) the government's failure to properly regulate ICMA, ISDA and FINRA-Type Associations; (ii) the government's implied or express delegation of rule-making to ICMA, ISDA and FINRA-Type Associations; (iii) the government's implied or actual use of standards/regulations created by ICMA, ISDA and FINRA-Type Associations. The government's interest in regulating capital markets and inability to regulate these standards-setting organizations are far outweighed by the actual/potential harm that can result from the continuing existence and operations of these standards-setting organizations.

4.9.7 *The* Right-of-Association Doctrine

The well-documented politicization of the ICMA, ISDA and FINRA-Type Associations and the self-regulation by FINRA and Accounting/Derivatives Standards Setting process, and the government's

[41] *See*: *Energy Reserves Group, Inc. vs. Kansas Power and Light Co.*, _____ US ____ (US Supreme Court; 1983); and *Sveen vs. Melin*, ___ US ____ (US Supreme Court; 2018).

failure to adequately regulate the ICMA, ISDA and FINRA-Type Associations (and private trade groups such as FINRA in the US) constitute discriminatory and unwarranted interferences with the *Rights-of-Association* of the users of swaps/derivatives and accounting regulations around the world. Such persons are a protected class.[42] The *Substantial Control Theory*, the *Substantial Inducement Theory* and the *Substitution Theory apply*. The *State Action* is: (1) the government's failure to properly regulate ICMA, ISDA and FINRA-Type Associations; (2) the government's implied or express delegation of rule-making to ICMA, ISDA and FINRA-Type Associations; (3) the government's implied or actual use of standards/regulations created by ICMA, ISDA and FINRA-Type Associations. The government's interest in regulating capital markets and inability to regulate these standards-setting organizations are far outweighed by the actual/potential harm that can result from the continuing existence and operations of these standards-setting organizations.

4.9.8 The Separation of Powers Doctrine

As explained herein and above, ICMA, ISDA and FINRA-Type Associations perform rule-making functions: (i) that have been unconstitutionally delegated by national legislatures; (ii) that involve the exercise of powers and processes and influence reserved for both the legislative and executive branches of modern democratic governments. That constitutes a violation of the *Separation of Powers Doctrine*.[43]

The *Substantial Control Theory*, the *Substantial Inducement Theory* and the *Substitution Theory* apply. The *State Action is*: (i) the government's failure to properly regulate ICMA, ISDA and FINRA-Type Associations; (ii) the government's implied or express delegation of rule-making to ICMA, ISDA and FINRA-Type Associations; (iii) the government's implied or actual use of standards/regulations created by ICMA, ISDA and FINRA-Type Associations. The government's interest in regulating

[42] *See*: *Thomas More Law Center vs. Bonta*, ___ US ___ (No. 19-255; US Supreme Court; pending as of 2021).

[43] *See*: *Collins vs. Yellen*, ___ US ___ (No. 19-422; US Supreme Court; pending as of 2021); *Collins vs. Mnuchin*, ____ US _____ (Docket No. 19-422; US Supreme Court; pending as of 2021); *Seila Law LLC vs. Consumer Financial Protection Bureau*, ____ US ____ (Case#: No. 19-7; US Supreme Court; 2020); *Humphrey's Executor vs. United States*, 295 U.S. 602 (US Supreme Court; 1935); and *PHH Corp. vs. CFPB*, 839 F.3d 1 (2016) *on rehearing enbanc*, 881 F.3d 75 (D.C. Cir., 2018) (en banc).

capital markets far outweighs any benefits from the actual or implied delegation of accounting/derivatives standards-setting to ICMA, ISDA and FINRA-Type Associations.

4.10 Conclusion

The unconstitutionality of these "institutions" implies that they can reduce or distort competition and increase actual and potential *systemic risk* and *financial instability* because: (i) these institutions don't face meaningful government oversight which can result in *coordination problems* and *regulatory-biases*; and (ii) the lack of adequate government input and control can result in regulations that don't reduce or control systemic risk and financial instability; (iii) the lobbying impact of the private sector can significantly reduce social welfare while imposing bailout costs and enforcement burdens on governments. This chapter uses the "traditional tests" for unconstitutionality which are typical in the US, Commonwealth countries and common law countries. While US law is used, the same principles are applicable in most common law and Commonwealth countries.

References

Ahdieh, R. (2003). Making Markets: Network Effects and the Role of Law in the Creation of Strong Securities Markets. *Southern California Law Review, 76*, 277–348.

Allee, L., Maines, L. A., & Wood, D. A. (2008). Unintended Economic Implications of Financial Reporting Standards. *Business Horizons, 51*(5), 371–377.

Andrews, M., Pritchett, L., & Woolcock, M. (2017). *Building State Capability: Evidence, Analysis, Action.*

Arner, D. (2007). *Financial Stability, Economic Growth and the Role of Law.* Cambridge University Press.

Arner, D., & Taylor, M. (2009, June). *The Global Financial Crisis and the Financial Stability Board: Hardening the Soft Law of International Financial Regulation?* AIIFL Working Paper No. 6. Asian Institute of International Financial Law Faculty of Law, The University of Hong Kong. www.AIIFL.com. Retrieved from http://law.hku.hk/aiifl/documents/AIIFLWorkingPaper6June2009_000.pdf.

Awrey, D. (2014). The Limits of Private Ordering Within Modern Financial Markets. *Review of Banking & Financial Law, 34*, 186–196.

Bamberger, M., Vaessen, J., & Raimondo, E. (2016). *Dealing with Complexity in Development Evaluation: A Practical Approach.*

Banker, S., Bhanot, S., & Deshpande, A. (2020, in press). Poverty Identity and Preference for Challenge: Evidence from the U.S. and India. *Journal of Economic Psychology, 76.*

Barr, M., & Miller, G. (2006). Global Administrative Law: The View from Basel. *European Journal of International Law, 17*, 15–25.

Bayoumi, T., Pickford, S., & Subacchi, P. (2016). *Managing Complexity: Economic Policy Cooperation After the Crisis.* Brookings Institution Press.

Bertezzolo, G. (2009). The European Union Facing the Global Arena: Standard Setting Bodies and Financial Regulation. *European Law Review, 34*(2), 257–267.

Biggins, J., & Scott, C. (2012). Public-Private Relations in a Transnational Private Regulatory Regime: ISDA, the State and OTC Derivatives Market Reform. *European Business Law Review, 324.*

Birz, G. (2017). Stale Economic News, Media and the Stock Market. *Journal of Economic Psychology, 61*, 87–102.

Blaufus, K., Möhlmann, A., & Schwäbe, A. (2019). Stock Price Reactions to News About Corporate Tax Avoidance and Evasion. *Journal of Economic Psychology, 72*, 278–292.

Blomquist, W., & Ostrom, E. (2009). Deliberation, Learning, and Institutional Change: The Evolution of Institutions in Judicial Settings. *Constitutional Political Economy, 19*(3), 180–202.

Boettke, P., & Aligica, P. (2009). *Challenging Institutional Analysis and Development.* London: Routledge.

Botzem, S. (2012). *The Politics of Accounting Regulation: Organizing Transnational Standard Setting in Financial Reporting.* Edward Elgar.

Byrne, D., & Callaghan, G. (2014). *Complexity Theory and The Social Sciences: The State of The Art.*

Camfferman, K. (2020, in press). International Accounting Standard Setting and Geopolitics. *Accounting in Europe.*

Cassese, S. (2005). Administrative Law Without the State? The Challenge of Global Regulation. *New York University Journal of International Law and Politics, 37*, 663–673.

Cattaneo, O., Engman, M., Saez, S., & Stern, R. (Eds.). (2010). *International Trade in Services: New Trends and Opportunities for Developing Countries.* World Bank.

Chiapello, E., & Mediad, K. (2009). An Unprecedented Privatisation of Mandatory Standard-Setting: The Case of European Accounting Policy. *Critical Perspectives on Accounting, 20*(4), 448–468.

Cooper, M. (2011). Complexity Theory After the Financial Crisis—The Death of Neoliberalism or the Triumph the Triumph of Hayek. *Journal of Cultural Economy, 4*(4), 371–385.

Currie, D. (1986). Positive and Negative Constitutional Rights. *University of Chicago Law Review, 53*(3), 864–890.

Datz, G. (2013). The Narrative of Complexity in the Crisis of Finance: Epistemological Challenge and Macroprudential Policy Response. *New Political Economy, 18*(4), 459–479.

de Larosière, J., et al. (2009). *High Level Group on Financial Supervision in the EU: Report*. Brussels: European Commission.

De Luca, F., & Prather-Kinsey, J. (2018). Legitimacy Theory May Explain the Failure of Global Adoption of IFRS: The Case of Europe and the U.S. *Journal of Management & Governance, 22*, 501–534.

Debelle, G. (2004). Household Debt and the Macroeconomy. *BIS Quarterly Review*. Retrieved from SSRN http://ssrn.com/abstract=1968418.

Delimatsis, P. (2012). *Of Bailouts and Rescue Measures: Subsidies in Financial Services*. Working Paper No 2012/24. Swiss National Center of Competence in Research. Retrieved from http://www20.iadb.org/intal/catalogo/PE/2012/12020.pdf.

Dima, S., Dima, B., et al. (2014). A Discussion Over IFRS' Adoption in Islamic Countries. *Accounting and Management Information, 13*(1), 35–49.

Dinov, S. (2017). The Role and Function of Private Trade Associations as a Private Regulator in Making Markets More Efficient and Stable: The ISDA, The ICMA and The LMA in Comparative Review. *British Journal of Economics, Management & Trade, 16*(4), 1–10.

Dixon, R., Griffiths, W., & Lim, G. (2014). Lay People's Models of the Economy: A Study Based on Surveys of Consumer Sentiments. *Journal of Economic Psychology, 44*, 13–20.

Dobler, M., & Knospe, O. (2016). Constituents' Formal Participation in the IASB's Due Process: New Insights Into the Impact of Country and Due Process Document Characteristics. *Journal of Governance and Regulation*.

Doring, T., & Schnellenbach, J. (2010). A Tale of Two Federalisms: Germany, the United States and the Ubiquity of Centralization. *Constitutional Political Economy, 22*(1), 83–102.

Durlauf, S. (2012). Complexity, Economics, and Public Policy. *Politics, Philosophy & Economics*.

Durocher, S., Gendron, Y., & Picard, C. (2015). Waves of Global Standardization: Small Practitioners' Resilience and Intra-Professional Fragmentation within the Accounting Profession. *Auditing: A Journal of Practice & Theory*.

Economides, N. (1998). The Incentive for Non-Price Discrimination by an Input Monopolist. *International Journal of Industrial Organization, 16*, 271–284.

Economides, N. (2012a). Tying, Bundling, and Loyalty/Requirement Rebates. Book Chap. in E. Elhauge (Ed.), *Research Handbook of the Economics of Antitrust Law*. Edward Elgar. Retrieved from http://www.stern.nyu.edu/networks/Economides_Tying_Bundling_and_Loyalty_Requirement_Rebates.pdf.

Economides, N. (2012b). Antitrust Issues in Network Industries. Book Chap. in I. Kokkoris & I. Lianos (Eds.), *The Reform of EC Competition Law*. Kluwer. Retrieved from http://www.stern.nyu.edu/networks/Economides_Antitrust_in_Network_Industries.pdf.

Ellman, S. (2001). A Constitutional Confluence: American "State Action" Law, And The Application Of South Africa's Socio Economic Rights Guarantees To Private Actors. *New York law School Law Review, 45*, 21–75.

Finch, J. (Ed.). (2013). *Complexity and the Economy—Implications for Economic Policy*. Edward Elgar.

Fleckner, A. (2008). FASB and IASB: Dependence Despite Independence. *Virginia Law & Business Review, 3*, 275–295.

Freeman, R. (2011). What Can We Learn from the NLRA to Create Labor Law for the Twenty-First Century? *ABA Journal of Labor & Employment Law, 26*(2), 327–343.

Garcia, F., Opromolla, L., & Marques, A. (2020, in press). The Effects of Official and Unofficial Information on Tax Compliance. *Journal of Economic Psychology, 78*.

Gardbaum, G. (2003). The "Horizontal Effect" of Constitutional Rights. *Michigan Law Review, 102*, 387–398.

Gardbaum, S. (2006). Where the (State) Action Is. *International Journal of Constitutional Law, 4*(4), 760–779.

Gäumann, M., & Dobler, M. (2019). Formal Participation in the EFRAG's Consultation Processes: The Role of European National Standard-Setters. *Accounting in Europe, 16*(1), 44–81.

Giner, B., & Mora, A. (2019). *Political Interference in Financial Reporting in the Financial Industry: Evidence from Spain*. Retrieved from www.ssrn.com.

Go, J. (2003). A Globalizing Constitutionalism? Views from the Post-Colony, 1945–2000. *International Society, 18*, 71–78.

Gros, M., & Worret, D. (2016). Lobbying and Audit Regulation in the EU. *Accounting in Europe*.

Haferkamp, A., Fetchenhauer, D., et al. (2009). Efficiency versus Fairness: The Evaluation of Labor Market Policies by Economists and Laypeople. *Journal of Economic Psychology, 30*(4), 527–539.

Hamann, A., & Fabri, H. (2008). Transnational Networks and Constitutionalism. *International Journal of Constitutional Law, 6*, 481–491.

Hardardottir, H. (2017). Long Term Stability of Time Preferences and the Role of the Macroeconomic Situation. *Journal of Economic Psychology, 60*, 21–36.

Hoffmann, S., & Zülch, H. (2014). Lobbying on Accounting Standard Setting in the Parliamentary Environment of Germany. *Critical Perspectives on Accounting*.

International Institute For Sustainable Development. (2009, March). *Will Government Bailouts Lead to Trade Wars?* Retrieved from https://www.iisd.org/gsi/news/will-government-bailouts-lead-trade-wars.

Jamal, K., & Sunder, S. (2014). Monopoly Versus Competition in Setting Accounting Standards. *Abacus.*

Jorissen, A., Lybaert, N., Orens, R., & Van der Tas, L. (2013). A Geographic Analysis of Constituents' Formal Participation in the Process of International Accounting Standard Setting: Do We Have a Level Playing Field? *Journal of Accounting and Public Policy, 32*(4), 237–270.

Kingsbury, B. (2009). The Concept of "Law" in Global Administrative Law. *European Journal of International Law, 20*, 23–33.

Kingsbury, B., Krisch, N., & Stewart, R. (2005). The Emergence of Global Administrative Law. *Law and Contemporary Problems, 68*, 15–30.

Kingston, C., & Caballero, G. (2009). Comparing Theories of Institutional Change. *Journal of Institutional Economics, 5*, 151–181.

Kirman, A. (2016). Complexity and Economic Policy: A Paradigm Shift or a Change in Perspective? A Review Essay on David Colander and Roland Kupers's *Complexity and the Art of Public Policy. Journal of Economic Literature, 54*(2), 534–572.

Königsgruber, R. (2010). A Political Economy of Accounting Setting. *Journal of Management & Governance.*

Konigsgruber, R. (2013). Expertise-Based Lobbying and Accounting Regulation. *Journal of Management & Governance.*

Konigsgruber, R. (2014). Accounting Standard Setting in Two Political Contexts. Chapt. in R. DiPietra, S. McLeay, & J. Ronen (Eds.), *Accounting and Regulation. New Insights on Governance, Markets and Institutions* (pp. 59–78). Springer.

Konigsgruber, R. (2017). Lobbying and Accounting Standard Setting. A Literature Survey. *Journal of Business Economics.*

Konigsgruber, R., & Palan, S. (2015). Earnings Management And Participation In Accounting Standard-Setting. *Central European Journal of Operations Research.*

Kuhlman, C., & Mortveit, H. (2014). Attractor Stability in Non-Uniform Boolean Networks. *Theoretical Computer Science, 559*, 20–33.

Kunst, P., & Wagner, R. (2011). Choice, Emergence, and Constitutional Process: A Framework for Positive Analysis. *Journal of Institutional Economics, 7*, 131–145.

Law, D., & Versteeg, M. (2012). The Declining Influence of the United States Constitution. *NYU Law Review, 87*, 762–826.

Lawson, G. (2010). Burying the Constitution Under a TARP. *Harvard Journal of Law and Public Policy, 33.*

Li, X., & Soobaroyen, T. (2020, in press). Accounting, Ideological and Political Work and Chinese Multinational Operations: A Neo-Gramscian Perspective. *Critical Perspectives on Accounting.*

Lord Turner. (2009). *The Turner Review: A Regulatory Response to the Global Banking Crisis* (p. 2009). London: Financial Services Authority.

Melgarejo, M. (2017). Additional Evidence on the Impact of the International Financial Reporting Standards on Earnings Quality: Evidence from Latin America. *Journal of Applied Business and Economics.*

Melnik, S., Ward, J., Gleeson, J., & Porter, M. (2013). Multi-Stage Complex Contagions. *Chaos, 23*, 013124. https://doi.org/10.1063/1.4790836.

Menkes, M. (2019). ICMA, ISDA, Sovereign Debt Restructuring and the Rule of Law. *Zeitschrift für europarechtliche Studien, 22*(3).

Metelska-Szaniawska, K. (2010). Constitutions and Economic Reforms in Transition: An Empirical Study. *Constitutional Political Economy, 20*(1), 1–41.

Meyer, T. (2009). Soft Law as Delegation. *Fordham International Law Journal, 32*, 888–898.

Miklashevich, I. (2003). Mathematical Representation of Social Systems: Uncertainty and Optimization of Social System Evolution. *Non Linear Phenomena in Complex Systems, 6*(2), 678–686.

Milberg, W., & Piegler, P. (2009). The Taming of Institutions in Economics: The Rise and Methodology of the '*New* New Institutionalism'. *Journal of Institutional Economics, 5*(3), 289–313.

Mistri, M. (2007). Institutional Changes and Shifting Ideas: A Constitutional Analysis of the Euro. *Constitutional Political Economy, 18*(2), 107–126.

Mohammadrezaei, F., & Mohd-Saleh, N. (2012). Political Economy of Corporate Governance: The Case of Iran. *Journal of Business, 7*, 301–330.

Morley, J. (2016). Internal lobbying at the IASB. *Journal of Accounting and Public Policy.*

Mwakagali, M. (2018). *International Financial Institutions and Labor Standards: A Legal Study Into the Role of These Institutions in the Promotion and Implementation of Freedom of Association and Collective Bargaining*. PhD thesis, Stockholm University, Sweden. Retrieved from https://su.diva-portal.org/smash/get/diva2:1189029/FULLTEXT01.pdf.

Nguyen, V., & Claus, E. (2013). Good News, Bad News, Consumer Sentiment and Consumption Behavior. *Journal of Economic Psychology, 39*, 426–438.

Norton, J. (1995). *Devising International Bank Supervisory Standards.* Kluwer.

Norton, J. (2009). Comment on the Developing Transnational Network(s) in the Area of International Financial Regulation: The Underpinnings of a New Bretton Woods II Global Financial System Framework. *International Lawyer, 43*, 175–185.

Nwogugu, M. (2003). Corporate Governance, Credit Risk and Legal Reasoning: The Case of Encompass Services, Inc. *Managerial Auditing Journal, 18*(4), 270–291.

Nwogugu, M. (2012). *Risk In The Global Real Estate Markets* (Hoboken: John Wiley).

Nwogugu, M. (2015). Goodwill/Intangibles Rules and Earnings Management. *European Journal of Law Reform, 17*(1), 1–10.

Nwogugu, M. (2021). *Complex Systems and Sustainability in the Global Auditing, Consulting, and Credit Rating Agency Industries.* IGI Global Publishers.

Ochsen, C., & Welsch, H. (2012). Who Benefits from Labor Market Institutions? Evidence from Surveys of Life Satisfaction. *Journal of Economic Psychology, 33*(1), 112–124.

OECD. (2009). *Competition and Regulation in Auditing and Related Professions—2009.* Retrieved from https://www.oecd.org/competition/sectors/44762253.pdf.

OECD, Ed. (2016, September 29–30). *New Approaches to Economic Challenges—Insights Into Complexity and Policy.* Paris: OECD Headquarters. Retrieved from https://www.oecd.org/naec/insights%20into%20complexity%20and%20policy.pdf.

Pántya, J., Kovács, J., et al. (2016). Work Performance and Tax Compliance in Flat and Progressive Tax Systems. *Journal of Economic Psychology, 56*, 262–273.

Perc, M., Donnay, K., & Helbing, D. (2013). Understanding Recurrent Crime as System-Immanent Collective Behavior. *PLOS ONE, 8*(10), e76063.

Pererea, H., & Baydoun, N. (2007). Convergence with International Financial Reporting Standards: The Case of Indonesia. *Advances in International Accounting, 20*, 201–224.

Piccioto, S. (2008). Constitutionalizing Multilevel Governance? *International Journal of Constitutional Law, 6*, 457–467.

Poretti, P. (2009). *The Regulation of Subsidies Within the General Agreement on Trade in Services—Problems and Perspectives.* Kluwer Law International.

Post, D., & Eisen, M. (2000). How Long is the Coastline of the Law? Thoughts on the Fractal Nature of Legal Systems. *Journal Of Legal Studies, 29*, 545–555.

Prochazka, D. (2015). Is a Full International Accounting Convergence Desirable? [Je žádoucí úplná konvergence účetního výkaznictví?] Český finanční a účetní časopis. *Prague University of Economics and Business, 2015*(3), 7–23.

Ramanna, K. (2013). The International Politics of IFRS Harmonization. *Accounting, Economics & Law.*

Ramanna, K., & Sletten, E. (2014). Network Effects in Countries' Adoption of IFRS. *Accounting Review, 89*(4), 1517–1543.

Rehman, I., & Shahzad, F. (2014). The Economic Consequences of Mandatory IFRS Reporting: Emerging Market Perspective. *Engineering Economics, 25*(4).

Room, G. (2011). *Complexity, Institutions, and Public Policy.*

Salzano, M., & Colander, D. (2007). *Complexity Hints for Economic Policy.* Springer.

Schniter, E., Shields, T., & Sznycer, D. (2020, in press). Trust in Humans and Robots: Economically Similar But Emotionally Different. *Journal of Economic Psychology, 78.*

Sokolov, V. (2016). Russia: Can IFRS Be Considered Accounting? Chapter in: D. Bensadon & N. Praquin (Eds.), *IFRS in a Global World* (pp. 187–200). Springer.

Sunder, S. (2011). IFRS Monopoly: The Pied Piper of Financial Reporting. *Accounting and Business Research*.

Temiz, H., & Gulec, O. (2017). Mandatory Adoption of IFRS in Emerging Markets: The Case of Turkey. *Journal of Accounting and Management Information Systems, 16*(4), 560–580.

Torgler, B., & Schneider, F. (2009). The Impact of Tax Morale and Institutional Quality on the Shadow Economy. *Journal of Economic Psychology, 30*(2), 228–245.

Trujillo, E. (2010). International Trade and the Financial Crisis. *Proceedings of the Annual Meeting (American Society of International Law), 104*, 438–443.

Tushnet, M. (2003). The Issue of State Action/Horizontal Effect in Comparative Constitutional Law. *International Journal of Constitutional Law, 1*(1), 79–98.

Vanberg, V. (2005). Market and State: The Perspective of Constitutional Political Economy. *Journal of Institutional Economics, 1*, 23–49.

Verdier, P. (2009). Transnational Regulatory Networks and their Limits. *Yale Journal of International Law, 34*, 113–123.

Wagenhofer, A. (2011). Towards a Theory of Accounting Regulation: A Discussion of the Politics of Disclosure Regulation Along the Economic Cycle. *Journal of Accounting and Economics*.

Walton, P. (2020, in press). Accounting and Politics in Europe: Influencing the Standard. *Accounting in Europe*.

Weber, R., & Arner, D. (2008). Toward a New Design for International Financial Regulation. *University of Pennsylvania Journal of International Law, 29*, 391–401.

Weiss, K., & Gronewold, U. (2020). *Lobbying the IASB: The Role of EFRAG*. Retrieved from https://ssrn.com/abstract=3628437 or https://doi.org/10.2139/ssrn.3628437.

White, L. (2001). *Reducing the Barriers to International Trade in Accounting Services*. AEI Press. Retrieved from http://www.aei.org/press/reducing-the-barriers-to-international-trade-in-accounting-services/.

Williams, C., & Arrigo, B. (2002). *Law, Psychology And Justice: Chaos Theory and New (Dis)Order*. Albany: State University Of New York Press.

Witt, U., & Schubert, C. (2009). Constitutional Interests in the Face of Innovations: How Much Do We Need to Know About Risk Preferences? *Constitutional Political Economy, 9*(3), 203–225.

WTO. (2017). *Accountancy Services*. Retrieved from https://www.wto.org/english/tratop_e/serv_e/accountancy_e/accountancy_e.htm.

Yu, G., & Wahid, A. (2014). Accounting Standards and International Portfolio Holdings. *The Accounting Review, 89*(5), 1895–1930.

Zaring, D. (2005). Informal Procedure, Hard and Soft, in International Administration. *Chicago Journal of International Law, 5*, 547–557.

Zaring, D. (2008). Rulemaking and Adjudication in International Law. *Columbia Journal of Transnational Law, 46*, 563–573.

CHAPTER 5

Unconstitutionality and Failure of *Sarbanes-Oxley Act, and* the *PCAOB* (USA) and Similar Institutions

Sarbanes Oxley Act (SOX), the PCAOB and the Dodd-Frank Act have pervasive effects on accounting firms, consulting firms and Credit Rating Agencies (CRAs) in the US (i.e. disclosures, professional standards, regulation/compliance, labor issues, employee-costs, standard-of-care, legal liability, etc.), and can also have *Global Multiplier Effects* across countries and industries via US multinational corporations (MNCs) and foreign companies that do business in the US and/or list their shares/debts on US financial exchanges. This chapter explains why SOX and the PCAOB and are partly or wholly unconstitutional. The theories in this chapter can be extended to similar statutes in other countries. SOX was a *Bail-in* because it changed the allocation of resources, rights and obligations within the global accounting/auditing industry, and within exchange-traded companies that are listed in US exchanges. SOX was also a *Bail-out* because SOX made the US government to invest in the accounting/auditing industry in the following ways: i) the creation and funding of PCAOB, ii) expenditures for the enforcement of SOX, iii) other expenditures—including funding of additional responsibilities imposed on the US SEC by SOX, and iv) government expenditures that can be deemed to be *subsidies* to accounting/auditing firms—including the foregoing government expenses.

While SOX/PCAOB are increasingly pervasive around the world (via US Multinational Corporations; US international banks and insurance companies; cross-border swaps/derivatives; foreign companies whose shares/

M. I. C. Nwogugu, *Geopolitical Risk, Sustainability and "Cross-Border Spillovers" in Emerging Markets, Volume II*,
https://doi.org/10.1007/978-3-030-71419-2_5

bonds are listed in US financial exchanges; US accounting/auditing firms that work outside the US; foreign accounting/auditing firms that work inside the US; etc.), it isn't clear that the dynamics and *Multiplier Effects* of SOX/PCAOB are being fully incorporated into quantitative models in published academic and practitioner research (i.e. within the context of regulatory failure; Economic/Financial Crisis; sovereign debt crisis, Panel Vector Autoregressive models, Granger Causality, GARCH-type Models, financial markets regulation, Portfolio Management, Economic Modelling, Economic Forecasting, Political Decisions, Behavioral Macroeconomics, Behavioral Expectations, Behavioral Operations Research; sovereign debt crisis, VaR estimation; Tail Risk; etc.).

5.1 Existing Literature

There is relatively little literature on the constitutional political economy and unconstitutionality of PCAOB and SOX. Nwogugu (2015a, b) explained why the Dodd-Frank Act failed and is unconstitutional. Nwogugu (2008, 2021) developed new models of *willingness-to-comply* and critiqued SOX. Some researchers have found that the bailouts of financial institutions in the US during 2008–2010 were unconstitutional. Some researchers have also commented on the trade implications of accounting regulations and government bailouts—see comments in Trujillo (2010), Poretti (2009), Delimatsis (2012) and International Institute for Sustainable Development (March 2009). Baker et al. (2014), Gordon and Nazari (2018), Hoffman and Nagy (2016), Bhabra et al. (2019), Bhabra and Hossain (2018), Chang and Choy (2016) and Loehlein (2017) discussed various important *multiplier effects* of SOX. Bather and Burnaby (2006), Huang and Chong (2016), Chiu et al. (2013), Loehlein (2017), Baker et al. (2014), and Udeh (2017) analyzed various important *multiplier effects* of PCAOB and its regulatory functions.

Other countries and jurisdictions have enacted statutes that are very similar to SOX such as the following:

i) Many Emerging Markets countries have copied and enacted smaller sections of SOX such as: 1) CEO/CFO certification of financial statements and Internal Controls; 2) creation of entities such as PCAOB; 3) the roles/obligations of auditing firms; 4) the roles/obligations of boards of directors; 5)
ii) The EU enacted the Financial Services Action Plan (http://www.financial-services-action-plan.com/); and the European Union's 8th

Company Law Directive on Statutory Audit (Directive 2006/43/EC) (http://www.8th-company-law-directive.com/).

iii) India enacted Clause-49 in 2005.
iv) The China Securities Regulatory Commission (CSRC) passed the Company Law and the Securities Law, both of which became effective in May 2006.
v) Japan's Financial Instruments and Exchange Act was enacted on June 14th, 2006, and became effective in April 2008.
vi) The Canadian government enacted http://en.wikipedia.org/w/index.php?title=Policy_52-109&action=edit&redlink=1 Policy 52–109; and Ontario (Canada) enacted http://en.wikipedia.org/wiki/Keeping_the_Promise_for_a_Strong_Economy_Act_(Budget_Measures),_2002 Keeping The Promise For A Strong Economy Act (Budget Measures) of 2002.
vii) The United Kingdom's Companies (Audit, Investigations and Community Enterprise) Act of 2004.
viii) Germany enacted the German Corporate Governance Code in 2002. Germany also enacted the "MaRisk" which is the minimum requirements for risk management (German Mindestanforderungen an das Risikomanagement), which was issued by the German Federal Financial Supervisory Authority (Bundesanstalt für Finanzdienstleistungsaufsicht, BaFin) and provides processes for risk management of banks, insurances and other companies financially trading in Germany. The primary legal background for MaRisk is the Kreditwesengesetz (KWG), the secondary legal background is the Solvabilitätsverordnung SolvV.
ix) In South Africa, the "King Report on Corporate Governance" was released in 2002 (South African corporate governance code, King II Report, non-legislative).
x) France enacted the Financial Security Law of France ("Loi sur la Sécurité Financière") – the French equivalent of Sarbanes–Oxley Act.
xi) Italy enacted Italian Law 262/2005 ("Disposizioni per la tutela del risparmio e la disciplina dei mercati finanziari") in 2006.
xii) Isreal.
xiii) Turkey enacted "TC-SOX", the Turkish equivalent of Sarbanes–Oxley Act.
xiv) Netherlands issued the "Code Tabaksblat" in 2003 – which is the Dutch governance code.
xv) Australia's government enacted the "CLERP-9" (Corporate Law Economic Reform Program Act 2004) in 2004.

Collectively, these and other SOX-type statutes/regulations that were enacted by non-US countries are hereafter referred to as "World SOX".

The legal systems and constitutional principles of the US and most Commonwealth countries are based on the British legal system; and the governments and citizens of the UK, Canada, India and other Commonwealth countries have made significant investments in the US. US commercial and investment banks (which are subject to SOX) are very active in the capital markets in the UK and many Commonwealth countries. The shares of many companies based in the United Kingdom and Commonwealth countries are listed in the US. Furthermore, the Global Financial Crisis has significantly affected many Commonwealth countries (like the United Kingdom, India, Canada, Australia, Egypt).

However, the literature on associated institutional law and economics is well developed. See: Kunst and Wagner (2011), Metelska-Szaniawska (2010), Witt and Schubert (2009) and Blomquist and Ostrom (2009). Doring and Schnellenbach (2010) compared federalism in Germany and the US, and concluded that a constitutional framework of competitive federalism does not prevent the long-term centralization of competencies, that formal institutions affect the pathways of government centralization and that informal political institutions may have a substantial effect on the preservation of state and local autonomy. These informal political institutions include trade associations, standards organizations (such as PCAOB), specific statutes (such as Sarbanes Oxley Act and the Dodd-Frank Act) and quasi-government agencies, and so on. Mistri (2007) analyzed the constitutional political economy of the creation of the Euro, and noted that the inherent conflict among the monetary systems of the constituent countries has been acted out according to the single states' collective preference functions, wherein both employment and price stability are major elements of said preference functions.

Some sections of SOX have functioned as both formal and informal "taxes"[1] on both US and foreign companies partly because of costs imposed (implementation cost, compliance costs and levies)—on the constitutionality of various types of taxation; see Chap. 4 in this book, Dunbar (Feb. 1901) and Houghton and Hellertein (2000).

[1] *See:* "The SOX tax: Many companies find initial costs were high, but they decline in subsequent years". By Ann Bednarz. April 10, 2006.

Its notable that in the Labor Economics and Labor Regulation literatures, most studies have completely omitted (or didn't adequately analyze) constitutional analysis[2] of workers' *Right-to-Contract*, *Right-of-Association* and *Equal Protection* rights. These three constitutional rights are central to workers' rights and ability to negotiate working conditions and to push for implementation of Collective Bargaining agreements, both of which account for a significant percentage of Labor-related litigation and economic Multiplier Effects. Even studies such as Mwakagali (2018) that take the legal approach have failed to fully analyze the Constitutional Law and Constitutional Political Economy implications of workers' *Right-to-Contract* and *Right-of-Association*.

5.1.1 SOX and PCAOB Regulations (and Similar Statutes in Other Countries) as Significant Labor Regulation

Sarbanes-Oxley Act (SOX) applies to all US listed/public companies, as well as non-public companies with publicly traded debt securities in the US. As explained in Nwogugu (2021), the Dodd-Frank Act is major labor and employment regulation/statute. Since the enactment of SOX, both SOX and the PCAOB have continued to function as labor, corporate governance and economic/financial stability regulation that have or can have global *multiplier effects*. SOX and PCAOB function as quasi-labor regulations because the legislative-intent, history and

[2] *See: "Unions, retirees sue to block Chicago pension changes"*. By Karen Pierog. Dec. 16, 2014. https://www.reuters.com/article/usa-chicago-pensions-lawsuit/update-2-unions-retirees-sue-to-block-chicago-pension-changes-idUSL1N0U01MO20141216. (states in part: "........The lawsuit asks the court to declare the law void and illegal because pensions will be reduced in violation of a constitutional provision prohibiting the diminishment or impairment of public employee retirement benefits. A similar argument by unions and others led to a Nov. 21 Sangamon County Circuit Court ruling that tossed Illinois' 2013 pension reform law for being unconstitutional. The Illinois Supreme Court will hear arguments in March over the state's appeal of that ruling. Illinois has the worst-funded state pension fund, while Chicago is struggling with a huge pension funding burden. Moody's Investors Service has said the city is an "extreme outlier" among U.S. local governments it rates, citing a $32 billion adjusted net pension liability that is equal to eight times operating revenue. A hearing on a temporary restraining order to stop the Jan.1 implementation of Chicago's pension law is set for Dec. 29, according to AFSCME spokesman Anders Lindall. He said last month's ruling on Illinois' law, along with a state supreme court ruling in July over state retiree health care, have reinforced constitutional protections for retirement benefits........").

wording and application of SOX evince an intent to directly or indirectly affect, regulate or modify:

1. Labor mobility.
2. Accountants' working conditions.
3. Workers' rights (including complaints and appeals) and consumer financial protection (i.e. the Consumer Financial Protection Bureau).
4. Accounting firms' legal liability for labor-related issues.
5. Accounting/audit firms' and their client-firms' exposures to labor costs and labor unions.
6. Industry structure and function; and the role and effects of industry trade associations in the accounting/auditing industry.
7. SOX doesn't map or properly define the labor-requirements and labor-related disclosure requirements for Global Supply Chains[3] in the financial services industry.
8. Actual or perceived collusion by accounting/auditing firms (and informal "labor unionism").
9. Existing labor/employment regulations.
10. Employee costs (i.e. compliance costs, employee salaries, employee taxes, etc.) companies in some industries (including the financial services industry).
11. Increased compliance processes and documentation that pertain to work-processes and workers in several industries (including the financial services industry).
12. SOX contains both civil and criminal whistleblower provisions[4] that can protect whistleblowers. See Section 806 of Sarbanes-Oxley (18 U.S.C. § 1514A).
13. SOX contains an anti-retaliation provision which covers employees' complaints to the US Department of Labor (DOL), the Occupational Safety and Health Administration (OSHA), the Equal Employment Opportunity Commission (EEOC), the US Citizenship and

[3] *See:* Phillips, N., LeBaron, G. & Wallin, S. (June 2018). *Mapping and Measuring the Effectiveness of Labour-Related Disclosure Requirements For Global Supply Chains.* International Labour Office, Research Department Working Paper No. 32. https://www.ilo.org/wcmsp5/groups/public/%2D%2D-dgreports/%2D%2D-inst/documents/publication/wcms_632120.pdf.

[4] *See:* "Labor Department Issues Procedures For Handling SOX Whistleblower Complaints". *DLA Piper—Employment Alert*, March 12, 2015. By: Daniel Turinsky & Amanda Rooney. https://www.dlapiper.com/en/us/insights/publications/2015/03/labor-department-issues-procedures/.

Immigration Services (USCIS) and the National Labor Relations Board (NLRB).

14. SOX contains a *401(K) Plan Blackout Period Notice Requirement.* "A blackout period is any period of more than three consecutive business days during which participants or beneficiaries of a 401(k) plan cannot direct or diversify assets credited to their accounts, or obtain loans or distributions".
15. OSHA[5] has adopted parts of SOX. SOX substantially modifies and supplements OSHA[6] regulations. OSHA is a US federal agency that

[5] *See:* "DOL Adopts Strengthened Sarbanes-Oxley Whistleblower Regulations". By Jason Zuckerman. August 9th, 2020. https://www.zuckermanlaw.com/dol-adopts-strengthened-sarbanes-oxley-whistleblower-regulations/. (OSHA has adopted Sarbanes-Oxley whistleblower regulations implementing the Dodd-Frank Act amendments to the Sarbanes-Oxley whistleblower law. The regulations also clarify and improve OSHA's procedures for handling Sarbanes-Oxley whistleblower claims, as well as to set forth OSHA's interpretations of SOX. Some of the significant enhancements include the following:

- SOX complaints need not be in any particular form. They may be either oral or in writing. And when a complaint is made orally, OSHA will reduce the complaint to writing.
- Consistent with the ARB's decisions in *Sylvester Parexel Int'l LLC*, ARB No. 07–123, (ARB May 25, 2011), the federal court pleading standards established in *Bell Atlantic Corp. vs. Twombly*, 550 U.S. 544 (2007) and *Ashcroft vs. Iqbal*, 556 U.S. 662 (2009) do not apply to Sarbanes-Oxley whistleblower complaints filed with OSHA.
- The final rule clarifies that a SOX whistleblower "need not show that the conduct complained of constituted an actual violation of law. Pursuant to this standard, an employee's whistleblower activity is protected where it is based on a reasonable, but mistaken, belief that a violation of the relevant law has occurred or is likely to occur."
- OSHA notes that its current policy is to request that each party provide the other parties with a copy of all submissions to OSHA that are responsive to the whistleblower complaint. Where the parties do not so provide, OSHA will ensure that each party is provided with such information, redacted as appropriate. OSHA will also ensure that each party is provided with an opportunity to respond to the other party's submissions.
- A SOX whistleblower who is reinstated pursuant to an OSHA order of preliminary reinstatement but is subsequently unsuccessful at a hearing on the merits is not required to reimburse the employer for wages earned during the period of reinstatement: "Congress intended that employees be preliminarily reinstated to their positions if OSHA finds reasonable cause to believe that they were discharged in violation of Sarbanes-Oxley. However, the statutory procedural scheme does not allow for reimbursement to the employer if actual preliminary reinstatement was ordered and yet the employer ultimately prevailed. Thus, there is no statutory basis to reimburse an employer in that instance.")

[6] *See*: Malone, A., & Jones, R. (December 6, 2010). "Revealed: Inside the Chinese suicide sweatshop where workers toil in 34-hour shifts to make your iPod". *Daily Mail* (London). Available at: http://www.dailymail.co.uk/news/article-1285980/Revealed-Inside-Chinese-suicide-sweatshop-workers-toil-34-hour-shifts-make-iPod.html.

See: "*Chinese Factory asks for 'no suicide' vow*". MSNBC. May 26, 2010. Available at: http://www.msnbc.msn.com/id/37354853/ns/business-world_business/?ns=business-world_business.

See: Carlson, N. (April 7, 2010). "What It's Like To Work In China's Gadget Sweatshops Where Your iPhones And iPads Are Made". *Business Insider*. Available at: http://www.businessinsider.com/what-its-like-to-work-if-chinas-gadget-sweatshops-where-your-iphones-and-ipads-are-made-2010-4?utm_source=Daily+Buzz&utm_campaign=81432d578c-nl_emv_db_04082010_a&utm_medium=email.

See: "Apple denies claims it broke Chinese labor laws in iPhone factory". September 8, 2019. By Saheli Roy Choudhury.

https://www.cnbc.com/2019/09/09/apple-appl-claims-it-broke-china-labor-laws-at-iphone-factory-mostly-false.html.

See: "Apple's 2019 supplier report shows progress on labor and health issues". Jeremy Horwitz. March 6, 2019. https://venturebeat.com/2019/03/06/apples-2019-supplier-report-shows-progress-on-labor-and-health-issues/.

See: "*Apple and Foxconn broke Chinese Labour law to build new iPhones—US tech group and manufacturing partner admit using too many temporary workers*". Louise Lucas. September 9, 2019. https://www.ft.com/content/19fefd86-d2c3-11e9-8367-807ebd53ab77.

See: "Apple—Supplier Responsibility" (PDF). *Apple*. https://images.apple.com/supplier-responsibility/pdf/L418102A_SR_2010Report_FF.pdf

See: Chen, B. (May 14, 2010), "Workers Plan to Sue iPhone Contractor Over Poisoning". *Wired*. https://www.wired.com/gadgetlab/2010/05/wintek-employees-sue/.

See: "Apple under fire again for working conditions at Chinese factories". *The Guardian*. December 19, 2014. https://www.theguardian.com/technology/2014/dec/19/apple-under-fire-again-for-working-conditions-at-chinese-factories?CMP=EMCNEWEML661912.

See: "Study Casts Doubts on Apple's Ethical Standards". *China Labor Watch*. February 24, 2016. http://www.chinalaborwatch.org/report/113.

See: "Poor Working Conditions Persist at Apple Supplier Pegatron". *China Labor Watch*. October 22, 2015. http://www.chinalaborwatch.org/report/109.

See: Perlin, R. (2013). "Chinese Workers Foxconned". *Dissent. 60(2): 46–52.*

See: Armitage, J. (July 30, 2013). "'Even Worse Than Foxconn': Apple Rocked by Child Labour Claims". *The Independent*. London.

See: Mozur, P. (December 19, 2012). "Life Inside Foxconn's Facility in Shenzhen". *The Wall Street Journal*. https://blogs.wsj.com/chinarealtime/2012/12/19/life-inside-foxconns-facility-in-shenzhen/.

See: "Apple suppliers maintain tight security to avoid leaks: Foxconn said to have 'special status' in China". MacNN, February 17, 2010. Available at: http://www.macnn.com/articles/10/02/17/foxconn.said.to.have.special.status.in.china/.

See: *Apple's Recent Strike in Suzhou is Sign of Continued Bad Labor and CSR Practices in China*. *All Roads Lead to China*, January 21, 2010. Available at: http://www.allroadsleadtochina.com/2010/01/21/will-apple-be-the-next-nike-or-will-they-take-labor-compliance-seriously/.

See: "*Apple—Supplier Responsibility*" (PDF). Apple. Available at: http://images.apple.com/supplierresponsibility/pdf/L418102A_SR_2010Report_FF.pdf.

See: Blodget, H. (April 7, 2010). "*Apple-Supplier Factory Worker Tries To Kill Herself—That's 4 In 4 Weeks*". Business Insider. Available at: http://www.businessinsider.com/henry-blodget-another-apple-supplier-factory-worker-tries-to-kill-herself-thats-4-in-4-weeks-2010-4.

See: Apple Loses Lawsuit Over a Company Policy Tim Cook Didn't Know About. By Sissi Cao. Feb. 14, 2020. https://observer.com/2020/02/apple-lose-lawsuit-retail-employee-security-check-pay/. ("Apple has a lost a class-action lawsuit brought by its Apple store employees regarding a seemingly miscellaneous company policy at the retail level that CEO Tim Cook wasn't even aware of. The plaintiffs filed the class-action suit in 2013, revealing that Apple would require its retail employees to go through a security check after they clocked out every day to make sure that no company assets or trade secrets were stolen. The exit check would typically take 10 to 20 minutes and involved searches of employees' purses, briefcases and personal iPhones".)

See: Apple sued by employees over labor issues. by James O'Toole. July 23, 2014. https://money.cnn.com/2014/07/23/technology/apple-labor/. ("The company is facing a lawsuit certified as a class action this week from employees who say they were denied meal breaks and rest periods in violation of California labor law. Attorneys for the plaintiffs estimate that more than 20,000 current or former Apple employees from the retail to corporate level have been affected by the alleged violations. Among other things, the lawsuit claims Apple employees were forced to work for stretches of five hours or more without meals, and didn't get breaks on shorter shifts".)

See: "Class complaint for injunctive relief and damages, in the United States District Court for the District of Columbia, 15 Dec 2019; Major tech companies respond to lawsuit over mining deaths". *ComputerWeekly.com.* https://www.business-humanrights.org/en/latest-news/lawsuit-against-apple-google-tesla-and-others-re-child-labour-drc/. ("Snapshot: In 2019, IRAdvocates, a US-based NGO filed a class action lawsuit against Apple, Google, Tesla, Alphabet, Microsoft, and Dell alleging the corporations profited from child labour in their cobalt supply chains in the Democratic Republic of Congo. Plaintiffs are either guardians of children killed in cobalt mining tunnels or children who were maimed while working in the mines".)

See: *The Other Side of Apple II: Pollution Spreads Through Apple's Supply Chain.* Institute of Public and Environmental Affairs, August 31, 2011. http://www.ipe.org.cn/Upload/Report-IT-V-Apple-II.pdf.

See: Barboza, D. (2012). Apple Cited as Adding to Pollution in China. *The New York Times*, September 1, 2011. Accessed March 26, 2012. https://www.nytimes.com/2011/09/02/technology/apple-suppliers-causing-environmental-problems-chinese-group-says.html?_r=1.

See: Watts, Jonathan, Apple Secretive About 'Polluting and Poisoning' Supply Chain, Says Report. *The Guardian*, January 19, 2011. https://www.theguardian.com/environment/2011/jan/20/apple-pollution-supply-chain.

See: Jobs, Steve, *A Greener Apple.* Apple, Inc. https://www.apple.com/hotnews/agreenerapple/.

See: Greenpeace. "Hazardous Materials Found in Apple's iPhone: Chemicals Include those Banned in Children's Toys in EU". Greenpeace International. Greenpeace. http://www.greenpeace.org/usa/en/media-center/news-releases/hazardous-materials-found-in-a/.

regulates working conditions in both government and private work-places.

16. As explained in this chapter, sections of SOX are unconstitutional and infringe the Rights-of-Association of workers.
17. The criminal provisions of SOX can be used to prevent or hinder collective bargaining and unionization in organizations (i.e. false accusations, entrapment, etc.).
18. The Dodd-Frank Act amends SOX's anti-retaliation provisions in the following ways:

    a. The Dodd-Frank Act clarifies that SOX's whistleblower protections also apply to employees of subsidiaries and affiliates of a publicly traded company.
    b. The Dodd-Frank Act doubles the statute of limitations for filing an administrative complaint with the United States Department of Labor to the longer of: (i) 180 days after the adverse employment action violation or (ii) 180 days after the date on which the employee became aware of the adverse action.
    c. The Dodd-Frank Act amends SOX by affording aggrieved employees the right to a federal jury trial and, thereby, removes any confusion or judicial discretion for this issue.
    d. The Dodd-Frank Act invalidates any agreements (including Collective-Bargaining Agreements) that would require pre-dispute arbitration of a SOX civil whistleblower dispute; and also states that SOX's anti-retaliation provisions cannot be waived through private agreement between an employee and a covered entity.

Similar statutes in other countries also have the same or similar regulatory effects on labor markets. See the comments in: Ochsen and Welsch (2012), Haferkamp et al. (2009), Diamond et al. (2019), Torgler and Schneider (2009), and Pántya et al. (2016).

See: Chen, B. (May 14, 2010), "Workers Plan to Sue iPhone Contractor Over Poisoning", *Wired*. https://www.wired.com/gadgetlab/2010/05/wintek-employees-sue/.

5.1.2 *Omissions of In-Depth Analysis of Constitutionally Granted* Right-to-Contract, Equal Protection *and* Right-of-Association *in the Labor Regulation and Labor Economics Literatures*

It's notable that in the Labor Economics and Labor Regulation literatures, most studies have completely omitted (or didn't adequately analyze) constitutional analysis[7] of workers' *Right-to-Contract*, *Right-of-Association* and *Equal Protection* rights. These three constitutional rights are central to workers' rights and ability to negotiate working conditions and to push for implementation of Collective Bargaining agreements, both of which account for a significant percentage of labor-related litigation and economic Multiplier Effects.

Even studies such as Mwakagali (2018) that take the legal approach have failed to fully analyze the Constitutional Law and Constitutional Political Economy implications of workers' *Right-to-Contract* and *Right-of-Association*.

5.1.3 *The Traditional US-Type* Standards-of-Review *for Constitutional Review Have Been Omitted in This Chapter*

As in Nwogugu (2012), the constitutional law analysis in this chapter intentionally omits in-depth discussion of US-style *standards-of-review* for

[7] *See: "Unions, retirees sue to block Chicago pension changes"*. By Karen Pierog. Dec. 16, 2014. https://www.reuters.com/article/usa-chicago-pensions-lawsuit/update-2-unions-retirees-sue-to-block-chicago-pension-changes-idUSL1N0U01MO20141216. (states in part: "The lawsuit asks the court to declare the law void and illegal because pensions will be reduced in violation of a constitutional provision prohibiting the diminishment or impairment of public employee retirement benefits. A similar argument by unions and others led to a Nov. 21 Sangamon County Circuit Court ruling that tossed Illinois' 2013 pension reform law for being unconstitutional. The Illinois Supreme Court will hear arguments in March over the state's appeal of that ruling. Illinois has the worst-funded state pension fund, while Chicago is struggling with a huge pension funding burden. Moody's Investors Service has said the city is an "extreme outlier" among U.S. local governments it rates, citing a $32 billion adjusted net pension liability that is equal to eight times operating revenue. A hearing on a temporary restraining order to stop the Jan. 1 implementation of Chicago's pension law is set for Dec. 29, according to AFSCME spokesman Anders Lindall. He said last month's ruling on Illinois' law, along with a state supreme court ruling in July over state retiree health care, have reinforced constitutional protections for retirement benefits").

constitutional law issues (i.e. *Rational-Basis* versus *Intermediate Scrutiny* versus *Strict Scrutiny*) because:

1. such classifications by themselves are suspect and can introduce significant and unwarranted discretion and bias in judicial reasoning—the implication is that persons' rights should not be so varied in relevance or importance (that such rights require such classification), and any such differences can be (and are already) accommodated in *Balancing-of-Interests tests*;
2. many judges are not technical experts in the matters and statutes being litigated and without such knowledge, it can be difficult to assign a specific standard-of-review to a statute/regulation or procedure/process or event or transaction or a group of persons;
3. where a judge or a group of judges are not technical experts, they usually rely on experts who unfortunately, are or can be subject to lobbying, bias, coercion and other influences and don't have the same physical protections as judges;
4. the costs of *false-positives* and *false-negatives* in such classifications can be significant and very damaging (and far outweigh any benefits that arise from such suspect classifications);
5. such classifications don't always advance the public interest or individuals' rights.

5.2 Geopolitical Risk and Some Economic Psychology[8] and Cross-Border *Spillover Effects* of SOX, World-SOX and PCAOB (Spillovers into Emerging Markets)

5.2.1 Cross-Border Spillovers and Economic Psychology Effects

The significant literatures on social networks, social capital and cross-border *spillover effects* are summarized in Chap. 2 of this book. SOX, World-SOX and PCAOB had, and continue to have, worldwide *Multiplier Effects* because of the following in addition to other factors:

[8] On associated *Economic Psychology* and *Behavioral IPE* issues, see: Hardardottir (2017), Birz (2017), Dixon et al. (2014), Ochsen and Welsch (2012), Debelle (2004), Schniter et al. (2020), Garcia et al. (2020), Torgler and Schneider (2009), Nguyen and Claus (2013), Banker et al. (2020), and Blaufus et al. (2019).

1. The evolution of accounting regulators and derivatives standards-setting organizations in various countries can be deemed to constitute global structural changes in the financial services industry and other industries.[9]
2. Given the foregoing, SOX, World-SOX and PCAOB have become important institutions and mechanisms partly because: (1) they dictate the relationships among issuers and investors, and accounting firms; (2) they significantly affect the disintermediation of financial services companies; (3) they affect the relationships between companies, consumers and financial services companies; (4) they affect the savings rates, expenditures, risk-perception and investment patterns of households, companies and parties to derivatives contracts; (5) they have international Multiplier Effects (disclosure, international capital flows, international trade, international investment, etc.).
3. During 2002–2020, various new US, European, Latin American and Asian "institutions" emerged and, in combination with SOX, World-SOX and PCAOB, have created various categories of "regulatory fragmentation", "regulatory capture" and new "administrative laws".
4. The "modern administrative state" (as exemplified by PCAOB in the USA) in various countries has veered from their constitutions—as noted by Lawson (2010). See also: Norton (2009), Bertezzolo (2009), Meyer (2009), Verdier (2009), Hamann and Fabri (2008), and Piccioto (2008).
5. The Global Financial Crisis of 2007–2014 has highlighted the need for the re-evaluation and restructuring of incentives, traditional institutions and analysis of institutions. Analysis in Institutional Economics has been largely defined by formal models and cost-benefit analysis, which collectively have not solved many modern problems inherent in institutions.
6. The unconstitutionality of SOX, World-SOX and PCAOB can create *deadweight losses* in: (1) the demand and supply of legal and accounting enforcement around the world; (2) the demand and supply of auditing services around the world; (3) the pricing of securities; (4) the pricing of auditing services.
7. SOX, World-SOX and PCAOB directly and/or indirectly regulates US and EU and East Asian multinational corporations which have significant global operations and are influential in international

[9] *See*: Nwogugu (2013).

trade—and many of these US and EU and East Asian MNCs have major suppliers that are located in Emerging Markets countries (e.g. Mexico, Brazil, India, the Philippines, Chile, Peru, China, ASEAN countries) that essentially have to comply with US and/or EU or East Asian business/legal standards. Also, MNCs' operations in foreign countries are a transmission channel for cross-border *Corporate Governance Contagion* and *Operations Policies Contagion.* "SecondaryLevel Emerging Markets countries" such as Nigeria, Russia and Brazil benefit from these US-, EU- and East Asian–influenced international trade/financial relationships—for example Nigeria sells its petroleum products to India, imports large volumes of goods from China and borrows large amounts from China. Russia gets the largest amount of Chinese Foreign Aid, borrows from China and sells products to China. On some international *Multiplier Effects* and implications of SOX, World-SOX and PCAOB, see: Baker et al. (2014); Chang and Choy (2016); Bhabra and Hossain (2018), Hoffman and Nagy (2016), Bather and Burnaby (2006), Huang and Chong (2016), and Udeh (2017).

8. SOX, World-SOX and PCAOB standards/regulations are "core" regulations for the global capital markets and the global derivatives markets, and thus they can affect market volatility, pricing of financial instruments, market integration and spillovers.
9. Many countries have copied parts of SOX, World-SOX and PCAOB standards/regulations or have enacted statutes/regulations that are similar to them, or have the same objectives. Such *regulatory contagion* amplifies the effects of SOX, World-SOX and PCAOB and makes them more acceptable in emerging markets countries.
10. SOX, World-SOX and PCAOB directly and indirectly regulate foreign companies that do business in the US, EU and East Asia, and/or whose shares and/or debt are traded on US and EU financial exchanges; and those that raise money in the US or EU.
11. SOX, World-SOX and PCAOB have significant worldwide economic *Multiplier Effects* and *Spillover Effects* across national borders because they affect and regulate the financing of international trade, international capital flows, capital raising, financial regulation and so on.
12. During 2010–2020, more than 50% of international trade was conducted with the US dollar and an average of about 59% of government foreign currency reserves around the world were in US Dollars. The US dollar is managed by the US Federal Reserve and the large

international US banks, all of which are significantly affected by, and also affect, SOX, World-SOX and PCAOB. During 2005–2020, the US Federal Reserve emerged as the central bank to the world because of the worldwide impact of its activities and policies.

13. SOX, World-SOX and PCAOB directly and indirectly regulate and have substantial effects on non-financial industries that are global industries—such as hotel chains, restaurant chains, insurance, logistics/distribution, technology/Internet, and telecommunications.
14. Around the world, sustainability and ESG-investing standards and measurements are based in part on environmental audits, accounting audits and compliance with SOX, World-SOX and PCAOB regulations—all of which affect international capital flows, FDI (foreign direct investment), FI (foreign investment) and foreign aid.
15. The domestic and international capital flows that determine sustainability and economic growth around the world are partly based on ICMA/ISDA regulations/standards.
16. SOX, World-SOX and PCAOB directly and indirectly regulate and have substantial effects on non-financial industries that employ significant numbers of immigrants such as hotel-chains, restaurants, construction, retail-trade, business services and healthcare/home-health services. These immigrants send remittances to, and make investments in, Emerging Markets countries. Also, immigrant-expenditures are not tied to their countries-of-origin—for example Philippines/Filipino immigrants in the United Kingdom can send remittances to relatives in Sri Lanka or the UAE or South Africa; and/or make investments in Kenya or Uganda (where there are substantial immigrant communities). SOX, World-SOX and PCAOB regulate and have significant effects on the financing of construction activity around the world. Construction activity metrics are major economic indicators in most developed and developing countries. In many developed and developing countries, the global construction industry imports significant volumes of finished/semi-finished products from Emerging Markets countries, and employs a significant number of immigrants who, in turn, send remittances, investments and knowledge/human-capital to Emerging Markets countries, all of which affect the GDP/exports/productivity of those countries.
17. SOX, World-SOX and PCAOB are likely to be influential in Emerging Markets countries that use or have used the US dollar or the EU Euro as their official currencies—these countries include Poland, Ecuador,

El Salvador, Zimbabwe, Timor-Leste, Micronesia, Palau and the Marshall Islands. The following countries/regions also widely use the US Dollar and/or the Euro simultaneously with their own local currencies—Bahamas, Barbados, St. Kitts and Nevis, Belize, Costa Rica, Nicaragua, Panama, Myanmar, Cambodia, and Liberia, as well as several Caribbean territories; and British territories in the Caribbean (Turks and Caicos and the British Virgin Islands).

18. SOX, World-SOX and PCAOB have affected and are likely to continue to affect legislation and adjudication in many countries because many such countries' statutes/regulations expressly or impliedly incorporate SOX, World-SOX and PCAOB standards/regulations.
19. The literature notes that accounting regulations have significant effects on international trade—and thus have significant effects on Emerging Markets countries, many of whom have trade-based and/or commodities-based economies. During the last ten years, the WTO (World Trade Organization) created working committees to analyze accounting regulations and accounting standards setting.
20. SOX, World-SOX and PCAOB, social networks and social capital dynamics have or can have significant effects on government tax policies, perceived tax equity, tax-sensitivity and tax compliance (by individuals and companies), all of which can affect savings/investments, remittances (to Emerging Markets), loan-volumes (to Emerging Markets), FDI/foreign investment/foreign aid, consumer confidence, consumer expenditures, business confidence, corporate expenditures, government expenditures, risk-perception and so on.
21. SOX applies to: (1) foreign companies that list their securities and financial instruments on US financial exchanges; and (2) US multinational corporations, many of whom have extensive international operations, social capital and political capital in foreign countries.
22. SOX affects some of the regulations issued by the US government, some of which in turn are based on FASB/SASB accounting standards; and FASB accounting standards are very similar to IASB/IFRS standards. A significant percentage of international investors use FASB and IASB/IFRS accounting standards to evaluate investments and, thus, are indirectly affected by SOX and PCAOB. A significant portion of international derivatives transactions are documented and settled in US Dollars, and involve listed US financial services companies as counter-parties and thus implicate SOX. As explained herein, SOX directly/indirectly affects both fiscal policy and monetary policy

in the US (and other affected and/or dependent countries)—that is, SOX directly and indirectly affects fiscal policy (accurate disclosure of corporate tax and real estate tax liabilities; government's revenues from fees, fines and levies; costs of corporate financial distress and bankruptcy; litigation costs; regulation of accounting/audit firms; compliance reporting; etc.) and monetary policy (earnings management and market volatility; stock market crashes; money-supply; liquidity in financial markets; bubbles; stock-market driven inflation/deflation; risk-perception [corporate bonds, stocks, etc.]; economic models and capital-adequacy models; derivatives compliance reports; contagion; etc.), all of which can have cross-border *Multiplier Effects* in Emerging Markets countries through the channels explained in this book. The global dominance of the US Dollar was analyzed in Chap. 1 in this book.

23. The US has the most advanced and comprehensive financial regulations and creates some of the most sophisticated financial products in the world.
24. During the last twenty years, the US consistently had the largest national economy in the world; and the US economy directly/indirectly (through international trade, outsourcing, FDI, FI, foreign aid, etc.) supported the economies of other "First-Level Associated" countries (such as China, Japan, Brazil, Mexico, India) which, in turn, directly/directly supported (through international trade, outsourcing, loans, FDI, FI, foreign aid, etc.) the economies of other "Second-Level Associated" countries (such as Russia, Nigeria, the Philippines, Thailand, ASEAN countries, Pakistan, Central American countries, CIS countriesc). During 1980–2020, the US was a major participant in major multilateral and bilateral trade agreements; and the US-China trade war (2019–present) continues to have significant economic/social/psychological *Multiplier Effects* on many countries. The use of the terms "First-Level Associated" countries and "Second-Level Associated" countries is introduced here as a "mutual-dependency" classification of countries as a way to better reflect the often symbiotic relationships between countries with regard to international trade and international capital flows.
25. SOX, World-SOX and PCAOB are major geopolitical risk factors and their actual effects on a specific country can vary dramatically across countries due to several factors including but not limited to the following:

a. Whether the subject country is a member of the WTO.
b. The terms of any treaties between the US and EU on one hand, and the subject country.
c. The volume of trade and balance-of-trade between the US and EU on one hand, and the subject country.
d. The existing financial, derivatives and accounting regulation frameworks in the subject country.
e. Interpretations of international law and conflict of laws.
f. The volumes of FDI, FI and foreign aid and other international capital flows between the US, EU and China on one hand, and the subject country.
g. The political structure and processes in the subject country, and the relative power/influence of the top political parties.
h. The regulation, if any, of political lobbying in the country.

5.2.2 *SOX and Fiscal Policy, Monetary Policy, Trade Policy and Foreign Policy*

Nwogugu (2008) introduced a model of *willingness-to-comply* with SOX. SOX can directly/indirectly and jointly affect both fiscal policy and trade policy in the following ways:

1. Accurate and timely disclosures of corporate tax and real estate tax liabilities (i.e. tax avoidance, tax evasion, international taxation, etc.).
2. Government's revenues from fees, fines, taxes, permits and levies.
3. Costs of corporate financial distress and bankruptcy (most of which are borne by governments).
4. Governments' litigation costs (economic, legal, social, psychological, environmental and political costs).
5. Government's enforcement costs.
6. Accuracy of National Income Accounting.
7. Regulation of domestic and foreign accounting/audit firms.
8. Compliance reporting and compliance-monitoring costs.
9. Labor dynamics—OSHA adopted parts of SOX; for example.

SOX can directly and indirectly affect monetary policy in the following ways:

1. Earnings management and market volatility, which extends to crash-risk and bubbles in stock, bond and commodities markets—that is, compliance/non-compliance with SOX.
2. Money-supply and liquidity in financial markets—through non-compliance with SOX.
3. Validity and accuracy of the asset base of financial institutions, some of which is used as collateral for trading and loans.
4. International Contagion—through international implementation/propagation of SOX.
5. Economic models and capital-adequacy models for SIFIs, non-financial SIFIs and financial institutions—both of which are substantially affected by SOX provisions.
6. Collateral for Derivatives, derivatives compliance reports and verification of derivatives trading processes.
7. Stock market–driven inflation/deflation.
8. The risk-perception of domestic and international investors (corporate bonds, stocks, etc.).
9. Interest rates—through banks' and non-bank financial institutions' cost-of-operations and compliance costs (which are factored into lending rates); and so on.
10. The US Fed's Open market transactions such as *quantitative easing*—through compliance reports, accuracy of pricing of financial instruments and so on.
11. Compliance.
12. Earnings Management and Insider Trading—see: Nwogugu (2015c) and Kinnunen, Martikainen-Peltola, Kallunki & Mikkonen (2016).
13. FDI—see Hämäläinen & Martikainen (2015).
14. Accounting quality and SOX compliance/disclosure requirements directly and indirectly affects "Netting", the Liquidity Coverage Ratio; and The US FSOC's Non-SIFI Criteria—see Nwogugu (2014d).
15. Accounting quality and SOX compliance/disclosure requirements directly and indirectly affects REITs, and REIT Shares/Interests Are Derivatives Instruments, and REITs are SIFIs—see: Nwogugu (2014e).

SOX can directly and indirectly affect both US foreign policy[10] and trade policy in the following ways:

[10] *See*: "NOTE: International Law and the Ramifications of the Sarbanes-Oxley Act of 2002." (Spring 2004) *Boston College International & Comparative Law Review*.

1. US companies and foreign companies that are listed on US stock exchanges and/or that issue securities in US capital markets must comply with SOX. Many of these companies are MNCs that have significant international operations, and thus propagate SOX and US standards around the world.
2. International Financial Contagion—through international propagation/implementation of, or non-compliance with, SOX around the world.
3. Bubbles and the Crash-risk of stock markets, commodities markets and bond markets—through international propagation/implementation of, or non-compliance with, SOX around the world.
4. Money supply and liquidity in international financial markets—through international propagation/implementation of, or non-compliance with, SOX around the world.
5. Validity and accuracy of the asset base of financial institutions, some of which is used as collateral for trading and loans; and Collateral for Derivatives, derivatives compliance reports and verification of derivatives trading processes.
6. Stock market–driven inflation/deflation.
7. Risk-perception of international investors (corporate bonds, stocks, commodities, interest rate products, etc.).
8. Calculation of foreign aid, FDI, import taxes and export taxes; and compliance reporting in international trade.
9. Compliance reporting in international finance.
10. Through PCAOB, SOX affects the regulation of foreign accounting firms (Sections 102 and 106 of SOX address domestic and foreign registration of accounting firms).
11. International perceptions of the political capital and enforcement-commitment of the US government.
12. Earnings Management and Insider Trading – see: Nwogugu (2015c) and Kinnunen, Martikainen-Peltola, Kallunki & Mikkonen (2016).
13. FDI - see Hämäläinen & Martikainen (2015).
14. Accounting quality and SOX compliance/disclosure requirements directly and indirectly affects "Netting", the Liquidity Coverage Ratio; And The US FSOC's Non-SIFI Criteria – see Nwogugu (2014d).

See: "EDITORIAL COMMENT: Extraterritoriality and the Corporate Governance Law" (2003). *American Journal of International Law* (April, 2003).

See: Bather and Burnaby (2006).

This chapter explains how SOX can affect labor policy. All of the foregoing can have cross-border *Multiplier Effects* in Emerging Markets countries through the *channels* explained in this book.

5.3 The Failure and Unconstitutionality of Sarbanes Oxley Act of 2002 (SOX) and "World-SOX"

SOX and World-SOX impose substantial economic and psychological burdens on micro-cap and small publicly traded companies (which constitute more than 70% of the publicly traded companies in the US). SOX violates the US Constitution in various ways and the "State Actions" are as follows: (a) the enactment of SOX, (b) SOX's delegation of rule-making and adjudication powers to the SEC, (c) the requirement for mandatory compliance with SOX, (d) SOX's delegation of powers (search, reports, etc.) to external accounting firms and law firms, and (e) the creation and powers of the PCAOB. The following are summaries of various violations of the US Constitution.

5.3.1 *The* Substantive Due Process Doctrine

Section 404 of SOX imposes excessive costs on small public companies[11,12] and has caused some small companies to de-list from US stock exchanges.

[11] See: Freeman J (December 15, 2009). *The Supreme Case Against Sarbanes-Oxley*. Available at: http://online.wsj.com/article/NA_WSJ_PUB:SB10001424052748704431804574539921864252380.html.

See: Rezzy (2007).

See: Pollock, A. (2007). *Reforming Sarbanes-Oxley*. AEI (USA). http://www.aei.org/speech/25803.

See: Hunter, B. (2007). *Punishing the Innocent: The Sarbanes-Oxley Act: The Law Has Inflicted Endless Losses on Businesses in Time and Money*. Available at: http://www.thefreemanonline.org/featured/punishing-the-innocent-the-sarbanes-oxley-act/#.

See: John, D. C. & Marano, N. (May 16, 2007). *The Sarbanes-Oxley Act: Do We Need a Regulatory or Legislative Fix?* Heritage Foundation, USA. Available at: http://www.heritage.org/Research/Reports/2007/05/The-Sarbanes-Oxley-Act-Do-We-Need-a-Regulatory-or-Legislative-Fix; or http://s3.amazonaws.com/thf_media/2007/pdf/bg2035.pdf.

[12] The small- and micro-cap public companies that are adversely affected by SOX constitute less than 7% of the total US equity market capitalization, and at least 70% of all the publicly traded companies in the US.

Butler and Ribstein (2006)[13] recommended an overhaul or repeal of SOX. Zhang (2007) estimated that the costs of complying with SOX were as much as $1.4 trillion, by measuring changes in market value around key SOX legislative "events". The Foley & Lardner Survey (2007)[14] found that the total costs of being a US public company (e.g. external auditor fees, directors and officers [D&O] insurance, board compensation, lost productivity and legal costs) were significantly affected by SOX, and increased significantly between FY2001 and FY2006. About 70% of survey respondents agreed that public companies whose annual revenues are less than US$251 million should be exempt from Section-404.

As noted herein and above, the SOX requirement for certification of financial statements by top managers (Section 906) has not been very effective—companies that filed certified financial statements were later discovered to have engaged in earnings management.

Nwogugu (2008; 2021) noted that sections of SOX are vague and don't sufficiently address many important issues—and thus are unconstitutional (the US Supreme Court and some terminal US state courts have held that some non-criminal statutes are unconstitutionally vague).[15] Separately and in the US, the *void-for-vagueness doctrine* is usually applied only to criminal statutes and is discussed herein and below. The following are elements of a "Civil Vagueness Exception Doctrine": i) the nature, intent and widespread (domestic and international) effects of the SOX statutes justifies the use of a "vagueness standard/criteria" for non-criminal sections of SOX; ii) in the "non criminal law" context, many of the

[13] *See*: Butler, H. & Ribstein, L. (2006). *The Sarbanes-Oxley Debacle: What We've Learned; How to Fix It* (AEI Press, 2006).

[14] *See*: Foley & Lardner LLP (2007). *The Cost of Being Public in the Era of Sarbanes-Oxley*. Available at: http://www.foley.com/files/tbl_s31Publications/Fstudy.ileUpload137/3736/Foley2007SOXstudy.pdf.

[15] *See: Connally v. General Constr. Co,* 269 US 385 (1926; US Supreme Court) (wage law was vague, and thus unconstitutional); *Dombrowski v. Pfister*, 380 US 479 (1965; US Supreme Court); *Gooding v. Wilson*, 405 US 518 (1972; US Supreme Court); *Soglin v. Kauffman*, 418 F2d 163 (CA7, 1969); *Humanitarian Law Project v. Department Of Justice*, 352 F3d 382 (CA9, 2003); *Board Of Education Of The City of St. Louis v. State Of Missouri*, 47 SW3d 366 (Mo., 2001)(the process for electing board members was vague); *Margraves v. State*, 996 SW2d 302(Tx.Cr.App., 2000)(official misconduct statute was unconstitutionally void for vagueness); *Cantwell v. Connecticut*, 310 US 296 (1940; US Supreme Court); *Winters v. New York*, 333 US 507 (1948; US Supreme Court); *Kolender v. Lawson*, 461 US 352 (1983; US Supreme Court); *Shuttlesworth v. City Of Birmingham*, 3782 US 87 (1965; US Supreme Court).

issues, documents and contexts that SOX covers are broad, can vary widely across companies and can change quickly; iii) some of the "civil" sections of SOX that are vague can trigger criminal law causes-of-action.

The government's interest[16] in requiring companies to maintain effective controls is far outweighed by the many documented dis-advantages of SOX, and its significant compliance-costs and adverse effects on small companies.

5.3.2 The Procedural Due Process Doctrine

The relevant *State Action* is the enactment of SOX. SOX delegates some adjudicatory functions to the PCAOB and SEC, whereas such functions should be properly handled by courts. SOX does not require the rotation of audit *firms* but SOX directs the Comptroller General of the United States to study the pros and cons of rotating audit firms and to report to Congress—that is a major omission because such rotation will help reduce

[16] *See*: *Railway Express v. New York*, ____US___(1949; US Supreme Court); *Kotch v. Bd. of River Port Pilot Commissioners*, ___ US ___(1947; US Supreme Court); *Skinner v. Oklahoma*, ____ US ___(1942; US Supreme Court); *Korematsu v. United States*, ___ US ___(1944) (US Supreme Court); *Loving v. Virginia*, ____US ____(1967; US Supreme Court); *Washington v. Davis*, ____ US ___ (1976; US Supreme Court); *Arlington Heights v. MHDC*, _____US ____ (1977; US Supreme Court); *Washington v. Glucksberg*, 521 U.S. 702, 719 (US Supreme Court; 1997); *Obergefell vs. Hodges*, 576 U.S. 644 (US Supreme Court; 2015); *Lawrence vs. Texas*, 539 U.S. 558 (US Supreme Court; 2003); *United States vs. Vaello-Madero*, _____ US ____ (Case#: 20-303; US Supreme Court; pending as of 2021); *DeNolf vs. U.S.*, _____ US _____ (US Supreme Court; pending as of 2021) (https://static1.squarespace.com/static/5b660749620b85c6c73e5e61/t/608d544886d55300e492a619/1619874888658/2021-22+AMCA+Case.pdf); *DeNolf vs. U.S.* (Case#: 01-76320; US 14th Circuit, 2020) (https://static1.squarespace.com/static/5b660749620b85c6c73e5e61/t/608d544886d55300e492a619/1619874888658/2021-22+AMCA+Case.pdf); and Planned Parenthood of Southeastern *Pennsylvania v. Casey*, 505 U.S. 833, 848 (1992); *Washington v. Glucksberg*, 521 U.S. 702, 719 (US Supreme Court; 1997); *Obergefell vs. Hodges*, 576 U.S. 644 (US Supreme Court; 2015); *Lawrence vs. Texas*, 539 U.S. 558 (US Supreme Court; 2003); *United States vs. Vaello-Madero*, _____ US ____ (Case#: 20-303; US Supreme Court; pending as of 2021); *DeNolf vs. U.S.*, _____ US _____ (US Supreme Court; pending as of 2021) (https://static1.squarespace.com/static/5b660749620b85c6c73e5e61/t/608d544886d55300e492a619/1619874888658/2021-22+AMCA+Case.pdf); *DeNolf vs. U.S.* (Case#: 01-76320; US 14th Circuit, 2020) (https://static1.squarespace.com/static/5b660749620b85c6c73e5e61/t/608d544886d55300e492a619/1619874888658/2021-22+AMCA+Case.pdf); and *Planned Parenthood of Southeastern Pennsylvania v. Casey*, 505 U.S. 833, 848 (1992).

the effects of oligopoly by the Big-Four accounting firms, and can improve the quality of financial statements.

An "extreme" school-of-thought is that Section 404 of SOX constitutes a violation of the procedural due process clause because it effectively authorizes accounting firms to perform police-type and investigatory functions that can be deemed to be unreasonable "searches" given the significantly-proprietary nature of details of internal controls of firms[17]. When implementing Section 404, the external accounting firm is essentially acting as an agent of, and as an extension of the US government (as specifically required by Section 404). The *Substitution Theory* applies in such circumstances. SOX doesn't provide sufficient criminal punishment, economic penalties and deterrence effects for Auditing firms that intentionally or unintentionally disclose Internal Control details of their client companies to third-parties without written/verified permission. SOX prescribes regulations that directly affect procedures for enforcement of regulations and adjudication of claims in courts and government agencies—but SOX does not integrate such rules properly into existing enforcement processes.

The government's interest in requiring companies to maintain effective controls is far outweighed by the substantial procedural due-process and substantive due-process deficiencies of SOX, and the many documented disadvantages of SOX, and its adverse effects on small companies.

5.3.3 *The* Equal Protection Doctrine[18]

The relevant *State Action* is the enactment of SOX. SOX unfairly discriminates between public and non-public companies. SOX unfairly discriminates

[17] The Fourth Amendment of the US Constitution states, "The right of the people to be secure in their persons, houses, papers, and effects, against unreasonable searches and seizures, shall not be violated, and no Warrants shall issue, but upon probable cause, supported by Oath or affirmation, and particularly describing the place to be searched, and the persons or things to be seized".

See: Backer (2004) and Butler and Ribstein (2006).

[18] *See: United States vs. Vaello-Madero*, _____ US ____ (Case#: 20-303; US Supreme Court; pending as of 2021); *Espinoza vs. Montana* Department of Revenue, _____ US ____ (US Supreme Court; pending as of 2021); *FCC v. Beach Communications*, ___US ____ (1993; US Supreme Court); *Logan v. Zimmerman Brush Co.*, ___US ____ (1982; US Supreme Court); *Schweiger v. Wilson*, ___US ____ (1981; US Supreme Court); *U.S. Railroad Retirement Board v. Fritz*, ___US ____ (1980; US Supreme Court), *New Orleans v. Dukes*, ___US ____ (1976; US Supreme Court), *McDonald v. Board of Election Commissioners*, ___

between US corporate entities that can be traded publicly (such as C-Corporations and limited partnerships), and corporate entities that cannot be publicly traded (such as S-Corporations, LLCs, sole proprietorships and regular partnerships). SOX unfairly discriminates between small listed/public companies that can hardly afford SOX compliance costs (and thus have incentives to engage in fraud and improper disclosure) and medium/large listed companies that can afford SOX compliance costs. SOX unfairly discriminates between public foreign companies that are listed on US exchanges, and foreign companies that list their ADRs/GDRs (Global Depository Receipts) in US stock exchanges. SOX unfairly discriminates between people who commit the same crime but who are prosecuted under federal securities laws and those who are prosecuted under SOX criminal statutes—hence SOX provides unfair regulatory arbitrage and opportunities for forum-shopping. SOX unfairly discriminates between public companies on one hand, and non-profit organizations and government agencies on the other hand. SOX does not apply to non-profit organizations and government agencies[19]—this is error because

US ___ (1969; US Supreme Court); *U.S. Railroad Retirement Board v. Fritz*, ___US ___ (1980; US Supreme Court); *N.Y.C. Transit Authority v. Beazer*, ___US ___ (1979; US Supreme Court); *Massachusetts Board of Retirement v. Murgia*, ___US ___ (1976; US Supreme Court); *Dept. of Agriculture v. Moreno*, ___US ___ (1973; US Supreme Court); *Adarand Constructors, Inc. v. Pena*, ___US ___ (1995; US Supreme Court); *Metro Broadcasting, Inc. v. FCC*, ___US ___ (1990; US Supreme Court); *Richmond v. J.A. Croson Co.*, ___US ___ (1989; US Supreme Court); *Wygant v. Jackson Board of Education*, ___US ___ (1986; US Supreme Court); *Fullilove v. Klutznick*, ___US ___ (1980; US Supreme Court); *Bernal v. Fainter*, ___US ___ (1984; US Supreme Court), *Ambach v. Norwick* (1979; US Supreme Court); *United States v. Virginia (The VMI Case)* (1996); *Williamson v. Lee Optical Co*, 348 US 483 (1955; US Supreme Court); *Dandridge v. Williams*, 397 US 471 (1970; US Supreme Court); *FCC v. Beach Communication Inc.*, 508 US 307 (1993; US Supreme Court). *City of Phoenix v. Kolodziejski*, 399 U.S. 204 (1970; US Supreme Court); *Griffith v. Connecticut*, 218 US 563 (1910); *Cipriano v. City of Houma*, 395 U.S. 701 (1969).

See: Bard (1961).

19 *See*: Soederberg (2008), Reiser (2004), and Mulligan (2006).

See: Aprill (2009) (which stated in part: "According to the Final Report of the SEC Advisory Committee on Smaller Companies, there are fewer than 9,500 public companies subject to SOX. The report classified smaller public companies as those with equity capitalizations of $787 million or less. In contrast, the Internal Revenue Service (IRS) reports that for 2003 it received information returns from 211,858 charitable nonprofit organizations, and only 63,327, or 27%, of these organizations had assets over $1 million. The total number does not include the smallest of exempt organizations—those with annual gross receipts less than $25,000, since they are not required to file an information return. Thus, the public companies subject to SOX are a small number of entities, all of which have substantial

many non-profit organizations and government agencies not only have substantial economic impact on indigenes and private companies (such that their failure will cause systemic risk), but also affect the daily operations of for-profit companies. In many countries, many non-profit organizations and government agencies provide the same services as publicly traded companies.

These foregoing discriminatory classifications don't serve any meaningful purpose, and the government's interest in ensuring sound internal controls of companies is far outweighed by the adverse effects of the discriminatory classifications that are directly and indirectly imposed by SOX.

5.3.4 *Violation of the* **Separation of Powers Clause**[20]

Section-404 and large sections of SOX are enforced by the US SEC which also simultaneously performs adjudicative and rule-making functions.[21] The relevant *State Action* is the enactment of SOX.

5.3.5 *Violation of the* **Right-to-Contract Clause**[22]

The relevant *State Action* is the enactment of SOX. First, Section 404 effectively forces companies to contract with external advisors (accounting

resources"). In the US, the number of publicly traded companies (there are at least 8500 publicly traded companies in the United States, including companies traded in the Pink Sheets) constitutes less than 1% of all incorporated for-profit entities.

See: Pillard (2005).

[20] *See:* Katyal (2006).

See: Collins vs. Yellen, ___ US ___ (No. 19-422; US Supreme Court; pending as of 2021).

See: Collins vs. Mnuchin, ____ US _____ (Docket No. 19-422; US Supreme Court; pending as of 2021).

See: Seila Law LLC vs. Consumer Financial Protection Bureau, ____ US ____ (Case#: No. 19-7; US Supreme Court; 2020) (the Consumer Financial Protection Bureau's single-Director structure violates the *Separation of Powers Doctrine*, and the proper remedy is to sever the Director's statutory for-cause removal restriction).

See: Humphrey's Executor vs. United States, 295 U.S. 602 (US Supreme Court; 1935).

See: PHH Corp. vs. CFPB, 839 F.3d 1 (2016) *on rehearing enbanc*, 881 F.3d 75 (D.C. Cir., 2018) (en banc).

[21] Schaumann (2004: 1317) states in part: " As is common in securities law, large portions of the Act do not themselves create substantive regulation, but rather, authorize the S.E.C. to adopt implementing rules. At this writing, the S.E.C. has adopted rules addressing most areas under SOX, but more rules are pending".

[22] *See: Energy Reserves Group v. Kansas Power & Light* (KPL), _____US ____ (US Supreme Court); *Nollan vs. California Coastal Commission*, 483 US 825 (1987; US Supreme Court);

firms)—whereas some companies can review and improve their internal controls by themselves, Second, Section 404 limits companies' ability to consummate transactions because Section 404 imposes substantial and adverse *Reputation Penalties* on subject companies; and non-complying companies must comply with Section 404 before they can consummate certain transactions that are reported to the US SEC. This causes fatal delays and can substantially increase the operating costs and transaction costs of companies. SOX expressly prohibits auditors from performing certain services,[23] and there isn't adequate evidence that having auditors perform the barred services will be detrimental to the quality of financial statements or internal controls—and the government's interest in regulating internal controls for public welfare is far outweighed by the additional costs imposed on subject companies, and any actual or perceived incremental reduction in conflict of interests. SOX prohibits an accounting firms from auditing an issuer if the issuer's CEO, CFO, controller, or chief accounting officer was employed by the accounting firm and participated in the issuer's audit within the immediately preceding twelve months. This prohibition was designed to reduce conflict of interest but is meaningless because people that report to the CFO or COO or Controller or the Chief Accounting Officer also have in-depth knowledge of a company's internal controls and financial statements (and some are more knowledgeable than the CFO/COO/CAO/Controller)—and the SOX prohibition does not apply to these professionals and is thus discriminatory.

5.3.6 *Violation of the* Right-to-Privacy Clause

SOX violates company's rights to privacy by effectively forcing them to reveal their internal controls to outsiders. SOX violates company's

Dolan v. City Of Tigard, 512 US 374 (1994; US Supreme Court); *Energy Reserves Group, Inc. vs. Kansas Power and Light Co.*, _____ US ____ (US Supreme Court; 1983); *Sveen vs. Melin*, ___ US ____ (US Supreme Court; 2018).

Keystone Bituminous Coal Ass'n. vs. DeBenedictis, 480 U.S. 470, 505 (1987; US Supreme Court); *Boys Scout Of America vs. Dale*, 530 US 640 (2000; US Supreme Court); *Trustees of Dartmouth College vs. Woodward*, 17 U.S. (4 Wheat.) 518 (1819; US Supreme Court); *United States Trust Co. v. New Jersey*, 431 U.S. 1 (1977; US Supreme Court); *Energy Reserves Group vs. Kansas Power & Light* 459 U.S. 400 (1983; US Supreme Court).

[23] *See:* Schaumann (2004).

See: Gifford, R. & Howe, H. (2009). Regulation and Unintended Consequences: Thoughts on Sarbanes-Oxley. *The CPA Journal*. http://www.nysscpa.org/cpajournal/2004/604/perspectives/p6.htm.

Privacy-Rights in ways that don't ensure that "statutory advisors" (accounting/auditing firms and consulting firms) maintain strict confidentiality. For example, SOX doesn't provide sufficient criminal penalties and monetary fines (that provide significant deterrence effects) for accounting/auditing firms (and their principals/partners and mid-level staff) that intentionally or unintentionally disclose their corporate clients' Internal Controls and or Control Environment details to third parties without express written permission. The relevant *State Action* is the enactment of SOX. Internal controls are a major intangible asset of, and a critical component of, operations of a corporate entity. Internal controls are a privacy right which arises from state constitutional laws, expectations, culture and norms. There is no assurance that external accounting firms will not convey details of internal controls to a firm's competitors or other parties, to the detriment of the subject company. A person that has detailed information about the internal controls of a company can circumvent the company's risk controls and risk management systems. In industries that are considered sensitive to national security (defense, biotechnology, etc.), SOX can lead to illegal theft of vital information. As currently stated and construed, SOX represents an unwarranted and detrimental intrusion into a company operations. The government's interest in enacting effective regulations to ensure adequate internal controls is far outweighed by the potentially catastrophic losses that a company may incur if details of its internal controls are leaked or unintentionally conveyed to third parties.

5.3.7 Void-for-Vagueness

The relevant *State Action* is the enactment of SOX. The criminal sections of SOX are constitutionally void-for-vagueness because for many critical issues, SOX simply delegates congressional responsibility to the executive branch by authorizing either the US SEC or another government agency to create new rules which the SEC (or agency) will enforce (thus violating the Separation of Powers clause), or SOX requests that a government agency conduct further studies. This type of legislation creates detrimental uncertainty costs and information costs, and "regulation gaps" that foster Regulatory-Capture, political lobbying and regulatory arbitrage. *Kolender v. Lawson*[24] explains how the void-for-vagueness doctrine is applied.

[24] *See*: *Kolender vs. Lawson*, 461 U.S. 352, 357 (1983) (a criminal statute is unconstitutionally vague only if it: (1) fails to give fair notice of what conduct is forbidden; and (2) therefore, encourages arbitrary and discriminatory enforcement).

Many of the criminal penalties in SOX (e.g. Sections 906 and 901) are vague because they don't state the specific types of prohibited misconduct. SOX statutes are very likely to result in classification of potentially innocent conduct as criminal misconduct. As explained herein, SOX inhibits the exercise of constitutionally protected rights. Furthermore, the "obstruction of justice" provision of Section 802[25] is vague—Section 802 applies to corporate fraud and to "the investigation or administration of any matter within the jurisdiction of any department or agency of the United States". Section 802 punishes a person who "knowingly alters, destroys, mutilates, conceals, covers up, falsifies, or makes a false entry in any record, document or tangible object" with up to 20 years in prison, even if the record tamperer does not have "criminal intent" or a "corrupt" motive.

5.3.8 The Freedom-of-Speech Doctrine[26]

The relevant *State Action* is the enactment of SOX. SOX violates the Freedom-of-Speech Doctrine by forcing companies to disclose their

See: Village of Hoffman Estates vs. Flipside, 455 U.S. 489, 499 (1982) ("the most important factor affecting the clarity that the Constitution demands of a law is whether it threatens to inhibit the exercise of constitutionally protected rights. If, for example, the law interferes with the right of free speech or of association, a more stringent vagueness test should apply").

See: Salky, S. & Rosman, A. (2004). *Is Sarbanes Oxley Vulnerable To Constitutional Challenge*? Available at: http://www.zuckerman.com/files/Publication/375468a3-d518-43e5-a6da-63474799822c/Presentation/PublicationAttachment/50441453-cd29-4d49-8dae-b030df75c042/media.88.pdf.

[25] *See*: Berlau, J. (January 2006). *Sarbanes-Oxley vs. the Free Press: How the government used business regulations to strong-arm the media.* http://reason.com/archives/2006/01/01/sarbanes-oxley-vs-the-free-pre.

[26] *See: U.S. v. United Foods,* Inc., _____ S.Ct. _____(2001 WL 703953, Sup. Ct., 2001); *Greater New Orleans Broadcasting Assn. vs. U.S.*, 119 S.Ct. 1923 (1999; US Supreme Court); *Virginia Bd. of Pharmacy v. Virginia Citizens Consumer Council, Inc.*, 425 U.S. 765, (US Supreme Court); *City of Cincinnati v. Discovery Network*, Inc., 507 U.S. 410, 419–420 (1993; US Supreme Court); *Thompson v. Western States Medical Center*, 122 S.Ct. 1497, 1507 (2002; US Supreme Court); *City Of Boerne v. Flores*, 521 US 507 (1997; US Supreme Court); *Bartnicki v. Vopper*, 532 US 514 (2001; US Supreme Court); *National Endowment Of The Arts v. Finley*, 524 US 569 (1998; US Supreme Court); *Rosenberger v. University Of Virginia*, 515 US 819 (1995; US Supreme Court); *Rust v. Sullivan*, 5001 US 173 (1991; US Supreme Court); *44 Liquormart*, 517 U.S. 484 (1996; US Supreme Court); *Buckley v. Valeo*, 424 U.S. 1 (1976; US Supreme Court); *First National Bank Of Boston v. Belotti*, 435 US 765 (1978; US Supreme Court); *Austin v. Michigan Chamber of Commerce*, 494 U.S. 652 (1990; US Supreme Court); *FEC v. Massachusetts Citizens For Life Inc.*, 479 U.S. 238 (1986; US Supreme Court); *Nixon v. Shrink Missouri Government PAC*, 528

internal controls to third parties and to the government. The problem is that SOX Section 404 forces disclosure of elements and structure of internal controls rather than focusing only on perceived or actual internal control weaknesses and any remedial actions. A corporate entity's refusal to disclose its internal controls is a form of protected speech. As stated above, internal controls are an intangible asset and proprietary asset. Any third-party statements or opinions about internal controls are not protected speech because: (1) such statements (regardless of whether they are positive or negative) reduce the value of the intangible asset (internal controls), and thus harm the corporate entity and its shareholders; (2) such statements don't necessarily or always improve public welfare (such statements about only one company can substantially increase the overall volatility of stock markets).

SOX restricts companies from choosing certain accounting firms for certain types of work and that can constitute a violation of Free Speech Rights—various empirical studies have shown that there is substantial information content in the choice of external accounting firms for services, and, hence, such choice is a type of protected speech.

Furthermore, the "obstruction of justice" provision of Section 802[27] of SOX is a violation of Free Speech Doctrine because it imposes excessive restrictions on journalists who are not connected with company financial statements—Section 802 applies to "the investigation or administration of any matter within the jurisdiction of any department or agency of the

U.S. 377 (2000; US Supreme Court); *Pacific Gas & Electric v. Public Utilities Commission*, 475 US 1 (1986; US Supreme Court); *Lorillard Tobacco v. Reilly*, 533 U.S. 525 (2001; US Supreme Court); *Nike Inc. v. Kasky*, 539 U.S. 654 (2003; US Supreme Court); *BASF Corp v. Peterson*, 544 *U.S.* 1012 (2005; US Supreme Court); *Virginia Board of Pharmacy v. Virginia Citizen's Consumer Council Inc.*, 425 US 748 (1976; US Supreme Court); *Reno v. ACLU*, 521 U.S. 844 (1997; US Supreme Court); *Buckley v. American Constitutional Law Foundation*, 525 U.S. 182 (1999; US Supreme Court); *Americans for Prosperity Foundation vs. Bonta*,_____ US _____ (US Supreme Court; pending as of 2021); *Mahanoy Area School District vs. B.L.*, _____ US _____ (No. 20–255; US Supreme Court; pending as of 2021); *Houston Community College System vs. Wilson*, _____ US _____ (Case#: 20-804; US Supreme Court; pending as of 2021); *Fulton vs. City of Philadelphia*, _____ US _____ (US Supreme Court; pending as of 2021); *Thomas More Law Center vs. Bonta*, _____ US _____ (No. 19–255; US Supreme Court; pending as of 2021).

See: Butler and Ribstein (1994).

[27] *See*: Berlau, J. (January 2006). *Sarbanes-Oxley vs. the Free Press: How the government used business regulations to strong-arm the media*. Reason.com. http://reason.com/archives/2006/01/01/sarbanes-oxley-vs-the-free-pre.

United States". Section 802 punishes a person who "knowingly alters, destroys, mutilates, conceals, covers up, falsifies, or makes a false entry in any record, document or tangible object" with up to twenty years in prison, even if the record tamperer does not have "criminal intent" or a "corrupt" motive.

5.3.9 *The Cruel and Unusual Punishment Clause*[28]

SOX's targeting of, and penalties for, non-compliance with certification requirements for top corporate executive officers (CFO; CEO) constitutes a violation of the *Cruel & Unusual Punishment clause* of the US Constitution.[29] As explained herein, these top corporate officers are sometimes removed from the details of the daily operations of companies, and it's the mid-level managers who have day-to-day responsibilities for internal controls, the control environment and risk management (and that can be a significant and perhaps over-riding mitigating factor[30] that precludes the conviction of CEOs and CFOs in such circumstances). SOX doesn't expressly provide for consideration of "mitigating factors" in the enforcement of the CEO/CFO Certification requirements.

[28] *See*: *Moore vs. Texas,* 581 US _____ (US Supreme Court; 2017) (whether the use of outdated standards violates the *Cruel & Unusual Punishment Clause*)

See: Austin vs. United States, 509 US 602 (US Supreme Court; 1993) (consideration of mitigating factors).

See: Bosse vs. Oklahoma, 580 US _____ (US Supreme Court; 2016) (court held that *Payne v. Tennessee* did not overrule its prior decision in *Booth vs. Maryland*).

See: Enmund vs. Florida, 458 US 782 (US Supreme Court; 1982).

See: Harmelin vs. Michigan, 501 US 957 (US Supreme Court; 1991) (consideration of mitigating factors). *See: Kansas vs. Marsh*, 548 US 163 (US Supreme Court; 2006) (consideration of mitigating factors).*See: Lockett vs. Ohio*, 438 US 586 (US Supreme Court; 1978) (consideration of mitigating factors).*See: Penry vs. Johnson*, 532 US 782 (US Supreme Court; 2001) (consideration of mitigating factors).

[29] *See*: Salky, S., & Rosman, A. (2004). *Is Sarbanes Oxley Vulnerable To Constitutional Challenge?* http://www.zuckerman.com/files/Publication/375468a3-d518-43e5-a6da-63474799822c/Presentation/PublicationAttachment/50441453-cd29-4d49-8dae-b030df75c042/media.88.pdf.

[30] *See: Bosse vs. Oklahoma*, 580 US _____ (US Supreme Court; 2016) (court held that *Payne v. Tennessee* did not overrule its prior decision in *Booth vs. Maryland*.

See: Johnson vs. Texas, 509 US 350 (US Supreme Court; 1993) (whether statute/regulation/conduct that doesn't consider "mitigating factors" violates the *Cruel & Unusual Punishment Clause*).

SOX doesn't expressly/statutorily provide for consideration of the CEOs' and CFOs' health when enforcing the CEO/CFO Certification requirement—CEOs/CFOs that suffer from medical conditions that seriously impair their cognition[31] maybe or should be exempted from penalties for non-compliance with the certification requirement.

Furthermore, SOX's CEO/CFO Certification requirement (and similar statutes in other countries) is an outdated standard[32] because of the following reasons:

1. Today, a significant and increasing percentage of financial/economic/accounting transactions are automated, whereas most CEOs and CFOs are not knowledgeable about such computer algorithms/systems.
2. As mentioned, middle-level managers (such as the Controller, the Treasurer, the Chief Information Officer; the Vice President Of Finance) are more knowledgeable about, and more directly responsible for such computer systems for accounting and Internal Controls (i.e.. Accounting Information Systems and ERP systems).
3. Enforcing the CEO/CFO Certification requirement provides relatively low *deterrence effects* to mid-level managers.
4. In most MNCs (multinational corporations) and listed/public companies, CEOs and CFOs are responsible for a much broader scope of activities than only financial statements (which is handled by Controllers). In such companies and apart from financial statements, CFOs are responsible for human resources, employee-incentives, financial planning, budgeting, contract negotiations, Treasury Operations, legal/compliance, Information Systems, government/public affairs and so on. SOX-type CEO/CFO Certification penalties can create the wrong impression that there are many other problems (at the subject company) that aren't related to accounting-disclosure and Internal Controls.
5. The speed of worldwide dissemination of information (about companies and governments' regulatory decisions) is almost instanta-

[31] *See: Powell vs. Texas*, 392 US 514 (US Supreme Court; 1968) (whether a medical condition is a mitigating factor when considering the *Cruel & Unusual Punishment Clause*.

See: Robinson vs. California, 370 US 660 (1962) (whether a medical condition is a mitigating factor when considering the *Cruel & Unusual Punishment Clause*).

[32] *See: Moore vs. Texas*, 581 US ____ (US Supreme Court; 2017) (whether the use of outdated standards violates the *Cruel & Unusual Punishment Clause*).

neous, and more types of financial transactions have been moved to the internet, and internet/broadband penetration in many countries now exceeds 65% of the adult population. That is in contrast to 2002 (when SOX was enacted) when the internet wasn't as pervasive.

6. The often significant negative "*Information Content*" and "*Market-Impact*" (stock and bond markets) of penalizing CEOs/CFOs under the SOX Certification requirements isn't justified by, or outweighs any benefits—(1) such penalties create long-term negative perceptions and can distort Risk Management processes (in banks and asset managers); and (2) the announcement and actual penalties most often negatively affect stocks/bonds of unrelated companies in the same industry and in related industries.

SOX's Section 302 can impose criminal penalties on individual corporate executives, while SOX's Section 404 applies only to the subject company. However, in some jurisdictions, non-compliance with statutory (SOX-type) CEO/CFO Certification requirements can generate separate criminal law causes—of-action. The SOX-type CEO/CFO Certification Requirement has been adopted/copied in many countries (especially in Emerging Markets countries).

Thus, the penalties for improper or fraudulent certification of financial statements should be directed to mid-level managers (or to both mid-level managers and senior executives such as the CEO and CFO), and should be amended to create both monetary penalties and non-monetary penalties. SOX doesn't expressly provide for the introduction of evidence of innocence during the pre-sentencing or sentencing phase of a trial of corporate executives that are convicted for improper/fraudulent disclosures.

5.3.10 *The* Takings Doctrine[33]

Section 404 and other parts of SOX constitutes violations of the *Takings Doctrine* of the US Constitution. The relevant *State Action* is the

[33] *See*: *Federal Republic of Germany et al.* vs. *Philipp et al.* (No. 19–351; February 3, 2021; US Supreme Court). https://www.supremecourt.gov/opinions/20pdf/19-351_o7jp.pdf.

See: Republic of Austria vs. Altmann, 541 U. S. 677 (US Supreme Court).

See: Bolivarian Republic of Venezuela vs. Helmerich & Payne Int'l Drilling Co., 581 U.S. ____ (2017; US Supreme Court).

See: *Kelo vs. City Of New London*, ____ US ____ (2005; US Supreme Court).

See: *Lingle vs. Chevron*, 544 US ____ (2005; US Supreme Court).

enactment of SOX. As mentioned, internal controls are an intangible asset and proprietary asset of corporate entities, and mandatory disclosure of internal controls and/or revelation of internal controls to third parties constitutes a *Taking* for which public companies are not compensated. As mentioned, SOX deprives corporate entities and their shareholders of certain rights for which they are not compensated. Regular audits by external accounting firms involve testing of internal controls. There is no evidence that in all or in most cases, the additional benefits obtained by additional internal controls testing (as required by SOX) by audit firms will exceed the benefits from the regular traditional auditing, or the risk of potential losses from unauthorized or unintentional dissemination of details of internal controls of a company.

5.3.11 Violations of the Interstate Commerce Clause and the Foreign Commerce Clause of the US Constitution

As explained in Colangelo (2010)[34] and Muth (2009), SOX violates the *Foreign Commerce clause* of the US Constitution. SOX violates the Interstate Commerce clause[35] because SOX burdens interstate commerce

See: *Monterrey vs. Del Monte Dunes at Monterrey*, 526 US 687 (1999; US Supreme Court).
See: *Dolan vs. City Of Tigard*, 512 US 374 (1994; US Supreme Court).
See: *Nollan vs. California Coastal Commission*, 483 US 825 (1987; US Supreme Court).
See: *Kaiser Aetna vs. United States*, 444 US 164 (1979; US Supreme Court).
See: *Williamson County Regional Planning Commission vs. Hamilton Bank Of Jefferson City*, 473 US 172 (1985; US Supreme Court).
See: *Palazzolo vs. Rhode Island*, 533 US 606 (2001; US Supreme Court).
See: *Lucas vs. South Carolina Coastal Council*, 505 US 1003 (1992; US Supreme Court).
See: *Cedar Point Nursery vs. Hassid*, _____ US _____ (US Supreme Court; pending as of 2021).
See: *Cedar Point Nursery vs. Sheroma*, _____ F.3d. _____ (US Ninth Circuit Court of Appeals).
See: *PennEast Pipeline Co. vs. New Jersey*, _____ US _____ (US Supreme Court; pending as of 2021).
See: *Murr vs. Wisconsin*, 137 S.Ct. 1933 (US Supreme Court; 2017).
See: *California Bldg. Industry Ass'n vs. City of San Jose, Calif.*, 136 S.Ct. 928 (US Supreme Court; 2016).
See: *Koontz vs. St. Johns River Water Management District*, 570 U.S. 2588 (US Supreme Court; 2013).

[34] *See*: Colangelo (2010), Vancea (2005), Kim (2003), Ribstein (2002) and Govekar (2008).

[35] *See:* Tate (1990), Hellerstein (June 1996), Larbalestier (1990), Merrill (2000) and Sedler (1985).

and creates substantial compliance costs—that is, the costs of compliance with SOX exponentially increases as the subject company's volume of

See: Dennis vs. Higgins, 498 U.S. 439 (1991; US Supreme Court); *Moorman Mfg. Co. vs. Bair*, 437 U.S. 267, 280 (1978; US Supreme Court); *Metropolitan Life Ins. Co. vs. Ward*, 470 U.S. 869 (1985; US Supreme Court); *Oregon Waste Systems, Inc.* vs. *Department of Environmental Quality of Oregon*, 511 U. S. 93 (______; US Supreme Court); *Hughes* vs. *Alexandria Scrap Corp.*, 426 U.S. 794 (______); *Reeves, Inc.* vs. *Stake*, 447 U.S. 429 (______; US Supreme Court); *United Haulers Assn., Inc.* vs. *Oneida-Herkimer Solid Waste Management Authority*, 550 U.S. ______ (______; US Supreme Court); *DeNolf vs. U.S.*, ______ US ______ (US Supreme Court; pending as of 2021) (https://static1.squarespace.com/static/5b660749620b85c6c73e5e61/t/608d544886d55300e492a619/1619874888658/2021-22+AMCA+Case.pdfhttps://static1.squarespace.com/static/5b660749620b85c6c73e5e61/t/608d544886d55300e492a619/1619874888658/2021-22+AMCA+Case.pdf); *DeNolf vs. U.S.* (Case#: 01-76320; US 14th Circuit, 2020) (https://static1.squarespace.com/static/5b660749620b85c6c73e5e61/t/608d544886d55300e492a619/1619874888658/2021-22+AMCA+Case.pdfhttps://static1.squarespace.com/static/5b660749620b85c6c73e5e61/t/608d544886d55300e492a619/1619874888658/2021-22+AMCA+Case.pdf); *Perez vs. United* States, 402 U.S. 146, 150 (1971) (Congress can ban loansharking that threatens interstate commerce); *Gonzales vs. Raich*, 545 U.S. 1, 18 (US Supreme Court; 2005); United States vs. Lopez, 514 U.S. 549 (US Supreme Court; 1995) (under the Commerce Clause, the US Congress can't prohibit firearms at public schools); *Edgar vs. MITE*, 457 US 624 (state law declared unconstitutional); *Dynamics Corp. Of America vs. CTS Corp.*, 679 Fsupp 1022 (*affirmed*) 794 F2d 250 (*reversed*) 481 US 69 (state law declared unconstitutional); *Department of Revenue of Kentucky et al. vs. Davis et. al.*, (May 19, 2008; No. 06-666; US Supreme Court); *Pike vs. Bruce Church, Inc.*, 397 U. S. 137, 142; *New Energy Co. of Ind.* vs. *Limbach*, 486 U. S. 269 (1988; US Supreme Court); *Fulton Corp.* vs. *Faulkner*, 516 U. S. 325 (1996; US Supreme Court); *Oklahoma Tax Comm'n* v. *Jefferson Lines, Inc.*, 514 U. S. 175 (1995; US Supreme Court); *Hughes* vs. *Oklahoma*, 441 U. S. 322 (1979; US Supreme Court); *Garcia* vs. *San Antonio Metropolitan Transit Authority*, 469 U. S. 528 (1985; US Supreme Court); *Philadelphia* vs. *New Jersey*, 437 U. S. 617 (1978; US Supreme Court); *Alexandria Scrap,* 426 U.S., at 810 (the "*market participant*' exception); *Reeves,* 447 U.S. at 436 (the "market participant' exception); *White* vs. *Massachusetts Council of Construction Employers, Inc.*, 460 U. S. 204 (1983; US Supreme Court) (the "market participant" exception); *Fulton Corporation vs. Faulkner,* 516 U.S. 325 (struck down higher tax on the stock of corporations with little or no presence in the State); *Dean Milk Co.* vs. *Madison*, 340 U.S. 349 (1951; US Supreme Court); *Hunt* vs. *Washington State Apple Advertising Commission,* 432 U.S. 333 (1977; US Supreme Court); *Fort Gratiot Sanitary Landfill, Inc.* vs. *Michigan Dept. of Natural Resources*, 504 U.S. 353 (1992; US Supreme Court); *C & A Carbone, Inc.* vs. *Clarkstown*, 511 U.S. 383 (1994; US Supreme Court); *Philadelphia* vs. *New Jersey*, 437 U.S. 617 (1978; US Supreme Court); *Hughes* vs. *Oklahoma*, 441 U.S. 322 (1979; US Supreme Court); *New England Power Co.* vs. *New Hampshire*, 455 U.S. 331 (1982; US Supreme Court); *Bacchus Imports, Ltd.* vs. *Dias*, 468 U.S. 263 (1984; US Supreme Court).

Contrast: Bonaparte v. *Tax Court*, 104 U.S. 592 (______; US Supreme Court).

interstate commerce increases. Also, SOX applies only to exchange traded companies, who generally have larger volumes of interstate commerce than non-listed companies—and thus SOX is discriminatory. SOX violates the Interstate Commerce clause because it reduces or can reduce the number of audit firms that are willing and able to audit publicly traded companies[36]—SOX burdens interstate commerce by imposing onerous requirements on auditing/accounting firms and thus, reduces competition among auditing/accounting firms. SOX violates the Interstate Commerce Clause because it (Section 302 and SOX Certification requirements) makes it much more difficult for publicly traded firms to recruit independent directors, and SOX has drastically increased the costs of obtaining directors and officers' insurance coverage[37]—many insurance companies in the US will now offer only limited D&O insurance contracts (with limited pay-outs).

5.4 Failure and Unconstitutionality of the PCAOB (USA): Some of the US Supreme Court's Rulings in *Free Enterprise Fund vs. PCAOB* Were Error

The existence and current operations of the Public Company Accountability Oversight Board (the PCAOB in the US) is unconstitutional.[38] The PCAOB is a non-profit entity that was incorporated (pursuant to the

Compare: United Haulers Assn., Inc. vs. *Oneida-Herkimer Solid Waste Management Authority*, 550 U.S. ______, ______-______ (2007; US Supreme Court) (the *Pike* vs. *Bruce Church* scrutiny).

Compare: Northwest Central Pipeline Corp. v. *State Corporation Comm'n of Kansas*, 489 U.S. 493 (1989; US Supreme Court) (the *Pike* vs. *Bruce Church* scrutiny).

Compare: Minnesota v. *Clover Leaf Creamery Co.*, 449 U.S. 456 (1981; US Supreme Court) (the *Pike* vs. *Bruce Church* scrutiny).

[36] *See*: Gifford and Howe (2009).

[37] *See*: Gifford and Howe (2009).

[38] *See: Free Enterprise Fund vs. PCAOB*, _____ *US* ____ (2010; US Supreme Court). http://www.supremecourt.gov/opinions/09pdf/08-861.pdf. Justice Roberts delivered the, 5–4 opinion of the Court which states in part: "The Board's existence does not violate the separation of powers, but the substantive removal restrictions imposed do. Concluding that the removal restrictions here are invalid leaves the Board removable by the Commission at will ... The consequence is that the Board may continue to function as before, but its members may be removed at will by the [Securities and Exchange] Commission". *See*: *United States vs. Arthrex, Inc.*, ___ US ___ (No. 19–1434; US Supreme Court; pending as

Sarbanes Oxley Act of 2002 (SOX) in Washington D.C. PCAOB monitors and regulates the accounting firms that conduct external audits of companies in the US and indirectly affects foreign companies and international operations of such accounting firms. Thus, PCAOB has a significant effect on reported risk, regulation of risk and perceptions of risk in global markets. PCAOB oversees the audits of public companies, other issuers and broker-dealers (including compliance reports). All PCAOB rules and standards, and its annual budget, must be approved by the U.S. Securities and Exchange Commission (the SEC). The PCAOB is funded with fees paid by the companies and broker-dealers who rely on the audit/accounting firms that are managed by PCAOB. PCAOB is managed by a Board of Directors which has five Board members, all of whom are appointed by the US SEC. The PCAOB must consult with the US Secretary of the Treasury and the Chairman of the Board of Governors of the Federal Reserve System before each Board Member is appointed. No more than two Board members may be Certified Public Accountants.

Bader and Berlau (Competitive Enterprise Institute) (Oct. 2005),[39] Russell (June 28, 2010),[40] and Shapiro and Cushman (December 5, 2009)

of 2021).*See*: *Arthrex Inc. vs. Smith & Nephew Inc.*, ____ US ___ (No. 19–1458; US Supreme Court; pending as of 2021).

See: AccountingWeb. (2010). *Update: Supreme Court Rules PCAOB Violates Constitution's Separation of Powers Principle.* http://www.accountingweb.com/topic/accounting-auditing/supreme-court-rules-pcaob-unconstitutional.

See: Cutler, C. (June 10, 2010). *Despite Ruling on Constitutionality, PCAOB (and SoX) Wins at Supreme Court.* http://www.subjecttoinquiry.com/pcaob/news/the-us-supreme-court-today/.

See: *Memorandum of Proposed Intervenor United States in Opposition to Plaintiffs' Motion for Summary Judgment and in Support Of United States' Cross-Motion for Summary Judgment.* http://www.sec.gov/news/extra/2006/2006-147_brief.pdf.

See: King, R. (Oct. 2009). *The PCAOB Meets the Constitution: The Supreme Court to Decide on PCAOB's Conformity with the Separation of Powers Doctrine and Appointments Clause.* http://www.olin.wustl.edu/docs/Faculty/KingCommentaryPCAOBSubmission.pdf.

See: Public Company Accounting Oversight Board (PCAOB). http://www.sec.gov/answers/pcaob.htm. http://pcaobus.org/Pages/default.aspx.

See: PCAOB (USA) (Nov. 2009). *Board Approves Its 2010 Budget And Related Strategic Plan.* http://pcaobus.org/News/Releases/Pages/11302009_Approves_Budget.aspx.

[39] *See*: Bader, H. & Berlau, J. (Competitive Enterprise Institute) (Oct. 2005). *The Public Company Accounting Oversight Board: An Unconstitutional Assault on Government Accountability.* http://cei.org/pdf/4873.pdf.

[40] *See*: Russell, K. (June 28, 2010). *Provision Of Sarbanes-Oxley Un-Constitutionally Interferes With Presidential Authority.* http://www.scotusblog.com/2010/06/provision-of-sarbanes-oxley-unconstitutionally-interferes-with-presidential-authority/.

and other authors[41] explain how the existence and operations of PCAOB are unconstitutional (for reasons different from those mentioned in this chapter).

5.4.1 The Substantial Control Theory

The PCAOB (USA) is among a class of very powerful non-governmental organizations/associations that have "quasi-executive powers" (similar to powers of the executive branch of the federal government) even though they are not part of the government (but are implicitly supported and encouraged by governments). The diffusion of power inherent in these organizations/associations creates a diffusion of accountability and lack of appropriate oversight, which effectively subverts the powers of the executive branch of the federal government in many countries. Through its rule-making functions, the PCAOB (USA) has "quasi-executive powers" even though they are not part of the government (but are implicitly supported and encouraged by governments). PCAOB (USA) receives substantial input on accounting regulations from, and are lobbied by, the private sector. Thus, PCAOB (USA) has "federal-government type" power and control over capital markets, securities brokers and disclosure patterns, and such power is essentially the same as government control and/or "state-action" required to prove violations of the US Constitution. Hence a new doctrine of constitutional analysis named "Substantial Control" is introduced here an alternative to the "State-Action"[42] requirement of

[41] *See*: Shapiro, I. & Cushman, T. (Dec. 5, 2009). *Peekaboo, I See A Constitutional Violation*. http://www.cato.org/pub_display.php?pub_id=11033.

See: Birg, E. (2003). *Is the Public Company Accounting Oversight Board Constitutional?*, at pg. 6. Federalist Society for Law and Public Policy Studies, Corporate Responsibility Practice Group, 2003. http://www.fed-soc.org/Publications/Corpresp/ApptClauseFinal.pdf. ("Board members … are appointed by the SEC as a whole").

See: Wallison, R. (May 12, 2003). Rein In the Public Company Accounting Oversight Board; PCAOB Constitutionality Questioned. *Corporate Financing Week*, 29(19).

See: Nagy, D. (2005). *Playing Peekaboo with Constitutional Law: The PCAOB and Its Public/Private Status.* Notre Dame Law Review, 80, 975–1053 (noting that the PCAOB may violate the Appointments Clause and the constitutional separation of powers).

[42] *See: Evans v. Newton*, 382 U.S. 296 (1966; US Supreme Court).

See: Evans v. Abney, 396 US 435 (1970; US Supreme Court).

See: Burton v. Wilmington, 365 U.S. 715.

See: Moose Lodge v. Irvis, 407 U.S. 163 (1972; US Supreme Court).

constitutional law. The elements of the *Substantial Control* doctrine are as follows: (1) a private entity; (2) that is a national or international or local or state organization; and (3) market participants that are not affiliated with this organization will find it difficult, but not impossible, to conduct business in the industry; (4) the rules of the organization are binding on its members and/or on the general public; (5) the rules of the organization are implicitly or explicitly sanctioned by, and are often adopted by, federal, state or local governments. The *Substantial Control Theory* is an alternative to the *State Action* action requirement of constitutional law, and is different from the *Substantial Inducement Theory* and the *Substitution Theory* (both are alternatives to the *State Action* requirement) which were introduced in Nwogugu (2012).[43]

5.4.2 *Unconstitutionality of the PCAOB: The US Supreme Court's Ruling in* Free Enterprise Fund vs. PCAOB *Was Error*

The relevant *State Actions* are as follows: (a) the enactment of SOX, which, in turn, mandated the incorporation of PCAOB;[44] and (b) the executive branch of the US government appoints the officers of PCAOB and, in some cases, has the power to remove such officers; (c) SOX stipulates specific processes for challenging the decisions and activities of PCAOB.

The US Supreme Court's decision in *Free Enterprise Fund vs. PCAOB* was error and was limited to a narrow range of issues which are as follows. First, the dual for-cause limitations on the US President's power to remove Board members (substantive removal restrictions imposed by §§7211(e)(6) and 7217(d)(3)) contravenes the Constitution's *Separation of Powers*

See: *Edmonson v Leesville Concrete*, 500 US 614 (1991; US Supreme Court).

See: Marsh v. Alabama, 326 U.S. 501 (1946; US Supreme Court).

See: Screws v. US, 325 *U.S.* 91 (1945; US Supreme Court).

See: Ellman (2001), Gardbaum (2003), Tushnet (2003), Gardbaum (2006), and Currie (1986).

[43] *See*: Nwogugu (2012: 198).

[44] *See: Lebron*, 513 U.S. at 399 (US Supreme Court) ("a corporation is an agency of the government for purposes of the constitutional obligations of the government ... when the State has specifically created that corporation for the furtherance of governmental objectives and ... controls the operation of the corporation through its appointees").

See: Pennsylvania v. Bd. of Directors of City Trusts of Philadelphia, 353 U.S. 235 (1957) (*per curiam*) (College built and maintained pursuant to private trust was state actor because it was operated and controlled by a board of state appointees).

Doctrine.[45] Second, SOX's multilevel tenure protections provide a blueprint for the extensive and questionable expansion of legislative power. Third, the unconstitutional tenure provisions are severable from the remainder of the statute. Fourth, the processes for appointment of members of the Board of PCAOB is inconsistent with the Appointments Clause[46] of the US Constitution. Fifth, *Free Enterprise Fund vs. PCAOB* impliedly concurred with the enabling SOX statutes that created PCAOB, which was error.

The applicable enabling provisions of SOX and the existence of the PCAOB contravenes the *Separation of Powers Doctrine* (of the US Constitution) in at least two ways. First, SOX confers executive power on PCAOB Board members who are not controlled (cannot be appointed or removed by) by the US President because there are two layers of tenure protection. PCAOB Board members can only be removed by the US SEC for good cause, and the US SEC's Commissioners, in turn, can only be removed by the US President for good cause. Secondly, PCAOB performs legislative, investigative/enforcement and adjudicative functions simultaneously, all of which taken together constitute a violation of the Separation of Powers clause. The Dodd-Frank Act of 2010 (USA) did not amend the SOX to eliminate the constitutional violations inherent in the existence of the PCAOB (e.g. the Separation of Powers Clause). The PCAOB should not be a self-regulatory organization;[47] and should be a government agency, given the nature, scope, intensity and economic/political/social

[45] On the *Separation of Powers Doctrine*, see: *Collins vs. Yellen*, ___ US ___ (No. 19-422; US Supreme Court; pending as of 2021); *Collins vs. Mnuchin*, ____ US _____ (Docket No. 19–422; US Supreme Court; pending as of 2021); *Seila Law LLC vs. Consumer Financial Protection Bureau*, ____ US ____ (Case#: No. 19–7; US Supreme Court; 2020) (the Consumer Financial Protection Bureau's single-Director structure violates the *Separation of Powers Doctrine*, and the proper remedy is to sever the Director's statutory for-cause removal restriction); *Humphrey's Executor vs. United States*, 295 U.S. 602 (US Supreme Court; 1935); and *PHH Corp. vs. CFPB*, 839 F.3d 1 (2016) *on rehearing enbanc*, 881 F.3d 75 (D.C. Cir., 2018) (en banc).

[46] *See: United States vs. Arthrex, Inc.*, ___ US ___ (No. 19-1434; US Supreme Court; pending as of 2021); and *Arthrex Inc. vs. Smith & Nephew Inc.*, ____ US ___ (No. 19-1458; US Supreme Court; pending as of 2021).

[47] *See:* Schaumann (2004: 1319) states in part: " Formally, the Public Company Accounting Oversight Board (the "Board") is not an agency of the U.S. government; it is a nonprofit corporation organized under the District of Columbia Nonprofit Corporation Act. The Board comprises five members, of which two must—and only two may—be certified public accountants".

effects of its functions. The PCAOB is redundant because it performs and duplicates functions that are either currently being performed, or are best performed by the US SEC (and state securities agencies) and state accounting boards, and FINRA. The PCAOB does not have any powers that the US SEC does not already have either fully or in a form/amount that can be rapidly expanded. Thus, the PCAOB should be a division of the US SEC. The PCAOB is unconstitutional because it's a non-governmental monopoly that has been granted regulatory and taxing powers[48] by the US Congress.

The SOX enabling statutes that created PCAOB are unconstitutional because the sole mechanism in SOX for review of claims that challenge the PCAOB's adjudicative, enforcement and rule-making activities violate both the procedural and substantive due process clauses[49] of the US Constitution. Any such claims must first be made in a US SEC proceeding and, if the US SEC affirms the PCAOB's action, the aggrieved party can appeal the action to an appropriate US court of appeals (collectively, the "PCAOB Review Process"). First, the PCAOB Review Process can be very expensive and time consuming even for an administrative proceeding. US SEC adjudicative proceedings alone can last for eighteen months. Furthermore, the nature of the matters that are adjudicated and/or enforced by the PCAOB affects large numbers of people, and requires relatively very quick resolutions—for example, quality of external audits; accounting firms' ability to practice. Secondly, the PCAOB does not have

[48] *See*: Niskanen, W. (2006). *Congress Should Repeal the Sarbanes-Oxley Act.* Cato Institute. Available at: http://www.cato.org/pub_display.php?pub_id=6624.

[49] On the *Substantive Due Process Clause*, see: *Washington v. Glucksberg*, 521 U.S. 702, 719 (US Supreme Court; 1997) ("The Due Process Clause guarantees more than fair process, and the 'liberty' it protects includes more than the absence of physical restraint."); *Obergefell vs. Hodges*, 576 U.S. 644 (US Supreme Court; 2015); *Lawrence vs. Texas*, 539 U.S. 558 (US Supreme Court; 2003); *United States vs. Vaello-Madero*, ______ US ______ (Case#: 20-303; US Supreme Court; pending as of 2021); *DeNolf vs. U.S.*, ______ US ______ (US Supreme Court; pending as of 2021) (https://static1.squarespace.com/static/5b660749620b85c6c73e5e61/t/608d544886d55300e492a619/1619874888658/2021-22+AMCA+Case.pdf); *DeNolf vs. U.S.* (Case#: 01-76320; US 14th Circuit, 2020) (https://static1.squarespace.com/static/5b660749620b85c6c73e5e61/t/608d544886d55300e492a619/1619874888658/2021-22+AMCA+Case.pdf); and *Planned Parenthood of Southeastern Pennsylvania vs. Casey*, 505 U.S. 833, 848 (1992) ("Neither the Bill of Rights nor the specific practices of States at the time of the adoption of the Fourteenth Amendment marks the outer limits of the substantive sphere of liberty which the Fourteenth Amendment protects").

the procedural powers that will facilitate efficient fact finding and adjudication—such as summary proceedings. Thirdly, the Appellate Review is not de novo (the US Federal Appeals Court must give some deference to the findings of the PCAOB and the SEC). Fourth, in situations/disputes where extensive discovery is required for proof or absence of misconduct, the PCAOB Review Process does not provide sufficient discovery at any of the three levels of adjudication. Fifth, because as explained herein, the process for appointment of the PCAOB Board Members violates the Appointment Clause of the US Constitution, decisions and actions of the PCAOB can be overturned by federal courts solely because of such improper appointments[50] (courts can block enforcement of the PCAOB's rules that enforce portions of SOX).

The SOX enabling statutes that created PCAOB also violate both the procedural and substantive due process clauses of the US Constitution for other reasons. The PCAOB has extensive powers to interpret the portions of SOX such as those that pertain to internal controls, and such powers can conflict with those of the US SEC. The PCAOB's interpretation of the portions of SOX that pertain to internal controls has imposed substantial

[50] *See: FEC v. NRA Political Victory Fund*, 6 F.3d 821 (D.C. Cir., 1993).

See: Williams v. Phelps, 482 F.2d 669, 671 n.3 (D.C. Cir. 1973) (labor union could sue to challenge policies harming government employees carried out by improperly appointed head of agency).

See: Ryder v. United States, 515 U.S. 177, 182–183 (1995) (since "one who makes a timely challenge to the constitutional validity of an officer who adjudicates his case" can use the invalid appointment to obtain "whatever relief may be appropriate," the defendant could challenge the composition of the Coast Guard Court of Military Review, which violated the Appointments Clause, and use it to overturn his conviction).

See: Williams v. Phelps, 482 F.2d 669, 671 n.3 (D.C. Cir., 1973) (standing of labor union to bring action challenging appointment of head of agency not nominated by president and confirmed by Senate as required by Appointments Clause "rests on firm ground" because that agency head carried out policies that "directly affected" the jobs of government employees who belonged to the union).

See: Freytag vs. C.I.R., 501 U.S. 868, 879 (1991; US Supreme Court) (Supreme Court entertained a challenge to a disciplinary proceeding of the U.S. Tax Court even though the defendant had not raised an Appointments Clause challenge at trial).

See: FEC vs. NRA Political Victory Fund, 6 F.3d 821, 824 (D.C. Cir., 1993) (NRA could challenge presence of non-voting congressional officials on executive branch agency, even if they had no vote in its decision to prosecute the NRA and were silent).

See: Seila Law LLC vs. Consumer Financial Protection Bureau, ______ US ______ (Case#: No. 19-7; US Supreme Court; 2020) (the Consumer Financial Protection Bureau's single-Director structure violates the *Separation of Powers Doctrine*, and the proper remedy is to make the Director removable by the President at will).

additional costs on publicly traded US companies[51]—for example, by requiring audits. The PCAOB's regulations have increased concentration and reduced competition in the accounting industry because the costs of its regulations have caused many small accounting firms to stop auditing publicly traded companies. SOX prohibits accounting firms from providing eight designated forms of consulting for their audit clients; and SOX authorized the PCAOB to "prohibit any other service that the Board determines, by regulation, is impermissible".

The SOX enabling statutes that created PCAOB are unconstitutional for the following reasons. Although it appears that such statutes enable the US Congress to restrict the US President's "removal authority" (authority to appoint or remove those PCAOB board members or otherwise supervise or control their exercise of that power) in any way it "deems best for the public interest", the opposite is the case, and the reality, is as follows. The majority votes required in both the US Senate and the US House may not be feasible or may take a long time to obtain. Any congressional interference on the President's removal authority is also subject to judicial review in Article-Three courts[52] which may declare such interference to be unconstitutional. Any congressional interference on the President's "removal authority" is unconstitutional because it limits the powers granted to the US President and the executive branch by the US Constitution. Any congressional interference on the President's "removal authority" creates, or can create, a conflict of interest. Any congressional interference on the President's "removal authority" is unconstitutional because it violates substantive due process clauses given that the US Congress members are not experts in accounting regulation and the executive branch is arguably more knowledgeable about, and is better position to handle (through administrative agencies such as the US SEC, the US FTC, etc.) accounting regulation.

[51] *See*: Skouvakis, A. (2005). Note: Exiting the Public Markets—A Difficult Choice for Small Public Companies Struggling with Sarbanes-Oxley. *Penn State Law Review*, 109: 1279–1289.

See: Rose (2005); Grundfest and Bochner (2007); Backer (2004); Carney (2006); Gupta and Leech (2005); Engel et al. (2007); Bartlett (April 2008); Kamar and Karaca-Mandic (2006); Tackett et al. (2006).

[52] *See: United States vs. Arthrex, Inc.*, ______ US ______ (US Supreme Court; pending as of 2021).

See: California vs. Texas, ______ US ______ (No. 19–840; US Supreme Court; pending as of 2021).

Any congressional interference on the President's "removal authority" is unconstitutional because it violates the procedural due process clause. Such interference will likely take a long time to achieve, and may cause deep divisions within the US Congress, which will burden interstate commerce, and depends on which political party controls the US Senate and the US House of Representatives. The US Congress members are not experts in accounting regulation (and the executive branch is arguably more knowledgeable about accounting regulation than the US Congress).

The procedure for the appointment of PCAOB's Board members violates the Appointments Clause of the US Constitution. The Appointments Clause requires that the US Senate must consent to the US President's appointment of any officers (except "inferior Officers", who can be appointed by "the President alone, … the Courts of Law, or … the Heads of Departments," Art. II, §2, cl. 2[53]). Pursuant to SOX, the PCAOB board members are appointed by the US SEC (although they should be appointed as "officers" by the US President). Under US Supreme Court cases, the PCAOB Board members are "principal/senior officer" and *not* "inferior officers" (whose appointment the US Congress may delegate to a "Head of Department"). This is because of the scope and national/international importance of their functions and because they have "significant authority".[54] For example, under Section 105(c)(4)(D) of SOX, PCAOB Board Members can impose fines on accounting firms of up to $2 million and fines of up to $100,000 on individual accountants for violations of SOX and PCAOB Board rules. Also, the international headquarters of many accounting firms is in the US. The Appointments Clause of the US Constitution grants only the US President the power to appoint the US "principal officers". However, "Inferior officers" can be appointed

[53] *See:* GAO Report No. GAO-03-339, Securities and Exchange Commission: Actions Needed to Improve Public Company Accounting Oversight Board Selection Process, at "Highlights" (unnumbered), 3 (www.gao.gov/htext/d03339.html).

[54] *See: Buckley v. Valeo*, 424 U.S. 1, 126 (1976; US Supreme Court) (government employees with "significant authority" are officers of the United States).

See: Edmond v. United States, 520 U.S. 651, 662 (1997; US Supreme Court).

See: United States v. Germaine, 99 U.S. 508, 511 (1879; US Supreme Court) (officer's "emoluments" are relevant to whether he is a "principal" or "inferior" officer).

See: Nagy (2005) (given the sheer scope of their power, and their fixed five-year terms, there is a "strong argument" that PCAOB Board members are "principal officers").

See: Wallison, P. (2005). *Rein in the Public Company Accounting Oversight Board*. http://regulators.itgo.com/ Reports/PCAOB/PCAOB_2Feb05.pdf (the "President alone" must pick PCAOB members under the *Appointments Clause*).

only by the President, by a court or by a single head of a cabinet-level "department". The activities of the PCAOB Board Members are not always "directed and supervised at some level" by "principal officers" of the US. The PCAOB Board members make decisions independent of such "principal officers" and the SEC. Under Section 107(b)(2) of SOX, "no rule of the Board shall become effective without prior approval of the Commission"; and under Sections 107(c)(2)(A) and 105(e), any disciplinary action by the Board is automatically stayed by an appeal to the US SEC. Furthermore, there is a significant difference between the US SEC having the power to appoint or remove PCAOB Board Members on one hand, and actual supervision of the daily activities of Board Members and the PCAOB by the SEC. For example, the PCAOB's decision whether or not to initiate an investigation cannot be reviewed by the US SEC. Hence the SEC's "department" status and powers has limited effects on the PCAOB. Furthermore, under US Supreme Court precedent,[55] the SEC cannot be deemed to be a "Department" under the Appointments Clause, and, thus, should not have the power to appoint PCAOB officers. The PCAOB is a non-governmental entity that cannot be deemed to be an extension of the SEC, especially given the limited control that the SEC has over the PCAOB, and the legislative intent of SOX.

The enabling statutes in SOX that created PCAOB are unconstitutional because they constitute an illegal delegation of duties of the executive branch of the US government to the PCAOB. Thus the enabling statutes in SOX contravene the *Non-Delegation Doctrine* of the US Constitution.[56]

[55] *See: Freytag vs. Commissioner of Internal Revenue*, 501 U.S. 868, 886–887 (1991; US Supreme Court) *quoting United States v. Germaine*, 99 U.S. 508, 510–511.

[56] *See: Carter v. Carter Coal Co.*, 298 U.S. 238, 311 (1936; US Supreme Court) (invalidating delegation to coal producers and unions of the power to set wages and prices in their industry).

See: Sarbanes-Oxley Act, § 109(b), 15 U.S.C. § 7219(b) (PCAOB sets its own budget, subject to approval only by the SEC, not by Congress).

See: Wallison, P. (Feb. 2005). *Rein in the Public Company Accounting Oversight Board.* pp. 3–4 ("because the SEC does not set its own budget, and the PCAOB can perform functions on behalf of the SEC, the SEC has a built-in incentive to approve burgeoning PCAOB budgets to free up the use of its own budget, and it has in fact approved PCAOB budgets that are much more generous than the SEC's own on a per capita basis") (http://regulators.itgo.com/Reports/PCAOB/PCAOB_2Feb05.pdf).

See: Byrne, R. (Jan. 13, 2003). Accountants Board Tin Ear Now Golden. *The Street*, Jan. 13, 2003 (http://www.thestreet.com/markets/rebeccabyrne/10062297.html).

Such impermissible delegation is also not combined with effective judicial review, as explained herein.

The PCAOB's interpretation of SOX's Section-404 (internal controls) and that of the US SEC may conflict. Such conflict can produce different results for different classes of exchange-traded companies, and which can burden interstate commerce by increasing compliance costs. The PCAOB's interpretation of the internal control provisions of SOX unfairly discriminates: (1) between public and private companies of the same size/scope/ business; (2) between public companies that can afford

The unconstitutionality of the SOX and the PCAOB are an example of the far-reaching effects of state and federal constitutions on risk regulation. Many authors have documented many weaknesses inherent in the Sarbanes Oxley Act.[57] The Financial Stability Act of 2010 (FSA, which is part of the Dodd-Frank Act) did not amend the Sarbanes Oxley Act to eliminate the inherent violations of the *Separation of Powers clause*—for example, pertaining to the existence and functions of the PCAOB. It was error to designate the PCAOB as a self-regulatory organization[58]—the

See: Schaumann (2004: 1319) which states in part: "Formally, the Public Company Accounting Oversight Board (the 'Board') is not an agency of the U.S. government; it is a nonprofit corporation organized under the District of Columbia Nonprofit Corporation Act. The Board comprises five members, of which two must—and only two may—be certified public accountants".

[57] *See*: Nwogugu (2008).

See: Sarbanes-Oxley Act of 2002, Pub. L. No. 107-204, 116 Stat. 745 (codified at various sections of 11, 15, 18, 28, and 29 U.S.C. (Supp. III 2003)).

See: Butler, H., & Ribstein, L. (2006). *The Sarbanes Oxley Debacle: What We've Learned; How to Fix It* (AEI Press, 2006).

See: *FEI Survey: Management Drives Sarbanes-Oxley Compliance Costs Down by 23%, But Auditor Fees Virtually Unchanged.* Financial Executive International, May 16, 2007. Available at: http://fei.mediaroom.com/index.php?s=press_releases&item=187.

See: Ribstein (2002), Iliev (2007), Litvak (2007), Ribstein (Oct. 2003), Romano (2004), Bainbridge and Johnson (2004), Baynes (2002), Braddock (2006), Cherry (2004), Jain et al. (2006), Jain and Rezaee (2004), Kamar et al. (2008), Zhang (2007), Burks (2010), Dey (2010), Chang and Sun (2009), Kang et al. (2010), Bargeron et al. (2010), Wang (2010), Leech (Nov. 2003a, 2003b), Linck et al. (2009), Linsley (2003), McTamaney (August 2002), Nielsen and Main (Oct. 2004), Perino (October 2002), Recine (2002), Cunningham (2002), Coates (2007), Carrillo (2008), Unger (2007), Wade (2008), Schmidt (2005), Tackett et al. (2004), Soederberg (2008), Taylor (2006), Cowart (2004), Schiller (2008), and Pautz (2009).

[58] *See:* Schaumann (2004: 1319) which states in part: " Formally, the Public Company Accounting Oversight Board (the 'Board') is not an agency of the U.S. government; it is a

PCAOB should rightfully be an agency of the US government (and should have some Congressional Oversight), given the nature and potentially significant domestic/Cross-Border Multiplier-Effects of its functions.

5.5 Conclusion

Important sections of SOX and the PCAOB's enabling statutes are unconstitutional. That has or can have broad macrofinance, regulation and IPE implications because of the worldwide *Multiplier Effects* of SOX, World-SOX and PCAOB (especially in Emerging Markets countries where regulation and enforcement are weaker).

Bibliography

April, E. (2009). What Critiques of Sarbanes-Oxley Can Teach About Regulation of Non-profit Governance. *Fordham Law Review, 76*, 765–775.

Arora, S., & Gangopadhyay, S. (1995). Toward a Theoretical Model of Voluntary Overcompliance. *Journal of Economic Behavior & Organization, 28*(3), 289–299.

Backer, L. (2004). Surveillance and Control: Privatizing and Nationalizing Corporate Monitoring after Sarbanes Oxley Act. *Michigan State Law Review, 2004*, 327–370.

Bader, H., & Berlau, J. (Competitive Enterprise Institute). (2005, October). *The Public Company Accounting Oversight Board: An Unconstitutional Assault on Government Accountability*. Retrieved from http://cei.org/pdf/4873.pdf.

Bainbridge, S., & Johnson, C. (2004). Managerialism, Legal Ethics and Sarbanes-Oxley Section 307. *Michigan State Law Review, 2004*, 299–316.

Baker, R., Bédard, J., & Hauret, C. (2014). The Regulation of Statutory Auditing: An Institutional Theory Approach. *Managerial Auditing Journal, 29*(5), 371–391.

Banker, S., Bhanot, S., & Deshpande, A. (2020). Poverty Identity and Preference for Challenge: Evidence from the U.S. and India. *Journal of Economic Psychology, 76*, 102214.

Bard, S. (1961). State Action and the Equal Protection Clause: Status of Lessee of Public Property. *Michigan Law Review, 59*(3), 450–454.

nonprofit corporation organized under the District of Columbia Nonprofit Corporation Act. The Board comprises five members, of which two must—and only two may—be certified public accountants").

Bargeron, L. L., Lehn, K., & Zutter, C. (2010). Sarbanes-Oxley and Corporate Risk-Taking. *Journal of Accounting and Economics, 49*(1–2), 34–52.

Bartlett, R. (2008, April). *Going Private But Staying Public: Reexamining the Effect of Sarbanes-Oxley on Firms' Going-Private Decisions.* American Law & Economics Association Annual Meetings. Retrieved from http://law.bepress.com/cgi/viewcontent.cgi?article=2521&context=alea.

Bather, A., & Burnaby, P. (2006). The Public Company Accounting Oversight Board: National and International Implications. *Managerial Auditing Journal, 21*(6), 657–669.

Baynes, L. (2002). Just Pucker and Blow? An Analysis of Corporate Whistleblowers, the Duty of Care, the Duty of Loyalty and the Sarbanes-Oxley Act. *St. Johns Law Review, 76*, 875–895.

Berlau, J. (2006, January). *Sarbanes-Oxley vs. the Free Press: How the Government Used Business Regulations to Strong-Arm the Media.* Reason.com. Retrieved from http://reason.com/archives/2006/01/01/sarbanes-oxley-vs-the-free-pre.

Bertezzolo, G. (2009). The European Union Facing the Global Arena: Standard Setting Bodies and Financial Regulation. *European Law Review, 34*(2), 257–267.

Bhabra, H., & Hossain, A. (2018). SOX vs C-SOX: Which One Works Better? *Managerial Finance, 44*(8), 1031–1046.

Bhabra, H., Hossain, A., & Karmakar, V. (2019). An Overview of C-SOX and Directions for Future Research. *Managerial Finance, 46*(2), 254–266.

Birg, E. (2003). *Is the Public Company Accounting Oversight Board Constitutional?*, p. 6.

Birz, G. (2017). Stale Economic News, Media and the Stock Market. *Journal of Economic Psychology, 61*, 87–102.

Blaufus, K., Möhlmann, A., & Schwäbe, A. (2019). Stock Price Reactions to News about Corporate Tax Avoidance and Evasion. *Journal of Economic Psychology, 72*, 278–292.

Blomquist, W., & Ostrom, E. (2009). Deliberation, Learning, and Institutional Change: The Evolution of Institutions in Judicial Settings. *Constitutional Political Economy, 19*(3), 180–202.

Braddock, C. (2006). Pennywise and Pound Foolish: Why Investors Would be Foolish to Pay a Penny or a Pound for the Protections Provided by Sarbanes-Oxley. *Brigham Young University Law Review, 2006*, 175–208.

Brown, J. (2006). Criticizing the Critics: Sarbanes Oxley and Quack Corporate Governance. *Marquette Law Review, 90*, 309435.

Burks, J. (2010). Disciplinary Measures in Response to Restatements after Sarbanes–Oxley. *Journal of Accounting and Public Policy, 29*(3), 195–225.

Burrowees, A., Kastanin, J., & Novicevic, N. (2004). The Sarbanes-Oxley Act as a Hologram of Post-Enron Disclosure: A Critical Realist Commentary. *Critical Perspectives on Accounting, 15*, 797–781.

Butler, H., & Ribstein, L. (1994). Corporate Governance Speech and the First Amendment. *Kansas Law Review, 42*, 163.

Butler, H., & Ribstein, L. (2006). *The Sarbanes-Oxley Debacle: What We've Learned; How to Fix It*. AEI Press.

Carney, W. (2006). The Costs of being Public After the Sarbanes-Oxley Act: The Irony of "Going Private". *Emory Law Journal, 55*, 141–151.

Carrillo, D. (2008). Disgorgement Plans under the Fair Funds Provision of the Sarbanes-Oxley Act of 2002: Are Creditors and Investors Truly Being Protected. *DePaul Business & Commercial Law, 6*, 315–325.

Chang, H., & Choy, H. (2016). The Effect of the Sarbanes–Oxley Act on Firm Productivity. *Journal of Centrum Cathedra, 9*(2), 120–142.

Chang, J., & Sun, H. (2009). Crossed-Listed Foreign Firms' Earnings Informativeness, Earnings Management and Disclosures of Corporate Governance Information Under SOX. *The International Journal of Accounting, 44*(1), 1–32.

Cherry, M. (2004). Whistling in the Dark? Corporate Fraud Whistleblowers and the Implications of the Sarbanes Oxley Act for Employment Law. *Washington Law Review, 79*, 1029–1049.

Chiu, S., Chien, C., & Lin, H. (2013). Audit Quality Following the Public Company Accounting Oversight Board's Operation. *Corporate Governance: The International Journal of Business in Society, 17*(5), 9827–9946.

Coates, J. C. (2007). The Goals and Promise of the Sarbanes-Oxley Act. *The Journal of Economic Perspectives, 21*(1), 91–116.

Colangelo, A. (2010). The Foreign Commerce Clause. *Virginia Law Review, 96*(5), 949. Retrieved from http://www.virginialawreview.org/articles.php?article=.

Cowart, K. T. (2004). Sarbanes-Oxley Act: How a Current Model in the Law of Unintended Consequences May Affect Securities Litigation. *Duquesne Law Review, 42*, 293–303.

Cunningham, L. A. (2002). The Sarbanes-Oxley Yawn: Heavy Rhetoric, Light Reform (and It Just Might Work). *Connecticut Law Review, 35*, 915.

Currie, D. (1986). Positive and Negative Constitutional Rights. *University of Chicago Law Review, 53*(3), 864–890.

Cutler, C. (2010, June 10). *Despite Ruling on Constitutionality, PCAOB (and SoX) Wins at Supreme Court*. Retrieved from http://www.subjecttoinquiry.com/pcaob/news/the-us-supreme-court-today/.

Debelle, G. (2004). Household Debt and the Macroeconomy. *BIS Quarterly Review*. Retrieved from SSRN http://ssrn.com/abstract=1968418.

Delimatsis, P. (2012). *Of Bailouts and Rescue Measures: Subsidies in Financial Services*. Working Paper No 2012/24. Swiss National Center of Competence in Research. Retrieved from http://www20.iadb.org/intal/catalogo/PE/2012/12020.pdf.

Dey, A. (2010). The Chilling Effect of Sarbanes–Oxley: A Discussion of Sarbanes–Oxley and Corporate Risk-Taking. *Journal of Accounting and Economics, 49*(1–2), 53–57.

Diamond, R., McQuade, T., & Qian, F. (2019). The Effects of Rent Control Expansion on Tenants, Landlords, and Inequality: Evidence from San Francisco. *American Economic Review, 109*(9), 3365–3394.

Dixon, R., Griffiths, W., & Lim, G. (2014). Lay People's Models of the Economy: A Study Based on Surveys of Consumer Sentiments. *Journal of Economic Psychology, 44*, 13–20.

Doring, T., & Schnellenbach, J. (2010). A Tale of Two Federalisms: Germany, the United States and the Ubiquity of Centralization. *Constitutional Political Economy, 22*(1), 83–102.

Dunbar, W. (1901). The Constitutionality of the US Inheritance Tax. *Quarterly Journal of Economics, 15*(2), 92–298.

Ellman, S. (2001). A Constitutional Confluence: American "State Action" Law, and the Application of South Africa's Socio Economic Rights Guarantees to Private Actors. *New York Law School Law Review, 45*, 21–75.

Engel, E., Hayes, R., & Wang, X. (2007). The Sarbanes–Oxley Act and Firms' Going-Private Decisions. *Journal of Accounting and Economics, 44*, 116–145.

Foley & Lardner LLP. (2007). *The Cost of Being Public in the Era of Sarbanes-Oxley*. Retrieved from http://www.foley.com/files/tbl_s31Publications/Fstudy.ileUpload137/3736/Foley2007SOXstudy.pdf.

Garcia, F., Opromolla, L., & Marques, A. (2020). The Effects of Official and Unofficial Information on Tax Compliance. *Journal of Economic Psychology, 78*.

Gardbaum, G. (2003). The "Horizontal Effect" of Constitutional Rights. *Michigan Law Review, 102*, 387–398.

Gardbaum, S. (2006). Where the (State) Action is. *International Journal Of Constitutional Law, 4*(4), 760–779.

Gifford, R., & Howe, H. (2009). Regulation and Unintended Consequences: Thoughts on Sarbanes-Oxley. *The CPA Journal, 76*, 6. Retrieved from http://www.nysscpa.org/cpajournal/2004/604/perspectives/p6.htm.

Gordon, I., & Nazari, J. (2018). Review of SOX in the Business Ethics Literature. *Managerial Auditing Journal, 33*(5), 470–502.

Grundfest, J., & Bochner, S. (2007). Fixing 404. *Michigan Law Review, 105*, 1643–1666.

Gupta, P., & Leech, T. (2005). Making Sarbanes Oxley 404 Work: Reducing Cost, Increasing Effectiveness. *International Journal of Disclosure and Governance, 3*(1), 27–48.

Haferkamp, A., Fetchenhauer, D., et al. (2009). Efficiency Versus Fairness: The Evaluation of Labor Market Policies by Economists and Laypeople. *Journal of Economic Psychology, 30*(4), 527–539.

Hämäläinen, S., & Martikainen, M. (2015). Foreign Direct Investments Affecting Accounting Quality in Transitional Economies of Europe. *International Journal of Business Innovation and Research, 9*(3), 295–310.

Hamann, A., & Fabri, H. (2008). Transnational Networks and Constitutionalism. *International Journal of Constitutional Law, 6*, 481–491.

Hardardottir, H. (2017). Long Term Stability of Time Preferences and the Role of the Macroeconomic Situation. *Journal of Economic Psychology, 60*, 21–36.

Hellerstein, W. (1996, June). Commerce Clause Restraints on State Tax Incentives. *The Region*. Federal Reserve Bank of Minneapolis.

Hoffman, B., & Nagy, A. (2016). SOX 404(b) Exemption Effects on Auditor Changes. *Managerial Auditing Journal, 31*(4/5), 381–402.

Houghton, K., & Hellertein, W. (2000). State Taxation of Electronic Commerce: Perspectives on Proposals for Change and Their Constitutionality. *Brigham Young University Law Review, 1*, 9–76.

Huang, H., & Chong, G. (2016). Audit and Legal Implications of PCAOB's Inspections Among BRIC. *International Journal of Law and Management, 58*(2), 231–244.

Hunter, B. (2007). *Punishing the Innocent: The Sarbanes-Oxley Act: The Law Has Inflicted Endless Losses on Businesses in Time and Money*. Retrieved from http://www.thefreemanonline.org/featured/punishing-the-innocent-the-sarbanes-oxley-act/#.

Iliev, P. (2007). *The Effect of the Sarbanes-Oxley Act (Section 404) Management's Report on Audit Fees, Accruals and Stock Returns*. Brown University Working Paper. Retrieved from http://ssrn.com/abstract=983772 (Section 404 Management Reports Lower Share Prices).

International Institute For Sustainable Development. (2009, March). *Will Government Bailouts Lead to Trade Wars?*. Retrieved from https://www.iisd.org/gsi/news/will-government-bailouts-lead-trade-wars.

Jain, K., & Rezaee, Z. (2004). Industry-wide Effects of the Sarbanes Oxley Act of 2002. *Journal of Forensic Accounting, 6*, 147–162.

Jain, P., Kim, J., & Rezaee, Z. (2006). *Trends and Determinants of Market Liquidity in the Pre- and Post Sarbanes Oxley Act Periods*. Presented at the 14th Annual Conference In Financial Economics and Accounting.

John, D. C. & Marano, N. (2007, May 16). *The Sarbanes-Oxley Act: Do We Need a Regulatory or Legislative Fix?*. Heritage Foundation, USA. Retrieved from http://www.heritage.org/Research/Reports/2007/05/The-Sarbanes-Oxley-Act-Do-We-Need-a-Regulatory-or-Legislative-Fix; or http://s3.amazonaws.com/thf_media/2007/pdf/bg2035.pdf.

Kamar, E., & Karaca-Mandic, P. (2006). *Going-Private Decisions and the Sarbanes Oxley Act of 2002: A Cross Country Analysis*. University of Southern California, Law & Economics Working Paper Series, Paper 52.

Kamar, E., Karaca-Mandic, P., & Talley, E. (2008). Going-Private Decisions and the Sarbanes-Oxley Act of 2002: A Cross-Country Analysis. *Journal of Law, Economics & Organization, 25*, 107.

Kamar, E., Karaca-Mandic, P., & Talley, E. (2007). *Sarbanes-Oxley's Effects on Small Firms: What Is the Evidence?*. USC CLEO Research Paper No. C07-9; USC Law Legal Studies Paper No. 07-8; Harvard Law & Economics Discussion Paper No. 588 (2007). Retrieved from https://scholarship.law.columbia.edu/faculty_scholarship/1478.

Kang, Q., Liu, Q., & Qi, R. (2010). The Sarbanes-Oxley Act and Corporate Investment: A Structural Assessment. *Journal of Financial Economics, 96*(2), 291–305.

Kaplow, L. (1995). A Model of the Optimal Complexity of Legal Rules. *Journal of law, Economics & Organization, 11*(1), 150–163.

Katyal, N. (2006). Internal Separation of Powers: Checking Today's Most Dangerous Branch from Within. *Yale Law Journal, 115*, 2314–2320.

Kim, B. (2003). Sarbanes-Oxley Act. *Harvard Journal on Legislation, 40*, 235–248.

King, R. (2009, October). The PCAOB Meets the Constitution: The Supreme Court to Decide on PCAOB's Conformity with the Separation of Powers Doctrine and Appointments Clause. Retrieved from http://www.olin.wustl.edu/docs/Faculty/KingCommentaryPCAOBSubmission.pdf.

Kinnunen, J., Martikainen-Peltola, M., Kallunki, J.-P., & Mikkonen, J. (2016). *Insider Trading and Earnings Management: A Cross-Country Comparison.* Proceedings of Nordic Accounting Conference 2016.

Kunst, P., & Wagner, R. (2011). Choice, Emergence, and Constitutional Process: A Framework for Positive Analysis. *Journal of Institutional Economics, 7*, 131–145.

Larbalestier, P. (1990). Australian Corporations Act Held to be Unconstitutional. *International Financial Law Review, 9*(4), 11–12.

Lawson, G. (2010). Burying the Constitution Under a TARP. *Harvard Journal of Law and Public Policy, 33*, 23–34.

Pántya, J., Kovács, J., et al. (2016). Work Performance and Tax Compliance in Flat and Progressive Tax Systems. *Journal of Economic Psychology, 56*, 262–273.

Leech, T. (2003a). Sarbanes Oxley Act: Hidden Shoals for the Unwary. *Global Risk Regulator.*

Leech, T. (2003b). *Sarbanes Oxley Sections 302 & 404: A White Paper Proposing Practical Cost Effective Compliance Strategies.* Working Paper.

Linck, J., Netter, J., & Yang, T. (2009). The Effects and Unintended Consequences of the Sarbanes Oxley Act on Corporate Boards. *Review of Financial Studies, 22*(8), 3287–3328.

Linsley, C. (2003). Auditing, Risk Management and a Post-Sarbanes Oxley World. *Review of Business, 24*, 21–23.

Litvak, K. (2007). The Effect of the Sarbanes-Oxley Act on Non-US Companies Cross-Listed in the US. *Michigan Law Review*, 105, 1857–1867 (Compliance with SOX Has a Net Negative Effect on the Share Prices of Cross-Listed Foreign Companies).

Loehlein, L. (2017). Measuring the Independence of Audit Oversight Entities: A Comparative Empirical Analysis. *Accounting Research Journal, 30*(2), 125–152.

McTamaney, R. (2002, August). *The Sarbanes Oxley Act of 2002: Will It Prevent Future "Enrons ?"* Washington Legal Foundation, 17(32).

Merrill, T. (2000). The Landscape of Constitutional Property. *Virginia Law Review, 86*(5), 885–999.

Metelska-Szaniawska, K. (2010). Constitutions and Economic Reforms in Transition: An Empirical Study. *Constitutional Political Economy, 20*(1), 1–41.

Meyer, T. (2009). Soft Law as Delegation. *Fordham International Law Journal, 32*, 888–898.

Mistri, M. (2007). Institutional Changes and Shifting Ideas: A Constitutional Analysis of the Euro. *Constitutional Political Economy, 18*(2), 107–126.

Mulligan, L. (2006). What's Good for the Goose Is Not Good for the Gander: Sarbanes-Oxley-Style Nonprofit Reforms. *Michigan Law Review, 105*, 1981–2009.

Muth, K. (2009). Sarbanes-Oxley Writ Large: Sarbanes-Oxley and the Foreign Commerce Clause. *Journal of International Business & Law, 8*, 29–39. Retrieved from http://www.karlmuth.com/uploads/Sarbanes-Oxley.pdf.

Mwakagali, M. (2018). *International Financial Institutions and Labor Standards: A Legal Study Into the Role of These Institutions in the Promotion and Implementation of Freedom of Association and Collective Bargaining*. PhD thesis, Stockholm University, Sweden. https://su.diva-portal.org/smash/get/diva2:1189029/FULLTEXT01.pdf.

Nagy, D. (2005). Playing Peekaboo with Constitutional Law: The PCAOB and Its Public/Private Status. *Notre Dame Law Review, 80*, 975–1053.

Nguyen, V., & Claus, E. (2013). Good News, Bad News, Consumer Sentiment and Consumption Behavior. *Journal of Economic Psychology, 39*, 426–438.

Nielsen, P., & Main, C. (2004, October). Company Liability after the Sarbanes Oxley Act. *Insight: The Corporate & Securities Law Advisor, 18*(1), 1–10.

Niskanen, W. (2006). *Congress Should Repeal the Sarbanes-Oxley Act.* Cato Institute. Retrieved from http://www.cato.org/pub_display.php?pub_id=6624.

Norton, J. (2009). Comment on the Developing Transnational Network(s) in the Area of International Financial Regulation: The Underpinnings of a New Bretton Woods II Global Financial System Framework. *International Lawyer, 43*, 175–185.

Nwogugu, M. (2004). Corporate Governance, Legal Reasoning and Credit Risk: The Case of Encompass Services Inc. *Managerial Auditing Journal, 19*(9), 1078–1118.

Nwogugu, M. (2008). The Efficiency of Sarbanes-Oxley Act: Willingness to Comply and Agency Problems. *Corporate Control & Ownership, 5*(1), 449–454.

Nwogugu, M. (2010/2013). *Problems Inherent in the Compensation and Business Models of Credit Rating Agencies.* Working Paper.

Nwogugu, M. (2012). *Risk in the Global Real Estate Market.* John Wiley.

Nwogugu, M. (2013; revised 2019). *Complexity, Network-Decisions and Alternative Risk Premia: Some New Theories of Structural Change and Portfolio Decisions.* Retrieved from SSRN: https://ssrn.com/abstract=2991095 or https://doi.org/10.2139/ssrn.2991095.

Nwogugu, M. (2014d). "Netting", The Liquidity Coverage Ratio; and the US FSOC's Non-SIFI Criteria, And New Recommendations. *Banking Law Journal, 131*(6), 416–420.

Nwogugu, M. (2014e). REIT Shares/Interests are Derivatives Instruments; and REITs are SIFIs. *Pratt's Journal of Bankruptcy Law, 10*(3), 242–246.

Nwogugu, M. (2015a). Failure of the Dodd-Frank Act. *Journal of Financial Crime, 22*(4), 520–572.

Nwogugu, M. (2015b). Un-constitutionality of the Dodd-Frank Act. *European Journal of Law Reform, 17*, 185–190.

Nwogugu, M. (2015c). Real Options, Enforcement of Goodwill/Intangibles Rules and Associated Behavioral Issues. *Journal of Money Laundering Control, 18*(3), 330–351.

Nwogugu, M. (2021). Models of Willingness-to-Comply: Internal-Controls and the Failures of Sarbanes-Oxley Act, the Dodd-Frank Act, and the PCAOB (USA) and Similar Institutions. In M. Nwogugu (Ed.), *Complex Systems and Sustainability in the Global Auditing, Consulting, and Credit Rating Agency Industries.* IGI Global Publishers.

Ochsen, C., & Welsch, H. (2012). Who Benefits from Labor Market Institutions? Evidence from Surveys of Life Satisfaction. *Journal of Economic Psychology, 33*(1), 112–124.

Pautz, M. C. (2009). Sarbanes-Oxley and the Relentless Pursuit of Government Accountability: The Perils of 21st-Century Reform. *Administration & Society, 41*, 651–673.

PCAOB (USA). (2009, November). *Board Approves Its 2010 Budget and Related Strategic Plan.* Retrieved from http://pcaobus.org/News/Releases/Pages/11302009_Approves_Budget.aspx.

Perino, M. (2002, October). *Enron's Legislative Aftermath: Some Reflections on the Deterrence Aspects of the Sarbanes-Oxley Act of 2002.* Working Paper Series, Center for Law & Economic Studies, Columbia Law School.

Piccioto, S. (2008). Constitutionalizing Multilevel Governance? *International Journal of Constitutional Law, 6*, 457–467.

Pillard, C. (2005). The Un-fulfilled Promise of the Constitution in Executive Hands. *Michigan Law Review, 103*, 676–686.

Pollock, A. (2007). *Reforming Sarbanes-Oxley*. AEI (USA). Retrieved from http://www.aei.org/speech/25803.

Poretti, P. (2009). *The Regulation of Subsidies Within the General Agreement on Trade in Services—Problems and Perspectives*. Kluwer Law International.

Recine, J. (2002). Examination of the White Collar Crime Penalty Enhancements in the Sarbanes Oxley Act. *American Criminal Law Review, 39*, 1535–1570.

Reiser, D. (2004). *Enron.org: Why Sarbanes-Oxley Will Not Ensure Comprehensive Nonprofit Accountability*. Brooklyn Law School, Public Law Research Paper No. 6.

Rezzy, O. (2007). Sarbanes-Oxley: Progressive Punishment for Regressive Victimization. *Houston Law Review, 44*(1), 95–105.

Ribstein, L. (2002). Market versus Regulatory Responses to Corporate Fraud: A Critique of Sarbanes-Oxley Act of 2002. *Journal of Corporation Law, 28*(1), 56.

Ribstein, L. (2003, October). International Implications of Sarbanes Oxley: Raising the Rent on US Law. *Journal of Corporate Law Studies*, 299–309.

Romano, R. (2004). The Sarbanes-Oxley Act and the Making of Quack Corporate Governance. *Yale Law Journal, 114*, 1521.

Rose, P. (2005). Balancing Public Market Benefits and Burdens for Smaller Public Companies Post Sarbanes-Oxley. *Williamette Law Review, 41*, 707–736.

Russell, K. (2010, June 28). *Provision of Sarbanes-Oxley Un-constitutionally Interferes with Presidential Authority*. Retrieved from http://www.scotusblog.com/2010/06/provision-of-sarbanes-oxley-unconstitutionally-interferes-with-presidential-authority/.

Salky, S. & Rosman, A. (2004). *Is Sarbanes Oxley Vulnerable to Constitutional Challenge?* Retrieved from http://www.zuckerman.com/files/Publication/375468a3-d518-43e5-a6da-63474799822c/Presentation/PublicationAttachment/50441453-cd29-4d49-8dae-b030df75c042/media.88.pdf.

Sarbanes-Oxley Act of 2002, Pub. L. No. 107-204, 116 Stat. 745 (Codified at Various Sections of 11, 15, 18, 28, and 29 U.S.C. (Supp. III 2003)).

Schaumann, N. (2004). The Sarbanes Oxley Act: Bird's Eye View. *William Mitchell Law Review, 30*(4), 1316–1336. Retrieved from http://www.wmitchell.edu/lawreview/Volume30/Issue4/5Schaumann.pdf.

Schiller, J. (2008). Deterring Obstruction of Justice Efficiently: The Impact of Arthur Andersen and the Sarbanes-Oxley Act. *NYU Annual Survey of American Law, 63*, 267–277.

Schmidt, M. (2005). "Whistle Blowing Regulation" and Accounting Standards Enforcement in Germany and Europe: An Economic Perspective. *International Review of Law & Economics, 25*, 143–168.

Schniter, E., Shields, T., & Sznycer, D. (2020). Trust in Humans and Robots: Economically Similar but Emotionally Different. *Journal of Economic Psychology, 78*, 102253.

Sedler, R. A. (1985). The Negative Commerce Clause as a Restriction on State Regulation and Taxation: An Analysis in Terms of Constitutional Structure. *Wayne Law Review, 31*, 885–895.

Shapiro, I., & Cushman, T. (2009, December 5). *Peekaboo, I See a Constitutional Violation*. Retrieved from http://www.cato.org/pub_display.php?pub_id=11033.

Skouvakis, A. (2005). Note: Exiting the Public Markets—A difficult Choice for Small Public Companies Struggling with Sarbanes-Oxley. *Penn State Law Review, 109*, 1279–1289.

Soederberg, S. (2008). A Critique of the Diagnosis and Cure for 'Enronitis': The Sarbanes-Oxley Act and Neo-Liberal Governance of Corporate America. *Critical Sociology, 34*, 657–680.

Tackett, J., Wolf, F., & Claypool, G. (2004). Sarbanes-Oxley and Audit Failure. *Managerial Auditing Journal, 19*(3), 340–350.

Tackett, J., Wolf, F., & Claypool, G. (2006). Internal Control Under Sarbanes Oxley: A Critical Examination. *Managerial Auditing Journal, 21*(3), 317–323.

Tate, C. (1990). The Constitutionality of State Attempts to Regulate Foreign Investment. *Yale Law Journal, 99*, 2023–2042.

Taylor, C. R. (2006). Breaking the Bank: Reconsidering Central Bank of Denver after Enron and Sarbanes-Oxley. *Missouri Law Review, 71*, 368–388.

Torgler, B., & Schneider, F. (2009). The Impact of Tax Morale and Institutional Quality on the Shadow Economy. *Journal of Economic Psychology, 30*(2), 228–245.

Trujillo, E. (2010). International Trade and the Financial Crisis. *Proceedings of the Annual Meeting (American Society of International Law), 104*, 438–443.

Tushnet, M. (2003). The Issue of State Action/Horizontal Effect in Comparative Constitutional Law. *International Journal of Constitutional Law, 1*(1), 79–98.

Udeh, I. (2017). Disclosure Effects of the PCAOB Part II Reports. *Journal of Accounting & Organizational Change, 13*(4), 568–580.

Unger, C. J. (2007). Section 1103 of the Sarbanes-Oxley Act. *Western New England Law Review, 29*, 231–241.

Vancea, M. (2005). Exporting US Corporate Governance Standards Through the Sarbanes Oxley Act: Unilateralism or Cooperation ? *Duke Law Journal, 53*, 833–844.

Verdier, P. (2009). Transnational Regulatory Networks and Their Limits. *Yale Journal of International Law, 34*, 113–123.

Wade, C. L. (2008). The Sarbanes-Oxley Act and Ethical Corporate Climates: What the Media Reports; What the General Public Knows. *Brooklyn Journal of Corporate and Commercial Law, 2*, 421–431.

Wang, X. (2010). Increased Disclosure Requirements and Corporate Governance Decisions: Evidence from Chief Financial Officers in the Pre- and Post-Sarbanes-Oxley Periods. *Journal of Accounting Research, 48*, 885–920.

Witt, U., & Schubert, C. (2009). Constitutional Interests in the Face of Innovations: How Much Do We Need to Know About Risk Preferences? *Constitutional Political Economy, 9*(3), 203–225.

Zhang, I. (2007). Economic Consequences of the Sarbanes–Oxley Act of 2002. *Journal of Accounting & Economics, 44*(1–2), 74–115.

CHAPTER 6

Complex Systems, Pandemics/Epidemics and the *Welfare-State*, Part-1: "*Policy-Contagion*" And *Cross-Border Spillovers*

During the last four hundred years, different types of pandemics/epidemics have wreaked havoc on the health, psyche, politics and economies of regions, nations and continents—see Appendix-1 herein and below for a list of global and regional pandemics/epidemics that occurred during the last few centuries. The grossly inadequate healthcare facilities and total lack of readiness by most governments in the face of COVID-19 indicates significant failures of political, economic and social welfare systems around the world. This chapter: i) discusses policy responses and *Policy-Contagion* worldwide, ii) introduces new theories and critiques existing economic/public policy approaches; iii) introduces possible channels of *Cross-Border Spillovers* and *Market-Integration* in financial markets, Information Markets, Labor markets, Commodities Markets (eg. food/agric products, metals, oil/gas; etc.) and Finished-Commodity-Products markets (eg. consumer durables; equipment; machine-parts; etc.).

Most (more than 93%) of this chapter was completed during the first week of April 2020 (and some information has changed since then).[1]

[1] Most (93%+) of this chapter was completed during the first week of April 2020—see: Nwogugu (2020a) which is available at https://ssrn.com/abstract=3569636 or https://doi.org/10.2139/ssrn.3569636. The subsequent events during April–September 2020 around the world and especially in the USA have confirmed most of the theories in this chapter. The unprecedented rises in the stock markets in the US, Japan and Europe during

M. I. C. Nwogugu, *Geopolitical Risk, Sustainability and "Cross-Border Spillovers" in Emerging Markets, Volume II*,
https://doi.org/10.1007/978-3-030-71419-2_6

However, during and up to November 2020, many of the countries that implemented welfare programs in March 2020 granted additional welfare benefits to their indigenes and domestic companies.

6.1 Existing Literature

On international trade dimensions of COVID-19, see Gruszczynski (2020) and Torsello and Winkler (2020). On the transmission of economic/political shocks, see: De Ferra et al. (2020), Milesi-Ferretti and Lane (2017) and Bayer et al. (2020).

Makin and Layton (2021) discussed risks and implications of global fiscal responses to COVID-19.

Nwogugu (2017) analyzed the validity of pricing models for, and factors that influence the valuation of fixed-income instruments (and associated volatility and Systemic Risk). In the COVID-19 pandemic context, government bond markets are critical because: (i) they are a major source of capital for national/state governments (and indirectly, companies) for the elimination of COVID-19 effects; (ii) in many countries (and especially in Emerging Markets countries), government bond markets finance substantial percentages of government expenditures, which in turn, constitute the majority of economic activity and cash in the national economy; (iii) government bond yields and credit ratings are often used as benchmarks for pricing domestic corporate bonds in many countries; (iv) government bond dynamics are major economic indicators and can cause or amplify *Cross-Border Spillover* effects, and also affects FDI and Foreign Aid. Zaremba et al. (2021) analyzed the effect of policy responses to the COVID-19 pandemic on bond market volatility, and found that: (i) government interventions reduced local sovereign bond volatility and that was driven by economic support policies; (ii) containment and closure or health regulations didn't have any major effect.

Singh et al. (2021) analyzed the effectiveness of Chinese and Russian policy interventions during financial/economic crises, and implications/lessons for the COVID-19 pandemic. Nwogugu (2015a, b) critiqued the

April 2020 to September 2020 were unsupported by the economic facts (most of the major economic indicators in those countries were deteriorating—such as unemployment, GDP, consumer confidence, business confidence, consumer debt, corporate profits and exports). These trends could be deemed to be evidence of Cross-Border Spillovers and or *international market-integration* in financial markets, labor markets and finished-commodity products.

Dodd-Frank Act (enacted in USA in response to financial/economic stresses and *Multiplier Effects*).

Asia remains a major global economic hub and has global *Multiplier Effects*, but was significantly affected by COVID-19 during 2020–2021. Hossain et al. (2021) and Kusuma et al. (2021) analyzed behavior-modification efforts and mental health effects of COVID-19 in Asia. Lisle (2021) analyzed the effects of COVID-19 in the context of U.S.-China-East Asia relations. Djalante et al. (2020) and ESCAP (2021) studied ASEAN policy responses to COVID-19. Fan et al. (2021) and Rasul (2021) discussed Food Security and Climate Change in Asia during the COVID-19 pandemic. Babu et al. (2021) confirmed low pandemic preparedness and response to COVID-19 in South Asian countries.

Like most other regions, Europe was unprepared for the COVID-19 pandemic which exposed weaknesses in the legal/economic/political structure of the EU (European Union), and created what could be deemed as constitutional political economy crisis pertaining to the allocation of powers, obligations and resources within the EU, and also complicated the issue of EU sovereign debt resolution (many European countries borrowed to finance COVID-19 remediation efforts). See: Tesche (2020) and Schmidt (2020). On political economy and Law & Economics issues pertaining to Euro area sovereign debt defaults, see: Heinemann (2021), Basu (2016), Copelovitch et al. (2016), Bénassy-Quéré et al. (2018), Wasserfallen et al. (2019) and Muellbauer (2013).

COVID-19 pandemic and associated government policies and economic/political events have partly or wholly contravened theories and conclusions in many IPE, Public Policy, MacroFinance and International Finance academic articles such as Chang and Fernandez (2013), Arellano (2008), Bayer et al. (2019), Cugat (2019), Sunel (2018), Auclert (2019), Auclert et al. (2018) and Milesi-Ferretti and Lane (2017).

On Economic Psychology issues, see: Haferkamp et al. (2009), Birz (2017), Dixon et al. (2014), Ochsen and Welsch (2012), Bavetta et al. (2020) and Torgler and Schneider (2009).

While pre-2019 epidemics/pandemics and COVID-19 have inflicted extensive damage on national economies, sustainability and human psyche/aspirations (and such harmful impacts are likely to be propagated globally into the future),[2] there should be increased efforts by researchers

[2] Especially through Multinational Corporations; international banks and insurance companies; cross-border swaps/derivatives; foreign companies

to include the dynamics, Constitutional Political Economy factors and *Multiplier Effects* of pandemics in quantitative models in published academic and practitioner research (i.e.. within the context of Behavioral Operations Research; sovereign debt crisis, VaR estimation; regulatory failure; Economic/Financial Crisis; sovereign debt crisis, Panel Vector Autoregressive models, Granger Causality, GARCH-type Models, financial markets regulation, Portfolio Management, Economic Modelling, Political Decisions, Behavioral Macroeconomics, Behavioral Expectations, Tail Risk; etc.).

6.1.1 Government's Statutory Emergency Powers, *Executive-Orders and New* Emergency Statutes *(During Pandemics and Crises) as Labor Regulations*

As of 2020, and in many countries, it was clear that the *legislative-intent*, history and wording of various "Emergency Powers statutes", new *Emergency Statutes* (such as the CARES Act in the US) and Presidential/ Governors' Emergency Executive Orders (applicable during epidemics/ pandemics and crises) evinced an intent to regulate, directly/indirectly affect, enact or modify the following:

1. Labor statutes.
2. Workers' rights and working conditions (sanitation, inoculation, lock-downs, travelling, employee-benefits, compensation, telecommuting, etc.).
3. Labor unions, industry associations and collective bargaining processes. That is, labor unions and industry associations are subject to state/municipal Executive Orders, regulations and agreements that pertain to pandemics/epidemics and economic/financial crises.
4. Trade agreements that have labor-market components.
5. Existing federal/state/local regulations (such as OSHA and its state- and municipal-level equivalents in the USA).
6. Consumers' perceptions of economic/financial crisis and/or epidemics/pandemics—which, in turn, can affect employee

whose shares/bonds are listed in foreign financial exchanges; labor mobility; regulatory-convergence; financial contagion; Cross-Border Spillovers in various dimensions; and so on.

morale, tax compliance, employee motivation, consumer confidence, business confidence and so on.
7. Labor mobility.
8. Employers' ability to recruit employees.
9. Employers' exposure to labor costs (employee salaries/commissions, employee taxes, employee benefits, other employee payment/deductions, social security taxes, etc.)—all of which can also affect workers' morale and motivation.
10. Allocation of labor resources across industries and industry-sectors.

See the comments in: Ochsen and Welsch (2012), Haferkamp, Fetchenhauer, et al. (2009), Diamond, McQuade and Qian (2019), Torgler and Schneider (2009), and Pántya, Kovács, et al. (2016).

6.1.2 Estimated Costs of COVID-19

During the first half of 2020, Researchers estimated that COVID-19 will cost nations[3] more than US$4 trillion (including the costs of reconstructing national economies, fixing disrupted supply chains, the costs of

[3] *See*: "*Coronavirus: Half a billion people could be pushed into poverty, says UN study Comments*". By Alasdair Sandford. April 09, 2020. https://www.euronews.com/2020/04/09/coronavirus-half-a-billion-people-could-be-pushed-into-poverty-says--un-study?utm_source=newsletter&utm_medium=en&utm_content=coronavirus-half-a-billion-people-could-be-pushed-into-poverty-says-un-study&_ope=eyJndWlkIjoiNTE4MWFhOTZjZmY5NjUxMTAzZTE2Y2Y1MGU1NDAwYTcifQ%3D%3D.

See: Sumner, A., Hoy, C. & Ortiz-Juarez, E. (2020). *Estimates of the impact of COVID-19 on global poverty.*

WIDER Working Paper 43/2020. UNU-WIDER. https://doi.org/10.35188/UNU-WIDER/2020/800-9. The abstract of this report states: "we make estimates of the potential short-term economic impact of COVID-19 on global monetary poverty through contractions in per capita household income or consumption. Our estimates are based on three scenarios: low, medium, and high global contractions of 5, 10, and 20 per cent; we calculate the impact of each of these scenarios on the poverty headcount using the international poverty lines of US$1.90, US$3.20 and US$5.50 per day. Our estimates show that COVID poses a real challenge to the UN Sustainable Development Goal of ending poverty by 2030 because global poverty could increase for the first time since 1990 and, depending on the poverty line, such increase could represent a reversal of approximately a decade in the world's progress in reducing poverty. In some regions, the adverse impacts could result in poverty levels similar to those recorded 30 years ago. Under the most extreme scenario of a 20 per cent income or consumption contraction, the number of people living in poverty could increase by 420–580 million, relative to the latest official recorded figures for 2018".

borrowing, treatment costs, and assistance to families and businesses; and perhaps even the restructuring of international organizations such as World Health Organization). See the comments in Gruszczynski (2020), Torsello and Winkler (2020), and Broberg (2020). A March 2020 survey by Aljazeera[4] stated that 70% (seventy percent) of indigenes of G7 countries (Canada, France, Germany, Italy, Japan, the United Kingdom and the United States) expect that their household will lose income because of COVID-19. During March 2020, the OECD[5] warned that the COVID-19 pandemic is creating a global economic downturn and reduced economic growth not seen since 2009. During February–March 2020, large US retailing chains[6] laid off or furloughed hundreds of thousands of workers and closed more than 9300 stores.

6.2 Geopolitical Risks and Some *International Market-Integration* and *Cross-Border Spillover Effects* of Pandemics

Pandemics are major geopolitical risks because:

1. They can have significant negative social, economic, psychological, political and environmental consequences (as clearly illustrated by the COVID-19 pandemic of 2019–present, and other pandemics).
2. There are significant differences in compliance rates and penalties around the world (compliance with public health standards and statutes/regulations for emergencies and pandemics).

[4] *See*: "*70 percent of G7 households expect to be made poorer by virus—Household incomes are being affected as cities enforce lockdowns, shutting businesses and factories, a survey showed*". March 25, 2020. https://www.aljazeera.com/ajimpact/70-percent-g7-households-expect--poorer-virus-200325060436759.html?utm_source=website&utm_medium=article_page&utm_campaign=read_more_links

[5] *See*: "*Virus Plunging Economy Into Worst Downturn Since 2009, OECD warns—Ringing recession alarm, OECD Urges Coronavirus Affected Countries To Take Necessary Measures As Quickly As Possible*". https://www.aljazeera.com/ajimpact/virus-plunging-economy-worst-downturn-2009-oecd-warns-200302205312855.html

[6] *See*: Kelly, J. (March 31, 2020). *Hundreds Of Thousands Of Retail Workers Are Losing Their Jobs Due To Coronavirus*. https://www.forbes.com/sites/jackkelly/2020/03/31/hundreds-of-thousands-of-workers-are-losing-their-jobs-in-a-coronavirus-induced-retail-apocalypse/#3bf466113184

3. Countries and even states/regions respond differently to pandemics—in terms of regulations, economic policies, lock-downs, reactions of indigenes, constitutional law issues, and so on.
4. There are significant differences in regulation and new legislation around the world and that is sometimes a function of the existing political system in the country.
5. There can be different rates of mutation of viruses/bacteria around the world.
6. The impact of pandemics on infrastructure, quality-of-life, consumer confidence, business confidence, corporate expenditures, government expenditures and critical systems can vary dramatically around the world and is sometimes a function of the existing political system in the country.
7. There are, or there can be significant differences in the reactions of stock, bond, currency and commodity markets to pandemics in various countries.
8. Only the uncertainty and anxiety caused by a pandemic is sufficient to crash stock markets, bond markets and exchange rates, as illustrated by the COVID-19 pandemic of 2019-present (especially during January–April 2020).
9. Pandemics affect international capital flows, international trade, foreign aid, FDI and foreign investment.
10. Pandemic affect and sometimes temporarily shutdown large-scale computer systems—which in Epidemics/Pandemics, often break down because they are overloaded with requests, transactions and filings during pandemics.[7]

[7] See: "*Our Government Runs On A 60-Year-Old Coding Language, And Now It's Falling Apart—Retired Engineers Are Coming To The Rescue*". By Dave Gershgorn. April 8, 2020. https://onezero.medium.com/our-government-runs-on-a-60-year-old-coding-language-and-now-its-falling-apart-61ec0bc8e121.

See: "*Unemployment websites from Oregon to NY Are Crashing Under The Weight Of The Coronavirus Crisis*" *(USA)*. March 18, 2020. By Christopher Zara. https://www.fastcompany.com/90478927/unemployment-websites-from-oregon-to-ny-are-crashing-under-the-weight-of-the-coronavirus-crisis.

See: "*SBA Computer System Crash; Further Tangles PPP Loan Process*" *(USA)*. By PYMNTS. April 7, 2020. https://www.pymnts.com/loans/2020/sba-computer-system-crash-further-tangles-ppp-loan-process/

See: "*Will Coronavirus Crash the Internet?—With most of the world now working from home, an increased need for speed could break the whole system*". By Caroline Delbert. Mar 23, 2020. https://www.popularmechanics.com/science/a31862370/coronavirus-covid-19-crash-internet/.

The significant associated healthcare and public health issues are that: i) the frequency of pandemics has increased during the last few decades; and ii) modern germs have a higher probability of mutating into new and more drug-resistant types of germs due to their interactions with drugs and chemical-laden air/environment (air pollution has increased in most countries during the last fifty years); iii) populations and the percentage of the poor, and the percentages of people without access to proper healthcare, have increased in most countries during the last forty years, iv) the percentages of senior citizens (who are more susceptible to pandemics) and people that have pre-existing conditions have also increased during the last forty years in most countries; v) many or most countries still don't have adequate healthcare facilities that can handle emergencies and pandemics; vi) as of March 2020, more than 2.8 billion people around the world were subject to COVID-19 lock-downs or quarantines and that was likely to cause short-term and long-term psychological/psychiatric problems, economic losses and major changes in modes of socialization and communication. Figure 6.1 shows the number of people affected by COVID-19 Lock-Downs around the world as of March 2020—and those amounts have increased significantly since September 2020.

One would think that by the twenty-first century and in both developed and developing countries, corporate boards of directors, educational administrators, central planners and government regulators would have built pandemics into their economics models, legal/economic reforms, legal infrastructure, contingency plans, manpower/training plans, internet infrastructure plans, public physical visual-surveillance systems, insurance provisions/regulations and budgets. Sadly and shockingly, that has not occurred—if adequate plans were in place, there should not be any need to enact new legislation and/or draconian monetary/fiscal/social-welfare/labor policies in response to pandemics.

See: "Popular remote working tool Microsoft Teams Crashes in Europe on the first day millions of people login from home to prevent coronavirus spread" (UK). By Joe Pinkstone. March 16, 2020. https://www.dailymail.co.uk/sciencetech/article-8116325/Microsoft-Teams-CRASHES-Europe-millions-workers-work-home-avoid-coronavirus.html.

See: "European Green Deal suffers delays over COVID-19 impact: report". March 19, 2020 (European Union). https://balkangreenenergynews.com/european-green-deal-suffers-delays-over-covid-19-impact-report/.

See: "COVID-19 welfare splash crashes MyGov website, spurs frenzied back-pedalling". By David Binning. March 23, 2020 (Australia). https://www.cio.com/article/3533359/covid-19-welfare-splash-crashes-mygov-website-spurs-frenzied-backpedalling.html

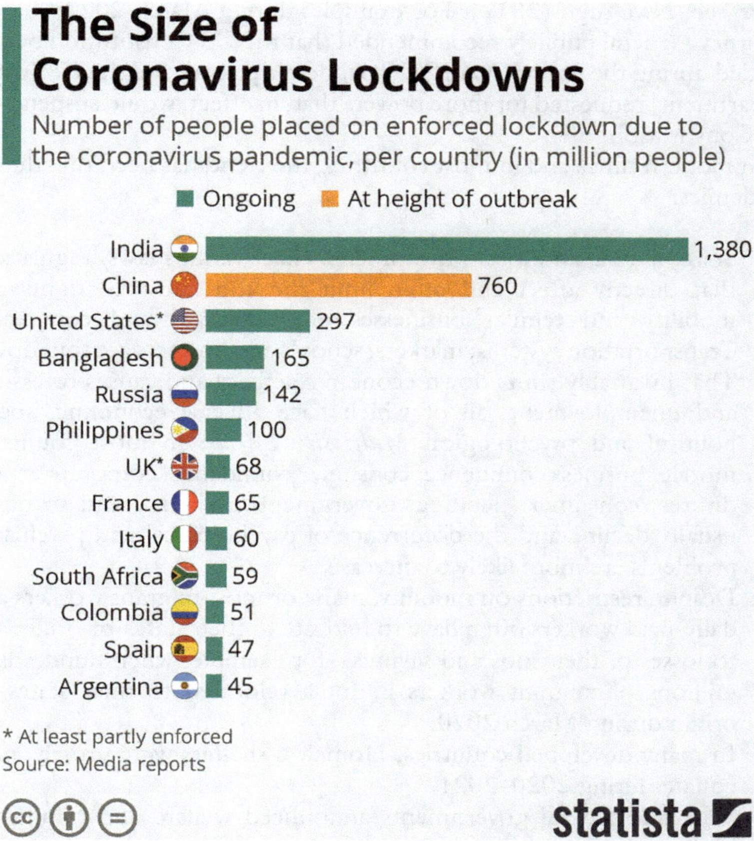

Fig. 6.1 Number of People Affected by COVID-19 Lock-Downs Around the World (in millions; March 2020). Source: https://www.weforum.org/agenda/2020/04/this-is-the-psychological-side-of-the-covid-19-pandemic-that-were-ignoring/?fbclid=IwAR0wbL-VSQUVeKybVsQZ2WrHXsrsI9h-ISDPNUqeqSbdh0X4Gqyp8lgPG4A

In modern times, most pandemics raise significant Constitutional Law and Constitutional Political Economy issues partly because of the resulting mandatory restrictions imposed by governments and businesses, the political negotiations and the resulting economic/financial damage. Such Constitutional Law problems can evolve into expensive *constitutional tort* claims against federal, state and/or local governments. On *Constitutional*

Torts, see: Nwogugu (2012). For example, during March 2020, the US Attorney General publicly recommended that the US Constitution be suspended during the entire COVID-19 pandemic period, and the US Justice Department[8] requested for more powers that, in effect, would suspend the US Constitution.

In modern times and in most countries, the trend has been that during pandemics:

- State, federal and local governments enact various laws/regulations that directly affect and often limit the constitutional rights and mobility and regular businesses of individuals and companies. Transportation systems, markets, schools and business are shut down.
- That invariably shuts down economic activity and causes recessions and unemployment, all of which have adverse economic, social, political and psychological *Multiplier Effects*. In most countries, morale, business confidence, consumer confidence, corporate expenditures, consumer spending, government credibility and so on all usually decline and the occurrence of psychological and psychiatric problems are more likely to increase.
- Despite restrictions on mobility, many or most migrant workers and daily-paid workers often have to relocate to their states-of-origin due to losses of their jobs and savings—for example, when hundreds of millions of migrant workers in India relocated to their states-of-origin during March 2020.
- In many developed countries, Homeless shelters were grossly inadequate during 2020–2021.
- State and federal governments announced welfare and "stimulus" packages, often without analyzing necessary pre-requisite economic and legal reforms, incentives, effectiveness of stimulus and long-term consequences.
- Central banks of many countries announced rate-cuts and bond purchase programs which usually have minimal positive effects, and

[8] *See*: "*DOJ Wants to Suspend Certain Constitutional Rights During Coronavirus Emergency—The Department of Justice has secretly asked Congress for the ability to detain arrested people "indefinitely" in addition to other powers that one expert called "terrifying""*. By Peter Wade. https://www.rollingstone.com/politics/politics-news/doj-suspend-constitutional-rights-coronavirus-970935/.

See: "*Justice Department Reportedly Asks Congress for Indefinite Detention Powers To Fight Coronavirus—Congress should loudly and unanimously reject this insanity*". By Eric Boehm. March 21, 2020. See:

most stock markets decline significantly due to uncertainty and perceived future negative effects on economic activity.

- The values of the currencies of many emerging markets countries (especially countries whose economies are linked to major economies such as the US or China) usually decline significantly.
- In most countries, the healthcare systems and facilities are almost always inadequate, overburdened and total unprepared.
- Supply chains and supplies of food and consumer durables are severely disrupted.
- Consumer debt and incidences of mental health problems usually increase.

6.3 The Welfare Packages of January–March 2020 (Which Affected Financial, Labor, Information, Commodities and Finished-Commodity-Goods Markets)

A summary of the economic stimulus packages[9] that were announced by various countries during January–March 2020 and in response to COVID-19 is listed herein and below (the data was current as of late March 2020, and after March 2020, the US government and other national governments enacted and implemented additional aid programs). These stimulus programs could have directly and indirectly affected financial, Labor, Information, commodities and Finished-Commodity-Goods markets around the world.

6.3.1 *Coordinated Economic Policy Responses*[10]

The following are summaries of some coordinated multi-nation and/or multi-organization stimulus packages that were announced during January–March 2020:

[9] *See*: "*Government Stimulus Efforts to Fight the COVID-19 Crisis—Here's what governments are doing to stimulate their economies*". By Gabe Alpert. Updated Mar 27, 2020. https://www.investopedia.com/government-stimulus-efforts-to-fight-the-covid-19-crisis-4799723

[10] *See*: European Central Bank (March 2020). "*Coordinated Central Bank Action To Enhance The Provision Of Global US Dollar Liquidity*". https://www.ecb.europa.eu/press/pr/date/2020/html/ecb.pr200315~1fab6a9f1f.en.html.

1. During March 2020, the central banks of Canada, the UK, Japan, the U.S., Switzerland and the European Central Bank all agreed to lower the price of US dollar liquidity swap line arrangements (which makes it easier and cheaper to borrow money in dollars outside the U.S.).
2. During March 2020, the IMF announced that it was ready to provide up to $1 trillion in loans to help its members.
3. During March 2020, the World Bank announced an initial package of up to $12 billion in loans for countries ($8 billion of the funding is new loans and the remaining $4 billion was re-allocated from current lines of credit).
4. During March 2020, the International Monetary Fund made $50 billion in loans available to deal with the coronavirus, including $10 billion of zero-interest loans to the poorest IMF member countries.
5. During March 2020, the US Federal Reserve announced that it is establishing dollar liquidity swaps with the central banks of Australia, Brazil, Denmark, South Korea, New Zealand, Singapore and Sweden.
6. During April 2020, Asian Development Bank announced that it had increased its reserves/provisions for the COVID-19 Pandemic to US$20 billion.

6.3.2 United States[11] (March 2020)

1. During March 2020, the US Federal Reserve announced the following monetary stimulus:

See: Federal Reserve, "*Federal Reserve Announces The Establishment Of Temporary U.S. Dollar Liquidity Arrangements With Other Central Banks*". https://www.federalreserve.gov/newsevents/pressreleases/monetary20200319b.htm.

See: International Monetary Fund (March 2020). "*IMF Makes Available $50 Billion to Help Address Coronavirus*". https://www.imf.org/en/News/Articles/2020/03/04/sp030420-imf-makes-available-50-billion-to-help-address-coronavirus.

See: IMF Blog (March 2020). "*Policy Action for a Healthy Global Economy*". https://blogs.imf.org/2020/03/16/policy-action-for-a-healthy-global-economy/.

See: The World Bank (March 2020). "World Bank Group Announces Up to $12 Billion Immediate Support for COVID-19 Country Response," https://www.worldbank.org/en/news/press-release/2020/03/03/world-bank-group-announces-up-to-12-billion-immediate-support-for-covid-19-country-response

[11] *See*: White House. "*Bill Announcement*". https://www.whitehouse.gov/briefings-statements/bill-announcement-84/.

See: Wall Street Journal (March 2020). "*President Trump Signs Coronavirus Spending Bill*". https://www.wsj.com/articles/trump-signs-8-3-billion-spending-bill-to-combat-coronavirus-11583506305?mod=article_inline.

See: New York Times (March 2020). "*House Passes Coronavirus Relief After Democrats Strike Deal With White House*". https://www.nytimes.com/2020/03/13/us/politics/trump-coronavirus-relief-congress.html.

See: Wall Street Journal (March 2020). "*Trump Declares National Emergency to Confront Coronavirus*". https://www.wsj.com/articles/coronavirus-strikes-key-figures-in-politics-sports-as-infections-spread-globally-11584093470?mod=hp_lead_pos1.

See: ABC News. "*Administration Announces 90-Day Delay For Many Tax Payments*". https://abcnews.go.com/US/wireStory/administration-announces-90-day-delay-tax-payments-69649907.

See: Wall Street Journal (March 2020). "*U.S. Seeks to Send Checks to Americans as Part of Stimulus Package*". https://www.wsj.com/articles/trump-administration-seeking-850-billion-stimulus-package-11584448802?mod=hp_lead_pos1.

See: Politico (March 2020). "*Democrats say Mnuchin squeezed paid sick leave program*". https://www.politico.com/news/2020/03/17/sick-leave-coronavirus-package-congress-134101.

See: CNN (March 2020). "*Trump Signs Coronavirus Relief Legislation Into Law*". https://www.cnn.com/2020/03/18/politics/coronavirus-congress-relief-senate-house/index.html.

See: Axios (March 2020). "*Senate passes House coronavirus relief package with no changes*". https://www.axios.com/senate-passes-house-coronavirus-relief-package-d0850224-11dc-44d9-84d8-929f2a1d6477.html.

See: Washington Post (March 2020). "*Senate Republicans Release Massive Economic Stimulus Bill For Coronavirus Response*". https://www.washingtonpost.com/business/2020/03/19/trump-coronavirus-economic-plan-stimulus/.

See: U.S. Department of Education (March 2020). "*Delivering on President Trump's Promise, Secretary DeVos Suspends Federal Student Loan Payments, Waives Interest During National Emergency*". https://www.ed.gov/news/press-releases/delivering-president-trumps-promise-secretary-devos-suspends-federal-student-loan-payments--waives-interest-during-national-emergency.

See: Speaker.Gov (March 2020). "*Pelosi Statement Ahead of Unveiling of Democrats' Third Coronavirus Response Bill*". https://www.speaker.gov/newsroom/32320.

See: Appropriations.House.Gov (March 2020). "*The Take Responsibility for Workers & Families Act*". https://appropriations.house.gov/sites/democrats.appropriations.house.gov/files/Take%20Responsibility%20for%20Workers%20%20Families%20Act%20one%20pager.pdf.

See: Wall Street Journal (March 2020). "*Historic $2 Trillion Coronavirus Aid Package Nears Finish Line in Congress*". https://www.wsj.com/articles/trump-administration-senate-democrats-said-to-reach-stimulus-bill-deal-11585113371.

See: NBC (March 2020). "*Senate passes massive $2 trillion coronavirus spending bill*". https://www.nbcnews.com/politics/congress/white-house-senate-reach-deal-massive-2-trillion-coronavirus-spending-n1168136.

See: New York Times (March 2020). "*Senate Approves $2 Trillion Stimulus After Bipartisan Deal*". https://www.nytimes.com/2020/03/25/us/politics/coronavirus-senate-deal.html.

- On March 3, 2020, the US Federal Reserve reduced the Fed funds rate by 0.5%, which was the largest cut since the 2008 financial crisis.

See: Wall Street Journal (March 2020). "*What's in the $2 Trillion Senate Coronavirus Bill*". https://www.wsj.com/articles/whats-in-the-2-trillion-senate-coronavirus-bill-11585185450?tesla=yamp;mod=article_inline.

See: Wall Street Journal (March 2020). "*House Passes $2 Trillion Coronavirus Stimulus Package*". https://www.wsj.com/articles/house-lawmakers-race-to-washington-to-ensure-coronavirus-stimulus-passes-11585318472.

See: New York Times (March 2020). "*Trump signs $2 trillion stimulus plan, clearing way for checks for Americans*". https://www.nytimes.com/2020/03/27/world/coronavirus-news.html?action=clickamp;module=Spotlightamp;pgtype=Homepage.

See: Federal Reserve (March 2020). "*Commercial Paper Funding Facility 2020: Program Terms and Conditions*". https://www.federalreserve.gov/newsevents/pressreleases/files/monetary20200317a1.pdf.

See: Federal Reserve (March 2020). "*Commercial Paper Funding Facility (CPFF)*". https://www.federalreserve.gov/regreform/reform-cpff.htm.

See: Federal Reserve (March 2020). "*Federal Reserve Board announces establishment of a Primary Dealer Credit Facility (PDCF) to support the credit needs of households and businesses*". https://www.federalreserve.gov/newsevents/pressreleases/monetary20200317b.htm.

See: Federal Reserve (March 2020). "*Term Sheet for Primary Dealer Credit Facility (PDCF)*". Pages 1 and 2. https://www.federalreserve.gov/newsevents/pressreleases/files/monetary20200317b1.pdf.

See: Federal Reserve (March 2020). "*Money Market Mutual Fund Liquidity Facility*". https://www.federalreserve.gov/newsevents/pressreleases/files/monetary20200318a1.pdf.

See: New York Fed (March 2020). "*Statement Regarding Treasury Securities and Agency Mortgage-Backed Securities Operations*". https://www.newyorkfed.org/markets/opolicy/operating_policy_200323.

See: Federal Reserve (March 2020). "*Federal Reserve announces extensive new measures to support the economy*". https://www.federalreserve.gov/newsevents/pressreleases/monetary20200323b.htm.

See: Federal Reserve (March 2020). "*Primary Market Corporate Credit Facility*". https://www.federalreserve.gov/newsevents/pressreleases/files/monetary20200323b1.pdf.

See: Federal Reserve (March 2020). "*Secondary Market Corporate Credit Facility*". https://www.federalreserve.gov/newsevents/pressreleases/files/monetary20200323b2.pdf.

See: Federal Reserve (March 2020). "*Term Asset-Backed Securities Loan Facility*". https://www.federalreserve.gov/newsevents/pressreleases/files/monetary20200323b3.pdf.

See: Board of Governors of the Federal Reserve System (March 2020). "*Federal Reserve issues FOMC statement*". https://www.federalreserve.gov/newsevents/pressreleases/monetary20200315a.htm.

See: Federal Reserve (March 2020). "*Federal Reserve Actions to Support the Flow of Credit to Households and Businesses*". https://www.federalreserve.gov/newsevents/pressreleases/monetary20200315b.htm.

See: Federal Reserve Bank of New York (March 2020). "Statement Regarding Repurchase Operations". https://www.newyorkfed.org/markets/opolicy/operating_policy_200316.

- On March 12, the US Fed massively expanded its reverse repo operations (added $1.5 trillion of liquidity to the banking system—extended short-term loans to banks to increase liquidity and stability).

2. During March 2020, the Federal Reserve announced the following additional monetary stimulus:

- Reduced interest rates by 1% to a range of 0.00% to 0.25%.
- Re-started quantitative easing (QE) with the purchase of $500 billion in US Treasury and $200 billion in mortgage-backed securities.
- Reduced the interest rate on the discount window by 1.5% to 0.25%.
- Reduced bank reserve requirements to zero.
- Encouraged banks to use their capital and liquidity buffers to lend.
- Increased its reverse repo operations by another $500 billion on March 16.
- On March 17, introduced two new programs to help preserve market liquidity:

  – The one-year *Commercial Paper Funding Facility* (CPFF) which allows the Fed to create a corporation which can purchase commercial paper, short-term, unsecured loans made by businesses for everyday expenses. The Treasury authorized up to $10 billion from the Treasury's Exchange Stabilization Fund (ESF) to help cover loan losses incurred under this program.
  – The six-month Primary Dealer Credit Facility (PDCF) which will offer short-term loans to banks secured by collateral such as municipal bonds or investment-grade corporate debt.

3. During March 18, the Federal Reserve announced the *Money Market Mutual Fund Liquidity Facility* (MMLF), to lend money to banks so they can purchase assets from money market funds (the

See: U.S. Treasury Department (March 2020). "*Statement from Secretary Steven T. Mnuchin on the Establishment of a Commercial Paper Funding Facility to Support the Flow of Credit to Households and Businesses*". https://home.treasury.gov/news/press-releases/sm944.

See: Federal Reserve Bank of New York (March 2020). "*Statement Regarding Treasury Reserve Management Purchases and Repurchase Operations*". https://www.newyorkfed.org/markets/opolicy/operating_policy_200312a

US Treasury offered up to $10 billion to cover loan losses that the US Fed will incur from the program).

4. On March 23, the Federal Reserve announced additional monetary stimulus including the following:

   - Expanded its asset purchases of both treasuries and mortgage-backed securities by an additional $625 billion.
   - Made agency commercial mortgage-backed securities eligible for purchase.
   - Creation of the *Primary Market Corporate Credit Facility* (PMCCF) to buy bonds and banks' corporate loans.
   - Creation of the *Secondary Market Corporate Credit Facility* (SMCCF) which will purchase bonds and bond ETFs (exchange-traded funds) in order to provide liquidity.
   - Re-establishment of the *Term Asset-Backed Securities Loan Facility* (TALF) to purchase asset-backed securities backed by auto loans, student loans or small business loans.
   - The foregoing special-purpose vehicles (CPFF, MMLF, TALF, SMCCF and PMCCF) would provide up to $300 billion in new financing and will operate until September 30, 2020, unless extended, and the US Treasury Department will cover up to $10 billion in loan losses by each of TALF, SMCCF or PMCCF from the ESF.
   - Expansion of the MMLF to include more different types of money market funds.
   - Expansion of the CPFF to include a wider variety of commercial paper assets, and a reduction in the interest rates for loans from the CPFF.
   - Creation of a "Main Street Business Lending Program" to support small and medium businesses.

5. On March 6, 2020, President Trump signed an $8.3 billion spending bill (the "Phase One" *stimulus package*) which consisted of the following:

   - Funds for vaccine research for COVID-19.
   - Funds for state and local governments to fight the spread of COVID-19.
   - Funds to help stop the spread of COVID-19 overseas.

6. On March 18, the US Congress enacted the "Phase Two" *stimulus package* that included, among other things:

   - Free testing for COVID-19.
   - Increased unemployment benefits.
   - Additional cash for the Medicaid insurance program.
   - A provision requiring paid sick leave for some workers affected by COVID-19.

7. During March 2020, President Trump announced a state of emergency, which made available up to $50 billion in aid to states, cities and territories.
8. During March 2020, Treasury Secretary Steven Mnuchin extended the deadline for filing individual and corporate tax returns by 90 days (he estimated that will free up $300 billion in extra liquidity during the ninety-day period) and individuals and companies can delay taxes up to $1 million and $10 million respectively.
9. During March 2020, the US Secretary of Education Betsy DeVos announced that "All borrowers with federally held student loans will automatically have their interest rates set to 0% for a period of at least 60 days. In addition, each of these borrowers will have the option to suspend their payments for at least two months."
10. On March 27, 2020, the President Trump and the US Congress enacted the *Phase-3 stimulus package*, and it included the following among other things:

    - $301 billion in direct cash payments, totaling $1200 for those earning up to $75,000 and $500 per child.
    - $600 a week in additional unemployment for 4 months.
    - $350 billion in small business loans.
    - Significantly greater oversight for the $500 billion in loans to corporations (which was originally to be disbursed at the discretion of the US Treasury Department). It will be overseen by an inspector general and a congressional panel.
    - $150 billion to state and local governments.
    - A ban on stock-buybacks and dividends for companies that receive government loans for as long as the loans last plus a year; and such companies shall not make layoffs for six months.

- $250 billion to expand unemployment insurance to include gig and freelance workers, increase the length of unemployment payments to thirty-nine weeks, and add $600 dollars a week for four months.
- $221 billion in business tax cuts (allows businesses to defer payroll taxes for the rest of 2020 and temporarily allows businesses to claim deductions for current losses against past profits to claim refunds).
- US$130 billion for hospitals and other healthcare providers.
- US$25 billion for public transit to make up for lost revenue.
- US$32 billion in cash grants to cover wages at airlines, airlines that that receive the money cannot issue dividends or make stock buybacks, in addition they cannot make furloughs or pay cuts through September. Executive pay is also capped.
- US$48 billion for agriculture and nutrition programs
- US$27 billion to fund drugs and vaccines for the coronavirus
- US$10 billion for the postal service to help cope with problems caused by the pandemic.
- The bill requires companies that service federally backed mortgages to grant a forbearance of up to 360 days to borrowers hurt by the virus, in addition they cannot start or process foreclosures or foreclosure-related evictions for a sixty-day period backdated to March.
- Owners of multifamily properties who have federally backed mortgages can get a forbearance for ninety days, on the condition that they do not evict tenants for nonpayment of rent or fees.
- Student loan payments will be suspended without interest accruing until September.
- The bill extends the repayment time people going through bankruptcy to repay part of their debt from five to seven years, and ensures that people filing for bankruptcy don't have to use their stimulus check to pay past debts.
- The bill delays a new accounting rule that would require banks to hold more capital and allows the comptroller of currency to allow banks to make larger loans than normal. Banks with under US$10 billion in assets will have a higher maximum leverage ratios.
- Banks will also get more leeway to work with borrowers who are falling behind on payments on consumer loans.
- Waives early withdrawal penalties for 401(k) of up to US$100,000.

6.3.3 *China*[12] *(March 2020)*

China's fiscal policy response to COVID-19 was far smaller (in scope and amount) than its response in 2008 during the global financial crisis or again in 2015 when its economic growth slowed substantially. During February–March 2020, the Chinese government announced an economic stimulus package that included the following:

1. The PBOC reduced one-year medium-term lending facility rate (for its loans to banks) by 0.10% in February 2020; and then reduced its one-year and five-year prime rates by 0.10% and 0.05%, respectively.
2. During February 2020, the PBOC expanded its reverse repo operations by US$174 billion (increased/extended loans to increase stability and liquidity in fixed income markets).
3. Again during February 2020, the PBOC expanded its reverse repo operations by another US$71 billion.
4. During March 2020, the PBOC lowered bank reserve requirements (increased bank lending capacity by about US$79 billion).
5. During March/April 2020, the Chinese government announced fiscal measures (a welfare package) of US$184 billion which includes additional healthcare spending, tax relief and unemployment insurance.

[12] *See*: Hong Kong (March 2020). The 2020–21 Budget. "Relieve Burden," https://www.budget.gov.hk/2020/eng/nt.html.

See: Xinhua. "China's central bank injects more liquidity into market amid Pandemic battle," http://www.xinhuanet.com/english/2020-02/03/c_138752041.htm.

See: The People's Bank of China (2020). "Announcement of Open Market Operations No.19 [2020]," http://www.pbc.gov.cn/en/3688110/3688181/3967540/index.html.

See: CNBC (Feb. 2020). "China cuts benchmark lending rates amid coronavirus outbreak," https://www.cnbc.com/2020/02/20/coronavirus-chinas-pboc-cuts-benchmark--lending-rate-loan-prime-rate.html.

See: Reuters (2020). "China pumps $79 billion into economy with bank cash reserve cut," https://www.reuters.com/article/us-china-economy-rrr-cut/china-pumps-79-billion-into-economy-with-bank-cash-reserve-cut-idUSKBN2101B3.

See: South China Morning Post (2020). "Coronavirus: China trying vouchers to boost consumer spending, but effort modest compared to HK, US," https://www.scmp.com/economy/china-economy/article/3075929/coronavirus-china-local-governments-try-boost-spending.

See: Wall Street Journal (2020). "China's Stimulus Strategy Faces New Test in Coronavirus," https://www.wsj.com/articles/chinas-stimulus-strategy-faces-new-test-in-coronavirus-11581616693

6. During January–March 2020, the Chinese government asked banks to extend the terms of business loans, and also asked commercial landlords to reduce rents.
7. Beginning from March 2020, many Chinese local governments were distributing prepaid spending vouchers for small amounts in order to increase consumer spending.
8. During February 2020, the Hong Kong government announced a significant fiscal stimulus package as part of its 2020–2021 budget and it included:

   - Low-interest, government-guaranteed loans for businesses.
   - Payment of one month's rent for public-housing tenants.
   - A US$1200 cash payment to all adult permanent residents.
   - Reduction of payroll, income, property and business taxes.
   - One month's worth of payments to citizens that collect pension or disability benefits.

6.3.4 Australia[13] *(March 2020)*

1. During March 2020, the Australian government announced an US$11.4 billion stimulus package including:

   - Payments to small businesses to encourage hiring.
   - A one-time payment to people collecting government benefits such as old-age or veterans' benefits.

[13] *See*: Prime Minister of Australia (March 2020). "Economic Stimulus Package," https://www.pm.gov.au/media/economic-stimulus-package.

See: The Guardian (March 2020). "Scott Morrison to announce $66 billion stimulus, including income support for workers," https://www.theguardian.com/business/2020/mar/22/scott-morrison-to-announce-66bn-stimulus-including-income-support-for-workers.

See: Reserve Bank of Australia (March 2020). "*Statement by Philip Lowe, Governor: Monetary Policy Decision*". https://www.rba.gov.au/media-releases/2020/mr-20-06.html.

See: Reserve Bank of Australia (March 2020). "*Statement by Philip Lowe, Governor*". https://www.rba.gov.au/media-releases/2020/mr-20-07.html.

See: Reserve Bank of Australia (March 2020). "*Statement by Philip Lowe, Governor: Monetary Policy Decision*". https://www.rba.gov.au/media-releases/2020/mr-20-08.html

- Business subsidies to businesses in industries which have been significantly affected by the coronavirus.

2. On March 22, 2020, the Australian government announced a second stimulus package worth US$54.2 billion including, among other things:

   - US$15.3 billion in cash payments equal to payroll withholdings for small businesses, up US$60,000 each.
   - US$24.3 billion in small business loans.

3. During March 2020, the Reserve Bank of Australia (Australia's central bank) implemented the following measures:

   - On March 3, it lowered interest rates by 0.25% to 0.50%.
   - On March 16, it announced the start of new types of repo operations.
   - On March 19, it again reduced benchmark interest rates by 0.25% to 0.25%.
   - On March 19, it started a $54 billion lending facility for small- and medium-sized business.
   - On March 19, it implemented bond purchases in order to reduce the yield of the three-year Australian treasury bond to 0.25%.

6.3.5 *Japan*[14] *(March 2020)*

1. During March 2020, the Bank of Japan announced a significant increase in *quantitative easing*, wherein it would double its purchases of ETFs (exchange-traded funds) from $56 billion a year to US$112 billion, and also increase purchases of corporate bonds and commercial paper.

[14] *See*: "*Japan stimulus highlight: $15bn small-biz loans*". *Asia Times*. https://asiatimes.com/2020/03/japan-stimulus-highlight-15bn-small-biz-loans/.

See: Bank of Japan (March 2020). "*Enhancement of Monetary Easing in Light of the Impact of the Outbreak of the Novel Coronavirus (COVID-19)*". https://www.boj.or.jp/en/announcements/release_2020/k200316b.pdf

2. During March 2020, the Bank of Japan announced a new program of offering 0% interest loans to increase lending to businesses affected by COVID-19.
3. The Japanese government enacted legislation for two new programs that offer small business loans (a US$4.6 billion package in February 2020, and a US$15 billion package in March 2020).
4. A legislative bill pending as of March 2020 included US$4 billion for COVID-19-related programs such as increasing mask production and prevent spread of COVID-19 to nursing homes.
5. During early April 2020, President Abe declared a one-month state of emergency that focused on Tokyo and six other prefectures (which collectively account for 44% of Japan's population). That amounted to a fiscal policy because it included shut-downs and restrictions on mobility.
6. During April 2020, the Japanese legislature enacted a US$993 billion stimulus package that included:
   (i) Aid for the aviation, travel and restaurant industries.
   (ii) Payment of 300,000 yen to households whose regular incomes declined.
   (iii) Payment of $18,000 each to affected SMEs.
   (iv) During April 2020, the Japanese government announced that it would pay US$930 (100,000 yen) to each of its citizens, and also expanded the state of emergency to the whole of Japan.

6.3.6 Philippines[15] (March 2020)

- During April 2020, the Philippines government reduced its benchmark interest rate by 50 basis points.
- During March 2020, the Philippines government announced that it would give cash grants to poor households that had been affected by COVID-19.

[15] *See*: "*Duterte's cash aid for poor Filipinos draws middle class pushback—Manila bracing for worst economic hit since 1998 as 1.2 million lose jobs*". By Cliff Venzon, April 17, 2020. https://asia.nikkei.com/Economy/Duterte-s-cash-aid-for-poor-Filipinos-draws-middle-class-pushback?utm_campaign=RN%20Free%20newsletteramp;utm_medium=daily%20 newsletter%20freeamp;utm_source=NAR%20Newsletteramp;utm_content=article%20 linkamp;del_type=1amp;pub_date=20200417190000amp;seq_num=4amp;si=%%user_id%%

- During April 2020, the Philippines central bank announced that it would reduce the reserve requirement ratio by at least 200 basis points; and that it would cut the benchmark interest rate.

6.3.7 Singapore[16] (March 2020)

- During March 2020, Singapore announced a US$33 billion welfare package.

6.3.8 Malaysia[17] (March 2020)

- During March 2020, Malaysia announced a US$53 billion welfare package.

6.3.9 Canada[18] (March 2020)

During March 2020, Bank of Canada announced a number of economic stimulus measures:

[16] *See*: "*Singapore unveils $33bn pandemic relief plan after GDP shrinks 2.2%—City-state forecasts 1–4% full-year contraction as ASEAN impact crystallizes*". By Dylan Loh amp; Masayuki Yuda. March 26, 2020. https://asia.nikkei.com/Economy/Singapore-unveils-33bn-pandemic-relief-plan-after-GDP-shrinks-2.2

[17] *See*: "*Malaysia adds $53 billion of coronavirus stimulus as fiscal pressure mounts—Indonesia also in tight spot while Singapore and others have wiggle room*". P. Kumar amp; D. Loh, March 27, 2020.

[18] *See*: Bank of Canada (March 2020). "*Bank of Canada lowers overnight rate target to 1¼ percent*". https://www.bankofcanada.ca/2020/03/fad-press-release-2020-03-04/.

See: Bank of Canada (March 2020). "*Bank of Canada Announces the Expansion of its Bond Buyback Program and Term Repo Operations*". https://www.bankofcanada.ca/2020/03/expansion-bond-buyback-term-repo/.

See: Bank of Canada (March 2020). "*Bank of Canada lowers overnight rate target to ¾ percent*".

See: Bank of Canada (March 2020). "*New Bank of Canada Measures to Support Key Funding Markets*". https://www.bankofcanada.ca/2020/03/market-notice-2020-03-16/.

See: Department of Finance Canada (March 2020). "*Canada outlines measures to support the economy and the financial sector*". https://www.canada.ca/en/department-finance/news/2020/03/canada-outlines-measures-to-support-the-economy-and-the-financial-sector.html.

See: Department of Finance Canada (March 2020). "*Canada outlines measures to support the economy and the financial sector*". https://www.canada.ca/en/department-finance/news/2020/03/canada-outlines-measures-to-support-the-economy-and-the-financial-sector.html

1. Bank of Canada cut the benchmark interest-rate twice by 0.50% on each occasion.
2. Bank of Canada announced the expansion of open-market bond purchases and repo operations.
3. The Canadian government announced that it would provide $7.1 billion in loans to businesses.
4. Bank of Canada announced it would expand the types of collateral used for repo operations, and would also increase purchases of mortgage-backed securities.
5. The Office of the Superintendent of Financial Institutions (OSFI) reduced bank reserve requirements (which increased bank lending capacity by US$214 billion).

6.3.10 *Russia*[19] *(March 2020)*

During March 2020, Russia announced it would create a US$4 billion fund to stimulate its economy to reduce the effects of COVID-19.

6.3.11 *India*[20] *(March 2020)*

During March 2020, India announced a US$22.5 billion stimulus package that consisted of the following:

1. Free cooking gas for rural women for three months.
2. Broadened insurance coverage for healthcare workers.
3. Three months of free grains and other staple foods for poor families.
4. A one-time cash payment to 30 million senior citizens.
5. Accelerated cash payments to eighty-seven million farmers as part of an existing program
6. Creating a new fund to help construction workers effected by the COVID-19 quarantine.

[19] *See*: The Moscow Times (March 2020). "***Russia to Launch $4 Billion Fund in Attempt to Shield Economy From Coronavirus Shock***". https://www.themoscowtimes.com/2020/03/16/russia-to-launch-4bln-fund-in-attempt-to-shield-economy-from-coronavirus-shock-a69633

[20] *See*: Wall Street Journal (March 2020). "***India to Spend $22.5 Billion to Help Poor Survive CoronavirusShutdown***".https://www.wsj.com/articles/india-to-spend-22-5-billion-to-help-poor-survive-coronavirus-shutdown-11585223446

During April 2020,[21] the Central Bank (Reserve Bank of India) cut reverse-repo rates by 25 basis points, to 3.75%, and announced a welfare package of $13 billion to help small businesses, shadow banks, farmers and the housing industry (e.g. new loans).

6.3.12 Brazil[22] (March 2020)

During March 2020, the Brazilian government announced a US$30 billion stimulus package which doesn't contain new spending, and consists of deferred payments and budget re-allocations:

1. Increased cash payouts to poor families.
2. Acceleration of payments for retirees.
3. Three-month deferral of debt payments SMEs.

6.3.13 European Union[23] (March 2020)

During March 2020, the European Central Bank (ECB) announced economic stimulus measures:

[21] *See*: "*India's central bank cuts deposit rates to ease coronavirus impact—$13 billion rupees injected to help shadow banks, agriculture and small businesses*". KIRAN SHARMA, April 17, 2020. https://asia.nikkei.com/Economy/India-s-central-bank-cuts-deposit-rates-to-ease-coronavirus-impact

[22] *See*: Reuters (March 2020). "*Brazil government to inject $30 billion into economy to combat coronavirus hit*". https://www.reuters.com/article/us-brazil-economy-budget/brazil-government-to-inject-30-billion-into-economy-to-combat-coronavirus-hit-idUSKBN21341I

[23] *See*: European Central Bank (March 2020). "*Monetary policy decisions*". https://www.ecb.europa.eu/press/pr/date/2020/html/ecb.mp200312~8d3aec3ff2.en.html.

See: European Central Bank (March 2020). "*ECB Banking Supervision provides temporary capital and operational relief in reaction to coronavirus*". https://www.ecb.europa.eu/press/pr/date/2020/html/ecb.pr200312~45417d8643.en.html.

See: European Central Bank (March 2020). "*ECB announces easing of conditions for targeted longer-term refinancing operations (TLTRO III)*". https://www.ecb.europa.eu/press/pr/date/2020/html/ecb.pr200312_1~39db50b717.en.html.

See: European Central Bank. "*ECB announces €750 billion Pandemic Emergency Purchase Programme (PEPP)*". https://www.ecb.europa.eu/press/pr/date/2020/html/ecb.pr200318_1~3949d6f266.en.html

1. Reduction of the interest rate for, and lending requirements for long term refinancing operations (TLTRO, long-term loans to banks).
2. The purchase of an additional $800 billion of bonds during 2020 (the *Pandemic Emergency Purchase Programme*, or PEPP)
3. An additional US$128 billion in bond purchases during 2020.
4. Reduced capital requirements for banks (which purportedly increases banks' lending capacity).

6.3.14 South Korea[24] *(April 2020)*

During March 2020:

- The South Korean government announced a US$49.8 billion economic stimulus package that includes:
  - Job retraining for unemployed persons.
  - Subsidies for SMEs to help them pay employees.
  - Child-care subsidies.
- The Bank of Korea's monetary policy board reduced the benchmark rate by 50 basis points to a record low of 0.75%.

6.3.15 Nigeria (April 2020)

- During March 2020, President Buhari invoked the Quarantine Act of 1926 (a statute enacted by the Nigerian federal legislature) pursuant to which the President can enact Executive Orders or new legislation pertaining to pandemics. President Buhari issued Executive Orders that shut down Lagos State, Ogun State and Federal Capital Territory (FCT).
- During March 2020, the federal government announced and disbursed N100 billion (roughly $265 million) in payments to poor families; and also distributed cash to 5000 households in FCT.

[24] *See*: Reuters (March 2020). "*South Korea unveils $9.8 billion stimulus to fight coronavirus*". https://www.reuters.com/article/us-southkorea-economy-budget/south-korea-unveils-9-8-billion-stimulus-to-fight-coronavirus-idUSKBN20R046

- During March 2020, the Central Bank of Nigeria (CBN) offered for sale, N98.51 billion (roughly US$260 million) of Nigeria treasury bills which were over-subscribed (announced total demand was N161 billion).
- During the third week of March 2020, CBN announced that the benchmark interest rate (monetary policy rate) would remain at 13.5%, and maintained the *Cash Reserve Ratio* and the *Liquidity Ratio* at 27.5% and 30% respectively.
- During March 2020, the Nigerian central bank announced a welfare package of N3.5 trillion (about US$9.2 billion including loans to businesses) and other policies including the following:

  - Reduce interest rates on central bank intervention facilities from 9% to 5%.
  - Increase financial inclusion.
  - Granting regulatory forbearance to banks to restructure loans in affected industries.
  - Improve FX supply to the central bank by instructing oil companies and oil services companies to sell FX to the Central Bank instead of NNPC.
  - Provide N100 billion of healthcare loans to the healthcare industry.
  - Request that banks implement business continuity measures.
  - Create a N50 billion targeted loan fund for affected households and SMEs.
  - Grant an additional moratorium of one year on Central Bank intervention facilities.
  - Improve the Loan-Deposit Ratio policy.
  - Provide N1 trillion of loans to boost local manufacturing/ production.

As of early April 2020, Nigeria had less than 600 cases of COVID-19 infections and less than thirty deaths from the pandemic.

6.3.16 United Kingdom[25] *(April 2020)*

During March 2020, the UK government announced the following economic stimulus measures:

1. The Bank of England announced it would buy US$228 billion worth of U.K. government bonds and corporate bonds and reduce interest rates by 0.15% to 0.1%.
2. The Bank of England further lowered benchmark interest rates again by 0.5%, reduced capital requirements for UK banks (permitted banks to use the "counter-cyclical capital buffer") and permitted banks to provide about US$390 billion in new loans.
3. Announced about US$37 billion in fiscal stimulus (*Phase-1 stimulus*) which included:

    - Expanded access to government benefits for the self-employed and unemployed.
    - A tax cut for retailers.
    - Cash payments to small businesses.
    - Aid to help sick persons pay for self-isolation.
    - A subsidy to help small businesses pay for sick pay.

4. On March 17, the UK announced a second and larger stimulus package (*Phase-2 stimulus*) that included:

[25] *See*: Bank of England (March 2020). "*Bank of England measures to respond to the economic shock from Covid-19*". https://www.bankofengland.co.uk/monetary-policy-summary-and-minutes/2020/monetary-policy-summary-for-the-special-monetary-policy-committee-meeting-on-19-march-2020.

See: Bank of England (March 2020). "Monetary Policy Summary for the special Monetary Policy Committee meeting on 19 March 2020". https://www.bankofengland.co.uk/monetary-policy-summary-and-minutes/2020/monetary-policy-summary-for-the-special-monetary-policy-committee-meeting-on-19-march-2020.

See: The Guardian (March 2020). "*Key points from budget 2020—at a glance*". https://www.theguardian.com/uk-news/2020/mar/11/key-points-from-budget-2020-at-a-glance.

See: Gov.UK. "*Chancellor announces additional support to protect businesses*". https://www.gov.uk/government/news/chancellor-announces-additional-support-to-protect-businesses.

See: The Guardian (March 2020). "*UK government to pay 80% of wages for those not working in coronavirus crisis*". https://www.theguardian.com/uk-news/2020/mar/20/government-pay-wages-jobs-coronavirus-rishi-sunak

- US$379 billion in business loan guarantees.
- US$23 billion in reduction of business taxes and payment of grants to businesses affected by COVID-19.

5. On March 20, the UK government announced a third set of fiscal stimulus (*Phase-3 stimulus*) measures including:

   - US$1.2 billion of aid to house renters.
   - A US$95.1 billion program to pay grants to companies (for to 80% of employed worker's salaries—and up to US$3046 a month per employee).
   - US$8.5 billion for an increase of $1200/person/year in safety net tax credits for unemployed people.
   - Deferment of payment of Q2–2020 Value Added tax (estimated at about US$36.6 billion).

6.3.17 Germany[26] (April 2020)

During March 2020, Germany announced a "stimulus" program:

1. Germany's state bank KfW (not the central bank) will lend up to US$610 billion to companies.
2. US$172 billion in increased spending including the following:

   - US$3.9 billion for personal protective equipment and vaccine research.
   - US$55 billion for cash payments to small businesses.
   - Cash payments up to $16,225/person for the self-employed.
   - US$60.7 billion for un-allocated fiscal measures.
   - US$8.5 billion for social security programs for the self-employed.

[26] *See*: Bloomberg News (March 2020). "*Borders Tighten Within EU as Germany Readies Virus Aid Package*". https://www.bloomberg.com/news/articles/2020-03-13/germany-will-provide-unlimited-liquidity-to-help-virus-hit-firms.

See: Reuters. "*Factbox: Germany's anti-coronavirus stimulus package*". https://www.reuters.com/article/us-health-coronavirus-germany-measures-f/factbox-germanys-anti-coronavirus-stimulus-package-idUSKBN21C26Y

6.3.18 France[27] *(April 2020)*

During March 2020, France announced a US$49 billion aid package that included the following:

1. The French government will guarantee bank loans of up to US$327 billion to help businesses affected by COVID-19.
2. The creation of a fund that will provide financial aid to shopkeepers and the self-employed.
3. Substantial reductions of social security taxes.
4. Unemployment benefits for people that are compelled to work part time.

6.3.19 Italy[28] *(April 2020)*

During March 2020, Italy announced a two-part US$28 billion stimulus package that included:

1. Financial and other aid for workers that are or may be laid off.
2. Adding cash to a fund that guarantees loans to SMEs.
3. Paying cash to companies that are affected by COVID-19.

6.3.20 Common Elements Among the Fiscal and Monetary Stimulus Programs of Various Countries (January–April 2020)

The monetary policies announced by most governments were very similar and consisted of reductions of benchmark interest rates and purchases of bonds, ETFs and MBS/ABS. The fiscal policies and welfare packages announced by national governments were similar across countries, and the common elements of these welfare packages are as follows:

[27] *See*: Politico (March 2020). "*France injects billions into stimulus plan amid coronavirus chaos*". https://www.politico.eu/article/france-injects-billions-into-stimulus-plan-amid-coronavirus-chaos-bruno-le-maire-economic-catastrophe/

[28] *See*: Bloomberg News (March 2020). "*Italy Announces $28 Billion Plan to Cushion Virus-Hit Economy*". https://www.bloomberg.com/news/articles/2020-03-10/conte-calls-on-ecb-to-do-whatever-it-takes-against-coronavirus

- Amounts were allocated for loans to, or investments in banks—presumably in the hope that such banks will increase their loan volumes to SMEs and individuals.
- Amounts were allocated as direct payments to qualifying households deemed to be at risk.
- Amounts were allocated as direct payments to qualifying SMEs and businesses deemed to be at risk.
- Amounts were allocated toward improving physical (not telemedicine) public health resources and facilities.
- Unemployment benefits were increased or extended—but without changing the structure unemployment insurance or adding re-insurance.
- Mortgage-backed securities and ETFs are increasingly being used in implementing monetary policies around the world.
- There are four classes of spender-countries: i) the super-large spenders (which include USA, Japan, the UK and the EU); ii) the large spenders (none), iii) the medium spenders (China); iv) the small spenders (South Korea, Italy and France); v) the micro spenders (which include India, Nigeria and Russia). Here spending is measured primarily on an adjusted per-capita basis.

6.4 The Welfare Packages Issued by Many Countries (January–April 2020) Didn't Address Key Solutions to Pandemics

Just like the $700 billion TARP rescue package in the USA, the welfare packages announced by many countries created significant opportunities for fraud, corruption, psychological problems, political influence and political lobbying. As of 2020, the US government was still prosecuting companies and individuals for filing (filed before 2014) fraudulent applications for TARP loans/benefits/grants.

The notable omissions in the COVID-19 welfare packages of most countries that announced them are as follows:

- Significant amounts that can be used to accelerate vaccine research.
- Programs and cash grants to build, maintain and expand national/international internet infrastructure which will enable more companies, individuals, SMEs, government agencies, educational institutions, retailing chains, business services companies, logistics

companies and healthcare facilities to do more of their business and transactions online.

- Cash grants to build and expand telemedicine facilities (to reduce costs and the exposures of healthcare workers) and automated analysis of lab tests, and to increase the number of medical labs.
- Cash grants for the online re-training of workers to give them new job skills.
- Cash grants for online training of workers on how to manage their income and to save. In many countries many households don't have more than 2–4.5 months' worth of monthly expenses as their lifetime savings. Mismanagement of income, bad habits, addictions and cravings are what rapidly increases consumer debt.
- Government agencies should take equity stakes in companies that receive government guarantees or participate in government-sponsored loan programs (such as those offered in most of the welfare packages).
- Creation of low-cost or zero-cost government-sponsored healthcare insurance coverage programs. It's clear that many private-insurance systems have failed or are inadequate.
- Grants and programs to fix disrupted supply chains.
- Grants and programs to increase the automation of factories in critical industries (to ensure that a specific minimum number of factories will operate at all times in all manufacturing sectors, and that such factories can increase their capacity during any pandemic or crisis).
- Creation of systems (taxation, fines, fees, credits, import duties, shut-downs, etc.) that will re-distribute the actual costs of pandemics and crises to offending and non-compliant companies, countries, groups and individuals.
- A specific minimum number of critical cities and large cities in each country must function normally during pandemics and crises in order to reduce economic, psychological and political damage (these cities should have priority in getting the automated pandemics surveillance systems mentioned herein).
- Programs to shift/re-distribute/re-allocate/re-insure unemployment insurance costs and other unemployment costs paid by companies and governments during pandemics and crises—in order to create cash reserves for future pandemics and to shift more of the private sector risks and burdens to private sector companies.
- Loans/investments/grants to build automated surveillance systems (for outdoors and public-assembly spaces, especially in large cities)

that can automatically identify people that are infected by COVID-19 and other infectious germs (e.g. by sensor analysis of body-temperatures and/or skin-condition and/or radio-signals).

- Issuance of non-transferable government food stamps that are redeemable at government-owned/-controlled food depots in large/medium cities. The government is best able to reduce the retail cost of food by coordinated large-scale purchases of food. The food stamps ensure that cash grants are used for intended purposes.
- Globalization (especially the movement of people) will have to be reduced substantially.
- Supply chains will have to be restructured substantially, and more production/manufacturing will have to be done locally or in regions where countries and multinational corporations (MNCs) have more direct or indirect control over policies.
- Programs to support issuance of: i) non-transferable private sector food stamps that are redeemable at government-owned/-controlled food depots or designated private food depots in large/medium/small cities; and ii) non-transferable private sector housing vouchers that redeemable at government-owned/-controlled housing projects and designated private housing projects in large/medium/small cities. The private sector food stamps and housing vouchers can be issued by consortiums of multinational corporations who in turn can get tax benefits from the government. The food stamps and housing vouchers ensure that cash grants are used for intended purposes.
- Changes in the funding, structure, rule-making, powers and operations of international organizations such as WHO (World Health Organization) and WTO (World Trade Organization) who were undoubtedly very unprepared to handle many aspects of COVID-19 and other pandemics. These two organizations can exert significant controls over the globalization, trade and movement that spreads pandemics across national boards (and even in-country regional borders).
- Long-term measures—most of the stimulus packages announced by many countries consisted of mostly short-term measures and benefits. If COVID-19 were to mutate into a different and more drug-resistant virus, or if COVID-19 were to last for more than nine months (i.e. beyond July 2020), most of these announced "stimulus" measures would be grossly deficient.
- Incentives for indigenes to get vaccinated if and when the anti-COVID-19 vaccines are developed.

In their 2020–2021 responses to the COVID-19 pandemic economic/ financial crises, most national governments didn't sufficiently address "*sub-markets*" for "*regulatory responses*", "*behavioral effects*" and "*firm-structure effects*". In the Nwogugu (2019a) suggested framework for policy-making, Labor and Environmental/Climate-Change issues are addressed under "*Trade Policies*"; while "*Healthcare Policies*" can be addressed under "*Fiscal Policy*" and or "*Behavioral Effects Policies*". By early April 2020, it had become clear that most monetary and fiscal policies implemented by governments around the world had failed or had started to fail. Many institutions and researchers drastically revised their growth estimates for various countries/regions downwards.[29] Many of the issues/omissions explained in Nwogugu (2019d) (especially Chaps. 2, 4, 6, 7, 8, 10 & 11), Nwogugu (2019d), Nwogugu (2015a, b) (the *Dodd Frank Act* in the USA was a response to similar economic/financial stresses), Nwogugu (2012: 17–77, 83–112, 249–316, 323–411), and Nwogugu (2019c: 565–691) should be considered by national and state governments.

[29] *See*: "*Pandemic to cut Asian growth to 2.2%, worst since 1998 crisis: ADB - Thailand, Hong Kong and seven other economies to shrink, China to slow sharply*". Cliff Venzon, April 03, 2020. https://asia.nikkei.com/Economy/Pandemic-to-cut-Asian-growth-to-2.2-worst-since-1998-crisis-ADB.

See: "*India's coronavirus lockdown spells disaster for struggling economy - Government can cut taxes and red tape to boost eventual return to growth*". Ritesh Kumar Singh, March 27, 2020. https://asia.nikkei.com/Opinion/India-s-coronavirus-lockdown-spells-disaster-for-struggling-economy.

See: "*Australia faces end of world's longest boom with recession coming - After 29 years, coronavirus puts stop to economic run*". Fumi Matsumoto, April 01, 2020. https://asia.nikkei.com/Economy/Australia-faces-end-of-world-s-longest-boom-with-recession-coming. *See*: "*Japan business sentiment plunges to 7-year low, BOJ Tankan shows Coronavirus hits economy reeling from sales tax increase and trade war*". Mitsuru Obe, April 01, 2020. https://asia.nikkei.com/Economy/Japan-business-sentiment-plunges-to-7-year-low-BOJ-Tankan-shows.

See: "*From New Delhi to Bangkok, Asia's megacities shackled - Travel bans to contain coronavirus sap region's economic lifeblood*". Takashi Nakano And Akira Hayakawa, March 24, 2020.https://asia.nikkei.com/Spotlight/Coronavirus/From-New-Delhi-to-Bangkok-Asia-s-megacities-shackled.

See: *"BREAKING: China GDP shrinks 6.8% in 1Q, first decline since 1992". Nikkei Asian Review*. Apr 17, 2020. https://asia.nikkei.com/Economy/Australia-faces-end-of-world-s-longest-boom-with-recession-coming.

See: "*Asia's reliance on trade, tourism weighs on COVID-19 recovery: IMF - Region lauded for swift responses but governments urged to restructure priorities*". Gwen Robinson. *Nikkei Asian Review* April 16, 2020. https://asia.nikkei.com/Editor-s-Picks/Interview/Asia-s-reliance-on-trade-tourism-weighs-on-COVID-19-recovery-IMF.

6.5 Failures of Economic Policy, Economic Systems and Government-Models: A Welfare State? Where Is the "Free Market"?

The COVID-19 pandemic clearly proved that most existing forms of government (ranging from the Chinese one-party communist model at one extreme, to the parliamentary democracies, parliamentary monarchies and to the US presidential democratic multi-party model at the other extreme) have failed; and that most economic systems and economic policies are also highly inefficient and problematic:

- Given the number of global pandemics that have occurred during the last sixty years and their often profound negative economic impact, national governments should by now have devised appropriate legal infrastructure, health policies and economic/financial policies, but that wasn't the case during before COVID-19.
- Instead and around the world and in both developed and developing countries, what we have seen is almost totally unprepared national, local and state governments, overburdened and inadequate health systems even in "developed" countries", inadequate medical research, ineffective regulations, disrupted supply chains and so on.
- Households faced significant psychological distress and uncertainty and many had minimal savings.
- Transportation systems were limited or shut down in many countries.
- Telecomm companies' infrastructure seems inadequate.
- Consumer durables and food were inadequate.
- Airlines, restaurants, hotels, cabs/livery, entertainment companies and many companies were shut down in many countries. In the US alone, more than seven million jobs had been lost from January to March 2020.
- Manufacturing supply chains were completely disrupted, leading to billions of dollars of losses around the world. Factories were shut down.

During January to April 2020, the welfare packages announced by many national governments (and the *political securitization* of the COVID-19 pandemic) revealed the true nature of different types of national governments around the world. The fact is that as of 2020/2021, most existing types/models of government were fundamentally welfare-oriented mechanisms:

- That will resort to welfare/charity policies in violation of their stated economic principles and political foundations, when pandemics occur.
- That will resort to welfare/charity policies in order to gather or consolidate political power.
- That will resort to welfare policies upon failure of traditional monetary and fiscal policies due to lack of knowledge of what else to do.
- That will resort to welfare/charity policies to boost their perceived image, credibility and standing in international circles.
- That have historically used "traditional" monetary and fiscal policies primarily as "welfare-state" tools and as political tools.

The US and Western Europe were built on a purported philosophy of free markets and capitalism. However, a closer look reveals that for the last century, the US has used a system of welfare policies, government charity and convoluted regulation to support its indigenes and companies—such as housing vouchers, food stamps, transportation vouchers, school lunch vouchers, tax credits, low-income housing credits, location credits, bailouts, low-interest loans, government guarantees of debt and defense contracts. Thus, the US has really been a convolutely regulated (complex regulations) *welfare state* that has significant *inequality* and is not a true capitalist economy. The same or similar condition exists in many Western European countries that profess to be capitalist economies—they impose relatively high personal taxes, are convolutely regulated and they are also *welfare states*. In addition and as explained in Nwogugu (2015a), *National Income Accounting* methods (and "earnings management" by national governments—over-statement of economic performance) hide and distort true economic activity and welfare in the US, China, India and Europe.

Given the structure of its economy and its centralized command-and-control communist party politics and policies, its explicit and hidden grants/transfers to households and companies, its tacit state support and subsidization of the government-owned companies that dominate the Chinese economy, China is also a *welfare state*. There is significant Inequality in China, and China has been reported to have repeatedly falsified its economic data, and its National Income Accounting methods hide and distort its true economic activity.

What remains surprising is that such government support does not emerge in most of the trade negotiations and WTO disputes of the US and European countries.

Figures 6.2–6.5 illustrate some of the effects of the failed economic policies. Figure 6.2 indicates that the significant rise in US stock market

Fig. 6.2 US Equities, Margin Debt and Composite Valuation Indices (2019–2020)

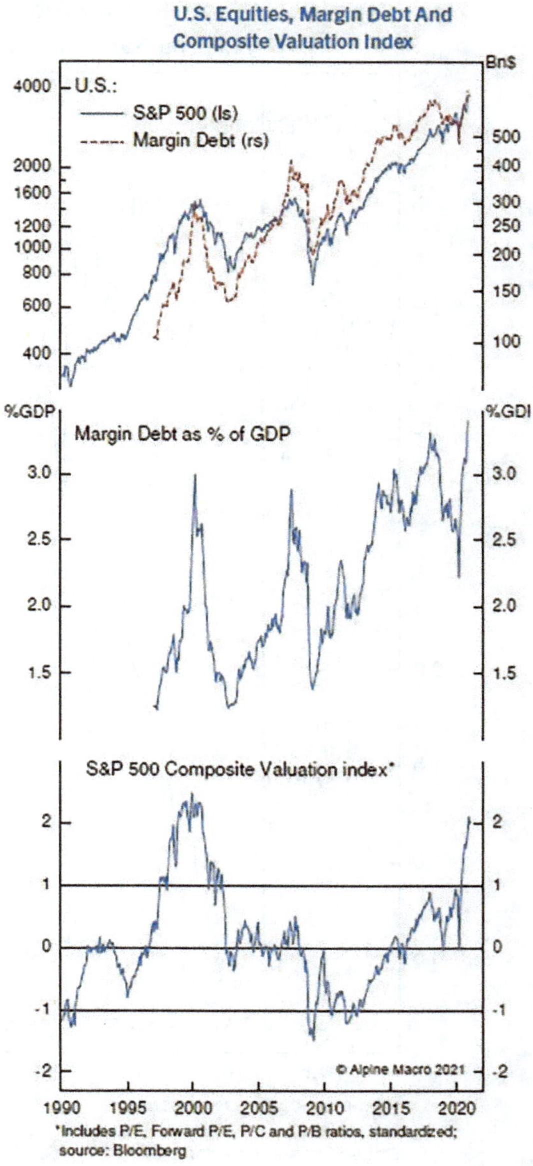

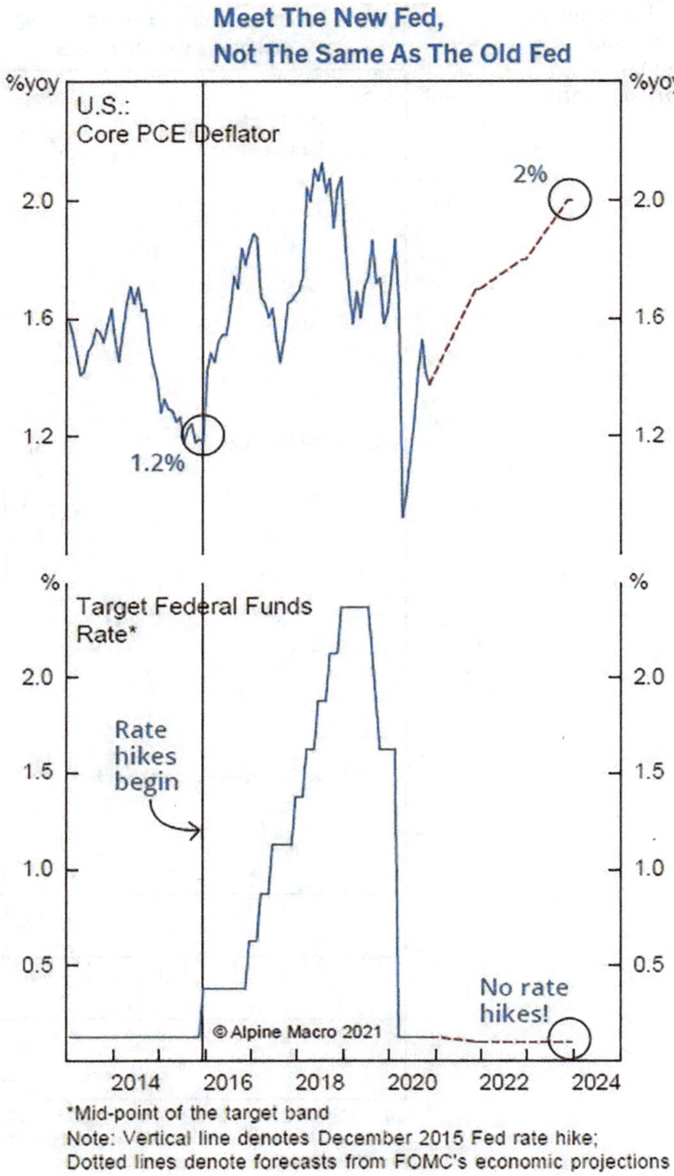

Fig. 6.3 Current and Forecasted US Interest Rates (2014–2024). Source: Alpine Macro 2021

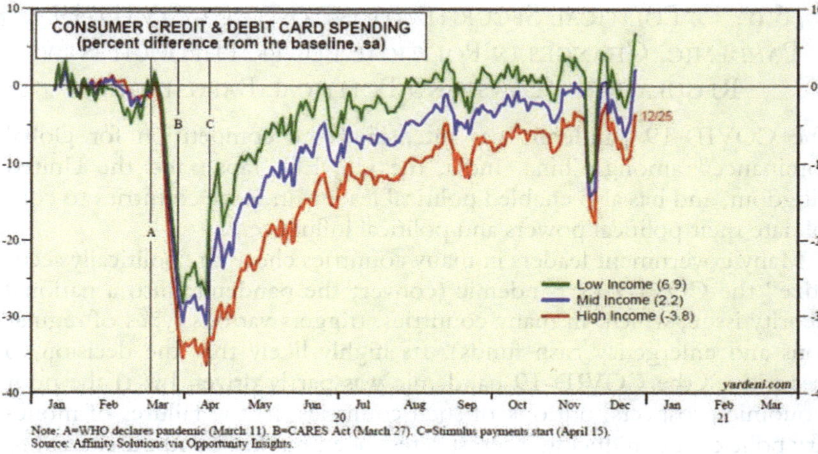

Fig. 6.4 US Consumer Credit and Debit Card Spending (2019–2020)

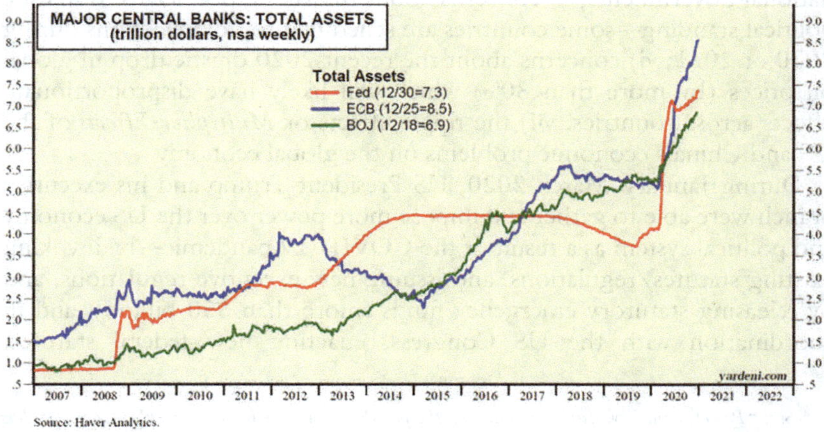

Fig. 6.5 Total Assets of Major Central Banks (2007–2020)

values during January–April 2020 was supported by significant increases in margin debt, matching levels seen around the 2000 US stock market crash—also the economic stimulus cash granted by the US government and other governments may have boosted stock markets during 2020.

6.6 "Political Securitization" of the COVID-19 Pandemic, Changes in Political Power Through New Regulations/Laws, and Political Bargaining

The COVID-19 pandemic has intensified the competition for global dominance[30] among China, India, the US, EU, Japan and the United Kingdom, and has also enabled political leaders in some countries to consolidate their political powers and political influence.

Many government leaders in many countries chose to "politically securitize" the COVID-19 pandemic (convert the pandemic into a national security issue, which, in many countries, triggers various types of regulations and emergency cash funds). Its highly likely that the decision to "securitize" the COVID-19 pandemic was partly driven by: i) the poor economic prospects/outlook of such countries; ii) the failures of monetary policies (i.e. reducing interest rates; open market bond purchases) to stimulate economic growth in many countries, and iii) the risks/uncertainties of the ongoing China-US and US-Japan Trade Wars; iv) the continuing growth of nationalist and far-right elements and philosophies in national governments; v) concerns about the ruling politicians' domestic political standing—some countries are scheduled to hold elections during 2020 or 2021; vi) concerns about the recent 2020 drastic drop in global oil prices (by more than 30%) which will likely have disproportionate effects across countries; vii) the ripple effects or *Multiplier-Effects* of the US and China's economic problems on the global economy.

During January–March 2020, US President Trump and his executive branch were able to gather and impose more power over the US economy and political system as a result of the COVID-19 pandemic—by invoking existing statutes/regulations, and issuing new executive regulations, and by releasing statutory emergency funds (more than $50 billion), and in coordination with the US Congress, enacting new federal statutes.

[30] *See*: "*Power, equality, nationalism: how the pandemic will reshape the world: Covid-19 has intensified the rivalry between the US and China—but it has also strengthened international co-operation. Will nations be more united or divided, more—or less—free?*" By Simon Tisdall. March 28, 2020. https://www.theguardian.com/world/2020/mar/28/power-equality-nationalism-how-the-pandemic-will-reshape-the-world.

See: "*Analysis—COVID-19 pandemic as global political crisis—Amid crisis, US failed not only its rivals like Iran, but also allies such as Italy by ignoring their calls for help*". Ali Balci and Tuncay Kardas. March 24, 2020. https://www.aa.com.tr/en/analysis/analysis-covid-19-pandemic-as-global-political-crisis/1777581

Similarly, some US state governors issued Executive Orders that impliedly gave them new and additional political powers—the use of Executive Orders issued by state governors instead of new legislation may have drastically reduced political/election risk for the two major US political parties (the Democrats and the Republicans). The US held federal and state elections during fall 2020, and the handling of the COVID-19 pandemic by US President Trump, the state governors, state-level congresses and the US Congress were major campaign issues.

Malcolm (2020)[31] noted that in response to COVID-19, President Trump, US government agencies and some state governors invoked and/or enacted several statutes purportedly to limit COVID-19:

- During January–March 2020, the Trump administration invoked the Stafford Act pursuant to which the US federal government can use a $50 billion emergency fund for disaster relief. During 2019, Trump invoked that same statute in order to respond to flooding in Nebraska and Iowa. During 2000, President Bill Clinton invoked the Stafford Act to respond to an outbreak of the West Nile virus in New York and New Jersey.
- During January–March 2020, the Trump administration invoked the Public Health Service Act. For several decades, US federal health inspectors have relied upon the Public Health Service Act to inspect people, animals, plants, goods and cargo entering the US.
- During January–March 2020, the Trump administration invoked the Defense Production Act, pursuant to which the President can direct private industry to allocate raw materials and prioritize the production of medical supplies.
- The Tenth Amendment of the US Constitution reserves to the states broad police power to regulate behavior and enforce order within their territory in order to protect the health, safety and general welfare of their inhabitants. The US Supreme Court has held that states can invoke such authority to respond to a health crisis.
- During 2020, President Trump and the US Congress enacted the CARES Act of 2020, which provides a $2.2 trillion welfare package for affected households and businesses.

[31] *See*: Malcolm, J. (Mar 20th, 2020). *In Combating Coronavirus, Trump and Governors Act Constitutionally.* https://www.heritage.org/the-constitution/commentary/combating-coronavirus-trump-and-governors-act-constitutionally

- During 2020, the US Justice Department (DOJ)[32] asked for more powers that, in effect, suspend the US Constitution. The US DOJ can also invoke regulations that change the rights of indigenes.
- During 2020, many US federal government agencies[33] enacted new regulations and have changed their operating policies in response to COVID-19.
- During 2020, many US states[34] enacted new Executive Orders, regulations and statutes in response to COVID-19.

Similarly and during 2020–2021, the COVID-19 Pandemic enabled Chinese leader Xi Jing Ping and his cohorts to consolidate power in China, eliminate dissidents/opposition and enact more favorable laws (in China) that give them more control over the economy and politics of China[35] (including Hong Kong).

[32] *See*: "*Trump's DOJ Interference Is Actually Not Crazy—In Trump's Mind, He Is Not Politicizing Law Enforcement. On The Contrary, He Is Trying To Fight Politicization Coming From His Opponents Within The Department*". February 27, 2020. By Mario Loyola. https://www.theatlantic.com/ideas/archive/2020/02/trumps-doj-unitary-executive/607141/

[33] *See*: "*COVID-19: Daily Announcements From Federal Agencies*". March 27, 2020. https://www.ncsl.org/ncsl-in-dc/publications-and-resources/covid-19-daily-announcements-from-federal-agencies.aspx

[34] *See*: "*State Action on Coronavirus (COVID-19)*". March 27, 2020. https://www.ncsl.org/research/health/state-action-on-coronavirus-covid-19.aspx.

See: "*State Fiscal Responses to Coronavirus (COVID-19)*". March 27, 2020. https://www.ncsl.org/research/fiscal-policy/state-fiscal-responses-to-covid-19.aspx

[35] *See*: "*COVID-19 and Xi Jinping: How the Strongman Got Stronger—Surprisingly, China's Xi is poised to politically profit from the deadly outbreak, both at home and abroad*". By Thomas Reilly. March 19, 2020. https://thediplomat.com/2020/03/covid-19-and-xi-jinping-how-the-strongman-got-stronger/.

See: "*Covid-19 Reveals How China's Internal Politics Now Affect The Whole World—What Happens In Wuhan Doesn't Stay In Wuhan*". By Andrew Mertha. March 6, 2020. https://www.washingtonpost.com/politics/2020/03/06/covid-19-reveals-how-chinas-internal-politics-now-affect-whole-world/.

See: "*Coronavirus: China's Attempts To Contain The Outbreak Has Given It New Levels Of State Power*".

March 11, 2020. http://theconversation.com/coronavirus-chinas-attempts-to-contain-the-outbreak-has-given-it-new-levels-of-state-power-133285.

See: "*The Myth Of Authoritarian Coronavirus Supremacy—China Wants You Believe Its Political System Stopped Coronavirus. That's A Lie*". By Zack Beauchamp. Mar 26, 2020.

In Japan[36] and during 2020 and in response to COVID-19, the Japanese government issued Executive Orders (at the state and federal levels) that restricted mobility and commerce; and Prime Minister Shinzo Abe negotiated new laws with opposition parties which expanded the national government's emergency legal powers and restricted the daily activities of indigenes and businesses.

In India,[37] the union government and some state governments issued Executive Orders that restricted mobility and commerce, and invoked several pre-existing statutes which granted them more political and economic powers. The Indian union government invoked Section 69 of the Disaster Management Act of 2005 (to delegate powers of the Home Secretary to the secretary of the MoHFW), advised state governments to invoke the Pandemic Disease Act and triggered funds available from the *State Disaster Response Fund* (SDRF). Some Indian states enacted new regulations pursuant to the Pandemic Disease Act such as *The Delhi Pandemic Diseases, COVID-19 Regulations, 2020* (https://main.sci.gov.in/pdf/cir/covid19_14032020.pdf), *The Maharashtra Pandemic Diseases COVID-19 Regulations, 2020* (https://www.maharashtra.gov.in/Site/Upload/Acts Rules/English/Korona Notification 14 March 2020….pdf), the *Punjab Pandemic Diseases, COVID-19 Regulations, 2020* (http://www.diprpunjab.gov.in/?q=content/punjab-govt-announces-emergency-measures-combat-coronavirus-menace) and *The Himachal Pradesh Pandemic Disease (COVID-19) Regulations, 2020* (https://himachal.gov.in/showfile.php?lang=1&dpt_id=19&level=1&lid=20068&sublinkid=19621).

The common trends during December 2019 to April 2020 were that in many countries:

See: "*Is Political Change Coming to China?*" Feb 14, 2020. Yuen Yuen Ang. https://www.project-syndicate.org/commentary/china-coronavirus-xi-hold-on-power-by-yuen-yuen-ang-2020-02

[36] *See*: "*Abe reaches across aisle for COVID-19 Emergency Law As Japan Cases Top 1000*". By Reiji Yoshida and Satoshi Sugiyama. https://www.japantimes.co.jp/news/2020/03/04/national/politics-diplomacy/abe-opposition-coronavirus-emergency-law/#.XoCY4nIo_IU.

See: "*How Far Can Japan Go To Curb The Coronavirus Outbreak? Not As Far As You May Think*". By Tomohiro Osaki. https://www.japantimes.co.jp/news/2020/03/01/national/japan-coronavirus-outbreak/#.XoCZiXIo_IV

[37] *See*: "*FALQs: India's Government Response to COVID-19 (Novel Coronavirus)*". March 19, 2020. by Ruth Levush. https://blogs.loc.gov/law/2020/03/falqs-indias-government-response-to-covid-19-novel-coronavirus/

1. Indigenes were very unhappy about their government's handling of the COVID-19 pandemic.[38] The main issues were misinformation by, and/or lack of "adequate" information from, the government; unpreparedness of the government; inadequate healthcare resources; loss of income/wealth, and the restrictions on mobility and businesses. Authoritarian countries[39] (such as China) and authoritarian regimes (such as Hungary) are particularly susceptible to upheavals and drastic political changes that arise from perceived mismanagement of sensitive national problems. In China, more than 760 million people were subjected to lock-downs during January–March 2020. In India during February–March 2020, more than 150 million migrant workers and day-workers had to physically trek home to their states-of-origin because of loss of their jobs and income.
2. COVID-19 has become a controversial political issue that will continue to affect political outcomes, and is significant enough to motivate revolutionary changes in governments and/or changes in political systems.
3. State government politicians and local politicians misused the COVID-19 pandemic to gain national media attention and to advance their political fortunes.
4. The COVID-19 pandemic has changed law enforcement practices,[40] the behaviors of criminal groups and the allocation of law enforcement resources. Many police officers from small towns were being relocated to work in larger cities, and in some countries, the army and army-reserve have been fully or partly mobilized to help enforce

[38] *See*: *EU Science Chief Resigns With Blast At Coronavirus Response—European Research Council's Mauro Ferrari Hits Out At Lack Of Co-Ordinated Action On Covid-19*. By Clive Cookson in London and Michael Peel. April 7, 2020. https://www.ft.com/content/f94725c8-e038-4841-a5f6-2e046ae78e95?fbclid=IwAR3FIP6sTm47Kambi0vXRfZTS3TfoDp_0REgeG0seUoZUJ2wBmT3zfTrw2Q

[39] *See*: *Opinion: Coronavirus Has The Power To Topple China's One-Party Regime—Politicians Shouldn't Underestimate The Implications Of China's Biggest Public-Health Crisis In Recent History*. March 4, 2020. By Minxin Pei. https://www.marketwatch.com/story/coronavirus-has-the-power-to-topple-chinas-one-party-regime-2020-03-04?cx_testId=3&cx_testVariant=cx_2&cx_artPos=6#cxrecs_s

[40] *See*: "*How COVID-19 is changing law enforcement practices by police and by criminal groups*". By Vanda Felbab-Brown. Tuesday, April 7, 2020. https://www.brookings.edu/blog/order-from-chaos/2020/04/07/how-covid-19-is-changing-law-enforcement-practices-by-police-and-by-criminal-groups/?fbclid=IwAR0IwzTIiXdKc1PJ_A2w-3iEf0QtcrFrC0_wEo_CB4WpW6eEP-yEDfAlyAo

lock-downs. During most of 2020, criminal gangs had more opportunities for illegal activities because of the lock-downs.

6.7 "Traditional Western" Monetary Policy and Fiscal Policy Have Failed Once Again Around the World: The Nwogugu (2019a) Policy Framework And Other Possible But Omitted Government Policy-Responses

During January–April 2020, the central banks of many countries (USA, EU, Japan; Australia, China, UK, Germany, India, Argentina, Brazil, Canada, Egypt, Iceland; New Zealand, Morocco, Mauritius, Norway, Pakistan, Poland, Russia, Serbia, Turkey, Ukraine, etc.) responded to the COVID-19 pandemic primarily by reducing their benchmark interest rates, and to a lesser extent by implementing open-market bond purchase programs (designed to provide more cash/liquidity in the economy) in order to stimulate their economies. In most countries that used them during January–April 2020 and afterward, these two monetary policies failed woefully. Even the most stupid professional bond traders can anticipate such policies and take appropriate trading positions in bond markets (yield-spread trades, credit-spread trades, etc.) and stock markets (index-options spreads, index-futures spreads, etc.). Both monetary policies benefit: i) corporate executives who don't always deploy the extra cash in domestic expansion or debt reduction, and who use the extra cash to execute share repurchases and increases in dividend payments which improve their company's per-share performance metrics and share-prices and increase their executive compensation; ii) banks, who don't always use the extra cash to increase their lending volumes and who instead, execute share repurchases and increase executive compensation; iii) professional bond traders and a few institutional investors. See Nwogugu (2012: 83-85; 118-127; 152-165; 250-259; 323-341; 17-31; 37-52; 59-75) which explains some reasons for the inefficient (and sometimes harmful) transmission of both types of monetary policies—that is, both monetary policies are usually not sufficiently "transmitted" across the national economy (and to *lower-tier dependent* foreign countries) to:

1. households in the form of lower monthly loan payments, or lower prices of goods/services or increased retirement savings or signifi-

cantly increased access to loans (i.e. partly because of credit scores, improper financial records, insufficient collateral, behavioral analytics, etc.); or

2. SMEs in the form of lower monthly loan payments or lower prices of inputs/goods/services or lower labor costs, or significantly increased access to loans (i.e. partly because of credit scores; improper financial records, insufficient collateral, behavioral analytics, etc.).

Similarly, many countries used the same fiscal policies during January 2020 to May 2020, most of which failed (i.e. most major non-stock-market indicators continued to deteriorate after those fiscal policies were implemented).

The issue is that in both developed and developing countries, individuals and SMEs face barriers to capital that are structural problems that are not (and perhaps cannot be) resolved by ***traditional western*** monetary policies and fiscal policies. These structural problems include credit scores, inadequate borrower information, inadequate truth-telling by borrowers, fraud, predatory lending, biased behavioral analytics, insufficient or unmarketable collateral, inefficient collateral recording systems and so on. Making capital available to individuals and SMEs doesn't necessarily mean that such capital will be used efficiently in ways that benefit the regional or national economy (there are problems of "intra-household allocative capabilities" and "intra-SME allocative capabilities" partly due to inadequate information and knowledge-processing). Similarly, providing tax breaks, tax credits, cash supplements and home-rent abatements/deferrals to households doesn't always provide sufficient incentives for such households to make decisions that improve both their economic/psychological position and overall social welfare. Also, when combined with the psychological pressures, lay-offs, loss of customers and cognitive deficiencies caused by pandemics/emergencies, it's likely that such *allocative capabilities* will be lower during such times.

These events and trends in the global stock markets and currency markets (summarized herein and below) are significant evidence that "traditional western" monetary policy tools (which have been adopted by Japan, Russia and China) have become obsolete and ineffective.

Most of the comments in Nwogugu (2019a) about *Risk-Perception* and *Nonlinear Risk*, were confirmed by the failures of fiscal/monetary/trade policies implemented by most governments around the world during

2020-present in response to COVID-19 Pandemic. Nwogugu (2019a) stated that:

> One of the implications of the theories introduced in this book is that macroeconomic policy-making should consist of at least six strands which should be simultaneously analyzed and which are *monetary and fiscal policies*; "*trade policies*"; "*firm-structure policies*" (which will seek to manage macroeconomic issues that arise from the structure/nature/powers of organizations); "*regulatory-response and anti-regulatory-capture policies*" (which will manage responses to regulations, antitrust and regulatory-capture); and "*behavioural-effects policies*" (which will seek to manage behavioural biases and psychological responses and also develop and track indices of same). Indeed in most developed, developing and under-developed economies there are or can be distinct "sub-markets" for "*regulatory responses*", "*behavioral effects*" and "*firm-structure effects*". Although the discussions in Hosek (1975) are somewhat outdated, the book aptly made an observation which remains valid today, when it stated in part "*.... Unfortunately, many textbooks discuss macroeconomic policy in the context of only the product market (the 'Keynesian Cross') or only the product and money markets (the IS-LM model). The labor market and the determinants of aggregate supply are usually treated separately and are not integrated in the full model....Moreover, the linkages among the all three markets become important in transmitting policy changes*".

By early August 2020, it had become clear that most monetary and fiscal policies implemented by governments around the world had failed or had started to fail. Many institutions and researchers drastically revised their growth estimates for various countries/regions downwards.[41]

[41] *See*: "*Pandemic to cut Asian growth to 2.2%, worst since 1998 crisis: ADB—Thailand, Hong Kong and seven other economies to shrink, China to slow sharply*". Cliff Venzon, April 03, 2020. https://asia.nikkei.com/Economy/Pandemic-to-cut-Asian-growth-to-2.2-worst-since-1998-crisis-ADB.

See: "*India's coronavirus lockdown spells disaster for struggling economy—Government can cut taxes and red tape to boost eventual return to growth*". Ritesh Kumar Singh, March 27, 2020. https://asia.nikkei.com/Opinion/India-s-coronavirus-lockdown-spells-disaster-for-struggling-economy.

See: "*Australia faces end of world's longest boom with recession coming—After 29 years, coronavirus puts stop to economic run*". Fumi Matsumoto, April 01, 2020. https://asia.nikkei.com/Economy/Australia-faces-end-of-world-s-longest-boom-with-recession-coming.

See: "*Japan business sentiment plunges to 7-year low, BOJ Tankan shows Coronavirus hits economy reeling from sales tax increase and trade war*". Mitsuru Obe, April 01, 2020. https://asia.nikkei.com/Economy/Japan-business-sentiment-plunges-to-7-year-low-BOJ-Tankan-shows.

6.8 Increased Risks Of Global Asset-Bubbles and Stock Market Volatility

In addition and during January–April 2020, the stock-market broad-indices (in many such countries that reduced benchmark interest rates) declined significantly and by as much as 22% in some countries[42]; and bond yields increased. The then prevailing negative "benchmark" interest rates in Japan, Denmark, Sweden and Switzerland didn't prevent their stock markets from crashing (or their bond yields from rising) during January–April 2020. Such stock-market mini-crashes were in response to announced government monetary policies, and can also be attributed to the following: i) uncertainty and perceived/actual negative outcomes of the COVID-19 Pandemic; ii) a *flight-to-quality* wherein investors sold stocks and purchased bonds and fixed income instruments; iii) the ongoing US-China and US-Japan trade wars; iv) concerns about the drastic drop in global oil prices during 2020 (by more than 30% to US$20–US$24/barrel)—which will likely have a disproportionate effect on the US economy where US oil companies need oil prices to be at around US$50/barrel or more in order for them to remain solvent; v) actual and announced bond purchases by central banks; vi) the ripple effects or *Multiplier-Effects* of the US, EU's, India's and China's economic problems on the global economy.

During and after April 2020 and up to November 2020, there was a strange and global phenomenon (the "*COVID-19 Stock Rebound and Asset-Bubble*") wherein the stock markets of many developed countries recovered (from prior substantial declines in 2020) and increased

See: "*From New Delhi to Bangkok, Asia's megacities shackled—Travel bans to contain coronavirus sap region's economic lifeblood*". Takashi Nakano And Akira Hayakawa, March 24, 2020. https://asia.nikkei.com/Spotlight/Coronavirus/From-New-Delhi-to-Bangkok-Asia-s-megacities-shackled.

See: "*BREAKING: China GDP shrinks 6.8% in 1Q, first decline since 1992*". *Nikkei Asian Review*. Apr 17, 2020.

See: "*Asia's reliance on trade, tourism weighs on COVID-19 recovery: IMF—Region lauded for swift responses but governments urged to restructure priorities*". Gwen Robinson. *Nikkei Asian Review*. April 16, 2020. https://asia.nikkei.com/Editor-s-Picks/Interview/Asia-s-reliance-on-trade-tourism-weighs-on-COVID-19-recovery-IMF

[42] *See: "Indian Stocks Crash By 13% In One Day As Economic Activity Stops—City Life Ground To A Halt As Nonessential Services Shut Down For The Rest Of The Month*". By Kiran Sharma, March 23, 2020. https://asia.nikkei.com/Business/Markets/Indian-stocks-crash-by-13-in-one-day-as-economic-activity-stops

substantially in value despite the fact that: i) most economic indices (unemployment, consumer confidence, corporate expenditures, housing starts, etc.) were at historically troubling levels, and/or were deteriorating; ii) the significant amounts spent by governments on fiscal and monetary stimulus programs during 2020 caused concerns about government budget deficits and significant government debts; iii) there were ongoing *trade wars* that negatively affected many industries in many countries.

The notable non-lagged synchronized volatility of most developed stock markets in Japan, Western Europe, Canada and the US during April–September 2020 can be deemed to be significant evidence of Cross-Border Spillovers and *international market-integration*.

The *COVID-19 Stock Rebound and Asset-Bubble* can be attributed to various factors including but not limited to the following:

1. Political interference in capital markets.
2. Government intervention in capital markets—for example, QE; government-stimulus bond-buying programs that significantly increased cash holdings of companies, pension funds and investment funds; government stimulus loans to small businesses.
3. Financial institutions' fears of retribution by national governments, many of which had triggered and implemented "Emergency Powers" (during January 2020–May 2020) pursuant to their statutes and constitutions. Such fears can cause financial institutions to maintain and support artificially high stock prices and bond prices.
4. Perhaps misguided overestimations of the benefits of the various government economic-stimulus programs around the world.
5. Misguided optimism about the timing of development and distribution (and effectiveness) of anti-COVID-19 vaccines; and hopes that COVID-19 won't mutate into new and more deadly strains.

Figure 6.6 shows the history of asset-bubbles around the world during 1980–2020. As of December 2019, there was already an ongoing global asset-bubble that was caused by technology disruptors.

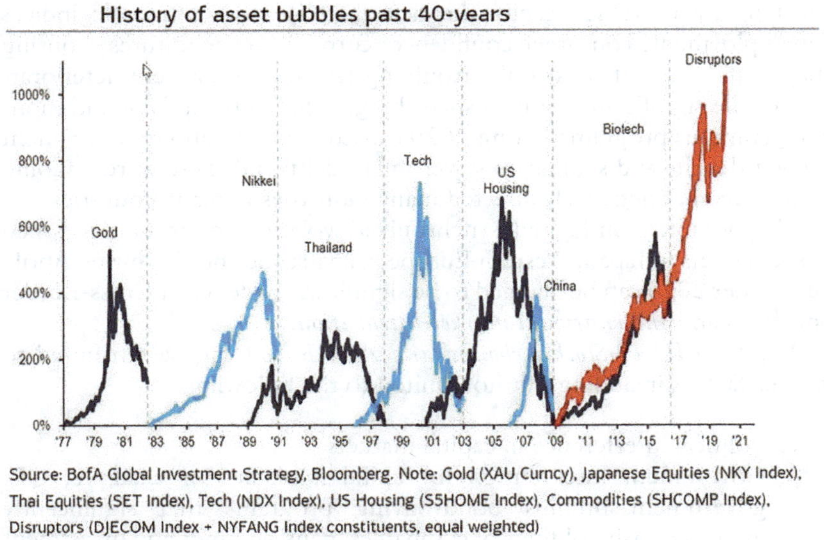

Fig. 6.6 Asset-Bubbles

6.9 Currency Markets, the Dominance of the US Economy and the SCO's (Shanghai Cooperation Organization) March 2020 Meeting And Resolution to Scrap the US Dollar

It's also noteworthy that during January–March 2020, the values of the currencies of many emerging markets countries (especially those countries whose economies were directly/indirectly linked to the US economy—i.e. indirectly linked through the China or Mexico connections/channels) declined against the US dollar and the euro (by up to 18% in some cases) even though some of these countries didn't reduce their benchmark interest rates. See Table 6.1 herein and below. Such currency devaluations can be attributed to the above-mentioned risk factors; and also make it much more difficult for such countries to reduce their benchmark interest rates. Thus, *interest rate parity* is probably wrong or doesn't exist in all circumstances. A March 2020 study by Bloomberg[43]:

[43] *See*: "*Emerging Currencies Face Losses of Up to 30% in Virus Sell-Down*". By Simon Flint. March 16, 2020. https://www.bloomberg.com/news/articles/2020-03-16/emerging-currencies-face-losses-of-up-to-30-in-virus-sell-down.

Table 6.1 Actual and Bloomberg-Forecasted Exchange Rate Movements (January–March 2020; and Post-March 2020)

Currency Pair	*Pair's Move During Jan. 20, 2020 to March 16, 2020*	*Predicted Future Move (After March 2020)*
US$/Turkish Lira	6.70%	39.30%
US$/Russian Ruble	18.00%	29.50%
US$/Colombia Peso	19.50%	23.10%
US$/South African Rand (South Africa, Lesotho; Namibia)	12.60%	22.40%
US$/Chilean Peso	8.90%	17.80%
US$/South Korean Won	5.30%	17.70%
US$/Mexican Peso	18.00%	16.10%
US$/Brazilian Lira	15.50%	16.10%
US$/Poland PZloty	3.00%	11.80%
US$/Indonesian Rupiah	8.10%	9.40%
USD/Indian Rupee	3.90%	8.70%
US$/Malaysian Ringgit	5.50%	8.50%
US$/Philippine Peso	0.10%	7.70%
US$/Taiwan $	0.70%	4.90%
US$/Thailand Baht	5.30%	3.40%
US$/Singapore $	5.30%	3.00%
US$/Chinese Yuan	2.10%	0.90%
AVERAGE	**8.50%**	**15.40%**
SPX (S&P 500 Index)	-25% (Feb. 19, 2020 to March 16, 2020)	-32.0%

Source: https://www.bloomberg.com/news/articles/2020-03-16/emerging-currencies-face-losses-of-up-to-30-in-virus-sell-down. In the case of exchange-rates, a positive percentage means that the currency's value fell/declined versus the US dollar (and vice versa for a negative percentage). In the case of the S&P 500 Index, a negative number means that the index value declined or will decline

1. estimated that the US dollar may appreciate an additional 30% against the Russian ruble and 23% versus the Chilean peso, and only 1% against the Chinese yuan during 2020.
2. Noted that the currency devaluations occurred simultaneously with declines in the US stock market in January–March 2020.

See: "*The Coronavirus Is The Biggest Emerging Markets Crisis Ever—The Pandemic Is Starting To Topple One Of The Pillars Of The Globalization Era*". By Adam Tooze. March 28, 2020. https://foreignpolicy.com/2020/03/28/coronavirus-biggest-emerging-markets-crisis-ever/.

See: "*Coronavirus' shadow looms over emerging market currencies*". By Gertrude Chavez-Dreyfuss. Reuters. March 5, 2020. https://www.nasdaq.com/articles/coronavirus-shadow-looms-over-emerging-market-currencies-2020-03-05

3. Stated that countries that have substantial current-account deficits and relatively illiquid financial markets are the most likely to lose value against the US dollar strength (e.g. South Africa, Indonesia, and India and some Latin American countries).

Chapter-1 (in this book) analyzed "US Dollar Dominance" and "US MNC Dominance".

The US has the most advanced and comprehensive financial regulations and creates some of the most sophisticated financial products in the world. The US has been at the forefront of enactment of financial/economic laws at both the federal and state levels. Many developing countries (and developed countries) copied their financial laws from US laws. For example, the Brazilian constitution is based on the US Constitution; and REIT statutes worldwide are based on US REIT laws. Many countries have created variants of the Dodd-Frank Act and the Sarbanes Oxley Act (SOX). Mortgage/foreclosure laws in many countries are very similar to US mortgage/foreclosure laws. Many developing countries and "transition" countries of Eastern Europe derived their mortgage/foreclosure laws from US laws.

During the last twenty years, the US consistently had the largest national economy in the world; and the US economy directly/indirectly (through international trade, outsourcing, FDI, FI, foreign aid, etc.) supported the economies of other "First-Level Associated" countries (such as China, Japan, Brazil, Mexico, India) which, in turn, directly/directly supported (through international trade, outsourcing, loans, FDI, FI, foreign aid) the economies of other "Second-Level Associated" countries (Russia, Nigeria, the Philippines, Thailand, ASEAN countries, Pakistan, Central American countries, CIS countries). During 1980–2020, the US was a major participant in major multilateral and bilateral trade agreements, and the US-China Trade War (2019–present) continues to have significant economic/social/psychological *Multiplier Effects* on many countries. The use of the terms "First-Level Associated" countries and "Second-Level Associated" countries is introduced here as a "mutual-dependency" classification of countries and a way to better reflect the often symbiotic relationships between countries with regard to international trade and international capital flows.

The US is a global technological innovation leader, and has consistently been a major contributor to, and beneficiary of the global digital economy. The US has the largest number of large MNCs (multinational corporations), many of which operate in more than five countries and are highly influential in international trade and finance.

The US economy (and US law) remains influential worldwide because:

- The US has a federal-presidential system of government (many developing countries are shifting to this system of government). Federalism is a big issue in US politics and economy, as well as in an increasing number of developed and developing countries (such as Germany, Russia, India, Nigeria and Brazil).
- US law was derived from English laws (which also form the basis for laws in Commonwealth countries).
- The US has a relatively diverse population; and relatively well developed and deep capital markets.
- The US has been at the forefront of mechanism design in both the private sector and in government.
- Securitization of assets/intangibles started in the US, and the securitization laws of many countries, were derived from US securitization laws—which include mortgage/foreclosure statutes.
- The US has one of the most advanced set of consumer protection laws in the world. The use of consumer credit is prevalent in the US economy—and is related to crime, willingness-to-comply and social order. Improper consumer credit was a major cause of the 2006–2009 Subprime Crisis in the US which ballooned into the Global Financial Crisis of 2007–2014.
- In the US, individual wealth, political capital and social capital are very much linked together. This seems to be a growing trend in some developing countries and in some "transition" countries of Eastern Europe.
- Labor unions have been a significant factor in the US economy, in US legislative processes and in US foreign policy; and have also shaped MNCs, which, in turn, sometimes propagated such influences and resultant effects around the world.
- Compared to other "developed" countries, US courts have been more willing to "experiment" in the areas of financial/economic regulation and the interpretation of the Constitution.
- US political/economic institutions and government agencies seem to be more concerned about various types of inequality (social, wealth, housing and income inequality) and sustainability (economic, environmental, etc.), compared to other countries.
- During 1980–2020, the US was a major cash contributor to, and exerted significant political influence at, international organizations such as the United Nations, World Bank, WTO and WHO.

During the March 2020 SCO meeting,[44] SCO members (Russia, China, India, Pakistan, Uzbekistan, Tajikistan, and Kyrgyzstan) resolved in principle to develop a framework (to be ratified at the next SCO meeting) to conduct their bilateral trade and settlements and to issue bonds and financial instruments in their national/local currencies instead of the US dollar. This move by the SCO will probably change all or some of the following:

1. Global economic power of nations and the SCO.
2. Global military alliances.
3. International capital flows and international trade.
4. Risk perceptions and perhaps credit ratings of SCO countries.
5. Foreign aid, FDI and FI in SCO countries.
6. The effectiveness of economic sanctions imposed by the UN and/or "western" countries.
7. The pace of economic development and trade in SCO countries and their lower-tier dependent countries.
8. Political power, political capital and influence in the US and the EU.
9. Foreign policies and international alliances of many countries.
10. The politics, structure and funding of international organizations such as the UN (United Nations), WTO (World Trade Organization), WHO (World Health Organization) and the World Bank.

Iran, Afghanistan, Belarus and Mongolia are SCO "observer-nations" that want to become regular members of SCO. Based on geographical coverage and population, the SCO is the largest regional organization in the world.

6.10 Government's *Emergency Powers* (During Pandemics and Crises) as Fiscal Policies That Have Repeatedly Failed

Around the world and during the last fifty years, governments' *Emergency Powers* (that automatically arise from existing statutes or are created through new statutes) during pandemics have usually been used to: i) restrict the mobility of indigenes and businesses; ii) shut down or limit

[44] *See*: "*Shanghai Cooperation Organization To Introduce 'Mutual Settlement In National Currencies' And Ditch US Dollar*". March 18, 2020. https://www.silkroadbriefing.com/news/2020/03/18/shanghai-cooperation-organisation-introduce-mutual-settlement-national-currencies-ditch-us-dollar/

businesses; iii) close schools and government offices; iv) grants cash payments to households and companies. These *Emergency Powers* have in effect become fiscal policies because:

1. As evidenced by the COVID-19 pandemic, the powers can cause significant economic and psychological harm (recessions).
2. The imposition of such powers often amounts to an implicit taxation on individuals and businesses who end up losing significant amounts of money.
3. Many state and federal governments subsequently have to spend additional money on "economic stimulus" to fix the damage done by the *Emergency Powers.*
4. These policies have significant effects on the budgets, spending and revenue sources of state, local and federal governments.
5. In many countries, they are government policies which are often widely announced and are enforced by the police and government officials.

In modern times, the exercise of such *Emergency Powers* has repeatedly led to costly failures (social, economic, psychological and political) as was the case during the Global Financial Crisis (in the USA and parts of Europe) and the 2020 COVID-19 pandemic (in the USA, China, Italy, Spain, etc.).

6.11 Reductions in Global Remittances, Foreign Aid, Foreign Direct Investment (FDI) and Foreign Investment (FI)

The COVID-19 pandemic will most probably reduce foreign investment, FDI, foreign aid and the $690+ billion (as of 2019/2020) in annual remittances[45] that immigrants send to their home countries (mostly

[45] *See*: World Bank (2020a). *Migration and Development Brief 33: COVID-19 Crisis Through a Migration Lens, October 2020.* World Bank, Washington, DC, USA.

See: *World Bank (2020b). Migration and Development Brief 32: COVID-19 Crisis Through a Migration Lens, April 2020.* World Bank, Washington, DC, USA.

See: World Bank (2019). *Migration and Remittances: Recent Developments and Outlook. Migration and Development Brief, No. 31, April 2019.* World Bank, Washington, DC, USA.

See: Migration Data Portal (2020). *Remittances.* 18 November 2020. https://migrationdataportal.org/themes/remittances. ("Remittance flows in 2020 to low- and middle-income countries (LMICs) are projected to fall by 7.2 per cent to USD 508 billion, followed by a

emerging markets countries). The main problems with remittances are as follows:

1. A significant percentage of such immigrants are not covered by, and won't benefit from, economic stimulus programs launched in their countries of residence.
2. A significant percentage of such immigrants either work in industries that were heavy affected by COVID-19 (hotels, tourism, restaurants, transportation, construction, automobiles, maintenance, agriculture, etc.) or are day-laborers (who earn income daily) or are part time workers, and thus lost their jobs or are likely to lose their jobs.
3. The emergency laws and associated border-closures and lock-downs in foreign countries will affect immigrants' access to payment systems and ability to find other sources of income.
4. Many of the immigrants are low-income or lower-middle-income earners and have relatively low savings.

Such reductions in global remittances may, in turn, have adverse social, economic and political ramifications in underdeveloped countries that are heavily dependent on remittances. Countries such as the Philippines

further decline of 7.5 per cent to USD 470 billion in 2021. These projected declines are among the sharpest in recent history (World Bank, 2020a). According to the World Bank, this fall is largely due to the economic crisis caused by the COVID-19 pandemic; for migrant workers, the pandemic has meant a fall in wages and employment (ibid.). The World Bank projects a decline of remittance flows in 2020 across all regions: Europe and Central Asia (-16%); Sub-Saharan Africa (-8.8%), South Asia (-4%), the Middle East and North Africa (-8%), Latin America and the Caribbean (-0.2%), and East Asia and the Pacific (-10.5%) (ibid.) ... This decline comes after remittances to LMICs reached a record USD 554 billion in 2019, overtaking Foreign Direct Investments (World Bank, 2020b). In 2019, in current USD, the top five remittance recipient countries were India (83.1 billion), China (68.4 billion), Mexico (38.5 billion), the Philippines (35.2 billion), and the Arab Republic of Egypt (26.8 billion) (ibid.). In relative terms, the top 5 countries which received the highest remittances as a share of gross domestic product (GDP) in 2019 were: Tonga (37.6% of GDP), Haiti (37.1%), South Sudan (34.1%), the Kyrgyz Republic (29.2%), and Tajikistan (28.2%) (ibid.). In the third quarter of 2020, the average costs of sending USD 200 to LMICs remained high at 6.8 per cent, well above the target of 3 per cent of the Sustainable Development Goal 10.c.1 (World Bank, 2020a). Sub-Saharan Africa continued to have the highest average remittance costs, at about 8.5 per cent; South Asia had the lowest average remittance costs at 5 per cent. The average remittance costs for the remaining regions were: Europe and Central Asia (6.5%); East Asia and Pacific (7.1%); Middle East and North Africa (7.5%); and Latin America and the Caribbean (5.8%) (ibid.)").

(2019/2018 remittances were about 9.8% of GDP), Lebanon (2019/2018 remittances were about 12.3% of GDP), Somalia, Sudan, Ukraine (11.8% of GDP), CIS countries (ex-Russia), Argentina, Venezuela, El Salvador (20.8%), Honduras (21.4%), Guatemala (13.0%), Pakistan (7.7% of GDP), Nicaragua (13%), Romania, and Egypt (8.5% of GDP) and many West African countries will likely be significantly affected because remittances accounted for 7%–35% of their annual 2018/2019 GDP.

The combination of Emergency Powers (granted to government agencies during pandemics or economic crisis and long-term effects of associated restrictions), uncertainty, actual/perceived political risk, increased credit risk around the world, domestically oriented economic stimulus programs launched by governments, stock market crashes during 2020, global reductions of labor force and so on will likely reduce both FDI and FI for the next few years.

These factors will probably change all or some of the following: i) global economic power and political influence; ii) international capital flows and international trade; iii) risk perceptions and perhaps credit ratings of developing countries; iv) FDI and FI in developing countries; v) the effectiveness of economic sanctions; vi) the pace of economic development and trade in emerging markets countries and their lower-tier dependent countries; vii) political power and influence in both developed and developing countries; v) foreign policies and international alliances of many countries; viii) the politics, structure and funding of international organizations such as the UN, WTO, IBRD, EBRD, WHO and the World Bank; and many NGOs that provide foreign aid in developing countries (Figs. 6.8 and 6.9).

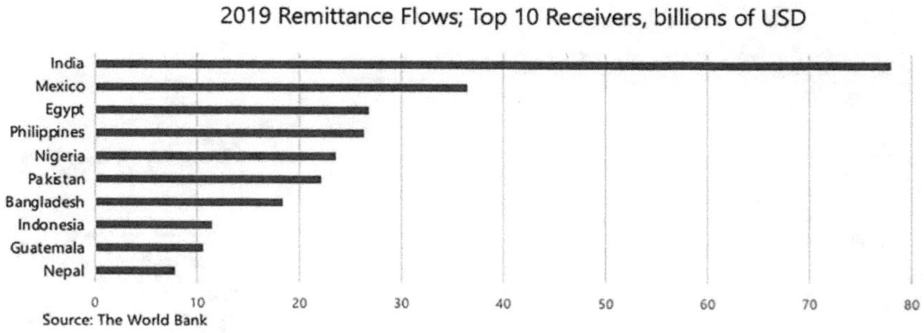

Fig. 6.8 Top-Ten Country-Receivers of Remittances (2019; in billions of US Dollars)

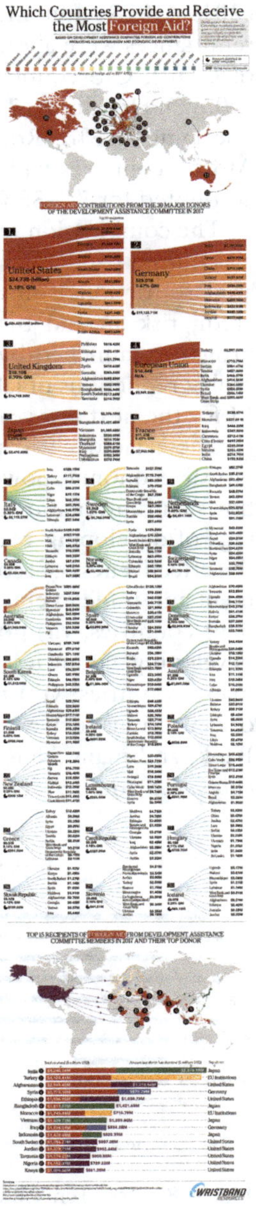

Fig. 6.9 Top Donors and Recipients of Foreign Aid (2017). Source: https://www.wristband.com/content/which-countries-provide-receive-most-foreign-aid/

6.12 The Failure of the "Financial Accelerator Theory" (Nwogugu [2012])

Nwogugu (2012: 126-127) explained why the "*Financial Accelerator Theory*" is wrong and won't work in most economies. The 2020 events, and the effects of the monetary/fiscal policies and government responses implemented by various countries (especially the US and the UK) in response to the COVID-19 pandemic of 2019–present, are additional evidence that the "*Financial Accelerator Theory*" doesn't work.

6.13 The *CoronaBond* Debate and the Fragile European Union (EU) Unity

Similar to most other prior crises, during January–April 2020, Europe took a very divided approach to battling COVID-19. Some European countries randomly enacted new laws and took decisions independent of both the EU and the *Schengen* frameworks, and some countries closed their national borders. *Schengen* was suspended during this period. The *Stability Pact* was also suspended. During January–April 2020, there were no coordinated responses to COVID-19 among European countries. When the Italian government activated the EU's solidarity mechanism during 2020 (in response to COVID-19), initially no EU country helped, and Germany and France implemented export bans on medical equipment. During March 2020, Italy accepted aid from both Russia and China, and Greece, Czech Republic and Serbia accepted aid from China. Russia and China have traditionally been stiff competitors to the European Union and NATO.

The EU and some EU countries chose to *politically securitize* the COVID-19 pandemic. Such action grants such EU countries new and greater domestic powers that may push them farther away from EU "central" control, policies and regulations. For example, on March 30, 2020, the Hungarian Parliament voted by 137–53 to accept the Hungarian government's request for the power to rule by decree during the COVID-19 pandemic, which literally converted Hungary into an authoritarian state with no specific time limits. More than 100,000 Hungarian residents had signed a petition against the new government powers.

Italy, Portugal, Greece and Spain have consistently expressed concerns that the EU abandons them during crises and emergencies, and that they have to frequently negotiate with the EU about resolving their domestic economic problems. Nationalist political parties in Greece, Portugal, Italy and Spain have raised the issue of leaving the EU. The way that the EU handles both the COVID-19 pandemic and its legal/economic relationships with these four countries will probably affect the political prospects of these nationalists. In the shadow of the UK's departure from the EU, the departure of Greece, Portugal, Italy, Hungary and/or Spain from the EU and/or the *Schengen* may trigger additional departures by other EU and/or *Schengen* countries that are dissatisfied with various elements of the EU and/or *Schengen* experiments. The reality is EU unity remains fragile and is more so in recent times. Some of the disputed issues are as follows:

1. Economic policy.
2. Implementation of the monetary union.
3. Immigration issues, security of borders and treatment and funding of migrants.
4. The "political union" remains weak and is almost distinct from, and not properly integrated into, the "monetary union".
5. Differential treatment of EU countries on similar issues.
6. EU aid to troubled EU countries in times of pandemics and crises.
7. The issuance of jointly backed debt by EU countries.

Thus the EU has been at a cross-roads since 2008 (when the Global Financial Crisis began) and has to decide to either: (i) come closer (i.e.. a much stronger economic and political bond among EU countries and more centralization of EU-related decisions; and eliminating political dominance by Germany and France), or (ii) become a loose federation of countries, with de-centralized decision-making for most issues. The longer it takes the EU to decide this issue, the more likely that other countries will leave the EU.

Despite opposition by Germany, Austria, Finland and the Netherlands (and assent by Spain, Italy, France, Belgium, Luxembourg, Ireland, Portugal, Greece and Slovenia), during and after 2020, the EU continued to debate the launch of the "CoronaBonds" which are debts that are backed by all EU countries and will be issued by EU institutions such as the European Investment Bank. The proceeds of the CoronaBonds will be used to fight COVID-19 pandemic and the associated reconstruction of national economies. The issuance of a jointly backed debt by EU countries has historically been a highly contentious issue, and had never been done as of March 2020. During the 2010–2012 sovereign debt crisis, France and Italy supported proposals to issue jointly backed EU bonds, but Germany opposed it.

The main alternatives to CoronaBonds are: i) the *European Stability Mechanism* (ESM), which was created during the 2008 (Global Financial Crisis) to provide financial assistance to EU countries and troubled EU banks; and ii) a proposed European Monetary Fund. Other insolvency solutions have been recommended as remedies for sovereign default in the EU. See: Rodden (2017), Wyplosz (2017), Fuest, Heinemann & Schröder (2016), Gasparotti, Minkina & Alice (2018) and Havlik & Heinemann (2020). All EU recipients of aid from the ESM can also receive additional aid in the form of open market purchases of their bonds by the European Central Bank (this bond buying program hasn't been used as of March 2020). The European Central Bank announced that it planned to spend at least €1 trillion in purchases of private and public debt in the EU during 2020.

Thus, the issuance of the CoronaBonds could mark a new beginning in intra-EU relations and politics, and may help heal the social and political divides in the European Union. The CoronaBonds signifies needed unity and will be the first of its kind in the EU in times of crises.

6.14 "*Adverse Policy Contagion*" and Risk Perception

The apparent *Adverse Policy Contagion* of 2020–present (i.e.. fiscal, monetary, social welfare and trade policies) across the world can increase the risks of Financial Instability, cross-border Systemic Risk Contagion, Cross-border Spillovers, Inflation and distorted Risk Perception (which affects expenditures, confidence, etc.). With regard to analytical, policy-making and policy-implementation approaches to *Risk Perception*, Nwogugu (2019a) noted that: "...The main problems with these different approaches are that: (i) they omit the nature/powers of the corporate entity; (ii) the analytical approaches have not been unified into a comprehensive approach; (iii) they omit the issues of adaptive systems (most treat the firm and its subsystems and constraints as near-static), Regret and Transferable Utilities; (iv) they don't consider the often significant and "dominant" relationship between financial risk on one hand and operational risk; and (v) they don't fully consider the effects of incentives (the incentives of employees, regulators, customers and the board of directors) ...".

Many theories and conclusions in articles such as Chang and Fernandez (2013), Arellano (2008), Bayer et al. (2019), Cugat (2019), Milesi-Ferretti and Lane (2017) and Sunel (2018) have been proven partly or wholly wrong by the COVID-19 pandemic.

6.15 The Non-Performing Loan (NPL) Crisis in Emerging Markets Countries; and the High-Consumer-Debt Crisis in USA, Europe, China, India, South Korea And Japan (2015–2021)

The vastly understated *NPL crisis* of 2017–2021 in Emerging Markets banks (e.g. in China, India, Nigeria) and the *High-Consumer-Debt Crisis* of 2015–2021 in USA, Europe, China, South Korea and Japan seem to be repeats of past trends and also pose significant Financial Instability risks, Inequality-Risks and *Cross-Border Spillover* Risks and will likely be exacerbated by COVID-19 (i.e. via lockdowns; job losses; corporate/personal financial distress; defaults; reduced income and revenues; reduced business confidence and Consumer Confidence; etc.). See: Garrido et al. (2020), Hossain et al. (2021), Torsello and Winkler (2020), De Ferra et al. (2020), Kusuma et al. (2021) and Bayer et al. (2020). These countries will have to take decisive measures such as the following:

1. Many of the issues/omissions explained in Nwogugu (2019c), Nwogugu (2012: 17–77; 83–112; 249–316; 323–411), Nwogugu (2015a, b), Nwogugu (2005a, b) and Nwogugu (2014; revised 2020) should be considered.
2. Enact and implement loan/debt resolution statutes and penalties; enforce statutes and implement strict penalties for inadequate financial disclosures, earnings management and asset-quality management—see Nwogugu (2020b).
3. Amend loan/bond pricing guidelines and financial statement disclosures because the COVID-19 pandemic, Trade Wars and economic conditions in Asia can distort the assumptions underlying most securities valuation methods—see the comments in Nwogugu (2017, 2020b).
4. Consider alternatives to "*Asset Management Corporations*" which have been used in USA, Singapore India, Malaysia, China and other countries with very limited success. Constitutionally credible variants of the Dodd Frank Act (USA) "*Orderly Liquidation*" provisions are viable options—see Nwogugu (2015a, b).
5. Planning and infrastructure development (at the state/municipal/federal levels) for future pandemics.

6.16 Key Success-Factors for Developing Policy Responses to COVID-19

Given that around the world, many large MNCs function like quasi-governments, the key success factors for governments' and MNCs' COVID-19 responses include but are not limited to the following:

1. Many of the issues/omissions explained in Nwogugu (2015a, b), Nwogugu (2019c), Nwogugu (2012: 17–77; 83–112; 249–316; 323–411), Nwogugu (2005a, b) and Nwogugu (2014; rev. 2020) should be considered.
2. Overall resource allocation—more resources should be allocated to measures and incentives that promote revenue generation, trade and good health/environmental compliance habits.
3. *Regulatory-Capture*, *Regulatory-Failures*, Corruption and Fraud in the allocation and distribution of social welfare and stimulus benefits.
4. Government budget deficits, and the financing of governments' current and future responses to COVID-19, and planning and infrastructure development (at the local/municipal/federal level) for future pandemics.
5. Mutation of COVID-19, and in-bound travelers that carry COVID-19 mutations into countries.
6. Changes in Healthcare policy, and enforcement of Public Health measures—for example, penalties and incentives (e.g. avoidance of overcrowding; masks/gloves; hand-washing), and providing healthcare services in rural areas; vaccines research and incentives for people to get vaccinated.
7. Restarting companies and domestic trade, and Community-based economic development. Economic Recovery in Asia will have to be built around companies (mostly Asian MNCs) and community-based cooperatives.
8. Social unrest, Compliance (by indigenes—as a physical phenomenon), public sentiment and responses of populations to announced/implemented government policies
9. Community-based food security and agriculture programs.
10. Assisting SMEs, educational institutions and government agencies to move their operations to the Internet.

11. In-country Migration Policy—especially incentives for low-income people to migrate to low-cost and less-densely-populated towns and agriculture-intensive areas (to reduce over-crowding in high-cost cities).

6.17 Some New Theories

6.17.1 ***The* Policy Contagion Theory**

During 2019–2020 and amid the COVID-19 pandemic, the economic and social welfare policies announced and implemented (somewhat sequentially or simultaneously) by many national governments were very similar, and most eventually failed or were only marginally successful. There seemed to be a *policy contagion* among national governments (but with relatively low coordinated action/policies among countries) which may have been driven by some of the following factors: i) similarities in educational training (i.e. training in "western" economic theory and models) of policy professionals; ii) use of similar macro and policy models (mainly "western" models); iii) direct and indirect influences of multilateral organizations—such as the World Bank, IMF, the European Central Bank, and EBRD; iv) many of the common policy processes/methods were routine and were typically used in non-crisis periods and, thus, there may have been an intentional aversion to new policy methods that would increase anxiety and perceived risk.

6.17.2 ***The* Truncated Integration Theory**

During the COVID-19 pandemic of 2019–present and around the world, market-integration (of financial, labor and finished-goods markets) seemed to increase in financial markets and commodities markets (2019–2020 data), but such international market-integration can be reduced/truncated by any of the following factors:

1. Government stimulus programs that conflict with other governments' stimulus programs.
2. Trade wars and trade tariffs (e.g. US-China trade war [2019–present]).
3. Immigration curbs by national governments.
4. Restrictions on remittances to foreign governments.
5. Consumer confidence and business confidence.

6.17.3 *The* Political Support Theory *(and the* Bifurcated Political Support Theory*)*

Political conditions often affect markets during pandemics and/or economic/financial shocks. During February to April 2020, the stock markets of many developed countries and some emerging markets countries (such as China) declined substantially due to concerns about COVID-19. However, beginning in April 2020 and as these same national governments announced new economic/financial and social welfare policies, their stock markets rebounded significantly and excessively (during April–November 2020) despite the fact that their economic data (such as business confidence, consumer confidence, GNP, unemployment; corporate profits; exports) were deteriorating badly. This phenomenon can be attributed to: i) anticipated or perceived "political support" of the economy by the national and state governments; ii) "expectations" of market participants—which are sometimes triggered by the implementation of "Emergency Statutes" by governments (which typically grant spending powers and special fiscal/monetary powers to such government); iii) fear of and/or perceived retribution by national governments against market-institutions such as banks and securities brokerages; iv) perceived or anticipated increased cooperation among competing political parties in order to resolve the ongoing crisis—such cooperation often resulted in economic aid packages that would normally be much more difficult to enact (collectively, the *political support theory*).

In democratic countries, the foregoing political support can be sometimes "bifurcated" by any of the following factors: i) political appointments, political appointees and their perceived powers/influence; ii) political donations and lobbying; iii) national debt and consumer/household debt; iv) availability and cost of both corporate and consumer credit; v) trade wars and trade tariffs (collectively, the *bifurcated political support theory*).

6.17.4 *The* Monetary-Fiscal Gap Theory

During the COVID-19 pandemic and beginning in January 2020 many national governments announced new economic/financial (monetary and fiscal) and social welfare policies, and their stock markets rebounded significantly (during April–October 2020) despite the fact that their economic data (such as business confidence, consumer confidence, GNP; unemployment; productivity; corporate profits; exports, etc.) were deteriorating badly. However, there was some evidence that in some countries such as the US and China, monetary policies and fiscal policies seemed to conflict and/or produce opposing results and harmful "gaps" in financial stability, economic growth and political power (the *monetary-fiscal gap*):

1. the cash stimulus provided by governments were often misspent and contributed to localized inflation and increased household debt;
2. the mandatory debt forbearances (real estate rents; interest payments for loans and mortgages, etc.) ordered by state and national governments led to the financial distress and bankruptcy of many landlords and financial institutions and losses for investment funds.
3. the "lock-downs" enacted by national and state governments drastically reduced economic activity and increased personal and corporate financial distress;
4. the "lock-downs" enacted by national and state governments created political conflicts (within and between political parties), *Costly Litigation* and *Costly Constitutional Controversies* (cost in terms of government administrative resource, litigation, effects of uncertainty on markets, reduced Consumer-confidence/Business-Confidence, etc.).

6.17.5 *The* Inefficient Re-Allocation Theory

What became apparent during 2020–2021 and around the world is that:

- In most democratic countries, pandemics, epidemics and economic/ financial crisis often require a re-alignment/re-allocation of power among the judiciary, the legislature and the executive branches of government at the state and federal levels.
- As of 2020–2021 and in some democratic countries like the USA, such re-alignment of power was sometimes achieved through "*Emergency Statutes*" (that are triggered by specific events/conditions), which have been very controversial as to their scope, intent and powers.
- As of 2020–2021, most democratic systems hadn't been able to develop or implement effective re-alignment/re-allocation of power among the judiciary, the legislature and the executive branches of

government at the state and federal levels in response to the COVID-19 pandemic—ie. lack of sufficient statutory power-reallocation that is required for economic growth/resiliency.
- This lack of effective re-alignment/re-allocation of power often results in ineffective public/economic/financial policies that eventually reduce social welfare and sustainable growth (as in the case of the USA and India during April–December 2020).

6.17.6 The Labor-Policy-Compliance Gap Theory

During the COVID-19 Pandemic and beginning in January 2020, there was some evidence that in some countries such as the USA, EU and China, some announced and implemented, Social-Welfare Policies, Labor Policies, and Fiscal Policies seemed to conflict and or produce opposing results and harmful "Gaps" (the *Labor-Monetary-Fiscal Gap*):

1. The cash stimulus provided to individuals and companies by governments were often mis-spent and may have increased actual unemployment (via fraudulent-claims; disincentives to work; companies reduced their actual head-counts in order to gain more fraudulent profits from false filings for stimulus cash; etc.).
2. The mandatory debt forbearances (e.g. Real estate rents; interest payments for loans and mortgages; etc.) ordered by municipal/ state and national governments led many landlords and financial institutions and investment funds to incur losses and caused these entities to reduce their staff, employee benefits, and to violate labor regulations (e.g. sanitation) and collective bargaining agreements.
3. The "Lock-downs" enacted by national and state governments drastically reduced economic activity and increased personal and corporate financial distress; they also reduced individuals' ability to re-train (obtain new skills) or re-locate to get new jobs.
4. The Lock-downs and implementation of fiscal policies and social-welfare created highly publicized and controversial power-conflicts among the national/state legislatures, courts and the executive branches of governments. Such conflicts can have negative effects on stock markets, bond markets currency markets and consumer confidence.
5. The Lock-downs increased under-employment in many cities (people were working part-time and some had to obtain lower-skill jobs).

6. The Lock-downs enacted by national and state governments created political conflicts (within and between political parties), *Costly Litigation* and *Costly Constitutional Controversies* (cost in terms of government administrative resource, litigation, effects of uncertainty on markets, reduced Consumer-confidence/Business-Confidence, etc.).
7. Some of the Social Welfare policies and the Lock-downs reduced compliance in many cities (e.g. fraudulent filings by individuals and companies for financial-aid and exemptions, violations of sanitation and or public health regulations, etc.).
8. In some countries (such as the USA, United Kingdom, European Union), the enactment and subsequent amendments and revocations of Executive Orders (pertaining to Labor and compliance) by Presidents/Prime-Ministers and the equivalent of state/regional governors in several countries amounted to policy-reversals and generated uncertainty, and affected or could have affected *Consumer-confidence, Business-Confidence*, Government *Confidence* and stock-market volatility.
9. COVID-19 caused many national and state governments to enact labor policies that significantly (and in some cases permanently) affected workers, employment contracts and collective-bargaining agreements, Risk-Perception, Fairness-Perceptions, *Propensity-To-Comply*, Consumer Confidence, Aspirations and prioritization of obligations and objectives.
10. In some countries (such as the USA, United Kingdom, European Union and China), COVID-19 caused many national/local/state governments to enact labor policies and compliance-policies that significantly (and in some cases permanently) changed the compliance-patterns, *Regret-Aversion* and Fairness-Perceptions of companies and individuals, and in ways that affected peoples' Aspirations, *Propensity-To-Comply*, Consumer Confidence and prioritization of obligations and objectives. That may have been manifested in the volumes of criminal activity, COVID-19 voluntary vaccination patterns, public protests (against government policies), ill-advised public gatherings, non-compliance with Anti-COVID19 policies, etc., in those countries.
11. In some countries (such as the USA) and during 2020–2021, the penalties for non-compliance with Emergency Statutes and Anti-COVID-19 protocols didn't seem to have sufficient deterrence effects.

12. In some countries (such as the USA) and during 2020–2021, courts focused on constitutional rights and labor rights, but didn't seem to attempt to control the timing, enforcement and legal-liability of economic/financial rights implicit in labor contracts and collective-bargaining agreements. That may have amounted to a "Judicial Moratorium" on rights (similar to debt forbearances ordered by the executive branches of state and federal governments). Any of those issues which could have had significant effects on regional/national economies, financial markets, Labor markets and commodity markets.

6.17.7 *The* Information-Confidence-Markets Gap Theory

During the COVID-19 Pandemic (2020–2021) and in the US, UK and China, there was some evidence that in those countries, government policies created "Gaps" in Markets, Information, Business/Consumer Confidence, "*Government Confidence*" and Labor practices (the *Information-Confidence-Markets Gap Theory*) such as the following:

1. Many companies changed their budgets, financial forecasts, employment practices, employee benefits and workers' rights in anticipation of resolution of COVID-19 based on disseminated information, but that wasn't the case because COVID-19 has lasted far longer than predicted by many.
2. The declining and lower Business Confidence and Consumer Confidence (and on occasion, lower "*Government Confidence*") were in stark contrast to the dynamics of Information Markets (news; financial indices; stock prices; financial disclosures by companies; etc.). There is the issue of the adequacy and timeliness of corporate disclosures of the effects of COVID-19. *Government Confidence* refers to confidence of government employees (and especially policy-makers) about current and future economic/social-welfare policies and the global economy.
3. In some countries (eg. USA, UK) and during 2020–2021, overall corporate compliance and individual-compliance with regulations seemed to have declined, and that conflicted with enforcement efforts, new regulations and Emergency Statutes, and dynamics of Information Markets (news; financial indices; stock prices; financial

disclosures by companies; etc.). In this context, non-compliance pertains to public health regulations, government processes and crime.

4. The mandatory debt forbearances (e.g. real estate rents, interest payments for loans and mortgages, etc.) ordered by state/local/national governments sent signals that often conflicted with the dynamics and trends of Information-Markets (news, financial indices, stock prices, financial disclosures by companies, etc. which indicated likelihood of improving conditions), and the trends in Labor markets (cash stimulus offered to companies to retain employees; layoffs, furloughs, government-sponsored loan programs that promoted employee-retention; employee-telecommuting; etc.).
5. The Lock-downs enacted by municipal/national/state governments drastically reduced economic activity and increased personal and corporate financial distress, and was in contrast to Information-Markets dynamics and trends, and also prevented/reduced Labor mobility and skills-acquisition.
6. The Lock-downs enacted by national/municipal/state governments created or could have created political conflicts (within and between political parties), *Costly Litigation* and *Costly Constitutional Controversies* (cost in terms of government administrative resources, litigation, effects of uncertainty on markets, reduced Consumer-confidence/Business-Confidence, etc.).
7. Some of the above-mentioned issues created and increased uncertainty in financial, labor, commodities and finished-goods markets around the world (partly due to the global economic power of the US, China and the EU and associated Cross-Border Spillovers).
8. During 2020–2021 and in some countries such as the US, UK and China, COVID-19 caused many governments to enact financial/social-welfare/information-dissemination policies that significantly (and in some cases permanently) affected employment contracts and collective-bargaining agreements, Risk-Perception, Fairness-Perceptions, Consumer Confidence, Aspirations and prioritization of obligations and objectives.
9. During 2020–2021, the enactment and subsequent amendments and revocations of Executive Orders (pertaining to government affairs, information and International Affairs) by Presidents/Prime-Ministers and the equivalent of state/regional governors in several countries (such as the USA) generated *uncertainty*, and

could have affected *Consumer-Confidence, Business-Confidence, Government Confidence* and stock-market volatility.

10. The patterns of dissemination of information by various national governments during 2020–2021 may have affected the policies, timing and announcements of governments of other countries (this may have been manifested in the *Constitutional-Contagion* and similarities of government policies noted in this chapter). The political and economic Opportunity-Costs of announcing "*non-standard*" policies (that differed substantially from those of other countries) may have been significant.
11. In some countries such as the US and the EU and during 2020–2021, there was the issue (and the gap) of the relationship between the impact and comprehension/understanding of Information (i.e. government policies/announcements; corporate disclosures; etc.) on one hand, and the dynamics of financial, commodities and Labor markets.
12. In some countries (such as the USA) and during 2020–2021, courts didn't seem to attempt to control the timing, legal-liability, amount and quality of announcements and information dissemination by state/national governments and large companies, any of which could have had significant effects on regional/national economies, financial markets, Labor markets and commodity markets. Rather, most courts focused on interpretations of constitutional rights and Labor rights.
13. In some countries (such as the USA) and during 2020–2021, many of the lower courts issued conflicting rulings on issues pertaining to COVID-19 and associated government policies.

6.17.8 The Relationship Between Currency Devaluation and Domestic Industrialization Does Not Apply in Some Emerging Markets Countries (Based on January–June 2020 Data)

Contrary to textbook theories, devaluation of an emerging market currency does not increase that country's industrialization, and does not reduce the country's dependence on imported goods. That became evident in some South Asian and Latin American countries whose currencies devalued against the US dollar during January–August 2020 (see the table above). Some of these affected countries still import substantial volumes of goods and or depend on sales of commodities for most of the foreign currency earnings—sometimes due to very high interest rates, endemic corruption, consumer preference for imported goods (which often convey social status); lack of entrepreneurship, inadequate protectionist statutes; relatively very low investment in technology and education; and so on.

6.17.9 *The Relationship Between GDP Growth and Increases in Exchange Rates Does Not Apply in Some Emerging Markets Countries (Based on January–June 2020 Data)*

The classic textbook economic/econometric theory is that the growth of a country's GDP causes increases in the country's currency exchange rates against major currencies—butt that wasn't the case in China during August 2020 to April 2021 when China's GDP unexpectedly grew but its currency lost value against the US dollar. Unfortunately, this false theory has caused many emerging markets countries to officially devalue their currencies with the hopes that their currency exchange rates will improve once: (i) there is import substitution in their economies; and (ii) when their manufacturing sector grows.

The viable alternatives to currency devaluation are: (i) impose direct import restrictions on foreign goods/services; (ii) impose heavy import taxes/duties on selected foreign goods and use the proceeds to subsidize domestic companies—that will also discourage consumption among the middle-class and lower classes.

6.17.10 *The Symbiotic Relationship Between Balance-Of-Trade and Exchange Rates Does Not Apply in Some Emerging Markets Countries; and the* Marshall-Lerner Conditions *Are Invalid (Based on January–November 2020 Data)*

Although China maintained positive Balances of Trade (Trade Surplus) during 2018–2021 and had historically relatively very high interest rates in 2018–2019 (which should have attracted foreign investors to China's bond markets), the market value of the Chinese Yuan continued to decline against many major currencies during 2018–2020. Thus, in some emerging markets, contrary to textbook macroeconomics theories, Balances of Trade (i.e. Trade Surplus) are or can be irrelevant to exchange rates; and currency devaluation does not always result in material increases in Trade Surpluses particularly when there are other conditions such as low credit quality (of domestic companies and governments), high consumer debt, perceived high political risk; and perceived corruption; economic sanctions.

The trading patterns of the Chinese Yuan and China's Balances-of-Trade during 2018–2020 are evidence that the *Marshall-Lerner Conditions* are invalid. The *Marshall-Lerner Conditions* theory is that when there is no capital mobility, and there is perfectly elastic supply of trade goods, full employment and unchanged stable income, and the relative price elasticity of import demand is greater than one and the initial balance of zero-recurring items, currency depreciation can increase export earnings and trade surplus will increase; while currency appreciation can reduce export earnings and increase import spending the trade-balance deficit. Chen and He (2011) also reached the same conclusion, and found that using the *Marshall–Lerner Conditions* for decision-making always leads to conclusions that are contrary to expectations and the *Marshall–Lerner Conditions* lack satisfactory technical demonstration effect.

6.17.11 Purchasing Power Parity *Does Not Apply in Some Emerging Markets Countries (Based on 2019–2020 Data)*

One of the lessons from COVID-19 2020 was that "*Purchasing Power Parity*" doesn't apply in many emerging markets. This has been manifested by: (i) the asymmetrical and disproportionate changes in exchange rates compared to changes in interest rates in the USA on one hand, and many of the countries listed in Table 6.1 herein and above; (ii) regionalized inflation/deflation; and iii) increased sensitivity of both the government and the private sector to changes in oil prices; and (iv) the asymmetrical and disproportionate changes in exchange rates compared to changes in inflation in the USA on one hand, and many of the countries listed in Table 6.1 herein and above. This can be attributed to distortions caused by perceived credit quality; perceived corruption; political risk; uneven unemployment; terrorism; perceived excessive state interference in the economy; differences between real and perceived inflation; economic sanctions; lack of, or inactivity of organized trade unions; un-developed retail markets; low education levels; high proportion of un-skilled labor; high-dependence on imported goods; high transaction costs; international trade restrictions; heavy dependence on exports of one or a few goods (e.g. oil/gas); high political risk; and so on.

6.17.12 The **Harrod-Balassa-Samuelson Effect** *Does Not Apply in Some Emerging Markets Countries (Based on 2019–2020 Data)*

The *Harrod-Balassa-Samuelson Effect* is defined as the following:

1. Consumer price levels in richer countries are systematically higher than in poorer ones (the "*Penn Effect*").
2. The assumption that productivity varies more by country in the traded goods' sectors than in other sectors (the *Balassa–Samuelson hypothesis*).

The *Harrod-Balassa-Samuelson Effect* is conjectured here not to exist in some emerging markets countries due to the following:

1. The effects of heavy dependence on imported goods.
2. Low manufacturing output and or quality.
3. Intense competition in industries in rich countries.
4. In many categories of consumer products (hotels; juices; household necessities; etc.), prices are the same in Nigeria, Germany and the US.
5. Productivity varies more in the banking and insurance industries in Nigeria on one hand and Germany and the US; than in the traded goods sectors of these countries. US imports significant volumes of products from China and other countries.

6.18 Conclusion

The COVID-19 Pandemic raises highly contentious Economic Policy, Social Welfare and International Political Economy problems that remain un-resolved in many countries, and requires: i) New (and perhaps more globally-coordinated) approaches to Monetary Policy, Fiscal Policy, Labor Policy, Trade Policy, Information-Flows Policy, Political Systems and Social Welfare policy. ii) The over-due recognition and harnessing of the quasi-government functions and status of MNCs (multinational corporations) in many countries and especially in emerging Markets Countries.

Appendix 1 List of Major Global Pandemics During the Last Four Hundred Years (as of March 26, 2020)

Fifteenth century and earlier				
Death toll (estimate)	*Location*	*Date*	*Event*	*Disease*
75,000–100,000	Greece	429–426 BC	Plague of Athens	Unknown, possibly typhus, typhoid fever or viral hemorrhagic fever
Unknown	Greece (Northern Greece, Roman Republic)	412 BC	412 BC Pandemic	Unknown, possibly influenza
5–10 million	Roman Empire	165–180 (possibly up to 190)	Antonine Plague	Unknown, possibly smallpox
1 million + (Unknown, but at least)	Europe	250–266	Plague of Cyprian	Unknown, possibly smallpox
25–100 million; 40–50% of population of Europe	Europe and West Asia	541–542	Plague of Justinian	Plague
	British Isles	664–689	Plague of 664	Plague
2 million (Approx. 1/3 of entire Japanese population)	Japan	735–737	735–737 Japanese smallpox pandemic	Smallpox

(*continued*)

(continued)

Fifteenth century and earlier				
Death toll (estimate)	*Location*	*Date*	*Event*	*Disease*
	Byzantine Empire, West Asia, Africa	746–747	Plague of 746–747	Plague
75–200 million (10–60% of European population)	Europe, Asia and North Africa	1331–1353	Black Death	Plague
10,000 +	Britain (England) and later continental Europe	1485–1551	Sweating sickness (multiple outbreaks)	Unknown, possibly an unknown species of hantavirus

Sixteenth and seventeenth centuries				
Death toll (estimate)	*Location*	*Date*	*Event*	*Disease*
5–8 million (40% of population)	Mexico	1520	1520 smallpox pandemic	Smallpox
5–15 million (80% of population)	Mexico	1545–1548	Cocoliztli pandemic of 1545–1548	Possibly *Salmonella enterica*
> 20,100 in London	London	1563–1564	1563 London plague	Plague
2–2.5 million (50% of population)	Mexico	1576–1580	Cocoliztli Pandemic of 1576	Possibly *Salmonella enterica*
	Seneca nation	1592–1596		Measles
3000	Malta	1592–1593	1592–1593 Malta plague Pandemic	Plague

(*continued*)

(continued)

Sixteenth and seventeenth centuries				
Death toll (estimate)	*Location*	*Date*	*Event*	*Disease*
> 19,900 in London and outer parishes	London	1592–1593	1592–1593 London plague	Plague
	Spain	1596–1602		Plague
	South America	1600–1650		Malaria
	England	1603		Plague
	Egypt	1609		Plague
30–90% of population	Southern New England, especially the Wampanoag people	1616–1620	1616 New England Pandemic	Unknown cause. Latest research suggests pandemic(s) of leptospirosis with Weil syndrome. Classic explanations include yellow fever, bubonic plague, influenza, smallpox, chickenpox, typhus, and syndemic infection of hepatitis B and hepatitis D.
280,000	Italy	1629–1631	Italian plague of 1629–1631	Plague
15,000-25,000	Wyandot people	1634		Smallpox
	Thirteen Colonies	1633	Massachusetts smallpox Pandemic	Smallpox
	England	1636		Plague
	China	1641–1644		Plague

(*continued*)

(continued)

Sixteenth and seventeenth centuries				
Death toll (estimate)	*Location*	*Date*	*Event*	*Disease*
	Spain	1647–1652	Great Plague of Seville	Plague
	Central America	1648		Yellow fever
	Italy	1656	Naples Plague	Plague
	Thirteen Colonies	1657		Measles
24,148	Netherlands	1663–1664		Plague
100,000	England	1665–1666	Great Plague of London	Plague
40,000	France	1668		Plague
11,300	Malta	1675–1676	1675–76 Malta plague Pandemic	Plague
	Spain	1676–1685		Plague
76,000	Austria	1679	Great Plague of Vienna	Plague
	Thirteen Colonies	1687		Measles
	Thirteen Colonies	1690		Yellow fever

Eighteenth century				
Death toll (estimate)	*Location*	*Date*	*Event*	*Disease*
	Canada, New France	1702–1703		Smallpox

(*continued*)

Eighteenth century				
Death toll (estimate)	*Location*	*Date*	*Event*	*Disease*
> 18,000 (36% of population)	Iceland	1707–1709	Great Smallpox Pandemic	Smallpox
	Denmark, Sweden	1710–1712	Great Northern War plague outbreak	Plague
	Thirteen Colonies	1713–1715		Measles
	Canada, New France	1714–1715		Measles
>100,000	France	1720–1722	Great Plague of Marseille	Plague
	Thirteen Colonies	1721–1722		Smallpox
	Thirteen Colonies	1729		Measles
	Spain	1730		Yellow fever
	Thirteen Colonies	1732–1733		Influenza
	Canada, New France	1733		Smallpox
> 50,000	Balkans	1738	Great Plague of 1738	Plague
	Thirteen Colonies	1738		Smallpox
	Thirteen Colonies	1739–1740		Measles
	Italy	1743		Plague
	Thirteen Colonies	1747		Measles
	North America	1755–1756		Smallpox

(*continued*)

(continued)

Eighteenth century				
Death toll (estimate)	*Location*	*Date*	*Event*	*Disease*
	North America	1759		Measles
	North America, West Indies	1761		Influenza
	North America, present-day Pittsburgh area.	1763		Smallpox
> 50,000	Russia	1770–1772	Russian plague of 1770–1772	Plague
	Pacific Northwest natives	1770s		Smallpox
	North America	1772		Measles
> 2000,000	Persia	1772	Persian Plague	Plague
	England	1775–1776		Influenza
	Spain	1778		Dengue fever
	Plains Indians	1780–1782	North American smallpox Pandemic	Smallpox
	Pueblo Indians	1788		Smallpox
	United States	1788		Measles

(*continued*)

(continued)

Eighteenth century				
Death toll (estimate)	*Location*	*Date*	*Event*	*Disease*
	New South Wales, Australia	1789–1790		Smallpox
	United States	1793		Influenza and Pandemic typhus
	United States	1793–1798	Yellow Fever pandemic of 1793, resurgences	Yellow fever

Nineteenth century				
Death toll (estimate)	*Location*	*Date*	*Event*	*Disease*
	Spain	1800–1803		Yellow fever
	Ottoman Empire, Egypt	1801		Bubonic plague
	United States	1803		Yellow fever
	Egypt	1812		Plague
	Ottoman Empire	1812–19	1812–1819 Ottoman plague Pandemic	Plague
4500	Malta	1813–1814	1813–14 Malta plague Pandemic	Plague
60,000	Romania	1813	Caragea's plague	Plague
	Ireland	1816–1819		Typhus

(*continued*)

(continued)

Nineteenth century				
Death toll (estimate)	*Location*	*Date*	*Event*	*Disease*
> 100,000	Asia, Europe	1816–1826	First cholera pandemic	Cholera
	United States	1820–1823		Yellow fever
	Spain	1821		Yellow fever
	New South Wales, Australia	1828		Smallpox
	Netherlands	1829	Groningen pandemic	Malaria
	South Australia	1829		Smallpox
	Iran	1829–1835		Bubonic plague
> 100,000	Asia, Europe, North America	1829–1851	Second cholera pandemic	Cholera
	Egypt	1831		Cholera
	Plains Indians	1831–1834		Smallpox
	England, France	1832		Cholera
	North America	1832		Cholera
	United States	1833		Cholera
	United States	1834		Cholera
	Egypt	1834–1836		Bubonic plague

(continued)

(continued)

Nineteenth century				
Death toll (estimate)	*Location*	*Date*	*Event*	*Disease*
	United States	1837		Typhus
	Great Plains	1837–1838	1837–38 smallpox Pandemic	Smallpox
	Dalmatia	1840		Plague
	South Africa	1840		Smallpox
	United States	1841		Yellow fever
> 20,000	Canada	1847–1848	Typhus Pandemic of 1847	Pandemic typhus
	United States	1847		Yellow fever
	Worldwide	1847–1848		Influenza
	Egypt	1848		Cholera
	North America	1848–1849		Cholera
	United States	1850		Yellow fever
	North America	1850–1851		Influenza
	United States	1851		Cholera
	United States	1852		Yellow fever
1000,000	Russia	1852–1860	Third cholera pandemic	Cholera
	Ottoman Empire	1853		Plague

(*continued*)

(continued)

Nineteenth century				
Death toll (estimate)	*Location*	*Date*	*Event*	*Disease*
4737	Copenhagen, Denmark	1853	Cholera Pandemic of Copenhagen 1853	Cholera
616	England	1854	Broad Street cholera outbreak	Cholera
	United States	1855		Yellow fever
>12 million in India and China	Worldwide	1855–1960	Third plague pandemic	Bubonic plague
	Portugal	1857		Yellow fever
	Victoria, Australia	1857		Smallpox
	Europe, North America, South America	1857–1859		Influenza
> 3000	Central Coast, British Columbia	1862–1863		Smallpox
	Middle East	1863–1879	Fourth cholera pandemic	Cholera
	Egypt	1865		Cholera
	Russia, Germany	1866–1867		Cholera
	Australia	1867		Measles
	Iraq	1867		Plague
	Argentina	1852–1871		Yellow fever
	Germany	1870–1871		Smallpox

(*continued*)

(continued)

Nineteenth century				
Death toll (estimate)	*Location*	*Date*	*Event*	*Disease*
40,000	Fiji	1875	1875 Fiji Measles outbreak	Measles
	Russian Empire	1877		Plague
	Egypt	1881		Cholera
> 9000	India, Germany	1881–1896	Fifth cholera pandemic	Cholera
3164	Montreal	1885		Smallpox
1000,000	Worldwide	1889–1890	1889–1890 flu pandemic	Influenza
	West Africa	1900		Yellow fever

Late nineteenth and twentieth centuries				
Death toll (estimate)	*Location*	*Date*	*Event*	*Disease*
	Congo Basin, Africa	1896–1906		Trypanosomiasis
> 800,000	Europe, Asia, Africa	1899–1923	Sixth cholera pandemic	Cholera
113	San Francisco	1900–1904		Bubonic plague
	Uganda	1900–1920		Trypanosomiasis
	Egypt	1902		Cholera
22	India	1903		Bubonic Plague
4	Fremantle	1903		Bubonic plague
40,000	China	1910–1912	1910 China plague	Bubonic plague

(*continued*)

(continued)

Late nineteenth and twentieth centuries				
Death toll (estimate)	*Location*	*Date*	*Event*	*Disease*
1.5 million	worldwide	1915–1926	1915 *Encephalitis lethargica* pandemic	*Encephalitis lethargica*
>7000	United States of America	1916		Poliomyelitis
17–100 million	worldwide	1918–1920	Spanish flu (pandemic)	Influenza A virus subtype H1N1
	Russia	1918–1922		Typhus
30	Los Angeles	1924	1924 Los Angeles pneumonic plague outbreak	Pneumonic plague
43	Croydon, UK	1937	Croydon pandemic of typhoid fever	Typhoid fever
	Egypt	1942–1944		Malaria
	China	1946		Bubonic plague
	Egypt	1946		Relapsing fever
1845	United States of America	1946		Poliomyelitis
	Egypt	1947		Cholera
2720	United States of America	1949		Poliomyelitis
3145	United States of America	1952		Poliomyelitis

(continued)

(continued)

Late nineteenth and twentieth centuries				
Death toll (estimate)	*Location*	*Date*	*Event*	*Disease*
2000,000	worldwide	1957–1958	Asian flu	Influenza A virus subtype H2N2
	worldwide	1961–1975	Seventh cholera pandemic	Cholera (El Tor strain)
500 million	worldwide	1877–1977		Smallpox
1000,000	worldwide	1968–1969	Hong Kong flu	Influenza A virus subtype H3N2
5	Netherlands	1971		Poliomyelitis
35	Yugoslavia	1972	1972 outbreak of smallpox in Yugoslavia	Smallpox
1027	United States	1972–1973	London flu	Influenza A virus subtype H3N2
15,000	India	1974	1974 smallpox Pandemic of India	Smallpox
> 32,000,000	worldwide	1920–present	HIV/AIDS pandemic	HIV/AIDS
	South America	1990s		Cholera
52	India	1994	1994 plague Pandemic in Surat	Plague
231	worldwide	1996–2001		vCJD
	West Africa	1996		Meningitis
105	Malaysia	1998–1999	1998–99 Malaysia Nipah virus outbreak	Nipah virus infection
	Central America	2000		Dengue fever

Twenty-first century				
Death toll (estimate)	*Location*	*Date*	*Event*	*Disease*
> 400	Nigeria	2001		Cholera
	South Africa	2001		Cholera
359	China	2002–2004	2002–2004 SARS outbreak	Severe acute respiratory syndrome (SARS)
299	Hong Kong			
37	Taiwan			
44	Canada			
33	Singapore			
	Algeria	2003		Plague
	Afghanistan	2004		Leishmaniosis
	Bangladesh	2004		Cholera
	Indonesia	2004		Dengue fever
	Senegal	2004		Cholera
7	Sudan	2004		Ebola
	Mali	2005		Yellow fever
27	Singapore	2005	2005 dengue outbreak in Singapore	Dengue fever
	Luanda, Angola	2006		Cholera
61	Ituri Province, Democratic Republic of the Congo	2006		Plague
17	India	2006		Malaria
> 50	India	2006	2006 dengue outbreak in India	Dengue fever

(*continued*)

(continued)

Twenty-first century				
Death toll (estimate)	*Location*	*Date*	*Event*	*Disease*
	India	2006	Chikungunya outbreaks	Chikungunya virus
> 50	Pakistan	2006	2006 dengue outbreak in Pakistan	Dengue fever
	Philippines	2006		Dengue fever
187	Democratic Republic of the Congo	2007	Mweka Ebola pandemic	Ebola
	Ethiopia	2007		Cholera
49	India	2008		Cholera
10	Iraq	2007	2007 Iraq cholera outbreak	Cholera
	Nigeria	2007		Poliomyelitis
	Puerto Rico; Dominican Republic; Mexico	2007		Dengue fever
	Somalia	2007		Cholera
37	Uganda	2007		Ebola
	Vietnam	2007		Cholera
	Brazil	2008		Dengue fever
	Cambodia	2008		Dengue fever
	Chad	2008		Cholera
	China	2008–2017		Hand, foot and mouth disease
	Madagascar	2008		Bubonic plague
	Philippines	2008		Dengue fever

(*continued*)

(continued)

Twenty-first century				
Death toll (estimate)	*Location*	*Date*	*Event*	*Disease*
	Vietnam	2008		Cholera
4293	Zimbabwe	2008–2009	2008–2009 Zimbabwean cholera outbreak	Cholera
18	Bolivia	2009	2009 Bolivian dengue fever Pandemic	Dengue fever
49	India	2009	2009 Gujarat hepatitis outbreak	Hepatitis B
	Queensland, Australia	2009		Dengue fever
	Worldwide	2009	Mumps outbreaks in the 2000s	Mumps
931	West Africa	2009–2010	2009–2010 West African meningitis outbreak	Meningitis
18,000+ (deaths confirmed by WHO).	Worldwide	2009–2010	2009 flu pandemic (informally called "swine flu")	Pandemic H1N1/09 virus
10,075 (May 2017)	Hispaniola	2010–present	Haiti cholera outbreak	Cholera (strain serogroup O1, serotype Ogawa)
> 4500 (February 2014)	Democratic Republic of the Congo	2011–present		Measles
170	Vietnam	2011–present		Hand, foot and mouth disease

(*continued*)

(continued)

Twenty-first century				
Death toll (estimate)	*Location*	*Date*	*Event*	*Disease*
> 350	Pakistan	2011	2011 dengue outbreak in Pakistan	Dengue fever
171 (as of January 10, 2013)	Darfur Sudan	2012	2012 yellow fever outbreak in Darfur, Sudan	Yellow fever
862 (as of January 13, 2020)	Worldwide	2012–present	2012 Middle East respiratory syndrome coronavirus outbreak	Middle East respiratory syndrome (MERS)
142	Vietnam	2013–2014		Measles
>> 11,300	Worldwide, primarily concentrated in West Africa	2013–2016	Ebola virus pandemic in West Africa	Ebola virus disease
183	Americas	2013–2015	2013–2014 chikungunya outbreak	Chikungunya
40	Madagascar	2014–2017	2014 Madagascar plague outbreak	Bubonic plague
36	India	2014–2015	2014 Odisha jaundice outbreak	Primarily hepatitis E, but also hepatitis A
2035	India	2015	2015 Indian swine flu outbreak	Influenza A virus subtype H1N1
~53	Worldwide	2015–2016	2015–2016 Zika virus pandemic	Zika virus

(*continued*)

(continued)

Twenty-first century				
Death toll (estimate)	*Location*	*Date*	*Event*	*Disease*
100 s (as of April 1, 2016)	Africa	2016	2016 yellow fever outbreak in Angola	Yellow fever
3886 (as of November 30, 2019)	Yemen	2016–present	2016–2020 Yemen cholera outbreak	Cholera
64 (as of August 16, 2017)	India	2017	2017 Gorakhpur Japanese encephalitis outbreak	Japanese encephalitis
18 (as of February 2020)	India	2018	2018 Nipah virus outbreak in Kerala	Nipah virus infection
2253 (as of February 20, 2020)	Democratic Republic of the Congo and Uganda	August 2018–present	2018–2020 Kivu Ebola Pandemic	Ebola virus disease
>5000 (by November 2019)	Democratic Republic of the Congo	2019–present	2019 measles outbreak in the Democratic Republic of the Congo	Measles
83	Samoa	2019–present	2019 Samoa measles outbreak	Measles
>2000 (Approx.)	Asia-Pacific, Latin America	2019–present	2019–2020 dengue fever Pandemic	Dengue fever
77,000+ dead; and 1,400,000+ infected worldwide as of March 2020	Worldwide	2019–present	2019–present coronavirus pandemic	Coronavirus disease 2019

Source: Wikipedia (as of March 26, 2020)

Bibliography

Arellano, C. (2008). Default Risk and Income Fluctuations in Emerging Economies. *American Economic Review, 98*(3), 690–712.

Auclert, A. (2019). Monetary Policy and the Redistribution Channel. *American Economic Review, 109*(6), 2333–2367.

Auclert, A., Rognlie, M., & Straub, L. (2018). *The Intertemporal Keynesian Cross.* National Bureau of Economic Research Working Paper No. 25020.

Babu, G., Khetrapal, S., et al. (2021). Pandemic Preparedness and Response to COVID-19 in South Asian Countries. *International Journal of Infectious Diseases, 104*, 169–174.

Basu, K. (2016). The Economics and Law of Sovereign Debt and Risk Sharing: Some Lessons from the Eurozone Crisis. *Review of Law & Economics, 12*(3), 495–506.

Bavetta, S., Li Donni, P., & Marino, M. (2020). How Consistent Are Perceptions of Inequality? *Journal of Economic Psychology, 78.*

Bayer, C., Born, B., & Luetticke, R. (2020). *Shocks, Frictions, and Inequality in US Business Cycles.* CEPR Discussion Paper No. 14364.

Bayer, C., Luetticke, E., Pham-Dao, L., & Tjaden, V. (2019). Precautionary Savings, Illiquid Assets, and the Aggregate Consequences of Shocks to Household Income Risk. *Econometrica, 87*(1), 255–290.

Bayer, C., & Luetticke, R. (2020). Solving Heterogeneous Agent Models in Discrete Time with Many Idiosyncratic States by Perturbation Methods. *Quantitative Economics, 11*, 1253–1288.

Bénassy-Quéré, A., Brunnermeier, M., Enderlein, H., Farhi, E., Fuest, C., Gourinchas, P.-O., et al. (2018). Reconciling Risk Sharing with Market Discipline: A Constructive Approach to Euro Area Reform. *CEPR Policy Insight*, 91

Birz, G. (2017). Stale Economic News, Media and the Stock Market. *Journal of Economic Psychology, 61*, 87–102.

Broberg, M. (2020). A Critical Appraisal of the World Health Organization's International Health Regulations (2005) in Times of Pandemic—It Is Time for Revision. *European Journal of Risk Regulation, 11*(2), 202–209.

Chang, R., & Fernandez, A. (2013). On the Sources of Aggregate Fluctuations in Emerging Economies. *International Economic Review, 54*(4), 1265–1293.

Chen, T., & He, S. (2011). The Differential Game Theory of RMB Exchange Rate Under Marshall-Lerner Conditions and Constraints. *European Journal of Business and Management, 3*(2).

Copelovitch, M., Frieden, J., & Walter, S. (2016). The Political Economy of the Euro Crisis. *Comparative Political Studies, 49*(7), 811–840.

Cugat, G. (2019). *Emerging Markets, Household Heterogeneity, and Exchange Rate Policy.* Society for Economic Dynamics 2019 Meeting Paper No. 526.

De Ferra, S., Mitman, K., & Romei, F. (2020). Household Heterogeneity and the Transmission of Foreign Shocks. *Journal of International Economics, 124*, 103–303.

Diamond, R., McQuade, T., & Qian, F. (2019). The Effects of Rent Control Expansion on Tenants, Landlords, and Inequality: Evidence from San Francisco. *American Economic Review, 109*(9), 3365–3394.

Dixon, R., Griffiths, W., & Lim, G. (2014). Lay People's Models of the Economy: A Study Based on Surveys of Consumer Sentiments. *Journal of Economic Psychology, 44*, 13–20.

Djalante, R., Nurhidayah, L., et al. (2020). COVID-19 and ASEAN Responses: Comparative Policy Analysis. *Progress in Disaster Science, 8*, 100129.

ESCAP (Economic & Social Commission For Asia And The Pacific). (2021). *Policy Briefs in Response to COVID-19*. Retrieved from https://www.unescap.org/covid19/policy-briefs.

Fan, S., Teng, P., et al. (2021). Food System Resilience and COVID-19—Lessons from the Asian Experience. *Global Food Security, 28*, 100501.

Fuest, C., Heinemann, F., & Schröder, C. (2016). A Viable Insolvency Procedure for Sovereigns in the Euro Area. *Journal of Common Market Studies, 54*(2), 301–317.

Garrido, J., Nadeem, S., et al. (2020). *Tackling Private Over-Indebtedness in Asia: Economic and Legal Aspects*. IMF Working Paper. Asia and Pacific Department. Washington, DC.

Gasparotti, A., Minkina, M. A., & Alice, Z. (2018). *The ESM and the Proposed EMF: A Tabular Comparison*. Euro Area Scrutiny: European Parliament.

Gruszczynski, L. (2020). The Covid-19 Pandemic and International Trade: Temporary Turbulences or Paradigm Shift ? *European Journal of Risk Regulation, 11*(2), 337–342.

Haferkamp, A., Fetchenhauer, D., et al. (2009). Efficiency versus Fairness: The Evaluation of Labor Market Policies by Economists and Laypeople. *Journal of Economic Psychology, 30*(4), 527–539.

Havlik, A., & Heinemann, F. (2020). *Sliding Down the Slippery Slope? Trends in the Rules and Country Allocations of the Eurosystem's PSPP and PEPP*. Econpol Policy Report 21.

Heinemann, F. (2021). The Political Economy of Euro Area Sovereign Debt Restructuring. *Constitutional Political Economy.*

Hong, S. (2020). *MPCs and Liquidity Constraints in Emerging Economies.* Working Paper.

Hossain, M., Rahman, M., et al. (2021). Prevalence of anxiety and depression in South Asia during COVID-19: A systematic review and meta-analysis. *Heliyon, 7*(4), e06677.

Kusuma, D., Pradeepa, R., et al. (2021). Low Uptake of COVID-19 Prevention Behaviors and High Socioeconomic Impact of Lockdown Measures in South

Asia: Evidence from a Large-Scale Multi-country Surveillance Program. *SSM—Population Health, 13*, 100751.

Lisle, J. (2021). When Rivalry Goes Viral: COVID-19, U.S.-China Relations, and East Asia. *Orbis, 65*(1), 46–74.

Makin, A., & Layton, A. (2021). The Global Fiscal Response to COVID-19: Risks and Repercussions. *Economic Analysis and Policy, 69*, 340–349.

Milesi-Ferretti, G., & Lane, P. (2017). *International Financial Integration in the Aftermath of the Global Financial Crisis.* Working Paper 115, International Monetary Fund.

Muellbauer, J. (2013). Conditional Eurobonds and the Eurozone Sovereign Debt Crisis. *Oxford Review of Economic Policy, 29*(3), 610–645.

Nwogugu, M. (2005a). *Legal, Economic and Corporate Strategy Issues In Housing in the 'New' Economy': New Theories of Industrial Organization and Structural Change.* Working paper. Retrieved from https://www.researchgate.net/publication/228163582_Legal_Economic_and_Strategy_Issues_in_Housing_in_the_New_Economy.

Nwogugu, M. (2005b). *Structural Changes in the US Retailing Industry: Legal, Economic and Strategic Implications for the US Real Estate Sector.* Working paper. Retrieved from www.ssrn.com

Nwogugu, M. (2012). *Risk in the Global Real Estate Market.* John Wiley.

Nwogugu, M. (2014; revised 2020). *Group-Decisions, Systemic Risk and Politics: The Case of Asset Management Corporation of Nigeria (AMCON); and the Malaysian and Indian Models of NPL-Resolution.* Working paper. Retrieved from https://www.researchgate.net/publication/315334141_Group-Decisions_Systemic_Risk_and_Politics_The_Case_of_Asset_Management_Corporation_of_Nigeria_AMCON_and_the_Malaysian_and_Indian_Models_of_NPL-Resolution.

Nwogugu, M. (2015a). Failure of the Dodd-Frank Act. *Journal of Financial Crime, 22*(4), 520–572.

Nwogugu, M. (2015b). Un-constitutionality of the Dodd-Frank Act. *European Journal of Law Reform, 17*, 185–190.

Nwogugu, M. (2017). *Anomalies in Net Present Value, Returns and Polynomials; and Regret Theory in Decision-Making.* Palgrave Macmillan.

Nwogugu, M. (2019a). Introduction. In *Complex Systems, Multi-Sided Incentives and Risk Perception in Companies.* Palgrave Macmillan.

Nwogugu, M. (2019b). Complex Adaptive Systems, Sustainable Growth and Securities Law: On Inequality and the "Optimal Design of Financial Contracts". In *Earnings Management, Fintech-Driven Incentives and Sustainable Growth: On Complex Systems, Legal and Mechanism Design Factors.* Routledge/Ashgate.

Nwogugu, M. (2019c). *Indices, Index Funds and ETFs HCI: Exploring HCI, Nonlinear Risk and Homomorphisms.* Palgrave Macmillan.

Nwogugu, M. (2019d). *Complex Systems, Multi-sided Incentives and Risk Perception in Organizations*. Palgrave Macmillan.

Nwogugu, M. (2020a). *Chapter-7: Complex Systems Challenges: Epidemics, the Welfare-State and the Constitution*. Working Paper. Retrieved from https://papers.ssrn.com/sol3/papers.cfm?abstract_id=3569636.

Nwogugu, M. (2020b). *Earnings Management, Incentives and Sustainable Growth: Complex-Systems, Legal and Mechanism Design Factors*. Routledge.

Ochsen, C., & Welsch, H. (2012). Who Benefits from Labor Market Institutions? Evidence from Surveys of Life Satisfaction. *Journal of Economic Psychology, 33*(1), 112–124.

Pántya, J., Kovács, J., et al. (2016). Work Performance and Tax Compliance in Flat and Progressive Tax Systems. *Journal of Economic Psychology, 56*, 262–273.

Rasul, G. (2021). Twin Challenges of COVID-19 Pandemic and Climate Change for Agriculture and Food Security in South Asia. *Environmental Challenges, 2*, 100027.

Rodden, J. (2017, May). An Evolutionary Path for a European Monetary Fund? A Comparative Perspective. European Parliament In-Depth Analysis.

Schmidt, V. A. (2020). Theorizing Institutional Change and Governance in European Responses to the Covid-19 Pandemic. *Journal of European Integration, 42*(8), 1177–1193.

Singh, V., Roca, E., & Li, B. (2021). Effectiveness of Policy Interventions During Financial Crises in China and Russia: Lessons for the COVID-19 Pandemic. *Journal of Policy Modeling, 43*, 253–277.

Sunel, E. (2018). Welfare Consequences of Gradual Disinflation in Emerging Economies. *Journal of Money, Credit and Banking, 50*(4), 705–755.

Tesche, T. (2020). The European Union's Response to the Coronavirus Emergency: An Early Assessment. *LSE Europe in Question Discussion Paper Series,* 157(157).

Torgler, B., & Schneider, F. (2009). The Impact of Tax Morale and Institutional Quality on the Shadow Economy. *Journal of Economic Psychology, 30*(2), 228–245.

Torsello, M., & Winkler, M. (2020). Coronavirus-Infected International Business Transactions: A Preliminary Diagnosis. *European Journal of Risk Regulation, 11*(2), 396–401.

Wasserfallen, F., Leuffen, D., Kudrna, Z., & Degner, H. (2019). Analysing European Union Decision-Making During the Eurozone Crisis with New Data. *European Union Politics, 20*(1), 3–23.

Wyplosz, C. (2017, May). A European Monetary Fund? European Parliament In-Depth Analysis.

Zaremba, A., Kizys, R. et al. (2021). Volatility in International Sovereign Bond Markets: The Role of Government Policy Responses to the COVID-19 Pandemic. *Finance Research Letters.*

CHAPTER 7

Complex Systems, Pandemics and the Welfare State, Part-2: Constitutional Political Economy, Compliance and *Constitutional Contagion* Issues

At least fifty percent chapter was completed at the beginning of April 2020[1] (and some information may have changed since then). As mentioned in Chaps. 1 and 6 in this book, Pandemics/epidemics are major geopolitical risks.[2] This chapter: (i) analyzes some of the constitutional political econ-

[1] *See*: Nwogugu, M. (April 2020). "*Chapter-7: Complex Systems Challenges: Epidemics, the Welfare-State and the Constitution (2020)*". Available at SSRN: https://ssrn.com/abstract=3569636 or https://doi.org/10.2139/ssrn.3569636.

[2] *See*: "*Coronavirus: Half a billion people could be pushed into poverty, says UN study Comments*". By Alasdair Sandford. April 09, 2020. https://www.euronews.com/2020/04/09/coronavirus-half-a-billion-people-could-be-pushed-into-poverty-says-un-study?utm_source=newsletter&utm_medium=en&utm_content=coronavirus-half-a-billion-people-could-be-pushed-into-poverty-says-un-study&_ope=eyJndWlkIjoiNTE4MWFhOTZjZmY5NjUxMTAzZTE2Y2Y1MGU1NDAwYTcifQ%3D%3D.

See: Sumner, A., Hoy, C. & Ortiz-Juarez, E. (2020). *Estimates of the impact of COVID-19 on global poverty.*

WIDER Working Paper 43/2020. UNU-WIDER. https://doi.org/10.35188/UNU-WIDER/2020/800-9. The abstract of this report states: "we make estimates of the potential short-term economic impact of COVID-19 on global monetary poverty through contractions in per capita household income or consumption. Our estimates are based on three scenarios: low, medium and high global contractions of 5, 10 and 20%; we calculate the impact of each of these scenarios on the poverty headcount using the international poverty lines of US$1.90, US$3.20 and US$5.50 per day. Our estimates show that COVID poses a real challenge to the UN Sustainable Development Goal of ending poverty by 2030 because global poverty could increase for the first time since 1990 and, depending on the poverty

M. I. C. Nwogugu, *Geopolitical Risk, Sustainability and "Cross-Border Spillovers" in Emerging Markets, Volume II*,
https://doi.org/10.1007/978-3-030-71419-2_7

omy, compliance (compliance with government regulations/statutes, tax laws, etc.) and *Constitutional Contagion* problems created by epidemics/ Pandemics and associated responses (using US case law and statutes); (ii) introduces new theories and critiques existing Constitutoinal Political Economy theories; iii) introduces possible channels of *Cross-Border Spillovers* and *Market-Integration* in financial markets, Information Markets, Labor markets, Commodities Markets (eg. food/agric products, metals, oil/gas; etc.) and Finished-Commodity-Products markets (eg. consumer durables; etc.).

7.1 Existing Literature

In modern times, most Pandemics and Epidemics raise significant Constitutional Law, IPE and Constitutional Political Economy issues partly because of the resulting new statutes, mandatory restrictions imposed by governments and businesses, the political negotiations and the resulting economic/financial damage. Some Constitutional Law problems can evolve into expensive *Constitutional Tort* claims against federal, state and or local governments. For example, during March 2020, the US Attorney General publicly recommended that the US Constitution be suspended during the entire COVID-19 Epidemic period, and the US Justice Department[3] requested for more powers that in effect, would suspend the US constitution. On *Constitutional Torts*, see: Nwogugu (2012).

During 2020–2021, Researchers estimated that COVID-19 will cost nations more than US$4 trillion dollars (including the costs of reconstructing national economies, fixing disrupted supply chains, the costs of borrowing; treatment costs; and assistance to families and businesses; and perhaps even the restructuring of International Organizations such as

line, such increase could represent a reversal of approximately a decade in the world's progress in reducing poverty. In some regions the adverse impacts could result in poverty levels similar to those recorded 30 years ago. Under the most extreme scenario of a 20 per cent income or consumption contraction, the number of people living in poverty could increase by 420–580 million, relative to the latest official recorded figures for 2018".

[3] *See*: "*DOJ Wants to Suspend Certain Constitutional Rights During Coronavirus Emergency—The Department of Justice has secretly asked Congress for the ability to detain arrested people 'indefinitely' in addition to other powers that one expert called 'terrifying'*". By Peter Wade. https://www.rollingstone.com/politics/politics-news/doj-suspend-constitutional-rights-coronavirus-970935/.

See: "*Justice Department Reportedly Asks Congress for Indefinite Detention Powers To Fight Coronavirus—Congress should loudly and unanimously reject this insanity*". By Eric Boehm. March 21, 2020.

WHO). See the comments in Gruszczynski (2020), Torsello and Winkler (2020) and Broberg (2020). A March 2020 survey by Aljazeera[4] stated that 70% of indigenes of G7 countries (Canada, France, Germany, Italy, Japan, the UK and the United States) expect that their household will lose income because of COVID-19. During March 2020, the OECD[5] warned that the COVD-19 Pandemic is creating a global economic downturn and reduced economic growth not seen since 2009. During Feb–March 2020, large US retailing chains[6] laid-off or furloughed hundreds of thousands of workers and closed more than 9300 stores.

Chapter 6 of this book summarized the economic stimulus packages[7] and some new statutes that were announced by various countries in response to COVID-19 and during January–April 2020. Many of these countries subsequently announced additional stimulus and welfare packages for households and private companies.

7.2 Evolution and Emergence: *Intra-Constitution Conflict*, *Preemption Doctrines* and *Preemption Criteria as Economic Policy*

In some common-law countries (and even in some civil law countries), *preemption doctrines* have evolved into major monetary policies, fiscal policies and labor policies (or determinants of same) partly because of the following reasons:

[4] *See*: "*70 percent of G7 households expect to be made poorer by virus—Household incomes are being affected as cities enforce lockdowns, shutting businesses and factories, a survey showed*". March 25, 2020. https://www.aljazeera.com/ajimpact/70-percent-g7-households-expect-poorer-virus-200325060436759.html?utm_source=website&utm_medium=article_page&utm_campaign=read_more_links.

[5] *See*: "*Virus Plunging Economy Into Worst Downturn Since 2009, OECD warns—Ringing recession alarm, OECD Urges Coronavirus Affected Countries To Take Necessary Measures As Quickly As Possible*". https://www.aljazeera.com/ajimpact/virus-plunging-economy-worst-downturn-2009-oecd-warns-200302205312855.html.

[6] *See*: Kelly, J. (March 31, 2020). *Hundreds Of Thousands Of Retail Workers Are Losing Their Jobs Due To Coronavirus.* https://www.forbes.com/sites/jackkelly/2020/03/31/hundreds-of-thousands-of-workers-are-losing-their-jobs-in-a-coronavirus-induced-retail-apocalypse/#3bf466113184.

[7] *See*: "*Government Stimulus Efforts to Fight the COVID-19 Crisis—Here's what governments are doing to stimulate their economies*". By Gabe Alpert. Updated March 27, 2020. https://www.investopedia.com/government-stimulus-efforts-to-fight-the-covid-19-crisis-4799723.

1. *Preemption doctrines* determine the allocation of fiscal powers and enforcement powers between state and federal governments; and also affects the efficiency of transmissoin of monetary policy and labor policy through various channels.
2. *Preemption doctrines* greatly affect the allocation of capital and resources among local, state and federal governments. Thus government budgets and spending are implicated.
3. In countries that regulate financial services at both the state and federal levels, *preemption doctrines* have significant, if not dominant, effects on such regulation (i.e. banks, insurance companies, finance companies, pension funds, investment funds, capital raising, securities laws, enforcement, etc.), and, thus, *preemption doctrines* affect or can affect capital markets, interest rates, perceived credit quality, financial stability and international capital flows.
4. *Preemption doctrines* can have significant effects on the main and traditional sources of revenues for state governments and local governments such as real estate taxes, fees, fines, sales taxes, corporate taxes and personal taxes.
5. *Preemption doctrines* have significant effects on the normal and extraordinary powers of state and federal governments during Pandemics/epidemics and crises, which ultimately affect labor, fiscal and monetary policies.

Some of the major consequences of the invocation of existing laws and the enactment of new "emergency" laws/regulations by national/state/local governments in many countries are *conflicts-of-laws* and *preemption* problems (among conflicting federal, state and local regulations), both of which typically generate significant volumes of annual litigation and political lobbying in many countries. In many countries, public health, natural disaster and emergency-response issues are regulated by both the state and federal governments (and also by local governments in some countries).

Preemption is likely to remain a big issue in the European Union, USA, Canada, Australia, Brazil, Nigeria, South Africa, India and China, and in countries that are either loose federations (such as Spain) or that don't have strong central governments (i.e. where most of the legislative philosophy and activity aren't driven by the central government—the opposite of China). It's also likely that *preemption* will continue to be analyzed within the same narrow political and constitutional frameworks partly because of the political pressures and political lobbying involved.

Nwogugu (2012: 127–132) summarized the *preemption criteria* that was developed by US Bankruptcy Courts. Nwogugu (2012: 132–135) summarized the *preemption criteria* that was developed by the US Supreme Court. Nwogugu (2012: 135–138) introduced some new *preemption criteria* that reflect changes in modern commerce, technology and investigation/enforcement methods.

One major issue is whether the US President's Executive Orders and statutory Emergency Powers[8] and/or any statute enacted by the US Congress can preempt US state governors' Executive Orders during public health emergencies and other crises—that is, whether the US President or the US Congress could cancel the lock-down Orders that were issued by state governors and mayors of cities. First, the Tenth Amendment to the US Constitution grants to US state governments (and, indirectly, municipal governments) the state police power and the rights and powers "not delegated to the United States". Police powers statutorily granted to US state governors are broad and include the rights to enact laws and statutes that pertain to public health and other emergencies, and general welfare. Thus, during emergencies, the US President's Executive Orders that pertain to Public Health and general welfare are applicable to only federal government employees; and the US Presidential Executive Orders or congressionally enacted[9] statutes (that pertain to public health) can only be advisory with regard to US state governments.[10] Furthermore, US Supreme Court rulings have clearly established that when the US Congress enacts a statute that imposes conditions on economic/financial aid it offers to state governments (and by extension local governments) and such statutes are coercive or can cause coercion, then such federal statutes are inherently unconstitutional.[11] The US Constitution doesn't contain any *Emergency Powers Clause* and does not specifically bestow the US

[8] and associated states such as the Stafford Act, the Defense Production Act, the Public Health Service Act and the various statutes triggered by a declaration of an emergency.

[9] *See*: *Printz* vs. *United States*, 521 US 898 (1997; US Supreme Court).

See: *Youngstown Sheet & Tube Co.* vs. *Sawyer*, 343 US 579 (1952; US Supreme Court).

[10] *See*: *New York* vs. *United States*, 505 US 144 (1992; US Supreme Court).

See: *Youngstown Sheet & Tube Co.* vs. *Sawyer*, 343 US 579 (1952; US Supreme Court).

[11] *See*: *National Federation of Independent Business v. Sebelius*, 567 U.S. 519 (2012; US Supreme Court).

Contrast: South Dakota vs. *Dole*, 483 US 203 (1987; US Supreme Court).

See: *Rutledge vs. Pharmaceutical Care Management Association*, _____ US _____ (No. 18-540; US Supreme Court; pending as of 2021).

President with any powers during national emergencies—any such powers are granted only by statutes enacted by the US Congress which remain subject to the *Tenth Amendment* and the *Police Powers Clause* of the US Constitution. The *National Emergencies Act of 1976* (which grants the US President the power to declare a national emergency without the prior approval of Congress) is still subject to the *Tenth Amendment* of the US Constitution. Given the foregoing, the US President's ordinary or statutory *Emergency Powers* cannot preempt state governors Executive Orders or state legislatures' statutes/regulations during public health crises and other emergencies. State governments and local/municipal governments are much closer to the population, local trends and problems that occur during emergencies, and thus are better positioned to supervise recovery efforts during emergencies.

Second, under the *"Vertical" Separation of Powers Doctrine*, the US Constitution essentially divided power between the US government and the US states (which by themselves are distinct federations that are not controlled by the US government).[12] The *"Horizontal" Separation of Power Doctrine* deals with separation of the legislative, judicial and executive branches of the federal government (or separately, those of the state government) and any perceived delegation of power among them. The *Supremacy Clause of the US Constitution* grants the US Congress the power to preempt state laws, but the *Supremacy Clause*[13] doesn't grant similar powers to the US President acting alone. Also the US Supreme Court case *Printz* vs. *United States*[14] implies that in emergencies or interim situations, the US Congress cannot preempt state laws or control state government officials. In *Edgar* vs. *MITE Corp*,[15] the US Supreme Court created standards for application of the *Supremacy Clause*.

[12] *See*: *Printz* vs. *United States*, 521 US 898 (1997; US Supreme Court) ("The Constitution's structure reveals a principle that controls these cases: the system of 'dual sovereignty.' See, e. g., *Gregory* vs. *Ashcroft*, 501 U. S. 452, 457. Although the States surrendered many of their powers to the new Federal Government, they retained a residuary and inviolable sovereignty that is reflected throughout the Constitution's text").

[13] *See: California* vs. *ARC America Corp.*, 490 U.S. 93 (1989; US Supreme Court) (US Congress can invoke *Supremacy Clause* if it intended to enact laws about a specific matter).

See: Crosby vs. *National Foreign Trade Council*, 530 U.S. 363 (2000; US Supreme Court).

See: Lawson, G. (_____). "*Essays On Article VI: Supremacy Clause*" (Washington D.C.: The Heritage Foundation).

[14] *See*: *Printz* vs. *United States*, 521 US 898 (1997; US Supreme Court).

[15] *See*: *Edgar* vs. *MITE Corp.*, 457 U.S. 624 (1982) (a state law violates the *Supremacy Clause* when the conflicting federal statute is constitutionally valid and: (1) "State law stands

Third, the *Interstate Commerce Clause* may seem to provide the US Congress with the powers to preempt the state governors' lock-down orders, but it doesn't. For a long time, the US Supreme Court has rejected *Interstate Commerce Clause* challenges against quarantines. Specifically, in *Oregon-Washington Railroad v. Washington* (1926; US Supreme Court), the US Supreme Court stated that "it is well settled that a state, in the exercise of its police power, may establish quarantines against human beings, or animals, or plants".[16]

Fourth, the right to travel is usually protected under the *Privileges and Immunities Clause*, but as the US Supreme Court noted in *Saenz* vs. *Roe*, 526 U.S. 489 (1999; US Supreme Court), such protection is conditional.

Thus, it appears that there is a conflict between the *Supremacy Clause*, the Fourteenth Amendment's *Privileges and Immunities Clause* and the *Interstate Commerce Clause* (of the US Constitution) on one hand, and on the other hand, the *Police Powers* of the Tenth Amendment (of the US Constitution); and it's not clear whether and which side preempts the other.

7.3 Executive Orders: Legitimacy, *Constitutional Contagions* and the *Separation of Powers Doctrine*

In many democracies, Executive Orders are widely used by Presidents, Prime Ministers and state/regional governors and thus have or can have significant effects on allocations of government powers, government expenditures (which often account for a significant percentage of both cash and economic activity in some Emerging Markets countries), government budgets/deficits and contracting, corporate expenditures, business

as an obstacle to the accomplishment and execution of the full purposes and objectives of Congress", and/or (2) persons cannot comply with both the federal law and the State law).

[16] On the Interstate Commerce Clause, see: *DeNolf vs. U.S.*, _____ US _____ (US Supreme Court; pending as of 2021) (https://static1.squarespace.com/static/5b660749620b85c6c73e5e61/t/608d544886d55300e492a619/1619874888658/2021-22+AMCA+Case.pdf); *DeNolf vs. U.S.* (Case#: 01-76320; US 14th Circuit, 2020) (https://static1.squarespace.com/static/5b660749620b85c6c73e5e61/t/608d544886d55300e492a619/1619874888658/2021-22+AMCA+Case.pdf); *Perez vs. United States*, 402 U.S. 146, 150 (1971) (Congress can ban loansharking that threatens interstate commerce); *Gonzales vs. Raich*, 545 U.S. 1, 18 (US Supreme Court; 2005); and *United States vs. Lopez*, 514 U.S. 549 (US Supreme Court; 1995).

confidence, consumer confidence, foreign aid, FDI, foreign investment, trade imbalances, remittances to emerging markets, construction activities, social welfare, education; healthcare and so on. In many commonwealth countries, UK-style parliamentary monarchies and parliamentary democracies (especially Canada, Australia and New Zealand), an *Order-in-Council* or the *Order-Of-Council* are the equivalents of an Executive Order (in US-style presidential governments), and are types of legislation. Cohn (2015), Harris (1992), and Lester and Weait (2003) analyzed the sources, nature and uses of unilateral, non-statutory executive powers in various countries. A major distinction is that in many parliamentary democracies (and unlike many presidential democracies), the legislative branch directly controls/governs the executive branch and, in some cases, indirectly controls the judiciary through legislative appropriations, budgets and protective-services for judges.

In the USA, presidential Executive Orders[17] are strange constitutional objects because they are usually not specifically/expressly authorized by the US Constitution, but are generally accepted as appropriate exercise of presidential power. See: Bolton and Thrower (2015), and Sunshine (2017). The constitutional power for the issuance of presidential or prime ministerial Executive Orders can be implied from any of the following main sources:

1. The national constitution—for example, *Article Two of the United States Constitution*[18] which grants the president broad discretionary

[17] *See*: Chu, V. & Garvey, T. (2014). *Executive Orders: Issuance, Modification, and Revocation*. US Congressional Research Service, Washington D.C., USA. The Chu & Garvey (2014) abstract stated that "..............Executive orders, presidential memoranda, and proclamations are used extensively by Presidents to achieve policy goals, set uniform standards for managing the executive branch, or outline a policy view intended to influence the behavior of private citizens. The U.S. Constitution does not define these presidential instruments and does not explicitly vest the President with the authority to issue them. Nonetheless, such orders are accepted as an inherent aspect of presidential power. Moreover, if they are based on appropriate authority, they have the force and effect of law".

See: New York University Law Review Online, "*Sources of Law (Part One): Executive Orders, Unilateral Executive Action, and Faithful Execution of the Laws*". https://www.nyulawreview.org/online-features/sources-of-law-part-one-executive-orders-unilateral-executive-action-and-faithful-execution-of-the-laws/.

[18] But see: *Youngstown Sheet & Tube Co.* vs. *Sawyer*, 343 US 579 (1952; US Supreme Court) (noting that " the President's power to see that the laws are faithfully executed refutes the idea that he is to be a lawmaker").

executive and enforcement authority—and states in part: "The executive Power shall be vested in a President of the United States of America".

2. Express or implied statutes of the national legislature (e.g. US Congress) that delegate discretionary power to the president or prime minister (i.e. "delegated" legislation).
3. New legislation or "Emergency Statutes" (triggered by emergencies or public health problems) that authorizes the president or prime minister to take action.
4. Court judgments that specifically require action by the president or prime minister.
5. Administrative law statutes or regulations that are enacted by government administrative agencies and require specific action by the president or prime minister.

In the US (and some common-law countries), the constitutional power/authority[19] for state governors' Executive Orders are usually based on any of the following:

[19] Gakh et al. (2013) noted that: ".........Federal or state laws may permit the issuance of a GEO (Gubernatorial Executive Order). The power to issue a GEO may arise from a federal law that requires action at the state level. ... Various state laws and cases also authorize governors to issue executive orders, and some states authorize GEOs using more than one legal mechanism. According to a survey conducted by the Council of State Governments, among the fifty states, twenty-six have explicit GEO authority in their state constitutions and thirty-seven authorize GEOs through legislation. Governors' authority to issue GEOs is also recognized in the case law of seven states. Furthermore, in eighteen states the governor's general responsibility to execute the state's laws includes the ability to issue GEOs. Through these varied legal mechanisms, governors issued more than 3,400 executive orders from 2004 to 2005. Many GEOs are not specifically relevant to public health. For example, during 2004 and 2005, 33% of all GEOs consisted of appointments, 6% ordered flying of flags at half-mast, 3% ordered pardons, and 1% established state holidays. Other types of GEOs directly affect the public's health...........".

See: Council of State Governments (2010). *Book of the states—table 4.5: gubernatorial executive orders: authorization, provisions, procedures* (Lexington, Kentucky: Council of State Governments; 2010).

See: Council of State Governments (2014). *The Book of States 2014*. Council of State Governments. USA. http://knowledgecenter.csg.org/kc/category/content-type/bos-2014.

1. The actual or implied constitutional powers of the state governors[20] that are granted by state constitutions.
2. Statutes (enacted by federal or state legislatures) that require specific action by state governors (that delegate discretionary power to the governor).
3. Court judgments that require action by the state governor.
4. Administrative law statutes or regulations enacted by government administrative agencies that require specific action by the state governor.
5. New legislation or "Emergency Statutes" (triggered by emergencies or public health problems) that authorizes the state governors to take action.
6. Constitutional powers that are granted by federal constitutions to state governors—for example, the Tenth Amendment to the US Constitution grants to US state governments, the state's *police power* and the rights and powers "not delegated to the United States". In most common-law countries, *police power* refers to the health, safety, morals and general welfare of indigenes.

US state governors' historical uses of Executive Orders for public health emergencies have generated significant legal and public policy controversies—see: Gakh et al. (2013), Sunshine (2017), Haffajee and al (2014) and Gakh et al. (2019). Sunshine (2017) argued the case for changing the criteria for authority for emergency declaration for public health threats—the use of such authority/power can trigger other legal issues (and perhaps constitutional law issues) including the legal framework for participating volunteers. Hodge et al. (2005) and Orenstein (2013) noted that the dual declaration of public health emergencies and general emergencies can create legislative confusion and duplication of efforts.

[20] *See*: *About Executive Orders of the State of Georgia*. https://gov.georgia.gov/executive-orders.

See: *About Executive Orders of the State of Florida*. https://www.flgov.com/all-executive-orders.

See: *About Executive Orders of the State of Utah*. https://rules.utah.gov/executive-documents.

See: *About Executive Orders of the State of Washington*. https://www.governor.wa.gov/office-governor/official-actions/executive-orders.

See: *About Executive Orders of the State of Colorado*. https://www.colorado.gov/governor/executive-orders.

On US state governors' use of Executive Orders, see: Ouyang and Carpentier (2018), Ferguson and Bowling (2008), Bernick (2016) and Sellers (2017). On the political powers of US state governors and some institutional economics ramifications, see: Redlawsk (2015), Bernick (2016) and Lewis et al. (2015).

In most commonwealth countries and common-law countries, Executive Orders are inherently assumed not to include or permit any discretion on the part of the issuing president or state governor (in the US, the sources of power for Executive Orders don't specifically address the issue of discretion). Such assumptions are reinforced by: (i) the threat of judicial review; (ii) the existence of the traditional federal or state legislatures, and threat of their veto powers; (iii) the potentially significant loss of political power and/or social capital by the issuing president or state governor.

Executive Orders raise the specter of abusive[21] laws, but state and federal Executive Orders are subject to judicial review[22] in most commonwealth and common-law countries. See: Branum (2002), Calabresi and Prakash (1994), Deering and Maltzman (1999), and Fatovic (2004). In the UK, *Orders-in-Council* have been used to overturn court rulings.[23] Historically, US Presidents have used Executive Orders to enact what amounts to legislation for highly sensitive issues for which the *Political Costs*" are significant or potentially significant, or for which the traditional legislative process would be too cumbersome, hostile or untimely. Similarly, US state governors have used Executive Orders to, in essence, legislate measures

[21] *See*: Gaziano, T. (February 21, 2001). "*The Use and Abuse of Executive Orders and Other Presidential Directives*". Legal Memorandum #2. The Heritage Foundation.

See: Edwards, C. (August 23, 1999). "Emergency Rule, Abuse of Power?" *Insight on the News*, p. 18.

[22] *See*: *Chamber of Commerce of the United States*, et al., vs. *Reich*, 74 F.3d 1322 (D.C. Cir. 1996; US Court Of Appeals).

See: *Trump, President Of The United States*, et al. vs. *Hawaii*, et al., U.S. Supreme Court Docket No. 17–965. (decided June 26, 2018; USA). https://www.supremecourt.gov/opinions/17pdf/17-965_h315.pdf.

See: *Khadr* vs. *Canada (Attorney General)*, 2006 F.C. 727, [2007] 2 F.C.R. 218 (Canada).

See: *Independent Meat Packers* vs. *Butz*, 526 F2d 228, 236 (CA8; 1975; US Court Of Appeals) (Executive Order requiring agencies to conduct impact analysis prior to the making of regulations wasn't enforceable by private civil action and was primarily "a managerial tool").

[23] *See*: *R (Bancoult)* vs. *Secretary of State For Foreign and Commonwealth Affairs* [2008] UKHL 61 (UK).

See: *R* vs. *Secretary of State for Foreign and Commonwealth Affairs, ex parte Bancoult* (No 2)) (UK).

for highly sensitive issues for which the "Political Costs" and/or social capital risks are significant or potentially significant, or for which the traditional legislative process would be too cumbersome, or hostile or untimely.

7.3.1 The Separation-of-Powers *Problem*

Given the foregoing, and because of its nature and scope, Executive Orders raise the problem or potential problem of violations of the *Separation of Powers* (SOP) clauses of national/state constitutions. See: Bradley and Morrison (2012).[24] As noted by Alvey (2017) and French (2018), *Separation of Powers (SOP) Doctrines* are similar only to some extent among common-law countries, and the US SOP is not exactly the same as the Australian and UK SOPs. See also: Prabhakar (2008).

The extent to which the *Separation of Powers Doctrine* is violated by the issuance of an Executive Order by a president or prime minister or state governor depends on the following factors among others:

1. The nature and urgency of the "emergency" that prompted the Executive Order.
2. The extent to which the traditional legislature could have issued similar legislation (and any extraordinary factors that could have prevented the legislature from doing so).
3. Whether the subject matter is highly specialized.
4. The potential economic/financial and/or public health damage that can result from issuing or not issuing the Executive Order.
5. The scope, number and location of persons affected by the issuance or non-issuance of the Executive Order.
6. Whether the constitution or the legislature has specifically or impliedly or historically delegated such matters to the issuer of the Executive order (president or state governor).

[24] *See*: *Collins vs. Yellen*, ____ US ____ (No. 19-422; US Supreme Court; pending as of 2021); *Collins vs. Mnuchin* ____ US ____ (Docket No. 19-422; US Supreme Court; pending as of 2021); *Seila Law LLC vs. Consumer Financial Protection Bureau*, ____ US ____ (Case#: No. 19-7; US Supreme Court; 2020); *Humphrey's Executor vs. United States*, 295 U.S. 602 (US Supreme Court; 1935); and *PHH Corp. vs. CFPB*, 839 F.3d 1 (2016) *on rehearing enbanc*, 881 F.3d 75 (D.C. Cir., 2018; USA) (en banc).

The probability of subsequent legal challenges of Executive Orders depends on the following factors among others:

1. The nature and urgency of the "emergency" that prompted the Executive Order.
2. The political standing and political capital of the issuer of the Executive Order.
3. The political party that controls the legislature.
4. The extent to which the traditional legislature could have issued similar legislation (and any extraordinary factors that could have prevented the legislature from doing so).
5. Whether the subject matter is highly specialized.
6. The degree of "emergency" involved and whether there was sufficient time for due process or for the legislature to enact new statutes.
7. The potential economic/financial and/or public harm damage that can result from issuing or not issuing the Executive Order.
8. The scope, number and location of persons affected by the issuance or non-issuance of the Executive Order.
9. Whether the constitution or the legislature has specifically or impliedly or historically delegated such matters to the issuer of the Executive Order (president or state governor).
10. The implicit "legislative intent" of the Executive Orders.
11. Whether the Executive Order violates any clauses of the constitution, or infringes any property interests of protected persons.

7.3.2 "Constitutional Contagion"

One of the major problems inherent in the use of Executive Orders by both state governors and president/prime-ministers is the risk of *Constitutional Contagion* across state borders or across national borders—wherein state governors, courts or law-makers or theorists adopt constitutional theories, statutes and legal mechanisms from other countries or states. Examples include but are not limited to the following: (i) the similarities of the Executive Orders issued by US state governors during January–April 2020 in response to the COVID-19 epidemic—see Appendix 1 herein and below; (ii) the similarities among the new emergency powers enacted by various national presidents and prime ministers through Executive Orders during January–April 2020 in response to the COVID-19 epidemic. *Constitutional Contagion* is more likely in federation countries (the US, Canada, EU, Spain, etc.), and Commonwealth countries. On cross-border "contagions" and spillovers in constitutional law judgments and theories, see: Groppi and Ponthoreau (2013), Choudhry (2006), Jackson (2010), and Law and Versteeg (2011).

7.3.3 *Labor-Regulation, Efficiency-of-Government and the Constitutionality of Executive Orders*

In most democratic systems, Executive Orders (by Presidents, Prime Ministers and Governors) can have significant effects on Government-Size through the following: (i) the classification of government employees (temporary vs. political vs. career government employees); (ii) hiring/firing processes for government workers; (iii) collective bargaining processes; (iv) labor union activities; (v) whistleblower activities; (vi) pre- and post-retirement benefits for government workers; and so on. Thus, the ability of government agencies to efficiently respond to Economic Crisis and or Pandemics can be significantly affected by Executive Orders that regulate Labor matters. These Executive Orders can typically be challenged in court[25] or revoked by subsequent Executive Officers. That raises the issue of the constitutionality of Executive Orders.

[25] *See*: "*Agencies Cleared to Apply Trump's Orders on Federal Labor Relations*". https://www.shrm.org/resourcesandtools/legal-and-compliance/employment-law/pages/agencies-cleared-to-apply-trump-orders-on-federal-labor-relations.aspx ("...The Federal Service Labor-Management Relations Statute allows federal employees to unionize and requires federal agencies to bargain in good faith with those unions. In May 2018, Trump issued three Executive Orders that instructed agencies:

- Not to negotiate with unions over permissive subjects—meaning that they should negotiate only items that are mandatory bargaining topics.
- To limit in collective bargaining agreements how much work time employees can spend on union business.
- To exclude from grievance proceedings any dispute over a decision to remove an employee for misconduct or unacceptable performance.

Agencies were instructed to "commit the time and resources necessary" to achieve these goals and to notify the Office of Personnel Management (OPM) if the goals were not met, according to court documents. Agencies were also ordered to continue meeting their obligation to bargain in good faith with labor unions. More than a dozen unions challenged the Executive Orders, asserting, among other claims, that Trump didn't have the authority to issue Executive Orders regarding federal labor relations. In August 2018, a federal district judge struck down parts of the orders. However, a three-judge panel of the US Court of

A prime example of the potentially extensive effect of Executive Orders on *Government-Efficiency* is the three Presidential Orders that were issued by US President Trump in 2018,[26] and an associated Memorandum[27] that

Appeals for the District of Columbia Circuit reversed the ruling in July, finding that the lower court didn't have jurisdiction over the disputed topic. But the orders remained on hold while the unions sought a ruling by the full panel of judges on the appeals court. On Sept. 25, the DC Circuit declined to revisit the ruling and the lower court ultimately lifted the injunction. …)

[26] *See*: *Executive Order 13836 of May 25, 2018* (Developing Efficient, Effective, and Cost-Reducing Approaches to Federal Sector Collective Bargaining).

See: *Executive Order 13837 of May 25, 2018* (Ensuring Transparency, Accountability, and Efficiency in Taxpayer-Funded Union Time Use).

See: *Executive Order 13839 of May 25, 2018* (Promoting Accountability and Streamlining Removal Procedures Consistent with Merit System Principles).

[27] *See*: *US President Trump (Oct. 11, 2019). "Presidential Memorandum on Executive Orders 13836, 13837, and 13839. BUDGET & SPENDING"*. Issued on: October 11, 2019. https://www.whitehouse.gov/presidential-actions/presidential-memorandum-executive-orders-13836-13837-13839/. (This Memorandum stated as follows: "…On May 25, 2018, I signed three Executive Orders requiring executive departments and agencies (agencies) to negotiate collective bargaining agreements that will reduce costs and promote government performance and accountability. These Executive Orders, Executive Order 13836 of May 25, 2018 (Developing Efficient, Effective and Cost-Reducing Approaches to Federal Sector Collective Bargaining), Executive Order 13837 of May 25, 2018 (Ensuring Transparency, Accountability, and Efficiency in Taxpayer-Funded Union Time Use), and Executive Order 13839 of May 25, 2018 (Promoting Accountability and Streamlining Removal Procedures Consistent with Merit System Principles), were partially enjoined by the United States District Court for the District of Columbia on August 25, 2018. The District Court's injunction barred enforcement of sections 5(a), 5(e), and 6 of Executive Order 13836, sections 3(a), 4(a), and 4(b) of Executive Order 13837, and sections 3, 4(a), and 4(c) of Executive Order 13839. On July 16, 2019, the United States Court of Appeals for the District of Columbia Circuit held that the District Court lacked jurisdiction and vacated its judgment, and the Court of Appeals has now issued the mandate making its judgment effective. Provisions of the Executive Orders that had been subject to the District Court's injunction set presumptively reasonable goals that agencies must pursue during bargaining; directed agencies to refuse to bargain over permissive subjects of negotiation; and established Government-wide rules that displace agencies' duty to bargain with unions over contrary matters, regardless of whether the Federal Service Labor-Management Relations Statute would otherwise require bargaining absent those rules. Sections 4(c)(ii) and 8(a) of Executive Order 13837 and section 8(b) of Executive Order 13839, however, recognized agencies' ability to comply with collective bargaining agreements containing prohibited terms so long as such agreements were effective on the date of the Executive Orders. While the District Court's injunction remained in effect, agencies retained the ability to bargain over subjects covered by the enjoined provisions. The Executive Orders, however, did not address collective bargaining agreements entered into during this period. As a result, it is necessary to clarify agencies' obligations with respect to such collective bargaining agreements. Agencies

he issued in 2019 (collectively, the "*Trump Labor Orders*"). The Trump Labor Orders changed the worker classification systems, the ability to hire/fire government workers, collective bargaining and accountability/transparency all of which affect Government-Size. The legality and constitutionality of the *Trump Labor Orders* were challenged in the US District Court and also litigated at the US Court of Appeals which ruled the US District Court didn't have the jurisdiction to consider such lawsuits.

However, during January 2021, President Biden[28] revoked the *Trump Labor Orders* and parts of other Executive Orders that were issued by

shall adhere to the terms of collective bargaining agreements executed while the injunction was in effect. Agencies that remain engaged in collective bargaining negotiations, to the extent consistent with law, shall comply with the terms of the Executive Orders. However, where, between the date of the Executive Orders and the date of the Court of Appeals's mandate, the parties to collective bargaining negotiations have executed an agreement to incorporate into a new collective bargaining agreement specific terms prohibited by the Executive Orders, an agency may execute the new collective bargaining agreement containing such terms, and terms ancillary to those specific terms, notwithstanding the Executive Orders. To the extent it is necessary, this memorandum should be construed to amend Executive Orders 13836, 13837, and 13839. The Director of the Office of Personnel Management is hereby authorized and directed to publish this memorandum in the Federal Register ... DONALD J. TRUMP...").

[28] *See*: The White House (USA) (Jan. 22, 2021). *Executive Order on Protecting the Federal Workforce (Presidential Actions)*. https://www.whitehouse.gov/briefing-room/presidential-actions/2021/01/22/executive-order-protecting-the-federal-workforce/.

See: "*Biden Revokes Trump Executive Orders on Federal Workforce*". https://sflerp.org/biden-revokes-trump-executive-orders-on-federal-workforce/. This article stated in part, "On Friday, January 22, 2021, President Biden issued an Executive Order revoking the Trump Administration's Executive Orders pertaining to the Federal Workforce and issues related to collective bargain in the Federal sector. The new Executive Order revoked the creation of a new Schedule F excepted service category in *Executive Order 13957* of October 21, 2020. In addition, the new order stipulates that *Executive Order 13836* of May 25, 2018 (Developing Efficient, Effective, and Cost-Reducing Approaches to Federal Sector Collective Bargaining), is also revoked and directs the Interagency Labor Relations Working Group to disband. It instructs the Director of OPM to withdraw all materials issued by this working group that are inconsistent with the policy set forth in section 1 of the new order. It also revokes the following orders and memo issued by the Trump Administration:

- *Executive Order 13837* of May 25, 2018 (Ensuring Transparency, Accountability, and Efficiency in Taxpayer-Funded Union Time Use),
- *Executive Order 13839* of May 25, 2018 (Promoting Accountability and Streamlining Removal Procedures Consistent with Merit System Principles),
- The *Presidential Memorandum* of October 11, 2019 (Executive Orders *13836*, *13837*, and *13839*).

President Trump. President Biden also subsequently revoked more Executive Orders[29] that were issued by President Trump including those

In addition to revoking certain portion of other orders, the new order instructs the head of each agency subject to the provisions of chapter 71 of title 5, United States Code, to elect to negotiate over the subjects set forth in 5 U.S.C. 7106(b)(1) and to instruct subordinate officials to do the same. The Director of OPM shall provide a report to the President with recommendations to promote a $15/hour minimum wage for Federal employees".

[29] *See:* "*Biden Revokes More Trump Executive Orders, Including One On New Green Cards—The Revoked Orders And Memos Include Those On Financial Regulation. Biden Targeted Some Of The Most Controversial Executive Actions Trump Took During His Final Months In Office*". February 25, 2021. https://theprint.in/world/biden-revokes-more-trump-executive-orders-including-one-on-new-green-cards/611421/. This article stated in part, "The actions were Biden's latest to erase Trump's legacy and reset the nation's course, without any involvement by Congress. In Biden's first week in office alone, he issued thirty-nine executive actions, many of which overturned Trump Orders…. The orders revoked by Biden include a 2017 measure signed by Trump directing the government to streamline regulations affecting the financial services industry, part of an effort to roll back the impact of the Dodd-Frank Act. Biden also targeted some of the most controversial executive actions Trump took during his final months in office. Among them is the withdrawal of an executive order that used the coronavirus pandemic to halt the issuance of new green cards, a move that drastically cut legal immigration to the U.S. Trump—who unveiled the changes after originally tweeting that he would act to prohibit "immigration into our Country"—had argued the measures were necessary to protect the American economy as it recovered from the pandemic… Biden also eliminated Trump's effort to identify cities he claimed were "permitting anarchy, violence and destruction" following anti-police brutality protests last summer, some of which involved violence and property destruction. Trump sought to cut federal funding to New York City, Seattle and Portland, Oregon…. And Biden scrapped a lame duck executive order that made classical architecture the preferred style for federal buildings in Washington. Trump's order stopped short of mandating that all new buildings conform to a classical style, but did require that they be "beautiful."… Finally, the president withdrew two Trump-era moves affecting federal workers: a 2018 executive order that allowed Pentagon leadership to limit the ability of civilian Department of Defense employees from collective bargaining, and a 2021 executive order that restricted the ability of career staff at government agencies from issuing regulations. "Any federal positions, committees and task forces created in association with the orders would also be eliminated, the White House said".

See: The White House (Feb. 24, 2021). *Executive Order on the Revocation of Certain Presidential Actions.* February 24, 2021. https://www.whitehouse.gov/briefing-room/presidential-actions/2021/02/24/executive-order-on-the-revocation-of-certain-presidential-actions/. This Executive Order Stated in part:

> …By the authority vested in me as President by the Constitution and the laws of the United States of America, it is hereby ordered as follows:

Section 1. Revocation of Presidential Actions. The following Presidential actions are revoked: Executive Order 13772 of February 3, 2017 (Core Principles for Regulating the United States Financial System), Executive Order 13828 of April 10, 2018 (Reducing

pertaining to Labor (collective-bargaining by US government employees), "anarchist-cities", financial regulations and immigration into the US.

Table 7.1 below summarizes the executive actions taken by President Biden during the first one-hundred days of his administration, and many of them: (1) reversed or amended Trump Administration's policies; (2) enacted new critical guidelines that were essentially omitted by the Trump Administration. These new and amending Executive Orders illustrate the potentially far-reaching effects of Executive Orders on government affairs, International Affairs, Labor markets, interstate commerce, justice, international financial markets and the global economy (sometimes encroaching on areas that are constitutionally allocated to the federal legislature).

7.4 The United States Case

This section analyzes the Government, Constitutional Law and Constitutional Economics implications of new statutes and government directives that were enacted in the US during January–April 2020 in response to the COVID-19 epidemic.

7.4.1 Constitutionality of the Executive Orders Issued by Some US State Governors During January–April 2020 in Response to COVID-19

During January–March 2020, almost all US state governors issued Executive Orders that prohibited public assembly, closed schools, limited movement of persons and required many businesses to close their operations for a while. Appendix 1 herein and below lists the various US state

Poverty in America by Promoting Opportunity and Economic Mobility), Memorandum of January 29, 2020 (Delegation of Certain Authority Under the Federal Service Labor-Management Relations Statute), Executive Order 13924 of May 19, 2020 (Regulatory Relief To Support Economic Recovery), Memorandum of September 2, 2020 (Reviewing Funding to State and Local Government Recipients of Federal Funds That Are Permitting Anarchy, Violence, and Destruction in American Cities), Executive Order 13967 of December 18, 2020 (Promoting Beautiful Federal Civic Architecture), and Executive Order 13979 of January 18, 2021 (Ensuring Democratic Accountability in Agency Rulemaking)....

See: "*Here Are The Executive Actions Biden Signed In His First 100 Days*". By Christopher Hickey, Curt Merrill, Richard J. Chang, Kate Sullivan, Janie Boschma and Sean O'Key, CNN. Updated April 30, 2021. https://edition.cnn.com/interactive/2021/politics/biden-executive-orders/.

Table 7.1 Executive actions by President Biden during his first one hundred days in office

Date of presidential executive-action	*Topic*	*Type of presidential action*	*Reversal (from Trump administration's policies)?*	*Summary*
04/27/2021	Labor	Executive order	No	Raises the minimum wage of federal contract workers to $15 an hour in early 2022, up from the current $10.95. Eliminates the tipped minimum wage, $7.65 an hour, by 2024. Requires a $15 minimum wage for federal contract workers with disabilities.
04/16/2021	Immigration	Memo	Yes	Reverses the Trump policy banning refugees from key regions and enables flights from those regions to begin within days. Declares that the 15,000 annual refugee cap set by Trump will be raised to a number to be determined by May 15.
04/15/2021	National security	Executive order	No	Imposes sanctions and diplomatic expulsions on Russia in response to the country's interference in the 2020 US election and the SolarWinds cyberattack; formally names the Russian Foreign Intelligence Service as the force behind SolarWinds; blocks US financial institutions from trading in Russian bonds
04/09/2021	Other	Executive order	No	Forms the Presidential Commission on the Supreme Court of the United States, which is intended to provide an analysis of the principal arguments for and against Supreme Court reform.
04/01/2021	Other	Executive order	Yes	Revokes a Trump executive order that authorized sanctions on International Criminal Court officials
03/08/2021	Equity	Executive order	No	Establishes a White House Gender Policy Council, which will submit a government-wide plan within 200 days with recommendations to "advance gender equity and equality in the United States and around the world"

(*continued*)

Table 7.1 (Continued)

Date of presidential executive-action	*Topic*	*Type of presidential action*	*Reversal (from Trump administration's policies)?*	*Summary*
03/08/2021	Equity	Executive order	No	Reaffirms as a policy of the Biden administration that "all students should be guaranteed an educational environment free from discrimination on the basis of sex, including discrimination in the form of sexual harassment, which encompasses sexual violence, and including discrimination on the basis of sexual orientation or gender identity." Directs the education secretary to review all department policies and actions to identify those that may be inconsistent with the stated policy.
03/07/2021	Equity	Executive order	No	Directs each agency to evaluate and submit a strategic plan within 200 days on opportunities to promote and expand access to voter registration and participation; directs the General Services Administration to modernize and improve vote.gov; calls for strategies to expand policies allowing federal employees time off to vote and to expand employees' ability to serve as nonpartisan poll workers or observers; requires a review of barriers to voting for individuals with disabilities and of the Federal Voter Registration Form to ensure it is accessible; requires the defense secretary to review the feasibility of providing an online system for military personnel serving abroad to manage their voter registration and request absentee ballots; directs the attorney general to require jails to provide educational materials on voting and voter registration; establishes the Interagency Steering Group on Native American Voting Rights

(*continued*)

Table 7.1 (Continued)

Date of presidential executive-action	*Topic*	*Type of presidential action*	*Reversal (from Trump administration's policies)?*	*Summary*
02/24/2021	Economy	Executive order	Yes	Revokes a series of seven Trump administration actions that had eased regulatory requirements, as well as actions that called for withholding funding from cities for allowing protests in support of Black Lives Matter, that imposed stricter work requirements to be eligible for federal welfare and that promoted "beautiful federal civic architecture"
02/24/2021	Immigration	Proclamation	Yes	Revokes a Trump-era proclamation that limited legal immigration during the Covid-19 pandemic
02/24/2021	National security	Executive order	No	Launches a 100-day review of US supply chains for pharmaceuticals, critical minerals, semiconductors and large-capacity batteries, directing agencies to identify opportunities to secure and invest in those supply chains. It also calls for a year-long review into six sectors: Defense, public health and biological preparedness, information and communications technology, energy, transportation, and agricultural commodities and food preparation
02/17/2021	Labor	Executive order	Yes	Revokes a Trump administration order creating an industry-led apprenticeship program
02/14/2021	Other	Executive order	No	Establishes a White House Office of Faith-Based and Neighborhood Partnerships to coordinate providing community services in partnership with federal, state and local governments and with other private organizations

(*continued*)

Table 7.1 (Continued)

Date of presidential executive-action	*Topic*	*Type of presidential action*	*Reversal (from Trump administration's policies)?*	*Summary*
02/11/2021	National security	Executive order	No	Sanctions Myanmar military leaders, blocking property ownership in the United States by any foreign person associated with those leaders, their business interests or those undermining democracy or human rights in Myanmar
02/04/2021	Immigration	Executive order	Yes	Expands the United States Refugee Admissions Program and rescinds Trump policies that limited refugee admissions and required additional vetting
02/04/2021	Immigration	Memo	Yes	Directs relevant agencies to ensure LGBTQI+ refugees and asylum seekers have equal access to protections, requires the Department of State to lead a standing group to respond quickly to international LGBTQI+ human rights abuses and to report annually to Congress on global LGBTQI+ abuses, directs agencies to review Trump administration policies and rescind those that are inconsistent with this memo within 100 days
02/04/2021	National security	Memo	No	Establishes an interagency working group to propose improvements for recruiting, retaining and supporting national security professions
02/04/2021	National security	Memo	No	Outlines the structure of the National Security Council, incorporates more regular participation from Cabinet officials focused on domestic policy that influences national security
02/02/2021	Immigration	Executive order	Yes	Revokes Trump's order justifying separating families at the border and creates a task force that recommends steps to Biden to reunite separated families

(*continued*)

Table 7.1 (Continued)

Date of presidential executive-action	*Topic*	*Type of presidential action*	*Reversal (from Trump administration's policies)?*	*Summary*
02/02/2021	Immigration	Executive order	Yes	Aims to address economic and political causes of migration, works with organizations to provide protection to asylum seekers and ensures Central American asylum seekers have legal access to the United States. Rescinds Trump administration policies and guidelines and also initiates a review of policies "that have effectively closed the U.S. border to asylum seekers"
02/02/2021	Immigration	Executive order	Yes	Rescinds Trump's memo requiring immigrants to repay the government if they receive public benefits. Elevates the role of the executive branch in promoting immigrant integration and inclusion, including reestablishing a Task Force on New Americans. Requires agencies to review immigration regulations and policies
02/02/2021	Coronavirus	Memo	No	Extends the timeline from his Jan. 21 memo, which directed FEMA to reimburse states to fully cover the cost for National Guard personnel and emergency supplies. Now states will also be reimbursed for emergency purchases made since the beginning of the pandemic
02/01/2021	Economy	Proclamation	Yes	Reinstates tariffs applied under the Trump administration to aluminum imports from the United Arab Emirates, citing the need for domestic production of aluminum for national security and reviving industry

(*continued*)

Table 7.1 (Continued)

Date of presidential executive-action	*Topic*	*Type of presidential action*	*Reversal (from Trump administration's policies)?*	*Summary*
01/28/2021	Health care	Executive order	No	Reopens enrollment on HealthCare.gov from Feb. 15 through May 15, and directs federal agencies to reexamine policies that may reduce or undermine access to the Affordable Care Act
01/28/2021	Health care	Memo	Yes	Rescinds the "Mexico City Policy," a ban on US government funding for foreign nonprofits that perform or promote abortions
01/27/2021	Environment	Executive order	No	Elevates climate change as an essential element of US foreign policy and national security and kicks off development of a new emissions reduction target, which will be announced by April 22
01/27/2021	Environment	Executive order	No	Reestablishes the President's Council of Advisors on Science and Technology
01/27/2021	Environment	Memo	No	Charges the director of the Office of Science and Technology Policy with responsibility for ensuring scientific integrity across federal agencies
01/26/2021	Equity	Memo	No	Directs the Department of Housing and Urban Development to review the Trump administration's regulatory actions for their effects on fair housing and to then "take steps necessary" to comply with the Fair Housing Act
01/26/2021	Equity	Executive order	No	Directs the attorney general not to renew federal contracts with private prisons
01/26/2021	Equity	Memo	No	Recommits federal agencies to "engage in regular, robust and meaningful consultation with Tribal governments"

(*continued*)

Table 7.1 (Continued)

Date of presidential executive-action	*Topic*	*Type of presidential action*	*Reversal (from Trump administration's policies)?*	*Summary*
01/26/2021	Equity	Memo	No	Acknowledges the rise in discrimination against Asian Americans and Pacific Islanders in the past year, directing the Department of Health and Human Services to consider issuing guidance on best practices to improve "cultural competency, language access and sensitivity toward AAPIs" in the federal government's Covid-19 response, and directs the Department of Justice to partner with AAPI communities to prevent hate crimes and harassment
01/25/2021	Economy	Executive order	No	Strengthens Buy American rules by closing loopholes and reducing waivers granted on federal purchases of domestic goods
01/25/2021	Coronavirus	Proclamation	Yes	Reinstates Covid-19 travel restrictions for individuals traveling to the United States from the Schengen Area, the United Kingdom, Ireland and South Africa
01/25/2021	Equity	Executive order	Yes	Reverses the Trump administration's ban on transgender Americans joining the military
01/22/2021	Economy	Executive order	Yes	Restores collective bargaining power and worker protections for federal workers, and lays the foundation for $15 minimum wage
01/22/2021	Economy	Executive order	No	Calls for assistance to those who are struggling to buy food, missed out on stimulus checks or are unemployed
01/21/2021	Coronavirus	Executive order	No	Accelerates manufacturing and delivery of supplies for vaccination, testing and Personal Protective Equipment

(*continued*)

Table 7.1 (Continued)

Date of presidential executive-action	*Topic*	*Type of presidential action*	*Reversal (from Trump administration's policies)?*	*Summary*
01/21/2021	Coronavirus	Memo	No	Directs FEMA to expand reimbursement to states to fully cover the cost for National Guard personnel and emergency supplies
01/21/2021	Coronavirus	Executive order	No	Establishes the Pandemic Testing Board to expand US coronavirus testing capacity
01/21/2021	Coronavirus	Executive order	No	Establishes a preclinical program to boost development of therapeutics in response to pandemic threats
01/21/2021	Coronavirus	Executive order	No	Enhances the nation's collection, production, sharing and analysis of coronavirus data
01/21/2021	Coronavirus	Executive order	No	Directs the Department of Education and HHS to provide guidance for safely reopening and operating schools, childcare providers and institutions of higher education
01/21/2021	Coronavirus	Executive order	No	Calls on the Occupational Safety and Health Administration to release clear guidance on Covid-19, decide whether to establish emergency temporary standards, and directs OSHA to enforce worker health and safety requirements
01/21/2021	Coronavirus	Executive order	No	Requires mask wearing in airports and on certain modes of transportation, including many trains, airplanes, maritime vessels and intercity buses. International travelers must provide proof of a negative Covid-19 test prior to coming to the US
01/21/2021	Coronavirus	Executive order	No	Creates the Covid-19 Health Equity Task Force to help ensure an equitable pandemic response and recovery

(*continued*)

Table 7.1 (Continued)

Date of presidential executive-action	*Topic*	*Type of presidential action*	*Reversal (from Trump administration's policies)?*	*Summary*
01/21/2021	Coronavirus	Memo	No	Promotes restoring America's leadership, supports the international pandemic response effort, promotes resilience for future threats and advance global health security and the Global Health Security Agenda
01/20/2021	Coronavirus	Executive order	No	Launches a "100 Days Masking Challenge" asking Americans to wear masks for 100 days. Requires masks and physical distancing in federal buildings, on federal lands and by government contractors, and urges states and local governments to do the same.
01/20/2021	Coronavirus	Other	Yes	Stops the United States' withdrawal from the World Health Organization, with Dr. Anthony Fauci becoming the head of the delegation to the WHO
01/20/2021	Coronavirus	Executive order	No	Creates the position of Covid-19 Response Coordinator, reporting directly to Biden and managing efforts to produce and distribute vaccines and medical equipment
01/20/2021	Economy	Directive	No	Extends the existing nationwide moratorium on evictions and foreclosures until at least March 31
01/20/2021	Economy	Directive	No	Extends the existing pause on student loan payments and interest for Americans with federal student loans until at least September 30
01/20/2021	Environment	Other	Yes	Rejoins the Paris climate accord, a process that will take 30 days
01/20/2021	Environment	Executive order	Yes	Cancels the Keystone XL pipeline and directs agencies to review and reverse more than 100 Trump actions on the environment

(*continued*)

Table 7.1 (Continued)

Date of presidential executive-action	*Topic*	*Type of presidential action*	*Reversal (from Trump administration's policies)?*	*Summary*
01/20/2021	Equity	Executive order	Yes	Rescinds the Trump administration's 1776 Commission, directs agencies to review their actions to ensure racial equity
01/20/2021	Equity	Executive order	No	Prevents workplace discrimination on the basis of sexual orientation or gender identity
01/20/2021	Census	Executive order	Yes	Requires non-citizens to be included in the Census and apportionment of congressional representatives
01/20/2021	Immigration	Memo	No	Fortifies DACA after Trump's efforts to undo protections for undocumented people brought into the country as children
01/20/2021	Immigration	Proclamation	Yes	Reverses the Trump administration's restrictions on US entry for passport holders from seven Muslim-majority countries
01/20/2021	Immigration	Executive order	Yes	Undoes Trump's expansion of immigration enforcement within the United States
01/20/2021	Immigration	Proclamation	Yes	Halts construction of the border wall by terminating the national emergency declaration used to fund it
01/20/2021	Immigration	Memo	No	Extends deferrals of deportation and work authorizations for Liberians with a safe haven in the United States until June 30, 2022
01/20/2021	Ethics	Executive order	No	Requires executive branch appointees to sign an ethics pledge barring them from acting in personal interest and requiring them to uphold the independence of the Department of Justice
01/20/2021	Regulation	Memo, executive order	Yes	Directs OMB director to develop recommendations to modernize regulatory review and undoes Trump's regulatory approval process

Source: https://edition.cnn.com/interactive/2021/politics/biden-executive-orders/

governors' 2020 COVID-19-related Executive Orders as of March 2020. While the US state governors' Executive Orders seemed to mimic the Chinese government's command-and-control-based COVID-19-related broad and intense restrictions of 2020, the US is a fundamentally different society with a very different set of Constitutional Law philosophies.

In the United States and during the COVID-19 era, various parties challenged the constitutionality[30] of states' emergency management stat-

[30] *See*: *Free Minn. Small Bus. Coalition vs. Walz*, 2020 Minn. Dist. LEXIS 256 (Minn. Dist. Ct. September 1, 2020) (court found that the Executive Orders did not violate the *non-delegation clause*; but the court rejected claims by individual legislators).

See: *Wisconsin Legislature vs. Palm*, 2020 WI 42 (2020) (the Wisconsin Legislature challenged the statutory authority of the state's Department of Health Services (DHS) to issue emergency orders; and the court held that the emergency order was a regulation that should emerge from the legislative rulemaking process in order for its civil and criminal provisions to be enforcable).

See: *Wolf vs. Scarnati*, 233 A.3d 679 (Pa. 2020) (the Pennsylvania Supreme Court held that the state legislature didn't have the power to cancel the governor's state of emergency declaration because the state constitution required that the state legislature first present the concurrent resolution for the governor to veto).

See: *County of Butler vs. Wolf*, No. 2:20-CV-677, 2020 WL 5510690 (US District Court; W.D. Pa.; Sept. 14, 2020) (could held that Pennsylvania's stay at home orders were unconstitutional).

See: *Robinson vs. Murphy*, No. CV 20-5420, 2020 WL 5884801 (US District Court; D.N.J.; Oct. 2, 2020) (court rejected the decision/reasoning in *County of Butler vs. Wolf*).

See: *Forrer vs. Alaska* (August 7, 2020, Juneau Superior Court, Alaska) (state government's appropriation of federal funds received per the Coronavirus Aid, Relief, and Economic Security Act didn't violate Alaska's Constitution).

See: *Barnes vs. Ahlman* (US Supreme Court; August 5, 2020) (case was returned to US Ninth Circuit Court of Appeals) (US Supreme Court stayed a district court's order that required an Orange County Sheriff to implement multiple COVID-19 safety precautions at the county jail, pending an appeal in the US Ninth Circuit Court of Appeals).

See: *Gateway City Church vs. Newsom* (US Supreme Court; February 26, 2021) (heightened restrictions on religious gatherings must be stopped because they violated an earlier ruling that struck down Governor Gavin Newsom's prohibition against indoor church services).

See: *Elim Romanian Pentecostal Church vs. Pritzker* (May 16, 2020; US Court of Appeals for the Seventh Circuit) (court rejected a motion for a temporary stay against the state governor's Executive Order 2020-32 that prohibited gatherings of more than ten people).

See: *South Bay United Pentecostal Church, et al. vs. Newsom* (US Supreme Court; May 29, 2020) (US Supreme Court rejected a challenge to California's religious gathering regulation which limited attendance in churches or places of worship to a maximum of 25% or 100 attendees).

utes and state governors' Executive Orders that pertained to emergencies and COVID-related regulations and the powers of the state legislatures but many US lower courts have ruled differently.

See: *Tandon vs. Newsom* (US Supreme Court; April 9, 2021) (US Supreme Court invalidated California's prohibition against religious gatherings of people from more than three households).

See: *Neville vs. Polis* (August 28, 2020; Colorado Supreme Court, United States) (court rejected challenge against more than three dozen Executive Orders issued by Colorado governor including a statewide mask mandate; and also rejected claim that the *Colorado Disaster Emergency Act* was an unconstitutional violation of the *Separation of Powers Doctrine*).

See: *Calvary Chapel Dayton Valley vs. Sisolak* (July 24, 2020; US Supreme Court) (US Supreme Court rejected a challenge by a Nevada church against the Nevada state governor's order that imposed COVID-19 capacity limits).

See: *Kelly vs. Legislative Coordinating Council* (Kansas Supreme Court, April 2020) (court ruled that Kansas's Legislative Coordinating Council did not have the power to revoke the state governor's Executive Order limiting religious gatherings to ten individuals—plaintiff state governor argued that only the full state legislature had the power to revoke the Executive Order).

See: *Roberts vs. Neace* (May 4, 2020, United States District Court for the Eastern District of Kentucky) (court enjoined the state government from enforcing its ban on interstate travel because of COVID-19).

See: *Beshear vs. Acree* (November 12, 2020; Kentucky Supreme Court) (court upheld state governor's COVID-19 emergency orders).

See: *4 Aces Enterprises, LLC vs. Edwards* (August 17, 2020; US District Court for the Eastern District of Louisiana) (appeal filed) (court rejected denied request by local bar owners to declare as unconstitutional, the state governor's Executive Order that closed bars in response to the COVID-19 pandemic).

See: *Big Tyme Investments, LLC vs. Edwards & 910 E Main, LLC vs. Edwards* (January 13, 2020; US Court of Appeals for the Fifth Circuit) (appeals court upheld state governor's authority to order COVID-19-related closures of bars and alcohol restrictions; and rejected arguments that the governor's order violated the *Equal Protection Clause* of the Fourteenth Amendment).

See: *Antietam Battlefield KOA vs. Hogan* (November 18, 2020; US District Court for the District of Maryland) (US District Court rejected challenge to state governor's COVID-19 related Executive Order restrictions; and rejected plaintiffs' allegations that the orders violated the First Amendment rights of free exercise of religion, freedom of assembly, and free speech, and violated the *equal protection clause*, the *interstate commerce clause* and the Takings Clause).

See: *Michigan House of Representatives and Michigan Senate vs. Gretchen Whitmer* (October 2, 2020; Michigan Supreme Court) (Michigan Supreme Court ruled that the Michigan state governor didn't have any authority to issue or renew Executive Orders relating to COVID-19 after April 30, 2020).

Napolitano (2020)[31] noted that:

> The governors of New York, New Jersey, Pennsylvania and Connecticut have all issued decrees closing most retail establishments, particularly all restaurants, bars and theaters. The governor of New Jersey is threatening to ban all travel after dark. And the mayor of New York City is threatening to ban all travel all the time. The fulfillment of these totalitarian impulses has put more than one million folks out of work, closed thousands of businesses and impaired the fundamental rights of tens of millions of persons—all in violation of numerous sections of the Constitution. The *Contracts Clause* of the Constitution prohibits the states from interfering with lawful contracts, such as leases and employment agreements. And the *Due Process Clause* of the Fourteenth Amendment prohibits the states from interfering with life, liberty or property without a trial at which the state must prove fault. The *Takings Clause* of the Fifth Amendment requires just compensation when the state meaningfully interferes with an owner's chosen lawful use of his property. Taken together, these clauses reveal the significant protections of private property in the Constitution itself. Add to this the threat of punishment that has accompanied these decrees and the fact that they are executive decrees, not legislation, and one can see the paramount rejection of basic democratic and constitutional principles in the minds and words and deeds of those who have perpetrated them.

It's noteworthy that in Nigeria and during 2016, in *Okafor* vs. *Governor of Lagos State*,[32] the Nigerian Federal Court of Appeals ruled that the Lagos State Governor's order/directive that limited the movement of people on each of Lagos State's monthly environmental cleanup day was unconstitutional. In Lagos State, the environmental cleanup day was held on one day during each calendar month.

The following section discusses the constitutionality of the US state governors' Executive Orders (that were issued during 2020 in response to the COVID-19 Pandemic).

[31] *See*: Napolitano, A. (2020). "*Judge Andrew Napolitano: Coronavirus Fear Lets Government Assault Our Freedom In Violation Of Constitution*". https://www.foxnews.com/opinion/judge-andrew-napolitano-liberty-coronavirus.

[32] *See*: *Okafor* vs. *Governor of Lagos State* (2016), LPELR-41066 (CA) (Nigerian Federal Court of Appeals court case).

7.4.1.1 The *Right-to-Contract Doctrine (*Contracts Clause *of the US Constitution)*

Napolitano (2020) noted that the US state Governors' Executive Orders infringed the *Right-to-Contract* of many persons and businesses. The affected classes of persons (the "Restricted Persons") were as follows:

1. Businesses and schools that were forced to close, and thus could not perform, enforce or enter into new contracts.
2. Individuals whose movements were restricted and thus could not perform, enforce or enter into new contracts.
3. Students who could not attend schools that were closed.

The public interest and the need to control the rapid spread of COVID-19 may or may not outweigh the personal rights of the affected/limited classes of persons and the potentially large economic harm that such Executive Orders can cause. See Nwogugu (2012).[33] The obvious *State Action* is the Executive Order. The issues are that:

1. The Executive Orders can be construed as "over-broad" and were not narrowly tailored to serve the intended purpose of promoting public health. The Executive Orders illegally interfere with lawful contracts, such as leases, sales contracts and employment agreements.
2. The Executive Orders didn't specifically provide viable alternatives for the "Restricted Persons" who most likely lost money and jobs—but internet commerce and web-based contracting provided a viable alternative to in-person contracting for some classes of Restricted Persons.
3. Such *Restricted Persons* had a constitutionally guaranteed *Property Interest* in valid statutes and in the right to move around, enter into contracts and conduct their normal daily activities. Such *Property Interests* arose from the US Constitution, state constitutions, expectations, norms/culture and usage-of-trade.
4. The Executive Orders increased or could have increased unemployment and social unrest, and had negative *Multiplier Effects* (economics, social, psychological and environmental) and

[33] *See*: *Energy Reserves Group, Inc. vs. Kansas Power and Light Co.*, _____ US ____ (US Supreme Court; 1983); and *Sveen vs. Melin*, _____ US ____ (US Supreme Court; 2018).

Emergence properties (i.e. new adverse economic, social, psychological and/or environmental phenomena can emerge as a result).

5. The Executive Orders unfairly discriminated between Restricted Persons that know how to, or could afford to obtain, or could hire political lobbyists to obtain exemptions from such Executive Orders, and those that couldn't. That can create various opportunities for *quid-pro-quo deals* and political lobbying. It's not clear whether such discrimination advances the public interest in the case of epidemics.
6. The Executive Orders unfairly discriminated between Restricted Persons that had significant cash reserves (or whose owners had cash reserves), and those that didn't. That can create various opportunities for crime. It's not clear whether such discrimination advances the public interest in the case of epidemics.
7. The Executive Orders unfairly discriminated between Restricted Persons that could easily postpone or transfer/assign or cancel their contracts and those that couldn't. That can create various opportunities for crime. It's not clear whether such discrimination advances the public interest in the case of epidemics.
8. The Executive Orders unfairly discriminated between Restricted Persons that could easily apply for announced federal government aid (for individuals and SMEs), and those that couldn't. That can create various opportunities for crime. It's not clear whether such discrimination advances the public interest in the case of epidemics.
9. The rapid, evolving and significant changes in online/offline *Social Networks* and *Social Capital* was likely to have lasting negative psychological, social and political effects on indigenes.
10. Some public health experts and researchers[34] noted that the then prevailing emphasis on restrictions on movement of people and closures of businesses wasn't helpful and, instead, governments and the public should have focused more resources on identifying and isolating infected persons.

[34] *See*: "*Virus Travel Bans Are Inevitable But Ineffective—Experts Can't Stop Restrictions, But They Can Mitigate Them*". By Mara Pillinger. February 23, 2020. https://foreignpolicy.com/2020/02/23/virus-travel-bans-are-inevitable-but-ineffective/.

See: "*How To Stop The Next Pandemic Before It Starts—It May Be Too Late To Contain The New Coronavirus. But We Can Safeguard The World Against The Next One*". By Annie Sparrow. https://foreignpolicy.com/2020/02/23/virus-travel-bans-are-inevitable-but-ineffective/.

11. Given the foregoing, the Executive Orders could have created *Price-Contagions* (unjustified, coordinated/replicated and uniform price increases in neighborhoods/towns), *Uncertainty-and-Inertia Contagions* (replicated and/or coordinated inertia and uncertainty in neighborhoods/towns) and *Deadweight Losses* in the demand/supply of goods and services, and in the demand/supply of government services.

For example the following could have been included in the state governors' Executive Orders:

1. Restaurants, SMEs and shops could conceivably remain open to serve verified uninfected people within a 200- to 500-meter radius (where the restaurants/shops check for guest-addresses, COVID-19 and other infectious diseases at their doors). Their staff must wear protective gear and must be tested every 15–24 hours for COVID-19 and infectious diseases and their premises must be disinfected daily.
2. Some SMEs, restaurants and shops could have remained open and sell only by take-out and personal delivery (no in-store visitors). Their staff must wear protective gear and must be tested regularly for COVID-19 and infectious diseases, and their premises must be disinfected daily.
3. Some physicians' and dentists' offices could conceivably remain open to serve people within a 2- to 3-kilometer radius (where these medical establishments check for COVID-19 and other infectious diseases at their doors). Their staff must wear protective gear and must be tested every 10 hours for COVID-19 and infectious diseases and their premises must be disinfected daily.

7.4.1.2 Substantive and Procedural Due Process (Due Process Clause *of the US Constitution)*

Napolitano (2020) correctly noted that the state Governors' Executive Orders infringed the *Due Process* rights of many persons and businesses. The affected classes of persons (the "Restricted Persons") were as follows:

1. Businesses and schools that were forced to close, and lost revenues as a result.

2. Individuals whose movements were restricted and thus could not earn income.
3. Students who could not attend schools that were closed.

However, the public interest and the need to control the rapid spread of COVID-19 may or may not outweigh the personal rights of the affected/limited classes of persons and the potentially large economic harm that such Executive Orders can cause. Perhaps the *balancing-of-interests* should be supported by economic studies. See Nwogugu (2012).[35] The obvious *State Action* were the Executive Orders and the enforcement of same. As above, the problems are that:

1. The Executive Orders can be construed as "over-broad" and they were not sufficiently and narrowly tailored to serve the intended purpose of promoting public health.
2. The Executive Orders didn't specifically provide viable alternatives for the "Restricted Persons" who will most likely lose money and jobs—but internet commerce and web-based contracting provides a viable alternative to in-person interactions/transactions for some classes of Restricted Persons.
3. Such *Restricted Persons* had a constitutionally guaranteed *Property Interest* in valid statutes, equitable procedures and in the right to move around and conduct their normal daily activities. Such *Property Interests* arise from the US Constitution, state constitutions, expectations, norms/culture and usage-of-trade.
4. There wasn't sufficient time for required procedural Due Process and litigation. Ordinarily the state government was required to provide evidence for its Executive Orders.

[35] On *Substantive Due Process*, see: *Washington v. Glucksberg*, 521 U.S. 702, 719 (US Supreme Court; 1997); *Obergefell vs. Hodges*, 576 U.S. 644 (US Supreme Court; 2015); *Lawrence vs. Texas*, 539 U.S. 558 (US Supreme Court; 2003); *United States vs. Vaello-Madero*, _____ US ____ (Case#: 20-303; US Supreme Court; pending as of 2021); *DeNolf vs. U.S.*, _____ US _____ (US Supreme Court; pending as of 2021) (https://static1.squarespace.com/static/5b660749620b85c6c73e5e61/t/608d544886d55300e492a619/1619874888658/2021-22+AMCA+Case.pdf); *DeNolf vs. U.S.* (Case#: 01-76320; US 14th Circuit, 2020) (https://static1.squarespace.com/static/5b660749620b85c6c73e5e61/t/608d544886d55300e492a619/1619874888658/2021-22+AMCA+Case.pdf); and *Planned Parenthood of Southeastern Pennsylvania v. Casey*, 505 U.S. 833, 848 (1992).

5. The Executive Orders unfairly discriminated between companies that knew how to, or could afford to obtain, or could hire consultants and political lobbyists to obtain exemptions from such Executive Orders, and the many small/medium businesses that couldn't. That created all sorts of opportunities for *quid-pro-quo* deals and political lobbying. It's not clear whether such discrimination advanced the public interest in the case of epidemics.
6. The Executive Orders unfairly discriminated between persons and companies that had significant cash reserves (or whose owners had cash reserves), and those that didn't. That created up all sorts of opportunities for crime. It's not clear whether such discrimination advances the public interest in the case of epidemics.
7. The Executive Orders unfairly discriminated between Restricted Persons that could easily postpone or transfer/assign or cancel their contracts and who could easily challenge the Executive Orders in court on one hand, and those that couldn't as a result of such Executive Orders. That can create various opportunities for crime. It's not clear whether such discrimination advances the public interest in the case of epidemics.
8. The Executive Orders unfairly discriminated between Restricted Persons that could easily apply for announced federal government aid (for individuals and SMEs), and those that couldn't as a result of such Executive Orders. That can create various opportunities for crime. It's not clear whether such discrimination advances the public interest in the case of crisis or pandemics/epidemics.
9. As explained herein and above, some public health experts have noted that the current emphasis on restrictions on movement and closures of businesses won't be helpful and, instead, governments and the public should focus more resources on identifying and isolating infected persons.
10. The cost of enforcing the Executive Orders can be very high, and compliance low.
11. The Executive Orders increased or could have increased unemployment and social unrest, and had negative *Multiplier Effects* (economics, social, psychological and environmental) and *Emergence properties* (i.e. new adverse economic, social, psychological and/or environmental phenomena can emerge as a result).
12. The Executive Orders unfairly discriminated between Restricted Persons that know how to, or could afford to obtain, or could hire

political lobbyists to obtain exemptions from such Executive Orders, and those that can't. That can create various opportunities for *quid-pro-quo deals* and political lobbying. It's not clear whether such discrimination advances the public interest in the case of crisis or pandemics/epidemics.

13. The Executive Orders unfairly discriminated between Restricted Persons that had significant cash reserves (or whose owners had cash reserves), and those that didn't. That can create various opportunities for crime. It's not clear whether such discrimination advances the public interest in the case of epidemics.
14. The rapid, evolving and significant changes in online/offline *Social Networks* and *Social Capital* are likely to have lasting negative psychological, social and political effects on indigenes.
15. Given the foregoing, the Executive Orders could have created *Price-Contagions* (unjustified, coordinated/replicated and uniform price increases in neighborhoods/towns), *Uncertainty-and-Inertia Contagions* (replicated and/or coordinated inertia and uncertainty in neighborhoods/towns) and *Deadweight Losses* in the demand/supply of goods and services, and in the demand/supply of government services.

7.4.1.3 The Takings Clause *of the Fifth Amendment and Fourteenth Amendment*[36] *of the US Constitution*

Napolitano (2020) made a good point by noting that the state Governors' Executive Orders constituted an illegal *Takings* against the restricted persons and businesses. The classes of "Restricted Persons" are as follows:

[36] The Fourteenth Amendment of the US Constitution doesn't formally include a *Takings* provision, but in its rulings, the US Supreme Court included such *Takings* provision in the Fourteenth Amendment. *Webb's Fabulous Pharmacies* vs. *Beckwith*, 449 U.S. 155, 159 (1980).

See: *Atlantic Coast Line R.R.* vs. *City of Goldsboro*, 232 U.S. 548 (1914; US Supreme Court). https://www.law.cornell.edu/supremecourt/text/232/548. This US Supreme Court case stated in part: "And any enactment, from whatever source originating, to which a state gives the force of law, is a statute of the state, within the meaning of the pertinent clause of § 709, Rev. Stat., Judicial Code, § 237; which confers jurisdiction on this court. *Williams v. Bruffy*, 96 U.S. 176, 183. We must therefore treat the ordinances as legislation enacted by virtue of the lawmaking power of the state. They are manifestly an exertion of the police power, and the question is whether, viewed in that light, they run counter to the 'contract' or 'due process' clauses ... For it is settled [however] that neither the 'contract' clause nor the 'due process' clause had the effect of overriding the power of the state

1. Businesses in the state who were forced to close or limit their operations and their businesses cannot be easily done over the Internet or by proxy (and lost revenues and/or clients as a result); and
2. Individuals in the state whose income and earning-capacity depended heavily on their ability to move around (e.g. their jobs or personal businesses cannot be done over the Internet), but were prohibited from doing do so (and lost revenues and/or clients as a result).

   However, the public interest and the need to control the rapid spread of COVID-19 may or may not outweigh the personal rights of the affected/limited classes of persons and the potentially large economic harm that such Executive Orders can cause. Perhaps the balancing-of-interests should be supported by economic studies. See Nwogugu (2012). The obvious *State Action* were the governors' Executive Orders and implementation of same. The state governments effected *Takings* on the Restricted Persons by ordering them to closes their businesses and to limit their physical movements within the state, all of which caused them to incur significant economic losses. However, such *Takings* were effected through the state governors' Executive Orders and not by state-law *Eminent Domain* statutes—that doesn't change the fact that there were *Takings*. Most US states have *Eminent Domain* statutes. As above, the problems are that:

to establish all regulations that are reasonably necessary to secure the health, safety, good order, comfort, or general welfare of the community; that this power can neither be abdicated nor bargained away, and is inalienable even by express grant; and that all contract and property [or other vested] rights are held subject to its fair exercise … And the enforcement of uncompensated obedience to a regulation established under this power for the public health or safety is not an unconstitutional taking of property without compensation or without due process of law".

See: *Cedar Point Nursery vs. Hassid*, ____ US ____ (US Supreme Court; pending as of 2021).

See: *Cedar Point Nursery vs. Sheroma*, ____ F.3d. ____ (US Ninth Circuit Court of Appeals).

See: *PennEast Pipeline Co. vs. New Jersey*, _____ US _____ (US Supreme Court; pending as of 2021).

See: *Murr vs. Wisconsin*, 137 S.Ct. 1933 (US Supreme Court; 2017).

See: *California Bldg. Industry Ass'n vs. City of San Jose, Calif.*, 136 S.Ct. 928 (US Supreme Court; 2016).

See: *Koontz vs. St. Johns River Water Management District*, 570 U.S. 2588 (US Supreme Court; 2013).

See: *Lucas vs. South Carolina Coastal Council*, 505 U.S. 1003 (US Supreme Court; 1992).

1. It's highly probable that the state governments could not afford to compensate the affected Restricted Persons for their *Takings* losses which were significant. There wasn't sufficient time for the required judicial "processes", appraisals and negotiation of compensation.
2. The Executive Orders can be construed as "over-broad" and they were not sufficiently and narrowly tailored to serve the intended purpose of promoting public health and eliminating COVID-19 and associated economic losses.
3. Such *Restricted Persons* have a constitutionally guaranteed *Property Interest* in valid statutes and in the right to move around, do business and earn money, and conduct their normal daily activities. Such *Property Interests* arise from the US Constitution, state constitutions, expectations, norms/culture and usage-of-trade.
4. The Executive Orders didn't specifically provide viable alternatives for the "Restricted Persons" who will most likely lose money and jobs—but the internet commerce and web-based contracting provides a viable alternative to in-person interactions for some classes of Restricted Persons.
5. The Executive Orders unfairly discriminated between Restricted Persons that know how to, or could afford to obtain, or could hire political lobbyists to obtain exemptions from such Executive Orders, and those that couldn't. That can create various opportunities for *quid-pro-quo deals* and political lobbying. It's not clear whether such discrimination advances the public interest in the case of crisis or pandemics/epidemics.
6. The Executive Orders unfairly discriminated between Restricted Persons that had significant cash reserves (or whose owners had cash reserves), and those that didn't. That can create various opportunities for crime. It's not clear whether such discrimination advances the public interest in the case of crisis or pandemics/epidemics.
7. The Executive Orders unfairly discriminated between Restricted Persons that could easily postpone or transfer/assign or cancel their contracts and who could easily challenge the Executive Orders in court on one hand, and those that couldn't as a result of such Executive Orders. That can create various opportunities for crime. It's not clear whether such discrimination advances the public interest in the case of crisis or pandemics/epidemics.
8. The Executive Orders unfairly discriminated between Restricted Persons that could easily apply for announced federal government

aid (for individuals and SMEs), and those that couldn't as a result of such Executive Orders. That can create various opportunities for crime. It's not clear whether such discrimination advances the public interest in the case of epidemics.

9. As stated herein and above, some public health experts have noted that the current emphasis on restrictions on movement and closures of businesses won't be helpful and, instead, governments and the public should focus more resources on identifying and isolating infected persons.
10. The cost of enforcing such Executive Orders was high, and compliance was likely to be low.
11. The Executive Orders could have increased unemployment, social unrest, and negative *Multiplier Effects* (economics, social, psychological and environmental) and *Emergence properties* (i.e. new adverse economic, social, psychological and/or environmental phenomena can emerge as a result).
12. The rapid, evolving and significant changes in online/offline *Social Networks* and *Social Capital* are likely to have lasting negative psychological, social and political effects on indigenes.
13. Given the foregoing, the Executive Orders could have created *Price-Contagions* (unjustified, coordinated/replicated and uniform price increases in neighborhoods/towns), *Uncertainty-and-Inertia Contagions* (replicated and/or coordinated inertia and uncertainty in neighborhoods/towns) and *Deadweight Losses* in the demand/supply of goods and services, and in the demand/supply of government services.

7.4.1.4 The Establishment Clause *and the* Free Exercise Clause *of the US Constitution*

On the surface, the US state Governors' Executive Orders constituted an infringement of *Establishment Clause* and The *Free Exercise Clause* rights of at least the following classes of persons (the "*Restricted Persons*"):

1. businesses that focus on religious activities incorporated churches, entities those that sell religiously prepared food or religious books, etc.) and who were forced to shut down their operations and thus could not profess, practice or advertise any religious affiliations or processes; and

2. individuals whose mobility and right to profess their religions were inadvertently restricted.

However, the public interest and the need to control the rapid spread of COVID-19 may or may not outweigh the personal rights of the affected/limited classes of persons and the potentially large economic harm that such Executive Orders can cause. Perhaps the balancing-of-interests should be supported by economic studies. See Nwogugu (2012).[37] The obvious *State Action* is the governors' Executive Orders. As above, the problems are that:

1. Allowing such *Establishment Clause* and *Free Exercise Clause* rights in any way may cause more people to move around and thus increase the spread of COVID-19.
2. The Executive Orders can be construed as "over-broad" and they were not sufficiently and narrowly tailored to serve the intended purpose of promoting public health.
3. Such *Restricted Persons* have a constitutionally guaranteed *Property Interest* in valid statutes and in the right to move around, practice their religion/beliefs freely and conduct their normal daily activities. Such *Property Interests* arise from the US Constitution, state constitutions, expectations, norms/culture and usage-of-trade.
4. The Executive Orders didn't specifically provide viable alternatives for the "Restricted Persons" who will most likely lose money and jobs—but the internet provides a viable alternative to physical "speech" for some classes of Restricted Persons.
5. The Executive Orders unfairly discriminated between Restricted Persons that know how to, or can afford to, obtain exemptions from such Executive Orders, and Restricted Persons that can't. That opens up all sorts of opportunities for quid-pro-quo deals and political lobbying. It's not clear whether such discrimination advances the public interest in the case of crisis or pandemics/epidemics.

[37] On the *Free Exercise Clause*, see: *Americans for Prosperity Foundation vs. Bonta*, _____ US _____ (US Supreme Court; pending as of 2021); *Mahanoy Area School District vs. B.L.*, _____ US _____ (No. 20-255; US Supreme Court; pending as of 2021) (free speech that occurs outside area-of-influence); *Houston Community College System vs. Wilson*, _____ US _____ (Case#: 20-804; US Supreme Court; pending as of 2021); *Fulton vs. City of Philadelphia*, _____ US _____ (US Supreme Court; pending as of 2021); and *Thomas More Law Center vs. Bonta*, _____ US ____ (No. 19-255; US Supreme Court; pending as of 2021).

6. As explained herein and above, some public health experts have noted that the current emphasis on restrictions on movement and closures of businesses won't be helpful and, instead, governments and the public should focus more resources on identifying and isolating infected persons.
7. The cost of enforcing such Executive Orders was high, and compliance was likely to be low.
8. The Executive Orders could have increased unemployment and social unrest, and have negative *Multiplier Effects* (economics, social, psychological and environmental) and *Emergence properties* (i.e. new adverse economic, social, psychological and/or environmental phenomena can emerge as a result).
9. The Executive Orders unfairly discriminated between Restricted Persons that could easily practice or profess their religion with no or limited mobility, and those that couldn't as a result of such Executive Orders. It's not clear whether such discrimination advances the public interest in the case of crisis or pandemics/epidemics.
10. The Executive Orders unfairly discriminated between Restricted Persons that could easily apply for announced federal government aid (for individuals and SMEs), and those that couldn't as a result of such Executive Orders. It's not clear whether such discrimination advances the public interest in the case of crisis or pandemics/epidemics.
11. Given the foregoing, the Executive Orders could have created *Price-Contagions* (unjustified, coordinated/replicated and uniform price increases in neighborhoods/towns), *Uncertainty-and-Inertia Contagions* (replicated and/or coordinated inertia and uncertainty in neighborhoods/towns) and *Deadweight Losses* in the demand/supply of goods and services, and in the demand/supply of government services.

7.4.1.5 The Equal Protection Clause *of the* Fourteenth Amendment *to the US Constitution*

The US state Governors' Executive Orders violated the *Equal Protection Clause* with respect to at least the following classes of persons:

1. Companies located in states that forced companies to shut down their operations; and

2. individuals who are located in subject-states whose governments prohibited them from gathering in crowds or participating in some types of meetings or going to public assembly spaces (restaurants, malls, movie theatres, etc.).

These *Restricted Persons* are also members of a protected class. However, the public interest and the need to control the rapid spread of COVID-19 may or may not outweigh the personal rights of the Restricted Persons and the potentially large economic harm that such Executive Orders can cause. Perhaps the balancing-of-interests should be supported by economic studies. See Nwogugu (2012).[38] The obvious *State Action* is the Executive Orders. As above, the problems are that:

1. Allowing such freedom of association in any way can cause or increase the spread of COVID-19.
2. The Executive Orders can be construed as "over-broad" and they were not sufficiently and narrowly tailored to serve the intended purpose of promoting public health.
3. Such *Restricted Persons* have a constitutionally guaranteed *Property Interest* in valid statutes and in the right to move around and conduct their normal daily activities, and to equitable delivery of services/benefits by the government. Such *Property Interests* arise from the US Constitution, state constitutions, expectations, norms/culture and usage-of-trade.
4. The Executive Orders didn't specifically provide viable alternatives for the "Restricted Persons" who will most likely lose money and jobs—but the internet provides a viable alternative to in-person physical meetings for some classes of Restricted Persons.
5. The Executive Orders unfairly discriminated between Restricted Persons that could afford to, or knew how to, or had the political influence to obtain exemptions from such Executive Orders, and those that couldn't. It's not clear whether such discrimination advances the public interest in the case of *crisis* or pandemics/epidemics.
6. The Executive Orders unfairly discriminated between Restricted Persons that had significant cash reserves (or whose owners have cash reserves), or could do a substantial percentage of their usual

[38] *See*: *United States vs. Vaello-Madero*, _____ US ____ (Case#: 20-303; US Supreme Court; pending as of 2021); and *Espinoza vs. Montana Department of Revenue*, _____ US ____ (US Supreme Court; pending as of 2021).

business over the Internet; and those that didn't or couldn't. It's not clear whether such discrimination advances the public interest in the case of crisis or pandemics/epidemics.

7. The Executive Orders unfairly discriminated between Restricted Persons that could easily postpone or transfer/assign or cancel their contracts and who could easily challenge the Executive Orders in court on one hand, and those that couldn't as a result of such Executive Orders. That can create various opportunities for crime. It's not clear whether such discrimination advances the public interest in the case of crisis or pandemics/epidemics.
8. The Executive Orders unfairly discriminated between Restricted Persons that could easily apply for announced federal government aid (for individuals and SMEs), and those that couldn't as a result of such Executive Orders. That can create various opportunities for crime. It's not clear whether such discrimination advances the public interest in the case of pandemics/epidemics.
9. The Executive Orders unfairly discriminated between Restricted Persons that are subject to the Dodd-Frank Act (Consumer Protection statutes and Orderly Liquidation provisions) and Restricted Persons that aren't. It's not clear whether such discrimination advances the public interest in the case of pandemics/epidemics. The Dodd-Frank Act Orderly Liquidation provisions provide the US government with powers to shut down companies (after a summary court procedure) that are deemed a threat to financial stability (the COVID-19 pandemics is clearly a threat to financial stability). Thus, the governors' Executive Orders and the Dodd-Frank Act take two different approaches to the same issue. The Consumer Protection statutes in the Dodd-Frank Act provide a wide array of solutions. The COVID-19 pandemics has generated new types of financial fraud and unfair business practices that are covered by the Consumer Protection sections of the Dodd-Frank Act.
10. The Executive Orders unfairly discriminate between: (i) US residents that are drug addicts and victims of the opioid epidemic of 2016–present in the US, for which the state governments haven't shut down many business establishments that sell or facilitate the sales of un-prescribed opioids and other illegal drugs; and (ii) US residents that are threatened (but not infected) by COVID-19, for which the Executive Orders imposed blanket lock-downs of towns/neighborhoods and shut-downs of businesses. The discrimination does not advance the public interest.

11. As explained herein and above, some public health experts have noted that the current emphasis on restrictions on movement and closures of businesses won't be helpful and, instead, governments and the public should focus more resources on identifying and isolating infected persons.
12. The cost of enforcing such Executive Orders was high, and compliance was likely to be low.
13. The Executive Orders could have increased unemployment and social unrest, and had negative *Multiplier Effects* (economics, social, psychological and environmental) and *Emergence properties* (i.e. new adverse economic, social, psychological and/or environmental phenomena can emerge as a result).
14. The rapid, evolving and significant changes in online/offline *Social Networks* and *Social Capital* are likely to have lasting negative psychological, social and political effects on indigenes.
15. Given the foregoing, the Executive Orders could have created *Price-Contagions* (unjustified, coordinated/replicated and uniform price increases in neighborhoods/towns), *Uncertainty-and-Inertia Contagions* (replicated and/or coordinated inertia and uncertainty in neighborhoods/towns) and *Deadweight Losses* in the demand/supply of goods and services, and in the demand/supply of government services.

7.4.1.6 The Free Speech Clause *of the US Constitution*

The state Governors' Executive Orders constituted an infringement of *the Free Speech* rights (distinct from other rights granted by the Free Exercise Clause) of at least the following classes of persons (the "Restricted Persons"):

1. businesses that were forced to shut down their operations (and thus couldn't advertise, conduct business, sell or exhibit their products/services all of which are types of *Protected Speech*); and
2. individuals whose mobility and professional activities were inadvertently restricted or banned; and who normally earn their living from activities that involve public speaking, personal expressions, public performances and/or advertising of their personal services (all of which are types of *Protected Speech*).

However, the public interest and the need to control the rapid spread of COVID-19 may or may not outweigh the personal rights of the affected/limited classes of persons and the potentially large economic harm that such Executive Orders could have caused. Perhaps the balancing-of-interests should be supported by economic studies. See Nwogugu (2012). The obvious *State Action* is the Executive Order. As above, the problems are that:

1. Allowing such *Speech* in any way (advertising, public displays) may cause more people to move around and thus cause or increase the spread of COVID-19 or other infectious diseases.
2. The Executive Orders can be construed as "over-broad" and they were not sufficiently and narrowly tailored to serve the intended purpose of promoting public health.
3. Such *Restricted Persons* have a constitutionally guaranteed *Property Interest* in valid statutes and in the right to move around, to speak freely and conduct their normal daily activities, to equitable delivery of aid/services by the government. Such *Property Interests* arise from the US Constitution, state constitutions, expectations, norms/culture and usage-of-trade.
4. The Executive Orders didn't specifically provide viable alternatives for the "Restricted Persons" who will most likely lose money and jobs—but the internet provides a viable alternative to physical "speech" for some classes of Restricted Persons.
5. The Executive Orders unfairly discriminated between Restricted Persons that knew how to, or could afford to, or could hire lobbyists to obtain exemptions from such Executive Orders, and Restricted Persons that couldn't. That created all sorts of opportunities for *quid-pro-quo* deals and political lobbying. It's not clear whether such discrimination advances the public interest in the case of pandemics/epidemics.
6. The Executive Orders unfairly discriminated between Restricted Persons that had significant cash reserves (or whose owners had cash reserves), and those that didn't. That created opportunities for crime. It's not clear whether such discrimination advances the public interest in the case of crisis or pandemics/epidemics.
7. The Executive Orders unfairly discriminated between Restricted Persons that could easily apply for announced federal government aid (for individuals and SMEs), and those that couldn't as a result

of such Executive Orders. That can create various opportunities for crime. It's not clear whether such discrimination advances the public interest in the case of crisis or pandemics/epidemics.

8. As explained herein and above, some public health experts have noted that the current emphasis on restrictions on movement and closures of businesses won't be helpful and, instead, governments and the public should focus more resources on identifying and isolating infected persons.
9. The cost of enforcing such Executive Orders was high, and compliance was likely to be low.
10. The Executive Orders could have increased unemployment and social unrest, and have negative *Multiplier Effects* (economics, social, psychological and environmental) and *Emergence properties* (i.e. new and harmful economic, social, psychological and/or environmental phenomena can emerge as a result).
11. The rapid, evolving and significant changes in online/offline *Social Networks* and *Social Capital* are likely to have lasting negative psychological, social and political effects on indigenes.
12. Given the foregoing, the Executive Orders could have created *Price-Contagions* (unjustified, coordinated/replicated and uniform price increases in neighborhoods/towns), *Uncertainty-and-Inertia Contagions* (replicated and/or coordinated inertia and uncertainty in neighborhoods/towns) and *Deadweight Losses* in the demand/supply of goods and services, and in the demand/supply of government services.

7.4.1.7 The Right-of-Association Clause *and* First Amendment Gatherings *(the First Amendment of the US Constitution)*

The state Governors' Executive Orders constituted an infringement of *the Rights-of-Association* and First Amendment gathering rights (distinct from other rights granted by the First Amendment) to gather in public, and to petition their state or local governments of the following classes of persons (the "*Restricted Persons*"):

1. businesses that were forced to shut down their operations; and
2. individuals who were prohibited from gathering in crowd or participating in some types of meetings or going to public assembly spaces (restaurants, malls, movie theatres, etc.).

3. businesses that want to gather for meetings (e.g. trade associations), or to create interest groups to petition the government or to seek concessions from the government; and whose right to gather and/ or to petition tribunals has been severely limited by the Executive Orders; and
4. Individuals that want to gather for meetings (e.g. trade associations) or to create interest groups to petition the government or to seek concessions from the government; and whose right to gather and/ or to petition tribunals has been severely limited by the Executive Orders.

However, the public interest and the need to control the rapid spread of COVID-19 may or may not outweigh the personal rights of the affected/limited classes of persons and the potentially large economic harm that such Executive Orders can cause. Perhaps the balancing-of-interests should be supported by economic studies. See Nwogugu (2012). The obvious *State Action* is the Executive Order. As above, the problems are that:

1. Allowing such *freedom of association* in any way can cause or increase the spread of COVID-19.
2. Allowing such *First Amendment gathering* rights in any form may cause more people to move around and thus increase the spread of COVID-19.
3. Such *Restricted Persons* have a constitutionally guaranteed *Property Interest* in valid statutes and in the right to move around, associate with whomever they want but in legal ways, and conduct their normal daily activities. Such *Property Interests* arise from the US Constitution, state constitutions, expectations, norms/culture and usage-of-trade.
4. The Executive Orders can be construed as "over-broad" and they were not sufficiently and narrowly tailored to serve the intended purpose of promoting public health.
5. The Executive Orders didn't specifically provide viable alternatives for the "Restricted Persons" who will most likely lose money and jobs—but the internet provides a viable alternative to in-person physical meetings/gatherings for some classes of Restricted Persons.
6. The Executive Orders unfairly discriminated between Restricted Persons that knew how to, or could afford to, or had the political

connections/influence to obtain exemptions from such Executive Orders, and Restricted Persons that couldn't. That created up all sorts of opportunities for *quid-pro-quo* deals and political lobbying. It's not clear whether such discrimination advances the public interest in the case of crisis or pandemics/epidemics.

7. The Executive Orders unfairly discriminated between Restricted Persons that had significant cash reserves (or whose owners had cash reserves), and those that didn't. That opens up all sorts of opportunities for crime. It's not clear whether such discrimination advances the public interest in the case of crisis or pandemics/epidemics.
8. The Executive Orders unfairly discriminated between Restricted Persons that could easily apply for announced federal government aid (for individuals and SMEs), and those that couldn't as a result of such Executive Orders. That can create various opportunities for crime. It's not clear whether such discrimination advances the public interest in the case of crisis or pandemics/epidemics.
9. As explained herein and above, some public health experts have noted that the current emphasis on restrictions on movement and closures of businesses won't be helpful and, instead, governments and the public should focus more resources on identifying and isolating infected persons.
10. The cost of enforcing such Executive Orders can be high, and compliance is likely to be low.
11. The Executive Orders could have increased unemployment and social unrest, and had negative *Multiplier Effects* (economics, social, psychological and environmental) and *Emergence properties* (i.e. new adverse economic, social, psychological and/or environmental phenomena can emerge as a result).
12. The resulting rapid, evolving and significant changes in online/offline *Social Networks* and *Social Capital* are likely to have lasting negative psychological, social and political effects on indigenes.
13. Given the foregoing, the Executive Orders could have created *Price-Contagions* (unjustified, coordinated/replicated and uniform price increases in neighborhoods/towns), *Uncertainty-and-Inertia Contagions* (replicated and/or coordinated inertia and uncertainty in neighborhoods/towns) and *Deadweight Losses* in the demand/supply of goods and services, and in the demand/supply of government services.

7.4.1.8 The Dormant Commerce Clause Doctrine *of the US Constitution*

The state Governors' Executive Orders constituted an infringement of *the Dormant Commerce Clause Doctrine* with respect to at least the following classes of persons (the "Restricted Persons"):

1. Companies located in states that forced companies to shut down their operations; and
2. Companies located in other states but do business in states that forced companies to shut down their operations; and
3. individuals who are located in states whose governments prohibited them from gathering in crowds or participating in some types of meetings or going to public assembly spaces (restaurants, malls, movie theatres, etc.).
4. Individuals who are located in other states but regularly visit or do business in states whose governments prohibited them from gathering in crowds or participating in some types of meetings or going to public assembly spaces (restaurants, malls, movie theatres, etc.).

However, the public interest and the need to control the rapid spread of COVID-19 may or may not outweigh the personal rights of the affected/limited classes of persons and the potentially large economic harm that such Executive Orders can cause. Perhaps the balancing-of-interests should be supported by economic studies. See Nwogugu (2012). The obvious *State Action* is the Executive Orders. As above, the problems are that:

1. Eliminating such restrictions (on physical mobility and commerce) can cause or increase the spread of COVID-19 epidemic across state lines. One critical issue is the definitions of "public health emergencies" and "essential businesses" under different state laws.
2. The Executive Orders can be construed as "over-broad" and they were not sufficiently and narrowly tailored to serve the intended purpose of promoting public health.
3. Such *Restricted Persons* have a constitutionally guaranteed *Property Interest* in valid statutes and in the right to move around and conduct their normal daily activities, and to equitable delivery of aid/services by the government. Such *Property Interests* arise from the US Constitution, state constitutions, expectations, norms/culture and usage-of-trade.

4. The Executive Orders didn't specifically provide viable alternatives for the "Restricted Persons" who will most likely lose money and jobs—but the internet provides a viable alternative to in-person physical meetings for some classes of Restricted Persons.
5. The cost of enforcing such Executive Orders was high, and compliance was likely to be low.
6. The Executive Orders could have increased unemployment and social unrest, and have negative *Multiplier Effects* (economics, social, psychological and environmental) and *Emergence properties* (i.e. new adverse economic, social, psychological and/or environmental phenomena can emerge as a result).
7. The rapid, evolving and significant changes in online/offline *Social Networks* and *Social Capital* are likely to have lasting negative psychological, social and political effects on indigenes.
8. The Executive Orders unfairly discriminated between Restricted Persons (in the subject state) that do substantial business in other states where such restrictions don't exist, and/or whose state's (law) definitions of "public health emergencies" and "essential businesses" vary unfavorably from other states; on one hand, and Restricted Persons that do most of their business in the subject/offending state. Such discrimination doesn't advance the public interest in the case of crisis or pandemics/epidemics.
9. The Executive Orders unfairly discriminated between Restricted Persons (in the subject state) that had significant cash reserves (or whose owners had cash reserves), and did or could do a substantial percentage of their usual business over the Internet; and those that didn't or couldn't. It's not clear whether such discrimination advances the public interest in the case of crisis or pandemics/epidemics.
10. The Executive Orders unfairly discriminated between Restricted Persons (in the subject state) that did substantial business in other states where such restrictions didn't exist and/or whose state's (law) definitions of "public health emergencies" and "essential businesses" vary unfavorably from other states, on one hand, and Restricted Persons that did most of their business in the subject/offending state. It's not clear whether such discrimination advances the public interest in the case of pandemics/epidemics.

11. The Executive Orders unfairly discriminated between aid applicants (businesses/individuals) whose cost-of-doing business across state lines was inadvertently increased because of provisions of the CARES Act, and/or because their state's laws' definitions of "public health emergencies" and "essential businesses" vary unfavorably from other states when read together with the CARES Act; on one hand, and businesses/individuals whose cost-of-doing business are the same or lower because of the CARES Act. Such discrimination doesn't advance the public interest in the case of crisis or pandemics/epidemics.
12. The Executive Orders unfairly discriminated between Restricted Persons that could easily postpone or transfer/assign or cancel their interstate contracts and who could easily challenge the Executive Orders in court on one hand, and those that couldn't as a result of such Executive Orders. That can create various opportunities for crime. Such discrimination doesn't advance the public interest in the case of crisis or pandemics/epidemics.
13. The Executive Orders unfairly discriminated between Restricted Persons that could easily apply for announced federal government and/or state government COVID-19-related aid (for individuals and SMEs) in other states; and those that couldn't as a result of such Executive Orders. For example, their state's (law) definitions of "public health emergencies" and "essential businesses" vary unfavorably from other states. That can create various opportunities for crime. Such discrimination doesn't advance the public interest in the case of crisis or pandemics/epidemics.
14. As explained herein and above, some public health experts have noted that the current emphasis on restrictions on movement and closures of businesses won't be helpful and, instead, governments and the public should focus more resources on identifying and isolating infected persons.
15. Given the foregoing, the Executive Orders could have created *Price-Contagions* (unjustified, coordinated/replicated and uniform price increases in neighborhoods/towns), *Uncertainty-and-Inertia Contagions* (replicated and/or coordinated inertia and uncertainty in neighborhoods/towns) and *Deadweight Losses* in the demand/supply of goods and services, and in the demand/supply of government services.

7.4.2 *Constitutionality of the US Department of Justice's (DOJ) 2020 Requests for Extraordinary Powers*

As mentioned above, during 2020, the US Justice Department (DOJ) asked the US Congress to statutorily grant it:

1. The power to request that US district court judges stop court proceedings during a national emergency (such as natural disasters and episodes of "civil disobedience").
2. The power to detain individuals without trial during government-declared "emergencies".

If granted by the US Congress, the DOJ's request would likely be unconstitutional because:

1. It violates the procedural *Due Process rights* of persons subjected to such powers.
2. It constitutes a *Takings* against persons subjected to such powers.
3. It violates the criminal procedure rights of persons (subjected to such powers) to a *speedy and public trial.*
4. It violates the *Equal Protection Clause rights* of persons subjected to such powers
5. It violates the *Right-of-Association Clause rights* and *First Amendment gathering rights* of persons subjected to such powers

See Nwogugu (2012). Some of the problems with the US DOJ's request are as follows:

1. Such powers may not slow or eliminate the spread of COVID-19 epidemic.
2. Such powers can be construed as "over-broad" and they were not sufficiently and narrowly tailored to serve the intended purpose of promoting public health.
3. The *Subject Persons* (i.e. the accused suspects; prisoners; the public and so on) have a constitutionally guaranteed *Property Interest* in valid statutes and in the right to move around and conduct their normal daily activities, and to equitable delivery of aid/services by the government. Such *Property Interests* arise from the US Constitution, state constitutions, expectations, norms/culture and usage-of-trade.

4. There are viable alternative to the US DOJ's requested powers.
5. The economic, social and psychological costs of enforcing such requested powers is likely to be significant.
6. The requested US DOJ powers can increase unemployment and social unrest, and have negative *Multiplier Effects* (economics, social, psychological and environmental) and *Emergence properties* (i.e. new adverse economic, social, psychological and/or environmental phenomena can emerge as a result).
7. The resulting rapid, evolving and significant changes in online/offline *Social Networks* and *Social Capital* are likely to have lasting negative psychological, social and political effects on indigenes.

7.4.3 Constitutionality and Economic Efficiency of the $2.2 Trillion Stimulus Package in the CARES Act *Enacted by the US Congress: A Repeat of the Mistakes of the US Government's $700 Billion Stimulus Package of 2009–2014?*

The Coronavirus Aid, Relief, and Economic Security Act (CARES Act)[39] amounts to discriminatory government welfare/charity that is bound to fail in both the short term and long term. See Nwogugu (2012, 2015a, 2015b).

US courts have ruled on the constitutionality of the CARES Act and COVID-related regulations but there have been divergent opinions by many lower courts—for example, on the constitutionality of the US CDC's moratorium on evictions.[40]

[39] *See*: https://www.uschamber.com/co/start/strategy/cares-act-small-business-guide.

[40] *See*: *Terkel vs. Centers for Disease Control and Prevention* (US District Court; No. 20-cv-564-JCB; E.D. Tex. Feb. 25, 2021) (appeal docketed, Mar. 3, 2021) (federal district court held that US Congress exceeded its authority by mandating a national eviction moratorium in response to the COVID-19 pandemic).

See: *Chambless Enterprises vs. Redfield*, No. 20-cv-01455 at 16 (US District Court; E.D. La. Dec. 22, 2020) (lower court upheld the constitutionality of the CDC's eviction moratorium based on the *Commerce Clause*on the basis that the "rental of real estate" was the regulated activity, and that under US Supreme Court precedent, the rental of real estate affects interstate commerce).

See: *Skyworks, Ltd. vs. Centers for Disease Control and Prevention*, No. 20-cv-02407 at 31 (US District Court; N.D. Ohio Mar. 10, 2021) (court held that the CDC's eviction moratorium orders "exceed the agency's statutory authority under [the Public Health Act's Quarantine and Inspection provision].").

See: *Brown vs. Azar* (US District Court; No. 20-cv-03702; N.D. Ga.; Oct. 29, 2020) (appealed docketed, Nov. 9, 2020) (court upheld the validity of the eviction moratorium).

By enacting the CARES Act, the US government is repeating the same mistakes and failures of its $700 billion TARP stimulus package of 2019–2014 (which was reduced to $475 billion in 2010 by the US Congress), some of which are as follows:

1. Under the CARES Act, the US government will dole out free or ridiculously cheap government money to inefficient companies and government agencies (that instead should be allowed to fail or should be substantially restructured or sold). Such charity doesn't provide the necessary incentives to the recipient companies and doesn't promote competition (it's anti-competitive).
2. The US government will not take equity stakes in companies that receive loans, government guarantees and other aid pursuant to the CARES Act. That doesn't provide the necessary incentives to the recipient companies and their competitors and doesn't promote competition (it's almost anti-competitive). No personal guarantee or collateral is required for most of such loans, and in some cases, a portion of the loans can be forgiven.
3. The US government's $700 billion stimulus package of 2008–2014 caused a "me-too" effect wherein companies that really didn't need the financial aid inadvertently filed false and fraudulent applications just because their more troubled competitors had filed applications for loans/guarantees or other aid.
4. More than $1 trillion of aid under the CARES Act (loans, government guarantees, etc., including the $500 billion corporate relief fund and $367 billion in loans to small businesses) requires that companies and individuals file applications at banks, financial institutions or government agencies. That creates opportunities for fraudulent applications, collusion, corruption and political lobbying. Aid can be conditioned on political affiliation. Its notable that as of 2020, the US Justice Department was still prosecuting individuals and companies that filed fraudulent applications for loans and aid under the $ billion TARP program which ended in 2014.
5. For the loans and guarantees that will be available under the CARES Act, the US government didn't issue a set of uniform specific application and approval criteria/standards that will be applied by banks

See: *Alabama Association of Realtors vs. US Department of Health and Human Services* (May 5, 2021; US District Court for the District of Columbia) (*appeal filed*) (court vacated the nationwide eviction moratorium issued by the US Centers for Disease Control).

and other entities that disburse such aid. That creates opportunities for fraud, collusion, corruption and political lobbying.

6. As explained in Nwogugu (2019b), the US government's $700 billion stimulus package of 2008–2014 failed woefully and didn't sufficiently stimulate the US economy primarily because of inadequate incentives, use of badly structured financial instruments, lack of uniform standards/criteria for providing aid/loans, fraud and corruption. More than 50% of the $700 billion stimulus package consisted of loans to companies and individuals.

In response to the Global Financial Crisis that worsened in 2007 and 2008, the US Congress enacted the Emergency Economic Stabilization Act of 2008[41] (the EESA), wherein the US Treasury, the US Federal Reserve and the US FDIC implemented several economic/financial aid programs for financial institutions, households and companies[42] in order to stabilize the US economy. As part of that, the TARP/CPP (Capital Purchase Program) Instruments program was launched by the US Treasury Department in 2008 in order to boost the US economy by investing in US entities (mostly financial institutions that in turn, would provide loans, guarantees, loan-restructuring and other economic/financial aid to

[41] *See*: *The Emergency Economic Stabilization Act of 2008*. http://www.house.gov/financialservices/EESABill_section-by-section.pdf.

Section 111(e) of the EESA, as amended by the American Recovery and Reinvestment Act on February 17, 2009, requires any entity that has received financial assistance under the Troubled Asset Relief Program (or TARP) to permit an annual advisory shareholder vote to approve the compensation of executives, as disclosed pursuant to the Commission's rules. This shareholder vote on executive compensation is non-binding and is required as long as obligations under the TARP remain outstanding. Section 111(e)(3) of the EESA directs the Commission to issue any required final rules not later than February 17, 2010.

[42] *See*: US Treasury Department (2009). *United States Department of The Treasury Section 105(a) Troubled Assets Relief Program—Report To Congress For The Period February 1, 2009 To February 28, 2009.*

See: Cadwalader, Wickersham & Taft (April 23, 2009). *Treasury, Federal Reserve and FDIC Credit and Liquidity Programs.* www.cadwalader.com/assets/client_friend/042309_Treasury,_Federal_Reserve,_FDIC.pdf.

See: A. M. Best (Stephanie McElroy & Rosemary Mirabella) (January 19, 2009). *Analyzing Securities Issued Under the US Treasury's Capital Purchase Program* (USA).

See: US Government Accountability Office (2016). *Troubled Asset Relief Program: Capital Purchase Program Largely Has Wound Down.* https://www.gao.gov/assets/680/676954.pdf.

companies and individuals). The Dodd-Frank Act of 2010[43] reduced the authorized TARP amount (including CPP) from $700 billion to $475 billion. The US Treasury invested about US$420 billion through the TARP/CPP Program during 2008–2014 (see: https://www.treasury.gov/initiatives/financial-stability/TARP-Programs/bank-investment-programs/cap/Pages/cpp-results.aspx?Program=Capital+Purchase+Program). The US Treasury ended the TARP Program in December 2014 and recovered $441.7 billion from $426.4 billion invested, (with a $15.3 billion profit or an annualized rate of return of 0.6%).

Nwogugu (2019b)[44] noted that " the TARP/CPP program was inefficient and failed as confirmed by many reports (see: Calabresi and Prakash (1994); Black and Hazelwood (2013); Farruggio et al. (2013); Song and Uzmanoglu (2016), and Semaan and Drake (2016))".

[43] On the Dodd-Frank Act, see Nwogugu (2015a, b), and Omarova (2011).

[44] *See*: "*SIGTARP report reveals massive failure of HAMP—'Massive lost opportunity for an emergency program'* ". July 29, 2015. By Brena Swanson. https://www.housingwire.com/articles/34609-sigtarp-report-reveals-massive-failure-of-hamp.

See: "*SIGTARP: HAMP's failure 'devastating,' permanent mods flat in December*". January 26, 2011. By Jon Prior. https://www.housingwire.com/articles/sigtarp-hamps-failure-devastating-permanent-mods-flat-december.

See: "*SIGTARP alleges Hardest Hit Fund failures—Participating states spent only 22% of the funds in three years*". October 29, 2013. By Kerri Ann Panchuk. https://www.housingwire.com/articles/27681-sigtarp-details-hardest-hit-fund-failures.

See: "Obama Program That Hurt Homeowners and Helped Big Banks Is Ending". By David Dayen. December 282,015. https://theintercept.com/2015/12/28/obama-program-hurt-homeowners-and-helped-big-banks-now-its-dead/.

See: SIGTARP (July 2015). *Quarterly Report to Congress—July 29, 2015*. https://www.sigtarp.gov/Quarterly%20Reports/July_29_2015_Report_to_Congress.pdf.

See: SIGTARP (2018). *Congressional Justification for Appropriations and Annual Performance Report and Plan—FY 2018*. https://www.treasury.gov/about/budget-performance/CJ18/11.%20SIGTARP%20-%20FY%202018%20CJ.pdf.

See: US Treasury Department (2009). United States Department of The Treasury Section 105(a) Troubled Assets Relief Program—Report To Congress For The Period February 1, 2009 To February 28, 2009.

See: A. M. Best (Stephanie McElroy & Rosemary Mirabella) (January 19, 2009). *Analyzing Securities Issued Under The US Treasury's Capital Purchase Program*. A. M. Best (USA).

See: *Hunton & Williams: Term Sheet For TARP CPP Program From Private Companies*. http://www.hunton.com/files/tbl_s10News%5CFileUpload44%5C15799%5Ctarp_capital_purchase_program_term_sheet_for_privately_held_companies.pdf.

See: *United States Department Of The Treasury Tranche Report To Congress*; NOVEMBER 4, 2008 (Accessible at: http://www.financialstability.gov/docs/TrancheReports/TrancheReportfinal.pdf).

As stated in Nwogugu (2019b), some of the specific failures of TARP/CPP Program were as follows:

1. Many of the investee-banks didn't materially increase their lending volumes.
2. The TARP/CPP investments increased bankers' and corporate executives' compensation without achieving the desired objectives.
3. The TARP/CPP Program caused *Inefficient Continuance* of some investee banks and companies.
4. There were many fraudulent applications for TARP/CPP funds.
5. Many of the participating banks and companies were weaker after the TARP/CPP investment.
6. TARP/CPP may have caused *Credit Contagions* and *Spillovers*.
7. The financial contracts used in the TARP/CPP program caused *Negative Externalities*.
8. HASP, HAMP and HARP failed woefully.
9. The US Treasury Department mis-classified the TARP/CPP financial instruments (some debt were really equity and vice versa; and the warrants were debt).
10. The program increased *Income/Wealth Inequality*, *Social Inequality* and *Housing Inequality*, and could have reduced financial stability, economic growth and economic/urban sustainability.

As explained in Nwogugu (2019a), some of the continuing negative effects of the TARP/CPP Program are as follows:

1. Continued civil and criminal prosecutions of persons that defrauded the TARP/CPP Program.
2. Changes in the internal controls, "internal capital markets", capital structures, accounting policies and lending policies of banks, insurance companies and finance companies.
3. Changes in the executive compensation systems and recruitment priorities/policies of participants.
4. Changes in the strategy and corporate governance policies of participants.
5. Changes in risk metrics and valuation metrics.
6. The "stigma" associated with receiving TARP/CPP funds.

7. Long-term changes in measures implemented by banks and insurance companies to comply with capital requirements which were triggered by and maintained because of the TARP/CPP program.
8. The nature and objectives of political lobbying by financial services companies (which were triggered by and maintained because of the TARP/CPP program).
9. The research studies that are statutorily required by the Dodd-Frank Act had not been completed as of 2019.
10. Many of the foregoing factors seem to have spilled over among foreign investors that invest in the US, and to foreign countries where many TARP/CPP investee-companies do business.

7.4.3.1 *The CARES Act Conflicts with Some* Legislative Intent *of the Current US Federal Competition Law Framework*

The CARES Act definitely doesn't promote competition but rather reduces competition in the following ways:

1. See the critiques of the CARES Act herein and above—most of those weaknesses of CARES Act can reduce competition.
2. *Inefficient Continuance* (of companies that should be allowed to fail or should be restructured or sold).
3. Introducing *political lobbying* or the possibility of same into business processes (firms, SMEs and even individuals will probably have to lobby or hire politically connected consultants in order to get financial aid from government agencies).
4. Introducing the risk of *Regulatory Capture.*
5. Introducing the risk of *State Capture* at the state level (i.e. Republican Party– and Democratic Party–controlled states).
6. Changing the nature of competition in industries (through the activities of banks selected to disburse loans and guarantees—e.g. approvals/rejections, loan terms for distressed companies, due diligence, actual loans, loan workouts).
7. Compelling selected manager-banks and the US Treasury Department to in effect serve as *quasi-competition* regulators through their lending and monitoring activities without sufficient Congressional oversight (approvals/rejections, loan-terms for distressed companies, due diligence, actual loans, loan workouts; etc.).

8. Giving cash to households (instead of redeemable non-transferable vouchers)—which indirectly and directly favors some industries whose products/services will be almost immediately and unnecessarily purchased by scared, uninformed, worried and depressed US households (many of whom are, or will soon be, unemployed) often at inflated prices (because of both hoarding and opportunistic price increases).
9. Compelling or tempting US hospitals to apply for $120 billion in loans, guarantees and grants during the COVID-19 epidemic will probably change their priorities, recruiting, service quality, incentive systems, and competition among hospitals.
10. Providing loans and guarantees through banks will most probably cause or increase *Deadweight Losses* in: (1) the demand/supply for loans to SMEs and individuals; (2) demand/supply and prices in specific industries that benefit from or are significantly harmed by COVID-19 (3) demand/supply for legal enforcement.
11. Providing loans and guarantees through banks will most probably cause or increase the same types of, fraudulent practices, consumer abuses and unfair business practices that the Dodd-Frank Act seeks to eliminate. As of 2020–2021, there was increasing incidence of COVID-19-related financial fraud in the USA.
12. The CARES Act favors companies that do or can do most of their businesses online.
13. the CARES Act generally increases transaction costs.
14. It's very likely that as explained herein, the implementation of the CARES Act will result in unfair business practices and fraud that will be reported to, and adjudicated or prosecuted by, the US FTC (US Federal Trade Commission).
15. It's arguably more difficult for the US FTC to develop or implement fair merger/acquisition criteria under the CARES Act regime than before, partly because of the issues mentioned herein.
16. The effectiveness and relevance of the US FTC's Franchising and Business Opportunity statutes are more likely to decline under the CARES Act regime than before.
17. The number of US indigenes that are eligible for protection under the US FTC regulations has increased under the CARES Act regime, even though it may be more difficult to prove that such persons have been negatively affected or have standing.

7.4.3.2 *The CARES Act* Conflicts with Some of the Legislative Intent *of the* Dodd-Frank Act

In enacting the Dodd-Frank Act,[45] the US government emphasized several principles/philosophies—and some of those regulatory and enforcement philosophies/principles and why they conflict with the CARES Act:

1. *Not-too-big-to-fail*—inherently weak corporate entities will be allowed to fail regardless of their size and without government intervention.
2. The *Orderly Liquidation* powers—the use of specified (but unconstitutional) procedures to liquidate private companies that supposedly threaten financial stability. While the COVID-19 epidemic is a financial stability threat, the same principle hasn't been applied in a constitutionally credible manner to companies that facilitate the spread of COVID-19 or other major epidemics.
3. *Consumer Protection statutes and initiatives*—the Dodd-Frank Act contains a broad range of statutes designed to protect consumers from various financial fraud, abusive practices/procedures and corruption including the types that have arisen or will arise from the COVID-19 epidemic and the disbursement of CARES Act aid. The CARES Act doesn't contain much of that, and, instead, increases the possibility of occurrence of such misconduct.
4. *Intense surveillance of financial and non-financial SIFIs* (systemically important financial institutions)—during January–March 2020, the federal government's intense surveillance wasn't officially extended to: (i) companies that facilitated or could facilitate the spread of COVID-19 and other epidemics through their policies and procedures; (ii) public assembly spaces such as airports, train stations and shopping malls.
5. *Turning the largest financial institutions in the US into quasi-regulators, tax collectors and police* (US banks and insurance companies are now responsible for implementing/enforcing more regulations, now collect more taxes and now have more compliance reporting requirements than before Dodd-Frank Act)—these institutions (and some US hospital chains) haven't helped much in epidemics.

[45] On the Dodd-Frank Act, see Nwogugu (2015a, b), Baily et al. (2017) and Omarova (2011). The Financial Services Committee of the US House of Representatives has introduced its alternative to the Dodd-Frank Act which is named "*Financial Choice 2.0*".

6. *Limited government intervention*—the opposite has been the case during the COVID-19 epidemic.
7. *Extending and broadening regulation and government oversight to most aspects of financial services*—on the contrary, the CARES Act creates situations that are either unregulated or are difficult to regulate.
8. *Shifting the cost of corporate financial distress and misconduct in the private sector to banks and private companies* (e.g. financial services companies bear some or all of the costs of bank failures)—the CARES Act does almost the opposite.
9. *Increased accountability and transparency of private companies and banks in times of financial/economic crisis* (i.e. apportionment of legal liability, fines and penalties, and new disclosure requirements)—the CARES Act does almost the opposite.
10. *Shifting rule-making from the US Congress to federal government agencies that are specialized and have more knowledge and experience than the US Congress*—the CARES Act does the opposite and statutorily requires some minimal congressional oversight.

All of these objectives and philosophies seem to have disappeared overnight in the face of the COVID-19 epidemic and the 2020 national and state-wide elections in the US!! The CARES Act takes an almost opposite approach.

7.4.3.3 The CARES Act Doesn't Sufficiently Address the Structural Causes of, and Required Solutions to, Pandemics/Epidemics

Some solutions to these problems are as follows:

- Automated and rapid identification (AI/ML, sensors, image-analysis and radio-waves) and isolation of infected persons.
- Online job re-training for both employed and unemployed persons.
- Online income-management and expense-control training for households and SMEs.
- Expansion of Internet infrastructure and capabilities so that more companies and persons can do more transactions/filings online.
- Fixing disrupted supply chains.
- Maintaining a minimum volume of manufacturing activity and critical services (and increased use of automation in manufacturing and services).

- Re-allocations/insurance/re-insurance of losses/costs incurred or to be incurred by SMEs as a result of epidemics/crisis—in order to "spread" the costs of harm to the private sector and to build cash reserves for future epidemics.
- Increased vaccine research.

Other problems inherent in the CARES Act are as follows:

1. The US government's direct payments of cash to US taxpayers is not realistic because there is an ongoing and severe opioid epidemic in the US (which has had disproportionately larger negative effects on the same low-income and lower-middle-income households that are most affected by COVID-19) and there is no guarantee that such cash will be used appropriately.
2. Inadequate long-term measures—the CARES Act focuses too much on COVID-19, and doesn't really address future epidemics and potential mutations of COVID-19. If COVID-19 were to mutate into a more drug-resistant version or if there is another epidemic during the seven-month period after the enactment of CARES Act, most of the provisions of the CARES Act will be useless.
3. The CARES Act should have explicitly stated the names of companies that are or were crucial to national security and for whom $17 billion was set aside.
4. The significant extension of unemployment benefits without sufficiently addressing the re-training of workers is unrealistic and provides the wrong incentives. Such unemployment benefits should have been tied to specific job re-training efforts or relocation efforts.
5. Loans to small businesses (the loans, which total more than $367 billion, would be made by community banks and federally insured banks). The loans will have a nominal interest rate, but any portion used to keep employees on staff or to pay critical costs like rent or utilities would be forgiven.
6. Small businesses got new tax incentives to keep people on their payroll—which provided the wrong incentives for them and creates opportunities for fraud (many of such business are or will shut down, or will drastically reduce the scope of their businesses because of government lock-down orders and lack of customers and thus would have laid off or need to lay off employees).

7. As mentioned, compelling US hospitals to compete for $100 billion (for the coronavirus outbreak) plus almost $20 billion (to stockpile medical equipment) will most probably change their priorities, service quality and incentives.
8. The $150 billion of funding for state and local governments should have been conditioned on specific objectives. Many US state and local governments have been insolvent for years. Borrowing is not the answer. The states governments and local governments need to structurally re-align their activities/services and their sources of revenues.

7.4.3.4 The Equal Protection Clause *of the* Fourteenth Amendment *to the US Constitution*

The CARES Act violated the *Equal Protection Clause* with respect to at least the following classes of "Affected Persons":

1. Companies that apply for economic/financial aid, government-backed grants, loans and government guarantees pursuant to the CARES Act; and
2. Individuals that apply for economic/financial aid, government-backed grants, loans and government guarantees pursuant to the CARES Act.

These *Affected Persons* are also members of a protected class. However, the public interest and the need to control and manage the economic/financial harm caused by COVID-19 may or may not outweigh the personal rights of the Affected Persons and the potentially large economic harm that both COVID-19 and CARES Act can cause. Perhaps the *balancing-of-interests* should be supported by economic studies. The obvious *State Action* is the CARES Act. See Nwogugu (2012). As above, the problems are that:

1. See the critique of the CARES Act herein and above.
2. The CARES Act can be construed as "over-broad" and was not sufficiently and narrowly tailored to serve the intended purpose of promoting economic growth and stability.

3. Such *Affected Persons* have a constitutionally guaranteed *Property Interest* in valid statutes and in fair application criteria and in equitable disbursement of economic/financial aid from the government, and in equitable delivery of aid/services. Such *Property Interests* arise from the US Constitution, state constitutions, expectations, norms and usage-of-trade.
4. The cost of enforcing such CARES Act can be high, and compliance is likely to be low because of such violations of the *Equal Protection Clause.*
5. The CARES Act could increase unemployment and social unrest, and have negative *Multiplier Effects* (economics, social, psychological and environmental) and *Emergence properties* (i.e. new adverse economic, social, psychological and/or environmental phenomena can emerge as a result) because of such violations of the *Equal Protection Clause.*
6. The resulting rapid, evolving and significant changes in online/offline *Social Networks* and *Social Capital* are likely to have lasting negative psychological, social and political effects on indigenes.
7. The CARES Act didn't issue a standard set of criteria to banks for the disbursement loans (or loan restructuring or loan guarantees), or to government agencies for cash grants and all aid decisions are or can be highly subjective—that is a major due process problem.
8. The CARES Act unfairly discriminated between sophisticated *Affected Persons* that knew how to "game" the application process, or could afford to hire consultants to navigate the application process, or had the political connections to get approvals for loans/guarantees/grants on one hand, and *Affected Persons* that couldn't do all that. Such discrimination doesn't advance the public interest in the case of crises and pandemics/epidemics.
9. The CARES Act unfairly discriminated between *Affected Persons* that filed applications for CARES Act benefits at banks that use wrong or overly discretionary application/approvals criteria or politically influenced approval-criteria, and *Affected Persons* that filed applications at banks that used more "normal" approval criteria. Such discrimination doesn't advance the public interest in the case of crises and pandemics/epidemics.
10. The CARES Act unfairly discriminated between *Affected Persons* that had significant cash reserves (or whose owners have cash reserves), and do or could do a substantial percentage of their

usual business over the Internet; and those that didn't or couldn't. Such discrimination doesn't advance the public interest in the case of crises and pandemics/epidemics.

11. The CARES Act unfairly discriminated between *Affected Persons* that were truly and significantly harmed by COVID-19 and thus needed economic/financial assistance and couldn't or didn't apply for aid on one hand, and *Affected Persons* that weren't harmed (or significantly harmed) that chose to apply for economic/financial aid under the CARES Act. The CARES Act didn't make adequate provisions to reduce or eliminate *false positives* and *false negatives.* Such discrimination doesn't advance the public interest in the case of crises and pandemics/epidemics.
12. The CARES Act unfairly discriminated between *Affected Persons* that are subject to the Dodd-Frank Act (Consumer Protection statutes and Orderly Liquidation provisions) and *Affected Persons* that aren't. Such discrimination doesn't advance the public interest in the case of epidemics. The Dodd-Frank Act Orderly Liquidation provisions provide the US government with powers to shut down companies (after a summary court procedure) that are deemed a threat to financial stability (the COVID-19 epidemic is clearly a threat to financial stability). Thus, the CARES Act and the Dodd-Frank Act take two different approaches to the same issue. The Consumer Protection statutes in the Dodd-Frank Act provide a wide array of solutions. The COVID-19 pandemic has generated new types of financial fraud and unfair business practices that are covered by the Consumer Protection sections of the Dodd-Frank Act.
13. The CARES Act unfairly discriminated between: (i) US residents that are drug addicts and victims of the *opioid epidemic* of 2016–present in the US, for which the US government hasn't provided sufficient economic aid and medical support on one hand; and (ii) Affected Persons that are threatened (but not infected) by COVID-19, for which the CARES Act provides unemployment, cash grants, loans, loan guarantees and other support. The discrimination does not advance the public interest.
14. Given the foregoing, the CARES Act can cause or increase *Deadweight Losses* in the demand/supply of loans and other aid, and in fees charged by banks, and in interest rates.

7.4.3.5 Substantive and Procedural Due Process Doctrines

The CARES Act violated the *Substantive And Procedural Due Process* rights of at least the following classes of *Affected Persons*:

1. Companies that apply for government-backed grants, loans and government guarantees pursuant to the CARES Act; and
2. Individuals that apply for government-backed grants, loans and government guarantees pursuant to the CARES Act.

These *Affected Persons* are also members of a protected class. However, the public interest and the need to control and manage the economic/financial harm caused by COVID-19 may or may not outweigh the personal rights of the Affected Persons and the potentially large economic harm that both COVID-19 and CARES Act can cause. Perhaps the balancing-of-interests should be supported by economic studies. The obvious *State Action* is the CARES Act. See Nwogugu (2012). As above, the problems are as follows:

1. See the critique of the CARES Act herein and above.
2. The CARES Act can be construed as "over-broad" and was not sufficiently and narrowly tailored to serve the intended purpose of promoting economic growth and stability.
3. Such *Affected Persons* have a constitutionally guaranteed *Property Interest* in valid statutes and in fair application criteria, and in equitable disbursement of economic/financial aid from the government, and in equitable delivery of aid/services. Such *Property Interests* arise from the US Constitution, state constitutions, expectations, norms and usage-of-trade.
4. The CARES Act didn't issue a standard set of criteria to banks for the disbursement loans (or loan restructuring or loan guarantees), or to government agencies for cash grants and all aid decisions are or can be highly subjective—that is a major Due Process problem.
5. The CARES Act unfairly discriminated between sophisticated *Affected Persons* that knew how to "game" the application process, or could afford to hire consultants to navigate the application process, or had the political connections to get approvals for loans/guarantees/grants on one hand, and *Affected Persons* that couldn't do all that. Such discrimination doesn't advance the public interest in the case of crises and pandemics/epidemics.

6. The CARES Act unfairly discriminated between *Affected Persons* that filed applications for CARES Act benefits at banks that use wrong or overly discretionary application/approvals criteria or politically influenced approval-criteria, and *Affected Persons* that filed applications at banks that used more "normal" approval criteria. Such discrimination doesn't advance the public interest in the case of crises and pandemics/epidemics.
7. The CARES Act unfairly discriminated between *Affected Persons* that had significant cash reserves (or whose owners have cash reserves), and do or could do a substantial percentage of their usual business over the Internet; and those that didn't or couldn't. Such discrimination doesn't advance the public interest in the case of crises and pandemics/epidemics.
8. The CARES Act unfairly discriminated between *Affected Persons* that were truly and significantly harmed by COVID-19 and thus needed economic/financial assistance and couldn't or didn't apply for aid on one hand, and *Affected Persons* that weren't harmed (or significantly harmed) that chose to apply for economic/financial aid under the CARES Act. The CARES Act didn't make adequate provisions to reduce or eliminate *false positives* and *false negatives.* Such discrimination doesn't advance the public interest in the case of crises and pandemics/epidemics.
9. The CARES Act unfairly discriminated between Restricted Persons that were subject to the Dodd-Frank Act (Consumer Protection statutes and Orderly Liquidation provisions) and Restricted Persons that weren't. Such discrimination doesn't advance the public interest in the case of epidemics. The Dodd-Frank Act Orderly Liquidation provisions provide the US government with powers to shut down companies (after a summary court procedure) that are deemed a threat to financial stability (the COVID-19 epidemic is clearly a threat to financial stability). Thus, the federal government's CARES Act and the Dodd-Frank Act take two different approaches to the same issue. The Consumer Protection statutes in the Dodd-Frank Act provide a wide array of solutions. The COVID-19 epidemic has generated new types of financial fraud and unfair business practices that are covered by the Consumer Protection sections of the Dodd-Frank Act.
10. Some public health experts have noted that governments' 2020–2021 emphasis on restrictions on movement and closures of

businesses won't be helpful and, instead, governments and the public should focus more resources on identifying and isolating infected persons.

11. The cost of enforcing such CARES Act can be high, and compliance is likely to be low because of such violations of the *Due Process Clause.*
12. The CARES Act could have increased unemployment and social unrest, and have negative *Multiplier Effects* (economics, social, psychological and environmental) and *Emergence properties* (i.e. new adverse economic, social, psychological and/or environmental phenomena can emerge as a result) because of such violations of the *Due Process Clause.*
13. The resulting rapid, evolving and significant changes in online/offline *Social Networks* and *Social Capital* are likely to have lasting negative psychological, social and political effects on indigenes.
14. Given the foregoing, the CARES Act can cause or increase *Deadweight Losses* in the demand/supply of loans and other aid, and in fees charged by banks, and in interest rates.

7.4.3.6 The Non-Delegation Doctrine

The *Non-Delegation Doctrine* (of Section-1 Of the US Constitution) means that the Congress of the United States cannot delegate its legislative powers to anyone else. The CARES Act violated the *Non-Delegation Doctrine* with respect to at least the following classes of *Affected Persons*:

1. Companies that apply for economic/financial aid, government-backed grants, loans and government guarantees pursuant to the CARES Act; and
2. Individuals that apply for economic/financial aid, government-backed grants, loans and government guarantees pursuant to the CARES Act.

These *Affected Persons* are also members of a protected class. However, the public interest and the need to control and manage the economic/financial harm caused by COVID-19 may or may not outweigh the personal rights of the Affected Persons and the potentially large economic harm that both COVID-19 and CARES Act can cause. Perhaps the *balancing-of-interests* tests should be supported by economic studies. The obvious *State Action* is the CARES Act. See Nwogugu (2012). As above, the problems are as follows:

1. See the critique of the CARES Act herein and above.
2. The wording of the CARES Act effectively and unconstitutionally transfers to banks (community banks; money center banks; federally chartered banks), the duty of legislating the application criteria and the approval criteria for Affected Persons that apply for economic/financial aid through such banks pursuant to the CARES Act. The CARES Act doesn't issue a standard set of criteria to banks for loans and loan-guarantees, or to agencies for cash grants and all aid decisions are highly subjective—that is a major problem.
3. Such *Affected Persons* have a constitutionally guaranteed *Property Interest* in valid statutes and in fair application criteria and in equitable disbursement of economic/financial aid from the government, and in equitable delivery of aid/services. Such *Property Interests* arise from the US Constitution, state constitutions, expectations, norms and usage-of-trade.
4. The CARES Act was enacted by the US Congress and approved by President Trump in March 2020. The wide scope and significant economic, social and political impact of the CARES Act grants the executive branch excessive powers in enactment, monitoring, enforcement and prosecution pertaining to CARES Act issues and that contravenes the legislative intent of the US Constitution (especially the checks-and-balances principle). The obvious lack of sufficient Congressional oversight in sections of the CARES Act remains a major costly mistake. However, some academics have rejected the *Non-Delegation doctrine*.[46]

[46] *See*: Mortenson, J. & Bagley, N. (2020). "There's No Historical Justification for One of the Most Dangerous Ideas in American Law—The Founders didn't believe that broad delegations of legislative power violated the Constitution, but conservative originalists keep insisting otherwise". *The Atlantic*. https://www.theatlantic.com/ideas/archive/2020/05/nondelegation-doctrine-orliginalism/612013/. This article stated in part: "…Most government activity in the United States rests on a simple idea: that it's okay for the legislature to authorize the executive branch to regulate basically anything the legislature itself could reach—working conditions, pollution, elections, financial products, mask wearing, you name it. That idea is now under attack. Relying on a so-called nondelegation doctrine, conservative originalists insist that the Founders never intended for government to work this way. They call for courts to strike down any laws that delegate too much power—and much of the federal bureaucracy along with them…. The nondelegation doctrine didn't exist at the

5. The inherent violations of the *Non-Delegation Doctrine* by the CARES Act unfairly discriminated between sophisticated Affected Persons that knew how to "game" the application process, or could afford to hire consultants/lawyers to navigate the application process, or had the political connections to get approvals for loans/guarantees/grants on one hand, and *Affected Persons* that couldn't. Such discrimination doesn't advance the public interest in the case of epidemics.
6. The inherent violations of the *Non-Delegation Doctrine* by the CARES Act unfairly discriminate between *Affected Persons* that file applications for CARES Act benefits at banks that use wrong or overly discretionary application/approvals criteria or politically influenced approvals criteria, and *Affected Persons* that file applications at banks that use more "normal" approval criteria. Such discrimination doesn't advance the public interest in the case of epidemics.
7. The inherent violations of the *Non-Delegation Doctrine* by the CARES Act unfairly discriminated between *Affected Persons* that had significant cash reserves (or whose owners have cash reserves), and do or can do a substantial percentage of their usual business over the Internet; and those that didn't or couldn't. Such discrimination doesn't advance the public interest in the case of crisis and pandemics/epidemics.
8. The inherent violations of the *Non-Delegation Doctrine* by the CARES Act unfairly discriminated between *Affected Persons* that have been truly and significantly harmed by COVID-19 and thus need economic/financial assistance and cannot apply for aid or don't apply for aid on one hand, and Affected Persons that haven't been harmed that chose to apply for economic/financial aid under the CARES Act. The CARES Act doesn't make adequate provisions to reduce or eliminate *false positives* and *false negatives.* Such discrimination doesn't advance the public interest in the case of crisis and pandemics/epidemics.

founding. It's a fable that originalists tell themselves about how enlightened people must have thought about the Constitution. For those suspicious of agency authority and centralized government, it makes for a comforting story. But it's just not true...".

9. The cost of enforcing such CARES Act can be high, and compliance is likely to be low because of such violations of the *Non-Delegation Doctrine*.
10. The CARES Act and its inherent violations of the *Non-Delegation Doctrine* can increase unemployment and social unrest, and have negative *Multiplier Effects* (economics, social, psychological and environmental) and *Emergence properties* (i.e. new adverse economic, social, psychological and/or environmental phenomena can emerge as a result) because of false negatives and false positives in the aid application/approval processes.
11. The CARES Act unfairly discriminated between: (i) US residents that are drug addicts and victims of the *opioid epidemic* of 2016–present in the US, for which the US government hasn't provided much needed economic aid and medical support on one hand; and (ii) Affected Persons that are threatened (but not infected) by COVID-19, for which the CARES Act provides unemployment, cash grants, loans, loan guarantees and other support. The discrimination does not advance the public interest.
12. The resulting rapid, evolving and significant changes in online/offline *Social Networks* and *Social Capital* are likely to have lasting negative psychological, social and political effects on indigenes.
13. Given the foregoing, the CARES Act can cause or increase *Deadweight Losses* in the demand/supply of loans and other aid, and in fees charged by banks, and in interest rates.

7.4.3.7 The Free Speech Doctrine

The CARES Act violates the *Free Speech Clause* with respect to at least the following classes of *Affected Persons*:

1. Companies and individuals that apply for government-backed grants, loans and government guarantees pursuant to the CARES Act (such applications are *Protected Speech*); and
2. Banks that apply to manage or disburse government-backed grants, loans and government guarantees pursuant to the CARES Act (such applications are *Protected Speech*).

These *Affected Persons* are also members of a protected class. However, the public interest and the need to control and manage the economic/

financial harm caused by COVID-19 may or may not outweigh the personal rights of the Affected Persons and the potentially large economic harm that both COVID-19 and CARES Act can cause. Perhaps the balancing-of-interests should be supported by economic studies. The obvious *State Action* is the CARES Act. See Nwogugu (2012). As above, the problems are as follows:

1. See the critique of the CARES Act herein and above.
2. The wording of the CARES Act effectively and unconstitutionally transfers to banks (community banks; money center banks; federally chartered banks), the duty of legislating the application criteria and the approval criteria for Affected Persons that apply for economic/financial aid through such banks pursuant to the CARES Act. The CARES Act doesn't issue: (1) a standard set of sufficient criteria for selection of "manager" banks; or (2) a standard set of sufficient criteria for banks for loans and loan-guarantees, or (3) a standard set of sufficient criteria for government agencies for cash grants. All aid decisions are or can be highly subjective—that is a major problem.
3. Such *Affected Persons* have a constitutionally guaranteed *Property Interest* in valid statutes and in fair application criteria and in equitable disbursement of economic/financial aid from the government, and in equitable delivery of aid/services. Such *Property Interests* arise from the US Constitution, state constitutions, expectations, norms and usage-of-trade.
4. The CARES Act can be construed as "over-broad" and was not sufficiently and narrowly tailored to serve the intended purpose of promoting economic growth and stability.
5. The inherent violations of the *Free Speech Clause* by the CARES Act unfairly discriminate between aid applicants (businesses/individuals) that know how to "game" the application process, or can afford to hire consultants/lawyers to navigate the application process, or have the political connections to get approvals for loans/guarantees/grants on one hand, and businesses/individuals that can't and whose applications are wrongly rejected or who are wrongly informed that they cannot apply when in reality they qualify. Such discrimination doesn't advance the public interest in the case of epidemics.

6. The inherent violations of the *Free Speech Clause* by the CARES Act unfairly discriminate between banks whose applications to manage/disburse or CARES Act benefits are successful because of their political connections, ability to hire consultants/lawyers, and/or because of excessive discretion and the lack of uniform selection standards and specificity of the CARES Act on one hand, banks whose applications are unsuccessful because they don't have such capabilities or because of excessive discretion and the lack of uniform selection standards and specificity of the CARES Act. Such discrimination doesn't advance the public interest in the case of epidemics.
7. The inherent violations of the *Free Speech Clause* by the CARES Act unfairly discriminate between banks whose applications to manage/disburse or CARES Act benefits are successful because they are located in US states whose state banking laws are more amenable to the CARES Act and the fiduciary functions of selected banks on one hand, and banks who are located in states whose state banking laws are not amenable. Such discrimination doesn't advance the public interest in the case of epidemics.
8. The cost of enforcing such CARES Act can be high, and compliance is likely to be low because of such violations of the *Free Speech Clause.*
9. The CARES Act and the inherent violations of the *Free Speech Clause* can increase unemployment and social unrest, and have negative *Multiplier Effects* (economics, social, psychological and environmental) and *Emergence properties* (i.e. new adverse economic, social, psychological and/or environmental phenomena can emerge as a result) because of false negatives and false positives in the aid application/approval processes.
10. The resulting rapid, evolving and significant changes in online/offline *Social Networks* and *Social Capital* are likely to have lasting negative psychological, social and political effects on indigenes.
11. Given the foregoing, the CARES Act can cause or increase *Deadweight Losses* in the demand/supply of loans and other aid, and in fees charged by banks, and in interest rates.

7.4.3.8 The Takings Doctrine

The CARES Act violates the *Takings Clause* with respect to at least the following classes of *Affected Persons*:

1. Companies and individuals that apply for government-backed grants, loans and government guarantees pursuant to the CARES Act; and
2. Banks that apply to manage or disburse government-backed grants, loans and government guarantees pursuant to the CARES Act.

These *Affected Persons* are also members of a protected class. However, the public interest and the need to control and manage the economic/financial harm caused by COVID-19 may or may not outweigh the personal rights of the Affected Persons and the potentially large economic harm that both COVID-19 and CARES Act can cause. Perhaps the balancing-of-interests should be supported by economic studies. The obvious *State Action* is the CARES Act. See Nwogugu (2012). As above, the problems are as follows:

1. See the critique of the CARES Act herein and above.
2. Such *Affected Persons* have a constitutionally guaranteed *Property Interest* in valid statutes and in fair application criteria and in equitable disbursement of economic/financial aid from the government, and in equitable delivery of aid/services. Such *Property Interests* arise from the US Constitution, state constitutions, expectations, norms and usage-of-trade.
3. The wording of the CARES Act effectively and unconstitutionally transfers to banks (community banks; money center banks; federally chartered banks), the duty of legislating the application criteria and the approval criteria for Affected Persons that apply for economic/financial aid through such banks pursuant to the CARES Act. The CARES Act doesn't issue: (1) a standard set of sufficient criteria for selection of "manager" banks; or (2) a standard set of sufficient criteria for banks for loans and loan-guarantees, or (3) a standard set of sufficient criteria for government agencies that disburse cash grants. All aid decisions are highly subjective—that is a major problem.

4. The CARES Act can be construed as "over-broad" and was not sufficiently and narrowly tailored to serve the intended purpose of promoting economic growth and stability.
5. The CARES Act unfairly discriminates between aid applicants (businesses/individuals) whose applications are wrongly denied because of insufficient specificity of the CARES Act and improper delegation of aid/loan management to banks on one hand, and businesses/individuals whose applications are wrongly approved because of insufficient specificity of the CARES Act and improper delegation of aid/loan management to banks. Such discrimination doesn't advance the public interest in the case of epidemics. Such improper denials of applications are *Takings* because such Affected Persons have constitutionally guaranteed property interests in valid statutes and in fair application criteria and in equitable disbursement of economic/financial aid from the government.
6. The inherent violations of the *Takings Clause* by the CARES Act unfairly discriminate between banks whose applications to manage/disburse or CARES Act benefits are successful because of their political connections, ability to hire consultants/lawyers, and/or because of excessive discretion and the lack of uniform selection standards and specificity of the CARES Act on one hand, banks whose applications are unsuccessful because they don't have such capabilities/connections or because of excessive discretion and the lack of uniform selection standards and specificity of the CARES Act. Such discrimination doesn't advance the public interest in the case of epidemics.
7. The inherent violations of the *Takings Clause* by the CARES Act unfairly discriminate between banks whose applications to manage/disburse or CARES Act benefits are successful because they are located in US states whose state banking laws are more amenable to the CARES Act and the fiduciary functions of selected "manager" banks on one hand, and banks who are located in states whose state banking laws are not amenable. Such discrimination doesn't advance the public interest in the case of epidemics.
8. The cost of enforcing such CARES Act can be high, and compliance is likely to be low because of such violations of the *Takings Clause*.
9. The CARES Act and its inherent violations of the *Takings Clause* can increase unemployment and social unrest, and have negative

Multiplier Effects (economics, social, psychological and environmental) and *Emergence properties* (i.e. new adverse economic, social, psychological and/or environmental phenomena can emerge as a result) because of false negatives and false positives in the aid application/approval processes.
10. The resulting rapid, evolving and significant changes in online/offline *Social Networks* and *Social Capital* are likely to have lasting negative psychological, social and political effects on indigenes.
11. Given the foregoing, the CARES Act can cause or increase *Deadweight Losses* in the demand/supply of loans and other aid, and in fees charged by banks, and in interest rates.

7.4.3.9 *The* Dormant Commerce Clause Doctrine

The US government's CARES Act constitutes an infringement of *the Dormant Commerce Clause Doctrine* with respect to at least the following classes of persons:

1. Companies that do business, or want to do business across state lines; and
2. Individuals that do business across or want to do business state lines.

These *Affected Persons* are also members of a protected class. However, the public interest and the need to control and manage the economic/financial harm caused by COVID-19 may or may not outweigh the personal rights of the Affected Persons and the potentially large economic harm that both COVID-19 and CARES Act can cause. Perhaps the balancing-of-interests should be supported by economic studies. The obvious *State Action* is the CARES Act. See Nwogugu (2012). As above, the problems are as follows:

1. See the critique of the CARES Act herein and above. One major problem is that different states have different definitions of "public health emergencies" and "essential businesses".
2. Such *Affected Persons* have a constitutionally guaranteed *Property Interest* in valid statutes and in fair application criteria and in equitable disbursement of economic/financial aid from the government, and in equitable delivery of aid/services. Such *Property Interests* arise from the US Constitution, state constitutions, expectations, norms/culture and usage-of-trade.

3. The wording of the CARES Act effectively and unconstitutionally transfers to banks (community banks; money center banks; federally chartered banks), the duty of legislating the application criteria and the approval criteria for Affected Persons that apply for economic/financial aid through such banks pursuant to the CARES Act. The CARES Act doesn't issue: (1) a standard set of sufficient criteria for selection of "manager" banks; or (2) a standard set of sufficient criteria for banks for loans and loan-guarantees, or (3) a standard set of sufficient criteria for government agencies that disburse cash grants. All aid decisions are highly subjective—that is a major problem.
4. The CARES Act can be construed as "over-broad" and was not sufficiently and narrowly tailored to serve the intended purpose of promoting economic growth and stability.
5. The inherent violations of the *Dormant Commerce Clause Doctrine* by the CARES Act unfairly discriminate between aid applicants (businesses/individuals) whose applications are wrongly denied or who cannot apply because their state banking laws limit the applicability and/or participation in CARES Act aid programs; and/or whose state's laws' definitions of "public health emergencies" and "essential businesses" vary unfavorably from other states; and/or whose state laws facilitate improper delegation of aid/loan management to banks on one hand; and businesses/individuals who are located in states where the state banking laws are amendable to CARES Act or whose state laws facilitate proper delegation of aid/loan management to banks. Such discrimination doesn't advance the public interest in the case of epidemics.
6. The inherent violations of the *Dormant Commerce Clause Doctrine* by the CARES Act unfairly discriminate between aid applicants (businesses/individuals) whose cost-of-doing business across state lines is inadvertently increased because of provisions/implementation of the CARES Act and/or because their state's laws' definitions of "public health emergencies" and "essential businesses" vary unfavorably from other states, on one hand, and businesses/individuals whose cost-of-doing business are the same or lower because of the implementation of the CARES Act. Such discrimination doesn't advance the public interest in the case of epidemics.
7. The inherent violations of the *Dormant Commerce Clause Doctrine* by the CARES Act unfairly discriminate between banks whose appli-

cations to manage/disburse or CARES Act benefits are successful because of their in-state political connections, ability to hire lobbyists/consultants/lawyers, and/or because of their local state banking laws on one hand; and banks whose applications are unsuccessful because they are located in states where such capabilities/connections don't exist or are expensive, or because their state banking laws promote excessive discretion and the lack of uniform selection standards and low-specificity of the CARES Act. Such discrimination doesn't advance the public interest in the case of epidemics.

8. The CARES Act unfairly discriminates between banks whose applications to manage/disburse or CARES Act benefits are successful because they are located in US states whose state banking laws are more amenable to the CARES Act and the fiduciary functions of selected "manager" banks on one hand, and banks who are located in states whose state banking laws are not amenable. Such discrimination doesn't advance the public interest in the case of epidemics.
9. The cost of implementing CARES Act can be higher, and compliance is likely to be low because of such violations of the *Dormant Commerce Clause Doctrine*.
10. The CARES Act and the inherent violations of the *Dormant Commerce Clause Doctrine* can increase unemployment and social unrest, and have negative *Multiplier Effects* (economics, social, psychological and environmental) and *Emergence properties* (i.e. new adverse economic, social, psychological and/or environmental phenomena can emerge as a result) because of false negatives and false positives in the bank-selection process and in aid application/approval processes.
11. The CARES Act unfairly discriminates between: (i) US residents that are drug addicts and victims of the *opioid epidemic* of 2016–present in the US (and live in states where local/state/federal assistance for drug-addicts is low and/or whose state's laws' definitions of "public health emergencies" and "essential businesses" vary unfavorably from other states) for which the US government hasn't provided much needed economic aid and medical support on one hand; and (ii) Affected Persons that are threatened (but not infected) by COVID-19 (and live in states where state/local/federal assistance for COVID-19 is significant), for which the CARES Act provides unemployment benefits, cash grants, loans, loan-guarantees and other support. The discrimination does not advance the public interest.

12. The resulting rapid, evolving and significant changes in online/offline *Social Networks* and *Social Capital* are likely to have lasting negative psychological, social and political effects on indigenes.
13. Given the foregoing, the CARES Act can cause or increase *Deadweight Losses* in the demand/supply of enforcement, loans and other economic aid, and in fees charged by banks, and in interest rates.

7.4.3.10 *The CARES Act* Violates the Spending Powers Clause[47] and the Twenty-first Amendment *of the US Constitution*

The CARES Act violates the Spending Powers *Clause* and the *Twenty-first Amendment* with respect to at least the following classes of *Affected Persons*:

1. State governments that apply for economic/financial aid pursuant to the CARES Act.
2. Local governments which are direct subsidiaries of such "applicant" state governments and/or depend on such federal government aid.
3. Companies and individuals that directly or indirectly benefit from or depend on such federal government aid to be granted to "applicant" state governments.

These *Affected Persons* are also members of a protected class. However, the public interest and the need to control and manage the economic/financial harm caused by COVID-19 may or may not outweigh the tenth Amendment rights of state governments (and the "derivative" rights of other and indirectly Affected Persons) and the potentially large economic harm that both COVID-19 and CARES Act can cause. Perhaps the balancing-of-interests should be supported by economic studies. The obvious *State Action* is the CARES Act. See Nwogugu (2012). As above, the problems are as follows:

[47] *Contrast: South Dakota* vs. *Dole*, 483 US 203 (1987; US Supreme Court) (the US Supreme Court announced a four-part test for reviewing the constitutionality of conditions attached to federal spending programs).

See: Mayer Brown (April 2, 2020). *Summary of CARES Act State and Local Government Relief Provisions.* https://www.mayerbrown.com/en/perspectives-events/publications/2020/04/summary-of-cares-act-state-and-local-government-relief-provisions.

See: Article I, Section 9, Clause 7, of the US Constitution.

1. See the critique of the CARES Act herein and above.
2. Such *Affected Persons* have a constitutionally guaranteed *Property Interest* in valid statutes and in fair application criteria and in equitable disbursement of economic/financial aid from the government, and in equitable delivery of aid/services. Such *Property Interests* arise from the US Constitution, state constitutions, expectations, norms and usage-of-trade.
3. The CARES Act is unconstitutional because it:

    a. *Imposes conditions on such aid* by not specifying adequate criteria for disbursement of such aid. The affected provisions/appropriations include but are not limited to the following: (i) $1 billion to the Community Services Block Grant; (ii) $750 million is reserved for payments to programs under the Head Start Act; (iii) $3.5 billion to the Child Care and Development Block Grant; (iv) an appropriation of over $30 billion to the Department of Education to provide relief to states, school districts and higher education institutions.
    b. *Compels* (or provides significant incentives for) *desperate state governments and their associated local governments to falsify data* in their applications and reports. The amounts disbursed are heavily dependent on reported populations of the state and its cities. The relief fund covers only necessary expenditures related to COVID-19 that were not included in that government's budget and were incurred between March 1 and December 30, 2020. That also introduces opportunities for lobbying and bribery.
    c. *Grants to the Department of the Treasury's Inspector General (a political appointee that can be removed by the US President), the sole power to determine whether or not federal funds have been used by state/local governments for "permitted" purposes* under the CARES Act—and if such aid is deemed used for non-permitted purposes, the aid will be converted into debt. In such circumstances, the Inspector General functions by filing periodic evaluation reports. All that gives the federal government the implicit power to directly or indirectly coerce state governments to follow its policies for COVID-19 epidemic. That also introduces opportunities for harmful lobbying and bribery.
    d. *Provides significant incentives for fraudulent reporting of unemployment benefits*—under the CARES Act, the federal government will reimburse half of the amounts paid by the state governments

for unemployment benefits during March–December 2020. It compels desperate state governments and their associated local governments to: (i) falsify data in their applications and reports; (ii) encourage or permit companies (including companies that have permanently lost significant revenues and have laid off or want to lay off staff) to file fraudulent applications for unemployment benefits and reimbursements. The reality is that in many states, unemployment benefits are subject to state and local income taxes and state governments depend on such taxes and thus have significant incentive to engage in misconduct.

e. The CARES Act sections that pertain to federal economic/financial aid for state governments can be construed as "over-broad" and was not sufficiently and narrowly tailored to serve the intended purpose of promoting economic growth and stability.
f. The inherent violations of the *Spending Powers Clause* by the CARES Act unfairly discriminate between state governments that have significant cash reserves and/or are politically connected, and/or can hire consultants/lawyers on one hand, state governments that don't have such resources. Such discrimination doesn't advance the public interest in the case of epidemics.
g. The CARES Act and its inherent violations of the *Spending Powers Clause* can increase unemployment and social unrest, and have negative *Multiplier Effects* (economics, social, psychological and environmental) and *Emergence properties* (i.e. new adverse economic, social, psychological and/or environmental phenomena can emerge as a result) because of false negatives and false positives in the aid application, approval and oversight processes.
h. Given the foregoing, the CARES Act can cause or increase *Deadweight Losses* in the demand/supply of enforcement and economic/financial aid.

7.5 Conclusion

The COVID-19 pandemic raises highly contentious Constitutional Law and Political Economy problems that remain unresolved in many countries, and may complicate and/or deter economic growth, sustainability efforts, and government/public and private responses to future emergencies and epidemics/pandemics.

Appendix 1: Executive Orders Issued by US State Governors (January 2020 to March 2020) in Response to the COVID-19 Epidemic (https://web.csg.org/covid19/executive-orders/)

Alabama

- State of Emergency Declared. https://governor.alabama.gov/newsroom/2020/03/state-of-emergency-coronavirus-covid-19/
- Gov. Kay Ivey establishes Coronavirus Task Force. https://governor.alabama.gov/newsroom/2020/03/governor-ivey-establishes-coronavirus-covid-19-task-force/
- Department of Public Health Order
- Supplemental State of Emergency: Coronavirus COVID-19. https://governor.alabama.gov/newsroom/2020/03/supplemental-state-of-emergency-coronavirus-covid-19/
- Governor Ivey Issues Statement on Updated Public Health Precautionary Guidelines. https://governor.alabama.gov/newsroom/2020/03/governor-ivey-issues-statement-on-updated-public-health-precautionary-guidelines/
- Governor Ivey Issues Statement on Statewide Public Health Order. https://governor.alabama.gov/newsroom/2020/03/governor-ivey-issues-statement-on-statewide-public-health-order/
- Governor Ivey Issues Statement on Updated Statewide Public Health Order. https://governor.alabama.gov/newsroom/2020/03/governor-ivey-issues-statement-on-updated-statewide-public-health-order/
- Second Supplemental State of Emergency
- Third Supplemental State of Emergency. https://governor.alabama.gov/newsroom/2020/03/third-supplemental-state-of-emergency-coronavirus-covid-19/
- Executive Order 2020-15 Expansion of Telemedicine. https://azgovernor.gov/executive-orders
- Governor Ducey Signs Legislation to Increase Resources for Arizona Hospitals. https://azgovernor.gov/governor/news/2020/03/governor-ducey-signs-legislation-increase-resources-arizona-hospitals
- Fourth Supplemental State of Emergency. https://governor.alabama.gov/newsroom/2020/03/fourth-supplemental-state-of-emergency-coronavirus-covid-19/

Alaska

- State of Emergency Declared. https://gov.alaska.gov/wp-content/uploads/sites/2/COVID-19-Disaster-Packet.pdf
- Administrative Order No. 315 directs the Department of Health and Social Services regarding COVID-19. https://gov.alaska.gov/admin-orders/administrative-order-no-315-2/
- COVID-19 Health Mandate. https://gov.alaska.gov/wp-content/uploads/sites/2/03132020-COVID-19-Health-Mandate-001.pdf
- Health Mandate Issued on March 16: Libraries, Archives and Museums, Residential Schools. Governor Dunleavy announces Alaska Economic Stabilization Team. https://gov.alaska.gov/wp-content/uploads/sites/2/03.16.20-COVID-19-Health-Mandate-002.pdf

(*continued*)

Appendix 1 (continued)

- Health Mandate 003: Statewide Closure Restaurants, Bars, Entertainment. https://gov.alaska.gov/home/covid19-healthmandates/
- Health Mandate 004: Travel. https://gov.alaska.gov/home/covid19-healthmandates/
- Health Mandate 005: Elective Medical Procedures. https://gov.alaska.gov/home/covid19-healthmandates/
- Health Mandate 006—Elective Oral Health Procedures. https://gov.alaska.gov/home/covid19-healthmandates/
- Health Mandate 007 Fairbanks North Star Borough & Ketchikan Gateway Borough—Personal Care Services and Gatherings. https://gov.alaska.gov/home/covid19-healthmandates/
- Health Mandate 008 Public and Private Schools. https://gov.alaska.gov/home/covid19-healthmandates/
- Alaska COVID-19 Economic Stabilization Plan Released. https://gov.alaska.gov/wp-content/uploads/sites/2/Alaska-Economic-Stabilization-Plan-FINAL-3.20.2020.pdf
- Health Mandate 009 Personal Care Services and Gatherings. https://gov.alaska.gov/home/covid19-healthmandates/
- Health Mandate 010 International and Interstate Travel—Order for Self-Quarantine. https://gov.alaska.gov/home/covid19-healthmandates/
- Governor Signs Legislation Expanding Unemployment Benefits and Increasing Internet Speeds for Alaska's Schools. https://gov.alaska.gov/home/covid19-healthmandates/

Arizona

- State of Emergency Declared. https://azgovernor.gov/sites/default/files/declaraton_0.pdf
- 2020-07 Proactive Measures to Protect Against COVID-19. https://azgovernor.gov/sites/default/files/eo_2020-07.pdf
- Governor Doug Ducey, Boys & Girls Clubs Announce Partnership to Help Address Impacts of COVID-19. https://azgovernor.gov/news-releases
- Executive Order 2020-08 Limiting In-Person Motor Vehicle Division Visits for Driver License Renewals. https://azgovernor.gov/executive-orders
- Executive Order 2020-09 Limiting the Operations of Certain Businesses to Slow the Spread of COVID-19. https://azgovernor.gov/executive-orders
- Executive Order 2020-10 Delaying Elective Surgeries to Conserve Personal Protective Equipment Necessary to Test and Treat Patients with COVID-19. https://azgovernor.gov/executive-orders
- Executive Order 2020-11 Ensuring Individuals Whose Employment Is Affected by COVID-19 Have Access to Unemployment Insurance. https://azgovernor.gov/executive-orders
- Governor Ducey Expands Access to Unemployment Insurance and Extends Income Tax Deadline. https://azgovernor.gov/governor/news/2020/03/governor-ducey-expands-access-unemployment-insurance-and-extends-income-tax
- Executive Order 2020-12 Prohibiting the Closure of Essential Services. https://azgovernor.gov/executive-orders

(*continued*)

Appendix 1 (continued)

- Executive Order 2020-13 Enhanced Surveillance Advisory. https://azgovernor.gov/executive-orders
- Executive Order 2020-14 Postponement of Eviction Actions. https://azgovernor.gov/executive-orders
- Governor Ducey and Superintendent Hoffman Announce Childcare for COVID-19 Frontline Workers. https://azgovernor.gov/governor/news/2020/03/governor-ducey-and-superintendent-hoffman-announce-childcare-covid-19
- Governor Ducey Takes Steps to Free Up More Physicians to Address COVID-19. https://azgovernor.gov/governor/news/2020/03/governor-ducey-takes-step-free-more-physicians-address-covid-19
- Governor Ducey Announces Public-Private Partnership to Secure Additional Medical Equipment. https://azgovernor.gov/governor/news/2020/03/governor-ducey-announces-public-private-partnership-secure-additional-medical
- Governor Ducey Announces Arizona Together Initiative, Linking Arizonans to Resources During COVID-19 Outbreak. https://azgovernor.gov/governor/news/2020/03/governor-ducey-announces-arizona-together-initiative-linking-arizonans
- Executive Order 2020-16 Increasing Hospital Capacity for COVID-19 Preparedness
- Executive Order 2020-17 Continuity of Work. https://azgovernor.gov/executive-orders
- Governor Ducey Announces Electric Utility Relief Package. https://azgovernor.gov/governor/news/2020/03/governor-ducey-announces-electric-utility-relief-package
- Arizona Waives Emissions Testing for Seniors to Reduce COVID-19 Risk. https://azgovernor.gov/governor/news/2020/03/arizona-waives-emissions-testing-seniors-reduce-covid-19-risk

Arkansas

- State of Emergency Declared. https://governor.arkansas.gov/images/uploads/executiveOrders/EO_20-03.__1.pdf
- EO 20-04 Authorizes Funds from Governor's Disaster Fund to be Used at discretion of Arkansas Division of Emergency Management. https://governor.arkansas.gov/images/uploads/executiveOrders/EO_20-04._.pdf
- EO 20-05 Suspends Telemedicine Provisions. https://governor.arkansas.gov/images/uploads/executiveOrders/EO_20-05.pdf
- Executive Order 20-06 to Amend Executive Order 20-03 Regarding the Public Health Emergency. https://governor.arkansas.gov/images/uploads/executiveOrders/EO_20-06._.pdf
- Governor Hutchinson Expedites Unemployment Benefits for Those Impacted by COVID-19. https://governor.arkansas.gov/news-media/press-releases/governor-hutchinson-expedites-unemployment-benefits-for-those-impacted-by
- Governor Hutchinson Announces Relief for Businesses, Child-care Providers to Ease COVID-19 Impact. https://governor.arkansas.gov/news-media/press-releases/governor-hutchinson-announces-relief-for-businesses-child-care-providers-to-ease-covid-19-impact

(*continued*)

Appendix 1 (continued)

- EO 20-08 Ordering Funds Released to Defray Program and Administrative Costs Associated with COVID-19. https://governor.arkansas.gov/images/uploads/executiveOrders/EO_20-08._.pdf
- EO 20-09 To Amend EO 20-03 for the Purpose of Extending the State Individual Tax Filing Deadline as a Result of COVID-19. https://governor.arkansas.gov/images/uploads/executiveOrders/200325_EO_20-09.pdf
- Proclamation: Governor Issues Call for Special Legislative Session of the 92nd General Assembly. https://governor.arkansas.gov/images/uploads/proclamations/2020_First_Extraordinary_Call_to_Special_Session.pdf
- EO 20-10 To Amend EO 20-03 for the Purpose of Restricting Gatherings to Prevent the Spread of COVID-19. https://governor.arkansas.gov/images/uploads/executiveOrders/EO_20-10._.pdf
- Governor Hutchinson Announces Proposal to Protect and Support Health Care Professionals, Public, and Providers. https://governor.arkansas.gov/news-media/press-releases/governor-hutchinson-announces-proposal-to-protect-and-support-health-care

California

- State of Emergency Declared. https://www.gov.ca.gov/wp-content/uploads/2020/03/3.4.20-Coronavirus-SOE-Proclamation.pdf
- Executive Order N-25-20 Further Enhancing State and Local Government's Ability to Respond to COVID-19 Pandemic. https://www.gov.ca.gov/wp-content/uploads/2020/03/3.12.20-EO-N-25-20-COVID-19.pdf
- Executive Order N-26-20 Ensuring State Funding for Schools Even in Event of Physical Closure. https://www.gov.ca.gov/wp-content/uploads/2020/03/3.13.20-EO-N-26-20-Schools.pdf
- Executive Order N-27-20 to Protect the Health and Safety of Californians Most Vulnerable. https://www.gov.ca.gov/wp-content/uploads/2020/03/3.15.2020-COVID-19-Facilities.pdf
- Department of Public Health Issues Guidance on Closure of Restaurants/Bars/Wineries. https://www.cdph.ca.gov/Programs/OPA/Pages/NR20-024.aspx
- Executive Order N-28-20 to Protect Renters and Homeowners During COVID-19 Pandemic. https://www.gov.ca.gov/wp-content/uploads/2020/03/3.16.20-Executive-Order.pdf
- Executive Order N-31-20 to Allow Timely Delivery of Vital Goods During COVID-19 Outbreak. https://www.gov.ca.gov/wp-content/uploads/2020/03/3.17.20-EO-motor.pdf
- Governor Newsom Signs Emergency Legislation to Fight COVID-19. https://www.gov.ca.gov/2020/03/17/governor-newsom-signs-emergency-legislation-to-fight-covid-19/
- Executive Order N-29-20 to Protect Ongoing Safety Net Services for Most Vulnerable Californians During COVID-19 Outbreak. https://www.gov.ca.gov/wp-content/uploads/2020/03/3.17.20-N-29-20-EO.pdf

(*continued*)

Appendix 1 (continued)

- Executive Order N-30-20 to Suspend Standardized Testing for Students in Response to COVID-19 Outbreak. https://www.gov.ca.gov/wp-content/uploads/2020/03/3.17.18-N-30-20-Schools.pdf
- California Launches New Comprehensive, Consumer-Friendly Website and Public Service Announcements to Boost COVID-19 Awareness. https://www.gov.ca.gov/2020/03/18/california-launches-new-comprehensive-consumer-friendly-website-and-public-service-announcements-to-boost-covid-19-awareness/
- Governor Newsom Takes Emergency Actions and Authorizes $150 Million in Funding to Protect Homeless Californians from COVID-19. https://www.gov.ca.gov/2020/03/18/governor-newsom-takes-emergency-actions-authorizes-150-million-in-funding-to-protect-homeless-californians-from-covid-19/
- Executive Order N-32-20 Local Flexibility. https://www.gov.ca.gov/wp-content/uploads/2020/03/3.18.20-EO.pdf
- Executive Order N-33-20 Stay at Home Order. https://covid19.ca.gov/img/Executive-Order-N-33-20.pdf
- Executive Order N-34-20 to Protect Public Health by Expanding Vote-by-Mail Options and Extending Deadlines for Presidential Primary Canvass. https://www.gov.ca.gov/wp-content/uploads/2020/03/3.20.20-N-34-20.pdf
- Executive Order N-35-20 Expands the State's Response to the COVID-19 Outbreak. https://www.gov.ca.gov/wp-content/uploads/2020/03/3.21.20-EO-N-35-20-text.pdf
- California Secures Presidential Major Disaster Declaration to Support State's COVID-19 Emergency Response. https://www.gov.ca.gov/2020/03/22/california-secures-presidential-major-disaster-declaration-to-support-states-covid-19-emergency-response/
- Governor Newsom Takes Action to Strengthen California's Health Care Delivery System to Respond to COVID-19. https://www.gov.ca.gov/2020/03/21/governor-newsom-takes-action-to-strengthen-californias-health-care-delivery-system-to-respond-to-covid-19/
- Executive Order N-36-20 State Prisons and Juvenile Facilities. https://www.gov.ca.gov/wp-content/uploads/2020/03/3.24.20-EO-N-36-20.pdf
- Governor Newsom Announces Major Financial Relief Package: 90-Day Mortgage Payment Relief During COVID-19 Crisis. https://www.gov.ca.gov/2020/03/25/governor-gavin-newsom-announces-major-financial-relief-package-90-day-mortgage-payment-relief-during-covid-19-crisis/

Colorado

- State of Emergency Declared. https://drive.google.com/file/d/1szJfU9WF36-lCVgRhXMAnJdlQyTSG83e/view
- D 2020 003 Declaring a Disaster Emergency due to the Presence of Coronavirus Disease 2019 in Colorado. https://drive.google.com/file/d/1szJfU9WF36-lCVgRhXMAnJdlQyTSG83e/view
- Notice of Public Health Order 20-22 Closing Bars, Restaurants, Theaters, Gymnasiums, and Casinos Statewide. https://www.colorado.gov/pacific/sites/default/files/atoms/files/BarsRestaurantsPHorder.pdf

(*continued*)

Appendix 1 (continued)

- Executive Order 2020-004 Ordering Closure of Downhill Ski Resorts due to the Presence of COVID-19 in the State of Colorado. https://drive.google.com/file/d/18ZabTj82DItSKzY9iZ3fDk-BPJWZNPOj/view
- Executive Order 2020-005 Directing State Parties and Secretary of State to Amend Rules Regarding In-Person Gatherings to Allow the 2020 Primary Election to Proceed Without Interruption, in light of the Disaster Declaration set forth in Executive Order D 2020 003. https://drive.google.com/file/d/1sF4zVsr-lePUcBTq9gkp_dERchD4g4jM/view
- 2020-007 Ordering Suspension of Normal In-Person Instruction at All Public and Private Elementary and Secondary Schools in the State of Colorado due to the Presence of COVID-19. https://drive.google.com/file/d/1ecMEQj3F3qeEl3qNMtLkAlk3ya3FbVH3/view
- Governor Polis, Coloradans, Launch COVID Relief Fund. https://www.colorado.gov/governor/news/gov-polis-coloradans-launch-covid-relief-fund
- Executive Order 2020-006 Amending Executive Order 2020-004. https://drive.google.com/file/d/1Y0_4CiFPPR7Tc66CS6fKCy97iBgkg3MD/view
- Executive Order 2020-008 Amending Executive Order 2020-005. https://drive.google.com/file/d/1a9SK1IpmUbhFZaC9Vv_Zf_YAtXLkckg8/view
- Executive Order 2020-009 Ordering the Temporary Cessation of All Elective and Non-Essential Surgeries and Procedures and Preserving Personal Protective Equipment and Ventilators. https://drive.google.com/file/d/1Sp3le5zUavA3GKM_omeDXpm7FNfL-wSt/view
- Executive Order 2020-010 Ordering the Suspension of Statute to Extend the Income Tax Payment Deadlines due to the COVID-19 Disaster Emergency. https://drive.google.com/file/d/1UKokz3ug7x7aBAKQxON8K7J6pCyxfvUq/view
- Executive Order 2020-011 Ordering the Temporary Suspension of Regulatory Statutes due to the Presence of COVID-19. https://drive.google.com/file/d/1HXTMP8E5KF9ppvusW4kAJIIDQrdHckqQ/view
- Executive Order 2020-012 Ordering Limiting Evictions, Foreclosures, and Public Utility Disconnections an Expediting Unemployment Insurance Claim Processing to Provide Relief to Coloradans Affected by COVID-19. https://drive.google.com/file/d/1mMCRLb6PxMPI680_THFn4nqLGAty1jq9/view
- Polis Announces Emergency Economic Advisory Council to Shepherd Colorado's Post-Coronavirus Recovery. https://www.cpr.org/2020/03/20/polis-announces-emergency-economic-advisory-council-to-shepherd-colorados-post-coronavirus-recovery/
- Executive Order 2020-013 Ordering Colorado Employers to Reduce In-Person Workforce by Fifty Percent due to the Presence of COVID-19 in the State. https://drive.google.com/file/d/1LQpL1oDurg4Iiasq_d6Cu_v2zM_0IMd3/view
- Executive Order 2020-17 Ordering Coloradans to Stay at Home due to the Presence of COVID-19 in the State. https://drive.google.com/file/d/1rv-4MmdsXja5VEPHV8_ber4Sk7QnhII3/view

(*continued*)

Appendix 1 (continued)

- Executive Order 2020-15 Authorizing the Executive Directors of Certain State Agencies to Promulgate and Issue Emergency Rules Extending the Expiration Date of Licenses and Other Documents due to the Presence of COVID-19. https://drive.google.com/file/d/1rv-4MmdsXja5VEPHV8_ber4Sk7QnhII3/view
- Executive Order 2020-16 Temporarily Suspending Certain Regulatory Statutes Concerning Criminal Justice. https://drive.google.com/file/d/18o0yWHzZleHJ87hmgLuBmXwpM8R74Q5x/view
- Updated Public Health Order 20-24 Implementing Stay at Home Requirements. https://drive.google.com/file/d/1GjiohfHn3BP10UxifTQLfgfdw0Twrut_/view

Connecticut

- State of Emergency Declared. https://portal.ct.gov/-/media/Office-of-the-Governor/News/20200310-declaration-of-civil-preparedness-and-public-health-emergency.pdf?la=en
- Executive Order No. 7 Protection of Public Health and Safety During COVID-19 Pandemic and Response. https://portal.ct.gov/-/media/Office-of-the-Governor/Executive-Orders/Lamont-Executive-Orders/Executive-Order-No-7.pdf
- Executive Order No. 7A Protection of Residents of Nursing Home Facilities, Residential Care Homes and Chronic Disease Hospitals During COVID-19 Pandemic. https://portal.ct.gov/-/media/Office-of-the-Governor/Executive-Orders/Lamont-Executive-Orders/Executive-Order-No-7A.pdf
- Executive Order 7B Protection of Public Health and Safety During COVID-19 Pandemic and Response Suspension or Modifications of Statutes. https://portal.ct.gov/-/media/Office-of-the-Governor/Executive-Orders/Lamont-Executive-Orders/Executive-Order-No-7B.pdf
- Executive Order No. 7C Protection of Public Health and Safety during COVID-19 Pandemic and Response—Further Suspension or Modification of Statutes. https://portal.ct.gov/-/media/Office-of-the-Governor/Executive-Orders/Lamont-Executive-Orders/Executive-Order-No-7C.pdf?la=en
- Executive Order No. 7D Protection of Public Health and Safety During COVID-19 Pandemic and Response—Crowd Reduction and Social Distancing. https://portal.ct.gov/-/media/Office-of-the-Governor/Executive-Orders/Lamont-Executive-Orders/Executive-Order-No-7D.pdf?la=en
- Executive Order No. 7E Takes Several Emergency Actions in Response to the COVID-19 Outbreak and the Governor's Civil Preparedness and Public Health Declarations. https://portal.ct.gov/-/media/Office-of-the-Governor/Executive-Orders/Lamont-Executive-Orders/Executive-Order-No-7E.pdf
- Executive Order No. 7F To Mitigate the Spread of COVID-19. https://portal.ct.gov/-/media/Office-of-the-Governor/Executive-Orders/Lamont-Executive-Orders/Executive-Order-No-7F.pdf?la=en
- Executive Order No. 7G Takes Several Emergency Actions. https://portal.ct.gov/-/media/Office-of-the-Governor/Executive-Orders/Lamont-Executive-Orders/Executive-Order-No-7G.pdf

(*continued*)

Appendix 1 (continued)

- Executive Order No. 7H Restrictions on Workplaces for Non-Essential Businesses, Coordinated Response Effort. https://portal.ct.gov/-/media/Office-of-the-Governor/Executive-Orders/Lamont-Executive-Orders/Executive-Order-No-7H.pdf
- Executive Order No. 7I Municipal Operations and Availability of Assistance and Healthcare. https://portal.ct.gov/-/media/Office-of-the-Governor/Executive-Orders/Lamont-Executive-Orders/Executive-Order-No-7I.pdf
- Executive Order No. 7J Clarifying EO No. 7H Regarding Operations at Non-Essential Businesses and Providing for Rapid State Government Emergency Response. https://portal.ct.gov/-/media/Office-of-the-Governor/Executive-Orders/Lamont-Executive-Orders/Executive-Order-No-7J.pdf
- Governor Lamont Uses CTAlert System to Urge Connecticut Residents to 'Stay Safe, Stay Home'. https://portal.ct.gov/Office-of-the-Governor/News/Press-Releases/2020/03-2020/Governor-Lamont-Uses-CTAlert-System-to-Urge-Connecticut-Residents-to-Stay-Safe-Stay-Home
- Executive Order No. 7K Remote Notarization, Suspension of Non-Critical Probate and Workers' Compensation Operations, and Various Public Health Measures. https://portal.ct.gov/-/media/Office-of-the-Governor/Executive-Orders/Lamont-Executive-Orders/Executive-Order-No-7K.pdf
- Executive Order No. 7L Extension of School Cancellation, Municipal Retiree Reemployment, Open Fishing Season and Additional Public Health Measures. https://portal.ct.gov/-/media/Office-of-the-Governor/Executive-Orders/Lamont-Executive-Orders/Executive-Order-No-7L.pdf
- Executive Order No. 7M Extension of Agency Administrative Deadlines. https://portal.ct.gov/-/media/Office-of-the-Governor/Executive-Orders/Lamont-Executive-Orders/Executive-Order-No-7M.pdf
- Governor Lamont Launches Emergency No-Interest Loan Program for Connecticut Small Businesses and Nonprofits Impacted by COVID-19. https://portal.ct.gov/Office-of-the-Governor/News/Press-Releases/2020/03-2020/Governor-Lamont-Launches-Emergency-No-Interest-Loan-Program-for-Small-Businesses-and-Nonprofits
- Executive Order No. 7N Increased Distancing, Expanded Family Assistance, and Academic Assessment Suspension. https://portal.ct.gov/-/media/Office-of-the-Governor/Executive-Orders/Lamont-Executive-Orders/Executive-Order-No-7N.pdf

Delaware

- State of Emergency Declared. https://governor.delaware.gov/wp-content/uploads/sites/24/2020/03/State-of-Emergency_03122020.pdf
- Governor Modified March 12 Emergency Declaration to Limit Delaware Restaurants, Taverns and Bars to Take-out and Delivery Only and Also Bans Public Gatherings of 50 or More People. https://governor.delaware.gov/state-of-emergency_modified-03162020/
- Governor Carney Announces HELP Program to Support Delaware Small Businesses. https://news.delaware.gov/2020/03/18/governor-carney-announces-help-program-to-support-delaware-small-businesses/

(*continued*)

Appendix 1 (continued)

- Governor Carney Issues Second Update to Emergency Declaration. https://governor.delaware.gov/wp-content/uploads/sites/24/2020/03/Second-Modification-to-the-State-of-Emergency.pdf
- Executive Order No. 38 Child Care. https://governor.delaware.gov/wp-content/uploads/sites/24/2020/03/EO-38_Expand-Access-to-Child-Care.pdf
- Governor Carney Issues Third Update to State of Emergency. https://news.delaware.gov/2020/03/21/governor-carney-issues-third-update-to-state-of-emergency/
- Fourth Modification of the Declaration of a State of Emergency (Closing Non-essential Businesses). https://governor.delaware.gov/wp-content/uploads/sites/24/2020/03/Fourth-Modification-to-State-of-Emergency-03222020.pdf
- Fifth Modification of the Declaration of a State of Emergency (Stay-at-Home Order). https://governor.delaware.gov/wp-content/uploads/sites/24/2020/03/Fifth-Modification-to-State-of-Emergency-03222020.pdf
- Governor Carney Declares Public Health Emergency. https://governor.delaware.gov/wp-content/uploads/sites/24/2020/03/Public-Health-Emergency-Order-03.23.20.pdf
- Sixth Modification of the Declaration of a State of Emergency. https://governor.delaware.gov/wp-content/uploads/sites/24/2020/03/Sixth-Modification-to-State-of-Emergency-03242020.pdf
- Governor Carney Closes Delaware Schools Through May 15. https://news.delaware.gov/2020/03/23/governor-carney-closes-delaware-schools-through-may-15/
- Governor Carney Announces Request for Assistance from Vendors. https://news.delaware.gov/2020/03/25/governor-carney-announces-request-for-assistance-from-vendors/
- Governor Carney Expands Hospital Emergency Loan Program. https://news.delaware.gov/2020/03/26/governor-carney-expands-hospitality-emergency-loan-program-h-e-l-p/
- Governor Carney and DSHA Announce Housing Assistance Program. https://news.delaware.gov/2020/03/26/governor-carney-and-dsha-announce-housing-assistance-program/

Florida

- Executive Order 20-51 Re: Public Health Emergency. https://www.flgov.com/wp-content/uploads/orders/2020/EO_20-51.pdf
- Executive Order 20-52 Re: Public Health Emergency. https://www.flgov.com/wp-content/uploads/orders/2020/EO_20-52.pdf
- Executive Order Number 20-68 re: Emergency Management—COVID-19 Regarding Bars, Beaches, and Restaurants. https://www.flgov.com/wp-content/uploads/orders/2020/EO_20-68.pdf
- Executive Order Number 2020-69 Local Government Public Meetings. https://www.flgov.com/wp-content/uploads/orders/2020/EO_20-69.pdf
- Executive Order Number 20-70 Broward and Palm Beach County Closures. https://www.flgov.com/wp-content/uploads/orders/2020/EO_20-70.pdf
- Executive Order 20-71 Alcohol Sales, Restaurants, and Gyms. https://www.flgov.com/wp-content/uploads/orders/2020/EO_20-71.pdf
- Executive Order Number 20-72 Non-essential Elective Medical Procedures. https://www.flgov.com/wp-content/uploads/orders/2020/EO_20-72.pdf

(*continued*)

Appendix 1 (continued)

- Governor DeSantis Announces First Two Emergency Bridge Loans for Small Businesses Impacted by COVID-19. https://www.flgov.com/2020/03/20/governor-ron-desantis-announces-first-two-emergency-bridge-loans-for-small-businesses-impacted-by-covid-19/
- Executive Order Number 20-80 Airport Screening and Isolation. https://www.flgov.com/wp-content/uploads/orders/2020/EO_20-80.pdf
- Executive Order Number 20-82 Isolation of Individuals Traveling to Florida. https://www.flgov.com/wp-content/uploads/orders/2020/EO_20-82.pdf
- Executive Order 20-83 Protective Measures for Vulnerable Populations, Gatherings of Private Citizens and Density of the Workforce. https://www.flgov.com/wp-content/uploads/orders/2020/EO_20-83.pdf

Georgia

- State of Emergency Declared. https://gov.georgia.gov/document/2020-executive-order/03142001/download
- 03.14.20.01 Declaration of Public Health State of Emergency. https://gov.georgia.gov/document/2020-executive-order/03142001/download
- 03.14.30.02 Authorizing the call of the Georgia National Guard to State Active Duty for Preparation and Response for Novel Coronavirus (COVID-19). https://gov.georgia.gov/document/2020-executive-order/3142002/download
- 03.16.20.01 Closing Public Elementary, Secondary, and Post-secondary Schools from March 18, 2020 to March 31, 2020 to Stop the Spread of COVID-19. https://gov.georgia.gov/executive-action/executive-orders-0/2020-executive-orders
- Governor Kemp Announces Coronavirus Task Force Subcommittees. https://gov.georgia.gov/press-releases/2020-03-12/gov-kemp-urges-calm-announces-coronavirus-task-force-subcommittees
- 03.20.20.02 Reducing Regulations to Assist the State's Response to the Spread of COVID-19. https://gov.georgia.gov/executive-action/executive-orders/2020-executive-orders
- 03.20.20.01 Authorizing a Transfer from the Governor's Emergency Fund. https://gov.georgia.gov/executive-action/executive-orders/2020-executive-orders
- 03.23.20.02 Expanding Temporary Licensing of Certain Medical Professions to Assist State's Response to the Spread of COVID-19. https://gov.georgia.gov/executive-action/executive-orders/2020-executive-orders
- 03.23.20.01 Limiting Large Gatherings Statewide, Ordering "Shelter in Place" for Specific Populations, and Closing Bars and Nightclubs in Georgia for Fourteen Days. https://gov.georgia.gov/executive-action/executive-orders/2020-executive-orders
- 03.24.20.01 Reducing Restrictions for Child Care Learning Centers and Family Child Learning Homes to Assist in the State's Response to COVID-19
- 03.25.20.01 Regarding Georgia's Driver's Licenses and Identification Cards, Ignition Interlock Device Requirements. https://gov.georgia.gov/executive-action/executive-orders/2020-executive-orders

(*continued*)

Appendix 1 (continued)

- 03.26.20.02 Closing Public Elementary and Secondary Schools Through April 24, 2020 to Stop the Spread of COVID-19
- 03.26.20.01 Regarding Unemployment Insurance Claims to Assist in the State's Response to COVID-19. https://gov.georgia.gov/executive-action/executive-orders/2020-executive-orders

Hawaii

- State of Emergency Declared. https://dod.hawaii.gov/hiema/emergency-proclamation-covid-19/
- Governor Ige Issues Supplemental Emergency Proclamation to Fight COVID-19. https://governor.hawaii.gov/wp-content/uploads/2020/03/2003109-ATG_COVID-19-Supplementary-Proclamation-signed.pdf
- Governor Ige Announces State Actions to Slow the Spread of COVID-19. https://governor.hawaii.gov/newsroom/latest-news/proper-use-of-covid-19-tests-imperative-there-is-a-current-shortage-of-hand-sanitizers-and-toilet-paper-in-hawaii-in-part-because-of-the-publics-over-reaction-to-covid-19-the-hawai/
- Governor Ige Urges Visitors to Stay Away for 30 Days; All Non-Essential State Workers to Stay Home
- Governor Ige Announces Measures to Address Economic Impact of COVID-19. https://governor.hawaii.gov/newsroom/latest-news/governors-office-gov-ige-announces-measures-to-address-economic-impact-of-covid-19/
- Second Supplementary Proclamation. https://governor.hawaii.gov/wp-content/uploads/2020/03/2003152-ATG_Second-Supplementary-Proclamation-for-COVID-19-signed.pdf
- Governor Ige Orders Mandatory 14-Day Quarantine for All Individuals Arriving or Returning to the State of Hawaii. https://governor.hawaii.gov/newsroom/latest-news/governors-office-news-release-gov-ige-orders-mandatory-14-day-quarantine-for-all-individuals-arriving-or-returning-to-the-state-of-hawai%ca%bbi/
- Third Supplementary Proclamation. https://governor.hawaii.gov/wp-content/uploads/2020/03/2003162-ATG_Third-Supplementary-Proclamation-for-COVID-19-signed.pdf
- Executive Order 20-01. https://governor.hawaii.gov/wp-content/uploads/2020/03/2003177.pdf

IDAHO

- State of Emergency Declared. https://gov.idaho.gov/wp-content/uploads/sites/74/2020/03/covid-19-declaration_final.pdf
- Governor, Legislature Advance Additional $1.3 million to Ensure Continuity of Essential Government Services amid Coronavirus Concerns. https://gov.idaho.gov/pressrelease/governor-legislature-advance-additional-1-3-million-to-ensure-continuity-of-essential-government-services-amid-coronavirus-concerns/

(*continued*)

Appendix 1 (continued)

- Proclamation Waiving 125 Agency Rules. https://coronavirus.idaho.gov/wp-content/uploads/sites/127/2020/03/proclamation_agency-rules_032320.pdf
- Proclamation Extending State Income Tax Filing Deadline. https://coronavirus.idaho.gov/wp-content/uploads/sites/127/2020/03/proclamation_tax-deadline_032320.pdf
- Governor Little Signs Extreme Emergency Declaration. https://coronavirus.idaho.gov/wp-content/uploads/sites/127/2020/03/proclamation_extreme-emergency-declaration_032520.pdf
- Governor Little Issues Statewide Stay-home Order. https://gov.idaho.gov/pressrelease/governor-little-issues-statewide-stay-home-order-signs-extreme-emergency-declaration/

Illinois

- State of Emergency Declared. https://www2.illinois.gov/sites/gov/Documents/APPROVED-CoronavirusDisasterProcWORD.pdf
- Executive Order 2020-03 Executive Order to Extend Application Deadline for Adult-Use Applications Due to COVID-19. https://www2.illinois.gov/Documents/ExecOrders/2020/ExecutiveOrder-2020-03.pdf
- Executive Order 2020-04 Cancelling of Large Gatherings. https://www2.illinois.gov/Documents/ExecOrders/2020/ExecutiveOrder-2020-04.pdf
- Executive Order 2020-05 Order Closing Public and Private Schools. https://www2.illinois.gov/Documents/ExecOrders/2020/ExecutiveOrder-2020-05.pdf
- Executive Order 2020-06 Closure of Schools. https://www2.illinois.gov/Documents/ExecOrders/2020/ExecutiveOrder-2020-06.pdf
- Executive Order 2020-07 Closure of Restaurants and Bars Through March 30. https://www2.illinois.gov/Documents/ExecOrders/2020/ExecutiveOrder-2020-07.pdf
- Executive Order 20-08. https://www2.illinois.gov/Documents/ExecOrders/2020/ExecutiveOrder-2020-08.pdf
- Executive Order No. 20-09. https://www2.illinois.gov/Documents/ExecOrders/2020/ExecutiveOrder-2020-09.pdf
- Governor Pritzker Waives Overweight Permit Fees for Transportation of Emergency Relief Supplies. https://www2.illinois.gov/Pages/news-item.aspx?ReleaseID=21265
- Governor Pritzker Announces Series of New Measures to Help Illinoisans Affected by COVID-19. https://www2.illinois.gov/Pages/news-item.aspx?ReleaseID=21284
- Executive Order 20-10 (Stay at Home Order). https://www2.illinois.gov/Documents/ExecOrders/2020/ExecutiveOrder-2020-10.pdf
- Executive Order 20-11 Essential Human Services Operations. https://www2.illinois.gov/Pages/Executive-Orders/ExecutiveOrder2020-11.aspx
- Executive Order 20-12 Suspends Healthcare Worker's Background Checks. https://www2.illinois.gov/Pages/Executive-Orders/ExecutiveOrder2020-12.aspx
- Governor Pritzker Announces Income Tax Filing Extension, More Than $90 Million in Small Business Aid. https://www2.illinois.gov/Pages/news-item.aspx?ReleaseID=21301

(*continued*)

Appendix 1 (continued)

- Executive Order 20-13 Suspends Admissions to IDOC From County Jails. https://www2.illinois.gov/Pages/Executive-Orders/ExecutiveOrder2020-13.aspx
- Executive Order 20-14 Notary and Witness Guidelines. https://www2.illinois.gov/Pages/Executive-Orders/ExecutiveOrder2020-14.aspx
- Governor Pritzker Partners with United Way of Illinois, Alliance of Illinois Community Foundations to Launch Illinois COVID-19 Response Fund. https://www2.illinois.gov/Pages/news-item.aspx?ReleaseID=21306

Indiana

- State of Emergency Declared. https://www.in.gov/gov/files/20-02ExecutiveOrder(DeclarationofPublicHealthEmergencyforCOVID-19)FINAL.pdf
- Executive Order 20-02 Declaration of Public Health Emergency for Coronavirus Disease 2019 Outbreak. https://www.in.gov/gov/files/20-02ExecutiveOrder(DeclarationofPublicHealthEmergencyforCOVID-19)FINAL.pdf
- Executive Order 20-03 Waiver of Hours of Service Regulations Relating to Motor Carriers and Drivers of Commercial Vehicles Transporting Good to Indiana Business. https://www.in.gov/gov/files/ExecutiveOrder20-03(WaiverofMotorCarrierHoursduetoPublicHealthEmergency).pdf
- Restaurants and bars closed to in-person customers. https://calendar.in.gov/site/gov/event/gov-holcomb-announces-more-steps-to-slow-the-spread-of-covid-19/
- Executive Order 20-04 Further Orders and Directives in Response to the Coronavirus Disease 2019 Epidemic. https://www.in.gov/gov/files/ExecutiveOrder20-04FurtherOrdersforPublicHealthEmergency.pdf
- Executive Order 20-05 Helping Hoosiers During the Public Health Emergency Declared for the Coronavirus 2019 Disease Outbreak. https://www.in.gov/gov/files/EO_20-05.pdf
- Executive Order 20-06 Temporary Prohibition on Eviction and Foreclosures. https://www.in.gov/gov/files/EO_20-06.pdf
- Executive Order 20-07 Rescheduling the Primary Election Due to Public Health Emergency. https://www.in.gov/gov/files/EO_20-07_Rescheduling_Primary.pdf
- Executive Order 20-08 Directive for Hoosiers to Stay at Home. https://www.in.gov/gov/files/Executive_Order_20-08_Stay_at_Home.pdf
- Executive Order 20-09 Relating to the Continuity of Operation of Government. https://www.in.gov/gov/files/ExecutiveOrder20-09(ContinuityofGovernmentOperations).pdf
- Executive Order 20-10 Enforcement Directive Regarding Prohibition of In-Person Dining. https://www.in.gov/gov/files/ExecutiveOrder20-10(EnforcementofIn-PersonDiningProhibition).pdf
- Executive Order 20-11 Relating to Carryout Consumption of Alcohol. https://www.in.gov/gov/files/ExecutiveOrder20-11(CarryoutConsumptionofAlcohol).pdf
- Executive Order 20-12 Further Provisions for Helping Hoosiers During the COVID-19 Public Health Emergency. https://www.in.gov/gov/files/EO_20-12_Further_Directives_Helping_Hoosiers.pdf

(*continued*)

Appendix 1 (continued)

Iowa

- State of Emergency Declared. https://www.homelandsecurity.iowa.gov/documents/disasters/Proclamations/2020/PROC_2020_32_COVID-19_March9.pdf
- Proclamation of Disaster Emergency—Suspending Provisions Restricting the Movement of Oversize and Overweight Loads of Food, Medical Supplies, Cleaning Products, etc. https://governor.iowa.gov/sites/default/files/documents/20200313162458165.pdf
- Governor Reynolds Signs Legislation to Fund Key Services, Combat COVID-19 Spread. https://governor.iowa.gov/press-release/gov-reynolds-signs-legislation-to-fund-key-services-combat-covid19-spread
- Governor Reynolds Signs Legislation Expanding Roles for physician Assistants. https://governor.iowa.gov/press-release/gov-reynolds-signs-legislation-expanding-roles-for-physician-assistants
- Governor Reynolds Signs Additional State Public Health Emergency Declaration. https://governor.iowa.gov/sites/default/files/documents/PublicHealthProclamation-2020.03.19.pdf
- Governor Reynolds Signs New Proclamation Continuing State Public Health Declaration. https://governor.iowa.gov/sites/default/files/documents/PublicHealthProclamation-2020.03.22.pdf
- Governor Reynolds Announces Unemployment Insurance Tax Extension to Assist Small Businesses. https://governor.iowa.gov/press-release/gov-reynolds-announces-unemployment-insurance-tax-extension-to-assist-small
- Governor Reynolds Signs New Proclamation Continuing State Public Health Emergency Declaration. https://governor.iowa.gov/sites/default/files/documents/PublicHealthProclamation-2020.03.26.pdf

Kansas

- State of Emergency Declared. https://governor.kansas.gov/wp-content/uploads/2020/03/2020-03-12-Proclamation.pdf
- Executive Order No. 20-03 Extending States of Local Disaster Emergency Relating to COVID-19. https://governor.kansas.gov/wp-content/uploads/2020/03/20-03-Executed.pdf
- Executive Order No. 20-04 Temporarily Prohibiting Mass Gatherings to Limit the Spread of COVID-19. https://governor.kansas.gov/wp-content/uploads/2020/03/20-04-Executed.pdf
- Executive Order No. 20-05 Temporarily Prohibiting Utility and Internet Disconnects. https://governor.kansas.gov/wp-content/uploads/2020/03/20-05-Executed.pdf
- Executive Order No. 20-06 Temporarily Prohibiting Evictions and Foreclosures.
- Executive Order 20-07 Temporarily Closing K-12 Schools to Slow the Spread of COVID-19. https://governor.kansas.gov/executive-order-20-07/
- Governor Signs Bipartisan Bills to help Kansans During COVID-19 Pandemic. https://governor.kansas.gov/governor-signs-bipartisan-bills-to-help-kansans-during-covid-19-pandemic/

(*continued*)

Appendix 1 (continued)

- Governor Laura Kelly Announces Disaster Assistance for Kansas Businesses and Discusses Banks, Unemployment. https://governor.kansas.gov/governor-laura-kelly-announces-disaster-assistance-for-kansas-businesses-and-discusses-banks-unemployment/
- Executive Order 20-08 Temporarily Expanding Telemedicine and Addressing Certain Licensing Requirements to Combat the Effects of COVID-19. https://governor.kansas.gov/wp-content/uploads/2020/03/E.O.-20-08.pdf
- Executive Order 20-09 Conditional and Temporary Relief from Certain Motor Carrier Rules and Regulations in Response to the COVID-19 Pandemic. https://governor.kansas.gov/wp-content/uploads/2020/03/E.O.-20-09.pdf
- Executive Order 20-10 Rescinding EO 20-06 and Temporarily Prohibiting Certain Foreclosures and Evictions. https://governor.kansas.gov/wp-content/uploads/2020/03/EO-20-10-Executed.pdf
- Executive Order 20-11 Temporarily Requiring Continuation of Waste Removal and Recycling Services. https://governor.kansas.gov/wp-content/uploads/2020/03/EO-20-11-Executed.pdf
- Executive Order 20-12 Drivers' License and Vehicle Registration and Regulation During Public Health Emergency. https://governor.kansas.gov/wp-content/uploads/2020/03/EO-20-12-Executed.pdf
- Executive Order 20-13 Allowing Certain Deferred Tax Deadlines and Payments During the COVID-19 Pandemic. https://governor.kansas.gov/wp-content/uploads/2020/03/EO-20-13-Executed.pdf
- Executive Order 20-14 Temporarily Prohibiting Mass Gatherings of 10 or More People to Limit the Spread of COVID-19 and Rescinding Executive Order 20-04. https://governor.kansas.gov/wp-content/uploads/2020/03/EO-20-14-Executed.pdf
- Executive Order 20-15 Establishing the Kansas Essential Function Framework for COVID-19 Response Efforts. https://governor.kansas.gov/wp-content/uploads/2020/03/EO-20-15-Executed.pdf

Kentucky

- State of Emergency Declared. https://governor.ky.gov/attachments/20200306_Executive-Order_2020-215.pdf
- Executive Order 2020-0215 State of Emergency due to the Novel Corona Virus. https://governor.ky.gov/attachments/20200306_Executive-Order_2020-215.pdf
- Executive Order 2020-0220 State of Emergency Relating to Insurance. http://apps.sos.ky.gov/Executive/Journal/execjournalimages/2020-MISC-2020-0220-266317.pdf
- Executive Order 2020-0224 State of Emergency Relating to the Dispensing of Pharmaceuticals. http://apps.sos.ky.gov/Executive/Journal/execjournalimages/2020-MISC-2020-0224-266318.pdf
- Executive Order 2020-0216 State of Emergency Relating to the Prohibition Against Price Gouging. http://apps.sos.ky.gov/executive/journal/(S(bbwhi1yjweblaikprwv01f0v))/journal2.aspx

(*continued*)

Appendix 1 (continued)

- Outlining Specific Steps All Public-facing Businesses Should Take Regarding Closures Executive Order 2020-215. https://governor.ky.gov/attachments/20200317_Order_Public-Facing-Businesses.pdf
- Executive Order 2020-0243 State of Emergency Relating to Social Distancing. http://apps.sos.ky.gov/executive/journal/(S(5boylojbklxcqggx4nql5tl2))/journal2.aspx
- Executive Order 2020-0317 Public-Facing Business Closure. https://governor.ky.gov/attachments/20200317_Order_Public-Facing-Businesses.pdf
- Letter Prohibiting Mass Gatherings. https://governor.ky.gov/attachments/20200319_Order_Mass-Gatherings.pdf
- Executive Order 2020-246 Closing Nonessential Retail. https://governor.ky.gov/attachments/20200322_Executive-Order_2020-246_Retail.pdf
- Executive Order 2020-00319 Order Permitting Carryout and Drive Thru Sales. https://governor.ky.gov/attachments/20200319_Order_Permitting-Carryout-and-Drive-Thru-Sales.pdf
- Ordering Ceasing all Elective Medical Procedures. https://governor.ky.gov/attachments/20200323_Directive_Elective-Procedures.pdf
- Executive Order 2020-257 Closing all but Life-Sustaining Business. https://governor.ky.gov/attachments/20200325_Executive-Order_2020-257_Healthy-at-Home.pdf

Louisiana

- State of Emergency Declared ()
- Proclamation No. JBE 2020-28- Elections Rescheduled due to COVID-19. https://gov.louisiana.gov/assets/Proclamations/2020/28-JBE-2020-Special-Elections-COVID-19-Postponement.pdf
- Proclamation No. JBE 2020-29 COVID 19 Additional Measures RE: Transportation. https://gov.louisiana.gov/assets/Proclamations/2020/29-JBE-2020-Public-Health-Emergency-COVID-19.pdf
- Proclamation No. JBE-2020-30 COVID-19 Additional Measurers. https://gov.louisiana.gov/assets/Proclamations/2020/Proc-No-30-updTED.pdf
- Proclamation No. JBE 2020-32 Additional Measures for COVID-19 Public Health Emergency. https://gov.louisiana.gov/assets/Proclamations/2020/32-JBE-2020-Public-Health-Emergency.pdf
- Proclamation No. JBE 2020-23 Additional Measures for COVID-19 Stay at Home. https://gov.louisiana.gov/assets/Proclamations/2020/33-JBE-2020-Public-Health-Emergency.pdf
- Proclamation No. 33 JBE 2020 Additional Measures for COVID-19 Stay at Home. https://gov.louisiana.gov/assets/Proclamations/2020/modified/33-JBE-2020-Public-Health-Emergency-COVID.pdf

Maine

- State of Emergency Declared. https://www.maine.gov/governor/mills/sites/maine.gov.governor.mills/files/inline-files/ProclamationofStateofCivilEmergencyToFurtherProtectPublicHealth.pdf

(*continued*)

Appendix 1 (continued)

- Proclamation of Insurance Emergency. https://www.maine.gov/governor/mills/sites/maine.gov.governor.mills/files/inline-files/ProclamationofInsuranceEmergency-March12th.pdf
- Proclamation Declaring Abnormal Market Disruption Caused by COVID-19 Emergency. https://www.maine.gov/governor/mills/sites/maine.gov.governor.mills/files/inline-files/ProclamationDeclaringAbnormalMarketDisruptionEmergency-March17th.pdf
- Vehicle Weights Limits. https://governor.maryland.gov/2020/03/19/vehicle-weights-limits/
- Executive Order 14: An Order to Protect Public Health. https://www.maine.gov/governor/mills/sites/maine.gov.governor.mills/files/inline-files/EO14AnOrdertoProtectPublicHealth.pdf
- Executive Order 15: An Order Regarding School Readiness. https://www.maine.gov/governor/mills/sites/maine.gov.governor.mills/files/inline-files/EO15AnOrderRegardingSchoolReadiness.pdf
- Executive Order 16: An Order Suspending Provisions of Certain Health Care Professional Licensing Statutes and Rules in Order to Facilitate the Treatment and Containment of COVID-19. https://www.maine.gov/governor/mills/sites/maine.gov.governor.mills/files/inline-files/EO16AnOrderSuspendingProvisionsofCertainHCProfessionalLicensing.pdf
- Executive Order 17: An Order Regarding Certain Laws Enforced by Inland Fish & Wildlife. https://www.maine.gov/governor/mills/sites/maine.gov.governor.mills/files/inline-files/EO17AnOrderRegardingCertainLawsEnforcedbyIFW.pdf
- Executive Order 18: An Order Extending Compliance Dates Under Certain Motor Vehicle Laws. https://www.maine.gov/governor/mills/sites/maine.gov.governor.mills/files/inline-files/EO18AnOrderExtendingComplianceDatesUnderCertainMotorVehicleLaws.pdf
- Executive Order 19: An Order Regarding Essential Businesses and Operations. https://www.maine.gov/governor/mills/sites/maine.gov.governor.mills/files/inline-files/AnOrderRegardingEssentialBusinessesandOperations_0.pdf

Maryland

- State of Emergency Declared. https://governor.maryland.gov/wp-content/uploads/2020/03/Proclamation-COVID-19.pdf
- Ordering Extending Certain Licenses, Permits, Registrations, and Other Governmental Authorizations, and Authorizing Suspension of Legal Time Requirements. https://governor.maryland.gov/wp-content/uploads/2020/03/Licenses-Permits-Registration.pdf
- Order Calling the Maryland National Guard into State Active Duty. https://governor.maryland.gov/wp-content/uploads/2020/03/National-Guard.pdf
- Order for Implementation of Elevated Level II of Pandemic Flu and Other Infectious Diseases Attendance and Leave Policy for Executive Branch Employees. https://governor.maryland.gov/wp-content/uploads/2020/03/Elevated-Level-II.pdf

(*continued*)

Appendix 1 (continued)

- Order Prohibiting the Movement of Persons to and from Certain Vessels Berthing at Terminals and Port Facilities in the Ports and Harbors of the State. https://governor.maryland.gov/wp-content/uploads/2020/03/Prohibiting-Movement.pdf
- Order Prohibiting Large Gatherings and Events and Closing Senior Centers. https://governor.maryland.gov/wp-content/uploads/2020/03/Prohibiting-Large-Gatherings.pdf
- Emergency Order Closing Casinos, Racetracks and Simulcast Betting Facilities. https://governor.maryland.gov/wp-content/uploads/2020/03/Casino-Racetrack-OTB-Closure-Order-1.pdf
- Emergency Order Expanding Child Care Access. https://governor.maryland.gov/wp-content/uploads/2020/03/Day-Care-Order.pdf
- Order Amending Prohibition of Large Gatherings. https://governor.maryland.gov/wp-content/uploads/2020/03/Executive-Order-Amending-Large-Gatherings.pdf
- Order Relating to Various Health Care Matters. https://governor.maryland.gov/wp-content/uploads/2020/03/Executive-Order-Health-Care-Matters.pdf
- Prohibiting Termination of Residential Services and Late Fees. https://governor.maryland.gov/category/executiveorders/
- Temporarily Prohibiting Evictions. https://governor.maryland.gov/wp-content/uploads/2020/03/Executive-Order-Temp-Evictions-Prohibiting.pdf
- Emergency Medical Services. https://governor.maryland.gov/wp-content/uploads/2020/03/Emergency-Medical-Services.pdf
- Beverage Delivery. https://governor.maryland.gov/wp-content/uploads/2020/03/Beverage-Delivery.pdf
- Restricting Gatherings Amended. https://governor.maryland.gov/wp-content/uploads/2020/03/Amending-Gatherings.pdf
- Lab Authorization. https://governor.maryland.gov/wp-content/uploads/2020/03/Lab-Authorization-3.23.20.pdf
- Price Gouging. https://governor.maryland.gov/wp-content/uploads/2020/03/Price-Gouging-3.23.20.pdf
- Essential Businesses. https://governor.maryland.gov/wp-content/uploads/2020/03/Gatherings-THIRD-AMENDED-3.23.20.pdf
- Authorizing Reimbursement for Telehealth. https://governor.maryland.gov/wp-content/uploads/2020/03/Medicaid-Telehealth-3.20.20.pdf
- Prohibiting Price Gouging. https://governor.maryland.gov/wp-content/uploads/2020/03/Price-Gouging-3.23.20.pdf
- Child Care for Essential Personnel. https://governor.maryland.gov/wp-content/uploads/2020/03/Child-Care-Access.pdf

Massachusetts

- State of Emergency Declared. https://archives.lib.state.ma.us/bitstream/handle/2452/824410/ocn456714827-2019-eo591.pdf?sequence=1&isAllowed=y
- Order Prohibiting Gatherings of More than 250 People. https://www.mass.gov/doc/order-prohibiting-gatherings-of-more-than-250-people/download

(*continued*)

Appendix 1 (continued)

- Order Extending the Registration of Certain Licensed Health Care Professionals. https://www.mass.gov/doc/march-17-2020-registration-of-health-care-professionals-order/download
- Order Expanding Access to Physician Services. https://www.mass.gov/doc/march-17-2020-expand-access-to-physician-services-order/download
- Order of the Commissioner of Public Health Regarding the Administration of Certain Medications for the Treatment of Opioid Use Disorder. https://www.mass.gov/doc/march-18-2020-pharmacist-opioid-misuse-disorder-medication/download
- Order of the Commissioner of Public Health Regarding the Flexible Reassignment of Physician Assistants. https://www.mass.gov/doc/march-18-2020-physician-assistant-order/download
- Order of the Commissioner of Public Health Providing for Continuity of Emergency Medical Services Care. https://www.mass.gov/doc/march-17-2020-ems-care-order/download
- Order Temporarily Closing All Public and Private Elementary and Secondary Schools. https://www.mass.gov/doc/march-16-2020-k-12-school-closing-order/download
- Order Expanding Access to Telehealth Services and to Protect Health Care Providers. https://www.mass.gov/doc/march-15-2020-telehealth-order/download
- Order Suspending Certain Provisions of the Open Meeting Law. https://www.mass.gov/doc/open-meeting-law-order-march-12-2020/download
- Sharing of Critical Information with First Responders
- Temporarily Closing all Child Care Programs. https://www.mass.gov/doc/order-of-the-commissioner-of-public-health-regarding-the-sharing-of-critical-information-with/download
- Ordering Nonessential Businesses and Organizations to Close Their Physical Workspaces and Facilities to Customers, Workers and the Public. https://www.mass.gov/doc/march-23-2020-essential-services-and-revised-gatherings-order
- Ordering Permitting the Temporary Conditional Deferral of Certain Inspections of Residential Real Estate.
- Order Authorizing Actions to Reduce In-Person Transactions Associated with the Licensing, Registration and Inspection of Motor Vehicles. https://www.mass.gov/doc/march-20-2020-rmv-order/download
- Department of Public Health Order Regarding Modification of Certain Requirements for Inspections by the Chief Medical Examiner. https://www.mass.gov/doc/cremation-viewing-order/download
- Department of Public Health Order Permitting Facilities Licensed by the Massachusetts Cannabis Control Commission to Create and Donate Hand Sanitizer to Certain Entities. https://www.mass.gov/doc/ccc-hand-sanitizer-order/download
- Emergency Order Ordering Nonessential Businesses and Organizations to Close their Physical Workspaces and Facilities to Customers, Workers and the Public. https://www.mass.gov/info-details/covid-19-state-of-emergency
- Department of Public Health Emergency Order Regarding Provision of Day Program Services Provided in Group Settings. https://www.mass.gov/doc/order/download

(*continued*)

Appendix 1 (continued)

- Department of Public Health Issued an Emergency Order Regarding Provision of Day Program Services Provided in Group Settings. https://www.mass.gov/doc/order/download
- Department of Public Health Issued an Emergency Order Regarding Modifications to Pharmacy Practice. https://www.mass.gov/doc/pharmacy-practice-order/download
- Department of Public Health Issued an Emergency Order Exempting Certain Activities from Determination of Need Approval, that are Necessary to Address COVID-19. https://www.mass.gov/doc/don-order/download
- Department of Public Health Issued an Emergency Order Exempting Hospitals from the Nurse Staffing Requirements of M.G.L. c. 111, §231. https://www.mass.gov/doc/nursing-staff-order/download
- Department of Public Health Issued an Emergency Order Addressing Operation of Grocery Stores and Pharmacies. https://www.mass.gov/doc/grocery-and-pharmacy-store-order/download

Michigan

- State of Emergency Declared. https://www.michigan.gov/whitmer/0,9309,7-387-90499_90705-521576--,00.html
- Executive Order No. 2020-5 Temporary Prohibition on Large Assemblages and Events, Temporary School Closures. https://www.michigan.gov/whitmer/0,9309,7-387-90499_90705-521595--,00.html
- Executive Order No. 2020-7 Temporary Restrictions on Entry into Health Care Facilities, Residential Care Facilities, Congregate Care Facilities and Juvenile Justice Facilities ()
- Executive Order No. 2020-8 Enhanced Restrictions on Price Gouging ()
- Executive Order No. 2020-9 Temporary Restrictions on the Use of Places of Public Accommodation ()
- Executive Order 2020-10 Temporary Expansions in Unemployment Eligibility and Cost-sharing ()
- Executive Order 2020-11 Temporary Prohibition on Large Assemblages and Events, Temporary School Closures ()
- Executive Order 2020-12 Enhanced Support for Deliveries ()
- Temporary Enhancements to Operational Capacity and Efficiency of Health Care Facilities ()
- Executive Order 2020-14 Temporary Extension of Deadline to Redeem Property for Nonpayment of Delinquent Property Taxes ()
- Executive Order 2020-15 Temporary Authorization of Remote Participation in Public Meetings and Hearings and Temporary Relief from Monthly Meeting Requirements for School Boards ()
- No. 2020-16 Expanding Child Care Access During the COVID-19 Emergency ()
- Executive Order No. 2020-17 Temporary Restrictions on Non-essential Medical and Dental Procedures ()
- Executive Order No. 2020-18 Enhanced Restrictions on Price Gouging ()

(*continued*)

Appendix 1 (continued)

- Executive Order No. 2020-19 Temporary Prohibition Against Entry to Premises for the Purpose of Removing or Excluding a Tenant or Mobile Home Owner from Their Home ()
- Executive Order No. 2020-20 Temporary Restrictions on the Use of Places of Public Accommodation ()
- No. 2020-21 Temporary Requirement to Suspend Activities That Are Not Necessary to Sustain or Protect Life ()
- No. 2020-22 Extension of County Canvass Deadlines for the March 10, 2020 Presidential Primary Election ()
- No. 2020-23 Enhanced Authorization of Remote Means for Carrying out State Administrative Procedures ()
- No. 2020-24 Temporary Expansions in Unemployment Eligibility and Cost-sharing Rescission of Executive Order 2020-10 ()

Minnesota

- State of Emergency Declared ()
- Emergency Executive Order 20-02 Authorizing and Directing the Commissioner of Education to Temporarily Close Schools to Plan for a Safe Educational Environment ()
- Executive Order 20-03 Protecting Residents of Minnesota Veterans Homes during the COVID-19 Peacetime Emergency ()
- Executive Order 20-04 Providing for Temporary Closure of Bars, Restaurants and Other Places of Public Accommodation ()
- Executive Order 20-05 Providing Immediate Relief to Employers and Unemployed Workers During the COVID-19 Peacetime Emergency ()
- Executive Order 20-06 Providing for Emergency Relief from Regulations to Motor Carriers and Drivers Operating in Minnesota ()
- Executive Order 20-07 Providing for State Workforce Needs During the COVID-19 Peacetime Emergency ()
- Executive Order 20-08 Clarifying Public Accommodations Subject to Executive Order 20-04 ()
- Executive Order 20-09 Directing Delay of Inpatient and Outpatient Elective Surgery and Procedural Cases during COVID-19 Peacetime Emergency ()
- Executive Order 20-10 Combatting Price Gouging During the COVID-19 Peacetime Emergency ()
- Executive Order 20-11 Securing Federal Authority to Continue Human Services Programs During the COVID-19 Peacetime Emergency ()
- Executive Order 20-12 Preserving Access to Human Services Programs During the COVID-19 Peacetime Emergency ()
- Emergency Executive Order 20-13 Authorizing National Guard Assistance to COVID-19 Response ()
- Emergency Executive Order 20-14 Suspending Evictions and Writs of Recovery During the COVID-19 Peacetime Emergency ()
- Emergency Executive Order 20-15 Providing Immediate Relief to Small Businesses During the COVID-19 Peacetime Emergency ()

(*continued*)

Appendix 1 (continued)

- Emergency Executive Order 20-16 Directing Non-Hospital Entities to Inventory and Preserve Vital Medical Equipment During the COVID-19 Peacetime Emergency ()
- Emergency Executive Order 20-17 Clarifying Application of Executive Order 20-09 to Veterinary Surgeries and Procedures ()
- Emergency Executive Order 20-18 Continuing the Closure of Bars, Restaurants, and Other Places of Public Accommodation ()
- Emergency Executive Order 20-19 Authorizing and Directing the Commissioner of Education to Implement a Distance Learning Period and Continue to Provide a Safe Learning Environment for Minnesota's Students ()
- Emergency Executive Order 20-20 Directing Minnesotans to Stay at Home ()

Mississippi
- State of Emergency Declared ()
- Executive order No. 1457 Mississippi COVID-19 Preparedness and Response Planning Steering Committee ()
- Executive Order No. 1458 Ensures Paid Leave for State/Local Employees and Determines Essential Employees and Also Directs MDE to Work on Distance Learning Solutions ()
- Executive Order No 1459 Activates the Mississippi National Guard to Support Mobile Testing Units ()
- Executive Order No. 1460 Closure of Public School ()
- Executive Order No. 1461 Congressional Elections Postponement ()
- Executive Order 1462 Tax Deadline Extension, Unemployment ()
- Executive Order 1463 Non-essential Gatherings, Restaurants, Nursing Homes ()

Missouri
- State of Emergency Declared ()
- EXECUTIVE ORDER NO. 20-04 CORONA VIRUS—EMERGENCY UNEMPLOYMENT INSURANCE BENEFIT RELIEF ()
- EXECUTIVE ORDER No. 20–05 CORONA VIRUS—MOTOR VEHICLE TITLING, REGISTRATION & DRIVER LICENSE WAIVER ()
- EXECUTIVE ORDER No. 20-06 CORONA VIRUS—RELIEF FOR RESTAURANT & BAR OPERATIONS ()
- EXECUTIVE ORDER 20-03 Postpones the General Municipal Election scheduled for April 7, 2020 until June 2, 2020 ()
- Executive Order 4 Suspends Certain Agency Regulations to Allow Them to Address the Current State of Emergency ()
- Executive Order 5 Suspends the Prohibition of the Sale of Unprepared Food by Restaurants to the Public During the Current State of Emergency ()

Montana
- State of Emergency Declared ()
- Executive Order 3-2020 Amending Executive Order 2-2020 and Providing that the State of Emergency Runs Concurrent with the President's Emergency Declaration ()

(*continued*)

Appendix 1 (continued)

Nebraska
- State of Emergency Declared ()
- Executive Order 20-01—Emergency Relief Due to COVID-19 ()
- Executive Order 20-02 Out of State Travel Ban ()
- EXECUTIVE ORDER NO. 20-03 CORONA VIRUS- PUBLIC MEETINGS REQUIREMENT LIMITED WAIVER ()
- Executive Order 20-07 Corona Virus—Temporary Residential Eviction Relief ()

Nevada
- State of Emergency Declared ()
- COVID-19 Declaration of Emergency Director 001—School Closure for K-12 COVID-19 ()
- Declaration of Emergency Directive 002—Closing of Gaming Establishments ()
- Declaration of Emergency Directive 003—Closing of Non-Essential Businesses ()
- Declaration of Emergency Directive 004–Closing of DMV and Licensing Regulations ()
- Declaration of Emergency Directive 005—Closing of All Schools Until April 16 ()
- Declaration of Emergency Directive 006—Restrictions on Gatherings ()

New Hampshire
- State of Emergency Declared ()
- Emergency Order #1 Temporary Remote Instruction and Support for Public K-12 School Districts ()
- Emergency Order #3 Temporary Prohibition on Disconnection of Certain Services ()
- Emergency Order #4 Temporary Prohibition on Evictions and Foreclosures ()
- Emergency Order #5 Access to Unemployment Benefits ()
- Emergency Order #6 Temporary authorization for take-out or delivery beer or wine ()
- Emergency Order 7—Temporary modification of data and privacy governance plans ()
- Emergency Order 8—Temporary expansion of access to Telehealth Services to protect the public and health care providers ()
- Emergency Order 9—Establishes the COVID-19 Emergency Healthcare System Relief Fund ()
- Emergency Order 9—Establishes the COVID-19 Emergency Healthcare System Relief Fund ()
- Emergency Order 10—Requiring all Sellers of Groceries to Temporarily Transition to Use of Single Use Paper or Plastic Bags. ()
- Emergency Order #11: Temporary Authority to Perform Secure Remote Online Notarization. ()
- Emergency Order #12: Temporary Modification of Public Access to Meetings under RSA 91-A. ()
- Emergency Order #13: Temporary Allowance for New Hampshire Pharmacists and Pharmacies to Compound and Sell Hand Sanitizer Over the Counter (OTC) and to Allow Pharmacy Technicians to Perform Non-dispensing Tasks Remotely. ()
- Emergency Order #14: Temporary Authorization for Out-of-State Pharmacies to Act as a Licensed Mail-order Facility within the State of New Hampshire ()

(*continued*)

Appendix 1 (continued)

- Emergency Order #15: Temporary Authorization for Out-of-State Medical Providers to Provide Medically Necessary Services and Provide Services Through Telehealth. ()
- Emergency Order #16: Temporary Prohibition of Scheduled Gatherings of 10 or More Attendees. ()
- Emergency Order 17: Closure of Non-essential Businesses and Requiring Granite Staters to Stay at Home ()

New Jersey

- State of Emergency Declared ()
- Executive Order No. 102 Executive Order Establish Coronavirus Task Force ()
- Executive Order No. 103 Declares State of Emergency and a Public Health Emergency, Effective Immediately ().
- Executive Order 104 Limits on Gatherings of 50 or More; Closure of All Schools, Closure of Racetracks, Casinos, etc.; Restaurant Restrictions ()
- Executive Order 105 Governor Murphy Announces Changes to Upcoming New Jersey Elections in Response to COVID-19 ()
- Executive Order 106 Governor Murphy Enacts Moratorium on Removals of Individuals Due to Evictions or Foreclosures ()
- Executive Order 107 Governor Murphy Directs All Residents to Stay at Home Until Further Notice ()
- Executive Order 108 Governor Murphy Invalidates Any County or Municipal Restriction That in Any Way Will or Might Conflict with any of the Provisions of Executive Order No. 107 ()
- Executive Order 109 Governor Murphy Suspends All Elective Surgeries, Invasive Procedures to Preserve Essential Equipment and Hospital Capacity ()
- Executive 110 Governor Murphy Signs Executive Order Requiring Child Care Centers Close on April 1 Unless Serving Children of Essential Workers ()

New Mexico

- State of Emergency Declared ()
- Executive Order 2020-004 Declares a State of Public Health Emergency and Invoking the Power Provided by the All Hazard Emergency Management Act and the Emergency Licensing Act ()
- Executive Order 2020-005 Order Directing the Closure of all Public School Until April 6, 2020 ()
- Executive Order 2020-006 Authorizes Money to National Guard ()
- Executive Order 2020-007 Authorizes Money for the Department of Homeland Security & Emergency Management ()
- Executive Order 2020-008 Authorizes Money to the Department of Health ()
- Executive Order 2020-009 Authorizes Money to the Public Education Department ()
- Executive Order 2020-010 Authorizes Money to the Children, Youth & Families Department ()

(*continued*)

Appendix 1 (continued)

- Public Health Emergency Order Closing All Businesses and Non-Profit Entities Except for those Deemed Essential and Providing Additional Restrictions on Mass Gatherings Due to COVID-19 ()
- Executive Order 2020-011 Authorizing Additional Emergency Funds for the New Mexico National Guard to Provide Humanitarian Assistance During the Statewide Public Health Emergency ()

New York

- State of Emergency Declared ()
- Executive Orders 202.3 and 202.4 ()
- No. 202.5: Continuing Temporary Suspension and Modification of Laws Relating to the Disaster Emergency ()
- No. 202.6: Continuing Temporary Suspension and Modification of Laws Relating to the Disaster Emergency ()
- No. 202.7: Continuing Temporary Suspension and Modification of Laws Relating to the Disaster Emergency ()
- No. 202.8 Continuing Temporary Suspension and Modification of Laws Relating to the Disaster Emergency ()
- No. 202.9 Continuing Temporary Suspension and Modification of Laws Relating to the Disaster Emergency ()
- No. 202.10: Continuing Temporary Suspension and Modification of Laws Relating to the Disaster Emergency ()

North Carolina

- State of Emergency Declared ()
- Executive Order No. 116 Declaration of a State Emergency to Coordinate Response and Protective Actions to Prevent the Spread of COVID-19 ()
- Executive Order No. 117 Prohibiting the Mass Gatherings and Directing the Statewide Closure of K-12 Public Schools to Limit the Spread of COVID-19 ()
- Forthcoming Executive Order will close Restaurants and Bars for Dine-In ()
- Executive Order No. 118 Limiting Operations of Restaurants and Bars and Broadening Unemployment Insurance Benefits in Response to COVID-19 ()
- Executive Order No. 119 Facilitating Critical Motor Vehicle Operations and Delegating Authority to the Secretary of the Department of Health and Human Services to Waive Regulations in Order to Expand Access to Child Care and Support Local Health Departments ()
- Executive Order No. 120 Additional Limitations on Mass Gatherings, Restrictions on Venues and Long Term Care Facilities and Extension of School Closure Date ()

North Dakota

- Executive Order 2020-03 Declares a State of Emergency in Response to Public Health Crisis of COVID-19 ()
- Executive Order 2020-04 Orders Schools to Close for One Week to Slow the Spread of COVID-19 ()

(*continued*)

Appendix 1 (continued)

- Executive Order 2020-04.1 Amends School Closure Order ()
- Executive Order 2020-05 Temporarily Suspending Certain Licensure Requirements ()
- Executive Order 2020-06 Closing Restaurants/Bars On-Site Dining and Recreational Facilities, Health Clubs, Theaters and Entertainment Venues through April 6 ()
- Executive Order 2020-05.1 Amending Order 2020-05 to Allow for Expanded Telehealth Services ()
- Executive Order 2020-07 Asking State Agencies to Identify State Laws, Rules or Regulations that Hinder or Delay their Ability to Render Maximum Assistance ()
- Executive Order 2020-08 Requiring Immediate Changes to Unemployment Insurance Process ()
- Executive Order 2020-09 Expanding Testing Locations, Eliminating Proof-of-Delivery Requirements for Pharmacies and Allowing Pharmacists to Provide Emergency Refills ()
- Executive Order 2020-10 Giving K-12 School Districts until March 27 to Submit Plans for Resuming Instruction with Age-Appropriate, Distance Learning Methods ()
- Executive Order 20-11 Suspends In-Person NDDOT Administrative Hearings, Removes Load Restrictions on State Highways ()
- Executive Order 20-12 Extends Workers' Compensation to First Responders, Health Workers Who Contract COVID-19 ()
- Executive Order 2020-13 Giving Counties the Option of Mail Ballot-Only Elections to Protect Public Health During the Coronavirus Emergency ()

Ohio

- State of Emergency Declared ()
- Department of Health Director Ordered Polling Locations Closed for 3/17 Primary ()
- Director of Health Orders Non-Essential or Elective Surgeries to Cease Effective March 18 ()
- Executive Order 2020-02D The Emergency Amendment of Rules ()
- Executive Order 2020-03D Lifting Certain Unemployment Compensation Benefit Restrictions ()
- Executive Order 2020-04D Establishing a Temporary Pandemic Child Care License ()
- Executive Order 2020-05D Expands Telehealth Services ()
- Health Director's Order on Sale of Food and Beverage ()
- Health Director's Order on Limited Access to Nursing Homes ()
- Health Director's Order to Limit Mass Gatherings ()
- Governor Orders Temporary Closure of Barbershops, Hair Salons, Nail Salons and Tattoo Parlors ()
- Health Director's Order to Cease Business Operations and Close Venues ()
- Health Director's Order to Prohibit Adult Day Support or Vocational Habilitation Services in Congregate Setting ()
- Health Director's Order to Close Facilities Providing Older Adult Day Care Services and Senior Centers ()
- Health Director's Order to Stay at Home Unless Engaged in Essential Work or Activity ()

(*continued*)

Appendix 1 (continued)

- Executive Order 2020-06D The Emergency Adoption of Rule 4729-5-30.2 of the Ohio Administrative Code by the State of Ohio Board of Pharmacy ()
- Executive Order 2020-07D The Emergency Adoption of Rule 5101:2-12-02.1, 5101:2-13-02.1 and 5101:2-14-02.1 of the Ohio Administrative Code by the Ohio Department of Job and Family Services ()
- Heath Director's Order to Close Facilities Providing Child Care Services ()
- Health Director's Amended Order to Close Facilities Providing Older Adult Day Care Services and Senior Centers ()

Oklahoma
- State of Emergency Declared ()
- Executive Order 2020-06 All State Agencies to Take Necessary Steps to Protect Vulnerable Populations ()
- Amended Executive Order 2020-07 (State of Emergency Declaration) ()
- Executive Order 2020-08 Urging Oklahomans to Follow CDC Guidelines ()
- Third Amended Executive Order 2020-07 Amended to Allow Labs at Oklahoma State University and University of Oklahoma to Conduct COVID-19 testing. ()
- Fourth Amended Executive Order 2020-07 Amended to Issue Statewide "Safer at Home" for Certain Citizens; Limits Gatherings; Postpones Elective Surgeries; Closes Some Businesses ()

Oregon
- State of Emergency Declared ()
- Executive Order 20-05 Prohibiting Large Gatherings due to Coronavirus (COVID-19) Outbreak in Oregon ()
- Executive Order 20-07 Prohibiting On-Premises Consumption of Food or Drink and Gatherings of More than 25 People ()
- Executive Order 20-08 School Closures and the Provision of School-Based and Child Care Services ()
- Executive Order 20-09 Suspension of In-Person Instructional Activities at Higher Education Institutions in Response to Coronavirus (COVID-19) Outbreak ()
- Executive Order 20-10 Preserving Personal Protective Equipment and Hospital Beds, Protecting Health Care Workers, Postponing Non-urgent Health Care Procedures, and Restricting Visitation in Response to Coronavirus (COVID-19) Outbreaks ()
- Executive Order 20-11 Temporary Moratorium on Residential Evictions for Nonpayment, in Response to Coronavirus ()
- Executive Order 20-12 Stay Home, Save Lives: Ordering Oregonians to Stay at Home, Closing Specified Retail Businesses, Requiring Social Distancing Measures for Other Public and Private Facilities, and Imposing Requirements for Outdoor Areas and Licensed Childcare Facilities ()

Pennsylvania
- State of Emergency Declared ()
- Governor Ordered all Restaurants and Bars in Allegheny, Bucks, Chester, Delaware and Montgomery Counties to Close their Dine-In Services for 14 Days ()

(*continued*)

Appendix 1 (continued)

- Governor Announced Statewide Mitigation Efforts ()
- Governor Requests the US Small Business Administration Implement a Disaster Declaration ()
- Governor Orders Closure of Non-Life-Sustaining Businesses ()
- Secretary of Health's Stay at Home Order ()
- Governor's Amended Stay at Home Order ()
- Secretary of Health's Amended Stay at Home Order ()
- Governor Wolf Announces Funding for Small Businesses through the new COVID-19 Working Capital Access Program ()
- Governor Wolf Urges FDA to Waive Eligibility Requirements for the Emergency Food Assistance Program ()

Rhode Island

- State of Emergency Declared ()
- Executive Order 20-04 Second Supplemental Declaration—Restaurants, Bars, Entertainment Venues, and Public Gatherings ()
- Executive Order 20-05 Third Supplemental Emergency Declaration—Public Meetings and Public Records Requests ()
- Executive Order 20-06 Fourth Supplemental Declaration—Expanding Access to Telemedicine Services ()
- Executive Order 20-07 Fifth Supplemental Declaration—Extension of Time for Weapon and Firearm Background Checks ()
- Executive Order 20-08 Sixth Supplemental Declaration—Economic Support for Restaurants, Bars and Establishments that Offer Food ()
- Executive Order 20-09 Seventh Supplemental Declaration—Public Gatherings, Close-Contact Businesses, Public Recreation and Business Service Providers ()
- Executive Order 20-10 Eighth Supplemental Emergency Declaration—Quarantine Restrictions on Domestic Air Travelers ()
- Executive Order 20-11 Ninth Supplemental Emergency Declaration—Delaying the Primary Elections and Preparing for a Predominantly Mail Ballot Election ()
- Executive Order 20-12 Tenth Supplemental Emergency Declaration—Quarantine Restrictions on Travelers from New York State ()

South Carolina

- State of Emergency Declared ()
- Executive Order No. 2020-06 Declaring State of Emergency in Response to COVID-19 ()
- Executive Order No. 2020-07 Declaring State of Emergency in Response to COVID-19 ()
- Executive Order No. 2020-08 Declaring State of Emergency in Response to COVID-19 ()
- Executive Order No. 2020-09 Closing Schools, Other Provisions in Response to COVID-19 ()

(*continued*)

Appendix 1 (continued)

- Executive Order No. 2020-10 Closing Dine-In Restaurants and Other Provisions in Response to COVID-19 ()
- Executive Order 2020-11 Regarding Working from Home for State Employees; Unemployment Claims ()
- Executive Order 2020-12 Allows Restaurants to Include Sealed Containers of Beer and Wine for Curbside Pickup or To-Go Orders ()
- Executive Order 2020-13 Authorizing Law Enforcement to Maintain Order, Ensure Public Safety, and Preserve Public Health During the State of Emergency ()

South Dakota

- State of Emergency Declared ()
- Governor Noem Statement Regarding Coronavirus in South Dakota ()
- Governor Noem Works to Activate Small Business Administration's Economic Injury Disaster Loan Fund Program in South Dakota ()
- Executive Order 2020-06 Extends Order for all Non-Essential Government Personnel to Work from Home ()
- Executive Order 2020-07 COVID-19 Medical Assistance ()
- Executive Order 2020-08 COVID-19 Personal, Business and Healthcare Precautions ()
- Executive Order 2020-09 Extends Order for All Non-Essential Government Personnel to Work from Home ()

Tennessee

- State of Emergency Declared ()
- Executive Order 14 AN ORDER SUSPENDING PROVISIONS OF CERTAIN STATUTES AND RULES IN ORDER TO FACILITATE THE TREATMENT AND CONTAINMENT OF COVID-19 ()
- Executive Order 15 AN ORDER SUSPENDING PROVISIONS OF CERTAIN STATUTES AND RULES AND TAKING OTHER NECESSARY MEASURES IN ORDER TO FACILITATE THE TREATMENT AND CONTAINMENT OF COVID-19 ()
- Executive Order 16 AN ORDER ENSURING GOVERNMENT CONTINUES TO FUNCTION OPENLY AND TRANSPARENTLY DURING THE COVID-19 EMERGENCY WHILE TAKING APPROPRIATE MEASURES TO PROTECT THE HEALTH AND SAFETY OF CITIZENS AND GOVERNMENT OFFICIALS ()
- Executive Order 17 AN ORDER TO MITIGATE THE SPREAD OF COVID-19 BY LIMITING SOCIAL GATHERINGS, DINE-IN SERVICE, AND GYM USE, AND EXPOSURE AT NURSING AND RETIREMENT HOMES, AND PROVIDING FLEXIBILITY FOR RESTAURANTS REGARDING THE SALE OF ALCOHOL ()
- Governor Lee Establishes COVID-19 Unified Command ()
- Executive Order 18 AN ORDER TO REDUCE THE SPREAD OF COVID-19 BY LIMITING NON-EMERGENCY HEALTHCARE PROCEDURES ()

(*continued*)

Appendix 1 (continued)

- Executive Order 19 AN ORDER AMENDING EXECUTIVE ORDER NO. 15 SUSPENDING PROVISIONS OF CERTAIN STATUTES AND RULES AND TAKING OTHER NECESSARY MEASURES IN ORDER TO FACILITATE THE TREATMENT AND CONTAINMENT OF COVID-19 ()
- Executive Order 20 AN ORDER AMENDING EXECUTIVE ORDER NO. 15 SUSPENDING PROVISIONS OF CERTAIN STATUTES AND RULES AND TAKING OTHER NECESSARY MEASURES IN ORDER TO FACILITATE THE TREATMENT AND CONTAINMENT OF COVID-19 ().

Texas
- State of Emergency Declared ()
- Governor Abbott Declares State of Disaster in Texas due to COVID-19 ()
- Governor Abbott Waives Certain State Trucking Regulations to Expedite Delivery of Resources Around Texas ()
- Governor Abbott Fast Tracks Licensing for Out-of-State Medial Professionals ()
- Governor Abbott Waives Laws to Allow Trucks from Alcohol Industry to Deliver Grocery Supplies ()
- Governor Abbott Waives Regulations to Ensure Students in Work Study Programs Receive Critical Funding During School Closures ()
- Governor Abbott Waives STAAR Testing Requirements ()
- Governor Abbott Allows Virtual and Telephonic Open Meetings to Maintain Government Transparency ()
- Governor Abbott Waives Certain Vehicle Registration, Titling and Parking Placard Regulations ()
- Executive Order GA-8 Regarding Social Gatherings, Closure of Restaurants, Bars, Gyms and Schools ()
- Health Commissioner's Declaration of Public Health Disaster ()
- Governor Abbott Waives Health Care Fees for Incarcerated Texans ()
- Texas Supreme Court Suspends Residential Eviction Proceedings ()
- Governor Abbott Waives Regulations to Support Pharmacy Operations ()
- Governor Abbott Takes Action to Expand Nursing Workforce ()
- Executive Order GA-09 Relating to Hospital Capacity During the COVID-19 Disaster ()
- Governor Abbott Requests Major Disaster Declaration from White House ()
- Governor Abbott Authorizes Restaurants to Sell Bulk Retail Product to the Public ()
- Executive Order to Strengthen Reporting Capabilities ()
- Executive Order GA-11 Relating to Airport Screening and Self-Quarantine During the COVID-19 Disaster ()

UTAH
- State of Emergency Declared
- Utah Executive Order 2020-1 Declaring a State of Emergency
- Recommendations on slowing the spread of COVID-19

(*continued*)

Appendix 1 (continued)

- Statement on Statewide Closure of Public Schools
- Governor Announces Recommendations to Help Slow the Spread of Novel Coronavirus
- Executive Order 2020-2 Suspending the Enforcement of Code Due to COVID-19
- Executive Order 2020-3 Temporarily Suspending Utah Code Regarding Public Access to Board of Pardons & Parole Hearings
- Executive Order 2020-4 Temporarily Suspending Utah Code Regarding Liquor Returns, Refunds and Exchanges
- Executive Order 2020-5 Suspending the Enforcement of Provisions of Utah Code and Related State Agency Orders Due to COVID-19
- Department of Health and Governor Order Restaurants and Bars to Suspend Dine-In Services for Two Weeks
- Governor Issues Executive Orders to Help Government Function Optimally Amid Adjustments to Slow Spread of COVID-19
- State Public Health Order Restricting Non-Urgent Medical Procedures
- Executive Order 2020-07 Suspending Enforcement of Statutes Relating to Telehealth Services
- Executive Order 2020-08 Suspending Certain Provisions of the Utah Election Code Regarding Signature Gathering

Vermont

- State of Emergency Declared
- Executive Order 01-20 Declaration of State of Emergency in Response to COVID-10 and National Guard Call-Out
- Addendum to Executive Order 01-20
- Addendum to Executive Order 01-20—Restricts gatherings to Less Than 50 people; Closure of Dine-In for Restaurants and Bars
- Gubernatorial Directive on Provision of Services to Children of Essential Persons During Closure Period in Response to COVID-19
- Gubernatorial Directive 3—Department of Motor Vehicles Suspension of In-Person Transactions
- Gubernatorial Directive 4—Department of Liquor and Lottery—Malt and Vinous Product Delivery and Take Out
- Addendum 3 to Executive Order 01-20 Suspension of all Non-Essential Adult Elective Surgery and Medical and Surgical Procedures
- Addendum 5 to Executive Order 01-20 Order to Work From Home for all Businesses and Non-Profits
- Addendum 6 to Executive Order 01-20 Stay Home/Stay Safe
- Gubernatorial Directive 5—Continuity of Learning Plan

VIRGINIA

- State of Emergency Declared
- Health Emergency Order Prohibiting More Than 10 Patrons in Restaurants, Fitness Centers and Theaters

(continued)

Appendix 1 (continued)

- Governor Northam Announces Additional Actions to Address COVID-19
- Executive Order 52 Increases in Hospital Bed Capacity in Response to Novel Coronavirus
- Amended Order of the Governor and State Health Commissioner Declaration of Public Health Emergency
- Executive Order 53 Temporary Restrictions on Restaurants, Recreational, Entertainment, Gatherings, Non-essential Retail Businesses, and Closure of K-12 Schools Due to Novel Coronavirus (COVID-19)
- Order of Public Health Emergency Two

Washington

- State of Emergency Declared
- Proclaiming a State of Emergency, February 29
- Proclaiming an Amendment to the State of Emergency, March 10
- Proclaiming Additional Amendments to the State of Emergency, March 11
- Proclamation for COVID-19 School Closures
- Proclamation for Statewide K-12 School Closures
- Proclamation for Long-Term Care Workers
- Proclamation for Gatherings Amendment
- Proclamation for College Closures
- Proclamation for Closure of Food and Beverage Services/Limiting Areas of Congregation
- Governor Signs COVID-19 Bill Package
- Amending Proclamation 20-05 Restrictions on Non Urgent Medical Procedures
- Governor Requests the USS *Mercy* to Be Sent to the Puget Sound
- Governor Requests Federal Major Disaster Declaration
- Proclamation for State Home—Stay Healthy
- Proclamation for Moratorium on Evictions
- Proclamation for Open Public Meetings Act and Public Records Act
- Proclamation Waiving Washington State Liquor and Cannabis Board Penalties
- Proclamation on Telemedicine
- Proclamation on Unemployment Benefits Job Search Requirements

West Virginia

- State of Emergency Declared
- Proclamation on State Preparedness
- Announcement of Statewide School Closures
- Governor Announces Closure of Restaurants and Bars
- Executive Oder 2-20
- Executive Order 3-20 Closure of Gyms and Recreational Facilities
- Executive Order 4-20 Providing Unemployment Benefits
- Executive Order 5-20 Declaring Counties Have Authority to Evaluate Courthouse Services
- Executive Order 6-20 Closure of Barbershops and Salons

(*continued*)

Appendix 1 (continued)

- Executive Order 7-20 Suspending Specified Statutory Regulations for the Duration of the State of Emergency
- Executive Order 8-20 Statewide Closure of all State Park Lodges and Closure of Hatfield McCoy Trail to the General Public
- Executive Order 9-20 Declare And Order: Stay At Home Or Your Place Of Residence; Non-Essential Businesses And Operations Must Temporarily Cease Operations; Essential Businesses And Operations Shall Continue to Operate; Prohibited Activities; Avoid Social Gatherings
- Governor Justice Appoints Clay Marsh as COVID-19 Czar

Wisconsin

- State of Emergency Declared
- Executive Order 72, Relating to Declaring a Health Emergency in Response to the COVID-19 Coronavirus
- Order for Statewide School Closure
- Department of Health Services Secretary Prohibits Gatherings of 50 or More
- Department of Health Emergency Order #5 Prohibiting Mass Gatherings of 10 People or More
- Emergency Order Restricting the Size of Child Care Settings
- Emergency Order to the Department of Workforce Development Regarding Unemployment Insurance
- Emergency Order #8 Updated Mass Gathering Ban
- Emergency Order #10 Department of Public Instruction Administrative Rule Suspension and Emergency
- Emergency Order #11 Public Service Commission Administrative Rules Suspension SUSPENSIONS
- Emergency Order #12 Safer at Home Order
- Emergency Order #9 Order to the Department of Corrections
- Governor Evers Launches Wisconsin's COVID-19 PPE Program

Wyoming

- State of Emergency Declared
- Executive Order 2020-2 Declaration of a State of Emergency and a Public Health Emergency
- Governor Announces Coronavirus Task Forces
- Governor and State Health Officer Issue Statewide Closure for Public Spaces
- Executive Order 2020-3 Emergency Exemption from Permissible Operating Time Regulations and Waiver of
  Allowable Size and Weight Permit Fees
- Statewide Public Health Order #2 Forbidding Gatherings of Ten People or More
- Executive Order 2020-04 Suspension of Provisions of Certain Statutes and Rules Related to Driver Licenses Due to a Public Health Emergency

(*continued*)

Appendix 1 (continued)

America Samoa
- Governor Announces Code Blue: School Closure, Gatherings Restricted to 10 People or Less

District of Columbia
- State of Emergency Declared
- Mayor's Order 2020-045 & 46 Declaration of Public Health Emergency: Coronavirus (COVID-19)
- Mayor's Order 2020-035 District Government Preparations for the Coronavirus (COVID-19)
- Mayor Adjusts DC Government's Operating Status
- Mayor's Order 2020-048 Prohibition on Mass Gatherings During Public Health Emergency
- Department of Transportation Suspends DC Circulator Fares
- Mayor Extends Modified District Operating Status
- Mayor's Order 2020-050 Extensions of Public Emergency and Public Health Emergency: Coronavirus
- Mayor's Order 2020-051 Prohibition on Mass Gatherings During Public Health Emergency: Coronavirus
- Mayor's Order 2020-053 Closure of Non-Essential Businesses and Prohibition on Large Gatherings During Public Health Emergency

American Samoa
- State of Emergency Declared
- Response and Action Plan

Guam
- State of Emergency Declared
- Executive Order 2020-04 Relative to Responding to Confirmed Cases of Novel Coronavirus
- Executive Order 2020-05 Relative to Mandating Social Isolation, Lifting Restrictions on Health Care Licensure and Clarifying Status on Non-Essential Government of Guam Operations
- Governor Implements a 14-Day Suspension of Non-Essential Government of Guam Operations Effective March 16
- Governor Extends Social Isolation Mandate and Limitation on Non-Essential Businesses and Government Operations

Northern Mariana Islands
State of Emergency Declared

(*continued*)

Appendix 1 (continued)

Puerto Rico
- State of Emergency Declared
- Executive Order 2020-22
- Executive Order 2020-23
- Executive Order 2020-24
- Executive Order 2020-25
- Executive Order 2020-026

US Virgin Islands
- State of Emergency Declared
- Governor's address on COVID-19
- Supplemental Executive Order Establishing Prohibitions and Restrictions to Movement, Gatherings, and Operations of Businesses, Government and Schools

References

Alvey, J. (2017, September 27–29). *The Separation of Powers Between The Executive And The Judiciary*. Paper presented to the Australasian Study of Parliament Conference, Parliament House, Hobart, Tasmania.

Baily, R., Klein, A., & Schardin, J. (2017). The Impact of the Dodd-Frank Act on Financial Stability and Economic Growth. *RSF: The Russell Sage Foundation Journal of the Social Sciences, 3*(1), 20–47.

Bernick, L. (2016). Studying Governors Over Five Decades: What We Know and Where We Need to Go? *State and Local Government Review, 48*(2), 132–146.

Black, L., & Hazelwood, L. (2013). The Effect of TARP on Bank Risk-Taking. *Journal of Financial Stability, 9*(4), 790–803.

Bolton, A., & Thrower, S. (2015). Legislative Capacity and Executive Unilateralism. *American Journal of Political Science, 60*(3), 649–663.

Bradley, C., & Morrison, T. (2012). Historical Gloss and the Separation of Powers. *Harvard Law Review, 126*, 411–431.

Branum, T. (2002). President or King? The Use and Abuse of Executive Orders in Modern-Day America. *Journal of Legislation, 28*, 1–6.

Broberg, M. (2020). A Critical Appraisal of the World Health Organization's International Health Regulations (2005) in Times of Pandemic—It Is Time for Revision. *European Journal of Risk Regulation.*

Calabresi, S., & Prakash, S. (1994). The President's Power to Execute the Laws. *Yale Law Journal, 104*, 541–551.

Choudhry, S. (Ed.). (2006). *The Migration of Constitutional Ideas.* CUP.

Cohn, M. (2015). Non-Statutory Executive Powers: Assessing Global Constitutionalism In A Structural-Institutional Context. *International & Comparative Law Quarterly, 64*(1), 65–102.

Deering, C., & Maltzman, F. (1999). The Politics of Executive Orders: Legislative Constraints on Presidential Power. *Political Research Quarterly, 52*(4), 767–783.

Farruggio, C., Michalak, T., & Uhde, A. (2013). The Light and Dark Side of TARP. *Journal of Banking & Finance, 37*(7), 2586–2604.

Fatovic, C. (2004). Constitutionalism and Presidential Prerogative: Jeffersonian and Hamiltonian Perspectives. *American Journal of Political Science, 48*, 429–439.

Ferguson, M., & Bowling, C. (2008). Executive Orders and Administrative Control. *Public Administration Review, 68*(Suppl. 1), S20–S28.

French, R. (2018). Executive Power In Australia—Nurtured And Bound In Anxiety. *University of Western Australia Law Review, 43*(2), 16–36.

Gakh, M., Vernick, J., & Rutkow, L. (2013). Using Gubernatorial Executive Orders to Advance Public Health. *Public Health Report, 128*(2), 127–130.

Gakh, M., Callahan, K., & al, e. (2019). How Have States Used Executive Orders to Address Public Health? *Journal of Public Health Management and Practice, 25*(1), 78–80.

Groppi, T., & Ponthoreau, M. (Eds.). (2013). *The Use of Foreign Precedents by Constitutional Judges.* (Hart).

Gruszczynski, L. (2020). The Covid-19 Pandemic and International Trade: Temporary Turbulences or Paradigm Shift? *European Journal of Risk Regulation.*

Haffajee, R., & al, e. (2014). What Is a Public Health "Emergency"? *New England Journal of Medicine, 371*, 986.

Harris, B. (1992). The "Third Source" of Authority for Government Action. *Law. Quarterly Review, 109*, 626–636.

Hodge, J., et al. (2005). The Legal Framework for Meeting Surge Capacity Through the Use of Volunteer Health Professionals During Public Health Emergencies and Other Disasters. *Journal of Contemporary Health Policy, 22*(5), 23–27.

Jackson, V. (2010). *Constitutional Engagement in a Transnational Era.* Oxford University Press.

Law, D., & Versteeg, M. (2011). The Evolution and Ideology of Global Constitutionalism. *Commonwealth Law Review, 99*, 1163–1183.

Lester, A., & Weait, M. (2003). The Use of Ministerial Powers without Parliamentary Authority: The Ram Doctrine. *Public Law*, 415–420.

Lewis, D., Schneider, C., & al, e. (2015). Institutional Characteristics and State Policy Priorities: The Impact of Legislatures and Governors. *State Politics and Policy Quarterly, 15*, 447–475.

Nwogugu, M. (2012). *Risk In The Global Real Estate Market.* Hoboken: John Wiley.

Nwogugu, M. (2015a). Failure of the Dodd-Frank Act. *Journal of Financial Crime, 22*(4), 520–572.

Nwogugu, M. (2015b). Un-Constitutionality of the Dodd-Frank Act. *European Journal of law Reform, 17*, 185–190.

Nwogugu, M. (2019a). *Introduction.* Chap. 1 in M. Nwogugu (Ed.), *Complex Systems, Multi-Sided Incentives and Risk Perception in Companies.* Palgrave Macmillan.

Nwogugu, M. (2019b). *Complex Adaptive Systems, Sustainable Growth And Securities Law: On Inequality And The "Optimal Design Of Financial Contracts".* Chap. 5 in M. Nwogugu (Ed.), *Earnings Management, Fintech-Driven Incentives and Sustainable Growth: On Complex Systems, Legal and Mechanism Design Factors.* Routledge/Ashgate.

Omarova, S. (2011). The Dodd-Frank Act: A New Deal for a New Age? *North Carolina Banking Institute Journal, 15*, 83–98.

Orenstein, D. (2013). When Law is not Law: Setting Aside Legal Provisions During Declared Emergencies. *Journal of Law & Medical Ethics, 41*, 73–76.

Ouyang, Y., & Carpentier, C. (2018). The (Lack of) Gender Dynamics of Gubernatorial Executive Orders. *Journal of the Indiana Academy of the Social Sciences, 21*(1), Article 43.

Prabhakar, M. (2008). *Separation of Powers: Global Perspectives* (pp. 1–26). Hyderabad: Amicus Books.

Redlawsk, D. (2015). *The American Governor: Power, Constraint, and Leadership in the States.* Basingstoke: Palgrave Macmillan.

Sellers, M. (2017). Gubernatorial Use of Executive Orders: Unilateral Action and Policy Adoption. *Journal of Public Policy, 37*(3), 315–339.

Semaan, E., & Drake, P. (2016). TARP and the Long-Term Perception of Risk. *Journal of Banking & Finance, 68*(C), 216–235.

Song, W., & Uzmanoglu, C. (2016). TARP Announcement, Bank Health, and Borrowers' Credit Risk. *Journal of Financial Stability, 22*(C), 22–32.

Sunshine, G. (2017). The Case For Streamlining Emergency Declaration Authorities And Adapting Legal Requirements To Ever-Changing Public Health Threats. *Emory Law Journal, 67*(3), 397–414.

Torsello, M., & Winkler, M. (2020). Coronavirus-Infected International Business Transactions: A Preliminary Diagnosis. *European Journal of Risk Regulation.*

Index[1]

[1] Note: Page numbers followed by 'n' refer to notes.

M. I. C. Nwogugu, *Geopolitical Risk, Sustainability and "Cross-Border Spillovers" in Emerging Markets, Volume II*, https://doi.org/10.1007/978-3-030-71419-2